STORAGE

3x 10/98 5/02

Art ✓

JUL 1997

D1791030

NINETEENTH CENTURY BASEBALL

To Jane,
for all of your love
and support

NINETEENTH CENTURY BASEBALL

Year-by-Year Statistics for the Major League Teams, 1871 through 1900

by MARSHALL D. WRIGHT

McFarland & Company, Inc., Publishers
Jefferson, North Carolina, and London

British Library Cataloguing-in-Publication data are available

Library of Congress Cataloguing-in-Publication Data

Wright, Marshall D.
      Nineteenth century baseball : year-by-year statistics for the
   major league teams, 1871 through 1900 / by Marshall D. Wright.
         p.   cm.
      Includes bibliographical references (p.   ) and index.
      ISBN 0-7864-0181-8 (library binding : 50# alk. paper) ∞
      1. Baseball — United States — History — 19th century —
   Statistics.   2. Baseball players — United States — History — 19th
   century — Statistics.   I. Title.
   GV863.A1W752   1996
   796.357'0973'09034021; sj04 05-07-96 — dc20   96-19833
                                                           CIP

©1996 Marshall D. Wright. All rights reserved

No part of this book, specifically including the table of contents and index, may be reproduced or transmitted in any form or by any means, electronic or mechanical, including photocopying or recording, or by any information storage and retrieval system, without permission in writing from the publisher.

Manufactured in the United States of America

McFarland & Company, Inc., Publishers
   Box 611, Jefferson, North Carolina 28640

ACKNOWLEDGMENTS

A book of this magnitude and scope owes a lot to many.

For the statistical tables, I am indebted to Macmillan's *The Baseball Encyclopedia* (especially the 1st, 4th and 9th editions), and to the 3rd and 4th editions of John Thorn's and Pete Palmer's *Total Baseball*. A special thanks to the National Baseball Library for their copies of the ICI computer printouts as well as a timely explanation of early baseball statistics. I am grateful to Howe Sportsdata for granting me access to their vast collection of *Spalding* and *Reach Baseball Guides*. I am also grateful to William Ryczek for his monumental work on the National Association, *Blackguards and Red Stockings*. And finally a big thanks to S. C. Thompson's pioneering classic *All Time Rosters of Major League Baseball Clubs*.

The text portion owes a lot to the fine researchers of SABR, including: Arthur Ahrens, Bob Bailey, Frederick Ivor-Campbell, Jerry Malloy, Jim Miller, Frank Phelps, Robert Shipley, Robert Tiemann, and David Voight. The text's final gloss is due to the fine polishing of my wife, Jane.

On a personal level, I would like to thank my family for their encouragement and support, and my colleagues at Howe Sportsdata and HST, who helped more than they realized. Finally, a very special thank you to my son Denny who kept me company many a long afternoon, while inputting a few verses of his own.

TABLE OF CONTENTS

ACKNOWLEDGMENTS v
INTRODUCTION ix

Prelude	*Amateurs and Professionals*	1
1871 National Association	*A New Configuration*	6
1872 National Association	*Expansion*	12
1873 National Association	*Ross Barnes*	19
1874 National Association	*The Boston Red Stockings*	25
1875 National Association	*Imbalance*	31
1876 National League	*The Owners Take Control*	39
1877 National League	*The Louisville Four*	45
1878 National League	*Survival*	50
1879 National League	*Reserved*	55
1880 National League	*The Chicago White Stockings*	61
1881 National League	*Cap Anson*	67
1882 National League	*Competition*	73
1882 American Association	*The Beer and Whiskey Circuit*	79
1883 National League	*The Return of the Prodigals*	85
1883 American Association	*The National Agreement*	91
1884 National League	*Old Hoss*	97
1884 American Association	*Equality*	104
1884 Union Association	*One Man's Dream*	114
1885 National League	*The Best Second*	124
1885 American Association	*The World Series*	131
1886 National League	*The King*	138
1886 American Association	*The $15,000 Slide*	145
1887 National League	*A Walk Is as Good as a Hit*	152

1887 American Association	*The St. Louis Browns*	159
1888 National League	*The Giants*	166
1888 American Association	*Giving Away the Store*	173
1889 National League	*The Very Last Day*	180
1889 American Association	*A New Champion*	187
1890 Players' League	*The Brotherhood*	194
1890 National League	*The Remnants*	201
1890 American Association	*The Last Shall Be First*	208
1891 National League	*Payback*	216
1891 American Association	*The Last Gasp*	223
1892 National League	*Monopoly*	231
1893 National League	*Moving Back*	241
1894 National League	*Hotter Than Blazes*	251
1895 National League	*Mr. Temple's Cup*	261
1896 National League	*The Baltimore Orioles*	271
1897 National League	*The Beaneaters Prevail*	281
1898 National League	*Willie Keeler*	290
1899 National League	*Winners and Losers*	300
1900 National League	*Consolidation*	311
1900 American League	*A New Threat*	318
Epilogue	*The Century Turns*	326

SELECTED BIBLIOGRAPHY 327
INDEX 329

INTRODUCTION

Some twenty years ago, I chanced upon a new baseball reference book. It was an encyclopedia which arranged the players by team, rather than individually, in a chronological index. I immediately saw the potential of such a listing. At a brief glance, one could see the relative strengths and weaknesses of each team while retaining the individual statistics of each player. As I thumbed through the volume, I noticed that something was missing. This book started its listings in 1901, and I well knew that major league baseball had started much earlier. I wondered to myself, why were those early years missing? Why were they not included in the book? Did players of the nineteenth century not deserve to be included too? The statistics for these nineteenth century players were already listed alphabetically in the major encyclopedias, but were not listed by team.

Twenty years later, while in the process of creating a table-top baseball game utilizing some nineteenth century teams, I needed to find a source for all nineteenth century players listed by team. Not knowing of any reference book like this to draw on, I decided to compile one myself.

What follows is the result. In the pages to come is a complete listing of the over 2,000 nineteenth century major league baseball players, listed by team, in chronological order. Preceding each chapter is a brief explanatory text highlighting some facet of that particular year.

In addition, I have included two groups of teams in this encyclopedia that the governors of baseball do not consider major: 1) the National Association (1871–1875), and 2) the first year of the American League (1900). In my mind, the truest definition of a major league is a league that contains the highest level of baseball being played. Both the National Association, and the American League's first year fit the description. The National Association contained all of the top players in the land, and when the "major" National League was formed in 1876, virtually all of their players and teams came from the National Association. Over half of the players participating in the first year of the American League were former major league stars. This certainly measures up to the record of the "major" American Association in 1882, and the Union Association of 1884.

A second definition of a major league concerns scheduling. The charge against the

National Association is that some of the teams did not schedule and play many games during the course of a season. There is no disputing the truth of that statement.

Several teams of the National Association played fewer than 15 games each year. What is also true is that much the same happened in the "major" Union Association in 1884. Five teams in that circuit played fewer than 30 games — in fact, one (St. Paul) played only nine. It is for these two reasons that I have included the National Association and the American League in this major league encyclopedia.

The chapters in this book each cover one league per year. The teams within each year are arranged in the order of their rank at the end of the season. That is, the team that finished in first place according to the rules governing their particular league appears first. For each team the data includes: games won and lost, winning percentage, games back, place in the standings, and the name of the manager. If the team had more than one manager, only the last names are given.

For the batters, the following data are included: games played at each position, total games played, at bats, runs, hits, runs batted in, doubles, triples, home runs, bases on balls, strikeouts, batting average, and slugging average.

For the pitchers, the following data are included: games won, games lost, winning percentage, games pitched, games started, complete games, shutouts, saves, innings pitched, hits allowed, bases on balls, strikeouts, and earned run average.

Under each category, for both hitting and pitching, are the team's totals.

The batters are arranged in roster order, starting with the eight players on each team who played the most games for each position, exclusive of the pitchers. The only exceptions occur when a player participated in the most games for a particular team in two different positions. The remaining players on each team are ranked according to most games played. The pitchers are ranked in the order of most games won.

Preceding some of the players is a numerical notation in parentheses. This indicates that the player was employed by more than one team. The first number indicates if it is his first, or second, etc., team for the season, while the second number tells how many total teams he played on that year.

In a couple of dozen cases, complete data are not available for a given player. In those few instances, the area is left blank. This is especially true for the American League of 1900, where the official statistics are skimpy. In some other cases, team totals are not available for runs batted in. The total for the data present is then underlined.

As stated before, the statistics for these players for the most part have been already published in the major baseball encyclopedias. What I have done is to arrange the statistics in a different format, as well as adding new features not found in most of the standard reference books. For example, with the exception of the first edition of Macmillan's *Baseball Encyclopedia*, most baseball reference books give short shrift to pitcher's batting statistics. In this volume they are included.

With the addition of the nineteenth century teams and players, the complete team by team story of the major leagues is ready. These early teams and players, as you will see, have very important and interesting stories to tell.

PRELUDE

Amateurs and Professionals

During the early years of the nineteenth century, the game of baseball emerged gently from a variety of bat and ball games such as the English game of rounders. The variety and forms of the game varied greatly from year to year and from town to town. One of these varieties was codified by a New Yorker named Alexander Cartwright in 1845. His version of "base ball" called for four bases set 90 feet apart, with a thrower 45 feet inside one of the corners. Furthermore, the Cartwright game consisted of nine men on a side, with three outs per side. This version is easily recognized as our game of baseball.

Cartwright wanted to test his new rules, so he and his club, the Knickerbockers, played over a dozen matches during the fall of 1845 with other clubs. However, it was not until the following spring that the game got much notice. The Knickerbocker club and a team calling itself the New York Base Ball Club met on June 19, 1846, at Elysian Fields in Hoboken, New Jersey, with the New York club prevailing 23 to 1. This landmark game in baseball history was the first one chronicled to any degree. Most date the beginning of organized baseball from this date.

In a few years, several other clubs were formed in the greater New York area, mostly between the years 1854–1857. The more noteworthy of them were the Excelsior club of New York (1854), the Eckford club of Brooklyn (1855), and the Atlantic club of Brooklyn (1856). In 1857, twenty-four of the clubs met and formed the National Association of Base Ball Players.

Many of the important matches of the day were between "picked" nines, that is to say, all-star teams. One of the most important of these groups of games occurred in 1858 at the Fashion Race Course on Long Island. In a series of three games, a picked nine from New York faced a picked nine from Brooklyn. On July 20, New York beat Brooklyn 22–15, a rematch on August 17 saw Brooklyn prevail 29–8, and in the rubber game New York won again 29–18. These games were important for another reason. This was the first recorded instance of someone having to pay to see a baseball game. The several thousand people attending these games had to pay 50 cents each for the privilege.

Another important picked nine match was played in 1861, again involving teams from New York and Brooklyn. At stake was the Silver Ball Trophy, put forth by the newspaper *The New York Clipper*. In the game, Brooklyn prevailed 18–6.

Meanwhile, the National Association was growing. From its start of 24 teams in 1857, it expanded to 62 teams by 1860. After a brief dip in membership due to the Civil War, the growth continued to 91 teams by 1865, and 237 by 1867. A natural outgrowth of all this expansion was some method of measurement — some way of deciding who was the best player, or which was the best team. To address the former issue, baseball statistics were born.

Henry Chadwick, a newspaper reporter and a native Englishman, was the driving force behind baseball statistics. Ever since seeing the Fashion Course matches in 1858, Chadwick had been enamored of baseball. In 1860 he started a yearly publication known as the *Beadle's Dime Base Ball Player*. In it he published a chronicle of the teams and their players, compiled painstakingly from the accounts of the games sent in by the various clubs. Thus, one could determine who were the best players — they were listed for all to see in black and white. Following is a list of the top three batters for each year from 1859 to 1870 together with their statistics:

Year	Player	Team	Outs		Runs	
1859	Burr	Putnam	1	3	4	2
	Morris	Star	1	4	4	2
	Grum	Eckfords	2	7	4	1
1860	Leggett	Excelsiors	2	6	3	10
	Grum	Eckfords	2	13	3	9
	Burtis	Gotham	2	0	3	2
1861	Start	Enterprise	2	1	4	1
	Campbell	Eckfords	2	2	4	1
	Pearce	Atlantics	2	7	3	7
1862	Creighton	Excelsiors	0	0	4	2
	Morris	Star	1	7	4	2
	Bell	H. Eckfords	1	8	4	2
1863	Wood	Eckfords	2	2	3	5
	Sprague	Eckfords	2	1	3	1
	Manolt	Eckfords	2	5	3	0
1864	C. Smith	Atlantics	2	12	5	5
	Galvin	Atlantics	2	6	5	2
	Pearce	Atlantics	3	2	4	14
1865	Mitchell	Star	1	3	5	1
	Start	Atlantics	2	3	4	10
	Bell	Eclectic	1	3	4	3
1866	McBride	Athletics	2	3	6	10
	Berthrong	Nationals	2	2	5	2
	Smith	Unions	2	10	4	26

(Year)	(Player)	(Team)	(Outs)		(Runs)	
1867	Wright	Nationals	2	6	6	8
	Reach	Athletics	2	22	6	0
	Start	Athletics	2	2	4	7
1868	Reach	Atlantics	2	37	5	6
	Radcliffe	Athletics	2	31	5	0
	Fisler	Athletics	2	17	4	43

			GP	H	HPG	TB	TBG
1869	Wright	Reds	57	304	5.19	614	10
	Waterman	Reds	57	226	3.55	377	6
	Allison	Reds	53	210	3.51	331	6
1870	Wright	Reds	58	248	4.27	411	7.08
	Waterman	Reds	72	278	3.86	414	5.75
	Leonard	Reds	74	269	3.63	424	5.70

These statistics look like nothing used today. They did, however, emphasize the most fundamental aspects of the game — outs and runs. Here is how they work: Using the example of Leggett of the 1860 Excelsior Club, you will notice the numbers 2 and 6 under the outs column, and 3 and 10 under the runs column. The first number of each column indicates the average per game, followed by any left over. The Excelsiors played in 21 games in 1860, and Leggett played in all of them. Leggett made (as a batter) two outs per game, plus six left over. That means he was put out 48 times in 1860. Likewise, using the same formula, Leggett scored three runs a game, with ten left over, equaling 73 runs scored for the year. Teams routinely scored twenty to thirty runs a game, explaining his high total.

In 1869 and 1870, a new wrinkle was added to the statistics — hits. The Beadle's Guide for 1870 stated that a player's clean hits was the true indicator of his ability. In the statistics for 1869 and 1870, the first column of numbers indicates how many games each played, the second indicates how many hits in those games. The columns under the heading of HPG are how many hits each got per game (using the same principles discussed above). The next two columns indicate how many total bases those hits manufactured — i.e., extra base hits. Although difficult to translate to modern terms without knowing a player's at bats, George Wright's five plus hits per game in 1869 would give him a batting average somewhere around .700. The figures for 1870 show exact percentages in the per game totals.

With that in mind, two different players' totals jump out of the chart. In 1862, Jim Creighton, in his outs column, shows two zeros. That means, if interpreted accurately, he was not retired once during the year. Creighton was one of the superstars of the era. He was a pitcher that overpowered the batters in an age when that was not the point of the game. Tragically, his best year in 1862 was also his last year. In October 1862, Creighton suffered an injury while batting and died a few days later. He was only 21.

The second statistic worth noting is the run scoring of George Wright for 1867. According to the chart, he scored more than six runs per game — an astounding total in any age.

The other side of the statistical coin, the determination of the best team, was not as easy. Teams did not play consistent schedules. Scheduling was handled on a club by club basis. Thus a team might have a gaudy record, but many of their wins would be at the expense of poor teams. Nevertheless, the best teams of the National Association between 1863 and 1868 were considered to be: 1863 — Eckfords, 1864 — Atlantics, 1865 — Atlantics, 1866 — Atlantics, 1867 — Unions, and 1868 — Atlantics. The 1863–1865 champions had undefeated seasons.

By 1868, the era of the amateur was changing. A new phenomenon was making itself more and more prevalent. This was the ballplayer who played for money — a professional. During the 1860s, if a baseball club wanted to succeed it would have to obtain the best players. If the club wanted the best players, it would have to pay them. The teams were circumspect about these practices — most everybody thought the idea of a "professional" ball player crude and crass. The payments usually took the form of a lucrative job (requiring little or no work), or some percentage of the money collected from the paying customers. In 1869, this all changed. The Cincinnati Reds, under the direction of Harry Wright, openly admitted to paying its players. The first professional team was born.

The Cincinnati baseball club was formed in July 1866. In November 1867, the club hired Harry Wright to run its operations. Not content to field a team of locals, Harry Wright ventured far and wide in search of baseball talent, in order to create the best team possible. The end result was a team consisting mostly of players from the New York area. In 1868, four of the players were paid, in 1869 all of them were.

Cincinnati began their season in 1869 with a 45–9 thumping of the Great Westerns on May 4. Sixty games later on November 5, they ended it the same way by besting the Mutual Green Stockings of New York 17–8. The remarkable feat for this team is that it did not lose any games in between. The Reds toured from coast to coast during the summer and fall of 1869, winning 60, and losing none (there was one tie on August 17 with the Troy Haymakers 17–17).

Cincinnati's success on the field did not translate to monetary success. As a matter of fact they barely finished in the black. But this did not diminish their accomplishment. A team of professionals, hand picked and well rewarded, could beat just about anybody.

The success of the Reds galvanized many other teams into action. By the start of the 1870 season, more than 15 teams scattered from Illinois to Maryland had admittedly turned professional. Most of these teams payed their players outright — others were cooperative ventures who paid each player a share of the gate money.

As the season progressed, the Reds continued their winning ways. Cincinnati came to Brooklyn on June 14 riding an 84-game winning streak. Nine thousand spectators witnessed what some call the greatest game ever played. Tied at the end of regulation 5–5, Cincinnati could have let the game end there with their unbeaten streak intact. But they decided to press on. And when they scored two in the top of the eleventh inning, the decision appeared to have been a wise one. But in the bottom of the inning after several hits and an error, Brooklyn pushed across three runs to win 8–7. The most spectacular winning streak in baseball history was over. Before June 1870, the Cincinnati Reds were unbeaten and thus unique. After their trip to Brooklyn, they were just like any other beaten team. They were still the best team in the land, but their mystique had vanished, forever lost.

Cincinnati still finished the season with 68 wins in 74 games. Against the amateurs they were undefeated; their six losses came against professional teams, like the Atlantics. The Athletics of Philadelphia finished with 66 wins, 24 against professionals. Further down the list of professional teams were the Atlantics, Haymakers, Olympics, White Stockings, and Forest Citys of Cleveland who each won more than they lost.

Although the professionals captured the attention and money of the baseball hungry public, an overwhelmingly large majority of the teams in the National Association were still considered amateur. These teams rebelled against the commercialism of the game, and their growing lack of influence in its government. It was obvious that the two, professionals and amateurs, could not exist in the same organization.

1871 NATIONAL ASSOCIATION

A New Configuration

To resolve the issue of professional versus amateur, ten of the more powerful professional clubs met in Brooklyn in March 1871 and formed the National Association of Professional Baseball Players. The teams were: the Athletics of Philadelphia, the Mutuals of New York, the Haymakers of Troy, the Olympics of Washington, the Red Stockings of Boston, the White Stockings of Chicago, the Kekiongas of Fort Wayne, the Forest Citys of Rockford (Illinois), the Forest Citys of Cleveland, and the Nationals of Washington. Nine of these teams (all but the Nationals) would compete for the pennant in 1871. Conspicuously absent from this group were the Cincinnati Reds. For financial reasons, the team had disbanded following the 1870 season. Most of their vaunted players would don the uniform of Boston, with the remainder going to Washington.

Rebuffed, the amateur teams met and formed the National Association of Amateur Base Ball Players. This organization never really jelled, and it disbanded in 1874. It was clear that the power in baseball was in the hands of the professionals.

Scheduling during this time was generally handled on a club by club basis. The clubs would arrange through their secretaries for a championship series, a three to five game affair, with every other team. Most of the eastern teams took two trips to the west, and the western teams did likewise, but not all teams participated to this degree and some played in significantly fewer games. To decide a true pennant winner, the rules of the National Association stated that the team winning the most games would be declared the winner. This would certainly favor the team that played a more complete schedule.

The championship season of 1871 started with the May 5 game between Cleveland and Fort Wayne. In late August, this same Fort Wayne team dropped out of the league (after only seven wins) and was replaced by the Eckfords of Brooklyn, who did not participate in the pennant race. As the season was winding down, three teams (Philadelphia, Boston, and Chicago) were clustered near the top. But it took a major conflagration to decide the final order. On October 8, the city of Chicago suffered one of the worst fires ever to hit an American city. The White Stockings lost their ballpark and all their equipment in this inferno. As a result, they were forced to play their remaining games on the road.

Due to the closeness of the pennant race, the Championship Committee (arbiter of all disputes) decided the October 30 game between Philadelphia and Chicago (in Brooklyn) would decide the pennant. Playing in an unfamiliar setting with borrowed uniforms and equipment, Chicago dropped the game 4–1, and lost the pennant. Chicago, along with Boston, finished two games behind the Athletics. With the loss of their ballpark, Chicago would not rejoin the National Association until 1874.

The Philadelphia Athletics boasted of some fine individual performances on their way to the inaugural National Association championship. None was more essential than third baseman Levi Meyerle. He hit the ball at an astounding .492 clip, a total that has yet to see its equal in major league baseball. In addition, Meyerle also tied for the circuit lead with four home runs. With their third baseman leading the way, the Athletics led the league in hitting (.320), but the second place Red Stockings (.310) were not far behind. This was a hard hitting team led by a trio of .400 hitters: second baseman Ross Barnes (.401), shortstop George Wright (.412), and catcher Cal McVey (.431). Pitcher Al Spalding of the Red Stockings finished first in wins (19) and second in the ERA race (3.36) while teammate Harry Wright became the first relief specialist by posting three saves. These two teams won on their hitting. Not so for the ill-fated White Stockings. Pitcher George Zettlein had a superb year finishing with a fine 2.73 ERA, which was more than half a run better than his closest competitor. Their hitting, though, was generally weak. Only Jimmy Wood (.378) finished among the league leaders.

Another three teams (New York, Washington, and Troy) were clustered near the middle of the pack. New York's Rynie Wolter was a one-man team. Not only was he the team's leading pitcher with 16 wins and a fine (3.43) ERA, but he was also the team's best hitter (.370), and the league's leading RBI man with 44. Washington had a balanced club, featuring three .300 hitters, while Troy had an unbalanced team that collectively hit .308. Steve King (.396) and Lip Pike (.377, 4 HR) led the way, but the pitching staff generously gave most of it back. Haymaker pitcher John McMullin gave up the most walks and hits and had the highest ERA (5.53) of any starting pitcher in the league.

The three teams that finished on the bottom (Cleveland, Fort Wayne, and Rockford) featured some fine performances. Pitcher Al Pratt of Cleveland led the league with 33 strikeouts, while 19-year-old Cap Anson of Rockford led the league with eleven doubles.

On the surface, there was not much difference between the baseball in the years leading to 1870, versus 1871. The teams were the same — the players too. Only the organization governing them differed.

The legacy of 1871 was to endure. The National Association would prove over time to be a viable organization which gave the game of baseball an excellent start for league play. Most importantly, for the first time, a logical champion could be crowned. It was unfortunate that fate stepped in and altered the pennant race, while depriving the city of Chicago of its team for the next two years.

PHILADELPHIA Athletics

21-7   .750   1st   Hicks Hayhurst

BATTERS	POS/GAMES	GP	AB	R	H	BI	2B	3B	HR	BB	SO	SB	BA	SA
Wes Fisler	1B26,2B2	28	147	43	41	16	8	2	0	3	2	6	.279	.361
Al Reach	2B26	26	133	43	47	34	7	6	0	5	6	2	.353	.496
John Radcliff	SS28	28	145	47	44	22	7	5	0	6	1	5	.303	.421
Levi Meyerle	3B26,P1	26	130	45	64	40	9	3	4	2	1	4	.492	.700
George Heubel	OF16,1B1	17	75	18	23	13	4	2	0	2	0	1	.307	.413
Count Sensenderfer	OF25	25	127	38	41	23	5	2	0	0	1	5	.323	.394
Ned Cuthbert	OF27	28	150	47	37	30	7	5	3	10	2	16	.247	.420
Fergy Malone	C27	27	134	33	46	33	7	1	1	9	4	9	.343	.433
Dick McBride	P25	25	132	36	31		3	0	0	7	1	4	.235	.257
George Bechtel	OF15,P3,3B2	20	94	24	33	21	9	1	1	2	2	4	.351	.500
Tom Pratt	1B1	1	6	2	2	1	0	0	0	0	0	0	.333	.333
Tom Berry	OF1	1	4	0	1	0	0	0	0	0	0	0	.250	.250
Nate Berkenstock	OF1	1	4	0	0	0	0	0	0	0	3	0	.000	.000
		28	1281	376	410	233	66	27	9	46	23	56	.320	.435

PITCHERS	W	L	PCT	G	GS	CG	SH	SV	IP	H	BB	SO	ERA
Dick McBride	18	5	.783	25	25	25	0	0	222	285	40	15	4.58
George Bechtel	1	2	.333	3	3	2	0	0	26	43	11	1	7.96
Levi Meyerle	0	0	----	1	0	0	0	0	1	1	2	0	9.00
	21	7	.750	28	28	27	0	0	249	329	53	16	4.95

BOSTON Red Stockings

20-10   .667   -2   2nd   Harry Wright

BATTERS	POS/GAMES	GP	AB	R	H	BI	2B	3B	HR	BB	SO	SB	BA	SA
Charlie Gould	1B30,OF1	31	151	38	43	32	9	2	2	3	1	6	.285	.411
Ross Barnes	2B16,SS15,3B1	31	157	66	63	34	10	9	0	13	1	11	.401	.580
George Wright	SS15,1B1	16	80	33	33	11	7	5	0	6	1	9	.412	.625
Harry Schafer	3B31,2B1	31	149	38	42	28	7	5	0	3	1	13	.282	.396
Fred Cone	OF19	19	77	17	20	16	3	1	0	8	2	12	.260	.325
Dave Birdsall	OF26,C3	29	152	51	46	24	3	3	0	4	4	6	.303	.362
Harry Wright	OF30,P9,SS1	31	147	42	44	26	5	2	0	13	2	7	.299	.361
Cal McVey	C28,OF1	29	153	43	66	43	9	5	0	1	2	6	.431	.556
Al Spalding	P31,OF9	31	144	43	39	31	10	1	1	8	1	2	.271	.375
Frank Barrows	OF15,2B1	18	86	13	13	11	2	1	0	0	0	1	.151	.198
Sam Jackson	2B14,OF1	15	76	17	17	11	5	3	0	1	4	0	.224	.368
		31	1372	401	426	267	70	37	3	60	19	73	.310	.422

PITCHERS	W	L	PCT	G	GS	CG	SH	SV	IP	H	BB	SO	ERA
Al Spalding	19	10	.655	31	31	22	1	0	257	333	38	23	3.36
Harry Wright	1	0	1.000	9	0	0	0	3	19	34	4	0	6.27
	20	10	.667	31	31	22	1	3	276	367	42	23	3.55

CHICAGO White Stockings

19-9   .679   -2   3rd   Jimmy Wood

BATTERS	POS/GAMES	GP	AB	R	H	BI	2B	3B	HR	BB	SO	SB	BA	SA
Bub McAtee	1B26	26	135	34	37	10	8	2	0	5	2	5	.274	.363
Jimmy Wood	2B28	28	135	45	51	29	10	6	1	11	3	13	.378	.563
Ed Duffy	SS25,3B1	26	121	30	28	15	5	0	0	3	2	11	.231	.273
Ed Pinkham	3B16,OF7,P3	24	95	27	25	17	5	5	1	18	3	5	.263	.453
Tom Foley	OF14,C3,3B1	18	84	18	22	13	3	1	0	3	2	1	.262	.321
Joe Simmons	OF25,1B2	27	129	29	28	17	6	1	0	1	0	4	.217	.279
Fred Treacey	OF25	25	124	39	42	33	7	5	4	2	5	13	.339	.573
Charlie Hodes	C18,3B7,OF2,SS1	28	130	32	36	25	4	1	2	7	0	3	.277	.369
George Zettlein	P28,OF3	28	128	24	32		3	0	0	2	4	4	.250	.273
Mart King	OF10,C7,SS3	20	101	23	21	16	1	0	2	8	1	5	.208	.277
Mike Brannock	3B3	3	14	2	1	0	0	0	0	0	0	0	.071	.071
		28	1196	302	323	175	52	21	10	60	22	69	.270	.374

PITCHERS	W	L	PCT	G	GS	CG	SH	SV	IP	H	BB	SO	ERA
George Zettlein	18	9	.667	28	28	25	0	0	241	298	25	22	2.73
Ed Pinkham	1	0	1.000	3	0	0	0	1	10	10	3	0	3.48
	19	9	.679	28	28	25	0	1	251	308	28	22	2.76

1871 NATIONAL ASSOCIATION

NEW YORK Mutuals

16-17   .485   -7.5   4th   Bob Ferguson

BATTERS	POS/GAMES	GP	AB	R	H	BI	2B	3B	HR	BB	SO	SB	BA	SA
Joe Start	1B33	33	161	35	58	34	5	1	1	3	0	4	.360	.422
Dick Higham	2B11,OF8,C1,3B1	21	94	21	34	9	3	1	0	2	0	3	.362	.415
Dickey Pearce	SS33	33	163	31	44	20	5	0	0	4	1	0	.270	.301
Bob Ferguson	3B19,2B10,C4,P1	33	158	30	38	25	6	1	0	3	2	4	.241	.291
Dave Eggler	OF33	33	147	37	47	18	7	3	0	4	3	14	.320	.408
Dan Patterson	OF31,2B1	32	151	31	31	13	2	0	0	1	0	2	.205	.219
John Hatfield	OF24,2B7,3B2	33	168	41	43	22	3	2	0	4	0	10	.256	.298
Charlie Mills	C28,OF3,2B1	32	146	27	36	22	4	3	0	1	0	2	.247	.315
Rynie Wolters	P32,OF1	32	138	33	51	44	6	9	0	10	8	1	.370	.543
Charlie Smith	3B11,2B3	14	72	15	19	5	2	1	0	1	1	6	.264	.319
Frank Fleet	P1	1	6	1	2	1	0	0	0	0	0	0	.333	.333
		33	1402	302	403	213	43	21	1	33	15	46	.287	.350

PITCHERS	W	L	PCT	G	GS	CG	SH	SV	IP	H	BB	SO	ERA
Rynie Wolters	16	16	.500	32	32	31	1	0	283	345	39	22	3.43
Frank Fleet	0	1	.000	1	1	1	0	0	9	20	3	0	10.00
Bob Ferguson	0	0	----	1	0	0	0	0	1	8	0	0	27.00
	16	17	.485	33	33	32	1	0	293	373	42	22	3.72

WASHINGTON Olympics

15-15   .500   -7   5th   N. Young

BATTERS	POS/GAMES	GP	AB	R	H	BI	2B	3B	HR	BB	SO	SB	BA	SA
Everett Mills	1B32	32	157	38	43	24	6	4	1	3	1	2	.274	.382
Andy Leonard	2B20,OF10,SS1	31	148	33	43	30	8	3	0	3	1	14	.291	.385
Davy Force	SS31,3B1	32	162	45	45	29	9	4	0	4	0	8	.278	.383
Fred Waterman	3B27,C6	32	158	46	50	17	7	4	0	10	0	11	.316	.411
George Hall	OF32	32	136	31	40	17	3	3	2	8	0	2	.294	.404
John Glenn	OF26	26	120	25	37	21	3	2	0	3	1	1	.308	.367
Harry Berthrong	OF12,2B4,3B1	17	73	17	17	8	1	0	0	4	2	3	.233	.246
Doug Allison	C27	27	133	28	44	27	10	2	2	0	2	1	.331	.481
Asa Brainard	P30	30	134	24	30	21	4	0	0	7	2	4	.224	.254
Henry Burroughs	OF8,3B5	12	63	11	15	14	2	3	1	1	1	0	.238	.413
Tommy Beals	OF8,2B2	10	36	6	7	1	0	0	0	2	0	2	.194	.194
Charlie Sweasy	2B5	5	19	5	4	4	1	0	0	1	0	0	.211	.263
William Stearns	P2	2	9	1	0		0	0	0	2	2	0	.000	.000
Warren White	2B1	1	4	0	0	0	0	0	0	0	0	0	.000	.000
Pete Norton	OF1	1	1	0	0	0	0	0	0	0	1	0	.000	.000
		32	1353	310	375	213	54	26	6	48	13	48	.277	.369

PITCHERS	W	L	PCT	G	GS	CG	SH	SV	IP	H	BB	SO	ERA
Asa Brainard	12	15	.444	30	30	30	0	0	264	361	37	13	4.50
William Stearns	2	0	1.000	2	2	2	0	0	18	10	8	0	2.50
	15	15	.500	32	32	32	0	0	282	371	45	13	4.37

TROY Haymakers

13-15   .464   -8   6th   Pike - Craver

BATTERS	POS/GAMES	GP	AB	R	H	BI	2B	3B	HR	BB	SO	SB	BA	SA
Clipper Flynn	1B19,OF9,3B1	29	142	43	48	27	6	1	0	4	2	3	.338	.394
Bill Craver	2B18,SS4,C3,1B2	27	118	26	38	26	8	1	0	3	0	6	.322	.407
Dickie Flowers	SS20,P1,2B1	21	105	39	33	18	5	4	0	4	0	4	.314	.438
Steve Bellan	3B28,SS1	29	128	26	32	23	3	3	0	9	2	4	.250	.320
Tom York	OF29	29	145	36	37	23	5	7	2	9	1	2	.255	.428
Steve King	OF29	29	144	45	57	34	10	6	0	1	1	3	.396	.549
Lip Pike	OF18,2B6,1B4	28	130	43	49	39	10	7	4	5	7	3	.377	.654
Mike McGeary	C26,SS3	29	148	42	39	12	4	0	0	6	0	20	.264	.291
John McMullin	P29	29	136	38	38	32	0	5	0	8	6	11	.279	.353
Ned Connors	1B4,OF2,2B1	7	33	6	7	2	0	0	0	0	0	0	.212	.212
E.P. Bevens	2B3	3	15	7	6	5	0	0	0	0	0	0	.400	.400
Dave Abercrombie	SS1	1	4	0	0	0	0	0	0	0	0	0	.000	.000
		29	1248	351	384	241	51	34	6	49	19	62	.308	.417

1871 NATIONAL ASSOCIATION

TROY (cont.)
Haymakers

PITCHERS	W	L	PCT	G	GS	CG	SH	SV	IP	H	BB	SO	ERA
John McMullin	12	15	.444	29	29	28	0	0	249	430	75	12	5.53
Dickie Flowers	0	0	----	1	0	0	0	0	1	1	0	0	0.00
	13	15	.464	29	29	28	0	0	250	431	75	12	5.51

CLEVELAND
Forest Citys

10-19 .345 -11.5 7th Charlie Pabor

BATTERS	POS/GAMES	GP	AB	R	H	BI	2B	3B	HR	BB	SO	SB	BA	SA
Jim Carleton	1B29	29	127	31	32	18	8	1	0	8	3	2	.252	.331
Gene Kimball	2B17,SS6,OF6	29	131	18	25	9	1	0	0	3	2	5	.191	.198
John Bass	SS22	22	89	18	27	18	1	10	3	3	4	0	.303	.640
Ezra Sutton	3B29	29	128	35	45	23	3	7	3	1	0	3	.352	.555
Art Allison	OF29	29	137	28	40	19	4	5	0	2	5	3	.292	.394
Charlie Pabor	OF28	29	142	24	42	18	2	4	0	1	3	1	.296	.366
Elmer White	OF13,C2	15	70	13	18	9	2	0	0	1	6	0	.257	.286
Deacon White	C27,2B2	29	146	40	47	21	6	5	1	4	1	2	.322	.452
Al Pratt	P28,OF7	29	130	31	34		6	8	0	1	0	1	.262	.431
Caleb Johnson	2B8,OF7,SS1	16	67	10	15	7	1	0	0	0	1	1	.224	.239
Joe Quest	2B2,SS1	3	13	1	3	2	1	0	0	1	0	0	.231	.308
G. Ewell	OF1	1	3	0	0	0	0	0	0	0	0	0	.000	.000
Joe Battin	OF1	1	3	0	0	0	0	0	0	1	0	0	.000	.000
		29	1186	249	328	144	35	40	7	26	25	18	.277	.391

PITCHERS	W	L	PCT	G	GS	CG	SH	SV	IP	H	BB	SO	ERA
Al Pratt	10	17	.370	28	28	22	0	0	225	296	47	34	3.77
Charlie Pabor	0	2	.000	7	1	1	0	0	29	50	6	0	6.75
	10	19	.345	29	29	23	0	0	254	346	53	34	4.11

FORT WAYNE
Kekiongas

7-12 .368 -9.5 8th Lennon - Deane

BATTERS	POS/GAMES	GP	AB	R	H	BI	2B	3B	HR	BB	SO	SB	BA	SA
Jim Foran	1B15,OF4	19	89	21	31	18	1	3	1	2	1	1	.348	.461
Tom Carey	2B18,SS1	19	87	16	20	10	2	0	0	2	1	5	.230	.253
Wally Goldsmith	SS12,3B5,C1,2B1	19	88	8	18	12	1	0	0	4	2	0	.205	.216
Frank Selman	3B13,C2,SS1	14	65	14	15	10	3	0	1	4	0	1	.231	.323
Bill Kelly	OF17,1B1	18	67	16	15	7	1	1	0	6	1	0	.224	.306
Sam Armstrong	OF12	12	49	9	11	5	2	1	0	0	1	0	.224	.269
Ed Mincher	OF9	9	36	4	8	5	0	0	0	0	0	1	.222	.222
Bill Lennon	C12	12	48	5	11	5	3	0	0	1	0	1	.229	.292
Bobby Mathews	P19	19	89	15	24	10	3	1	0	2	0	2	.270	.326
Peter Donnelly	OF9,3B1	9	34	7	7	3	1	1	0	1	2	0	.206	.294
Harry Deane	OF6	6	22	3	4	2	0	1	0	2	0	0	.182	.273
Jim Hallinan	SS5	5	25	7	5	2	0	0	0	2	0	1	.200	.200
Joe Quinn	C5	5	17	8	4	2	0	0	0	4	0	3	.235	.235
Henry Kohler	1B2,3B1	3	12	0	2	1	1	0	0	0	0	0	.167	.250
Joe McDermott	OF2	2	8	3	2	1	0	0	0	1	1	1	.250	.250
Bill Barrett	C1,3B1	1	5	1	1	1	1	0	0	0	0	0	.200	.200
Neal Phelps	1B1	1	3	0	0	0	0	0	0	1	0	0	.000	.000
Charlie Bierman	1B1	1	2	0	0	0	0	0	0	0	1	0	.000	.000
		19	746	137	178	94	19	8	2	33	9	16	.239	.294

PITCHERS	W	L	PCT	G	GS	CG	SH	SV	IP	H	BB	SO	ERA
Bobby Mathews	6	11	.353	19	19	19	1	0	169	261	21	17	5.17
	7	12	.368	19	19	19	1	0	169	261	21	17	5.17

ROCKFORD
Forest Citys

4-21 .160 -15.5 9th Scott Hastings

BATTERS	POS/GAMES	GP	AB	R	H	BI	2B	3B	HR	BB	SO	SB	BA	SA
Denny Mack	1B24,P1,SS1	25	122	34	30	17	8	1	0	8	7	12	.246	.320
Bob Addy	2B22,SS3	25	118	30	32	13	6	0	0	4	0	8	.271	.322

ROCKFORD (cont.)
Forest Citys

BATTERS	POS/GAMES	GP	AB	R	H	BI	2B	3B	HR	BB	SO	SB	BA	SA
Chick Fulmer	SS15,1B1	16	63	11	17	3	1	3	0	5	1	0	.270	.381
Cap Anson	3B20,C3,2B2,OF1	25	120	29	39	16	11	3	0	2	1	6	.325	.467
Gat Stines	OF25	25	110	23	30	24	4	6	2	7	5	3	.273	.473
George Bird	OF25	25	106	19	28	13	2	5	0	3	2	1	.264	.377
Ralph Ham	OF18,3B7,SS2	25	113	25	28	12	4	0	0	1	7	6	.248	.283
Scott Hastings	C23,2B2,OF1	25	118	27	30	20	6	4	0	2	4	11	.254	.373
Cherokee Fisher	P24,SS1	25	123	24	28	22	3	3	1	3	1	1	.228	.325
Pony Sager	OF4,SS4	8	39	9	11	5	0	0	0	2	2	5	.282	.282
Al Barker	OF1	1	4	0	1	2	0	0	0	1	0	0	.250	.250
		25	1036	231	274	147	44	25	3	38	30	53	.264	.364

PITCHERS		W	L	PCT	G	GS	CG	SH	SV	IP	H	BB	SO	ERA
Cherokee Fisher		4	20	.167	24	24	22	1	0	213	295	31	15	4.35
Denny Mack		0	1	.000	3	1	1	0	0	13	20	3	1	3.46
		4	21	.160	25	25	23	1	0	226	315	34	16	4.30

1872 NATIONAL ASSOCIATION

Expansion

Most participants were pleased with the organization of the National Association in 1871. A logical sequence of games had been played — logically determining the champion. Naturally, more teams wanted to be a part of this new-fangled operation. And for a fee of only ten dollars, admission was yours.

Six of the nine teams from 1871 started play in 1872. The three westernmost 1871 entrants (Chicago, Rockford, and Fort Wayne) did not compete, but they were more than replaced by five additional teams, all from cities on the eastern seaboard. They were: Brooklyn (the Atlantics and Eckfords), Washington (the Nationals), Baltimore, and Middletown (Connecticut). These 11 teams would comprise the National Association circuit in 1872.

The Red Stockings of Boston quickly moved to the head of the class. They finished with a 39-8 record and a seven and one-half game lead. They accomplished this by having the league's best hitter, Ross Barnes (.422), as well as the best pitcher, Al Spalding (38-8, 1.98 ERA). This team, as in 1871, was basically a reincarnation of the famous undefeated Cincinnati Reds of 1869. No fewer than seven players (including Barnes and Spalding) played for both teams.

Baltimore, New York and Philadelphia also had fine years, finishing in a group about eight games back with winning percentages in the .600's. Baltimore was led by Lip Pike's league leading six home runs, and by third baseman Davy Force (.419) who played well after arriving from the disbanded Troy franchise. For New York, Dave Eggler led the circuit in runs (95) and hits (97), while in Philadelphia, Cap Anson (.414) contributed to his team's league leading batting average (.317).

The rest of the teams played only a partial schedule. The Washington Olympics played their last game in late May, and their sister team, the Nationals, followed suit in June. Troy gave up the ghost in July, with most of their players going to the Eckfords. Middletown and Cleveland stopped their seasons in August. Troy was the only one of this group to win more than they lost, finishing with a record of 15 and 10. Their best player was the aforementioned Davy Force (.398) who later peddled his wares for Baltimore.

The teams from Brooklyn, Cleveland, and Middletown did little to distinguish themselves. Each of these teams managed at least one good hitter. They were: Tom

Barlow (.329) for the Atlantics, Deacon White (.343) for Cleveland, John Clapp (.330) for Middletown, and Doug Allison (.342) for the Eckfords.

The two teams from Washington finished on the bottom with particularly dismal records. The Olympics won two of nine, while the Nationals won none of 11.

Expansion was a mixed bag for the National Association. There were two more teams, but six of the 11 teams completed only a partial schedule. Another disturbing trend was the disparity of the records. The league leader, Boston, lost only eight games, while the bottom four teams totaled only ten wins among them. The league was to see in the coming years that this trend was to continue and flourish with one team making a mockery of each pennant race.

BOSTON Red Stockings — 39-8 .830 1st Harry Wright

BATTERS	POS/GAMES	GP	AB	R	H	BI	2B	3B	HR	BB	SO	SB	BA	SA
Charlie Gould	1B44,OF2	45	214	39	57	33	7	8	0	2	3		.266	.374
Ross Barnes	2B45	45	230	81	97	44	28	2	1	9	4		.422	.574
George Wright	SS48	48	255	87	87	33	16	5	2	3	1		.341	.467
Harry Schafer	3B43,OF5	48	226	50	66	37	12	5	1	0	8		.292	.403
Andy Leonard	OF37,3B6,2B3	46	243	59	84	44	8	2	2	0	2		.346	.420
Fraley Rogers	OF42,1B6	45	204	39	58	28	10	1	1	1	4		.284	.358
Harry Wright	OF48,P7	48	208	39	54	22	6	0	0	9	2		.260	.288
Cal McVey	C40,0F9	46	237	56	73	41	11	3	0	0	1		.308	.380
Al Spalding	P48,OF7	48	244	60	87	48	13	5	0	3	1		.357	.451
Dave Birdsall	C11,OF5	16	76	11	14	14	3	0	0	1	0		.184	.224
		48	2137	521	677	344	114	31	7	28	26	47	.317	.409

PITCHERS		W	L	PCT	G	GS	CG	SH	SV	IP	H	BB	SO	ERA
Al Spalding		38	8	.826	48	48	41	3	0	405	412	27	27	1.98
Harry Wright		1	0	1.000	7	0	0	0	1	26	26	0	1	2.10
		39	8	.830	48	48	41	3	1	430	438	27	28	1.99

BALTIMORE Lord Baltimores — 35-19 .648 -7.5 2nd Craver - Mills

BATTERS	POS/GAMES		GP	AB	R	H	BI	2B	3B	HR	BB	SO	SB	BA	SA
Everett Mills	1B55		55	267	55	76	35	13	3	0	3	2		.285	.356
Tom Carey	2B26,SS8,3B3,OF3,1B1		42	197	43	58	27	7	1	2	0	2		.294	.371
John Radcliff	SS48,3B5,2B1		56	298	70	87	46	10	4	1	0	2		.292	.362
Davy Force	3B19	(2-2)	19	96	29	40	13	3	2	0	1	0		.417	.490
Lip Pike	OF24,2B21,3B9		56	285	68	84	62	10	4	6	3	5		.295	.421
Tom York	OF51		51	249	65	64	42	8	4	1	3	1		.257	.333
George Hall	OF53,1B1		53	252	69	82	40	14	8	1	3	1		.325	.456
Bill Craver	C25,OF5,3B2,2B2		35	180	55	50	24	5	3	0	5	2		.278	.339
Dick Higham	C21,OF18,2B6,1B1		50	244	72	85	40	9	2	2	2	3		.348	.426
Bobby Mathews	P49,OF3,3B2		50	221	35	50	21	2	1	0	3	2		.226	.244
Cherokee Fisher	P19,3B17,OF16		46	226	40	52	39	10	2	1	2	5		.230	.305
Scott Hastings	C9,2B2	(2-2)	13	61	16	19	4	3	1	0	1	2		.311	.393
			58	2576	617	747	393	94	35	14	27	28	35	.290	.370

PITCHERS		W	L	PCT	G	GS	CG	SH	SV	IP	H	BB	SO	ERA
Bobby Mathews		25	18	.581	49	47	39	0	0	405	477	52	55	3.15
Cherokee Fisher		10	1	.909	19	11	9	1	1	110	89	11	20	2.53
		35	19	.648	58	58	48	1	1	515	566	63	75	3.02

NEW YORK Mutuals — 34-20 .630 -8.5 3rd Pearce - Hatfield

BATTERS	POS/GAMES	GP	AB	R	H	BI	2B	3B	HR	BB	SO	SB	BA	SA
Joe Start	1B55	55	280	62	74	49	6	0	0	1	0		.264	.286
John Hatfield	2B56	56	287	75	91	45	12	2	1	9	5		.317	.383
Dickey Pearce	SS42,OF1	44	206	32	40	24	1	1	1	4	1		.194	.223
Bill Boyd	3B33,SS1,OF1	35	164	26	44	32	6	1	1	6	7		.268	.335
Dave Eggler	OF56	56	287	95	97	19	20	0	0	8	9		.338	.408
George Bechtel	OF51,1B1	51	246	60	74	39	11	2	0	6	3		.301	.362
John McMullin	OF53,P3	54	237	48	60	24	7	1	0	11	6		.253	.291
Nat Hicks	C55,OF2	56	266	55	81	35	12	2	0	5	3		.305	.365
Candy Cummings	P55	55	252	36	52		9	3	0	3	15		.206	.266
Chick Fulmer	3B23,SS13	36	167	28	51	12	2	1	1	2	3		.305	.347
Charlie Mills	OF5, C2	6	31	6	4	2	0	0	0	0	0		.129	.129
		56	2423	523	668	281	86	13	4	55	52	56	.276	.327

PITCHERS		W	L	PCT	G	GS	CG	SH	SV	IP	H	BB	SO	ERA
Candy Cummings		33	20	.623	55	55	53	3	0	497	600	30	43	2.52
John McMullin		1	0	1.000	3	1	1	0	0	15	18	2	1	3.60
		34	20	.630	56	56	54	3	0	512	618	32	44	2.55

1872 NATIONAL ASSOCIATION   15

PHILADELPHIA Athletics

30-14 .682 -7.5 4th Dick McBride

BATTERS	POS/GAMES	GP	AB	R	H	BI	2B	3B	HR	BB	SO	SB	BA	SA
Denny Mack	1B24,SS22	47	205	68	59	34	9	1	0	23	9		.288	.341
Wes Fisler	2B47	47	243	50	84	48	14	3	0	4	4		.346	.428
Mike McGeary	SS20,C25,OF1	47	226	68	81	35	9	2	0	2	1		.358	.416
Cap Anson	3B46	46	215	60	89	50	9	7	0	16	3		.414	.521
Fred Treacey	OF47	47	236	53	64	29	7	2	2	5	10		.271	.343
Ned Cuthbert	OF47	47	258	82	90	47	9	0	1	6	10		.349	.395
Levi Meyerle	OF25,SS1,3B1	27	146	31	48	31	7	6	1	0	1		.329	.479
Fergy Malone	C21,1B18	41	213	46	61	39	6	2	0	4	5		.286	.333
Dick McBride	P47	47	260	57	73		7	0	0	3	2		.281	.308
Al Reach	OF19,1B4	24	118	21	23	11	0	0	0	4	0		.195	.195
Dickie Flowers	SS3	3	15	1	4	4	0	0	0	2	2		.267	.267
Count Sensenderfer	OF1	1	5	2	2	1	0	0	0	0	0		.400	.400
		47	2140	539	678	329	77	23	4	69	47	58	.317	.380

PITCHERS		W	L	PCT	G	GS	CG	SH	SV	IP	H	BB	SO	ERA
Dick McBride		30	14	.682	47	47	47	1	0	419	513	26	44	3.01
		30	14	.682	47	47	47	1	0	419	513	26	44	3.01

TROY Haymakers

15-10 .600 -13 5th Jimmy Wood

BATTERS	POS/GAMES		GP	AB	R	H	BI	2B	3B	HR	BB	SO	SB	BA	SA
Bub McAtee	1B25		25	130	30	29	15	4	1	0	1	2		.223	.269
Jimmy Wood	2B25	(1-2)	25	116	40	38	27	9	3	2	2	1		.328	.509
Steve Bellan	SS9,3B8,OF6		23	118	22	30	16	4	1	0	0	0		.254	.305
Davy Force	3B16,SS9	(1-2)	25	133	40	53	16	7	1	0	1	0		.398	.466
Steve King	OF25		25	129	33	40	21	9	1	0	1	2		.310	.395
Phonney Martin	OF23,P8	(1-2)	25	120	27	34	14	3	1	0	0	1		.283	.325
Count Gedney	OF10	(1-2)	10	51	15	21	18	2	1	3	0	0		.412	.667
Doug Allison	C22,SS1		23	118	23	34	20	5	2	0	1	3		.288	.364
George Zettlein	P25,OF5	(1-2)	25	116	25	29		8	0	0	0	2		.250	.319
Charlie Hodes	SS5,OF4,C3,3B1		13	65	17	15	12	5	0	0	1	0		.231	.308
Candy Nelson	OF3,SS1	(1-2)	4	17	1	6	4	0	0	0	0	2		.353	.353
Mart King	OF3		3	11	0	0	1	0	0	0	0	1		.000	.000
			25	1124	273	329	148	56	11	5	7	14	9	.293	.375

PITCHERS			W	L	PCT	G	GS	CG	SH	SV	IP	H	BB	SO	ERA
George Zettlein		(1-2)	14	8	.636	25	22	17	2	0	188	209	8	17	2.54
Phonney Martin		(1-2)	1	2	.333	8	3	0	0	0	37	73	2	1	5.79
			15	10	.600	25	25	17	2	0	225	282	10	18	3.08

BROOKLYN Atlantics

9-28 .243 -25 6th Bob Ferguson

BATTERS	POS/GAMES		GP	AB	R	H	BI	2B	3B	HR	BB	SO	SB	BA	SA
Dutch Dehlman	1B37		37	164	30	36	15	3	0	0	3	1		.220	.238
Jim Hall	2B12,OF1		13	56	9	16	6	1	1	0	1	0		.286	.339
Jack Burdock	SS33,C2,2B1		37	174	26	45	15	2	1	0	1	1		.259	.282
Bob Ferguson	3B37		37	166	33	45	19	6	0	0	3	0		.271	.307
Jack Remsen	OF37		37	164	26	40	13	6	5	0	2	5		.244	.341
Al Thake	OF17,2B1		18	80	14	23	16	2	2	0	0	1		.287	.363
Jack McDonald	OF15		15	61	9	15	5	4	1	0	0	1		.246	.344
Tom Barlow	C34,SS2		37	170	34	56	10	2	0	0	3	2		.329	.341
Jim Britt	P37		37	157	24	39		7	0	0	5	7		.248	.293
Eddie Booth	OF13,2B1	(1-2)	15	62	11	18	8	5	0	0	0	0		.290	.371
E.P. Beavans	2B8,OF1,SS1		10	45	6	10	3	2	0	0	1	0		.222	.267
Bill Barrett	OF8	(1-2)	8	35	6	7	1	2	0	0	0	1		.200	.257
Charlie Lowe	2B7		7	32	1	5	2	0	0	0	0	2		.156	.156
Herm Doscher	OF6		6	25	4	9	5	1	0	0	0	1		.360	.400
John Kenney	2B3,OF2		5	19	0	0	1	0	0	0	0	1		.000	.000
Oliver Brown	OF4		4	16	0	1	0	0	0	0	0	1		.063	.063
Sam Jackson	OF3		3	12	0	2	0	1	0	0	0	0		.167	.250
Denny Clare	2B2		2	7	1	1	0	0	0	0	0	0		.143	.143
John Bass	OF2		2	7	0	1	1	1	0	0	0	0		.143	.286

BROOKLYN (cont.)
Atlantics

BATTERS	POS/GAMES		GP	AB	R	H	BI	2B	3B	HR	BB	SO	SB	BA	SA
Herb Worth	OF1		1	6	1	1	1	1	0	0	0	0		.167	.333
John Galvin	2B1		1	4	0	0	0	0	0	0	0	0		.000	.000
----- Higby	OF1		1	4	0	0	0	0	0	0	0	0		.000	.000
			37	1466	237	370	121	46	10	0	19	24	17	.252	.297

PITCHERS		W	L	PCT	G	GS	CG	SH	SV	IP	H	BB	SO	ERA
Jim Britt		9	28	.243	37	37	37	0	0	336	561	19	13	5.06
		9	28	.243	37	37	37	0	0	336	561	19	13	5.06

CLEVELAND
Forest Cities

6-16   .273   -20.5   7th   Hastings - White

BATTERS	POS/GAMES		GP	AB	R	H	BI	2B	3B	HR	BB	SO	SB	BA	SA
Joe Simmons	1B14,OF3		18	89	11	23	9	5	1	0	1	2		.258	.337
Charlie Sweasy	2B10,OF1		12	52	8	16	6	0	0	0	2	1		.308	.308
Jim Holdsworth	SS22	(1-2)	22	111	19	33	11	5	1	0	1	2		.297	.360
Ezra Sutton	3B22		22	108	30	30	10	8	1	0	1	1		.278	.370
Charlie Pabor	OF20,P2		21	90	12	19	7	0	0	0	0	0		.211	.211
Art Allison	OF19		19	85	13	23	8	6	0	0	0	2		.271	.341
Rynie Wolters	OF8,P12		16	69	7	16					0			.232	
Deacon White	C13,2B6,OF3		22	108	21	37	22	3	2	0	4	1		.343	.407
Scott Hastings	C11,OF7,2B	(1-2)	22	117	34	45	16	6	0	0	3	2		.385	.436
Al Pratt	P15,OF3		16	64	10	18					0			.281	
Jim Carleton	1B7		7	38	8	12	4	3	0	0	1	0		.316	.395
----- Mullen	OF1		1	4	1	0	0	0	0	0	0	0		.000	.000
			22	935	174	272	93	37	6	0	17	13	12	.291	.343

PITCHERS		W	L	PCT	G	GS	CG	SH	SV	IP	H	BB	SO	ERA
Rynie Wolters		3	6	.333	12	8	5	0	0	76	119	7	4	5.19
Al Pratt		2	9	.182	15	12	8	0	0	105	150	14	7	4.39
Charlie Pabor		1	1	.500	2	2	2	0	0	18	20	3	0	3.00
		6	16	.273	22	22	15	0	0	199	289	24	11	4.57

MIDDLETOWN
Mansfields

5-19   .208   -22.5   8th   John Clapp

BATTERS	POS/GAMES		GP	AB	R	H	BI	2B	3B	HR	BB	SO	SB	BA	SA
Tim Murnane	1B24		24	115	29	39	13	3	0	0	0	1		.339	.365
Eddie Booth	2B20,OF4	(1-2)	24	118	24	40	15	3	2	0	0	1		.339	.398
Jim O'Rourke	SS16,C5,3B2		23	100	27	33	15	3	0	0	2	0		.330	.360
George Fields	3B10,OF6,SS1		18	83	14	22	8	2	2	0	0	2		.265	.337
Frank McCarton	OF19		19	83	19	31	9	5	0	0	1	3		.373	.434
Jim Tipper	OF18,3B6		24	113	23	33	21	2	0	0	0	0		.292	.310
Ham Allen	OF10,SS6		15	59	8	15	11	2	0	0	0	1		.254	.288
John Clapp	C19		19	97	30	32	12	8	0	1	1	0		.330	.443
Cy Bentley	P18,OF8		23	115	26	27		3	4	0	0	2		.235	.330
Frank Buttery	P6,3B6,OF6		18	93	18	25	8	0	0	0	0	2		.269	.269
Asa Brainard	2B4,P2	(1-2)	6	25	2	5	0	0	0	0	1	0		.200	.200
Billy Arnold	OF2		2	8	2	1	0	0	0	0	0	0		.125	.125
Ralph Ham	SS1		1	5	0	2	1	0	0	0	0	0		.400	.400
			24	1014	220	305	113	31	8	1	5	12	5	.301	.350

PITCHERS		W	L	PCT	G	GS	CG	SH	SV	IP	H	BB	SO	ERA
Frank Buttery		3	2	.600	6	5	5	0	0	49	81	1	0	5.14
Cy Bentley		2	15	.118	18	17	16	0	0	154	273	12	5	6.15
Asa Brainard		0	2	.000	2	2	1	0	0	8	14	0	0	7.88
		5	19	.208	24	24	22	0	0	211	368	13	5	5.97

1872 NATIONAL ASSOCIATION

BROOKLYN Eckfords — 3-26 .103 -27 9th Jimmy Wood

BATTERS	POS/GAMES		GP	AB	R	H	BI	2B	3B	HR	BB	SO	SB	BA	SA
Andy Allison	1B23,OF2		24	99	11	15	7	2	0	0	0	3		.152	.172
Candy Nelson	2B8,OF8,3B2	(2-2)	18	76	12	19	7	2	0	0	2	2		.250	.276
Jim Snyder	SS22,OF3,C1		26	106	16	27	10	2	3	0	0	1		.255	.330
Frank Fleet	3B10,2B2,OF1		13	54	10	13	6	2	0	0	0	1		.241	.278
Count Gedney	OF18	(2-2)	18	72	4	11	5	1	0	0	0	0		.153	.167
Dan Patterson	OF11,1B1		12	47	6	8	3	1	0	0	0	1		.170	.191
Josh Snyder	OF9		9	42	3	6	1	2	0	0	1	1		.143	.190
Doug Allison	C18		18	79	18	27	6	2	1	0	1	2		.342	.392
Jim Clinton	3B9,OF8,SS4,2B3		25	97	13	23	7	2	1	0	0	2		.234	.277
Phonney Martin	P10,OF8	(2-2)	18	79	12	14	9	0	0	0	1	2		.177	.177
Marty Swandell	3B8,OF4,2B1,1B1		14	55	8	11	4	0	0	0	2	1		.200	.200
Dick Hunt	OF8,2B3		11	48	11	15	5	4	0	0	1	0		.313	.396
George Zettlein	P9	(1-2)	9	34		3		0	0	0	0	0		.088	
Joe McDermott	P7		7	33	3	9	3	3	0	0	1	2		.273	.364
Jimmy Wood	2B7	(2-2)	7	30	10	6	0	1	1	0	4	1		.200	.300
----- Kavanaugh	1B4,OF1		5	22	3	6	2	1	0	0	0	0		.273	.318
Al Martin	2B4		4	18	2	5	2	0	0	0	0	0		.278	.278
----- Malone	P3,OF1		4	16		5		0	0	0	0	0		.313	
---- Bestick	C4		4	14	0	3	1	0	0	0	0	0		.214	.214
----- Leutz	C4		4	13	2	1	0	0	0	0	0	0		.077	.077
Bill Allison	OF2,2B1		3	10	3	2	1	0	0	0	0	1		.200	.200
George Fletcher	OF2		2	8	1	3	1	0	0	0	0	0		.375	.375
Nat Jewett	C2		2	8	1	1	0	0	0	0	0	0		.125	.125
Jim Holdsworth	SS2	(2-2)	2	7	1	2	0	0	0	0	0	0		.286	.286
Jack McDonald	SS1	(1-2)	1	4	0	0	0	0	0	0	0	0		.000	.000
----- O'Rourke	P1		1	4	0	0	0	0	0	0	0	0		.000	.000
			29	1075	152	235	80	26	6	0	14	29	8	.219	.254

PITCHERS			W	L	PCT	G	GS	CG	SH	SV	IP	H	BB	SO	ERA
Phonney Martin		(2-2)	2	7	.222	10	9	9	0	0	85	142	4	2	4.45
George Zettlein		(2-2)	1	8	.111	9	9	8	0	0	75	105	6	8	2.99
----- O'Rourke			0	1	.000	1	1	1	0	0	9	16	2	0	6.00
----- Malone			0	3	.000	3	3	3	0	0	27	98	0	0	11.33
Joe McDermott			0	7	.000	7	7	7	0	0	63	142	12	1	8.29
			3	26	.103	29	29	28	0	0	259	503	23	11	5.73

WASHINGTON Olympics — 2-7 .222 -18 10th N. Young

BATTERS	POS/GAMES		GP	AB	R	H	BI	2B	3B	HR	BB	SO	SB	BA	SA
Clipper Flynn	1B9		9	40	4	9	2	1	0	0	0	0		.225	.250
Tommy Beals	2B5,SS2,OF2		9	36	7	12	5	0	2	0	1	1		.333	.444
Wally Goldsmith	SS5,2B4		9	40	4	10	5	0	0	0	0	0		.250	.250
Fred Waterman	3B7,C2		9	44	13	18	6	1	1	0	0	0		.409	.477
John Glenn	OF9	(1-2)	9	40	5	6	3	2	0	0	1	0		.150	.200
Val Robinson	OF7		7	32	6	6	4	0	0	0	1	1		.188	.188
George Heubel	OF5		5	23	2	3	1	1	0	0	0	0		.130	.174
Frank Selman	C7,3B2		9	41	3	10	1	3	0	0	0	0		.244	.317
Asa Brainard	P9	(1-2)	9	41	8	16	6	3	0	0	0	0		.390	.463
Bob Reach	SS2		2	8	1	2	0	0	0	0	0	0		.250	.250
Henry Burroughs	OF2		2	7	1	1	0	1	0	0	1	0		.143	.286
Dick Hurley	OF2		2	7	0	0	0	0	0	0	0	1		.000	.000
Bill Barrett	C1		1	4	0	0	0	0	0	0	0	0		.000	.000
			9	363	54	93	33	12	3	0	4	3	0	.256	.306

PITCHERS			W	L	PCT	G	GS	CG	SH	SV	IP	H	BB	SO	ERA
Asa Brainard			2	7	.222	9	9	9	0	0	79	147	5	1	6.38
			2	7	.222	9	9	9	0	0	79	147	5	1	6.38

WASHINGTON Nationals — 0-11 .000 -21 11th Paul Hines

BATTERS	POS/GAMES	GP	AB	R	H	BI	2B	3B	HR	BB	SO	SB	BA	SA
Paul Hines	1B10,3B1	11	50	10	12	4	1	1	0	0	0		.240	.300
John Hollingshead	2B9	9	46	12	15	5	0	1	0	1	0		.326	.370

WASHINGTON (cont.)
Nationals

BATTERS	POS/GAMES		GP	AB	R	H	BI	2B	3B	HR	BB	SO	SB	BA	SA
Joe Doyle	SS6,2B1,3B1		9	42	7	12	8	0	0	0	0	0		.286	.286
Warren White	3B9,SS1		10	45	7	12	3	0	0	0	0	0		.267	.267
Ed Mincher	OF11		11	54	4	5	3	0	0	0	0	1		.093	.093
Seem Studley	OF5		5	21	3	2	2	0	0	0	0	0		.095	.095
Oscar Bielaski	OF10		10	46	13	9	2	0	0	0	0	0		.196	.196
Bill Lennon	C11		11	55	11	12	5	2	0	0	0	0		.218	.255
William Stearns	P11		11	47	7	11		0	0	0	0	2		.234	.234
Dennis Coughlin	OF5,SS2,2B1	(2-2)	8	38	5	12	6	0	0	0	0	0		.316	.316
John Glenn	OF1		1	4	0	2	0	0	0	0	0	0		.500	.500
Joe Miller	1B1		1	4	0	1	0	0	0	0	0	0		.250	.250
----- Spencer	SS1		1	4	1	0	0	0	0	0	0	0		.000	.000
Bill Yeatman	OF1		1	4	0	0	0	0	0	0	0	0		.000	.000
			11	460	80	105	<u>38</u>	3	2	0	1	3		.228	.243

PITCHERS		W	L	PCT	G	GS	CG	SH	SV	IP	H	BB	SO	ERA
William Stearns		0	11	.000	11	11	11	0	0	99	194	3	2	6.91
		0	11	.000	11	11	11	0	0	99	194	3	2	6.91

1873 NATIONAL ASSOCIATION

Ross Barnes

There were plenty of good hitters in the National Association. Cap Anson of the Athletics, George Wright and Cal McVey of the Red Stockings, and Levi Meyerle of Philadelphia were just a few. However, this august group was surpassed by one man—Ross Barnes of the Red Stockings.

Barnes was not a physically imposing ball player. He stood 5' 8", and weighed 145 pounds—an average size for the nineteenth century. But he seemed a giant when he hit. Born in Mount Morris, Illinois in 1850, Barnes started his career with the Forest Citys club of Rockford, Illinois. In 1871, he and teammate Al Spalding joined Boston in the newly formed National Association. Here Barnes's career really took off. In his career in the Association, Barnes batted: .401, .422, .425, .344, and .361. The second and third years he led the league. His overall average of .388 for the five years was easily the best. In addition, he led his team to four pennants in five years.

In 1873, the league dropped from eleven to nine teams. One of the Brooklyn teams (Eckfords) and one of the Washington teams (Nationals) dropped out in addition to Cleveland and Middletown. In turn, a second team from Philadelphia (the Philadelphias), another team from Baltimore (the Marylands), and a team from Elizabeth (New Jersey) were added.

As the season progressed, the Red Stockings caught the front running Philadelphias in September, and passed them in October. Unsurprisingly, they were spearheaded by Ross Barnes who posted his finest year. He led the league in the following categories: batting average (.425), runs (125), hits (137), doubles (28), triples (10), and slugging percentage (.602). A notch below this performance were teammates George Wright (.388) and Deacon White (.390) who also had the most runs batted in finishing with 64. The team as a whole batted .338, which would prove to be the highest in Association history.

The new entrant from Philadelphia, the Philadelphias, came close, finishing only four games back. Their best players were Levi Meyerle (.349), and pitcher George Zettlein (36-15). Baltimore, New York, and the Athletics also enjoyed good seasons. Baltimore's Lip Pike led the league with four home runs, New York's pitcher Bobby Mathews had 75 strikeouts (almost double any other pitcher) and the Athletic's Cap Anson finished second in the batting race at .398.

The rest of the league did not have a good year. Only Brooklyn finished the season, their sole exceptional player being Charlie Pabor (.360). The bottom trio of teams, playing partial seasons, combined for ten wins — eight from Washington, two from Elizabeth, and none from Maryland. This was the second year in a row the league had an entrant with zero wins. The latter two teams finished their seasons early — the Marylands in July and Elizabeth in August.

Ross Barnes continued his torrid hitting in the National League in 1876, winning another batting title. His career then tailed off drastically due to injuries and rule changes which did not favor his hitting style. His baseball career came to an end in 1881 in the city where he achieved his most glory — Boston. Despite his lackluster end, Barnes showed the baseball world that one did not have to be a physical giant to rule the batter's box. And for the duration of the National Association, Ross Barnes did just that.

1873 NATIONAL ASSOCIATION

BOSTON Red Stockings
43-16 .729   1st   Harry Wright

BATTERS	POS/GAMES		GP	AB	R	H	BI	2B	3B	HR	BB	SO	SB	BA	SA
Jim O'Rourke	1B32,OF20,C5		57	280	79	98	46	22	3	1	14	1		.350	.461
Ross Barnes	2B47,3B13		60	322	125	137	61	28	10	3	18	2		.425	.602
George Wright	SS59		59	325	99	126	48	13	7	3	8	2		.388	.498
Harry Schafer	3B47,OF13		60	295	65	79	43	8	3	2	3	1		.268	.336
Harry Wright	OF55,P12		58	266	57	67	33	8	3	2	10	3		.252	.327
Andy Leonard	OF45,2B12,SS1		58	302	81	95	58	12	6	0	4	0		.315	.394
Bob Addy	OF31	(2-2)	31	152	37	54	36	6	2	1	1	0		.355	.441
Deacon White	C55,OF5		60	310	79	121	64	20	8	0	0	2		.390	.506
Al Spalding	P57,OF3		60	322	83	106	59	13	2	1	3	1		.329	.391
Jack Manning	1B28,OF5		32	159	29	43	22	5	2	0	1	11		.270	.327
Dave Birdsall	OF3		3	12	4	1	1	0	0	0	0	0		.083	.083
Fraley Rogers	1B1		1	6	1	2	2	2	0	0	0	0		.333	.667
Charlie Sweasy	2B1		1	4	0	1	0	0	0	0	0	0		.250	.250
			60	2755	739	930	473	137	46	13	62	24	39	.338	.435

PITCHERS		W	L	PCT	G	GS	CG	SH	SV	IP	H	BB	SO	ERA
Al Spalding		41	14	.745	60	55	48	1	2	498	643	28	31	2.46
Harry Wright		2	2	.500	12	5	0	0	1	38	65	7	0	4.23
		43	16	.729	60	60	48	1	3	536	708	35	31	2.59

PHILADELPHIA Philadelphias
36-17 .679 -4   2nd   Malone - Wood

BATTERS	POS/GAMES		GP	AB	R	H	BI	2B	3B	HR	BB	SO	SB	BA	SA
Denny Mack	1B40,OF4,2B1,SS1		48	205	55	60	19	5	0	0	15	9		.293	.317
Jimmy Wood	2B42		42	209	67	67	27	11	1	0	8	1		.321	.383
Chick Fulmer	SS48,C1,P1		49	236	42	66	37	11	3	1	2	3		.280	.364
Levi Meyerle	3B48		48	238	53	83	56	14	4	3	2	0		.349	.479
Fred Treacey	OF51		51	243	49	62	32	7	2	1	5	6		.255	.313
Ned Cuthbert	OF51		51	278	78	77	32	5	3	2	2	4		.277	.338
George Bechtel	OF50,P3		53	258	53	63	38	12	1	1	9	1		.244	.310
Fergy Malone	C52,SS1		53	259	59	75	42	11	2	0	14	7		.290	.347
George Zettlein	P51		51	241	39	50		2	0	0	1	4		.207	.216
Jim Devlin	1B12,3B5,SS3,OF2		23	99	18	24	9	4	4	0	2	4		.242	.364
Bob Addy	2B10	(1-2)	10	51	12	16	9	1	0	0	2	0		.314	.333
Johnny Ryan	OF1, 1B1		2	8	1	2	1	0	0	0	0	0		.250	.250
			53	2325	526	645	302	83	20	8	62	39	44	.277	.341

PITCHERS		W	L	PCT	G	GS	CG	SH	SV	IP	H	BB	SO	ERA
George Zettlein		36	15	.706	51	51	49	0	0	460	593	41	28	2.70
George Bechtel		0	2	.000	3	2	1	0	0	16	27	2	0	4.50
Chick Fulmer		0	0	----	2	0	0	0	0	5	7	1	0	3.60
		36	17	.679	53	53	50	0	0	481	627	44	28	2.77

BALTIMORE Lord Baltimores
34-22 .607 -7.5   3rd   McVey - Carey

BATTERS	POS/GAMES	GP	AB	R	H	BI	2B	3B	HR	BB	SO	SB	BA	SA
Everett Mills	1B52,OF1	54	263	64	87	57	16	6	0	2	1		.331	.437
Tom Carey	2B51,3B3,SS3	56	290	76	97	55	18	3	2	1	2		.334	.438
John Radcliff	SS22,3B22,2B1	45	245	59	70	33	10	1	0	3	2		.286	.335
Davy Force	3B32,SS15,P2	49	234	77	86	31	12	3	0	9	0		.368	.444
Tom York	OF57	57	277	70	84	49	10	5	2	3	3		.303	.397
Lip Pike	OF56,2B1	56	287	71	90	48	18	8	4	6	4		.314	.474
George Hall	OF35	35	168	44	58	30	8	4	1	2	0		.345	.458
Bill Craver	C20,SS12,OF3,1B1	41	196	45	57	27	7	4	0	2	3		.291	.367
Candy Cummings	P42	42	192	30	48		5	0	0	5	5		.250	.276
Cal McVey	C17,OF6,SS5,2B3,1B3,3B1	38	192	49	73	33	8	5	3	3	2		.380	.521
Scott Hastings	C19,OF10,2B1	30	146	41	41	12	5	0	0	4	1		.281	.315
Asa Brainard	P14,OF2,2B1	16	69	18	18	8	2	0	0	0	2		.261	.290
Bill Barrett	OF1,SS1	1	4	0	1	0	0	0	0	0	0		.250	.250
		57	2563	644	810	383	119	39	12	40	25	21	.316	.407

1873 NATIONAL ASSOCIATION

BALTIMORE (cont.)
Lord Baltimores

PITCHERS	W	L	PCT	G	GS	CG	SH	SV	IP	H	BB	SO	ERA
Candy Cummings	28	14	.667	42	42	42	1	0	382	475	33	31	2.66
Asa Brainard	5	7	.417	14	14	12	0	0	109	182	9	3	4.14
Davy Force	1	1	.500	3	1	1	0	0	18	23	0	0	3.50
	34	22	.607	57	57	55	1	0	509	680	42	34	3.01

NEW YORK
Mutuals

29-24 .547 -11 4th Hatfield - Start

BATTERS	POS/GAMES		GP	AB	R	H	BI	2B	3B	HR	BB	SO	SB	BA	SA
Joe Start	1B53		53	251	42	67	28	11	3	1	4	0		.267	.347
Candy Nelson	2B27,OF6,3B3		36	168	28	55	22	6	1	0	1	2		.327	.375
Jim Holdsworth	SS53		53	233	46	75	27	6	8	0	0	3		.322	.416
John Hatfield	3B42,2B10		52	255	54	78	45	6	7	2	3	2		.306	.408
Count Gedney	OF53		53	224	41	60	25	5	5	1	7	5		.268	.348
Dave Eggler	OF53		53	268	82	90	34	16	5	0	5	2		.336	.433
Phonney Martin	OF27,P6		31	139	12	30	14	2	0	0	0	4		.216	.230
Nat Hicks	C28		28	121	12	29	14	2	2	1	7	0		.240	.314
Bobby Mathews	P51,OF1		52	223	40	43	13	4	3	0	10	3		.193	.238
Dick Higham	OF18,2B16,C14,3B1		49	245	57	77	34	6	7	0	2	1		.314	.396
Doug Allison	C11,OF1	(2-2)	11	49	6	11	3	1	0	0	1	0		.224	.245
Steve Bellan	3B7,2B1		8	32	4	7	3	2	0	0	2	0		.219	.281
Neal Phelps	OF1		1	6	0	0	0	0	0	0	0	0		.000	.000
			53	2214	424	622	262	67	41	5	42	22	15	.281	.355

PITCHERS	W	L	PCT	G	GS	CG	SH	SV	IP	H	BB	SO	ERA
Bobby Mathews	29	23	.558	52	52	47	2	0	443	489	62	75	2.56
Phonney Martin	0	1	.000	6	1	1	0	0	34	50	7	1	3.44
	29	24	.547	53	53	48	2	0	477	539	69	76	2.62

PHILADELPHIA
Athletics

28-23 .549 -11 5th Dick McBride

BATTERS	POS/GAMES	GP	AB	R	H	BI	2B	3B	HR	BB	SO	SB	BA	SA
Cap Anson	1B36,3B10,2B4,C1,OF1	52	254	53	101	36	9	2	0	5	1		.398	.449
Wes Fisler	2B35,1B10	44	218	44	75	42	12	4	1	2	2		.344	.450
Mike McGeary	SS43,C10,3B1	52	275	63	83	30	9	1	0	1	1		.302	.342
Ezra Sutton	3B44,SS7,2B1	51	242	51	81	32	7	7	0	2	2		.335	.421
John McMullin	OF51,P1	52	227	54	62	29	8	1	0	8	4		.273	.317
Cherokee Fisher	OF45,P13,1B1,2B1	51	253	50	66	35	4	3	1	4	5		.261	.312
Tim Murnane	OF29,1B8,2B6	41	176	53	39	10	3	1	1	8	13		.222	.267
John Clapp	C42,SS2,2B1	45	204	36	62	28	11	2	1	2	2		.304	.392
Dick McBride	P46,OF8	46	253	41	71		7	0	0	2	0		.281	.308
Count Sensenderfer	OF19,1B1	20	86	12	24	8	1	0	0	0	2		.279	.291
Al Reach	OF8,2B5	13	73	13	16	9	5	1	0	0	0		.219	.315
Joe Battin	OF1	1	5	4	3	2	0	0	0	1	0		.600	.600
		52	2266	474	683	261	76	22	4	35	32	29	.301	.360

PITCHERS	W	L	PCT	G	GS	CG	SH	SV	IP	H	BB	SO	ERA
Dick McBride	24	19	.558	46	46	38	3	0	383	453	47	25	3.32
Cherokee Fisher	3	4	.429	13	5	5	0	1	84	90	10	14	1.81
John McMullin	1	0	1.000	1	1	1	0	0	8	10	1	2	2.25
	28	23	.549	52	52	44	3	1	475	553	58	41	3.03

BROOKLYN
Atlantics

17-37 .315 -23.5 6th Bob Ferguson

BATTERS	POS/GAMES	GP	AB	R	H	BI	2B	3B	HR	BB	SO	SB	BA	SA
Dutch Dehlman	1B54	54	221	50	52	17	5	2	0	9	7		.235	.276
Jack Burdock	2B55	55	245	56	62	33	9	2	2	7	4		.253	.331
Dickey Pearce	SS55	55	262	42	72	25	6	0	1	8	2		.275	.309
Bob Ferguson	3B50,P4	51	228	36	59	24	5	5	0	4	9		.259	.325
Charlie Pabor	OF55	55	228	36	82	41	7	4	0	6	3		.360	.425

1873 NATIONAL ASSOCIATION

BROOKLYN (cont.)
Atlantics

BATTERS	POS/GAMES		GP	AB	R	H	BI	2B	3B	HR	BB	SO	SB	BA	SA
Jack Remsen	OF50		50	207	29	61	29	7	6	1	2	2		.295	.401
Bill Boyd	OF43,3B5		50	228	31	63	30	10	5	1	2	2		.276	.377
Tom Barlow	C55		55	271	48	74	13	2	2	1	4	0		.273	.306
Jim Britt	P54,OF3		54	240	29	47		6	0	0	8	14		.196	.221
Eddie Booth	OF16	(2-2)	16	69	8	14	7	3	1	0	3	0		.203	.275
Herm Doscher	OF1		1	6	1	1	1	0	0	0	0	0		.167	.167
Henry Kessler	1B1		1	5	0	1	1	0	0	0	0	0		.200	.200
			55	2210	366	588	221	60	27	6	53	43	18	.266	.326

PITCHERS		W	L	PCT	G	GS	CG	SH	SV	IP	H	BB	SO	ERA
Jim Britt		17	36	.321	54	54	51	1	0	481	696	40	15	3.89
Bob Ferguson		0	1	.000	4	1	1	0	0	19	41	2	0	6.05
		17	37	.315	55	55	52	1	0	500	737	42	15	3.98

WASHINGTON
Washingtons

8-31 .205 -25 7th N. Young

BATTERS	POS/GAMES		GP	AB	R	H	BI	2B	3B	HR	BB	SO	SB	BA	SA
John Glenn	1B39		39	185	39	49	18	9	2	1	3	0		.265	.351
Tommy Beals	2B26,C11,OF1		37	169	35	46	20	8	6	0	1	1		.272	.391
Joe Gerhardt	SS13		13	56	6	12	6	2	1	0	0	5		.214	.286
Warren White	3B37,SS2		39	160	29	43	18	3	5	0	0	1		.269	.350
Oscar Bielaski	OF38		38	173	35	49	20	2	3	0	4	5		.283	.329
Paul Hines	OF36,2B2,C1		39	181	33	60	26	11	2	2	1	1		.331	.448
Holly Hollingshead	OF30,2B1		30	136	25	35	19	1	3	0	0	6		.257	.309
Pop Snyder	C28,OF1		28	108	16	21	3	2	0	0	3	3		.194	.213
William Stearns	P32		32	133	22	24		1	0	0	5	10		.180	.188
John Donnelly	SS13,2B11,OF6		30	137	15	35	17	3	0	0	1	0		.255	.277
Fred Waterman	SS9,OF4,3B2		15	80	20	28	10	3	3	0	1	1		.350	.463
----- Greyson	P7		7	28	4	4		0	0	0	0	0		.143	.143
Ed Atkinson	OF2		2	8	2	0	0	0	0	0	0	0		.000	.000
Bob Reach	SS1		1	5	1	1	0	0	0	0	0	0		.200	.200
Howard Wall	SS1		1	4	1	1	0	0	0	0	0	0		.250	.250
			39	1563	283	408	157	45	25	3	19	33	5	.261	.328

PITCHERS		W	L	PCT	G	GS	CG	SH	SV	IP	H	BB	SO	ERA
William Stearns		7	25	.219	32	32	32	0	0	283	481	15	4	4.55
----- Greyson		1	6	.143	7	7	7	0	0	63	112	7	3	5.43
		8	31	.205	39	39	39	0	0	346	593	22	7	4.71

ELIZABETH
Resolutes

2-21 .087 -23 8th J. Benjamin

BATTERS	POS/GAMES		GP	AB	R	H	BI	2B	3B	HR	BB	SO	SB	BA	SA
Mat Campbell	1B17,SS3,OF1		21	82	9	12	3	0	0	0	3	6		.146	.146
Ben Laughlin	2B12		12	50	3	12	6	1	0	0	0	0		.240	.260
Favel Wordsworth	SS11,OF1		12	42	5	10	3	1	0	0	2	1		.238	.262
Al Nevins	3B11,OF1		13	54	7	11	2	0	2	0	0	3		.204	.278
Henry Austin	OF23		23	101	10	25	11	3	3	0	0	4		.248	.337
Art Allison	OF20,1B2,C1		23	99	12	32	11	5	0	0	0	0		.323	.374
Eddie Booth	OF17,2B1	(1-2)	18	72	11	21	4	2	2	0	0	2		.292	.375
Doug Allison	C18,OF3	(1-2)	18	84	11	24	8	5	0	0	0	0		.286	.345
Frank Fleet	2B8,SS7,3B3,P3,1B1		22	90	11	23	10	2	0	0	1	2		.256	.278
Hugh Campbell	P19,2B1,OF1		20	86	10	13		0	1	0	2	1		.151	.174
John Farrow	C7,OF2,SS2,1B1		12	48	2	8	3	1	0	0	0	3		.167	.188
Jim Clinton	3B9		9	38	5	9	3	1	0	0	0	0		.237	.263
Marty Swandell	1B2		2	9	1	1	1	0	0	0	0	0		.111	.111
Len Lovett	P1		1	5	1	2	1	0	0	0	0	0		.400	.400
Fred Crane	2B1		1	4	0	1	1	0	0	0	0	0		.250	.250
Rynie Wolters	P1		1	4	0	0		0	0	0	0	0		.000	.000
			23	868	98	204	67	21	8	0	8	22	2	.235	.278

ELIZABETH (cont.)
Resolutes

PITCHERS	W	L	PCT	G	GS	CG	SH	SV	IP	H	BB	SO	ERA
Hugh Campbell	2	16	.111	19	18	18	0	0	165	250	7	5	2.84
Len Lovett	0	1	.000	1	1	1	0	0	9	22	1	1	7.00
Rynie Wolters	0	1	.000	1	1	1	0	0	9	13	1	1	0.00
Frank Fleet	0	3	.000	3	3	2	0	0	24	57	0	1	5.63
	2	21	.087	23	23	22	0	0	207	342	9	8	3.22

BALTIMORE   0-6   .000   -16.5   9th   Bill Smith
Marylands

BATTERS	POS/GAMES	GP	AB	R	H	BI	2B	3B	HR	BB	SO	SB	BA	SA
Bill Lennon	1B3,3B1,C1	5	19	2	4	0	1	0	0	0	0		.211	.263
Marty Simpson	2B2,C2	4	15	4	2	1	0	0	0	0	0		.133	.133
John Smith	SS2,OF2,2B1	5	19	2	2	1	0	0	0	0	0		.105	.105
Henry Kohler	3B5,C1	6	25	2	3	0	3	0	0	0	0		.120	.240
Bill French	OF2,1B2,3B1,P1	5	18	3	4	1	0	0	0	0	0		.222	.222
Mike Hooper	OF2,C1	3	14	3	3	0	0	0	0	0	0		.214	.214
John Sheppard	OF2,C1	3	11	1	0	0	0	0	0	0	0		.000	.000
Bill Smith	C1,OF3,2B2	6	23	2	4	1	0	0	0	0	0		.174	.174
Ed Stratton	OF1,P3	4	16	2	2		0	0	0	0	0		.125	.125
Louis Say	SS2,OF1	3	12	1	2	2	0	0	0	0	0		.167	.167
Joe Kernan	2B1,OF1	2	8	1	3	1	0	0	0	0	0		.375	.375
Red Woodhead	SS1	1	5	1	0	0	0	0	0	0	0		.000	.000
----- Jones	OF1	1	4	0	3	0	1	0	0	0	0		.750	1.000
George Popplein	3B1,OF1	1	4	0	0	0	0	0	0	0	0		.000	.000
Tom Johns	OF1	1	4	0	0	0	0	0	0	0	0		.000	.000
Wally Goldsmith	2B1	1	4	0	0	0	0	0	0	0	0		.000	.000
----- McDoolan	P1	1	4	1	0		0	0	0	0	0		.000	.000
Frank Selman	P1	1	3	1	1	0	0	0	0	0	0		.333	.333
----- Eland	OF1	1	3	0	0	0	0	0	0	0	0		.000	.000
		6	211	26	33	7	5	0	0	0	0		.156	.180

PITCHERS	W	L	PCT	G	GS	CG	SH	SV	IP	H	BB	SO	ERA
Frank Selman	0	1	.000	1	1	1	0	0	9	21	0	0	8.00
Bill French	0	1	.000	1	1	1	0	0	9	30	0	0	12.00
----- McDoolan	0	1	.000	1	1	1	0	0	9	18	0	0	3.00
Ed Stratton	0	3	.000	3	3	3	0	0	27	75	0	0	8.33
	0	6	.000	6	6	6	0	0	54	144	0	0	8.00

1874 NATIONAL ASSOCIATION

The Boston Red Stockings

The Boston Red Stockings were one of the founding members of the National Association. They were also the most fabulously successful of all the league's entrants. They won pennants four of the five years of the Association's existence. The year they did not win (1871) Boston finished second two games out. In none of their pennant winning years, except 1873, were they seriously threatened for the lead. Boston's aggregate record for the five-year period was 225-60, which translates to a .789 winning percentage. The Athletics of Philadelphia had the next best five-year record at 165-86, a .657 percentage. This was a fine record, but it was still 60 wins less than Boston. The Red Stockings' team batting average during these five years was equally impressive at .321, leading the league in all years but 1871. In reality, the Boston team simply outclassed the rest of the league so totally and completely, that the only real competition was for second place in all phases of the game.

In 1874, the league fell back to eight teams. Among them were two new teams — Chicago and Hartford. The teams from Washington, Elizabeth, and the Marylands dropped out. Although the league had fewer teams, the year was considered a success because all eight teams completed at least 45 games — a league first.

One interesting sidelight to the 1874 season, was the mid-season tour to England. In July, Al Spalding took two teams (Boston and Philadelphia Athletics) to England for the express purpose of introducing the national pastime to the mother country. The two teams played a series of 15 exhibition games in several different locales, but met only with middling success. Cricket fans of England thought of baseball as a mild curiosity, nothing more. The two teams returned to the states to resume their seasons.

Upon their return, Boston found that New York had fattened up on inferior opponents to climb back in the pennant race. But the pretender vanished when Boston resumed their winning ways, and in October they pulled away to win easily.

Boston's pennant winning team in 1874 did not feature an overpowering individual performance as in years past. Rather, they featured a balanced attack which led the league in every offensive category but most walks. Five of their starters, topped by Cal McVey (.364) hit over .320. Jim O'Rourke led the Association in home runs with five, while George Wright had the most triples (15), and Cal McVey had the most runs (91) and hits (124). Pitcher Al Spalding contributed by posting four shutouts to go with his 52 wins.

New York and the Athletics of Philadelphia finished second and third. New York's best player was pitcher Bobby Mathews who won the earned run average race (2.30), while the Athletics boasted of hitters Cap Anson (.331) and John McMullin (.340). Finishing a rung lower were the Philadelphias, Chicago (back after a two-year absence) and Brooklyn. The Philadelphias were led by Bill Craver (.352), Chicago by batting champion Levi Meyerle (.403), and Brooklyn by no one in particular — no one hit over .295.

Hartford and Baltimore finished at the rear, but each team had one good player. Hartford's Lip Pike led the Association with 24 doubles and a .496 slugging percentage, and Baltimore's Jack Manning hit .351.

Although Boston enjoyed unparalleled success in the National Association, the success did not rub off on the other teams. Despite good records, no other clubs, save one, could win the pennant. In each year of the Association, at least two other teams other than Boston finished with win-loss records better than .600. Unfortunately, good was not good enough against a truly great team like the Boston Red Stockings.

1874 NATIONAL ASSOCIATION

BOSTON Red Stockings
52-18 .743 1st Harry Wright

BATTERS	POS/GAMES	GP	AB	R	H	BI	2B	3B	HR	BB	SO	SB	BA	SA
Jim O'Rourke	1B70	70	332	82	105		12	6	5	2			.316	.434
Ross Barnes	2B51	51	259	72	89		12	4	0	8			.344	.421
George Wright	SS60	60	313	76	106		11	15	2	7			.339	.489
Harry Schafer	3B71	71	325	69	84		13	3	1	0			.258	.326
Cal McVey	OF55,C15	70	341	91	124		22	4	4	0			.364	.487
Andy Leonard	OF51,SS11,2B9	71	340	68	109		18	4	0	2			.321	.397
George Hall	OF47	47	222	58	64		11	7	1	2			.288	.414
Deacon White	C55,OF12,1B1,2B1	70	350	75	106		4	7	3	4			.303	.380
Al Spalding	P71	71	359	80	119		15	1	0	3			.331	.379
Harry Wright	OF38,P6,C1	40	184	44	56		9	2	2	4			.304	.408
Tommy Beals	2B11,OF8	19	97	20	19		3	4	0	0			.196	.309
		71	3122	735	981		130	57	18	32			.314	.410

PITCHERS		W	L	PCT	G	GS	CG	SH	SV	IP	H	BB	SO	ERA
Al Spalding		52	16	.765	71	69	65	4	0	616	753	23		2.35
Harry Wright		0	2	.000	6	2	0	0	3	17	24	4		2.70
		52	18	.743	71	71	65	4	3	633	777	27		2.36

NEW YORK Mutuals
42-23 .646 -7.5 2nd Carey - Higham

BATTERS	POS/GAMES		GP	AB	R	H	BI	2B	3B	HR	BB	SO	SB	BA	SA
Joe Start	1B63		63	306	67	94		14	4	2	4			.307	.399
Candy Nelson	2B51,SS14		65	295	55	71		8	5	0	9			.241	.302
Tom Carey	SS51,2B13		64	286	54	82		10	3	1	2			.287	.353
Jack Burdock	3B61		61	272	45	76		16	3	2	1			.279	.382
Jack Remsen	OF63,1B1		64	285	52	65		11	4	2	0			.228	.316
John Hatfield	OF59,3B4,1B1,P1		63	289	46	68		12	2	0	8			.235	.291
Doug Allison	OF41,C24		65	316	69	88		8	5	0	6			.278	.335
Dick Higham	C41,OF23,2B1		65	331	58	87		13	4	1	4			.263	.335
Bobby Mathews	P65		65	297	47	70		8	1	0	4			.236	.269
Neal Phelps	OF6		6	24	5	3		0	0	0	0			.125	.125
Billy Geer	OF2		2	8	0	2		0	0	0	0			.250	.250
Dan Patterson	1B1,OF1		1	5	1	2		0	0	0	0			.400	.400
Orator Shaffer	OF1	(2-2)	1	5	1	1		0	0	0	0			.200	.200
			65	2719	500	709		100	31	8	38			.261	.329

PITCHERS		W	L	PCT	G	GS	CG	SH	SV	IP	H	BB	SO	ERA
Bobby Mathews		42	22	.656	65	65	62	4	0	578	647	39		2.30
John Hatfield		0	1	.000	3	0	0	0	0	8	11	1		2.25
		42	23	.646	65	65	62	4	0	586	658	40		2.30

PHILADELPHIA Athletics
33-22 .600 -11.5 3rd Dick McBride

BATTERS	POS/GAMES	GP	AB	R	H	BI	2B	3B	HR	BB	SO	SB	BA	SA
Wes Fisler	1B28,2B9	37	179	26	59		12	1	0	0			.330	.408
Joe Battin	2B40,OF7,SS4	51	226	40	52		11	1	0	1			.230	.288
Mike McGeary	SS26,C24,OF4	54	270	61	87		11	2	0	2			.322	.378
Ezra Sutton	3B36,SS20	55	244	54	72		10	2	0	0			.295	.352
John McMullin	OF54,C1	55	262	61	89		10	2	2	7			.340	.416
Count Gedney	OF50,1B4	54	222	49	60		6	1	1	7			.270	.320
Al Reach	OF14	14	55	8	7		2	0	0	0			.127	.164
John Clapp	C26,OF13,SS1	39	165	46	48		8	4	3	1			.291	.442
Dick McBride	P55	55	264	30	57		7	1	0	1			.216	.250
Cap Anson	1B22,3B20,OF8,SS5	55	260	51	86		8	3	0	3			.331	.385
Tim Murnane	OF12,2B6,1B1	21	81	11	18		2	0	0	2			.222	.247
Count Sensenderfer	OF5	5	16	3	3		0	0	0	0			.188	.188
Reddy Miller	C4	4	16	1	8		0	0	0	0			.500	.500
		55	2260	441	646		87	17	6	24			.286	.347

PITCHERS		W	L	PCT	G	GS	CG	SH	SV	IP	H	BB	SO	ERA
Dick McBride		33	22	.600	55	55	55	0	0	487	514	29		2.55
		33	22	.600	55	55	55	0	0	487	514	29		2.55

1874 NATIONAL ASSOCIATION

PHILADELPHIA
Philadelphias   29-29   .500   -17   4th   Bill Craver

BATTERS	POS/GAMES	GP	AB	R	H	BI	2B	3B	HR	BB	SO	SB	BA	SA
Denny Mack	1B56	56	248	48	51		7	4	0	1			.206	.266
Bill Craver	2B53,C3	55	267	68	94		13	11	0	4			.352	.483
Chick Fulmer	SS31,3B26	57	259	49	72		5	3	0	1			.278	.320
Jim Holdsworth	3B31,SS23,OF4	57	286	60	97		8	9	0	1			.339	.430
Dave Eggler	OF56,2B2	58	296	71	96		14	7	0	6			.324	.419
Tom York	OF50	50	223	36	58		3	8	0	4			.260	.345
George Bechtel	OF28,P6	32	151	29	44		5	4	1	2			.291	.397
Nat Hicks	C56,OF2	58	264	50	74		8	2	0	5			.280	.326
Candy Cummings	P54	54	229	32	54		5	3	0	2			.236	.284
John Radcliff	OF16,2B3,SS2,1B1,3B1	23	102	20	26		6	0	1	2			.255	.343
Charlie Pabor	OF17	17	77	11	18		0	0	1	0			.234	.273
John Donnelly	OF2,SS2,2B1	6	22	2	5		0	0	0	0			.227	.227
----- Quinlan	SS1	1	4	0	1		0	0	0	0			.250	.250
Ed McKenna	1B1	1	4	0	0		0	0	0	0			.000	.000
		58	2432	476	690		74	51	3	28			.284	.360

PITCHERS		W	L	PCT	G	GS	CG	SH	SV	IP	H	BB	SO	ERA
Candy Cummings		28	26	.519	54	54	52	3	0	482	602	21		2.88
George Bechtel		1	3	.333	6	4	4	0	0	42	64	0		3.86
		29	29	.500	58	58	56	3	0	524	666	21		2.95

CHICAGO
White Stockings   28-31   .475   -18.5   5th   Malone - Wood

BATTERS	POS/GAMES	GP	AB	R	H	BI	2B	3B	HR	BB	SO	SB	BA	SA
John Glenn	1B38,1B17	55	235	33	66		8	0	0	6			.281	.315
Levi Meyerle	2B26,3B14,OF7,SS5	53	253	66	102		20	0	1	3			.403	.494
John Peters	SS32,2B21,3B1	55	240	39	69		10	0	1	2			.287	.342
Davy Force	3B38,SS20,OF1,P1	59	296	61	93		10	0	0	2			.314	.348
Ned Cuthbert	OF55,C3	58	293	65	81		6	1	1	7			.276	.314
Paul Hines	OF46,2B12,SS2	59	270	47	81		12	1	0	4			.300	.352
Fred Treacey	OF35	35	146	18	28		6	0	0	3			.192	.233
Fergy Malone	C47	47	222	32	55		5	0	0	5			.248	.270
George Zettlein	P57	57	244	26	47		6	0	0	0			.193	.217
Jim Devlin	1B22,OF16,3B6	45	203	26	59		5	1	0	2			.291	.325
----- Gilroy	C8	8	39	4	8		1	0	0	0			.205	.231
Dan Collins	OF2,P2,SS1	3	12	1	1		0	0	0	0			.083	.083
Terry Connell	C1	1	4	0	0		0	0	0	0			.000	.000
		59	2457	418	690		89	3	3	34			.281	.323

PITCHERS		W	L	PCT	G	GS	CG	SH	SV	IP	H	BB	SO	ERA
George Zettlein		27	30	.474	57	57	57	3	0	516	653	46		3.07
Dan Collins		1	1	.500	2	2	1	0	0	11	21	2		5.73
Davy Force		0	0	----	1	0	0	0	0	7	22	0		12.86
		28	31	.475	59	59	58	3	0	534	696	48		3.25

BROOKLYN
Atlantics   22-33   .400   -22.5   6th   Bob Ferguson

BATTERS	POS/GAMES		GP	AB	R	H	BI	2B	3B	HR	BB	SO	SB	BA	SA
Dutch Dehlman	1B53		53	216	40	50		5	1	0	7			.231	.264
John Farrow	2B12,C15		27	121	16	26		3	0	0	1			.215	.240
Dickey Pearce	SS56,3B2		56	254	48	75		4	0	0	7			.295	.311
Bob Ferguson	3B55,C2,P1		56	246	34	63		5	1	0	1			.256	.285
Jack Chapman	OF52,1B1		53	238	32	64		7	3	0	5			.269	.324
Eddie Booth	OF44		44	187	24	47		2	4	1	3			.251	.321
Bobby Clack	OF31,1B2		33	134	22	23		2	0	0	2			.172	.187
Jake Knowdell	C20,OF3		23	84	8	12		1	1	0	2			.143	.179
Tommy Bond	P55		55	247	25	54		11	0	0	1			.219	.263
Frank Fleet	C12,2B7,OF1		22	95	18	22		1	0	0	2			.232	.242
Charlie Hodes	OF19,2B2		22	82	8	13		2	1	0	0			.159	.207
Pat McGee	OF15,SS2,2B1		16	65	4	11		2	0	0	0			.169	.200
Henry Kessler	C8,2B4,OF2,3B1		14	57	8	16		2	0	0	0			.281	.316
Charlie Sweasy	2B10	(2-2)	10	44	4	5		1	0	0	0			.114	.136

BROOKLYN (cont.)
Atlantics

BATTERS	POS/GAMES	GP	AB	R	H	BI	2B	3B	HR	BB	SO	SB	BA	SA
Billy West	2B9	9	35	4	7		1	0	0	1			.200	.229
Al Martin	2B6,OF1	7	30	1	4		0	0	0	0			.133	.133
Jim Clinton	2B1,OF1	2	11	3	2		1	0	0	0			.182	.273
Jim Hall	2B2	2	9	0	1		0	0	0	0			.111	.111
Mike Ledwith	C1	1	4	1	1		0	0	0	0			.250	.250
---- Govern	2B1	1	4	1	0		0	0	0	0			.000	.000
Charlie Snow	OF1	1	2	0	1		0	0	0	0			.500	.500
		56	2165	301	497		50	11	1	32			.230	.264

PITCHERS		W	L	PCT	G	GS	CG	SH	SV	IP	H	BB	SO	ERA
Tommy Bond		22	32	.407	55	55	55	1	0	497	609	10		3.19
Bob Ferguson		0	1	.000	1	1	1	0	0	9	12	3		4.00
		22	33	.400	56	56	56	1	0	506	621	13		3.20

HARTFORD
Dark Blues

16-37   .302   -27.5   7th   Lip Pike

BATTERS	POS/GAMES		GP	AB	R	H	BI	2B	3B	HR	BB	SO	SB	BA	SA
Everett Mills	1B53		53	241	40	70		6	2	0	6			.290	.332
Bob Addy	2B45,3B4,SS1		50	211	25	50		9	2	0	2			.237	.299
Tom Barlow	SS32		32	156	37	44		4	1	0	1			.282	.321
Bill Boyd	3B25,OF1		26	116	22	41		9	4	0	2			.353	.500
Jim Tipper	OF45		45	197	35	60		10	0	0	0			.305	.355
Lip Pike	OF27,SS18,2B7		52	238	58	81		24	5	1	0			.340	.496
Billy Barnie	OF21,C23,SS1		45	188	21	34		3	2	0	0			.181	.218
Scott Hastings	C31,OF20,2B1		52	248	60	80		13	1	0	4			.323	.383
Cherokee Fisher	P39,OF10,3B6,SS1		52	242	28	54		8	0	0	0			.223	.256
William Stearns	P22,OF14		32	132	16	21		1	0	0	8			.159	.167
Steve Brady	3B17,OF8		27	115	19	38		5	2	0	3			.330	.409
Orator Shaffer	OF9	(1-2)	9	34	6	8		0	0	1	0			.235	.324
Jack Farrell	OF3		3	14	3	5		0	0	0	0			.357	.357
Jack Manning	3B1	(2-2)	1	5	1	1		0	0	0	0			.200	.200
---- O'Neal	OF1		1	3	0	0		0	0	0	0			.000	.000
			53	2140	371	587		92	19	2	26			.274	.338

PITCHERS		W	L	PCT	G	GS	CG	SH	SV	IP	H	BB	SO	ERA
Cherokee Fisher		14	23	.378	39	35	31	0	0	317	405	10		3.04
William Stearns		2	14	.125	22	18	14	0	1	164	255	13		4.50
		16	37	.302	53	53	45	0	1	481	660	23		3.54

BALTIMORE
Lord Baltimores

9-38   .191   -31.5   8th   Warren White

BATTERS	POS/GAMES		GP	AB	R	H	BI	2B	3B	HR	BB	SO	SB	BA	SA
Charlie Gould	1B32,C1		33	142	20	31		6	0	0	3			.218	.261
Jack Manning	2B20,P22,SS5	(1-2)	42	168	33	59		10	1	0	3			.351	.423
Louis Say	SS18		18	67	4	14		3	0	0	0			.209	.254
Warren White	3B45		45	212	20	56		1	0	0	1			.264	.269
Johnny Ryan	OF47,P1		47	184	29	33		7	1	0	5			.179	.228
Harry Deane	OF45,2B2		47	204	29	50		9	2	0	4			.245	.309
Oscar Bielaski	OF26,1B1,2B1		27	113	18	27		1	0	0	2			.239	.248
Pop Snyder	C39		39	152	24	33		4	2	1	2			.217	.289
Asa Brainard	P29,2B17,OF2		46	198	19	50		5	0	0	2			.253	.278
---- Barron	OF17		17	78	6	20		0	0	0	0			.256	.256
Joe Gerhardt	SS14		14	61	10	20		1	1	0	0			.328	.377
---- Taylor	1B13		13	48	3	13		1	0	0	0			.271	.292
Frank Selman	SS7,C6,OF1		12	54	9	16		4	1	0	0			.296	.407
Charlie Sweasy	2B7,OF1	(1-2)	8	33	2	8		0	0	0	2			.242	.242
John Smith	SS5,OF1		6	20	1	3		1	0	0	0			.150	.200
---- Brown	SS2		2	9	0	0		0	0	0	0			.000	.000
---- Jones	C1,OF1		2	7	0	1		0	0	0	0			.143	.143
Bill Smiley	3B2		2	7	0	0		0	0	0	0			.000	.000
Henry Kohler	1B2		2	4	0	0		0	0	0	0			.000	.000
---- Wood	2B1		1	6	0	0		0	0	0	0			.000	.000
Hugh Reed	OF1		1	4	0	0		0	0	0	0			.000	.000

BALTIMORE (cont.)
Lord Baltimores

BATTERS	POS/GAMES	GP	AB	R	H	BI	2B	3B	HR	BB	SO	SB	BA	SA
Henry Reville	OF1	1	4	0	0		0	0	0	0			.000	.000
Fred Boardman	OF1	1	3	0	1		0	0	0	0			.333	.333
Lew Carl	C1	1	3	0	0		0	0	0	0			.000	.000
		47	1781	227	435		53	8	1	24			.244	.285

PITCHERS	W	L	PCT	G	GS	CG	SH	SV	IP	H	BB	SO	ERA
Asa Brainard	5	22	.185	29	27	25	0	0	239	403	27		4.93
Jack Manning	4	16	.200	22	20	18	0	0	180	231	10		3.41
Johnny Ryan	0	0	----	1	0	0	0	0	1	9	0		13.50
	9	38	.191	47	47	43	0	0	420	643	37		4.31

1875 NATIONAL ASSOCIATION

Imbalance

The 1875 season epitomized the failures of the National Association in two significant areas. The first was the one-sided nature of the competition emphasized by the polyglot itinerary which saw six of the 13 participants play incomplete schedules, and secondly the problem of revolving. It was the former which reached heroic proportions in 1875.

The Boston Red Stockings had given the rest of the Association a terrific pounding during the previous three years. However, those years were a mere prelude to the shellacking the Red Stockings would dish out in 1875. Boston finished the season with a 71-8 record with an accompanying winning percentage of .899. This total has never been topped.

On the other side, the Brooklyn Atlantics finished with a 2-42 record and the lowest percentage (.045) of all time (among teams who played a semblance of a complete schedule). In any given year, one will find extremes — never before had such drastic examples of both extremes surfaced in one year. Brooklyn finished 51.5 games out of first. If they had lost all their games, and Boston had won all of theirs, the total would have been only 56.5 — not a great deal different than the actual total.

Another disturbing trend came to the forefront in 1875 — the problem of revolving. It was common practice for players to jump from one team to another during the era of the National Association. This tendency was called revolving. Before the 1875 season, second baseman Davy Force signed contracts with two different clubs, Chicago and the Philadelphia Athletics. At first, the Association's Judiciary committee ruled his Chicago contract valid. Later, that decision was overturned and Force was awarded to the Athletics. The decision outraged many — most specifically William Hulbert, owner of the Chicago club. Soon the baseball world would know how Hulbert would even the score.

Six new teams joined the Association fray in 1875. They were: 1) the St. Louis Browns, 2) the St. Louis Reds, 3) New Haven, 4) the Philadelphia Centennials, 5) Keokuk, Iowa, and 6) Washington. The team from Baltimore dropped out. None of these new entrants played more than 50 games — most played significantly less.

Boston used a balanced attack to throttle all comers. The team hit .320, thirty points higher than anyone else. They were paced by Deacon White's league-leading

.366 average, and by Ross Barnes's .361 average, 114 runs and 142 hits, the latter two leading the circuit. Pitcher Al Spalding finished with a fancy 55 wins and only five losses, a .917 win percentage, seven shutouts, eight saves and a 1.52 earned run average — all of these totals led the league.

Hartford and the Philadelphia Athletics finished second and third with records that would have placed them first in most seasons. Hartford's forte was pitching which featured curveball inventor Candy Cummings (35-12) who finished with the runner-up position in the ERA race (1.60). The Athletics featured league-leading triple hitters Bill Craver and George Hall who hit 13 a piece.

The St. Louis Brown Stockings, Philadelphias, New York and Chicago all finished in the middle of the pack. Their best players were Lip Pike of St. Louis (.343), and Levi Meyerle of Philadelphia (.320).

The rest of the teams played in few games, rarely posting a win. The Philadelphia Centennials dropped out in May, and Keokuk followed in June. In July, both Washington and the St. Louis Reds played their last games.

The bottom six won 21 and lost 143. Much of the blame falls to Brooklyn whose 2-42 record, and 31-game losing streak, will stand forever as a monument to futility.

The organization known as the National Association was by 1875 proving itself not strong enough to deal with the world of baseball. Something new needed to happen to return stability to the national pastime. And, in a short while, something did.

1875 NATIONAL ASSOCIATION

BOSTON Red Stockings — 71-8 .899 1st Harry Wright

BATTERS	POS/GAMES		GP	AB	R	H	BI	2B	3B	HR	BB	SO	SB	BA	SA
Cal McVey	1B54,OF17,C11,P3		82	389	88	137		33	9	3	1			.352	.506
Ross Barnes	2B78		78	393	114	142		22	6	1	7			.361	.455
George Wright	SS79,P2		79	406	105	135		18	7	1	2			.333	.419
Harry Schafer	3B50,OF1		51	216	47	62		9	0	0	0			.287	.329
Andy Leonard	OF73,3B3,SS3,2B1		80	394	87	127		14	6	1	1			.322	.396
Jack Manning	OF58,P17,1B2,3B2		77	343	71	94		8	2	1	2			.274	.318
Jim O'Rourke	OF45,3B27,1B3		75	364	98	106		16	8	6	10			.291	.429
Deacon White	C80,OF1,1B1		80	372	77	136		20	4	1	2			.366	.449
Al Spalding	P72,OF10,1B2		74	343	68	107		12	3	0	4			.312	.364
Tommy Beals	OF31,2B6		36	164	41	42		1	5	0	2			.256	.323
Juice Latham	1B16	(1-2)	16	77	23	21		4	1	0	0			.273	.351
Frank Heifer	1B7,OF5,P1		11	51	11	14		0	3	0	0			.275	.392
Harry Wright	OF1		1	4	1	1		0	0	0	0			.250	.250
			82	3516	831	1124		157	54	14	31			.320	.407

PITCHERS		W	L	PCT	G	GS	CG	SH	SV	IP	H	BB	SO	ERA
Al Spalding		55	5	.917	72	63	52	7	8	575	571	14		1.52
Jack Manning		15	2	.882	27	17	8	1	7	140	153	14		2.19
Cal McVey		1	0	1.000	3	2	0	0	1	11	15	1		3.27
George Wright		0	1	.000	2	0	0	0	0	4	5	0		2.25
Frank Heifer		0	0	----	2	0	0	0	1	2	7	0		7.71
		71	8	.899	82	82	60	10	17	732	751	29		1.70

HARTFORD Dark Blues — 54-28 .659 -18.5 2nd Bob Ferguson

BATTERS	POS/GAMES		GP	AB	R	H	BI	2B	3B	HR	BB	SO	SB	BA	SA
Everett Mills	1B80		80	341	59	91		10	4	1	0			.267	.328
Jack Burdock	2B72,3B1		74	347	72	102		14	5	0	5			.294	.363
Tom Carey	SS86		86	382	63	101		6	2	0	2			.264	.291
Bob Ferguson	3B85		85	366	66	88		12	4	0	2			.240	.295
Tom York	OF86		86	376	68	112		12	7	0	4			.298	.367
Jack Remsen	OF86		86	354	69	96		10	4	0	5			.271	.322
Art Allison	OF34,2B1	(2-2)	40	173	26	41		6	0	1	0			.237	.289
Doug Allison	C59,1B3		61	267	38	67		7	0	0	7			.251	.277
Tommy Bond	P40,OF29,1B2,2B2		71	289	32	78		12	3	0	0			.270	.332
Candy Cummings	P48,OF6		53	221	30	44		6	2	0	2			.199	.244
Bill Harbridge	C25,OF13,2B10,1B3		53	205	32	50		3	3	0	12			.244	.288
Joe Quinn	C2,OF1	(2-3)	5	13	1	3		0	0	0	1			.231	.231
Charlie Jones	OF1	(2-2)	1	4	1	0		0	0	0	0			.000	.000
Tom Brady	OF1		1	4	0	0		0	0	0	0			.000	.000
			86	3342	557	873		98	34	2	40			.261	.313

PITCHERS		W	L	PCT	G	GS	CG	SH	SV	IP	H	BB	SO	ERA
Candy Cummings		35	12	.745	48	47	46	7	0	417	396	6		1.60
Tommy Bond		19	16	.543	40	39	37	6	0	352	301	10		1.56
		54	28	.659	86	86	83	13	0	771	706	16		1.61

PHILADELPHIA Athletics — 53-20 .726 -15 3rd McBride - Anson

BATTERS	POS/GAMES		GP	AB	R	H	BI	2B	3B	HR	BB	SO	SB	BA	SA
Wes Fisler	1B44,OF9,2B4		58	267	55	74		14	3	0	4			.277	.352
Bill Craver	2B53,C1	(2-2)	54	260	71	83		11	11	2	4			.319	.469
Davy Force	SS77		77	384	78	120		21	6	0	8			.313	.398
Ezra Sutton	3B73,P2,1B1,OF1		75	358	83	116		11	7	2	1			.324	.411
George Hall	OF77		77	360	71	107		12	13	5	1			.297	.444
Dave Eggler	OF66		66	293	66	89		15	7	0	2			.304	.403
George Bechtel	OF30,P4	(2-2)	35	164	33	46		5	2	0	1			.280	.335
John Clapp	C60		60	291	65	77		7	8	0	8			.265	.344
Cap Anson	1B32,OF22,C11,3B4		69	324	84	105		17	4	1	6			.324	.410
Dick McBride	P60,OF1		60	269	42	73		9	0	0	5			.271	.305
John Richmond	2B16,OF11,C2		29	126	29	25		1	0	0	0			.198	.206
Adam Rocap	OF11,2B3		16	70	13	12		0	0	0	0			.171	.171

PHILADELPHIA (cont.)
Athletics

BATTERS	POS/GAMES		GP	AB	R	H	BI	2B	3B	HR	BB	SO	SB	BA	SA
Lon Knight	P13		13	47	4	6		2	0	0	0			.128	.170
Al Reach	OF2,2B1		3	14	4	4		1	0	0	0			.286	.357
William Coon	C3		3	12	1	2		0	0	0	0			.167	.167
Jim Gilroy	C1,OF1		2	6	0	1		0	0	0	0			.167	.167
			77	3245	699	940		126	61	10	40			.290	.375

PITCHERS		W	L	PCT	G	GS	CG	SH	SV	IP	H	BB	SO	ERA
Dick McBride		44	14	.759	60	60	59	6	0	538	602	25		1.97
Lon Knight		6	5	.545	13	13	12	0	0	107	114	12		2.44
George Bechtel	(2-2)	3	1	.750	4	4	4	0	0	36	45	3		2.25
Ezra Sutton		0	0	----	2	0	0	0	0	6	14	0		7.50
		53	20	.726	77	77	75	6	0	687	775	40		2.11

ST. LOUIS
Brown Stockings

39-29   .574   -26.5   4th   Dicky Pearce

BATTERS	POS/GAMES		GP	AB	R	H	BI	2B	3B	HR	BB	SO	SB	BA	SA
Dutch Dehlman	1B67		67	254	42	57		12	2	0	11			.224	.287
Joe Battin	2B60,3B6		67	284	31	71		7	3	0	0			.250	.296
Dickey Pearce	SS70,P2		70	312	51	77		5	3	0	7			.247	.282
Bill Hague	3B61,1B1		62	260	24	56		2	0	0	2			.215	.223
Ned Cuthbert	OF67,C2		68	318	68	77		9	2	0	3			.242	.283
Lip Pike	OF62,2B8		70	312	61	107		21	10	0	3			.343	.474
Jack Chapman	OF43		43	195	28	44		6	3	0	1			.226	.287
Reddy Miller	C52,3B3		55	212	17	34		2	0	0	2			.160	.170
George Bradley	P60,3B1,OF1		60	254	28	62		8	3	0	1			.244	.299
Charlie Waitt	OF29,1B2		31	118	14	25		9	0	0	2			.212	.288
George Seward	C17,OF5,2B2		25	97	13	24		2	0	0	1			.247	.268
Pud Galvin	P8,OF5		12	47	8	6		1	1	0	0			.128	.191
Frank Fleet	P3	(1-2)	4	16	1	1		0	0	0	0			.063	.063
			70	2679	386	641		84	27	0	33			.239	.291

PITCHERS		W	L	PCT	G	GS	CG	SH	SV	IP	H	BB	SO	ERA
George Bradley		33	26	.559	60	60	57	4	0	536	538	16		2.05
Pud Galvin		4	2	.667	8	7	7	1	1	62	53	1		2.18
Frank Fleet	(1-2)	2	1	.667	3	3	3	0	0	27	33	3		2.33
Dickey Pearce		0	0	----	2	0	0	0	0	5	10	0		6.75
		39	29	.574	70	70	67	5	1	630	634	20		2.11

PHILADELPHIA
Philadelphias

37-31   .544   -28.5   5th   McGeary - Addy

BATTERS	POS/GAMES		GP	AB	R	H	BI	2B	3B	HR	BB	SO	SB	BA	SA
Tim Murnane	1B31,OF26,2B12		69	311	70	85		4	0	1	8			.273	.296
Levi Meyerle	2B32,3B21,1B15		68	300	55	96		13	9	1	0			.320	.433
Chick Fulmer	SS54,3B14		69	293	50	65		5	1	0	0			.222	.246
Mike McGeary	3B24,2B23,SS18,OF3,C1		68	309	71	89		6	2	0	1			.288	.320
Bob Addy	OF66,2B3		69	311	60	79		11	4	0	0			.254	.315
John McMullin	OF53,P1		54	223	34	56		9	4	2	5			.251	.354
Fred Treacey	OF43	(2-2)	43	179	24	38		3	3	0	1			.212	.262
Pop Snyder	C65,OF1		66	263	37	64		7	2	1	4			.243	.297
Cherokee Fisher	P41,OF5		41	177	26	41		2	1	0	1			.232	.254
Fergy Malone	1B21,C4,OF2		29	122	15	28		2	1	0	1			.230	.262
George Zettlein	P21,1B1	(2-2)	21	84	11	15		1	0	0	0			.179	.190
Orator Shaffer	OF10,3B6,1B2		19	70	10	17		2	1	0	0			.243	.300
Bill Crowley	OF4,3B3,1B1,2B1		9	37	4	3		0	0	0	1			.081	.081
Joe Borden	P7		7	28	3	3		0	0	0	0			.107	.107
Bill Parks	OF2,P2	(2-2)	2	6	0	1		0	0	0	0			.167	.167
Sam Weaver	P1		1	4	0	1		0	0	0	0			.250	.250
			70	2717	470	681		65	28	5	22			.251	.301

PITCHERS		W	L	PCT	G	GS	CG	SH	SV	IP	H	BB	SO	ERA
Cherokee Fisher		22	19	.537	41	41	36	2	0	357	345	9		1.92
George Zettlein	(2-2)	12	8	.600	21	21	20	1	0	180	208	10		2.40

1875 NATIONAL ASSOCIATION

PHILADELPHIA (cont.)
Philadelphias

PITCHERS	W	L	PCT	G	GS	CG	SH	SV	IP	H	BB	SO	ERA
Joe Borden	2	4	.333	7	7	7	2	0	66	47	7		1.64
Sam Weaver	1	0	1.000	1	1	1	0	0	6	6	2		1.50
John McMullin	0	0	----	4	0	0	0	0	13	31	1		6.39
Bill Parks	0	0	----	2	0	0	0	0	5	13	1		6.75
	37	31	.544	70	70	64	5	0	627	650	30		2.15

NEW YORK
Mutuals

30-38 .441 -35.5 6th Nat Hicks

BATTERS	POS/GAMES		GP	AB	R	H	BI	2B	3B	HR	BB	SO	SB	BA	SA
Joe Start	1B68		68	309	56	87		9	5	4	3			.282	.382
Candy Nelson	2B47,3B22,OF1		70	276	29	56		8	0	0	10			.203	.232
Jim Hallinan	SS44	(2-2)	44	202	29	58		7	3	3	1			.287	.396
Joe Gerhardt	3B44,2B12,SS1		58	251	29	53		8	3	0	0			.211	.267
Count Gedney	OF66,P2		68	266	30	54		12	4	0	2			.203	.278
Eddie Booth	OF62,2B6		68	278	33	55		3	4	0	1			.198	.237
Jim Holdsworth	OF45,SS26		71	325	45	91		11	1	0	1			.280	.320
Nat Hicks	C59,OF3		62	269	32	67		11	2	0	2			.249	.305
Bobby Mathews	P70		70	268	23	47		5	2	0	0			.175	.209
Pat McGee	OF25	(1-2)	25	94	4	16		3	0	0	0			.170	.202
Dick Higham	C7,2B4,OF2,1B2	(2-2)	15	64	12	25		5	0	0	0			.391	.469
Billy Barnie	C5,OF5	(2-2)	9	35	1	5		1	0	0	0			.143	.171
Bob Metcalf	3B4,OF2,SS1		8	31	2	7		0	0	0	1			.226	.226
John Hatfield	OF2		2	9	2	3		1	0	0	0			.333	.444
Neal Phelps	OF2		2	6	1	2		0	0	0	0			.333	.333
			71	2683	328	626		84	24	7	21			.233	.290

PITCHERS		W	L	PCT	G	GS	CG	SH	SV	IP	H	BB	SO	ERA
Bobby Mathews		29	38	.433	70	70	69	2	0	627	709	23		2.41
Count Gedney		1	0	1.000	2	1	1	0	0	11	7	1		1.64
		30	38	.441	71	71	70	2	0	638	716	24		2.40

CHICAGO
White Stockings

30-37 .448 -35 7th J. Wood

BATTERS	POS/GAMES		GP	AB	R	H	BI	2B	3B	HR	BB	SO	SB	BA	SA
Jim Devlin	1B43,P28,OF3		69	315	60	92		18	5	0	5			.292	.381
Paul Hines	2B28,OF41		69	308	45	97		13	4	0	1			.315	.383
John Peters	SS66,2B4		69	298	40	86		18	0	0	0			.289	.349
Warren White	3B61,SS4,OF3,2B2		69	285	37	71		9	0	0	0			.249	.281
Oscar Bielaski	OF51		51	196	21	49		2	0	0	2			.250	.260
John Glenn	OF44,1B26		69	303	46	75		9	0	0	5			.248	.277
Scott Hastings	OF25,C39,2B2		65	284	43	73		9	0	0	9			.257	.289
Dick Higham	C23,2B15,OF	(1-2)	42	204	44	49		3	3	0	0			.240	.284
George Zettlein	P31,1B1	(1-2)	32	130	7	29		0	0	0	0			.223	.223
Mike Golden	OF24,P14,1B1	(2-2)	39	155	16	40		3	0	0	2			.258	.277
Joe Quinn	C10,OF8	(3-3)	17	59	12	14		0	0	0	0			.237	.237
Joe Miller	2B14,OF2	(2-2)	15	53	1	8		0	0	0	0			.151	.151
George Karl	2B6		6	23	2	3		0	0	0	0			.130	.130
Fred Waterman	3B4,2B1		5	20	2	6		0	0	0	0			.300	.300
Will Foley	3B3		3	12	0	3		1	0	0	0			.250	.250
Mike Brannock	3B2		2	9	2	1		0	0	0	0			.111	.111
----- Brady	OF1		1	4	1	1		0	1	0	0			.250	.750
			69	2658	379	697		85	13	0	24			.262	.304

PITCHERS		W	L	PCT	G	GS	CG	SH	SV	IP	H	BB	SO	ERA
George Zettlein	(1-2)	17	14	.548	31	31	29	6	0	282	269	6		1.82
Jim Devlin	(2-2)	7	16	.304	28	24	24	0	0	224	254	11		2.87
Mike Golden		6	7	.462	14	14	12	1	0	119	129	11		2.89
		30	37	.448	69	69	65	7	0	625	652	28		2.40

NEW HAVEN
Elm Citys

7-40 .149 -48 8th Gould - Latham - Pabor

BATTERS	POS/GAMES		GP	AB	R	H	BI	2B	3B	HR	BB	SO	SB	BA	SA
Charlie Gould	1B26,OF1		27	109	9	29		2	1	0	1			.266	.303
Ed Somerville	2B30,1B1,3B1,SS1	(2-2)	33	134	14	29		4	0	0	1			.219	.246
Sam Wright	SS33		33	128	10	24		4	0	0	1			.188	.219
Henry Luff	3B26,P10,OF4		38	165	15	46		11	3	2	0			.279	.418
Jim Tipper	OF41		41	158	10	25		0	0	0	0			.158	.158
John McKelvey	OF39,3B4		43	187	26	43		4	1	0	4			.230	.262
Johnny Ryan	OF29,P10,3B1,SS1		37	146	17	23		2	1	0	3			.158	.185
Tim McGinley	C32	(2-2)	32	130	13	36		3	1	0	1			.277	.315
Billy Geer	OF17,2B13,SS5,3B1,1B1		37	162	20	40		6	1	0	1			.247	.296
Tricky Nichols	P34,OF1		34	120	12	23		0	2	0	1			.192	.225
Juice Latham	1B13,SS4,3B3	(2-2)	20	76	6	15		1	0	0	0			.197	.211
Stud Bancker	C12,2B3,3B3,SS1		19	72	3	11		0	0	0	0			.153	.153
George Trenwith	3B6	(2-2)	6	25	1	6		2	0	0	0			.240	.320
Charlie Pabor	OF6	(2-2)	6	23	4	8		0	2	0	0			.348	.522
John Cassidy	1B6	(2-2)	6	22	3	3		1	0	0	0			.136	.182
Jim Keenan	3B2,C1		4	13	1	1		0	0	0	0			.077	.077
----- Sullivan	OF2		2	8	3	3		0	0	0	0			.375	.375
Tom Barlow	SS1	(1-2)	1	5	1	1		0	0	0	0			.200	.200
Rit Harrison	C1		1	4	0	2		1	0	0	0			.500	.750
Fred Goldsmith	2B1		1	4	0	2		0	0	0	0			.500	.500
----- Evans	OF1		1	4	1	2		1	0	0	0			.500	.750
Lester Dole	OF1		1	4	1	2		0	0	0	0			.500	.500
George Knight	P1		1	4	0	0		0	0	0	0			.000	.000
John Smith	SS1		1	3	0	0		0	0	0	0			.000	.000
----- Booth	SS1		1	2	0	0		0	0	0	0			.000	.000
			47	1708	170	374		42	12	2	13			.219	.261

PITCHERS		W	L	PCT	G	GS	CG	SH	SV	IP	H	BB	SO	ERA
Tricky Nichols		4	29	.121	34	33	30	0	0	288	319	10		3.03
George Knight		1	0	1.000	1	1	1	0	0	9	12	0		2.00
Johnny Ryan		1	5	.167	10	6	4	0	0	59	69	9		3.34
Henry Luff		1	6	.143	10	7	5	0	0	70	100	3		4.78
		7	40	.149	47	47	40	0	0	426	500	22		3.34

WASHINGTON
Washingtons

5-23 .179 -40.5 9th Hollingshead - Parks

BATTERS	POS/GAMES		GP	AB	R	H	BI	2B	3B	HR	BB	SO	SB	BA	SA
Art Allison	1B24,OF2,C1	(1-2)	26	110	18	24		3	1	0	1			.218	.264
Steve Brady	2B16,OF2,1B1		21	90	6	13		1	1	0	0			.144	.178
John Dailey	SS17,3B7,2B2	(1-2)	27	106	17	20		3	5	0	0			.189	.311
Herm Doscher	3B19,SS2		22	81	5	15		2	0	0	0			.185	.210
Larry Ressler	OF19,2B7		27	106	17	21		1	0	0	1			.198	.208
Holly Hollingshead	OF19		19	81	7	20		0	2	0	0			.247	.296
Bill Parks	OF15,P14	(1-2)	26	112	13	20		1	0	0	0			.179	.188
Andrew Thompson	C10,OF1		11	41	3	4		0	1	0	0			.098	.146
William Stearns	P17,OF6		23	77	10	20		1	0	0	1			.260	.273
----- McCloskey	C11		11	40	1	7		0	0	0	1			.175	.175
Louis Say	SS8,2B1,OF1		11	39	4	10		0	0	0	0			.256	.256
Charlie Mason	OF7,P1	(2-2)	8	34	2	3		0	0	0	0			.088	.088
----- Terry	OF4,1B2		6	22	0	4		0	1	0	0			.182	.273
John Laury	OF6		6	21	2	3		0	0	0	1			.143	.143
Sam Field	C4,OF1	(2-2)	5	17	0	5		0	0	0	0			.294	.294
Jim Gilmore	C2,2B1,3B1		3	12	2	3		0	0	0	0			.250	.250
----- Witherow	P1		1	5	0	0		0	0	0	0			.000	.000
Frank Selman	1B1		1	3	0	1		0	0	0	0			.333	.333
			28	997	107	194		12	11	0	5			.195	.229

PITCHERS		W	L	PCT	G	GS	CG	SH	SV	IP	H	BB	SO	ERA
Bill Parks	(1-2)	4	8	.333	14	11	9	0	0	107	146	6		4.05
William Stearns		1	14	.067	17	16	14	0	0	141	243	4		5.36
----- Witherow		0	1	.000	1	1	0	0	0	1	5	0		18.00
Charlie Mason	(2-2)	0	0	----	1	0	0	0	0	2	3	1		4.50
		5	23	.179	28	28	23	0	0	251	397	11		4.85

1875 NATIONAL ASSOCIATION

ST. LOUIS Reds
4-15 .211 -37 10th Charlie Sweasey

BATTERS	POS/GAMES	GP	AB	R	H	BI	2B	3B	HR	BB	SO	SB	BA	SA
Charlie Hautz	1B19	19	83	5	25		2	0	0	1			.301	.325
Charlie Sweasy	2B19	19	76	7	13		0	0	0	4			.171	.171
Billy Redmon	SS17,3B1,C1	19	82	12	16		2	0	0	2			.195	.220
Trick McSorley	3B8,OF6	15	52	4	11		0	0	0	0			.212	.212
Tom Oran	OF19	19	81	7	16		5	1	0	1			.198	.284
Art Croft	OF19	19	75	5	15		3	0	0	0			.200	.240
Bill Morgan	OF8,P7,3B6	19	69	11	18		4	0	0	5			.261	.319
Silver Flint	C15,3B1	17	61	4	5		0	0	0	1			.082	.082
Joe Blong	P14,OF3	16	68	3	10		2	0	0	0			.147	.176
Joe Ellick	3B3,OF2,SS1	7	27	1	6		1	0	0	0			.222	.259
Packy Dillon	C3	3	13	1	3		1	0	0	0			.231	.308
John Dillon	SS1	1	1	0	0		0	0	0	0			.000	.000
		19	688	60	138		20	1	0	14			.201	.233

PITCHERS		W	L	PCT	G	GS	CG	SH	SV	IP	H	BB	SO	ERA
Joe Blong		3	12	.200	15	15	12	1	0	129	169	2		3.35
Bill Morgan		1	3	.333	7	4	4	1	0	42	38	1		3.43
		4	15	.211	19	19	16	2	0	171	207	3		3.37

PHILADELPHIA Centennials
2-12 .143 -36.5 11th Bill Craver

BATTERS	POS/GAMES		GP	AB	R	H	BI	2B	3B	HR	BB	SO	SB	BA	SA
John Abadie	1B11	(1-2)	11	45	3	10		0	0	0	0			.222	.222
Ed Somerville	2B14	(1-2)	14	55	6	13		3	0	0	2			.236	.291
Bill Craver	SS9,3B4,1B1,C1	(1-2)	14	65	8	18		5	2	0	0			.277	.415
George Trenwirth	3B10		10	45	5	8		0	0	0	1			.178	.178
Fred Warner	OF14		14	57	11	14		1	0	0	1			.246	.263
Fred Treacey	OF11	(1-2)	11	46	9	12		2	0	0	2			.261	.304
Charlie Mason	OF10,1B2		12	47	5	11		1	0	0	0			.234	.255
Tim McGinley	C13,OF1	(1-2)	13	51	5	13		1	1	0	1			.255	.314
George Bechtel	P14	(1-2)	14	62	12	17		5	0	0	0			.274	.355
Len Lovett	OF6		6	21	2	5		1	0	0	1			.238	.286
John Radcliff	SS5		5	24	2	4		0	0	0	0			.167	.167
Sam Field	C2,OF1	(1-2)	3	11	2	1		0	0	0	0			.091	.091
			14	529	70	126		19	3	0	8			.238	.285

PITCHERS			W	L	PCT	G	GS	CG	SH	SV	IP	H	BB	SO	ERA
George Bechtel		(1-2)	2	12	.143	14	14	14	0	0	126	170	3		3.93
			2	12	.143	14	14	14	0	0	126	170	8		3.93

BROOKLYN Atlantics
2-42 .045 -51.5 12th Pabor - Boyd

BATTERS	POS/GAMES		GP	AB	R	H	BI	2B	3B	HR	BB	SO	SB	BA	SA
Fred Crane	1B20,OF1		21	80	7	17		1	0	0	0			.213	.225
Bill Boyd	2B15,OF11,3B9,1B1,P1		36	148	14	44		8	2	1	1			.297	.399
Henry Kessler	SS18,OF6,2B1,C1		25	104	17	26		2	0	0	1			.250	.269
Al Nichols	3B32		32	129	4	20		3	0	0	0			.155	.178
Charlie Pabor	OF41,P2	(1-2)	42	153	15	36		1	3	0	1			.235	.281
Bobby Clack	OF17		17	59	1	6		0	0	0	0			.102	.102
Pat McGee	OF13,2B5	(1-2)	18	63	3	9		4	1	0	1			.143	.238
Jake Knowdell	C33,SS8,OF3		43	161	17	32		3	0	0	2			.199	.217
John Cassidy	P27,OF10,1B7		41	165	14	29		3	2	1	1			.176	.236
Frank Fleet	2B11,C10,SS6,P2	(2-2)	26	112	13	25		1	0	0	1			.223	.232
Molly Moore	SS14,1B6,3B3		22	88	5	20		5	0	0	0			.227	.284
Jim Clinton	P17,OF5,1B4,2B1		19	81		10		0	0	0				.123	.123
Dan Patterson	2B5,OF5		11	41	3	8		0	0	0	0			.195	.195
Al Martin	OF6		6	26	1	3		0	0	0	0			.115	.115
J. O'Neill	P5,OF3		6	26		3		0	0	0				.115	.115
Tom Smith	2B3		3	12	0	1		0	0	0	0			.083	.083
Oliver Brown	1B3		3	10	0	0		0	0	0	0			.000	.000
----- Stoddard	OF2		2	9	1	1		1	0	0	0			.111	.222
John Dailey	1B1,OF1	(2-2)	2	8	3	1		0	0	0	0			.125	.125

1875 NATIONAL ASSOCIATION

BROOKLYN (cont.)
Atlantics

BATTERS	POS/GAMES		GP	AB	R	H	BI	2B	3B	HR	BB	SO	SB	BA	SA
Barney Gilligan	C1,OF1		2	8	2	2		0	0	0	0			.250	.250
Paddy Quinn	OF2		2	7	2	1		0	0	0	0			.143	.143
Doc Bushong	C1		1	5	0	3		0	1	0	0			.600	1.000
Frank Thompson	OF1		1	5	1	2		0	0	0	0			.400	.400
----- Edwards	P1,OF1		1	5	1	1		0	0	0				.200	.200
Washington Fulmer	3B1		1	4	1	2		0	0	0	0			.500	.500
John Abadie	1B1	(1-2)	1	4	1	1		0	0	0	0			.250	.250
----- Hellings	2B1		1	4	0	1		0	0	0	0			.250	.250
----- Sheridan	OF1		1	4	0	0		0	0	0	0			.000	.000
----- Shaffer	OF1		1	4	0	0		0	0	0	0			.000	.000
Bill Rexter	OF1		1	4	0	0		0	0	0	0			.000	.000
Horatio Munn	2B1		1	4	0	0		0	0	0	0			.000	.000
----- Boland	OF1		1	4	0	0		0	0	0	0			.000	.000
Tom Barlow	2B1	(2-2)	1	4	0	0		0	0	0	0			.000	.000
Harry Arundel	OF1		1	4	0	0		0	0	0				.000	.000
Oscar Walker	OF1		1	2	0	0		0	0	0	1			.000	.000
			44	1547	132	304		32	9	2	10			.197	.233

PITCHERS			W	L	PCT	G	GS	CG	SH	SV	IP	H	BB	SO	ERA
Jim Clinton			1	14	.067	17	14	9	0	0	123	146	8		3.22
John Cassidy		(1-2)	1	20	.048	30	22	18	0	0	215	278	12		3.98
Frank Fleet			0	1	.000	2	1	1	0	0	15	24	0		4.70
Charlie Pabor			0	1	.000	1	1	0	0	0	4	11	1		9.00
J. O'Neill			0	4	.000	5	4	3	0	0	34	56	0		4.76
----- Edwards			0	1	.000	1	1	0	0	0	2	6	0		9.00
Bill Boyd			0	0	----	1	0	0	0	0	2	4	0		5.40
			2	42	.045	44	44	31	0	0	396	531	22		3.95

KEOKUK
Westerns

1-12 .077 -37 13th J. Simmons

BATTERS	POS/GAMES		GP	AB	R	H	BI	2B	3B	HR	BB	SO	SB	BA	SA
Jack Carbine	1B10		10	36	0	3		0	0	0	0			.083	.083
Joe Miller	2B13	(1-2)	13	50	4	6		1	0	0	0			.120	.120
Jim Hallinan	SS13	(1-2)	13	51	12	14		1	1	0	0			.275	.333
Wally Goldsmith	3B13		13	51	3	6		0	0	0	0			.118	.118
Charlie Jones	OF12	(1-2)	12	47	5	13		2	4	0	0			.277	.489
Joe Simmons	OF10,1B3		13	53	5	9		1	0	0	0			.170	.189
Billy Riley	OF8		8	33	4	5		1	0	0	1			.152	.182
Joe Quinn	C7,OF4	(1-3)	11	43	4	14		2	0	0	0			.326	.372
Mike Golden	P13	(1-2)	13	46	5	6		0	0	0	0			.130	.130
Billy Barnie	C5,OF5	(1-2)	10	36	3	4		1	0	0	0			.111	.139
Jim Hall	OF1		1	3	0	1		0	1	0	0			.333	1.000
			13	449	45	81		9	6	0	1			.180	.227

PITCHERS			W	L	PCT	G	GS	CG	SH	SV	IP	H	BB	SO	ERA
Mike Golden		(1-2)	1	12	.077	13	13	13	0	0	112	110	14		2.81
			1	12	.077	13	13	13	0	0	112	110	14		2.81

1876 NATIONAL LEAGUE

The Owners Take Control

By 1875, the National Association was reeling. This player-run organization, as good as it was, was simply not strong enough to keep disreputable practices such as gambling and revolving (the term coined for players jumping teams) out of the game. One man sought a solution to these problems. His name: William Hulbert.

Hulbert was a Chicago businessman who had gained control of the Chicago Association team. During the summer of 1875, Hulbert met secretly with Al Spalding, star pitcher of the Boston Red Stockings, and convinced him to sign a contract with the Chicago team for the 1876 season. Spalding in turn convinced three of his teammates, Deacon White, Ross Barnes, and Cal McVey to sign with Chicago as well. Hulbert then turned to the Athletics of Philadelphia and signed Cap Anson to the growing Chicago roster.

Hulbert's aim was simple. He wanted a strong team in a strong league. If the eastern clubs of the National Association objected to his raiding policies, he would simply bypass them and form a new league. To prepare for this eventuality, Hulbert met with representatives from three western clubs in Cincinnati, Louisville, and St. Louis and received their firm backing. He then sent overtures to four eastern clubs in Hartford, New York, Boston, and Philadelphia and invited them to a meeting to be held in New York. On February 2, 1876, these representatives met and hammered out an agreement which formed the National League of Professional Baseball Clubs.

The difference between the National League and the National Association was clear. The players controlled the Association, while the owners controlled the League. The National League was designed to be a strong organization, holding total control over its members. Rules governed such things as territorial rights (only one club to a city), gate receipts, and the like. Annual dues were ten times ($100) the rate of the Association. A strict schedule was adopted requiring each member to play one another ten times during the course of the season. This point would be severely tested before the year was out.

On the field, Hulbert and Spalding's White Stockings clearly outclassed the league. The team hit a resounding .337, 67 points higher than anybody else. Chicago also scored nearly ten runs a game, totaling over 150 more than their nearest rival. One fifth of these runs (126) were scored by one man, second baseman Ross Barnes. Barnes, continuing his torrid Association hitting, led the league with a .429 mark, also leading with 21 doubles and 14 triples. Barnes finished tied for second (with teammates Cap Anson and Paul Hines) in the RBI race with 59, one behind another teammate, Deacon White. Chicago pitcher Al Spalding paced the league with 47 wins, and a winning percentage of .796.

The only reason the Chicagos did not spread-eagle the field was due to the fine pitching of St. Louis and Hartford who finished tied for second, six games out. St. Louis ace George Bradley won the ERA crown (1.23) while Tommy Bond (1.68) and curveball inventor Candy Cummings (1.67) of Hartford finished third and fourth. Mediocre hitting kept these two teams from making a run at the top.

Fourth place Boston was led offensively by shortstop George Wright (.299) and outfielder Jim O'Rourke (.327). But the most interesting wrinkle in this team was on its pitching staff. In an era of finish-it-yourself pitching, John Manning was an anomaly. Manning started 20 games as a pitcher that year, and also relieved in 14 others, picking up five saves along the way. He finished with an 18-5 record and a winning percentage (.783) second only to Spalding. If this was not enough, Manning was also the starting center fielder for the Red Stockings. A very busy year indeed!

The second division showcased some fine individual efforts. Pitcher Jim Devlin of fifth place Louisville kept his team flirting with the .500 mark. Although he and the team finished with a losing mark, Devlin finished second (1.56) in the ERA race, and led the league with 122 strikeouts. The seventh place Athletics of Philadelphia were a hard-hitting team paced by outfielder George Hall (.366) who was the only non-Chicagoan to crack the top five in the batting race. Hall also hit the most home runs (5), one more than Charlie Jones of last place Cincinnati.

As the season wound down, the National League faced its first crisis. For financial reasons, both New York and Philadelphia refused to go on their last western trip. This was a fairly common occurrence in the National Association, but not in the National League. Hulbert was outraged. He demanded, and got, an unanimous vote from the other owners which expelled the two recalcitrants from the league. Most critics thought this foolhardy, seeing that New York and Philadelphia were the two most populous cities gracing the circuit. But Hulbert had his way; neither team would rejoin the National League for another seven years.

The year 1876 saw the transition of baseball from a game controlled by the players, to one controlled by the owners. It constituted a new beginning with the game being brought under tight control for the first time. Consistent scheduling and controlled rosters were the most positive results. Tighter restrictions on the players was one of the drawbacks.

In February 1876, eight businessmen were faced with a choice: stick with a flawed, albeit comfortable status quo, or follow a new man with a new approach. Most agree the right choice was made.

1876 NATIONAL LEAGUE   41

CHICAGO
White Stockings 52-14   .788   1st   Al Spalding

BATTERS	POS/GAMES	GP	AB	R	H	BI	2B	3B	HR	BB	SO	SB	BA	SA
Cal McVey	1B55,P11,C6,OF1,3B1	63	308	62	107	53	15	0	1	2	4		.347	.406
Ross Barnes	2B66,P1	66	322	126	138	59	21	14	1	20	8		.429	.590
John Peters	SS66,P1	66	316	70	111	47	14	2	1	3	2		.351	.418
Cap Anson	3B66,C2	66	309	63	110	59	9	7	2	12	8		.356	.453
Bob Addy	OF32	32	142	36	40	16	4	1	0	5	0		.282	.324
Paul Hines	OF64,2B1	64	305	62	101	59	21	3	2	1	3		.331	.439
John Glenn	OF56,1B15	66	276	55	84	32	9	2	0	12	6		.304	.351
Deacon White	C63,OF3,1B3,3B1,P1	66	303	66	104	60	18	1	1	7	3		.343	.419
Al Spalding	P61,OF10,1B3	66	292	54	91	44	14	2	0	6	3		.312	.373
Oscar Bielaski	OF32	32	139	24	29	10	3	0	0	2	3		.209	.230
Fred Andrus	OF8	8	36	6	11	2	3	0	0	0	5		.306	.389
		66	2748	624	926	441	131	32	8	70	45		.337	.417

PITCHERS		W	L	PCT	G	GS	CG	SH	SV	IP	H	BB	SO	ERA
Al Spalding		47	12	.796	61	60	53	8	0	529	542	26	39	1.75
Cal McVey		5	2	.714	11	6	5	0	2	59	57	2	9	1.52
Deacon White		0	0	----	1	0	0	0	0	1	2	1	3	0.00
John Peters		0	0	----	1	0	0	0	1	1	1	1	0	0.00
Ross Barnes		0	0	----	1	0	0	0	0	1	7	0	1	20.25
		52	14	.788	66	66	58	8	4	592	608	29	51	1.76

ST. LOUIS
Brown Stockings 45-19   .703   -6   2nd   Graffen - McManus

BATTERS	POS/GAMES	GP	AB	R	H	BI	2B	3B	HR	BB	SO	SB	BA	SA
Dutch Dehlman	1B64	64	245	40	45	9	6	0	0	9	10		.184	.208
Mike McGeary	2B56,C5,OF1,3B1	61	276	48	72	30	3	0	0	2	1		.261	.272
Denny Mack	SS41,2B5,OF2,	48	180	32	39	7	5	0	1	11	5		.217	.261
Joe Battin	3B63,2B1	64	283	34	85	46	11	4	0	6	6		.300	.367
Joe Blong	OF62,P1	62	264	30	62	30	7	4	0	2	9		.235	.292
Lip Pike	OF62,2B2	63	282	55	91	50	19	10	1	8	9		.323	.472
Ned Cuthbert	OF63	63	283	46	70	25	10	1	0	7	4		.247	.290
John Clapp	C61,OF4,2B1	64	298	60	91	29	4	2	0	8	2		.305	.332
George Bradley	P64	64	265	29	66	28	7	6	0	3	12		.249	.321
Dickey Pearce	SS23,OF1,2B1	25	102	12	21	10	1	0	0	3	5		.206	.216
		64	2478	386	642	264	73	27	2	59	63		.259	.313

PITCHERS		W	L	PCT	G	GS	CG	SH	SV	IP	H	BB	SO	ERA
George Bradley		45	19	.703	64	64	63	16	0	573	470	38	103	1.23
Joe Blong		0	0	----	1	0	0	0	0	4	2	1	0	0.00
		45	19	.703	64	64	63	16	0	577	472	39	103	1.22

HARTFORD
Dark Blues 47-21   .691   -6   3rd   O'Leary - Crane

BATTERS	POS/GAMES	GP	AB	R	H	BI	2B	3B	HR	BB	SO	SB	BA	SA
Everett Mills	1B63	63	254	28	66	23	8	1	0	1	3		.260	.299
Jack Burdock	2B69,3B1	69	309	66	80	23	9	1	0	13	16		.259	.294
Tom Carey	SS68	68	289	51	78	26	7	0	0	3	4		.270	.294
Bob Ferguson	3B69	69	310	48	82	32	8	5	0	2	11		.265	.323
Dick Higham	OF59,C13,2B1,SS1	67	312	59	102	35	21	2	0	2	7		.327	.407
Jack Remsen	OF69	69	324	62	89	30	12	5	1	1	15		.275	.352
Tom York	OF67	67	263	47	68	39	12	7	1	10	4		.259	.369
Doug Allison	C40,OF6	44	163	19	43	15	4	0	0	3	9		.264	.288
Tommy Bond	P45	45	182	18	50	21	8	0	0	0	4		.275	.319
Bill Harbridge	C24,OF6,1B2	30	106	11	23	6	2	1	0	3	2		.217	.255
Candy Cummings	P24	24	105	14	17	7	3	0	0	0	3		.162	.190
John Cassidy	OF8,1B4	12	47	6	13	8	2	0	0	1	0		.277	.319
		69	2664	429	711	265	96	22	2	39	78		.267	.322

PITCHERS		W	L	PCT	G	GS	CG	SH	SV	IP	H	BB	SO	ERA
Tommy Bond		31	13	.705	45	45	45	6	0	408	355	13	88	1.68
Candy Cummings		16	8	.667	24	24	24	5	0	216	215	14	26	1.67
		47	21	.691	69	69	69	11	0	624	570	27	114	1.67

1876 NATIONAL LEAGUE

BOSTON Red Caps
39-31 .557 -15 4th Harry Wright

BATTERS	POS/GAMES	GP	AB	R	H	BI	2B	3B	HR	BB	SO	SB	BA	SA
Tim Murnane	1B65,OF3,2B1	69	308	60	87	34	4	3	2	8	12		.282	.334
John Morrill	2B37,C23,OF5,1B3	66	278	38	73	26	5	2	0	3	5		.263	.295
George Wright	SS68,2B2,P1	70	335	72	100	34	18	6	1	8	9		.299	.397
Harry Schafer	3B70	70	286	47	72	35	11	0	0	4	11		.252	.290
Jim O'Rourke	OF68,1B2,C1	70	312	61	102	43	17	3	2	15	17		.327	.420
Jack Manning	OF56,P34,SS1,2B1	70	288	52	76	25	13	0	2	7	5		.264	.330
Andy Leonard	OF35,2B30	64	303	53	85	27	10	2	0	4	6		.281	.327
Lewis Brown	C45,OF1	45	195	23	41	21	6	6	2	3	22		.210	.333
Frank Whitney	OF34,2B1	34	139	27	33	15	7	1	0	1	3		.237	.302
Joe Borden	P29,OF16	32	121	19	25	7	3	0	0	3	3		.207	.231
George Bradley	P22,OF4	22	82	12	19	8	2	1	0	2	3		.232	.280
Tim McGinley	OF6,C3	9	40	5	6	2	0	0	0	0	1		.150	.150
Dick McBride	P4,OF1	4	16	2	3	4	0	0	0	0	0		.188	.188
Sam Wright	SS2	2	8	0	1	0	0	0	0	0	0		.125	.125
Tricky Nichols	P1	1	4	0	0	0	0	0	0	0	0		.000	.000
William Parks	OF1	1	4	0	0	0	0	0	0	0	0		.000	.000
Harry Wright	OF1	1	3	0	0	0	0	0	0	0	1		.000	.000
		70	2722	471	723	281	96	24	9	58	98		.266	.328

PITCHERS		W	L	PCT	G	GS	CG	SH	SV	IP	H	BB	SO	ERA
Jack Manning		18	5	.783	34	20	13	0	5	197	213	32	24	2.14
Joe Borden		11	12	.478	29	24	16	2	1	218	257	51	34	2.89
George Bradley		9	10	.474	22	21	16	1	1	173	201	16	16	2.49
Tricky Nichols		1	0	1.000	1	1	1	0	0	9	7	0	0	1.00
Dick McBride		0	4	.000	4	4	3	0	0	33	53	5	2	2.73
George Wright		0	0	----	1	0	0	0	0	1	1	0	1	0.00
		39	31	.557	70	70	49	3	7	631	732	104	77	2.51

LOUISVILLE Grays
30-36 .455 -22 5th Jack Chapman

BATTERS	POS/GAMES	GP	AB	R	H	BI	2B	3B	HR	BB	SO	SB	BA	SA
Joe Gerhardt	1B54,2B5,SS3,3B2,OF2	65	292	33	76	18	10	3	2	3	5		.260	.336
Ed Somerville	2B64	64	256	29	48	14	5	1	0	1	6		.188	.215
Chick Fulmer	SS66	66	267	28	73	29	9	5	1	1	10		.273	.356
Bill Hague	3B67,SS1	67	294	31	78	22	8	0	1	2	10		.265	.303
Art Allison	OF23,1B8	31	130	9	27	10	2	1	0	2	6		.208	.238
Scott Hastings	OF65,C5	67	283	36	73	21	6	1	0	5	11		.258	.286
Johnny Ryan	OF64,P1	64	241	32	61	18	5	1	1	6	23		.253	.295
Pop Snyder	C55,OF4	56	224	21	44	9	4	1	1	2	7		.196	.237
Jim Devlin	P68	68	298	38	94	28	14	1	0	1	11		.315	.369
Jack Chapman	OF17,3B1	17	67	4	16	5	1	0	0	1	3		.239	.254
Jim Clinton	OF14,1B1,P1	16	65	8	22	0	2	0	0	0	0		.338	.369
George Bechtel	OF14	(1-2) 14	55	2	10	2	1	0	0	0	1		.182	.200
Bill Holbert	C12	12	43	3	11	5	0	0	0	0	3		.256	.256
Dan Collins	OF7	7	28	3	4	9	1	0	0	0	2		.143	.179
Jack Carbine	1B6,OF1	7	25	3	4	1	0	0	0	0	0		.160	.160
Frank Pearce	P1	1	2	0	0	0	0	0	0	0	0		.000	.000
		69	2570	280	641	191	68	14	6	24	98		.249	.294

PITCHERS		W	L	PCT	G	GS	CG	SH	SV	IP	H	BB	SO	ERA
Jim Devlin		30	35	.462	68	68	66	5	0	622	566	37	122	1.56
Jim Clinton		0	1	.000	1	1	1	0	0	9	12	0	1	6.00
Johnny Ryan		0	0	----	1	0	0	0	0	8	22	0	1	5.63
Frank Pearce		0	0	----	1	0	0	0	0	4	5	1	1	4.50
		30	36	.455	69	69	67	5	0	643	605	38	125	1.69

NEW YORK Mutuals
21-35 .375 -25 6th Bill Cammeyer

BATTERS	POS/GAMES	GP	AB	R	H	BI	2B	3B	HR	BB	SO	SB	BA	SA
Joe Start	1B56	56	264	40	73	21	6	0	0	1	2		.277	.299
Bill Craver	2B42,C11,SS6	56	246	24	55	22	4	0	0	2	7		.224	.240
Jim Hallinan	SS50,2B4,OF2	54	240	45	67	36	7	6	2	2	4		.279	.383
Al Nichols	3B57	57	212	20	38	9	4	0	0	2	3		.179	.198

1876 NATIONAL LEAGUE

NEW YORK (cont.)
Mutuals

BATTERS	POS/GAMES		GP	AB	R	H	BI	2B	3B	HR	BB	SO	SB	BA	SA
Eddie Booth	OF53,2B5,P1		57	228	17	49	7	2	1	0	2	4		.215	.232
Jim Holdsworth	OF49,2B3		52	241	23	64	19	3	2	0	1	2		.266	.238
Fred Treacey	OF57		57	256	47	54	18	5	1	0	1	5		.211	.238
Nat Hicks	C45		45	188	20	44	15	4	1	0	3	4		.234	.266
Bobby Mathews	P56,OF1		56	218	19	40	9	4	1	0	3	2		.183	.211
Mike Hayes	OF5		5	21	2	3	2	0	2	0	0	0		.143	.333
George Bechtel	OF2	(2-2)	2	10	2	3	0	0	0	0	0	0		.300	.300
Jim Shandly	OF2		2	8	0	1	0	0	0	0	0	0		.125	.125
John Maloney	OF2		2	7	1	2	2	0	1	0	0	1		.286	.571
Pete Treacey	SS2		2	5	1	0	0	0	0	0	1	0		.000	.000
John Hatfield	2B1		1	4	0	1	1	0	0	0	0	0		.250	.250
George Heubel	1B1		1	4	0	0	0	0	0	0	0	0		.000	.000
Terry Larkin	P1		1	4	0	0	0	0	0	0	0	0		.000	.000
John McGuiness	2B1,C1		1	4	0	0	0	0	0	0	0	0		.000	.000
Ed Thayer	2B1		1	4	0	0	0	0	0	0	0	0		.000	.000
Billy West	1B1		1	4	0	0	0	0	0	0	0	0		.000	.000
Davy Force	SS1	(2-2)	1	3	0	0	0	0	0	0	0	0		.000	.000
Neal Phelps	C1	(1-2)	1	3	0	0	0	0	0	0	0	1		.000	.000
George Seward	2B1		1	3	0	0	0	0	0	0	0	0		.000	.000
Bob Valentine	C1		1	3	0	0	0	0	0	0	0	0		.000	.000
			57	2180	260	494	161	39	15	2	18	35		.227	.261

PITCHERS		W	L	PCT	G	GS	CG	SH	SV	IP	H	BB	SO	ERA
Bobby Mathews		21	34	.382	56	55	55	2	0	516	693	24	37	2.86
Terry Larkin		0	1	.000	1	1	1	0	0	9	9	0	0	3.00
Eddie Booth		0	0	.000	1	0	0	0	0	5	16	0	0	10.80
		21	35	.375	56	56	56	2	0	530	718	24	37	2.94

PHILADELPHIA   14-45   .237   -34.5   7th   Al Wright
Athletics

BATTERS	POS/GAMES		GP	AB	R	H	BI	2B	3B	HR	BB	SO	SB	BA	SA
Ezra Sutton	1B29,2B15,3B8,OF4		54	236	45	70	31	12	7	1	3	2		.297	.419
Wes Fisler	2B21,OF24,1B14,SS1		59	278	42	80	30	15	1	1	2	4		.288	.360
Davy Force	SS60,3B2	(1-2)	60	284	48	66	17	6	0	0	5	3		.232	.254
Levi Meyerle	3B49,OF3,2B3,P2		55	256	46	87	34	12	8	0	3	2		.340	.449
William Coon	OF29,C18,3B4,2B4,P2		54	220	30	50	22	5	1	0	2	4		.227	.259
Dave Eggler	OF39		39	174	28	52	19	4	0	0	2	4		.299	.322
George Hall	OF60		60	268	51	98	45	7	13	5	8	4		.366	.545
Fergy Malone	C20,OF3,SS1		22	96	14	22	6	2	0	0	0	1		.229	.250
Lon Knight	P34,1B13,OF9,2B6		55	240	32	60	24	9	3	0	2	2		.250	.313
George Zettlein	P28,OF12,1B7,2B1		32	128	11	27	11	2	1	0	0	5		.211	.242
Bill Fouser	2B14,OF7,1B1		21	89	11	12	2	0	1	0	0	0		.135	.157
Whitey Ritterson	C14,OF4,3B1		16	52	8	13	4	3	0	0	0	2		.250	.308
Doc Bushong	C5		5	21	4	1	1	0	0	0	0	0		.048	.048
Pete Curren	C2,OF1		3	12	5	4	2	1	0	0	0	0		.333	.417
Lou Paul	C3		3	12	2	2	0	1	0	0	0	0		.167	.250
Jim Ward	C1		1	4	1	2	1	0	0	0	0	1		.500	.500
John Bergh	C1,OF1		1	4	0	0	0	0	0	0	0	2		.000	.000
Neal Phelps	C1	(2-2)	1	4	0	0	0	0	0	0	0	0		.000	.000
Fred Warner	OF1		1	3	0	0	0	0	0	0	0	0		.000	.000
Flip Lafferty	P1		1	3	0	0	0	0	0	0	0	0		.000	.000
John Mueller	C1		1	3	0	0	0	0	0	0	0	0		.000	.000
			60	2387	378	646	249	79	35	7	27	36		.271	.342

PITCHERS		W	L	PCT	G	GS	CG	SH	SV	IP	H	BB	SO	ERA
Lon Knight		10	22	.313	34	32	27	0	0	282	383	34	12	2.62
George Zettlein		4	20	.167	28	25	23	1	2	234	358	6	10	3.88
Flip Lafferty		0	1	.000	1	1	1	0	0	9	5	0	0	0.00
Levi Meyerle		0	2	.000	2	2	2	0	0	18	28	1	0	5.00
William Coon		0	0	----	2	0	0	0	0	7	9	0	0	5.14
		14	45	.237	60	60	53	1	2	550	783	41	22	3.22

1876 NATIONAL LEAGUE

CINCINNATI
Red Stockings   9-56   .138   -42.5   8th   Charlie Gould

BATTERS	POS/GAMES	GP	AB	R	H	BI	2B	3B	HR	BB	SO	SB	BA	SA
Charlie Gould	1B62,P2	61	258	27	65	11	7	0	0	6	11		.252	.279
Charlie Sweasy	2B55,OF1	56	225	18	46	10	5	2	0	2	5		.204	.244
Henry Kessler	SS46,OF16	59	248	26	64	11	5	0	0	7	10		.258	.278
Will Foley	3B46,C20	58	221	19	50	9	3	2	0	0	14		.226	.258
Dave Pearson	OF30,C31,SS1,2B1,3B1,P1	57	233	33	55	13	4	1	0	1	9		.236	.262
Charlie Jones	OF64	64	276	40	79	38	17	4	4	7	17		.286	.420
Redleg Snyder	OF55	55	205	10	31	12	3	1	0	1	19		.151	.176
Amos Booth	C24,3B24,SS22,OF3,P3	63	272	31	71	14	3	0	0	9	11		.261	.272
Cherokee Fisher	P28,OF11,SS1,1B1	35	129	12	32	4	1	0	0	0	8		.248	.256
Dory Dean	P30,OF5,SS2	34	138	9	36	4	3	1	0	2	13		.261	.297
Bobby Clack	OF17,2B8,1B5,3B3,P1	32	118	10	19	5	0	1	0	5	12		.161	.178
Dale Williams	P9	9	35	1	7	1	0	0	0	0	4		.200	.200
Sam Field	C3,2B2	4	14	2	0	0	0	0	0	1	3		.000	.000
		65	2372	238	555	132	51	12	4	41	136		.234	.271

PITCHERS		W	L	PCT	G	GS	CG	SH	SV	IP	H	BB	SO	ERA
Cherokee Fisher		4	20	.167	28	24	22	0	0	229	294	6	29	3.02
Dory Dean		4	26	.133	30	30	26	0	0	263	397	24	22	3.73
Dale Williams		1	8	.111	9	9	9	0	0	83	123	4	9	4.23
Amos Booth		0	1	.000	3	1	0	0	0	10	22	0	0	9.31
Dave Pearson		0	1	.000	1	1	0	0	0	0	2	0	0	inf.
Charlie Gould		0	0	----	2	0	0	0	0	4	10	0	0	0.00
Bobby Clack		0	0	----	1	0	0	0	0	2	2	0	0	4.50
		9	56	.138	65	65	57	0	0	591	850	34	60	3.64

1877 NATIONAL LEAGUE

The Louisville Four

During the summer of 1877, the Louisville Grays were proving themselves the toast of the National League. On the morning of August 13, they found themselves firmly in first place over the Boston nine by a three and one-half game margin. But then they began to lose. By the 25th, they came to Boston with only a one-game lead, which Louisville squandered by losing three straight. In this series, pitcher Jim Devlin threw particularly poorly, even committing a costly error in the first game. By September 17, Louisville had lost 11 of 14 to fall seven and one-half games behind. The Grays won seven of their last eight, but it was too late and they finished second, seven games out.

Teams go into slumps all too often, thus no one questioned Louisville's sudden decline. No one that is, but Louisville's biggest newspaper. The newspaper recalled shoddy play during the Grays' August swoon, which included poor fielding, pitching and hitting. Then four of the Grays' prominent players were seen sporting diamond stickpins. Gambling connections, and covert telegrams were recalled—and the four players, when pressed, confessed that they had deliberately lost games, paid to do so by gamblers. The four indicted were: Jim Devlin, pitcher; George Hall, outfielder; Bill Craver, shortstop; and Al Nichols, a utility infielder. All four were immediately banned from baseball.

The National League was down to six teams in 1877; for the New York and Philadelphia clubs had not been replaced. The remaining teams (Boston, Hartford, St. Louis, Chicago, Louisville, and Cincinnati) were all that were left.

There was no argument that Boston had help from Louisville in capturing the pennant. Equally helpful was their 20-1 spurt at the end of the season. As a matter of fact, if Louisville had won games during their last 22 as they had through their first 38 (through August 13) they would have still lost to Boston's final onslaught by two games. Boston first baseman, Deacon White, earned his best season ever. He hit .387, with 103 hits and 11 triples, all league-leading totals. Jim O'Rourke was not far behind at .362, leading the circuit with 68 runs. Tommy Bond won the pitching equivalent of the Triple Crown with forty wins, 170 strikeouts, and a 2.11 earned run average.

Despite going into the tank, Louisville finished with a fine year. George Hall (.323) played well as did Joe Gerhardt (.304). The pitching started and ended with Jim Devlin, who was the last of the one-man staffs. He finished second with 35 wins.

Hartford finished third, ten games out, while St. Louis finished fourth. Hartford featured Joe Start (.332) and runner-up batting champ John Cassidy (.378), while St. Louis showcased Mike Dorgan (.308), and John Clapp (.318).

Chicago plummeted from first to fifth mostly due to the unfortunate decision of manager Al Spalding to play first base instead of pitch. Also contributing was the injury to Ross Barnes, who saw his average dive to .272. Despite good years from Cal McVey (.368), Cap Anson (.337), and John Peters (.317), the White Stockings finished seven games under .500.

Once again, Cincinnati finished in the cellar. However, they were lucky to finish at all. The team went bankrupt in June and spent several days in limbo before new owners could be found. During this interregnum, Chicago brazenly snatched two of Cincinnati's best from the "defunct" team—Jim Hallinan and Charlie Jones. Amidst howls of protests from the new owners, Chicago returned Jones, but they kept Hallinan (who was hitting .370 at the time). Jones ended up with a good year at .310 and Jack Manning hit .317, while Lip Pike won the home run title with a modest total of four.

Of the Louisville four, only Jim Devlin made any serious efforts to return to organized baseball. Entreating the owners each and every year, he claimed severe financial hardship as his need to return. Finally, the president of the National League, William Hulbert, met with Devlin. After slipping him a fifty dollar bill he said, "Devlin, that is what I think of you personally; but damn you, you have sold a game, you are dishonest, and this National League will not stand for it." Hulbert was true to his word. Neither Jim Devlin nor any of his co-conspirators ever again appeared in a National League game.

1877 NATIONAL LEAGUE 47

BOSTON Red Caps

42-18   .700   1st   Harry Wright

BATTERS	POS/GAMES	GP	AB	R	H	BI	2B	3B	HR	BB	SO	SB	BA	SA
Deacon White	1B35,OF19,C7	59	266	51	103	49	14	11	2	8	3		.387	.545
George Wright	2B58,SS3	61	290	58	80	35	15	1	0	9	15		.276	.334
Ezra Sutton	SS36,3B22	58	253	43	74	39	10	6	0	4	10		.292	.379
John Morrill	3B30,1B18,OF11,2B3	61	242	47	73	28	5	1	0	6	15		.302	.331
Andy Leonard	OF37,SS21	58	272	46	78	27	5	0	0	5	5		.287	.305
Jim O'Rourke	OF60,1B1	61	265	68	96	23	14	4	0	20	9		.362	.445
Tim Murnane	OF30,1B5	35	140	23	39	15	7	1	1	6	7		.279	.374
Lewis Brown	C55,1B4	58	221	27	56	31	12	8	1	6	7		.253	.294
Tommy Bond	P58,OF3	61	259	32	59	30	4	3	0	1	15		.228	.266
Harry Schafer	OF23,3B9,SS1	33	141	20	39	13	5	2	0	0	7		.277	.340
Will White	P3	3	15	4	3	1	0	0	0	0	1		.200	.200
Harry Wright	OF1	1	4	0	0	0	0	0	0	0	1		.000	.000
		61	2368	419	700	291	91	37	4	65	121		.296	.370

PITCHERS		W	L	PCT	G	GS	CG	SH	SV	IP	H	BB	SO	ERA
Tommy Bond		40	17	.702	58	58	58	6	0	521	530	36	170	2.11
Will White		2	1	.667	3	3	3	1	0	27	27	2	7	3.00
		42	18	.700	61	61	61	7	0	548	557	38	177	2.15

LOUISVILLE Grays

35-25   .583   -7   2nd   Jack Chapman

BATTERS	POS/GAMES	GP	AB	R	H	BI	2B	3B	HR	BB	SO	SB	BA	SA
Juice Latham	1B59	59	278	42	81	22	10	6	0	5	6		.291	.371
Joe Gerhardt	2B57	59	250	41	76	35	6	5	1	5	8		.304	.380
Bill Craver	SS57	57	238	33	63	29	5	2	0	5	11		.265	.303
Bill Hague	3B59	59	263	38	70	24	7	1	1	7	18		.266	.312
Orator Shaffer	OF60,1B1	61	260	38	74	34	9	5	3	9	17		.285	.392
Bill Crowley	OF58,SS2,C2,3B1,2B1	61	238	30	67	23	9	3	1	4	13		.282	.357
George Hall	OF61	61	269	53	87	26	15	8	0	12	19		.323	.439
Pop Snyder	C61,OF1,SS1	61	248	23	64	28	7	2	2	3	14		.258	.327
Jim Devlin	P61	61	268	38	72	27	6	3	1	7	27		.269	.325
Al Nichols	2B3,SS1,3B1,1B1	6	19	1	4	0	0	1	0	0	2		.211	.316
Flip Lafferty	OF4	4	17	2	1	0	1	0	0	0	4		.059	.118
John Haldeman	2B1	1	4	0	0	0	0	0	0	0	0		.000	.000
Harry Little	2B1	(2-2) 1	3	0	0	0	0	0	0	0	0		.000	.000
		61	2355	339	659	248	75	36	9	58	140		.280	.354

PITCHERS		W	L	PCT	G	GS	CG	SH	SV	IP	H	BB	SO	ERA
Jim Devlin		35	25	.583	61	61	61	4	0	559	617	41	140	2.25
		35	25	.583	61	61	61	4	0	559	617	41	140	2.25

HARTFORD Dark Blues

31-27   .534   -10   3rd   Bob Ferguson

BATTERS	POS/GAMES	GP	AB	R	H	BI	2B	3B	HR	BB	SO	SB	BA	SA
Joe Start	1B60	60	271	55	90	21	3	6	1	6	2		.332	.399
Jack Burdock	2B55,3B3	58	277	35	72	9	6	0	0	2	16		.260	.282
Tom Carey	SS60	60	274	38	70	20	3	2	1	0	9		.255	.292
Bob Ferguson	3B56,P3	58	254	40	65	35	7	2	0	3	10		.256	.299
John Cassidy	OF58,P2	60	251	43	95	27	10	5	0	3	3		.378	.458
Jim Holdsworth	OF55	55	260	26	66	20	5	2	0	2	8		.254	.288
Tom York	OF56	56	237	43	67	37	16	7	1	3	11		.283	.422
Bill Harbridge	C32,OF5,2B4	41	167	18	37	8	5	2	0	3	6		.222	.275
Terry Larkin	P56,3B2,2B1	58	228	28	52	18	6	5	1	5	23		.228	.311
Doug Allison	C29	29	115	14	17	6	2	0	0	3	7		.148	.165
Oak Taylor	OF2	2	8	0	3	0	0	0	0	0	2		.375	.375
John Bass	OF1	1	4	1	1	0	0	0	0	0	0		.250	.250
John Maloney	OF1	1	4	0	1	0	0	0	0	0	0		.250	.250
Jay Pike	OF1	1	4	0	1	0	0	0	0	0	0		.250	.250
Josh Bunce	OF1	1	4	0	0	0	0	0	0	0	0		.000	.000
		60	2358	341	637	201	63	31	4	30	97		.270	.375

HARTFORD (cont.)
Dark Blues

PITCHERS	W	L	PCT	G	GS	CG	SH	SV	IP	H	BB	SO	ERA
Terry Larkin	29	25	.537	56	56	55	4	0	501	510	53	96	2.14
Bob Ferguson	1	1	.500	3	2	2	0	0	25	38	2	1	3.96
John Cassidy	1	1	.500	2	2	2	0	0	18	24	1	2	5.00
	31	27	.534	60	60	59	4	0	544	572	56	99	2.32

ST. LOUIS
Brown Stockings

28-32 .467 -14 4th George McManus

BATTERS	POS/GAMES		GP	AB	R	H	BI	2B	3B	HR	BB	SO	SB	BA	SA
Dutch Dehlman	1B31,OF1		32	119	24	22	11	4	0	0	7	21		.185	.218
Mike McGeary	2B39,3B19		57	258	35	65	20	3	2	0	2	6		.252	.279
Davy Force	SS50,3B8		58	225	24	59	22	5	3	0	11	15		.262	.311
Joe Battin	3B32,2B21,OF5,P1		57	226	28	45	22	3	7	1	6	17		.199	.288
Joe Blong	OF40,P25		58	218	17	47	13	8	3	0	4	22		.216	.280
Jack Remsen	OF33		33	123	14	32	13	3	4	0	4	3		.260	.350
Mike Dorgan	OF50,C12,3B2,SS1,2B1		60	266	45	82	23	9	7	0	9	13		.308	.395
John Clapp	C53,OF10,1B1		60	255	47	81	34	6	6	0	8	6		.318	.388
Art Croft	1B28,OF25,2B1		54	220	23	51	27	5	2	0	1	15		.232	.273
Tricky Nichols	P42,OF16		51	186	22	31	9	4	2	0	3	15		.167	.210
Dickey Pearce	SS8		8	29	1	5	4	0	0	0	1	4		.172	.172
Leonidas Lee	OF4,SS1		4	18	0	5	0	1	0	0	0	1		.278	.333
George Little	OF3	(1-2)	3	12	2	2	0	0	0	0	1	6		.167	.167
Tom Loftus	OF3		3	11	2	2	0	0	0	0	0	1		.182	.182
Ed McKenna	OF1		1	5	0	1	0	0	0	0	0	0		.200	.200
Jack Gleason	OF1		1	4	0	1	0	0	0	0	0	1		.250	.250
T.E. Newell	SS1		1	3	0	0	0	0	0	0	0	0		.000	.000
			60	2178	284	531	198	51	36	1	57	147		.244	.302

PITCHERS	W	L	PCT	G	GS	CG	SH	SV	IP	H	BB	SO	ERA
Tricky Nichols	18	23	.439	42	39	35	1	0	350	376	53	80	2.60
Joe Blong	10	9	.526	25	21	17	0	0	187	203	38	51	2.74
Joe Battin	0	0	----	1	0	0	0	0	4	3	1	1	4.91
	28	32	.467	60	60	52	1	0	541	582	92	132	2.66

CHICAGO
White Stockings

26-33 .441 -22.5 5th Al Spalding

BATTERS	POS/GAMES		GP	AB	R	H	BI	2B	3B	HR	BB	SO	SB	BA	SA
Al Spalding	1B45,2B13,P4,3B2		60	254	29	65	35	7	6	0	3	16		.256	.331
Ross Barnes	2B22		22	92	16	25	5	1	0	0	7	4		.272	.283
John Peters	SS60		60	265	45	84	41	10	3	0	1	7		.317	.377
Cap Anson	3B40,C31		59	255	52	86	32	19	1	0	9	3		.337	.420
Paul Hines	OF49,2B11		60	261	44	73	23	11	7	0	9	3		.280	.375
Dave Eggler	OF33		33	136	20	36	20	3	0	0	1	5		.265	.287
John Glenn	OF36,1B14		50	202	31	46	20	6	1	0	8	16		.228	.267
Cal McVey	C40,3B17,P17,2B1,1B1		60	266	58	98	36	9	7	0	8	11		.368	.455
George Bradley	P50,3B16,1B3,OF1		55	214	31	52	12	7	3	0	6	19		.243	.304
Harry Smith	2B14,OF10	(1-2)	24	94	7	19	3	1	0	0	4	6		.202	.213
Jim Hallman	OF19	(2-2)	19	89	17	25	11	4	1	0	4	2		.281	.348
Charles Eden	OF15		15	55	9	12	5	0	1	0	3	6		.218	.255
Charlie Waitt	OF10		10	41	2	4	2	0	0	0	0	3		.098	.098
Laurie Reis	P4		4	16	3	2	1	0	0	0	0	0		.125	.125
----- Quinn	OF4		4	14	1	1	0	0	0	0	1	0		.071	.071
Charlie Jones	OF2	(2-3)	2	8	1	3	2	1	0	0	1	0		.375	.375
Dave Rowe	OF2,P1		2	7	0	2	0	0	0	0	0	3		.286	.286
Cherokee Fisher	3B1		1	4	0	0	0	0	0	0	0	2		.000	.000
			60	2273	366	633	248	79	30	0	57	111		.278	.340

PITCHERS	W	L	PCT	G	GS	CG	SH	SV	IP	H	BB	SO	ERA
George Bradley	18	23	.439	50	44	35	2	0	394	452	39	59	3.31
Cal McVey	4	8	.333	17	10	6	0	2	92	129	11	20	4.50
Laurie Reis	3	1	.750	4	4	4	1	0	36	29	6	11	0.75
Al Spalding	1	0	1.000	4	1	0	0	1	11	17	0	2	3.27
Dave Rowe	0	1	.000	1	1	0	0	0	1	3	2	0	18.00
	26	33	.441	60	60	45	3	3	534	630	58	92	3.37

1877 NATIONAL LEAGUE

CINCINNATI
Red Stockings
15-42 .263 -25.5 6th Pike - Addy

BATTERS	POS/GAMES		GP	AB	R	H	BI	2B	3B	HR	BB	SO	SB	BA	SA
Charlie Gould	1B24,OF1		24	91	5	25	13	2	1	0	5	5		.275	.319
Jim Hallinan	2B16	(1-2)	16	73	18	27	7	1	1	0	1	1		.370	.411
Jack Manning	SS26,1B17,OF12,P10,2B2		57	252	47	80	36	16	7	0	5	6		.317	.437
Will Foley	3B56		56	216	23	41	18	5	1	0	4	13		.190	.222
Bob Addy	OF57		57	245	27	68	31	2	3	0	6	5		.278	.310
Lip Pike	OF38,2B22,SS2		58	262	45	78	23	12	4	4	9	7		.298	.420
Charlie Jones	OF46,1B10	(1,3-3)	55	232	52	72	36	11	10	2	14	25		.310	.470
Scott Hastings	C20,OF1		20	71	7	10	3	1	0	0	3	6		.141	.155
Amos Booth	SS13,C12,P12,2B1,3B3		44	157	16	27	13	2	1	0	12	10		.172	.197
Levi Meyerle	SS18,2B12,OF1		27	107	11	35	15	7	2	0	0	4		.327	.430
Candy Cummings	P19,OF3		19	70	6	14	4	1	2	0	4	6		.200	.271
Bobby Mathews	P15,OF1,SS1		15	59	5	10	2	5	0	0	1	2		.179	.268
Robert Mitchell	P12,OF2		13	49	5	10	5	3	0	0	1	2		.204	.265
Ned Cuthbert	OF12		12	56	6	10	2	5	0	0	1	2		.179	.268
George Miller	C11		11	37	4	6	3	1	0	0	5	2		.162	.189
Harry Smith	C8,2B3,OF1	(2-2)	10	36	4	9	3	2	1	0	1	5		.250	.361
Chub Sullivan	1B8		8	32	4	8	4	0	0	0	1	0		.250	.250
Nat Hicks	C8		8	32	3	6	3	0	0	0	1	2		.188	.188
Johnny Ryan	OF6		6	26	2	4	2	0	1	0	1	5		.154	.231
Henry Kessler	C5		6	20	0	2	0	0	0	0	2	1		.100	.100
Billy Redmon	SS3		3	12	1	3	3	1	0	0	1	1		.250	.333
			58	2135	291	545	224	72	34	6	78	110		.255	.329

PITCHERS		W	L	PCT	G	GS	CG	SH	SV	IP	H	BB	SO	ERA
Robert Mitchell		6	5	.545	12	12	11	1	0	100	123	11	41	3.51
Candy Cummings		5	14	.263	19	19	16	0	0	156	219	13	11	4.34
Bobby Mathews		3	12	.200	15	15	13	0	0	129	208	17	9	4.04
Amos Booth		1	7	.125	12	8	6	0	0	86	114	13	18	3.56
Jack Manning		0	4	.000	10	4	2	0	1	44	83	7	6	6.95
		15	42	.263	58	58	48	1	1	515	747	61	85	4.19

1878 NATIONAL LEAGUE

Survival

The National League was in trouble. The six teams staggered through 1877, only to be rocked by the gambling scandal which decimated the Louisville squad following the season. Thus it was no surprise when Louisville decided not to field a team in the National League in 1878. It was more of a surprise when Hartford, then St. Louis followed suit.

Financially, 1877 was not a successful year for baseball. All six clubs lost money — $20,000 in all, led by St. Louis's $8,000 loss. It was no wonder that three of the teams decided not to take a financial bath in 1878. It was a wonder that three decided to stick it out.

In another aspect of the game, 1877 was a success. That was the year that saw the birth of the minor leagues. Two minor league organizations — the League Alliance and the International Association — contained 29 teams. The best team in the International Association proved to be the Tecumsehs who won 14 of 18 league games, while the Indianapolis team of the League Alliance finished with the best winning percentage, winning 23 of 34. Interestingly, there was no clear-cut division between these minor leagues and the National League. Quite frequently, these teams would play one another. When comparing the records of their interlocking schedules, six of the so-called minor league teams (the Star, Indianapolis, Allegheny, Lowell, Tecumseh, and Cricket clubs), finished with better marks than did St. Louis, Chicago, and Cincinnati of the National League. When the season's statistics were published in the 1878 *Spalding's Baseball Guide*, all of the batting averages were put in the same sort. No differentiation was made between the different leagues.

When the National League needed to fill out its roster of teams, it naturally turned to these other leagues for a solution. The Milwaukee and Indianapolis clubs from the League Alliance were recruited, as well as a team from Providence which consisted largely of the old Hartford players. These three, along with Chicago, Cincinnati, and Boston made up the National League in 1878.

Boston, for the second straight year, finished with the best record. Using a compact roster which saw the use of only one substitute during the year, the team finished with 41 wins, four games ahead of Cincinnati. The club did not particularly hit well — their team average was only .241, and their best hitter, Jim O'Rourke only managed .278. Their forte was the strong arm of Tommy Bond who won a league-leading 40 games, while ringing up a league-leading 182 strikeouts. He pitched in all but 11 of his team's 544 innings.

Cincinnati had better hitting and pitching than Boston, yet they still finished second. It was a remarkable turnaround, though, for a team that had spent two dismal years in the cellar. Their 37 wins in 1878 were 13 more than the combined totals of their wins in 1876 and 1877. Their lineup in 1878 featured three .300 hitters, Cal McVey (.306), Charlie Jones (.310), and Deacon White (.310). Pitcher Will White (30-21, 1.79 ERA) anchored the league's best pitching staff.

Both third place Providence, and fourth place Chicago finished at the .500 mark or better. Providence was led by Triple Crown winner Paul Hines who paced the circuit in average (.358), home runs (4) and runs batted in (50). In Chicago, Al Spalding wisely gave up his first baseman duties to Joe Start who hit .351 while leading the league with 100 hits. His teammates, Bob Ferguson (.351) and Cap Anson (.341) also contributed.

Indianapolis and Milwaukee found the diet of pure National League competition to be a bit rich. Both struggled through lackluster seasons and finished with only 39 wins between them. However both showcased some fine talent. Milwaukee outfielder Abner Dalrymple finished second in the batting race (.354) while Orator Shaffer of Indianapolis finished sixth (.338).

The National League survived its tough times by dipping into the vast resource of baseball talent already in place — the other leagues. By recruiting two of their strongest teams, they were able to avoid disaster and completed their modest six-team league. However, things were beginning to look even better for the National League. Waiting in the wings were four new teams eager to join the league.

1878 NATIONAL LEAGUE

BOSTON Red Caps   41-19   .683   1st   Harry Wright

BATTERS	POS/GAMES		GP	AB	R	H	BI	2B	3B	HR	BB	SO	SB	BA	SA
John Morrill	1B59,3B1,1B1		60	233	26	56	23	5	1	0	5	16		.240	.270
Jack Burdock	2B60		60	246	37	64	25	12	6	0	3	17		.260	.358
George Wright	SS59		59	267	35	60	12	5	1	0	6	22		.225	.251
Ezra Sutton	3B59,SS1		60	239	31	54	29	9	3	1	2	14		.226	.301
Jack Manning	OF59,P3		60	248	41	63	23	10	1	0	10	16		.254	.302
Jim O'Rourke	OF57,1B2,C2		60	255	44	71	29	17	7	1	5	21		.278	.412
Andy Leonard	OF60		60	262	41	68	16	8	5	0	3	19		.260	.328
Pop Snyder	C58,OF2		60	226	21	48	14	5	0	0	1	19		.212	.235
Tommy Bond	P59,OF2		59	236	22	50	23	4	1	0	0	9		.212	.237
Harry Schafer	OF2		2	8	0	1	0	0	0	0	0	1		.125	.125
			60	2220	298	535	194	75	25	2	35	154		.241	.300

PITCHERS		W	L	PCT	G	GS	CG	SH	SV	IP	H	BB	SO	ERA
Tommy Bond		40	19	.678	59	59	57	9	0	533	571	33	182	2.06
Jack Manning		1	0	1.000	3	1	1	0	0	11	24	5	2	14.29
		41	19	.683	60	60	58	9	0	544	595	38	184	2.32

CINCINNATI Reds   37-23   .617   -4   2nd   Cal McVey

BATTERS	POS/GAMES		GP	AB	R	H	BI	2B	3B	HR	BB	SO	SB	BA	SA
Chub Sullivan	1B61		61	244	29	63	20	4	2	0	2	9		.258	.291
Joe Gerhardt	2B60		60	259	46	77	28	7	2	0	7	14		.297	.340
Billy Geer	SS60,2B2		61	237	31	52	20	13	2	0	10	18		.219	.291
Cal McVey	3B61,C3		61	271	43	83	28	10	4	2	5	10		.306	.395
King Kelly	OF47,C17,3B2		60	237	29	67	27	7	1	0	7	7		.283	.321
Lip Pike	OF31	(1-2)	31	145	28	47	11	5	1	0	4	9		.324	.372
Charlie Jones	OF61		61	261	50	81	39	11	7	3	4	17		.310	.441
Deacon White	C48,OF16,3B1		61	258	41	81	29	4	1	0	10	5		.314	.337
Will White	P52		52	197	15	28	9	1	1	0	8	41		.142	.157
Buttercup Dickerson	OF29		29	123	17	38	9	5	1	0	0	7		.309	.366
Robert Mitchell	P9,SS2,OF1		13	49	4	12	8	0	0	0	1	4		.245	.245
			61	2281	333	629	228	67	22	5	58	141		.276	.331

PITCHERS		W	L	PCT	G	GS	CG	SH	SV	IP	H	BB	SO	ERA
Will White		30	21	.588	52	52	52	5	0	468	477	45	169	1.79
Robert Mitchell		7	2	.778	9	9	9	1	0	80	69	18	51	2.14
		37	23	.617	61	61	61	6	0	548	546	63	220	1.84

PROVIDENCE Grays   33-27   .550   -8   3rd   Tom York

BATTERS	POS/GAMES		GP	AB	R	H	BI	2B	3B	HR	BB	SO	SB	BA	SA
Tim Murnane	1B48,OF1		49	188	35	45	14	6	1	0	8	12		.239	.282
Charlie Sweasy	2B55		55	212	23	37	8	3	0	0	7	23		.175	.189
Tom Carey	SS61		61	253	33	60	24	10	3	0	0	14		.237	.300
Bill Hague	3B62		62	250	21	51	25	3	0	0	5	34		.204	.216
Dick Higham	OF62,C1		62	281	60	90	29	22	1	1	5	16		.320	.416
Paul Hines	OF61,SS1		62	257	42	92	50	13	4	4	2	10		.358	.486
Tom York	OF62		62	269	56	83	26	19	10	1	8	19		.309	.465
Lewis Brown	C45,1B15,P1,OF1		58	243	44	74	43	21	6	1	7	37		.305	.453
Monte Ward	P37		37	138	14	27	15	5	4	1	2	13		.196	.312
Doug Allison	C19,P1		19	76	9	22	7	2	0	0	1	8		.289	.316
Tricky Nichols	P11		11	49	2	9	2	2	0	0	2	10		.184	.224
Harry Wheeler	P7		7	27	7	4	1	0	0	0	2	15		.148	.148
Fred Carey	P5,2B2,1B1		7	21	3	3	1	0	0	0	0	2		.143	.143
Lip Pike	2B5	(2-2)	5	22	4	5	4	0	1	0	1	1		.227	.318
Tom Healey	P3	(1-2)	3	9	0	2	0	1	0	0	0	4		.222	.333
Cherokee Fisher	P1		1	3	0	0	0	0	0	0	0	0		.000	.000
			62	2298	353	604	249	107	30	8	50	218		.263	.346

1878 NATIONAL LEAGUE

PROVIDENCE (cont.)
Grays

PITCHERS		W	L	PCT	G	GS	CG	SH	SV	IP	H	BB	SO	ERA
Monte Ward		22	13	.629	37	37	37	6	0	334	308	34	116	1.51
Harry Wheeler		6	1	.857	7	6	6	0	0	62	70	25	25	3.48
Tricky Nichols		4	7	.364	11	10	10	0	0	98	157	8	21	4.22
Fred Carey		1	2	.333	5	5	2	0	0	23	22	7	7	2.35
Cherokee Fisher		0	1	.000	1	1	1	0	0	9	14	0	2	4.00
Tom Healey	(1-2)	0	3	.000	3	3	3	0	0	24	27	7	2	3.00
Doug Allison		0	0	----	1	0	0	0	0	5	11	1	0	1.80
Lewis Brown		0	0	----	1	0	0	0	0	1	0	4	0	18.00
		33	27	.550	62	62	59	6	0	556	609	86	173	2.38

CHICAGO
White Stockings

30-30 .500 -11 4th Bob Ferguson

BATTERS	POS/GAMES		GP	AB	R	H	BI	2B	3B	HR	BB	SO	SB	BA	SA
Joe Start	1B61		61	285	58	100	27	12	5	1	2	3		.351	.439
Bill McClellan	2B42,SS5,OF1		48	205	26	46	29	6	1	0	2	13		.224	.263
Bob Ferguson	SS57,2B4,C1		61	259	44	91	39	10	2	0	10	12		.351	.405
Frank Hankinson	3B57,P1		58	240	38	64	27	8	3	1	5	36		.267	.338
John Cassidy	OF60,C1		60	256	33	68	29	7	1	0	9	11		.266	.301
Jack Remsen	OF56		56	224	32	52	19	11	1	1	17	33		.232	.304
Cap Anson	OF48,2B9,C3,3B3		60	261	55	89	40	12	2	0	13	1		.341	.402
Bill Harbridge	C50,OF8		54	240	32	71	37	12	0	0	6	13		.296	.346
Terry Larkin	P56,3B1,OF1		58	226	33	65	32	9	4	0	17	17		.288	.363
Jim Hallinan	OF11,2B5	(1-2)	16	67	14	19	2	3	0	0	5	6		.284	.328
Phil Powers	C8		8	31	2	5	2	1	1	0	1	5		.161	.258
Laurie Reis	P4,OF1		5	20	2	3	0	0	0	0	1	6		.150	.150
Bill Traffley	C2		2	9	1	1	1	0	0	0	0	1		.111	.111
Bill Sullivan	OF2		2	6	1	1	0	0	0	0	0	0		.167	.167
Al Spalding	2B1		1	4	0	2	0	0	0	0	0	0		.500	.500
			61	2333	371	677	284	91	20	3	88	157		.290	.350

PITCHERS		W	L	PCT	G	GS	CG	SH	SV	IP	H	BB	SO	ERA
Terry Larkin		29	26	.527	56	56	56	1	0	506	511	31	163	2.24
Laurie Reis		1	3	.250	4	4	4	0	0	36	55	4	8	3.25
Frank Hankinson		0	1	.000	1	1	1	0	0	9	11	0	4	6.00
		30	30	.500	61	61	61	1	0	551	577	35	175	2.37

INDIANAPOLIS
Hoosiers

24-36 .400 -17 5th John Clapp

BATTERS	POS/GAMES		GP	AB	R	H	BI	2B	3B	HR	BB	SO	SB	BA	SA
Art Croft	1B51,OF9		60	222	22	35	16	6	0	0	5	23		.158	.185
Joe Quest	2B62		62	278	45	57	13	3	2	0	12	24		.205	.230
Fred Warner	SS41,OF2		43	165	19	41	10	4	0	0	2	15		.248	.273
Ned Williamson	3B63		63	250	31	58	19	10	2	1	5	15		.232	.300
Orator Shaffer	OF63		63	266	48	90	30	19	6	0	13	20		.338	.455
Russ McKelvy	OF62,P4		63	253	33	57	36	4	3	2	5	38		.225	.289
John Clapp	OF44,1B12,C9,SS3,2B1		63	263	42	80	29	10	2	0	13	8		.304	.357
Silver Flint	C59,OF9		63	254	23	57	18	7	0	0	2	15		.224	.252
The Only Nolan	P38,OF1		38	152	11	37	16	8	0	0	2	10		.243	.296
Candy Nelson	SS19		19	84	12	11	5	1	0	0	5	11		.131	.143
Jim McCormick	P14,OF3		15	56	5	8	0	1	0	0	0	2		.143	.161
Tom Healey	P11,OF3	(2-2)	12	45	2	8		1	0	0	0	14		.178	.200
Jim Hallinan	OF3	(2-2)	3	12	0	3	1	2	0	0	0	2		.250	.417
			63	2300	293	542	193	76	15	3	64	197		.236	.286

PITCHERS		W	L	PCT	G	GS	CG	SH	SV	IP	H	BB	SO	ERA
The Only Nolan		13	22	.371	38	38	37	1	0	347	357	56	125	2.57
Tom Healey	(2-2)	6	4	.600	11	10	9	0	1	89	98	13	18	2.22
Jim McCormick		5	8	.385	14	14	12	1	0	117	128	15	36	1.69
Russ McKelvy		0	2	.000	4	1	1	0	0	25	38	3	3	2.16
		24	36	.400	63	63	59	2	1	578	621	87	182	2.32

1878 NATIONAL LEAGUE

MILWAUKEE
Cream Citys

15-45 .250 -26 6th Jack Chapman

BATTERS	POS/GAMES	GP	AB	R	H	BI	2B	3B	HR	BB	SO	SB	BA	SA
Jake Goodman	1B60	60	252	28	62	27	4	3	1	7	33		.246	.298
John Peters	2B34,SS22	55	246	33	76	22	6	1	0	5	8		.309	.341
Billy Redmon	SS39,OF7,3B3,C1	48	187	16	43	21	8	0	0	8	13		.230	.273
Will Foley	3B53,C7	56	229	33	62	22	8	5	0	7	14		.271	.349
Bill Holbert	OF30,C21	45	173	10	32	12	2	0	0	3	14		.185	.197
Mike Golden	OF39,P22,1B1	55	214	16	44	20	6	3	0	3	35		.206	.262
Abner Dalrymple	OF61	61	271	52	96	15	10	4	0	6	29		.354	.421
Charlie Bennett	C35,OF20	49	184	16	45	12	9	0	1	10	26		.245	.310
George Creamer	2B28,OF17,3B6	50	193	30	41	15	7	3	0	5	15		.212	.280
Sam Weaver	P45,OF9	48	170	15	34	3	4	1	0	11	14		.200	.235
Bill Morgan	OF13,3B3,2B1	14	56	2	11	5	0	0	0	3	9		.196	.196
Jake Knowdell	C2,OF1,SS1	4	14	2	3	2	1	0	0	0	3		.214	.286
Joe Ellick	C2,P1,3B1	3	13	2	2	1	0	0	0	0	1		.154	.154
Frank Bliss	3B1,C1	2	8	1	1	0	0	0	0	0	0		.125	.125
Al Jennings	C1	1	2	0	0	0	0	0	0	1	0		.000	.000
		61	2212	256	552	177	65	20	2	69	214		.250	.300

PITCHERS		W	L	PCT	G	GS	CG	SH	SV	IP	H	BB	SO	ERA
Sam Weaver		12	31	.279	45	43	39	1	0	383	371	21	95	1.95
Mike Golden		3	13	.188	22	18	15	0	0	161	217	33	52	4.14
Joe Ellick		0	1	.000	1	0	0	0	0	3	1	1	0	3.00
		15	45	.250	61	61	54	1	0	547	589	55	147	2.60

1879 NATIONAL LEAGUE

Reserved

A baseball player was an expensive investment for the owner of a team. One had to pay his salary, training, traveling, and eating expenses. And after all that, there was no guarantee that upon the expiration of his contract, he would not peddle his wares elsewhere. All too often, to keep him on your team you would have to outspend your rival owners for his services. To protect their investments, and to stop the escalating expenses of player salaries, the owners decided to take action.

In September 1879, the owners met and decided among themselves that they each could "reserve" five men on their rosters. These five players, under contract or not, could not be signed or tampered with by another league team. Thus each team could keep the nucleus of its team intact free from outside influences and temptations. Nowhere was this rule written down, it was merely a gentleman's agreement between the owners.

The upshot of this rule for the player was that he, once reserved, was forever bound to his team. He could not seek his true value as a player on the open market. Only through release or trade could he change clubs. Several methods of circumventing this rule were tried. Some players dropped out of baseball or switched leagues for a couple of years only to find that their original team had methodically kept their names on its reserve list, thus preventing them from going elsewhere. One player tried a more creative approach. Pat Deasley signed a contract one year with the stipulation that he would not be reserved for the following year. Much to his chagrin, he was overruled. The authorities stated that the terms of his contract were illegal because they tried to circumvent the binding rule of the reserve clause.

Before the start of the 1879 season, the two weakest teams of the National League — Milwaukee and Indianapolis — dropped out. They were replaced by four other teams — Buffalo, Cleveland, Syracuse, and Troy — giving the league eight members for the first time since 1876. The National League also expanded its schedule to 85 games.

Providence surprised every one by winning 59 games and winning their first pennant. Their outfielder, Paul Hines, won his second consecutive batting crown, finishing with a .357 average. Not far behind him was his teammate Jim O'Rourke at .348. To go with the league's best hitting attack (.296), Providence also had the best pitching (2.18) led by Monte Ward's 47 wins.

Boston slipped a notch into second place. Their best players were John O'Rourke (.341) and Charlie Jones (.315). Both shared the league lead with 62 runs batted in, while Jones also led with nine home runs. Pitcher Tommy Bond won the earned run average title with a mark of 1.96.

Buffalo finished third, one-half game better than Chicago who finished fourth. Buffalo used the strong pitching of Pud Galvin (37-27, 2.28 ERA), while Chicago used the strong bat of Cap Anson (.317) to finish in the first division. Partway through the season, Anson also took over the managerial chores of the Chicago team; a post he would not relinquish for another 18 years.

In 1878, Cincinnati pitcher Will White pitched in more than 90 percent of his team's 60 games. While the team's games increased to 81 in 1879, that percentage remained the same. The result was an astounding 76-game, 680-inning season for Mr. White, who won 43 of them. His teammate, the rising superstar King Kelly, contributed with a .348 average.

Three of the new teams, Cleveland, Syracuse, and Troy finished deep in the second division. Their only players of note were Charles Eden of Cleveland who hit 31 doubles and Jack Farrell of Syracuse who hit .303.

By the end of the 1880s, the reserve list had expanded to include 14 players per team, which was virtually each team's entire roster. To the owner's point of view, this was a necessity to keep the wealthy clubs from running roughshod over the game. To the player's point of view, it was a necessary evil, because they would certainly not be allowed to play the game without abiding by it. And for almost one hundred years, these were the rules by which the game off the field was played.

1879 NATIONAL LEAGUE

PROVIDENCE Grays
59-25 .702 1st George Wright

BATTERS	POS/GAMES		GP	AB	R	H	BI	2B	3B	HR	BB	SO	SB	BA	SA
Joe Start	1B65,OF1		66	317	70	101	37	11	5	2	7	4		.319	.404
Mike McGeary	2B73,3B12		85	374	62	103	35	7	2	0	5	13		.275	.305
George Wright	SS85		85	388	79	107	42	15	10	1	13	20		.276	.374
Bill Hague	3B51		51	209	20	47	21	3	1	0	3	19		.225	.249
Jim O'Rourke	OF56,1B20,C5,3B3		81	362	69	126	46	19	9	1	13	10		.348	.459
Paul Hines	OF85		85	409	81	146	52	25	10	2	8	16		.357	.482
Tom York	OF81		81	342	69	106	50	25	5	1	19	28		.310	.421
Lewis Brown	C48,OF6	(1-2)	53	229	23	59	38	13	4	2	4	24		.258	.376
Monte Ward	P70,3B16,OF8		83	364	71	104	41	9	4	2	7	14		.286	.349
Bobby Mathews	P27,OF21,3B5		43	173	25	35	10	2	0	1	7	12		.202	.231
Emil Gross	C30		30	132	31	46	24	9	5	0	4	8		.348	.492
Jack Farrell	2B12	(2-2)	12	51	5	13	5	2	0	0	0	0		.255	.294
Denny Sullivan	3B4,OF1		5	19	5	5	2	2	0	0	1	1		.263	.368
Dan O'Leary	OF2		2	7	1	3	2	0	0	0	0	0		.429	.429
Rudy Kemmler	C2		2	7	0	1	0	0	0	0	0	1		.143	.143
Doug Allison	C1		1	5	0	0	0	0	0	0	0	1		.000	.000
Bill White	1B1		1	4	1	1	0	0	0	0	0	1		.250	.250
			85	3392	612	1003	405	142	55	12	91	172		.296	.381

PITCHERS		W	L	PCT	G	GS	CG	SH	SV	IP	H	BB	SO	ERA
Monte Ward		47	19	.712	70	60	58	2	1	587	571	36	239	2.15
Bobby Mathews		12	6	.667	27	25	15	1	1	189	194	26	90	2.29
		59	25	.702	85	85	73	3	2	776	765	62	329	2.18

BOSTON Red Caps
54-30 .643 -5 2nd Harry Wright

BATTERS	POS/GAMES	GP	AB	R	H	BI	2B	3B	HR	BB	SO	SB	BA	SA
Ed Cogswell	1B49	49	236	51	76	18	8	1	1	8	5		.322	.377
Jack Burdock	2B84	84	359	64	86	36	10	3	0	9	28		.240	.284
Ezra Sutton	SS51,3B33	84	339	54	84	34	13	4	0	2	18		.248	.310
John Morrill	3B51,1B33	84	348	56	98	49	18	5	0	14	32		.282	.362
Sadie Houck	OF47,SS33	80	356	69	95	49	24	9	2	4	11		.267	.402
John O'Rourke	OF71	72	317	69	108	62	17	11	6	8	32		.341	.521
Charlie Jones	OF83	83	355	85	112	62	22	10	9	29	38		.315	.510
Pop Snyder	C80,OF2	81	329	42	78	35	16	3	2	5	31		.237	.322
Tommy Bond	P64,OF5,1B1	65	257	35	62	21	3	1	0	6	8		.241	.261
Bill Hawes	OF34,C5	38	155	19	31	9	3	3	0	2	13		.200	.258
Curry Foley	P21,OF17,1B2	35	146	16	46	17	3	1	0	3	4		.315	.349
Jim Tyng	P3	3	14	2	5	0	1	0	0	0	1		.357	.429
Lee Richmond	P1	1	6	0	2	1	0	0	0	0	1		.333	.333
		84	3217	562	883	393	138	51	20	90	222		.274	.368

PITCHERS	W	L	PCT	G	GS	CG	SH	SV	IP	H	BB	SO	ERA
Tommy Bond	43	19	.694	64	64	59	11	0	555	543	24	155	1.96
Curry Foley	9	9	.500	21	16	16	1	0	162	175	15	57	2.51
Lee Richmond	1	0	1.000	1	1	1	0	0	9	4	1	11	2.00
Jim Tyng	1	2	.333	3	3	3	0	0	27	35	6	7	5.00
	54	30	.643	84	84	79	13	0	753	757	46	230	2.19

BUFFALO Bisons
46-32 .590 -10 3rd John Clapp

BATTERS	POS/GAMES	GP	AB	R	H	BI	2B	3B	HR	BB	SO	SB	BA	SA
Oscar Walker	1B72	72	287	35	79	35	15	6	1	8	38		.275	.380
Chick Fulmer	2B76	76	306	30	82	28	11	5	0	5	34		.268	.337
Davy Force	SS78,3B1	79	316	36	66	8	5	2	0	13	37		.209	.237
Hardy Richardson	3B78,C1	79	336	54	95	37	18	10	0	16	30		.283	.396
Bill Crowley	OF43,C10,1B7,2B3	60	261	41	75	30	9	5	0	6	14		.287	.360
Dave Eggler	OF78	78	317	41	66	27	5	7	0	11	41		.208	.268
Joe Hornung	OF77,1B1	78	319	46	85	38	18	7	0	2	27		.266	.367
John Clapp	C63,OF7	70	292	47	77	36	12	5	1	11	11		.264	.349
Pud Galvin	P66,SS1	67	265	34	66	27	11	6	0	1	56		.249	.336
William McGunnigle	OF34,P14	47	171	22	30	5	0	1	0	5	24		.175	.187

1879 NATIONAL LEAGUE

BUFFALO (cont.)
Bisons

BATTERS	POS/GAMES		GP	AB	R	H	BI	2B	3B	HR	BB	SO	SB	BA	SA
Jack Rowe	C6,OF2		8	34	8	12	8	1	0	0	0	1		.353	.382
Stephen Libby	1B1		1	2	0	0	0	0	0	0	0	1		.000	.000
			79	2906	394	733	279	105	54	2	78	314		.252	.328

PITCHERS			W	L	PCT	G	GS	CG	SH	SV	IP	H	BB	SO	ERA
Pud Galvin			37	27	.578	66	66	65	6	0	593	585	31	136	2.28
William McGunnigle			9	5	.643	14	13	13	2	0	120	113	16	62	2.63
			46	32	.590	79	79	78	8	0	713	698	47	198	2.34

CHICAGO
White Stockings

46-33 .582 -10.5 4th Anson - Flint

BATTERS	POS/GAMES		GP	AB	R	H	BI	2B	3B	HR	BB	SO	SB	BA	SA
Cap Anson	1B51		51	227	40	72	34	20	1	0	2	2		.317	.414
Joe Quest	2B83		83	334	38	69	22	16	1	0	9	33		.207	.260
John Peters	SS83		83	379	45	93	31	13	2	1	1	19		.245	.298
Ned Williamson	3B70,1B6,C4		80	320	66	94	36	20	13	1	24	31		.294	.447
Orator Shaffer	OF72,3B1		73	316	53	96	35	13	0	0	6	28		.304	.345
George Gore	OF54,1B9		63	266	43	70	32	17	4	0	8	30		.263	.357
Abner Dalrymple	OF71		71	333	47	97	23	25	1	0	4	29		.291	.372
Silver Flint	C78,OF1		79	324	46	92	41	22	6	1	6	44		.284	.398
Terry Larkin	P58,OF3		60	228	26	50	18	12	2	0	8	24		.219	.289
Frank Hankinson	P26,OF14,3B5		44	171	14	31	8	4	0	0	2	14		.181	.205
Jack Remsen	OF31,1B11		42	152	14	33	8	4	2	0	2	23		.217	.270
Lewis Brown	1B6	(2-2)	6	21	2	6	3	1	0	0	1	4		.286	.333
Bill Harbridge	OF4		4	18	2	2	1	0	0	0	0	5		.111	.111
John Stedronsky	3B4		4	12	0	1	0	0	0	0	0	3		.083	.083
Herm Doscher	3B3	(2-2)	3	11	1	2	1	0	0	0	0	3		.182	.182
Tom Dolan	C1		1	4	0	0	0	0	0	0	0	2		.000	.000
			83	3116	437	808	293	167	32	3	73	294		.259	.336

PITCHERS			W	L	PCT	G	GS	CG	SH	SV	IP	H	BB	SO	ERA
Terry Larkin			31	23	.574	58	58	57	4	0	513	514	30	142	2.44
Frank Hankinson			15	10	.600	26	25	25	2	0	231	248	27	69	2.50
			46	33	.582	83	83	82	6	0	744	762	57	211	2.46

CINCINNATI
Reds

43-37 .538 -14 5th White - McVey

BATTERS	POS/GAMES		GP	AB	R	H	BI	2B	3B	HR	BB	SO	SB	BA	SA
Cal McVey	1B72,OF7,P3,3B1,C1		81	354	64	105	55	18	6	0	8	13		.297	.381
Joe Gerhardt	2B55,3B16,1B8,SS1		79	313	22	62	39	12	3	1	3	19		.198	.265
Ross Barnes	SS61,2B16		77	323	55	86	30	9	2	1	16	25		.266	.316
King Kelly	3B33,OF29,C21,2B1		77	345	78	120	47	20	12	2	8	14		.348	.493
Will Foley	OF25,3B29,2B3		56	218	22	46	25	5	1	0	2	16		.211	.243
Pete Hotaling	OF69,C8,2B6,3B3		81	369	64	103	27	20	9	1	12	17		.279	.390
Buttercup Dickerson	OF81		81	350	73	102	57	18	14	2	3	27		.291	.440
Deacon White	C59,OF21,1B2		78	333	55	110	52	16	6	1	6	9		.330	.423
Will White	P76		76	294	28	40	17	6	0	0	6	56		.136	.156
Mike Burke	SS19,3B5,OF5		28	117	13	26	8	3	0	0	2	5		.222	.248
Blondie Purcell	OF10,P2	(2-2)	12	50	10	11	4	0	0	0	0	3		.220	.220
John Neagle	P2,OF2		3	12	1	2	2	0	0	0	0	0		.167	.167
John Magner	OF1		1	4	0	0	1	0	0	0	0	1		.000	.000
Harry Wheeler	OF1,P1		1	3	0	0	0	0	0	0	0	2		.000	.000
			81	3085	485	813	364	127	53	8	66	207		.264	.347

PITCHERS			W	L	PCT	G	GS	CG	SH	SV	IP	H	BB	SO	ERA
Will White			43	31	.581	76	75	75	4	0	680	676	68	232	1.99
John Neagle			0	2	.000	2	2	1	0	0	13	13	5	4	3.46
Harry Wheeler			0	1	.000	1	1	0	0	0	1	6	4	0	81.00
Cal McVey			0	2	.000	3	1	1	0	0	14	34	2	7	8.36
Blondie Purcell			0	2	.000	2	2	2	0	0	18	27	2	3	4.00
			43	37	.538	81	81	79	4	0	726	756	81	246	2.29

1879 NATIONAL LEAGUE

CLEVELAND Blues — 27-55 .321 -31 6th — Jim McCormick

BATTERS	POS/GAMES		GP	AB	R	H	BI	2B	3B	HR	BB	SO	SB	BA	SA
Bill Phillips	1B75,C11,OF2		81	365	58	99	29	15	4	0	2	20		.271	.334
Jack Glasscock	2B66,3B14		80	325	31	68	29	9	3	0	6	24		.209	.255
Tom Carey	SS80		80	335	30	80	32	14	1	0	5	20		.239	.287
Fred Warner	3B54,OF21,1B1		76	316	32	77	22	11	4	0	2	20		.244	.304
Charles Eden	OF80,1B3,C1		81	353	40	96	34	31	7	3	6	20		.272	.425
George Strief	OF55,2B16		71	264	24	46	15	7	1	0	10	23		.174	.208
Billy Riley	OF43,1B1,C1		44	165	14	24	9	2	0	0	2	26		.145	.158
Doc Kennedy	C46,1B4		49	193	19	56	18	8	2	1	2	10		.290	.368
Jim McCormick	P62,OF13,1B4		75	282	35	62	20	10	2	0	1	9		.220	.270
Barney Gilligan	C27,OF23,SS2		52	205	20	35	11	6	2	0	0	13		.171	.220
Robert Mitchell	P23,OF9		30	109	11	16	6	2	2	0	0	14		.147	.202
Jack Allen	3B,OF	(2-2)	16	60	7	7	4	1	1	0	1	9		.117	.167
Hickey Hoffman	C2,OF1		2	6	0	0	0	0	0	0	0	3		.000	.000
Leonard Stockwell	OF2		2	6	0	0	0	0	0	0	0	2		.000	.000
Fred Gunkle	C1		1	3	1	0	0	0	0	0	0	1		.000	.000
			82	2987	322	666	229	16	29	4	37	214		.223	.285

PITCHERS		W	L	PCT	G	GS	CG	SH	SV	IP	H	BB	SO	ERA
Jim McCormick		20	40	.333	62	60	59	3	0	546	582	74	197	2.42
Robert Mitchell		7	15	.318	23	22	20	0	0	195	236	42	90	3.28
		27	55	.321	82	82	79	3	0	741	818	116	287	2.65

SYRACUSE Stars — 22-48 .314 -30 7th — Dorgan - Holbert Macullar

BATTERS	POS/GAMES		GP	AB	R	H	BI	2B	3B	HR	BB	SO	SB	BA	SA
Hick Carpenter	1B34,3B18,OF11,2B3		65	261	30	53	20	6	0	0	2	15		.203	.226
Jack Farrell	2B54	(1-2)	54	241	40	73	21	6	2	1	3	13		.303	.357
Jimmy Macullar	SS37,OF26,2B4,3B1		64	246	24	52	13	9	0	0	3	27		.211	.248
Red Woodhead	3B34		34	131	4	21	2	1	0	0	0	23		.160	.168
Blondie Purcell	OF47,P22,C	(1-2)	63	277	32	72	25	6	3	0	3	13		.260	.303
John Richmond	OF35,SS28,C2		62	254	31	54	23	8	4	1	4	24		.213	.287
Mike Mansell	OF67		67	242	24	52	13	4	2	1	5	45		.215	.260
Bill Holbert	C55,OF4	(1-2)	59	229	11	46	21	0	0	0	1	20		.201	.201
Mike Dorgan	1B21,OF16,3B11,SS6,C4,P2,2B1		59	270	38	72	17	11	5	1	4	13		.267	.356
Harry McCormick	P54,OF7		57	230	21	51	21	4	1	1	0	22		.222	.261
George Creamer	2B10,SS3,OF2		15	60	3	13	3	2	0	0	1	2		.217	.250
John McGuiness	1B12		12	51	7	15	4	1	1	0	0	6		.294	.353
Jack Allen	3B8,OF3	(1-2)	11	48	7	9	3	2	1	0	1	5		.188	.271
John Kelly	C8,1B2	(1-2)	10	36	4	4	2	1	0	0	0	6		.111	.139
George Adams	1B2,OF2		4	13	0	3	0	0	0	0	1	1		.231	.231
Frank Decker	C2,1B1,OF1		3	10	0	1	0	0	0	0	0	3		.100	.100
Charles Osterhout	C1,OF1		2	8	0	0	0	0	0	0	0	0		.000	.000
Tom Mansell	OF1	(2-2)	1	4	0	1	0	0	0	0	0	0		.250	.250
			71	2611	276	592	188	61	19	5	28	238		.227	.270

PITCHERS		W	L	PCT	G	GS	CG	SH	SV	IP	H	BB	SO	ERA
Harry McCormick		18	33	.353	54	54	49	5	0	457	517	31	96	2.99
Blondie Purcell	(1-2)	4	15	.211	22	17	15	0	0	180	245	19	28	3.76
Mike Dorgan		0	0	----	2	0	0	0	0	12	13	2	8	1.13
		22	48	.314	71	71	64	5	0	649	775	52	132	3.19

TROY Trojans — 19-56 .253 -35.5 8th — Phillips - Ferguson

BATTERS	POS/GAMES		GP	AB	R	H	BI	2B	3B	HR	BB	SO	SB	BA	SA
Dan Brouthers	1B37,P3		39	168	17	46	17	12	1	4	1	18		.274	.429
Thorny Hawkes	2B64		64	250	24	52	20	6	1	0	4	14		.208	.240
Ed Caskin	SS42,C22,2B6		70	304	32	78	21	13	2	0	2	14		.257	.313
Herm Doscher	3B47	(1-2)	47	191	16	42	18	8	0	0	2	10		.220	.262
Jake Evans	OF72		72	280	30	65	17	9	5	0	5	18		.232	.300
Al Hall	OF67		67	306	30	79	14	7	3	0	3	13		.258	.301
Tom Mansell	OF40	(1-2)	40	177	29	43	11	6	0	0	3	9		.243	.277
Charlie Reilley	C49,1B11,OF2		62	236	17	54	19	5	1	0	1	20		.229	.258

TROY (cont.)
Trojans

BATTERS	POS/GAMES		GP	AB	R	H	BI	2B	3B	HR	BB	SO	SB	BA	SA
George Bradley	P54,3B5,1B3,OF1,SS1		63	251	36	62	23	9	5	0	1	20		.247	.323
Aaron Clapp	1B25,OF11		36	146	24	39	18	9	3	0	6	10		.267	.370
Bob Ferguson	3B24,2B6		30	123	18	31	4	5	2	0	4	3		.252	.325
Candy Nelson	SS24,OF4		28	106	17	28	10	7	1	0	8	4		.264	.349
Sandy Taylor	OF24		24	97	10	21	8	4	0	0	1	8		.216	.258
John Sharpe	SS10,2B1		11	44	5	4	1	0	0	0	0	3		.091	.091
Harry Salisbury	P10,OF1		10	36	3	2	0	0	0	0	1	7		.056	.056
Fred Goldsmith	P8,1B1,OF2		9	38	6	9	2	1	0	0	1	3		.237	.263
John Cassidy	OF8,1B2		9	37	4	7	1	1	0	0	2	4		.189	.216
John Kelly	C3,OF2,3B1	(2-2)	6	22	1	5	0	0	0	0	0	1		.227	.227
Bill Holbert	C4	(2-2)	4	15	1	4	2	0	0	0	0	1		.267	.267
Pat McManus	P2		2	8	0	1	0	0	0	0	0	2		.125	.125
Gid Gardner	P2		2	6	1	1	0	0	0	0	0	0		.167	.167
			77	2841	321	673	206	102	24	4	45	182		.237	.294

PITCHERS	W	L	PCT	G	GS	CG	SH	SV	IP	H	BB	SO	ERA
George Bradley	13	40	.245	54	54	53	3	0	487	590	26	133	2.85
Harry Salisbury	4	6	.400	10	10	9	0	0	89	103	11	31	2.22
Fred Goldsmith	2	4	.333	8	7	7	0	0	63	61	1	31	1.57
Dan Brouthers	0	2	.000	3	2	2	0	0	21	35	8	6	5.57
Pat McManus	0	2	.000	2	2	2	0	0	21	24	1	6	3.00
Gid Gardner	0	2	.000	2	2	2	0	0	14	27	0	3	5.79
	19	56	.253	77	77	75	3	0	695	840	47	210	2.80

1880 NATIONAL LEAGUE

The Chicago White Stockings

The city of Chicago has a rich and storied tradition of baseball. And that story begins and ends with the White Stockings.

In 1870, the Chicago White Stockings were formed. As one of the country's first recognized professional teams, they counted as their contemporaries the Atlantics, Mutuals, Athletics, and even the famed Cincinnati Red Stockings. When the first professional league, the National Association, was formed in 1871, the White Stockings were one of its founding members. And when it was time to restructure baseball in 1876, it was the president of the team, William Hulbert, who spearheaded the foundation of the National League. Later, team president Al Spalding, would continue the influential role of the White Stockings in the world of baseball as the sport's most ardent and determined advocate.

On the field, the team's successes mirrored its powerful role off the field. Of the first 11 pennants awarded by the National League, the White Stockings won six. In 1876, the team finished six ahead; in 1880 it was a fifteen-game margin; 1881 saw them on top by nine; 1882 was closer at only three; 1885 still closer at two; and 1886 witnessed a two and one-half game bulge.

The 1880 edition was perhaps the strongest. Bolstered by the addition of King Kelly, the White Stockings steamrollered defending champion Providence by 15 games, finishing with a record .798 winning percentage, fourth best of all time. The team had the league's best hitter, George Gore (.360), as well as the second best, Cap Anson (.337), and the fourth best, Abner Dalrymple (.330). Dalrymple also had the most runs (91) and hits (126). On the pitching front, Larry Corcoran won 43, striking out a circuit topping 268. The backup pitcher, Fred Goldsmith won 21 of his 24 decisions.

Providence relied on its strong pitching staff to finish second. The team posted a team-earned run average of 1.64, good for third place on the all-time list. Monte Ward was the team's big winner with 39, fueled by eight shutouts. Only Paul Hines (.307) could dent the .300 barrier.

Both Cleveland and Troy improved dramatically over their 1879 showing. Cleveland boasted of the league's winningest pitcher, Jim McCormick, who finished with 45 on the strength of 658 innings pitched. Troy was paced by Roger Connor who batted .332, and by earned run average leader Tim Keefe. His minuscule 0.86 earned run average stands as the best of all time.

Worcester and Boston finished with nearly identical marks in fifth and sixth place. The Worcester Ruby Legs, which took the place of the defunct Syracuse Stars, unveiled a young slugger named Harry Stovey, who laced 14 triples and poked six home runs to lead the league in each category. Boston's plummet to the second division was primarily the story of mediocre pitching. Charlie Jones (.300) and Jim O'Rourke (6 HR) kept them within four games of .500.

Buffalo and Cincinnati finished on the bottom two rungs. There was nary a distinguishing hitter on either team, but Cincinnati pitcher Will White, despite a league-leading 42 losses, finished with a fine 2.14 earned run average.

Despite the leadership of the White Sox's management, what set the team apart from the league during the first decade of the National League was their record on the field. Out of the seven best records ever recorded in the major leagues from 1871 to the present day, the Chicago teams from this era own three of them.

1880 NATIONAL LEAGUE

CHICAGO White Stockings
67-17   .798   1st   Cap Anson

BATTERS	POS/GAMES		GP	AB	R	H	BI	2B	3B	HR	BB	SO	SB	BA	SA
Cap Anson	1B81,3B9,2B1,SS1		86	356	54	120	74	24	1	1	14	12		.337	.419
Joe Quest	2B80,SS2,3B1		82	300	37	71	27	12	1	0	8	16		.237	.283
Tom Burns	SS79,3B9,C2,P1		85	333	47	103	43	17	3	0	12	23		.309	.378
Ned Williamson	3B63,C11,2B3		75	311	65	78	31	20	2	0	15	26		.251	.328
King Kelly	OF64,C17,3B14,2B1,P1,SS1		84	344	72	100	60	17	9	1	12	22		.291	.401
George Gore	OF74,1B7		77	322	70	116	47	23	2	2	21	10		.360	.463
Abner Dalrymple	OF86		86	382	91	126	36	25	12	0	3	18		.330	.458
Silver Flint	C67,OF13		74	284	30	46	17	10	4	0	5	32		.162	.225
Larry Corcoran	P63,OF8,SS8		72	286	41	66	25	11	1	0	10	33		.231	.276
Fred Goldsmith	P26,OF10,1B4		35	142	24	37	15	4	2	0	2	15		.261	.317
Tommy Beals	OF10,2B3		13	46	4	7	3	0	0	0	1	6		.152	.152
Tom Poorman	OF7,P2	(2-2)	7	25	3	5	0	1	2	0	0	2		.200	.400
Charlie Guth	P1		1	4	0	1	0	0	0	0	1	2		.250	.250
			86	3135	538	876	378	164	39	4	104	217		.279	.360

PITCHERS			W	L	PCT	G	GS	CG	SH	SV	IP	H	BB	SO	ERA
Larry Corcoran			43	14	.754	63	60	57	4	2	536	404	99	268	1.95
Fred Goldsmith			21	3	.875	26	24	22	4	1	210	189	18	90	1.75
Tom Poorman		(2-2)	2	0	1.000	2	1	0	0	0	15	12	8	0	2.40
Charlie Guth			1	0	1.000	1	1	1	0	0	9	12	1	7	5.00
King Kelly			0	0	----	1	0	0	0	0	3	3	1	1	0.00
Tom Burns			0	0	----	1	0	0	0	0	1	2	2	1	0.00
			67	17	.798	86	86	80	8	3	774	622	129	367	1.93

PROVIDENCE Grays
52-32   .619   -15   2nd   McGeary - Ward Dorgan

BATTERS	POS/GAMES		GP	AB	R	H	BI	2B	3B	HR	BB	SO	SB	BA	SA
Joe Start	1B82		82	345	53	96	27	14	6	0	13	20		.278	.354
Jack Farrell	2B80		80	339	46	92	36	12	5	3	10	6		.271	.363
John Peters	SS86		86	359	30	82	24	5	0	0	5	15		.228	.242
George Bradley	3B57,P28,OF7,1B2		64	309	32	70	23	7	6	0	5	38		.227	.288
Mike Dorgan	OF77,3B2,P1		79	321	45	79	31	10	1	0	10	18		.246	.283
Paul Hines	OF75,2B6,1B4		85	374	64	115	35	20	2	3	13	17		.307	.396
Tom York	OF53		53	203	21	43	18	9	2	0	8	29		.212	.276
Emil Gross	C87		87	347	43	90	34	18	3	1	16	15		.259	.337
Monte Ward	P70,3B25,OF2		86	356	53	81	27	12	2	0	6	16		.228	.272
Sadie Houck	OF49	(2-2)	49	184	27	37	22	7	7	1	3	6		.201	.332
Mike McGeary	3B17,2B2,SS1	(1-2)	18	59	5	8	1	0	0	0	0	6		.136	.136
			87	3196	419	793	278	114	34	8	89	186		.248	.313

PITCHERS			W	L	PCT	G	GS	CG	SH	SV	IP	H	BB	SO	ERA
Monte Ward			39	24	.619	70	67	59	8	1	595	501	45	230	1.74
George Bradley			13	8	.619	28	20	16	4	1	196	158	6	54	1.38
Mike Dorgan			0	0	----	1	0	0	0	0	8	4	0	2	1.13
			52	32	.619	87	87	75	13	2	799	663	51	286	1.64

CLEVELAND Blues
47-37   .560   -20   3rd   Jim McCormick

BATTERS	POS/GAMES		GP	AB	R	H	BI	2B	3B	HR	BB	SO	SB	BA	SA
Bill Phillips	1B85		85	334	41	85	36	14	10	1	6	29		.254	.365
Fred Dunlap	2B85		85	373	61	103	30	27	9	4	7	32		.276	.429
Jack Glasscock	SS77		77	296	37	72	27	13	3	0	2	21		.243	.307
Frank Hankinson	3B56,OF12,P4		69	263	32	55	19	7	4	1	1	23		.209	.278
Orator Shaffer	OF83		83	338	62	90	21	14	9	0	17	36		.266	.361
Pete Hotaling	OF78,C2		78	325	40	78	41	17	8	0	10	30		.240	.342
Ned Hanlon	OF69,SS4		73	280	30	69	32	10	3	0	11	30		.246	.304
Doc Kennedy	C65,OF2		66	250	26	50	18	10	1	0	5	12		.200	.248
Jim McCormick	P74,OF5		78	289	34	71	26	11	0	0	5	5		.246	.284
Mike McGeary	3B29,OF2	(2-2)	31	111	14	28	6	2	1	0	4	3		.252	.288
Barney Gilligan	C23,OF4,SS4		30	99	9	17	13	4	3	1	6	12		.172	.303
Gid Gardner	P9,OF1		10	32	0	6	4	1	1	0	2	4		.188	.281

CLEVELAND (cont.)
Blues

BATTERS	POS/GAMES		GP	AB	R	H	BI	2B	3B	HR	BB	SO	SB	BA	SA
Al Hall	OF3		3	8	1	1	0	0	0	0	0	0		.125	.125
Harry Wheeler	OF1	(1-2)	1	4	0	1	0	0	0	0	0	0		.250	.250
			85	3002	387	726	273	130	52	7	76	237		.242	.327

PITCHERS		W	L	PCT	G	GS	CG	SH	SV	IP	H	BB	SO	ERA
Jim McCormick		45	28	.616	74	74	72	7	0	658	585	75	260	1.85
Frank Hankinson		1	1	.500	4	2	2	0	1	25	20	3	8	1.08
Gid Gardner		1	8	.111	9	9	9	0	0	77	80	20	21	2.57
		47	37	.560	85	85	83	7	1	760	685	98	289	1.90

TROY
Trojans

41-42   .494   -25.5   4th   Bob Ferguson

BATTERS	POS/GAMES		GP	AB	R	H	BI	2B	3B	HR	BB	SO	SB	BA	SA
Ed Cogswell	1B47		47	209	41	63	13	7	3	0	11	10		.301	.364
Bob Ferguson	2B82		82	332	55	87	22	9	0	0	24	24		.262	.289
Ed Caskin	SS82,C2		82	333	36	75	28	5	4	0	7	24		.225	.264
Roger Connor	3B83		83	340	53	113	47	18	8	3	13	21		.332	.459
Jake Evans	OF47,P1		47	180	31	46	22	8	1	0	7	15		.256	.311
John Cassidy	OF82,2B1		83	352	40	89	29	14	8	0	12	34		.253	.338
Pete Gillespie	OF82		82	346	50	84	24	20	5	2	17	35		.243	.347
Bill Holbert	C58,OF3		60	212	18	40	8	5	1	0	9	18		.189	.222
Mickey Welch	P65,OF2		66	251	25	72	27	20	3	0	5	24		.287	.390
Bill Tobin	1B33	(2-2)	33	136	14	22	8	1	1	0	4	20		.162	.184
Buttercup Dickerson	OF30,SS1	(1-2)	30	119	15	23	10	2	2	0	2	3		.193	.244
Buck Ewing	C10,OF4		13	45	1	8	5	1	0	0	1	3		.178	.200
Tim Keefe	P12		12	43	4	10	3	3	0	0	1	12		.233	.302
Bill Harbridge	C9,OF1		9	27	3	10	2	0	1	0	0	3		.370	.444
Terry Larkin	P5,OF2,SS1		6	20	1	3	1	1	0	0	3	4		.150	.200
Mike Lawlor	C4		4	9	1	1	0	0	0	0	1	1		.111	.111
Joe Straub	C3		3	12	1	3	3	0	0	0	1	3		.250	.250
Dan Brouthers	1B3		3	12	0	2	1	0	0	0	1	0		.167	.167
Frank Mountain	P2		2	9	1	2	0	0	0	0	0	4		.222	.222
Fred Haley	C2		2	7	0	0	0	0	0	0	1	2		.000	.000
Dick Higham	OF1,C1		1	5	1	1	0	0	0	0	0	0		.200	.200
Charles Ahearn	C1		1	4	1	1	0	0	0	0	0	0		.250	.250
Fatty Briody	C1		1	4	0	0	0	0	0	0	0	0		.000	.000
			83	3007	392	755	253	114	37	5	120	260		.251	.319

PITCHERS	W	L	PCT	G	GS	CG	SH	SV	IP	H	BB	SO	ERA
Mickey Welch	34	30	.531	65	64	64	4	0	574	575	80	123	2.54
Tim Keefe	6	6	.500	12	12	12	0	0	105	71	17	43	0.86
Frank Mountain	1	1	.500	2	2	2	0	0	17	23	6	2	5.29
Terry Larkin	0	5	.000	5	5	3	0	0	38	83	10	5	8.76
Jake Evans	0	0	---	1	0	0	0	0	4	11	0	0	13.50
	41	42	.494	83	83	81	4	0	738	763	113	173	2.74

WORCESTER
Ruby Legs

40-43   .482   -26.5   5th   Frank Bancroft

BATTERS	POS/GAMES		GP	AB	R	H	BI	2B	3B	HR	BB	SO	SB	BA	SA
Chub Sullivan	1B43		43	166	22	43	0	6	3	0	4	6		.259	.331
George Creamer	2B85		85	306	40	61	27	6	3	0	4	21		.199	.239
Art Irwin	SS82,3B3,C1		85	352	53	91	35	19	4	1	11	27		.259	.344
Art Whitney	3B76		76	302	38	67	36	13	5	1	9	15		.222	.308
Lon Knight	OF49		49	201	31	48	21	11	3	0	5	8		.239	.323
Harry Stovey	OF46,1B37,P2		83	355	76	94	28	21	14	6	12	46		.265	.454
George Wood	OF80,3B2,1B1		81	327	37	80	28	16	5	0	10	37		.245	.324
Charlie Bennett	C46,OF6		51	193	20	44	18	9	3	0	10	30		.228	.306
Lee Richmond	P74,OF20		77	309	44	70	34	8	4	0	9	32		.227	.278
Doc Bushong	C40,3B1,OF1		41	146	13	25	19	3	0	0	1	16		.171	.192
Fred Corey	OF29,P25,SS3,3B1,1B1		41	138	11	24	6	8	1	0	4	27		.174	.246
Buttercup Dickerson	OF31	(2-2)	31	133	22	39	20	8	6	0	1	2		.293	.444
Jerry Dorgan	OF9,C1		10	35	2	7	1	1	0	0	0	1		.200	.229
Joe Ellick	3B5		5	18	1	1	0	0	0	0	1	2		.056	.056
Bill Tobin	1B5	(1-2)	5	16	1	2	3	0	0	0	0	5		.125	.125

1880 NATIONAL LEAGUE 65

WORCESTER (cont.)
Ruby Legs

BATTERS	POS/GAMES		GP	AB	R	H	BI	2B	3B	HR	BB	SO	SB	BA	SA
Steve Dignan	OF3	(2-2)	3	10	1	3	2	0	1	0	0	1		.300	.500
Tricky Nichols	P2		2	7	0	0	0	0	0	0	0	0		.000	.000
Billy Geer	SS1,OF1		2	6	0	0	0	0	0	0	0	0		.000	.000
William McGunnigle	OF1	(2-2)	1	4	0	0	0	0	0	0	0	2		.000	.000
			85	3024	412	699	278	129	52	8	81	278		.231	.316

PITCHERS		W	L	PCT	G	GS	CG	SH	SV	IP	H	BB	SO	ERA
Lee Richmond		32	32	.500	74	66	57	5	3	591	541	74	243	2.15
Fred Corey		8	9	.471	25	17	9	2	2	148	131	16	47	2.43
Tricky Nichols		0	2	.000	2	2	2	0	0	18	29	4	4	4.08
Harry Stovey		0	0	----	2	0	0	0	0	6	8	3	3	4.50
		40	43	.482	85	85	68	7	5	763	709	97	297	2.27

BOSTON
Red Caps

40-44   .476   -27   6th   Harry Wright

BATTERS	POS/GAMES		GP	AB	R	H	BI	2B	3B	HR	BB	SO	SB	BA	SA
John Morrill	1B46,3B40,P3		86	342	51	81	44	16	8	2	11	37		.237	.348
Jack Burdock	2B86		86	356	58	90	35	17	4	2	8	26		.253	.340
John Richmond	SS31,OF1		32	129	12	32	9	3	1	0	2	18		.248	.287
Ezra Sutton	3B37,SS39		76	288	41	72	25	9	2	0	7	7		.250	.295
John O'Rourke	OF81		81	313	30	86	36	22	8	3	18	32		.275	.425
Jim O'Rourke	OF37,1B19,SS17,3B10,C9		86	363	71	100	45	20	11	6	21	8		.275	.441
Charlie Jones	OF66		66	280	44	84	38	15	3	5	11	27		.300	.429
Phil Powers	C37,OF2		37	126	11	18	10	5	0	0	5	15		.143	.183
Curry Foley	P36,OF35,1B25		80	332	44	97	31	13	2	2	8	14		.292	.361
Tommy Bond	P63,OF26,1B1,3B1		76	282	27	62	24	4	1	0	8	14		.220	.241
Sam Trott	C36,OF4		39	125	14	26	9	4	1	0	3	5		.208	.256
Sadie Houck	OF12	(1-2)	12	47	2	7	2	0	0	0	0	6		.149	.149
John Bergh	C11		11	40	2	8	0	3	0	0	2	5		.200	.275
Steve Dignan	OF8	(1-2)	8	34	4	11	4	1	0	0	0	3		.324	.353
Dan O'Leary	OF3		3	12	1	3	1	2	0	0	0	3		.250	.417
Denny Sullivan	C1		1	4	1	1	1	0	0	0	0	1		.250	.250
George Wright	SS1		1	4	2	1	0	0	0	0	0	0		.250	.250
Jack Leary	P1,OF1		1	3	1	0	0	0	0	0	1	0		.000	.000
			86	3080	416	779	314	134	41	20	105	221		.253	.343

PITCHERS		W	L	PCT	G	GS	CG	SH	SV	IP	H	BB	SO	ERA
Tommy Bond		26	29	.473	63	57	49	3	0	493	559	45	118	2.67
Curry Foley		14	14	.500	36	28	21	1	0	238	264	40	68	3.89
Jack Leary		0	1	.000	1	1	0	0	0	3	8	0	1	15.00
John Morrill		0	0	----	3	0	0	0	0	11	9	1	0	0.84
		40	44	.476	86	86	70	4	0	745	840	86	187	3.08

BUFFALO
Bisons

24-58   .293   -42   7th   Sam Crane

BATTERS	POS/GAMES		GP	AB	R	H	BI	2B	3B	HR	BB	SO	SB	BA	SA
Dude Esterbrook	1B47,OF15,2B6,C1,SS1		64	253	20	61	35	12	1	0	0	15		.241	.296
Davy Force	2B53,SS30		81	290	22	49	17	10	0	0	10	35		.169	.203
Mike Moynahan	SS27		27	100	12	33	14	5	1	0	6	9		.330	.400
Hardy Richardson	3B81,C5		83	343	48	89	17	18	8	0	14	37		.259	.359
Dan Stearns	OF20,C8,3B5,SS1		28	104	8	19	13	6	1	0	3	23		.183	.260
Bill Crowley	OF74,C22		85	354	57	95	20	16	4	0	19	23		.268	.336
Joe Hornung	OF67,1B18,2B5,P1		85	342	47	91	42	8	11	1	8	29		.266	.363
Jack Rowe	C60,OF25,3B3		79	326	43	82	36	10	6	1	6	17		.252	.328
Pud Galvin	P58,OF19		66	241	25	51	12	9	2	0	5	57		.212	.266
Oscar Walker	1B24,OF11		34	126	12	29	15	4	2	1	6	18		.230	.317
Stump Weidman	P17,OF13		23	78	8	8	3	1	0	0	2	11		.103	.115
Arlie Latham	SS12,OF10,C1		22	79	9	10	3	3	1	0	1	8		.127	.190
Tom Poorman	P11,OF	(1-2)	19	70	5	11	1	1	0	0	0	13		.157	.171
Denny Driscoll	OF14,P6		18	65	1	10	4	1	0	0	1	7		.154	.169
Denny Mack	SS16,2B1		17	59	5	12	3	0	0	0	5	7		.203	.203
Chick Fulmer	2B11		11	44	3	7	1	0	0	0	2	4		.159	.159
Sam Crane	2B10,OF1		10	31	4	4	2	0	0	0	1	8		.129	.129

1880 NATIONAL LEAGUE

BUFFALO (cont.)
Bisons

BATTERS	POS/GAMES		GP	AB	R	H	BI	2B	3B	HR	BB	SO	SB	BA	SA
William McGunnigle	P5,OF	(1-2)	7	22	0	4	1	0	0	0	0	4		.182	.182
Old Hoss Radbourn	OF3,2B3		6	21	1	3	1	0	0	0	0	1		.143	.143
Jim Keenan	C2		2	7	1	1	0	0	0	0	1	1		.143	.143
Tom Kearns	C2		2	7	0	0	0	0	0	0	0	0		.000	.000
			85	2962	331	669	240	104	37	3	90	327		.226	.289

PITCHERS			W	L	PCT	G	GS	CG	SH	SV	IP	H	BB	SO	ERA
Pud Galvin			20	35	.364	58	54	46	5	0	459	528	32	128	2.71
William McGunnigle			2	3	.400	5	5	4	1	0	37	43	8	3	3.41
Denny Driscoll			1	3	.250	6	4	4	0	0	42	48	9	17	3.89
Tom Poorman		(1-2)	1	8	.111	11	9	9	0	1	85	117	19	13	4.13
Stump Weidman			0	9	.000	17	13	9	0	0	114	141	9	25	3.40
Joe Hornung			0	0	----	1	0	0	0	0	3	2	1	0	6.00
			24	58	.293	85	85	72	6	1	739	879	78	186	3.09

CINCINNATI
Reds

21-59　.263　-44　8th　John Clapp

BATTERS	POS/GAMES		GP	AB	R	H	RBI	2B	3B	HR	BB	SO	SB	BA	SA
Long John Reilly	1B72,OF3		73	272	21	56	16	8	4	0	3	36		.206	.265
Pop Smith	2B83		83	334	35	69	27	10	9	0	6	36		.207	.290
Louis Say	SS48		48	191	14	38	15	8	1	0	4	31		.199	.251
Hick Carpenter	3B67,1B9,SS1		77	300	32	72	23	6	4	0	2	15		.240	.287
Jack Manning	OF47,P1		48	190	20	41	17	6	3	2	7	15		.216	.311
Blondie Purcell	OF55,P25,SS1		77	325	48	95	24	13	6	1	5	13		.292	.378
Mike Mansell	OF53		53	187	22	36	12	6	2	2	4	37		.193	.278
John Clapp	C73,OF10		80	323	33	91	20	16	4	1	21	10		.282	.365
Will White	P62,OF3		62	207	16	35	14	7	1	0	6	29		.169	.213
Deacon White	OF33,1B3,2B1		35	141	21	42	7	4	2	0	9	7		.298	.355
Andy Leonard	SS23,3B10		33	133	15	28	17	3	0	1	8	11		.211	.256
Charlie Reilley	OF16,C13,3B4,		30	103	8	21	9	1	0	0	0	5		.204	.214
Joe Sommer	OF22,3B1,C1,SS1		24	88	10	16	6	1	0	0	0	2		.182	.193
Harry Wheeler	OF17	(2-2)	17	65	1	6	2	2	0	0	0	15		.092	.123
Sam Wright	SS9		9	34	0	3	0	0	0	0	0	5		.088	.088
Amos Booth	OF1		1	2	0	0	0	0	0	0	0	0		.000	.000
			83	2895	296	649	209	91	36	7	75	267		.224	.288

PITCHERS		W	L	PCT	G	GS	CG	SH	SV	IP	H	BB	SO	ERA
Will White		18	42	.300	62	62	58	3	0	517	550	56	161	2.14
Blondie Purcell		3	17	.150	25	21	21	0	0	196	235	32	47	3.21
		21	59	.263	83	83	79	3	0	713	785	88	208	2.44

1881 NATIONAL LEAGUE

Cap Anson

A colossus strode across the baseball world during the latter part of the nineteenth century. He played hard for nearly 30 years, and managed hard for almost 20. He was revered by his fans, respected by his colleagues, and feared by his charges. This six-foot giant of a man was Adrian Constantine Anson, but most people called him Cap.

Born in Iowa in 1852, Anson burst on the baseball scene for the Forest Citys club of Rockford, Illinois. When his team joined the National Association as a charter member in 1871, Anson was their starting third baseman. After one year with Rockford, Anson jumped to the Athletics of Philadelphia club for the final four years of the Association. During his tenure in this league, Cap batted a robust .358, with a best year total of .414 in 1872. His overall average ranks him the top five of all National Association batters.

When William Hulbert was forming his first National League team, Cap Anson was one of his key desires, and he signed him away from the Athletics to be his third baseman. This proved to be a good choice, as Anson was a natural leader on and off the field. He was rewarded for his leadership by being made team manager midway through the 1879 season, when he also changed positions, becoming almost exclusively a first baseman.

Although he was hitting over .300 each year, 1881 proved to be his career year. In leading his White Stockings to their second consecutive pennant, Anson blistered the ball to the tune of .399, which would prove to be his personal National League best. In addition, he led the league with 137 hits and 82 runs batted in. He did have help in securing this pennant because three other White Stockings hit over .300, led by King Kelly at .323.

Providence, once again finished second. Led by Joe Start (.328), and by Tom York (.304), the club managed to finish closer this time, only nine games back. Despite these two good batting performances, their strength was once again pitching. Old Hoss Radbourn's leading .694 winning percentage, and 2.43 earned run average, helped pave the way to the team earned run average crown (2.40) once again.

Buffalo bounced back into third behind the bats of what was to be labeled the Big Four. The Big Four consisted of Dan Brouthers, Hardy Richardson, Jack Rowe and

Deacon White. These four played well this year, averaging over .300 as a group. In addition, Dan Brouthers won the home run title with eight.

The National League owners were tired of the hijinks perpetrated by the Cincinnati club. For years they had been selling beer in their ballpark and playing baseball on Sundays. Both these practices were frowned upon by the baseball magnates. Fed up at last, the rest of the owners expelled Cincinnati from the league following the 1880 season.

Their replacement, the Detroit Wolverines, finished fourth in 1881, two games under .500. Players they could boast of included: Martin Powell (.338) and earned run average champion Stump Weidman (1.80).

Finishing right behind Detroit were Troy and Boston. Troy's best player was once again Roger Connor (.292), while workhorse Jim Whitney of Boston led the league in wins and losses, while pitching in 552 innings.

Cleveland and Worcester finished in seventh and eighth. Cleveland's Fred Dunlap (.325), and Worcester's Pete Hotaling (.309) and Buttercup Dickerson (.316) were the only good hitters on either team.

After 1881, Cap Anson's career continued to flourish. Before the decade was out, he would lead his White Stockings to three more pennants while winning two more batting titles. His career came to an end in the late 1890s, after a serious flirtation with the .400 mark at the age of 42.

Anson stands alone as the supreme mark for quality and longevity in the nineteenth century. When all Cap's statistics were tabulated, he totaled over 3,400 hits in his career, finishing with a career average of .332. Out of his 27 years in professional baseball, he hit .300 in 24 of them, including the first 20 in a row. It was no wonder then, when the Baseball Hall of Fame was founded in 1939, that Cap Anson was selected as one of its first members.

1881 NATIONAL LEAGUE

CHICAGO White Stockings   56-28   .667   1st   Cap Anson

BATTERS	POS/GAMES		GP	AB	R	H	BI	2B	3B	HR	BB	SO	SB	BA	SA
Cap Anson	1B84,C2,SS1		84	343	67	137	82	21	7	1	26	4		.399	.510
Joe Quest	2B77,SS1		78	293	35	72	26	6	0	1	2	29		.246	.276
Tom Burns	SS80,2B3,3B3		84	342	41	95	42	20	3	4	14	22		.278	.389
Ned Williamson	3B76,2B4,P3,SS2,C1		82	343	56	92	48	12	6	1	19	19		.268	.347
King Kelly	OF72,C11,3B8		82	353	84	114	55	27	3	2	16	14		.323	.433
George Gore	OF72,1B1,3B1		73	309	86	92	44	18	9	1	27	23		.298	.424
Abner Dalrymple	OF82		82	362	72	117	37	22	4	1	15	22		.323	.414
Silver Flint	C80,OF8,1B1		80	306	46	95	34	18	0	1	6	39		.310	.379
Larry Corcoran	P45,SS2,OF1		47	189	25	42	9	8	0	0	5	22		.222	.265
Fred Goldsmith	P39,OF3		42	158	24	38	16	3	4	0	6	17		.241	.310
Hugh Nicol	OF26,SS1		26	108	13	22	7	2	0	0	4	12		.204	.222
Andy Piercy	2B1,3B1		2	8	1	2	0	0	0	0	0	1		.250	.250
			84	3114	550	918	400	157	36	12	140	224		.295	.380

PITCHERS		W	L	PCT	G	GS	CG	SH	SV	IP	H	BB	SO	ERA
Larry Corcoran		31	14	.689	45	44	43	4	0	397	380	78	150	2.31
Fred Goldsmith		24	13	.649	39	39	37	5	0	330	328	44	76	2.59
Ned Williamson		1	1	.500	3	1	1	0	0	18	14	0	2	2.00
		56	28	.667	84	84	81	9	0	745	722	122	228	2.43

PROVIDENCE Grays   47-37   .560   -9   2nd   Farrell - York

BATTERS	POS/GAMES		GP	AB	R	H	BI	2B	3B	HR	BB	SO	SB	BA	SA
Joe Start	1B79		79	348	56	114	29	12	6	0	9	7		.328	.397
Jack Farrell	2B82,OF3		84	345	69	82	36	16	5	5	29	23		.238	.357
Bill McClellan	SS50,OF17,2B1		68	259	30	43	16	3	1	0	15	21		.166	.185
Jerry Denny	3B85		85	320	38	77	24	16	2	1	5	44		.241	.313
Monte Ward	OF40,P39,SS13		85	357	56	87	53	18	6	0	5	10		.244	.328
Paul Hines	OF78,2B4,1B1		80	361	65	103	31	27	5	2	13	12		.285	.404
Tom York	OF85		85	316	57	96	47	23	5	2	29	26		.304	.427
Emil Gross	C50,OF1		51	182	15	50	24	9	4	1	13	11		.275	.385
Old Hoss Radbourn	P41,OF25,SS13		72	270	27	59	28	9	0	0	10	15		.219	.252
Barney Gilligan	C36,SS10,OF1		46	183	19	40	20	7	2	0	9	24		.219	.279
Lewis Brown	OF13,1B5	(2-2)	18	75	9	18	10	3	1	0	4	13		.240	.307
Bobby Mathews	P14,OF6	(1-2)	16	57	6	11	4	1	0	0	5	6		.193	.211
Henry Myers	SS1		1	4	0	0	0	0	0	0	0	2		.000	.000
			85	3077	447	780	322	144	37	11	146	214		.253	.335

PITCHERS			W	L	PCT	G	GS	CG	SH	SV	IP	H	BB	SO	ERA
Old Hoss Radbourn			25	11	.694	41	36	34	3	0	325	309	64	117	2.43
Monte Ward			18	18	.500	39	35	32	3	0	330	326	53	119	2.13
Bobby Mathews		(1-2)	4	8	.333	14	14	10	1	*0	102	121	21	28	3.17
			47	37	.560	85	85	76	7	0	758	756	138	264	2.40

BUFFALO Bisons   45-38   .542   -10.5   3rd   Jim O'Rourke

BATTERS	POS/GAMES		GP	AB	R	H	BI	2B	3B	HR	BB	SO	SB	BA	SA
Dan Brouthers	1B30,OF35		65	270	60	86	45	18	9	8	18	22		.319	.541
Davy Force	2B51,SS21,OF3,3B1		75	278	21	50	15	9	1	0	11	29		.180	.219
John Peters	SS53,OF1		54	229	21	49	25	8	1	0	3	12		.214	.258
Jim O'Rourke	3B56,OF18,C8,SS3,1B1		83	348	71	105	30	21	7	0	27	18		.302	.402
Curry Foley	OF55,1B27,P10		83	375	58	96	25	20	2	1	7	27		.256	.328
Hardy Richardson	OF79,2B5,SS1,3B1		83	344	62	100	53	18	9	2	12	27		.291	.413
Blondie Purcell	OF25,P9	(2-2)	30	113	15	33	17	7	2	0	8	8		.292	.389
Jack Rowe	C46,3B7,SS7,OF5		64	246	30	82	43	11	11	1	1	12		.333	.480
Deacon White	1B26,2B25,OF17,3B7,C4		78	319	58	99	53	24	4	0	9	8		.310	.411
Pud Galvin	P56,OF14,SS1		62	236	19	50	21	12	4	0	3	70		.212	.297
Sleeper Sullivan	C31,OF5		35	121	13	23	15	4	0	0	1	21		.190	.223
Jack Lynch	P20,OF6		23	78	6	13	3	3	0	0	4	8		.167	.205
John Morrissey	3B12		12	47	3	10	3	2	0	0	0	3		.213	.255
Pop Smith	2B3	(3-3)	3	11	3	0	1	0	0	0	3	5		.000	.000

BUFFALO (cont.)
Bisons

BATTERS	POS/GAMES		GP	AB	R	H	RBI	2B	3B	HR	BB	SO	SB	BA	SA
Ed Swartwood	OF1		1	3	0	1	0	0	0	0	1	0		.333	.333
Jack Manning	OF1		1	1	0	0	0	0	0	0	0	0		.000	.000
			83	3019	440	797	349	157	50	12	108	270		.264	.361

PITCHERS			W	L	PCT	G	GS	CG	SH	SV	IP	H	BB	SO	ERA
Pud Galvin			28	24	.538	56	53	48	5	0	474	546	46	136	2.37
Jack Lynch			10	9	.526	20	19	17	0	0	166	203	29	32	3.59
Blondie Purcell		(2-2)	4	1	.800	9	5	5	0	0	62	62	9	15	2.77
Curry Foley			3	4	.429	10	6	2	0	0	41	70	5	2	5.27
			45	38	.542	83	83	72	5	0	742	881	89	185	2.84

DETROIT
Wolverines
41-43   .488   -15   4th   Frank Bancroft

BATTERS	POS/GAMES		GP	AB	R	H	RBI	2B	3B	HR	BB	SO	SB	BA	SA
Martin Powell	1B55,C1		55	219	47	74	38	9	4	1	15	9		.338	.429
Joe Gerhardt	2B79,3B1		80	297	35	72	36	13	6	0	7	31		.242	.327
Sadie Houck	SS75		75	308	43	86	36	16	6	1	6	6		.279	.380
Art Whitney	3B58		58	214	23	39	9	7	5	0	7	15		.182	.262
Lon Knight	OF82,1B1,2B1		83	340	67	92	52	16	3	1	23	21		.271	.344
Ned Hanlon	OF74,SS2		76	305	63	85	28	14	8	2	22	11		.279	.397
George Wood	OF80		80	337	54	100	32	18	9	2	19	32		.297	.421
Charlie Bennett	C70,3B5,OF3		76	299	44	90	64	18	7	7	18	37		.301	.478
George Derby	P56,OF4		59	236	17	44	12	3	1	0	4	29		.186	.208
Lewis Brown	1B27	(1-2)	27	108	16	26	14	3	1	3	3	16		.241	.370
Charlie Reilley	C10,OF4,3B3,SS3,1B1	(1-2)	19	70	8	12	3	2	0	0	0	10		.171	.200
Stump Weidman	P13		13	47	8	12	5	1	0	0	2	2		.255	.277
Dasher Troy	3B7,2B4		11	44	2	15	4	3	0	0	3	8		.341	.409
Mike Dorgan	OF5,3B2,1B1	(2-2)	8	34	5	8	5	1	0	0	1	0		.235	.265
Frank Mountain	P7		7	25	0	4	4	1	1	0	2	8		.160	.280
Sam Trott	C6		6	25	3	5	2	2	1	0	1	3		.200	.360
Tony Mullane	P5		5	19	0	5	1	0	0	0	0	0		.263	.263
Will Foley	3B5		5	15	0	2	1	0	0	0	2	3		.133	.133
Jack Leary	P2,OF2		3	11	2	3	4	1	1	0	1	1		.273	.545
Dan Stearns	SS3		3	11	1	1	0	1	0	0	0	2		.091	.182
Dan O'Leary	OF2		2	8	0	0	0	0	0	0	0	2		.000	.000
Will White	P2		2	7	0	0	0	0	0	0	0	1		.000	.000
Sam Wise	3B1		1	4	0	2	0	0	0	0	0	2		.500	.500
Bill Taylor	3B1	(2-3)	1	4	0	2	1	2	0	0	0	0		.500	1.000
Mike Moynahan	3B1	(2-2)	1	4	1	1	0	0	0	0	0	1		.250	.250
George Bradley	SS1	(1-2)	1	4	0	0	0	0	0	0	0	0		.000	.000
			84	2995	439	780	351	131	53	17	136	250		.260	.357

PITCHERS			W	L	PCT	G	GS	CG	SH	SV	IP	H	BB	SO	ERA
George Derby			29	26	.527	56	55	55	9	0	495	505	86	212	2.20
Stump Weidman			8	5	.615	13	13	13	1	0	115	108	12	26	1.80
Frank Mountain			3	4	.429	7	7	7	0	0	60	80	18	13	5.25
Tony Mullane			1	4	.200	5	5	5	0	0	44	55	17	7	4.91
Will White			0	2	.000	2	2	2	0	0	18	24	2	5	5.00
Jack Leary			0	2	.000	2	2	1	0	0	13	13	2	2	4.15
			41	43	.488	84	84	83	10	0	745	785	137	265	2.65

TROY
Trojans
39-45   .464   -17   5th   Bob Ferguson

BATTERS	POS/GAMES	GP	AB	R	H	BI	2B	3B	HR	BB	SO	SB	BA	SA
Roger Connor	1B85	85	367	55	107	31	17	6	2	15	20		.292	.387
Bob Ferguson	2B85	85	339	56	96	35	13	5	1	29	12		.283	.360
Ed Caskin	SS63	63	234	33	53	21	7	1	0	13	29		.226	.265
Frank Hankinson	3B84,SS1	85	321	34	62	19	15	0	1	10	41		.193	.249
Jake Evans	OF83	83	315	35	76	28	11	5	0	14	30		.241	.308
John Cassidy	OF84,SS1	85	370	57	82	11	13	3	1	18	21		.222	.281
Pete Gillespie	OF84	84	348	43	96	41	14	3	0	9	24		.276	.333
Buck Ewing	C44,SS22,OF2,3B1	67	272	40	68	25	14	7	0	7	8		.250	.353

1881 NATIONAL LEAGUE

TROY (cont.)
Trojans

BATTERS	POS/GAMES		GP	AB	R	H	BI	2B	3B	HR	BB	SO	SB	BA	SA
Bill Holbert	C43,OF3		46	180	16	49	14	3	0	0	3	13		.272	.289
Tim Keefe	P45,OF1		46	152	18	35	19	7	1	0	21	26		.230	.289
Mickey Welch	P40		40	148	12	30	11	10	0	0	1	16		.203	.270
			85	3046	399	754	255	124	31	5	140	240		.248	.314

PITCHERS			W	L	PCT	G	GS	CG	SH	SV	IP	H	BB	SO	ERA
Mickey Welch			21	18	.538	40	40	40	4	0	368	371	78	104	2.67
Tim Keefe			18	27	.400	45	45	45	4	0	402	442	81	103	3.25
			39	45	.464	85	85	85	8	0	770	813	159	207	2.97

BOSTON
Red Caps

38-45 .458 -17.5 6th Harry Wright

BATTERS	POS/GAMES		GP	AB	R	H	BI	2B	3B	HR	BB	SO	SB	BA	SA
John Morrill	1B74,2B4,P3,3B2		81	311	47	90	39	19	3	1	12	30		.289	.379
Jack Burdock	2B72,SS1		73	282	36	67	24	12	4	1	7	18		.238	.319
Ross Barnes	SS63,2B7		69	295	42	80	17	14	1	0	16	16		.271	.325
Ezra Sutton	3B81,SS2		83	333	43	97	31	12	4	0	13	9		.291	.351
Fred Lewis	OF27		27	114	17	25	9	6	0	0	7	5		.219	.272
Bill Crowley	OF72		72	279	33	71	31	12	0	0	14	15		.254	.297
Joe Hornung	OF83		83	324	40	78	25	12	8	2	5	25		.241	.346
Pop Snyder	C60,2B1,OF1,SS1		62	219	14	50	16	8	0	0	3	23		.228	.265
Jim Whitney	P66,OF15,1B2		75	282	37	72	32	17	3	0	19	18		.255	.337
Pat Deasley	C28,SS7,OF7,1B2		43	147	13	35	8	5	2	0	5	10		.238	.299
John Fox	P17,OF12,1B6		30	118	8	21	4	0	0	0	0	11		.178	.178
John Richmond	OF25,SS2		27	98	13	27	12	2	2	1	6	7		.276	.367
Bobby Mathews	OF17,P5	(2-2)	19	71	2	12	4	2	0	0	0	5		.169	.197
George Wright	SS7		7	25	4	5	0	0	0	0	3	1		.200	.200
Tommy Bond	P3		3	10	0	2	0	0	0	0	0	0		.200	.200
Sam Wright	SS1		1	4	0	1	0	0	0	0	0	0		.250	.250
----- Quinn	1B1	(1-1)	1	4	0	0	0	0	0	0	0	0		.000	.000
			83	2916	349	733	252	121	27	5	110	193		.251	.317

PITCHERS			W	L	PCT	G	GS	CG	SH	SV	IP	H	BB	SO	ERA
Jim Whitney			31	33	.484	66	63	57	6	0	552	548	90	162	2.48
John Fox			6	8	.429	17	16	12	0	0	124	144	39	30	3.33
Bobby Mathews		(2-2)	1	0	1.000	5	1	1	0	*2	23	22	11	5	2.35
John Morrill			0	1	.000	3	0	0	0	1	6	9	1	0	6.35
Tommy Bond			0	3	.000	3	3	2	0	0	25	40	2	2	4.26
			38	45	.458	83	83	72	6	3	731	763	143	199	2.71

CLEVELAND
Blues

36-48 .429 -20 7th McGeary - Clapp

BATTERS	POS/GAMES		GP	AB	R	H	BI	2B	3B	HR	BB	SO	SB	BA	SA
Bill Phillips	1B85		85	357	51	97	44	18	10	1	5	19		.272	.387
Fred Dunlap	2B79,3B1		80	351	60	114	24	25	4	3	18	24		.325	.444
Jack Glasscock	SS79,2B6		85	335	49	86	33	9	5	0	15	8		.257	.313
George Bradley	3B48,P6,SS6,OF1	(2-2)	60	241	21	60	18	10	1	2	4	25		.249	.324
Orator Shaffer	OF85		85	343	48	88	34	13	6	1	23	20		.257	.338
Jack Remsen	OF48		48	172	14	30	13	4	3	0	9	31		.174	.233
Mike Moynahan	OF32,3B1	(1-2)	33	135	12	31	8	5	1	0	3	14		.230	.281
John Clapp	C48,OF21		68	261	47	66	25	12	2	0	35	6		.253	.314
Jim McCormick	P59,OF10,2B1,3B1		70	309	45	79	26	9	4	0	5	16		.256	.311
The Only Nolan	P22,OF14,3B6		41	168	12	41	18	5	1	0	4	13		.244	.286
Doc Kennedy	C35,OF3,3B1		39	150	19	47	15	7	1	0	5	13		.313	.373
Bill Taylor	OF23,P1,3B1	(3-3)	24	103	6	25	12	1	0	0	0	8		.243	.252
Blondie Purcell	OF20	(1-2)	20	80	3	14	4	2	1	0	5	8		.175	.225
Mike McGeary	3B11		11	41	1	9	5	0	0	0	0	6		.220	.220
Pop Smith	3B10	(1-3)	10	34	1	4	3	0	0	0	0	8		.118	.118
John Doscher	3B5		5	19	2	4	0	0	0	0	0	2		.211	.211
Phil Powers	C4,3B1		5	15	1	1	0	0	0	0	1	2		.067	.067
Rudy Kemmler	C1		1	3	0	0	0	0	0	0	0	1		.000	.000
			85	3117	392	796	277	120	39	7	132	224		.255	.326

1881 NATIONAL LEAGUE

CLEVELAND (cont.)
Blues

PITCHERS		W	L	PCT	G	GS	CG	SH	SV	IP	H	BB	SO	ERA
Jim McCormick		26	30	.464	59	58	57	2	0	526	484	84	178	2.45
The Only Nolan		8	14	.364	22	21	20	0	0	180	183	38	54	3.05
George Bradley	(2-2)	2	4	.333	6	6	5	0	0	51	70	3	6	3.88
Bill Taylor	(3-3)	0	0	.000	1	0	0	0	0	3	0	1	2	0.00
		36	48	.429	85	85	82	2	0	760	737	126	240	2.68

WORCESTER
Ruby Legs

32-50   .390   -23   8th   Dorgan - Stovey

BATTERS	POS/GAMES		GP	AB	R	H	BI	2B	3B	HR	BB	SO	SB	BA	SA
Harry Stovey	1B57,OF18		75	341	57	92	30	25	7	2	12	23		.270	.402
George Creamer	2B80		80	309	42	64	25	9	2	0	11	27		.207	.249
Art Irwin	SS50		50	206	27	55	24	8	2	0	7	4		.267	.325
Hick Carpenter	3B83		83	347	40	75	31	12	2	2	3	19		.216	.280
Mike Dorgan	OF,1B,SS	(1-2)	51	220	36	61	18	5	0	0	8	4		.277	.300
Pete Hotaling	OF74,C3		77	317	51	98	35	15	3	1	18	12		.309	.385
Buttercup Dickerson	OF80		80	367	48	116	31	18	6	1	8	8		.316	.406
Doc Bushong	C76		76	275	35	64	21	7	4	0	21	23		.233	.287
Lee Richmond	P53,OF11		61	252	31	63	28	5	1	0	10	10		.250	.278
Fred Corey	OF25,P23,SS7		51	203	22	45	10	8	4	0	5	10		.222	.300
Candy Nelson	SS24		24	103	13	29	15	1	0	1	5	6		.282	.320
Harry McCormick	P9,OF3		12	45	1	6	3	0	0	0	5	6		.133	.133
Pop Smith	OF8,2B3	(2-3)	11	41	1	3	2	0	0	0	3	5		.073	.073
Bill Taylor	OF5,P1	(1-3)	6	28	3	3	2	1	0	0	0	2		.107	.143
Lip Pike	OF5		5	18	1	2	0	0	0	0	4	3		.111	.111
Charlie Reilley	C2	(2-2)	2	8	2	3	1	0	0	0	0	1		.375	.375
----- Quinn	C2	(2-2)	2	7	0	1	1	0	0	0	1	2		.143	.143
Asa Stratton	SS1		1	4	0	1	0	0	0	0	0	2		.250	.250
Marty Flaherty	OF1		1	2	0	0	0	0	0	0	0	2		.000	.000
			83	3093	410	781	277	114	31	7	121	169		.253	.316

PITCHERS		W	L	PCT	G	GS	CG	SH	SV	IP	H	BB	SO	ERA
Lee Richmond		25	26	.490	53	52	50	3	0	462	547	68	156	3.39
Fred Corey		6	15	.286	23	21	20	1	0	189	231	31	33	3.72
Harry McCormick		1	8	.111	9	9	9	1	0	78	89	15	7	3.56
Bill Taylor	(1-3)	0	1	.000	1	1	1	0	0	8	15	6	0	7.88
		32	50	.390	83	83	80	5	0	737	882	120	196	3.54

1882 NATIONAL LEAGUE

Competition

By the beginning of the 1882 season, six charter National League cities were without major league teams. New York and Philadelphia were booted out in 1876 for failing to play out their schedule. St. Louis, Hartford, and Louisville left for financial reasons after the 1877 season. Cincinnati was expelled in 1880 for conduct unbecoming a National League franchise. These cities — populous and eager for baseball — were ripe for the picking.

The business of baseball was in excellent shape by the early 1880s. Unruly players had been brought into line by the reserve clause, and unruly clubs had been voted out. The National League was in position to be in full control. It was proving itself to be a lucrative business, with the financial losses of the 1870s nothing but a memory. Being lucrative, naturally more businessmen wanted a part of the action. What better place to start than in the cities conveniently vacated by the National League.

When talk of a new major league emerged, centered in Cincinnati and St. Louis, National League magnates scoffed at the idea. Much the same thing had happened in the late 1870s with the formation of the League Alliance and the International Association. Those two circuits proved to be too diffuse to pose any real threat to the National League. There was no indication that this new league would be any different. Also, with the monopoly they held on the top players, the league thought itself impregnable. Much to their shock and dismay, not only was the new league organized, it was up and running when the National League started its 1882 season.

On the field, for the third straight year, the Chicago White Stockings copped the pennant. This margin of victory, however, was down to three games. Their offensive stars included Cap Anson (.362) and a league-leading 83 runs batted in, King Kelly (.305) who hit a circuit best 37 doubles, and George Gore who scored a league best 99 runs to accompany his .319 average. Fred Goldsmith and Larry Corcoran split the pitching duties, winning all of the team's 55 victories. Corcoran also finished with the best earned run average at 1.95, and the best winning percentage (.692)

Thrice in a row a bridesmaid, Providence finished strong with 52 wins. Joe Start (.329) and Paul Hines (.309) were their offensive mainstays, while Old Hoss Radbourn helped with his dominating pitching. He finished with 33 wins, 201 strikeouts and six shutouts.

Buffalo and Boston finished tied for third. Dan Brouthers, of Buffalo, was quickly emerging as a superstar. In 1882, he led the league in three important categories: batting average (.368), slugging average (.547), and hits (129). Boston's Joe Hornung (.302) was their best player.

Cleveland and Detroit finished fifth and sixth, just a notch over the .500 mark. Cleveland was led by the league's winningest pitcher Jim McCormick, who finished with 36, while Detroit was paced by George Wood's league's best seven home runs, and by Charlie Bennett's .301 batting average.

Troy and Worcester finished at the bottom. The only player of note on either team was Troy's Roger Connor, who rapped out a league best 18 triples to go along with his .330 average.

Of the six original cities vacated by the National League, the new major league placed teams in four of them, with a fifth coming the next year. Cincinnati, St. Louis, Louisville, and Philadelphia were charter members of this new league, with New York joining the next year. Soon, the National League would have all the competition it could handle from this new league — the American Association.

1882 NATIONAL LEAGUE

CHICAGO
White Stockings

55-29   .655   1st   Cap Anson

BATTERS	POS/GAMES	GP	AB	R	H	BI	2B	3B	HR	BB	SO	SB	BA	SA
Cap Anson	1B82,C1	82	348	69	126	83	29	8	1	20	7		.362	.500
Tom Burns	2B43,SS41	84	355	55	88	48	23	6	0	15	28		.248	.346
King Kelly	SS42,OF38,C12,3B3,1B1	84	377	81	115	55	37	4	1	10	27		.305	.432
Ned Williamson	3B83,P1	83	348	66	98	60	27	4	3	27	21		.282	.408
Hugh Nicol	OF47,SS8	47	186	19	37	16	9	1	1	7	29		.199	.274
George Gore	OF84	84	367	99	117	51	15	7	3	29	19		.319	.422
Abner Dalrymple	OF84	84	397	96	117	36	25	11	1	14	18		.295	.421
Silver Flint	C81,OF10	81	331	48	83	44	18	8	4	2	50		.251	.390
Fred Goldsmith	P44,1B1	45	183	23	42	19	11	1	0	4	29		.230	.301
Joe Quest	2B41,SS1	42	159	24	32	15	5	2	0	8	16		.201	.258
Larry Corcoran	P39,3B1	40	169	23	35	24	10	2	1	6	18		.207	.308
Milt Scott	1B1	1	5	1	2	0	0	0	0	0	0		.400	.400
		84	3225	604	892	451	209	54	15	142	262		.277	.389

PITCHERS		W	L	PCT	G	GS	CG	SH	SV	IP	H	BB	SO	ERA
Fred Goldsmith		28	17	.622	45	45	45	4	0	405	377	38	109	2.42
Larry Corcoran		27	12	.692	39	39	38	3	0	356	281	63	170	1.95
Ned Williamson		0	0	----	1	0	0	0	0	3	9	1	0	6.00
		55	29	.655	84	84	83	7	0	764	667	102	279	2.22

PROVIDENCE
Grays

52-32   .619   -3   2nd   Harry Wright

BATTERS	POS/GAMES		GP	AB	R	H	BI	2B	3B	HR	BB	SO	SB	BA	SA
Joe Start	1B82		82	356	58	117	48	8	10	0	11	7		.329	.407
Jack Farrell	2B84		84	366	67	93	31	21	6	2	16	23		.254	.361
George Wright	SS46		46	185	14	30	9	1	2	0	4	36		.162	.189
Jerry Denny	3B84		84	329	54	81	42	10	9	2	4	46		.246	.350
Monte Ward	OF50,P33,SS4		83	355	58	87	39	10	3	1	13	22		.245	.299
Paul Hines	OF84		84	379	73	117	34	28	10	4	10	14		.309	.467
Tom York	OF81		81	321	48	86	40	23	7	1	19	14		.268	.393
Barney Gilligan	C54,SS2		56	201	32	45	26	7	6	0	4	26		.224	.318
Old Hoss Radbourn	P55,OF31,SS1		83	326	30	78	32	11	0	1	12	22		.239	.282
Sandy Nava	C27,OF1		28	97	15	20	7	2	0	0	1	13		.206	.227
Tim Manning	SS17,C4		21	76	7	8	8	0	0	0	5	13		.105	.105
Art Whitney	SS11	(1-2)	11	40	2	3	1	0	0	0	2	11		.075	.075
Cliff Carroll	OF10		10	41	4	5	2	0	0	0	0	4		.122	.122
Dasher Troy	SS4	(2-2)	4	17	1	4	1	0	0	0	0	1		.235	.235
Charlie Reilley	C3		3	11	0	2	2	0	0	0	1	2		.182	.182
Charlie Sweeney	OF1		1	4	0	0	0	0	0	0	0	1		.000	.000
			84	3104	463	776	322	121	53	11	102	255		.250	.334

PITCHERS		W	L	PCT	G	GS	CG	SH	SV	IP	H	BB	SO	ERA
Old Hoss Radbourn		33	20	.623	55	52	51	6	0	474	429	51	201	2.09
Monte Ward		19	12	.613	33	32	29	4	1	278	261	36	72	2.59
		52	32	.619	84	84	80	10	1	752	690	87	273	2.27

BUFFALO
Bisons

45-39   .536   -10   3rd   Jim O'Rourke
                      (tie)

BATTERS	POS/GAMES	GP	AB	R	H	BI	2B	3B	HR	BB	SO	SB	BA	SA
Dan Brouthers	1B84	84	351	71	129	63	23	11	6	21	7		.368	.547
Hardy Richardson	2B83	83	354	61	96	57	20	8	2	11	33		.271	.390
Davy Force	SS61,3B11,2B1	73	278	39	67	28	10	1	1	12	17		.241	.295
Deacon White	3B63,C20	83	337	51	95	33	17	0	1	15	16		.282	.341
Curry Foley	OF84,P1	84	341	51	104	49	16	4	3	12	26		.305	.402
Jim O'Rourke	OF81,C2,SS2,3B1	84	370	62	104	37	15	6	2	13	13		.281	.370
Blondie Purcell	OF82,P6	84	380	79	105	40	18	6	2	14	27		.276	.371
Jack Rowe	C46,SS22,3B7,OF1	75	308	43	82	42	14	5	1	12	0		.266	.354
Pud Galvin	P52,OF6	54	206	21	44		7	4	0	2	49		.214	.286
One Arm Daily	P29	29	110	10	18		6	1	0	2	28		.164	.236
Tom Dolan	C18,OF4,3B2	22	89	12	14	8	0	1	0	2	11		.157	.180
Walter Burke	P1,OF1	1	4	0	0	0	0	0	0	0	1		.000	.000
		84	3128	500	858	357	146	47	18	116	228		.274	.368

1882 NATIONAL LEAGUE

BUFFALO (cont.)
Bisons

PITCHERS	W	L	PCT	G	GS	CG	SH	SV	IP	H	BB	SO	ERA
Pud Galvin	28	23	.549	52	51	48	3	0	445	476	40	162	3.17
One Arm Daily	15	14	.517	29	29	29	0	0	256	246	70	116	2.99
Blondie Purcell	2	1	.667	6	3	2	0	0	31	44	4	9	4.94
Walter Burke	0	1	.000	1	1	0	0	0	4	10	0	0	11.25
Curry Foley	0	0	---	1	0	0	0	0	1	2	0	0	18.00
	45	39	.536	84	84	79	3	0	737	778	114	287	3.25

BOSTON
Red Caps

45-39 .536 -10 3rd (tie) John Morrill

BATTERS	POS/GAMES	GP	AB	R	H	BI	2B	3B	HR	BB	SO	SB	BA	SA
John Morrill	1B76,SS3,2B2,3B1,OF1,P1	83	349	73	101	54	19	11	2	18	29		.289	.424
Jack Burdock	2B83	83	319	36	76	27	6	7	0	9	24		.238	.301
Sam Wise	SS72,3B6	78	298	44	66	34	11	4	4	5	45		.221	.326
Ezra Sutton	3B77,SS4	81	319	44	80	38	8	1	2	24	25		.251	.301
Ed Rowen	OF48,C34,SS6,3B1	83	327	36	81	43	7	4	1	19	18		.248	.303
Pete Hotaling	OF84	84	378	64	98	28	16	5	0	16	21		.259	.328
Joe Hornung	OF84,1B1	85	388	67	117	50	14	11	1	2	25		.302	.402
Pat Deasley	C56,OF14,SS1	67	264	36	70	29	8	0	0	7	22		.265	.295
Jim Whitney	P49,OF9,1B6	61	251	49	81	48	18	7	5	24	13		.323	.510
Bobby Mathews	P34,OF13,SS1	45	169	17	38	13	6	0	0	8	18		.225	.260
Charles Buffinton	OF7,P5,1B4	15	50	5	13	4	1	0	0	2	3		.260	.280
Hal McClure	OF2	2	6	1	2	0	0	0	0	0	1		.333	.333
		85	3118	472	823	368	114	50	15	134	244		.264	.347

PITCHERS	W	L	PCT	G	GS	CG	SH	SV	IP	H	BB	SO	ERA
Jim Whitney	24	21	.533	49	48	46	3	0	420	404	41	180	2.64
Bobby Mathews	19	15	.559	34	32	31	0	0	285	278	22	153	2.87
Charles Buffinton	2	3	.400	5	5	4	1	0	42	53	14	17	4.07
John Morrill	0	0	---	1	0	0	0	0	2	3	0	2	0.00
	45	39	.536	85	85	81	4	0	749	738	77	352	2.80

CLEVELAND
Blues

42-40 .512 -12 5th McCormick - Dunlap

BATTERS	POS/GAMES		GP	AB	R	H	BI	2B	3B	HR	BB	SO	SB	BA	SA
Bill Phillips	1B78,C1		78	335	40	87	47	17	7	4	7	18		.260	.388
Fred Dunlap	2B84		84	364	68	102	28	19	4	0	23	26		.280	.354
Jack Glasscock	SS83,3B1		84	358	66	104	46	27	9	4	13	9		.291	.450
Mike Muldoon	3B61,OF23		84	341	50	84	45	17	5	6	10	28		.246	.378
Orator Shaffer	OF84		84	313	37	67	28	14	2	3	27	27		.214	.300
John Richmond	OF41	(1-2)	41	140	12	24	11	6	2	0	11	27		.171	.243
Dude Esterbrook	OF45,1B1		45	179	13	44	19	4	3	0	5	12		.246	.302
Fatty Briody	C53		53	194	30	50	13	13	0	0	9	13		.258	.325
Jim McCormick	P68,OF4		70	262	35	57	15	7	3	2	2	22		.218	.290
George Bradley	P18,OF9,1B6		30	115	16	21	6	5	0	0	4	16		.183	.226
John Kelly	C30		30	104	6	14	5	2	0	0	1	24		.135	.154
Herm Doscher	3B22,OF2,SS1		25	104	7	25	10	2	0	0	0	11		.240	.260
Dave Rowe	OF23,P1		24	97	13	25	17	4	3	1	4	9		.258	.392
John Tilley	OF15		15	56	2	5	4	1	1	0	2	11		.089	.143
Julius Willigrod	OF9		9	36	5	5	2	1	1	0	3	7		.139	.222
William McGunnigle	OF1		1	5	2	1	0	0	0	0	0	1		.200	.200
Doc Kennedy	C1		1	3	0	1	0	0	0	0	1	0		.333	.333
John Dwyer	C1,OF1		1	3	0	0	1	0	0	0	0	0		.000	.000
			84	3009	402	716	297	139	40	20	122	261		.238	.331

PITCHERS	W	L	PCT	G	GS	CG	SH	SV	IP	H	BB	SO	ERA
Jim McCormick	36	30	.545	68	67	65	4	0	596	550	103	200	2.37
George Bradley	6	9	.400	18	16	15	0	0	147	164	22	32	3.73
Dave Rowe	0	1	.000	1	1	1	0	0	9	29	7	0	12.00
	42	40	.512	84	84	81	4	0	752	743	132	232	2.75

1882 NATIONAL LEAGUE

DETROIT Wolverines
42-41 .506 -12.5 6th Frank Bancroft

BATTERS	POS/GAMES		GP	AB	R	H	BI	2B	3B	HR	BB	SO	SB	BA	SA
Martin Powell	1B80		80	338	44	81	29	13	0	0	19	27		.240	.278
Dasher Troy	2B31,SS11	(1-2)	40	152	22	37	14	7	2	0	5	10		.243	.316
Mike McGeary	SS33,2B3		34	133	14	19	2	4	1	0	2	20		.143	.188
Joe Farrell	3B42,2B18,SS9		69	283	34	70	24	12	2	1	4	20		.247	.314
Lon Knight	OF84,1B2		86	347	39	72	24	12	6	0	16	21		.207	.277
Ned Hanlon	OF82,2B1		82	347	68	80	38	18	6	5	26	25		.231	.360
George Wood	OF84		84	375	69	101	29	12	12	7	14	30		.269	.421
Charlie Bennett	C65,3B11,2B7,1B1,SS1		84	342	43	103	51	16	10	5	20	33		.301	.450
Stump Weidman	P46,OF6,SS1		50	193	20	42	20	7	1	0	2	19		.218	.264
George Derby	P40,OF2		40	149	13	29	8	2	1	0	7	23		.195	.221
Sam Trott	C23,1B3,SS3,2B3,OF2,3B1		32	129	11	31	12	7	1	0	0	13		.240	.310
Art Whitney	3B22,SS8,P3	(2-2)	31	115	10	21	4	0	0	0	1	12		.183	.183
Tom Forster	2B21		21	76	5	7	2	0	0	0	5	12		.092	.092
Walt Kinzie	SS13		13	53	5	5	2	0	1	0	0	8		.094	.132
Yank Robinson	SS10,OF1,P1		11	39	1	7	2	1	0	0	1	13		.179	.205
Bob Casey	3B8,2B1		9	39	5	9	7	2	1	1	0	15		.231	.410
Tom Kearns	2B4		4	13	2	4	1	2	0	0	0	4		.308	.462
Henry Luff	2B3,OF1	(1-2)	3	11	1	3	1	2	0	0	0	0		.273	.455
John Morrissey	3B2		2	7	1	2	0	0	0	0	0	2		.286	.286
Julius Willigrod	SS1	(1-2)	1	3	0	1	1	0	0	0	0	1		.333	.333
			86	3144	407	724	271	117	44	19	122	308		.230	.315

PITCHERS			W	L	PCT	G	GS	CG	SH	SV	IP	H	BB	SO	ERA
Stump Weidman			25	20	.556	46	45	43	4	0	411	391	39	161	2.63
George Derby			17	20	.459	40	39	38	3	0	362	386	81	182	3.26
Art Whitney		(2-2)	0	1	.000	3	2	1	0	0	18	31	8	11	6.00
Yank Robinson			0	0	----	1	0	0	0	0	2	0	1	0	0.00
			42	41	.506	86	86	82	7	0	793	808	129	354	2.98

TROY Trojans
35-48 .422 -19.5 7th Bob Ferguson

BATTERS	POS/GAMES		GP	AB	R	H	BI	2B	3B	HR	BB	SO	SB	BA	SA
John Smith	1B35	(1-2)	35	149	27	36	14	4	3	0	3	24		.242	.309
Bob Ferguson	2B79,SS2		81	319	44	82	33	15	2	0	23	21		.257	.317
Fred Pfeffer	SS83,2B2		85	330	26	72	31	7	4	1	1	24		.218	.273
Buck Ewing	3B44,C25,2B4,1B1,OF1,P1		74	328	67	89	29	16	11	2	10	15		.271	.405
Chief Roseman	OF82		82	331	41	78	43	21	6	1	3	41		.236	.344
Roger Conner	OF24,1B43,3B14		81	349	65	115	42	22	18	4	13	20		.330	.530
Pete Gillespie	OF74		74	298	46	82	32	5	4	2	9	14		.275	.339
Bill Holbert	C58,3B12,OF3		71	251	24	46	23	5	0	0	11	22		.183	.203
Tim Keefe	P43,OF8,3B3		53	189	24	43	19	8	7	1	17	46		.228	.360
Mickey Welch	P33,OF8		38	151	26	37	17	6	0	1	5	16		.245	.305
Bill Harbridge	OF23,1B6,C3		32	123	11	23	13	1	1	0	10	17		.187	.211
James Egan	OF18,P12,C2		30	115	15	23	10	3	2	0	1	21		.200	.261
John Cassidy	OF16,3B13		29	121	14	21	9	3	1	0	3	16		.174	.215
Jim Holdsworth	OF1		1	3	0	0	0	0	0	0	0	1		.000	.000
			85	3057	430	747	315	116	59	12	109	298		.244	.333

PITCHERS			W	L	PCT	G	GS	CG	SH	SV	IP	H	BB	SO	ERA
Tim Keefe			17	26	.395	43	42	41	1	0	375	368	81	116	2.50
Mickey Welch			14	16	.467	33	33	30	5	0	281	334	62	53	3.46
James Egan			4	6	.400	12	10	10	0	0	100	133	24	20	4.14
Buck Ewing			0	0	----	1	0	0	0	0	1	2	1	0	9.00
			35	48	.422	85	85	81	6	0	757	837	168	189	3.08

WORCESTER Ruby Legs
18-66 .214 -37 8th Brown - Bond Chapman

BATTERS	POS/GAMES	GP	AB	R	H	BI	2B	3B	HR	BB	SO	SB	BA	SA
Harry Stovey	1B43,OF41	84	360	90	104	26	13	10	5	22	34		.289	.422
George Creamer	2B81	81	286	27	65	29	16	6	1	14	24		.227	.336
Fred Corey	SS26,P21,OF15,3B6,1B5	64	255	33	63	29	7	12	0	5	31		.247	.369
Art Irwin	3B51,SS53	84	333	30	73	30	12	4	0	14	34		.219	.279

WORCESTER (cont.)
Ruby Legs

BATTERS	POS/GAMES		GP	AB	R	H	BI	2B	3B	HR	BB	SO	SB	BA	SA
Jake Evans	OF68,SS11,2B1,3B1,P1		80	334	33	71	25	10	4	0	7	22		.213	.266
Jack Hayes	OF58,C15,3B5,SS1		78	326	27	88	54	22	4	4	6	26		.270	.399
Jim Clinton	OF26		26	98	9	16	3	2	0	0	7	13		.163	.184
Doc Bushong	C69		69	253	20	40	15	4	1	1	5	17		.158	.194
Lee Richmond	P48,OF11		55	228	50	64	28	8	9	2	9	11		.281	.421
Frank Mountain	P18,OF,1B2,SS1	(1,3-3)	25	86	9	20	6	2	2	2	3	23		.233	.372
Tom O'Brien	OF20,2B2,3B1		22	89	9	18	7	1	1	0	1	10		.202	.236
Fred Mann	3B18,1B1	(1-2)	19	77	12	18	7	5	0	0	2	15		.234	.299
John Smith	1B19	(2-2)	19	70	10	17	5	3	2	0	5	10		.243	.343
Frank McLaughlin	SS14,OF1		15	55	7	12	4	0	2	1	0	11		.218	.345
Ed Cogswell	1B13		13	51	10	7	1	1	0	0	6	6		.137	.157
Tommy Bond	OF8,P2		8	30	1	4	2	0	0	0	2	3		.133	.133
Dan O'Leary	OF6		6	22	2	4	2	1	0	0	5	5		.182	.227
John Clarkson	P3,1B1		3	11	0	4	2	2	0	0	0	3		.364	.545
Ed Merrill	3B2		2	8	0	1	4	0	0	0	0	1		.125	.125
Jim Halpin	3B2		2	8	0	0	0	0	0	0	0	0		.000	.000
John Irwin	1B1		1	4	0	0	0	0	0	0	0	2		.000	.000
			84	2984	379	689	279	109	57	16	113	301		.231	.322

PITCHERS			W	L	PCT	G	GS	CG	SH	SV	IP	H	BB	SO	ERA
Lee Richmond			14	33	.298	48	46	44	0	0	411	525	88	123	3.74
Frank Mountain		(1,3-3)	2	16	.111	18	18	16	0	0	144	185	35	29	3.69
John Clarkson			1	2	.333	3	3	2	0	0	24	49	2	3	4.50
Fred Corey			1	13	.071	21	14	12	0	0	139	180	19	36	3.56
Tommy Bond			0	1	.000	2	2	0	0	0	12	12	7	2	4.38
Jake Evans			0	1	.000	1	1	1	0	0	8	13	0	2	5.63
			18	66	.214	84	84	75	0	0	738	964	151	195	3.75

1882 AMERICAN ASSOCIATION

The Beer and Whiskey Circuit

Many baseball fans in the early 1880s were disgruntled. Not only did the stodgy National League owners charge 50 cents for the privilege of attending a game, they did not allow any of these games to occur on a Sunday, nor did they allow the partaking of spirits at the ballpark. The one team that sometimes had lightened these restrictions, Cincinnati, had been shown the door by the other National League owners. To the middle class, beer drinking fans of America's heartland, it was an intolerable situation. However, a solution was in the offing.

Late in 1881, the backers of several independent clubs met in Cincinnati with the idea of forming a new major league. On November 2, the American Association was formed. The charter members included: St. Louis, Cincinnati, Pittsburgh, Philadelphia, Louisville, and Brooklyn. Later, after pleading insolvency, the Brooklyn team was dropped, to be replaced by Baltimore. Four of the teams (St. Louis, Cincinnati, Louisville, and Baltimore) were owned or backed by breweries, thus the moniker "the beer and whiskey circuit" was coined to describe the American Association.

The new league differed from the old in three key areas. 1) Sunday baseball was permitted; 2) only 25 cents admission would gain entrance to an Association ballpark; and 3) liquor would be sold on the premises. To stock their teams, the American Association at first signed players outside the jurisdiction of the National League. But when two players (Sam Wise and Dasher Troy) jumped their Association contracts to sign with National League teams, the gloves dropped. Soon, an all out war broke out between the two leagues for players. Contract jumping was rampant as all the teams struggled to fill their rosters. This war would not be resolved for more than a year.

In its inaugural season, Cincinnati proved itself to be the pick of the American Association. Winning the pennant by eleven and one-half games, the team boasted of the best hitting and pitching in the league. Third baseman Hick Carpenter (.342) finished second in the batting race, and first (120) in the most hits race. His teammate, Will White (who had pitched for the Cincinnati team a few years before) posted the most wins (40) and shutouts (8).

In second were the Philadelphia Athletics. Their offensive mainstays were catcher Jack O'Brien (.303) and first baseman Juice Latham (.285), while Sam Weaver (26-15) anchored the pitching staff.

Louisville, behind the big bat of batting champ Pete Browning, finished just behind Philadelphia in third. Browning, who batted .378, also finished second in the home run race with five. Louisville pitcher, Tony Mullane, won 30, while striking out a league best of 170.

Pittsburgh finished in fourth place right at the .500 mark. The team was distinguished by its extra base hitting, leading the league in all three categories. Ed Swartwood and Mike Mansell shared the lead with most doubles at eighteen, while Mansell hit 16 triples, also the season's best. Pitcher Denny Driscoll won the earned run average title at 1.21.

St. Louis and Baltimore finished at the bottom. St. Louis was led by home run champ Oscar Walker, who swatted seven. Baltimore, as a team, batted an abysmal .207, the third lowest of all time. Despite this, one of their regulars, Tom Brown (.304) managed to crack the .300 barrier.

Following the season, the two leagues buried the hatchet long enough to stage a series of games between each pennant winner—Cincinnati of the American Association, against Chicago of the National League. After two games, with each team having won once, American Association president Denny McKnight threatened Cincinnati with expulsion should the series continue. So the first attempt at a championship series ended after two games.

Despite its modest six-team roster of clubs, the American Association survived its inaugural season with ease. It had quickly proved itself to be a viable alternative to the old ways of the National League by showcasing several popular ideas. The American Association had gone from being a nuisance, to an actual threat to the National League. And soon, it would strive to be its equal.

1882 AMERICAN ASSOCIATION

CINCINNATI
Red Stockings 55-25 .687 1st Pop Snyder

BATTERS	POS/GAMES		GP	AB	R	H	BI	2B	3B	HR	BB	SO	SB	BA	SA
Dan Stearns	1B35,OF12,2B2,SS1		49	214	28	55		10	2	0	6			.257	.322
Bid McPhee	2B78		78	311	43	71		8	7	1	11			.228	.309
Chick Fulmer	SS79		79	324	54	91		13	4	0	10			.281	.346
Hick Carpenter	3B80		80	351	78	120		15	5	1	10			.342	.422
John McCuller	OF79		79	299	44	70		6	6	0	14			.234	.294
Joe Sommer	OF80		80	354	82	102		12	6	1	24			.288	.364
Harry Wheeler	OF64,1B12,P4		76	344	59	86		11	11	1	7			.250	.355
Pop Snyder	C70,1B2,OF1		72	309	49	90		12	2	1	9			.291	.353
Will White	P54,OF2		54	207	28	55		4	0	0	5			.266	.285
Henry Luff	1B27,OF1	(2-2)	28	120	16	28		2	2	0	2			.233	.283
Pat McCormick	P25,OF2		26	93	3	12		0	1	0	1			.129	.151
Phil Powers	C10,1B5,OF1		16	60	4	13		1	1	0	3			.217	.267
Rudy Kemmler	C3,OF1	(1-2)	3	11	0	1		1	0	0	0			.091	.182
John Thompson	OF1		1	5	0	1		0	0	0	0			.200	.200
William Tierney	1B1		1	5	1	0		0	0	0	0			.000	.000
			80	3007	489	795		95	47	5	102	165		.264	.332

PITCHERS		W	L	PCT	G	GS	CG	SH	SV	IP	H	BB	SO	ERA
Will White		40	12	.769	54	54	52	8	0	480	411	71	122	1.54
Pat McCormick		14	11	.560	25	25	24	3	0	220	177	42	33	1.51
Harry Wheeler		1	2	.333	4	1	1	0	0	22	21	12	10	5.73
		55	25	.687	80	80	77	11	0	721	609	125	165	1.65

PHILADELPHIA
Athletics 41-34 .547 -11.5 2nd Juice Latham

BATTERS	POS/GAMES		GP	AB	R	H	BI	2B	3B	HR	BB	SO	SB	BA	SA
Juice Latham	1B74		74	323	47	92		10	2	0	10			.285	.328
Cub Stricker	2B72,P2,OF1		72	272	34	59		6	1	0	15			.217	.246
Louis Say	SS49		49	199	35	45		4	3	1	8			.226	.291
Fred Mann	3B29	(2-2)	29	121	13	28		7	4	0	4			.231	.355
Bob Blakiston	OF38,3B34,2B1		72	281	40	64		4	1	0	9			.228	.249
John Mansell	OF31		31	126	17	30		3	1	0	4			.238	.278
Jud Birchall	OF74,2B1		75	338	65	89		12	1	0	8			.263	.305
Jack O'Brien	C45,OF18,3B1,1B1		62	241	44	73		13	3	3	13			.303	.419
Jerry Dorgan	C25,OF22		44	181	25	51		9	1	0	4			.282	.343
Sam Weaver	P42,OF2		43	155	19	36		3	0	0	12			.232	.252
Bill Sweeney	P20,OF5		23	88	8	14		4	0	0	4			.159	.205
Jim Say	SS22	(2-2)	22	82	12	17		2	0	1	1			.207	.268
Tom Smith	3B11,SS4,OF3,2B2		21	65	10	6		0	0	0	12			.092	.092
John Richmond	OF18	(2-2)	18	65	8	12		2	2	0	11			.185	.277
Frank Mountain	P8,OF1	(2-3)	9	36	5	12		3	0	0	2			.333	.417
Bill Keinzil	OF9		9	33	8	11		3	2	0	5			.333	.545
Joe Straub	C7,OF1		8	32	2	6		2	0	0	1			.188	.250
Bill Greenwood	OF7,2B2		7	30	8	9		1	0	0	1			.300	.333
Doc Landis	P2,OF1	(1-2)	3	12	1	2		0	0	0	0			.167	.167
Charlie Reynolds	P2,OF1		2	8	1	1		0	0	0	0			.125	.125
Bill Farrell	OF2,C1		2	7	2	2		1	0	0	1			.286	.429
Tug Arundel	C1		1	5	0	0		0	0	0	0			.000	.000
Ed Halbriter	P1		1	4	0	0		0	0	0	0			.000	.000
George Snyder	P1		1	3	2	1		0	0	0	0			.333	.333
			75	2707	406	660		89	21	5	125	164		.244	.298

PITCHERS		W	L	PCT	G	GS	CG	SH	SV	IP	H	BB	SO	ERA
Sam Weaver		26	15	.634	42	41	41	2	0	371	374	35	104	2.74
Bill Sweeney		9	10	.474	20	20	18	0	0	170	178	42	48	2.91
Frank Mountain	(2-3)	2	6	.250	8	8	8	0	0	69	72	11	15	3.91
Cub Stricker		1	0	1.000	2	0	0	0	0	7	3	1	2	1.29
George Snyder		1	0	1.000	1	1	1	0	0	9	4	2	0	0.00
Doc Landis	(1-2)	1	1	.500	2	2	2	0	0	17	16	1	13	3.18
Charlie Reynolds		1	1	.500	2	2	1	0	0	12	18	3	4	5.25
Ed Halbriter		0	1	.000	1	1	1	0	0	8	17	4	4	7.88
		41	34	.547	75	75	72	2	0	663	682	99	190	2.97

1882 AMERICAN ASSOCIATION

LOUISVILLE Eclipse   42-38   .525   -13   3rd   Denny Mack

BATTERS	POS/GAMES		GP	AB	R	H	BI	2B	3B	HR	BB	SO	SB	BA	SA
Guy Hecker	1B66,P13,OF2		78	340	62	94		14	4	3	5			.276	.378
Pete Browning	2B42,SS18,3B13		69	288	67	109		17	3	5	26			.378	.510
Denny Mack	SS49,2B24,OF5		72	264	41	48		3	1	0	16			.182	.201
Bill Schenk	3B58,P2,SS2		60	231	37	60		11	3	0	8			.260	.333
Chicken Wolf	OF70,SS9,1B1,P1		78	318	46	95		11	8	0	9			.299	.384
John Reccius	OF65,P13		74	266	46	63		12	3	1	23			.237	.316
Leech Maskrey	OF76,2B1		76	288	30	65		14	2	0	9			.226	.288
Dan Sullivan	C54,3B10,OF4,SS1		67	286	44	78		8	2	0	9			.273	.315
Tony Mullane	P55,1B13,OF12,2B2		77	303	46	78		13	1	0	13			.257	.307
John Strick	C21,2B6,OF6,1B1,SS1		32	110	17	18		6	1	0	9			.164	.236
Gracie Pierce	2B9	(1-2)	9	33	3	10		1	0	0	1			.303	.333
Joe Crotty	C5	(1-2)	5	20	1	2		0	0	0	0			.100	.100
Phil Reccius	OF4		4	15	0	2		0	0	0	0			.133	.133
Charlie Bohn	OF2,P2		4	13	0	2		0	0	0	0			.154	.154
Pop Smith	SS3	(2-2)	3	11	1	2		0	0	0	0			.182	.182
Harry McCaffery	2B1	(1-2)	1	4	1	1		0	0	0	0			.250	.250
Jim Say	3B1	(1-2)	1	4	1	1		0	0	0	0			.250	.250
Harry Maskrey	OF1		1	4	0	0		0	0	0	0			.000	.000
John Dyler	OF1		1	4	0	0		0	0	0	0			.000	.000
Amos Booth	2B1	(2-2)	1	3	0	0		0	0	0	0			.000	.000
			80	2806	443	728		110	28	9	128	193		.259	.328

PITCHERS			W	L	PCT	G	GS	CG	SH	SV	IP	H	BB	SO	ERA
Tony Mullane			30	24	.556	55	55	51	5	0	460	418	78	170	1.88
Guy Hecker			6	6	.500	13	11	10	0	0	104	75	5	33	1.30
John Reccius			4	6	.400	13	10	9	1	0	95	106	22	31	3.03
Bill Schenk			1	0	1.000	2	1	1	0	0	10	6	1	4	0.90
Charlie Bohn			1	1	.500	2	2	2	0	0	18	21	3	1	3.00
Chicken Wolf			0	0	----	1	0	0	0	0	6	11	3	1	9.00
			42	38	.525	80	79	73	6	0	693	637	112	240	2.03

PITTSBURGH Alleghenys   39-39   .500   -15   4th   Al Pratt

BATTERS	POS/GAMES		GP	AB	R	H	BI	2B	3B	HR	BB	SO	SB	BA	SA
Chappy Lane	1B43,OF13,C2		57	214	26	38		8	2	3	5			.178	.276
George Strief	2B78,SS1		79	297	45	58		9	6	2	13			.195	.286
John Peters	SS77,2B1		78	333	46	96		10	1	0	4			.288	.324
Joe Battin	3B34		34	133	13	28		5	1	1	3			.211	.286
Ed Swartwood	OF73,1B4		76	325	86	107		18	11	4	21			.329	.489
Mike Mansell	OF79		79	347	59	96		18	16	2	7			.277	.438
Jack Leary	OF27,3B33,P3,2B1,1B1	(1-2)	60	257	32	75		7	3	1	5			.292	.354
Bill Taylor	C27,1B23,3B14,OF8,P1		70	299	40	84		16	13	3	7			.281	.452
Harry Salisbury	P38,OF1		38	145	17	22		2	0	0	4			.152	.166
Charlie Morton	OF25,3B3,SS1	(1-2)	25	103	12	29		0	3	0	5			.282	.340
Jim Keenan	C22,OF3,SS1		25	96	10	21		7	0	1	1			.219	.323
Rudy Kemmler	C23,OF2		24	99	7	25		4	0	0	1			.253	.293
Denny Driscoll	P23		23	80	12	11		2	0	1	3			.138	.200
Bill Morgan	OF11,C7		17	66	10	17		2	1	0	4			.258	.318
Harry Arundel	P14,SS1		14	53	8	10		0	0	0	5			.189	.189
Jake Goodman	1B10		10	41	5	13		2	2	0	2			.317	.463
Morrie Critchley	P1	(1-2)	1	5	0	0		0	0	0	0			.000	.000
Russ McKelvy	OF1		1	4	0	0		0	0	0	0			.000	.000
Jake Seymour	P1		1	4	0	0		0	0	0	0			.000	.000
Ren Wylie	OF1		1	3	0	0		0	0	0	0			.000	.000
			79	2904	428	730		110	59	18	90	183		.251	.351

PITCHERS			W	L	PCT	G	GS	CG	SH	SV	IP	H	BB	SO	ERA
Harry Salisbury			20	18	.526	38	38	38	1	0	335	315	37	135	2.63
Denny Driscoll			13	9	.591	23	23	23	0	0	201	162	12	59	1.21
Harry Arundel			4	10	.286	14	14	13	0	0	120	155	23	47	4.65
Jack Leary			1	0	1.000	3	2	1	0	0	19	28	3	5	6.27
Morrie Critchley		(1-2)	1	0	1.000	1	1	1	1	0	9	7	1	3	0.00
Jake Seymour			0	1	.000	1	1	1	0	0	8	16	2	2	7.88
Billy Taylor			0	1	.000	1	0	0	0	0	5	11	4	1	16.20
			39	39	.500	79	79	77	2	0	697	694	82	252	2.79

1882 AMERICAN ASSOCIATION

ST. LOUIS 37-43   .463   -18   5th   Ned Cuthbert
Brown Stockings

BATTERS	POS/GAMES		GP	AB	R	H	BI	2B	3B	HR	BB	SO	SB	BA	SA
Charlie Comiskey	1B77,P2		78	329	58	80		9	5	1	4			.243	.310
Bill Smiley	2B58,OF2	(1-2)	59	240	30	51		4	2	0	6			.213	.246
Bill Gleason	SS79		79	347	63	100		11	6	1	6			.288	.363
Jack Gleason	3B73,OF6,2B1		78	331	53	84		10	1	2	27			.254	.308
George Seward	OF35,C5		38	144	23	31		1	1	0	12			.215	.236
Oscar Walker	OF75,2B1,1B1		75	318	48	76		15	7	7	10			.239	.396
Ned Cuthbert	OF60		60	233	28	52		16	5	0	17			.223	.335
Sleeper Sullivan	C50,P1		51	188	24	34		3	3	0	3			.181	.229
Jumbo McGinnis	P44,OF6,C1,2B1		51	203	17	44		6	4	0	3			.217	.286
Harry McCaffery	OF23,2B8,3B7,1B1	(2-2)	38	153	23	42		8	6	0	3			.275	.405
Ed Fusselbach	C19,OF15,P4		35	136	13	31		2	0	0	5			.228	.243
Ed Brown	OF15,2B2,P1		17	60	4	11		0	0	0	4			.183	.183
Jack Schappert	P15,OF1		15	50	7	9		1	0	0	7			.180	.200
Charlie Morton	2B7,OF3	(2-2)	9	32	2	2		0	1	0	2			.063	.125
Joe Crotty	C7,OF1	(2-2)	8	28	2	4		1	0	0	3			.143	.179
Bert Dorr	P8		8	26	2	4		0	0	0	0			.154	.154
Morrie Critchley	P4	(2-2)	4	14	0	3		0	0	0	0			.214	.214
Ed Doyle	P3		3	11	0	2		0	0	0	0			.182	.182
Frank Decker	2B2		2	8	0	2		0	0	0	0			.250	.250
John Shoupe	2B2		2	7	1	0		0	0	0	0			.000	.000
Robert Mitchell	OF1,P1		1	4	0	0		0	0	0	0			.000	.000
Eddie Hogan	P1		1	3	1	1		0	0	0	0			.333	.333
			80	2865	399	663		87	41	11	112	226		.231	.302

PITCHERS			W	L	PCT	G	GS	CG	SH	SV	IP	H	BB	SO	ERA
Jumbo McGinnis			25	18	.581	45	45	43	3	0	379	370	52	134	2.60
Jack Schappert			8	7	.533	15	14	13	0	0	128	131	32	38	3.52
Bert Dorr			2	6	.250	8	8	8	0	0	66	53	1	34	2.59
Ed Fusselbach			1	2	.333	4	2	2	0	1	23	34	2	3	4.70
Sleeper Sullivan			0	1	.000	1	1	1	0	0	9	15	1	0	8.00
Eddie Hogan			0	1	.000	1	1	1	0	0	8	10	0	4	1.13
Charlie Comiskey			0	1	.000	2	1	1	0	0	8	12	3	2	0.00
Robert Mitchell			0	1	.000	1	1	0	0	0	7	12	2	2	7.71
John Doyle			0	3	.000	3	3	3	0	0	24	41	3	5	2.63
Morrie Critchley			0	4	.000	4	4	4	0	0	34	43	7	2	4.24
Ed Brown			0	0	----	1	0	0	0	0	2	2	0	1	0.00
			37	43	.463	80	79	75	3	1	688	829	103	225	2.92

BALTIMORE 19-54   .260   -32.5   6th   Henry Myers
Orioles

BATTERS	POS/GAMES		GP	AB	R	H	BI	2B	3B	HR	BB	SO	SB	BA	SA
Charles Householder	1B74,C3		74	307	42	78		10	7	1	4			.254	.342
Gracie Pierce	2B38,OF3,SS1	(2-2)	41	151	8	30		2	1	0	3			.199	.225
Henry Myers	SS68,P6		69	294	43	53		3	0	0	12			.180	.190
John Shetzline	3B52,2B20,OF1,SS1		73	282	23	62		8	3	0	5			.220	.270
Tom Brown	OF45,P2		45	181	30	55		5	2	1	6			.304	.370
Monk Cline	OF39,SS8,2B2,3B1		44	172	18	38		6	2	0	3			.221	.279
Charlie Waitt	OF72		72	250	19	39		4	0	0	13			.156	.172
Ed Whiting	C72,1B3,OF2		74	308	43	80		14	5	0	7			.260	.338
Doc Landis	P42,OF14	(2-2)	50	175	9	29		1	0	0	3			.166	.171
Harry Jacoby	3B19,OF13		31	121	17	21		1	1	1	7			.174	.223
Tricky Nichols	P16,OF14	(1-2)	26	95	4	15		1	0	0	7			.158	.168
Bill Smiley	2B14,SS2	(2-2)	16	61	3	9		0	0	0	0			.148	.148
Emil Geis	P13,OF4		13	41	2	6		0	1	0	1			.146	.195
Nick Scharf	OF9,3B1		10	39	4	8		1	1	1	0			.205	.359
Frank Burt	OF10		10	36	2	4		2	1	0	1			.111	.222
Bill Wise	P3,OF2		5	20	2	2		1	0	0	0			.100	.150
Jack Leary	P3,OF1	(2-2)	4	18	3	4		1	0	0	0			.222	.278
Bill Jones	C2,OF2		4	15	1	1		0	0	0	0			.067	.067
Harry East	3B1		1	4	0	0		0	0	0	0			.000	.000
Tom Evers	2B1		1	4	0	0		0	0	0	0			.000	.000
----- Rust	OF1,P1		1	3	0	1		0	0	0	0			.333	.333
Amos Booth	3B1	(1-2)	1	3	0	0		0	0	0	0			.000	.000
Pop Smith	OF1	(1-2)	1	3	0	0		0	0	0	0			.000	.000
			74	2583	273	535		60	24	4	72	215		.207	.254

BALTIMORE (cont.)
Orioles

PITCHERS		W	L	PCT	G	GS	CG	SH	SV	IP	H	BB	SO	ERA
Doc Landis	(2-2)	11	27	.289	42	39	35	0	0	341	409	46	62	3.33
Emil Geis		4	9	.308	13	13	10	1	0	96	84	22	10	4.80
Jack Leary	(2-2)	2	1	.667	3	3	3	0	0	26	29	8	2	1.38
Bill Wise		1	2	.333	3	3	3	0	0	26	30	4	9	2.77
Tricky Nichols	(1-2)	1	12	.077	16	13	12	0	0	118	155	17	21	5.02
---- Rust		0	1	----	1	1	0	0	0	5	10	1	0	7.20
Henry Myers		0	2	----	6	2	1	0	0	26	30	4	7	6.58
Tom Brown		0	0	----	2	0	0	0	0	8	13	6	2	1.08
		19	54	.260	74	74	64	1	0	646	760	108	113	3.88

1883 NATIONAL LEAGUE

The Return of the Prodigals

When New York and Philadelphia were kicked out of the National League during the latter stages of the 1876 season, most thought the league would perish. New York and Philadelphia were, after all, the two largest cities in the league. But the league survived, and even prospered. By utilizing teams in medium-size cities such as Milwaukee, Troy, and Worcester, the National League continued intact. However, with the advent of the American Association, who by 1883 fielded teams in New York and Philadelphia, the National League was ready to welcome the prodigals home.

After their expulsion from organized baseball, the two cities did not just sit idly by, as both New York and Philadelphia fielded powerful, independent teams. In 1880, the New York Metropolitans were formed. Playing in the loosely organized Eastern Championship Association in 1881 and 1882, the Metropolitans finished with the best record in each year. In addition during 1881, they played 60 games against National League opponents of which they won eighteen. In Philadelphia, the expelled Athletics reorganized as an independent team in 1877 and finished with a 66 and 31 mark. In 1881 the team joined the Metropolitans in their Eastern Championship Association, after which they joined the American Association as a charter member. In 1883, the Metropolitans joined the Association as well.

With their arch rivals firmly ensconced in the country's two largest cities, the National League quickly acted. Rather than expanding to a ten team league to accommodate these desires, the league sought to transfer two franchises instead. Both Troy and Worcester needed financial help to finish the 1882 season. These two, then, were the logical choice to have the privilege of transferring to New York and Philadelphia. As it turned out, the Troy franchise shifted to New York, while the Worcester club moved to Philadelphia.

In 1883, after a five-year absence, Boston returned to the top rung of the National League standings. Jack Burdock (.330), Ezra Sutton (.324), and John Morrill (.319) were the team's three .300 hitters. Boston pitcher Jim Whitney also had a fine year, winning 37, while striking out a league best 345. Chicago, for the first time in four years, did not finish first. They finished second, four games out. Once again, Cap Anson (.308) and George Gore (.334) led the offense while pitchers Larry Corcoran, with 34 wins, and Fred Goldsmith with 25, claimed all of the team's 59 wins.

Providence slipped a notch to third place, while Cleveland jumped to fourth. Jack Farrell led Providence with a .305 average, and Fred Dunlap (.326) did the same for Cleveland. Both teams had outstanding pitching as well. Providence hurler Old Hoss Radbourn won a league best 48, and Cleveland pitcher Jim McCormick had the best earned run average (1.84).

Fifth place Buffalo featured two outstanding performances. Dan Brouthers won his second straight batting title with a mark of .374. He also topped the circuit with 159 hits and 97 runs batted in. His teammate, Pud Galvin, had his best year, posting 46 wins in 75 games, while pitching 656 innings.

New York finished sixth, while Detroit finished seventh. Roger Connor (.357), and Buck Ewing (.303, 10 HR) led New York, while George Wood (.302) and Charlie Bennett (.305) led Detroit.

In 1882, Worcester won only 18 games. Transplanted to Philadelphia in 1883, the team played 15 more games and won one less, finishing with a 17-81 record. The resulting win percentage (.173) ranks as the fourth worst of all time. Despite its dismal showing, the team had one good hitter, Emil Gross, who finished at .307. On the other hand, pitcher Jack Coleman was credited with 48 losses, the all time record.

In 1882, the population of the six cities affiliated with the American Association, was greater than the population of the eight cities affiliated with the National League. With the extra profits that resulted from a larger population base, it was a necessary step to court the once spurned largest cities, and invite them back. And that is just what the National League did in 1883.

1883 NATIONAL LEAGUE

BOSTON
Beaneaters

63-35 .643 1st Burdock - Morrill

BATTERS	POS/GAMES		GP	AB	R	H	BI	2B	3B	HR	BB	SO	SB	BA	SA
John Morrill	1B81,OF7,3B6,2B2,SS2,P2		97	404	83	129	68	33	16	6	15	68		.319	.525
Jack Burdock	2B96		96	400	80	132	88	27	8	5	14	35		.330	.475
Sam Wise	SS96		96	406	73	110	58	25	7	4	13	74		.271	.397
Ezra Sutton	3B93,OF1,SS1		94	414	101	134	73	28	15	3	17	12		.324	.486
Paul Radford	OF72		72	258	46	53	14	6	3	0	9	26		.205	.252
Charles Buffinton	OF51,P43,1B2		86	341	28	81	26	8	3	1	6	24		.238	.287
Joe Hornung	OF98,3B1		98	446	107	124	66	25	13	8	8	54		.278	.446
Mike Hines	C59,OF7		63	231	38	52	16	13	1	0	7	36		.225	.290
Jim Whitney	P62,OF40,1B2		96	409	78	115	57	27	10	5	25	29		.281	.433
Mert Hackett	C44,OF4		46	179	20	42	24	8	6	2	1	48		.235	.380
Edgar Smith	OF30,C1		30	115	10	25	16	5	3	0	5	11		.217	.313
Lewis Brown	1B14	(1-2)	14	54	5	13	9	4	1	0	3	6		.241	.352
			98	3657	669	1010	515	209	86	34	123	423		.276	.408

PITCHERS		W	L	PCT	G	GS	CG	SH	SV	IP	H	BB	SO	ERA
Jim Whitney		37	21	.638	62	56	54	1	2	514	492	35	345	2.24
Charles Buffinton		25	14	.641	43	41	34	4	1	333	346	51	188	3.03
John Morrill		1	0	1.000	2	1	1	0	0	13	15	4	5	2.77
		63	35	.643	98	98	89	6	3	860	853	90	538	2.55

CHICAGO
White Stockings

59-39 .602 -4 2nd Cap Anson

BATTERS	POS/GAMES	GP	AB	R	H	BI	2B	3B	HR	BB	SO	SB	BA	SA
Cap Anson	1B98,P2,C1,OF1	98	413	70	127	68	36	5	0	18	9		.308	.419
Fred Pfeffer	2B79,SS18,3B1,1B1	96	371	41	87	45	22	7	1	8	50		.235	.340
Tom Burns	SS79,2B19,OF1	97	405	69	119	67	37	7	2	13	31		.294	.435
Ned Williamson	3B97,C3,P1	98	402	83	111	59	49	5	2	22	48		.276	.438
King Kelly	OF82,C38,2B3,3B2,P1	98	428	92	109	61	28	10	3	16	35		.255	.388
George Gore	OF92	92	392	105	131	52	30	9	2	27	13		.334	.472
Abner Dalrymple	OF80	80	363	78	108	37	24	4	2	11	29		.298	.402
Silver Flint	C83,OF23	85	332	57	88	32	23	4	0	3	69		.265	.358
Larry Corcoran	P56,OF13,SS3,2B1	68	263	40	55	25	12	7	0	6	62		.209	.308
Fred Goldsmith	P46,OF16,1B2	60	235	38	52	16	12	3	1	4	35		.221	.311
Billy Sunday	OF14	14	54	6	13	5	4	0	0	1	18		.241	.315
		98	3658	679	1000	467	277	61	13	129	399		.273	.393

PITCHERS	W	L	PCT	G	GS	CG	SH	SV	IP	H	BB	SO	ERA
Larry Corcoran	34	20	.630	56	53	51	3	0	474	483	82	216	2.49
Fred Goldsmith	25	19	.568	46	45	40	2	0	383	456	39	82	3.15
Cap Anson	0	0	----	2	0	0	0	1	3	1	1	0	0.00
King Kelly	0	0	----	1	0	0	0	0	1	1	0	0	0.00
Ned Williamson	0	0	----	1	0	0	0	0	1	1	1	1	9.00
	59	39	.602	98	98	91	5	1	862	942	123	299	2.78

PROVIDENCE
Grays

58-40 .592 -5 3rd Harry Wright

BATTERS	POS/GAMES		GP	AB	R	H	BI	2B	3B	HR	BB	SO	SB	BA	SA
Joe Start	1B87		87	370	63	105	57	16	7	1	22	16		.284	.373
Jack Farrell	2B95		95	420	92	128	61	24	11	3	15	21		.305	.436
Art Irwin	SS94,2B4		98	406	67	116	44	22	7	0	12	38		.286	.374
Jerry Denny	3B98		98	393	73	108	55	26	8	3	9	48		.275	.443
John Cassidy	OF88,1B1,2B1		89	366	46	87	42	16	5	0	9	38		.238	.309
Paul Hines	OF89,1B9		97	442	94	132	45	32	4	4	18	23		.299	.416
Cliff Carroll	OF58		58	238	37	63	20	12	3	1	4	28		.265	.353
Barney Gilligan	C74		74	263	34	52	24	13	3	0	26	32		.198	.270
Old Hoss Radbourn	P76,OF20,1B2		89	381	59	108	48	11	3	3	14	16		.283	.352
Lee Richmond	OF41,P12		49	194	41	55	19	8	6	1	15	19		.284	.402
Sandy Nava	C27,OF2		29	100	18	24	16	4	2	0	3	17		.240	.320
Charlie Sweeney	P20,OF7		22	87	9	19	15	3	0	0	2	10		.218	.253
Joe Mulvey	SS4	(1-2)	4	16	1	2	2	1	0	0	0	1		.125	.188
Edgar Smith	1B2,OF2	(1-2)	2	9	2	2	1	1	0	0	0	2		.222	.333
			98	3685	636	1001	449	189	59	21	149	309		.272	.372

PROVIDENCE (cont.)
Grays

PITCHERS	W	L	PCT	G	GS	CG	SH	SV	IP	H	BB	SO	ERA
Old Hoss Radbourn	48	25	.658	76	68	66	4	1	632	563	56	315	2.05
Charlie Sweeney	7	7	.500	20	18	14	0	0	147	142	28	48	3.13
Lee Richmond	3	7	.300	12	12	8	0	0	92	122	27	13	3.33
	58	40	.592	98	98	88	4	1	871	827	111	376	2.37

CLEVELAND   55-42   .567   -7.5   4th   Frank Bancroft
Blues

BATTERS	POS/GAMES		GP	AB	R	H	BI	2B	3B	HR	BB	SO	SB	BA	SA
Bill Phillips	1B97		97	382	42	94	40	29	8	2	8	49		.246	.380
Fred Dunlap	2B93,OF1		93	396	81	129	37	34	2	4	22	21		.326	.452
Jack Glasscock	SS93,2B3		96	383	67	110	46	19	6	0	13	23		.287	.368
Mike Muldoon	3B98,OF2		98	378	54	86	29	22	3	0	10	39		.228	.302
Jake Evans	OF86,3B3,SS3,2B1,P1		90	332	36	79	31	13	2	0	8	38		.238	.289
Pete Hotaling	OF100		100	417	54	108	30	20	8	0	12	31		.259	.345
Tom York	OF100		100	381	56	99	46	29	5	2	37	55		.260	.318
Doc Bushong	C63		63	215	15	37	9	5	0	0	7	19		.172	.195
One Arm Daily	P45,OF1		45	142	18	18		1	0	0	10	36		.127	.134
Jim McCormick	P43,OF1		43	157	21	37		2	2	0	2	14		.236	.274
Fatty Briody	C33,2B4,1B2,3B1		40	145	23	34	10	5	1	0	3	13		.234	.283
Will Sawyer	P17		17	47	3	1		0	0	0	3	19		.021	.021
Bill Crowley	OF11	(2-2)	11	41	3	12	5	5	0	0	1	7		.293	.415
George Bradley	SS4	(1-2)	4	16	0	5	1	0	1	0	0	1		.313	.438
Cecil Broughton	C4	(1-2)	4	10	2	2	1	0	0	0	2	2		.200	.200
Charles Cady	OF2,P1		3	11	0	0	0	0	0	0	1	5		.000	.000
Lem Hunter	P1,OF1		1	4	1	1	0	0	0	0	0	2		.250	.250
			100	3457	476	852	285	184	38	8	139	374		.246	.329

PITCHERS	W	L	PCT	G	GS	CG	SH	SV	IP	H	BB	SO	ERA
Jim McCormick	28	12	.700	43	41	36	1	1	342	316	65	145	1.84
One Arm Daily	23	19	.548	45	43	40	4	1	379	360	99	171	2.42
Will Sawyer	4	10	.286	17	15	15	0	0	141	119	47	76	2.36
Charles Cady	0	1	.000	1	1	1	0	0	8	13	4	5	7.88
Lem Hunter	0	0	----	1	0	0	0	0	6	10	2	4	1.42
Jake Evans	0	0	----	1	0	0	0	0	3	0	0	1	0.00
	55	42	.567	100	100	92	5	2	879	818	217	402	2.22

BUFFALO   52-45   .536   -10.5   5th   Jim O'Rourke
Bisons

BATTERS	POS/GAMES		GP	AB	R	H	BI	2B	3B	HR	BB	SO	SB	BA	SA
Dan Brouthers	1B97,3B1,P1		98	425	85	159	97	41	17	3	16	17		.374	.572
Hardy Richardson	2B92		92	399	73	124	56	34	7	1	22	20		.311	.439
Davy Force	SS78,3B13,2B7		96	378	40	82	35	11	3	0	12	39		.217	.262
Deacon White	3B77,C22		94	391	62	114	47	14	5	0	23	18		.292	.353
Orator Shaffer	OF95		95	401	67	117	41	11	3	0	27	39		.292	.334
James Lillie	OF47,P3,C2,1B1,3B1,SS1		50	201	25	47	29	7	3	1	1	31		.234	.313
Jim O'Rourke	OF61,C33,3B8,SS3,P2		94	436	102	143	38	29	8	1	15	13		.328	.438
Jack Rowe	C49,OF28,SS18,3B3		87	374	65	104	38	18	7	1	15	14		.278	.372
Pud Galvin	P76,OF8		80	322	41	71		11	2	1	3	79		.220	.276
Dave Eggler	OF38	(2-2)	38	153	13	38	13	2	1	0	2	29		.248	.275
Curry Foley	OF23,P1		23	111	23	30	6	5	3	0	4	12		.270	.369
George Derby	P14,OF3		16	59	10	14		1	0	0	0	7		.237	.254
Ed Cushman	P7,OF1		7	23	3	5		0	0	0	2	7		.217	.217
Dell Darling	C6		6	18	1	3	1	0	0	0	2	5		.167	.167
Doc Kennedy	OF4,1B1		5	19	3	6	2	0	0	0	2	2		.316	.316
Tony Suck	C1,OF1		2	7	1	0	0	0	0	0	1	4		.000	.000
Art Hagan	P2,OF1	(1-2)	2	7	0	0		0	0	0	0	3		.000	.000
Walter Burke	P1,OF1		1	5	0	1	1	0	0	0	0	3		.200	.200
			98	3729	614	1058	404	184	59	8	147	342		.284	.371

PITCHERS	W	L	PCT	G	GS	CG	SH	SV	IP	H	BB	SO	ERA
Pud Galvin	46	29	.613	76	75	72	5	0	656	676	50	279	2.72
Ed Cushman	3	3	.500	7	7	5	0	0	50	61	17	34	3.93
George Derby	2	10	.167	14	13	12	0	1	108	173	15	34	5.85

1883 NATIONAL LEAGUE

BUFFALO (cont.)
Bisons

PITCHERS		W	L	PCT	G	GS	CG	SH	SV	IP	H	BB	SO	ERA
Curry Foley		1	0	1.000	1	0	0	0	0	1	0	4	0	0.00
Jim Lillie		0	1	.000	3	0	0	0	0	12	16	2	4	3.00
Art Hagan	(2-2)	0	2	.000	2	2	1	0	0	15	17	6	7	3.60
Walter Burke		0	0	----	1	1	0	0	0	8	9	3	1	5.63
Jim O'Rourke		0	0	----	2	0	0	0	1	7	10	1	1	6.43
Dan Brouthers		0	0	----	1	0	0	0	0	2	9	3	2	31.50
		52	45	.536	98	98	90	5	2	859	971	101	362	3.32

NEW YORK
Gothams

46-50 .479 -16 6th John Clapp

BATTERS	POS/GAMES		GP	AB	R	H	BI	2B	3B	HR	BB	SO	SB	BA	SA
Roger Connor	1B98		98	409	80	146	50	28	15	1	25	16		.357	.506
Dasher Troy	2B73,SS12		85	316	37	68	20	7	5	0	9	33		.215	.269
Ed Caskin	SS81,2B13,C1		95	383	47	91	40	11	2	1	14	25		.238	.285
Frank Hankinson	3B93,OF1		94	337	40	74	30	13	6	2	19	38		.220	.312
Mike Dorgan	OF59,C6,P1		64	261	32	61	27	11	3	0	2	23		.234	.299
Monte Ward	OF56,P33,3B5,SS2,2B1		88	380	76	97	54	18	7	7	8	25		.255	.395
Pete Gillespie	OF98		98	411	64	129	62	23	12	1	9	27		.314	.436
Buck Ewing	C63,OF14,2B11,SS4,3B1		88	376	90	114	41	11	13	10	20	14		.303	.481
Mickey Welch	P54,OF38		84	320	42	75		13	5	2	10	38		.234	.325
John Humphries	C20,OF12		29	107	5	12	4	1	0	0	1	22		.112	.121
Tip O'Neill	P19,OF7		23	76	8	15	5	3	0	0	3	15		.197	.237
John Clapp	C16,OF5		20	73	6	13	5	0	0	0	5	4		.178	.178
Gracie Pierce	OF18,2B1	(2-2)	18	62	3	5	2	0	1	0	1	9		.081	.113
Dick Cramer	OF2		2	6	0	0	0	0	0	0	1	5		.000	.000
Myron Allen	P1		1	4	0	0	1	0	0	0	0	2		.000	.000
Dave Orr	OF1	(2-3)	1	3	0	0	0	0	0	0	0	1		.000	.000
			98	3524	530	900	341	139	69	24	127	297		.255	.354

PITCHERS		W	L	PCT	G	GS	CG	SH	SV	IP	H	BB	SO	ERA
Mickey Welch		25	23	.521	54	52	46	4	0	426	431	66	144	2.73
Monte Ward		16	13	.552	34	25	24	1	0	277	278	31	121	2.70
Tip O'Neill		5	12	.294	19	19	15	0	0	148	182	64	55	4.07
Myron Allen		0	1	.000	1	1	1	0	0	8	8	3	0	1.13
Mike Dorgan		0	1	.000	1	1	1	0	0	7	8	6	3	3.86
		46	50	.479	98	98	87	5	0	866	907	170	323	2.94

DETROIT
Wolverines

40-58 .408 -23 7th Jack Chapman

BATTERS	POS/GAMES		GP	AB	R	H	BI	2B	3B	HR	BB	SO	SB	BA	SA
Martin Powell	1B101		101	421	76	115	48	17	5	1	28	23		.273	.344
Sam Trott	2B42,C34,OF6,1B1		75	295	27	72	29	14	1	0	10	23		.244	.298
Sadie Houck	SS101		101	416	52	105	40	18	12	0	9	18		.252	.353
Joe Farrell	3B101		101	444	58	108	36	13	5	0	5	29		.243	.295
Tom Mansell	OF34,P1		34	131	22	29	10	4	1	0	8	13		.221	.267
Ned Hanlon	OF90,2B11		100	413	65	100	40	13	2	1	34	44		.242	.291
George Wood	OF99,P1		99	441	81	133	47	26	11	5	25	37		.302	.444
Charlie Bennett	C72,2B15,OF12		92	371	56	113	55	34	7	5	26	59		.305	.474
Stump Weidman	P52,OF35,2B4		79	313	34	58	24	6	1	1	4	38		.185	.220
Dupee Shaw	P26,OF15		38	141	13	29		3	0	0	3	36		.206	.227
Dick Burns	OF24,P17		37	140	11	26	5	7	1	0	2	22		.186	.250
Joe Quest	2B37	(1-2)	37	137	22	32	25	8	2	0	10	18		.234	.321
Jack Jones	P12,OF3	(1-2)	12	42	3	8		1	0	0	1	11		.190	.214
George Radbourn	P3,OF1		3	12	2	2		0	0	0	0	5		.167	.167
Ben Quincy	OF1		1	5	1	1	0	0	0	0	0	1		.200	.200
Frank McIntyre	P1	(1-2)	1	4	1	0		0	0	0	1	1		.000	.000
			101	3726	524	931	359	164	48	13	166	378		.250	.330

PITCHERS		W	L	PCT	G	GS	CG	SH	SV	IP	H	BB	SO	ERA
Stump Weidman		20	24	.455	52	47	41	3	2	402	435	72	183	3.53
Dupee Shaw		10	15	.400	26	25	23	1	0	227	238	44	73	2.50
Jack Jones	(1-2)	6	5	.545	12	12	9	1	0	93	103	19	33	3.50
Dick Burns		2	12	.143	17	13	13	0	0	128	172	33	30	4.51

1883 NATIONAL LEAGUE

DETROIT (cont.)
Wolverines

PITCHERS			W	L	PCT	G	GS	CG	SH	SV	IP	H	BB	SO	ERA
Frank McIntyre		(1-2)	1	0	1.000	1	1	1	0	0	11	11	1	0	0.82
George Radbourn			1	2	.333	3	3	2	0	0	22	38	7	2	6.55
Tom Mansell			0	0	----	1	0	0	0	0	7	21	5	3	18.90
George Wood			0	0	----	1	0	0	0	0	5	8	3	0	7.20
			40	58	.408	101	101	89	5	2	894	1026	184	324	3.58

PHILADELPHIA
Quakers

17-81 .173 -46 8th Ferguson - Purcell

BATTERS	POS/GAMES		GP	AB	R	H	BI	2B	3B	HR	BB	SO	SB	BA	SA
Sid Farrar	1B99		99	377	41	88	29	19	8	0	4	37		.233	.326
Bob Ferguson	2B86,P1		86	329	39	85	27	9	2	0	18	21		.258	.298
Bill McClellan	SS78,OF2,3B1		80	326	42	75	33	21	4	1	19	18		.230	.328
Fred Warner	3B38,OF1		39	141	13	32	13	6	1	0	5	21		.227	.284
Jack Manning	OF98		98	420	60	112	37	31	5	0	20	37		.267	.364
Fred Lewis	OF38	(1-2)	38	160	21	40	18	7	0	0	4	13		.250	.294
Blondie Purcell	OF44,3B46,P11		97	425	70	114	32	20	5	1	13	26		.268	.346
Emil Gross	C55,OF2		57	231	39	71	25	25	7	1	12	18		.307	.489
Jack Coleman	P65,OF31,2B1		90	354	33	83	32	12	8	0	15	39		.234	.314
Bill Harbridge	OF44,SS11,2B9,C7,3B5		73	280	32	62	21	12	3	0	24	20		.221	.286
Frank Ringo	C39,OF11,SS6,3B5,2B2		60	221	24	42	12	10	1	0	6	34		.190	.244
John Neagle	OF12,P8	(1-3)	18	73	6	12	4	1	0	0	1	9		.164	.178
Art Hagan	P17,OF1	(2-2)	17	59	3	6		1	1	0	0			.102	.153
Connie Doyle	OF16		16	68	3	15	3	3	2	0	0	15		.221	.324
Dick Pierre	SS5		5	19	1	3	0	0	0	0	0	2		.158	.158
Art Benedict	2B3		3	15	3	4	4	1	0	0	0	4		.267	.333
Joe Mulvey	3B3	(2-2)	3	12	2	6	3	1	0	0	0	1		.500	.583
-----Wilsonholm	C2,OF1		3	11	0	1		1	0	0	0	0		.091	.182
Charles Hilsey	P3		3	10	0	1	1	0	0	0	0	4		.100	.100
Hardie Henderson	P1	(1-2)	2	8	1	2		1	0	0	0	1		.250	.375
Bill Gallagher	OF2	(1-2)	2	8	1	0	0	0	0	0	0	4		.000	.000
Charles Kelly	3B2		2	7	0	1	0	0	1	0	0	3		.143	.143
Piggy Ward	3B1		1	5	0	0	0	0	0	0	0	2		.000	.000
Edgar Smith	P1,OF1	(2-2)	1	4	1	3	1	0	0	0	0	0		.750	.750
Buck Gladman	3B1		1	4	1	0	0	0	0	0	0	2		.000	.000
Charlie Waitt	OF1		1	3	0	1	0	0	0	0	0	1		.333	.333
John Kelly	OF1	(2-2)	1	3	0	0	0	0	0	0	0	2		.000	.000
Alonzo Breitenstein	P1		1	2	0	0		0	0	0	0	1		.000	.000
C. B. White	3B1,SS1		1	1	0	0	0	0	0	0	0	0		.000	.000
			99	3576	437	859	295	181	48	3	141	355		.240	.320

PITCHERS		W	L	PCT	G	GS	CG	SH	SV	IP	H	BB	SO	ERA
Jack Coleman		12	48	.200	65	61	59	3	0	538	772	48	159	4.87
Blondie Purcell		2	6	.333	11	9	7	0	0	80	110	12	30	4.39
John Neagle	(1-2)	1	7	.125	8	7	6	0	0	61	88	21	13	6.90
Art Hagan	(1-2)	1	14	.067	17	16	15	0	0	137	207	33	39	5.45
Hardie Henderson	(1-2)	0	1	.000	1	1	1	0	0	9	26	2	2	19.00
Edgar Smith		0	1	.000	1	1	0	0	0	7	18	3	2	15.43
Alonzo Breitenstein		0	1	.000	1	1	0	0	0	5	8	2	0	9.00
Charles Hilsey		0	3	.000	3	3	3	0	0	26	36	4	8	5.54
Bob Ferguson		0	0	----	1	0	0	0	0	1	2	0	0	9.00
		17	81	.173	99	99	91	3	0	865	1267	125	253	5.34

1883 AMERICAN ASSOCIATION

The National Agreement

The National League had not enjoyed their first taste of the American Association. In 1882, the association had been an annoyance — by 1883, they were a threatening competitor, vying for the public's attention as a full-fledged baseball league. The two leagues were also vying with each other for the best players. All through the 1882 season no player contract was safe — no team was safe from their rival league's overtures.

The policy of raiding and player piracy was proving detrimental to both leagues. So, late in 1882, both leagues formed committees to seek an end to the hostilities. On February 15, 1883, the committees from the American Association and National League met in New York to discuss a peace agreement. The two committees hammered out a settlement called the National Agreement. The basic premises of the agreement were rules for teams to honor contracts and reserve lists. An arbitration committee (including members from both leagues) was formed to settle all disputes.

Another offshoot of the National Agreement was the provision made for the minor leagues. The minor Northwestern League was to be given protection under the agreement to preserve its territorial rights and players from tampering. When other minor leagues formed in the years to come, they too fell under the umbrella of protection given by the National Agreement.

With the agreement in place, the American Association went on to post a successful season in 1883. Two teams, New York and Columbus, were added to the previous six to round out the league at eight members. Every team, save New York, managed to post a profit for the season.

Philadelphia won the pennant in a thrilling manner by beating Louisville in extra innings on September 28, 7-6. This gave them a two-game bulge, with only one game left. A loss in their last game and a win by second place St. Louis in theirs, put the final margin of victory at one game, the closest race yet to date in the major leagues. The Athletics were carried by their big slugger Harry Stovey who led the league with a record 14 home runs. He also hit .302 to join teammate Mike Moynahan (.308) as the team's only .300 hitters.

St. Louis came within a whisker of their first pennant by riding the strong arm of Tony Mullane. He posted 35 wins and a 2.19 earned run average to lead his team to the ERA crown (2.23). Their best full-time hitter was their manager Charlie Comiskey who finished at .294.

Cincinnati, New York, and Louisville finished next in third, fourth and fifth. Cincinnati's best were hitter Long John Reilly (.311) and pitcher Will White who finished with 43 wins, the league's best. The Metropolitans were led by Candy Nelson (.307) and by Tim Keefe's 41 wins and the league's most strikeouts, 361. Louisville was paced by Pete Browning's .338 batting average.

Columbus, Pittsburgh, and Baltimore finished on the bottom. Columbus featured pitcher Frank Mountain who won 26 while losing a league-leading 33. Pittsburgh's noteworthy player was batting champion Ed Swartwood (.356). And, excelling for Baltimore was Dave Rowe (.313).

The National Agreement served both the American Association and the National League (along with their client minor leagues) for many years to come. The agreement provided a framework of authority that was essential for two rival leagues to peacefully coexist.

1883 AMERICAN ASSOCIATION

PHILADELPHIA Athletics   66-32   .673   1st   Lon Knight

BATTERS	POS/GAMES		GP	AB	R	H	BI	2B	3B	HR	BB	SO	SB	BA	SA
Harry Stovey	1B93,OF3,P1		94	421	110	127		31	6	14	26			.302	.504
Cub Stricker	2B88,C2		89	330	67	90		8	0	1	19			.273	.306
Mike Moynahan	SS95		95	400	90	123		18	10	1	30			.308	.410
George Bradley	3B44,P26,OF11,1B2	(2-2)	76	312	47	73		8	5	1	8			.234	.301
Lon Knight	OF93,3B3,2B2		97	429	98	108		23	9	1	21			.252	.354
Bob Blakiston	OF37,1B6,3B5		44	167	26	41		3	3	0	9			.246	.299
Jud Birchall	OF96		96	449	95	108		10	1	1	19			.241	.274
Jack O'Brien	C58,OF25,3B19,SS1		94	390	74	113		14	10	0	25			.290	.377
Fred Corey	3B34,P18,OF14,2B9,C1,SS1		71	298	45	77		16	2	1	12			.258	.336
Ed Rowen	C44,OF8,2B1,3B1		49	196	28	43		10	1	0	10			.219	.281
Bobby Mathews	P44,OF3		45	167	15	31		2	0	0	4			.186	.198
Bill Crowley	OF22,1B1	(1-2)	23	96	16	24		4	3	0	3			.250	.354
Jersey Bakely	P8,OF1		8	26	4	5		1	0	0	6			.192	.231
Jack Jones	P7	(2-2)	7	25	3	6		1	0	0	1			.240	.280
Allen Hubbard	SS1,C1		2	6	2	2		0	0	0	1			.333	.333
Charlie Mason	OF1		1	2	0	1		0	0	0	0			.500	.500
			98	3714	720	972		149	50	20	194	268		.262	.345

PITCHERS			W	L	PCT	G	GS	CG	SH	SV	IP	H	BB	SO	ERA
Bobby Mathews			30	13	.698	44	44	41	1	0	381	396	31	203	2.46
George Bradley		(2-2)	16	7	.696	26	23	22	0	0	214	215	22	56	3.15
Fred Corey			10	7	.588	18	16	15	0	0	148	182	24	42	3.40
Jack Jones		(2-2)	5	2	.714	7	7	7	0	0	65	58	6	28	2.63
Jersey Bakely			5	3	.625	8	8	7	0	0	61	65	12	14	3.23
Harry Stovey			0	0	----	1	0	0	0	0	3	5	0	4	9.00
			66	32	.673	98	98	92	1	0	873	921	95	347	2.88

ST. LOUIS Browns   65-33   .663   -1   2nd   Sullivan - Comiskey

BATTERS	POS/GAMES		GP	AB	R	H	BI	2B	3B	HR	BB	SO	SB	BA	SA
Charlie Comiskey	1B96,OF1		96	401	87	118		17	9	2	11			.294	.397
George Strief	2B67,OF15		82	302	22	68		9	0	1	12			.225	.265
Bill Gleason	SS98		98	425	81	122		21	9	2	16			.287	.393
Arlie Latham	3B98,C1		98	406	86	96		12	7	0	18			.236	.300
Hugh Nicol	OF84,2B11		94	368	73	106		13	3	0	18			.288	.340
Fred Lewis	OF49	(2-2)	49	209	37	63		8	4	1	1			.301	.392
Tom Dolan	OF40,C42,P1		81	295	32	63		9	2	1	9			.214	.268
Pat Deasley	C56,OF2		58	206	27	53		2	1	0	6			.257	.277
Tony Mullane	P53,OF30,2B3,1B2		83	307	38	69		11	6	0	13			.225	.300
Jumbo McGinnis	P45,OF4		45	180	20	36		4	2	0	0			.200	.244
Tom Mansell	OF28	(2-2)	28	112	23	45		8	1	0	7			.402	.491
Ned Cuthbert	OF20,1B1		21	71	3	12		1	0	0	4			.169	.183
Joe Quest	2B19	(2-2)	19	78	12	20		3	1	0	1			.256	.321
Jack Gleason	OF9	(1-2)	9	34	2	8		0	0	0	4			.235	.235
Sleeper Sullivan	C6,OF2		8	27	2	6		0	1	0	0			.222	.296
Tom Loftus	OF6		6	22	1	4		0	0	0	2			.182	.182
Harry McCaffery	OF5		5	18	0	1		0	0	0	1			.056	.056
Henry Oberbeck	OF4	(2-2)	4	14	0	0		0	0	0	0			.000	.000
Charles Hodnett	P4,OF1		4	11	3	2		0	0	0	2			.182	.182
John Ewing	OF1		1	5	0	0		0	0	0	0			.000	.000
John Gorman	OF1		1	4	0	0		0	0	0	0			.000	.000
			98	3495	549	892		118	46	7	125	240		.255	.321

PITCHERS			W	L	PCT	G	GS	CG	SH	SV	IP	H	BB	SO	ERA
Tony Mullane			35	15	.700	53	49	49	3	1	461	372	74	191	2.19
Jumbo McGinnis			28	16	.636	45	45	41	6	0	383	325	69	128	2.33
Charles Hodnett			2	2	.500	4	4	3	0	0	32	28	7	6	1.41
Tom Dolan			0	0	----	1	0	0	0	0	4	4	0	0	4.50
			65	33	.663	98	98	93	9	1	879	729	150	325	2.23

1883 AMERICAN ASSOCIATION

CINCINNATI Red Stockings
61-37   .622   -5   3rd   Pop Snyder

BATTERS	POS/GAMES	GP	AB	R	H	BI	2B	3B	HR	BB	SO	SB	BA	SA
Long John Reilly	1B98,OF1	98	437	103	136		21	14	9	9			.311	.485
Bid McPhee	2B96	96	367	61	90		10	10	2	18			.245	.343
Chick Fulmer	SS92	92	361	52	93		13	5	5	13			.258	.363
Hick Carpenter	3B95	95	436	99	129		18	4	3	18			.296	.376
Pop Corkhill	OF85,1B2,2B2,SS2	88	375	53	81		10	8	2	3			.216	.301
Charlie Jones	OF90	90	391	84	115		15	12	10	20			.294	.471
Joe Sommer	OF94,3B3,P1	97	413	79	115		5	7	3	20			.278	.346
Pop Snyder	C57,SS2	58	250	38	64		14	6	0	8			.256	.360
Will White	P65	65	240	38	54		4	3	0	16			.225	.267
Phil Powers	C17,OF13	30	114	16	28		1	4	0	3			.246	.325
Bill Traffley	C29,SS2	30	105	17	21		5	0	0	4			.200	.248
Ren Deagle	P18,OF1,SS1	19	70	9	9		2	0	0	1			.129	.157
Harry McCormick	P15	15	55	8	17		2	1	0	2			.309	.382
John Macullar	OF14,SS1	14	48	4	8		2	0	0	4			.167	.208
Podgie Weihe	OF1	1	4	1	1		0	0	0	0			.250	.250
Bill Mountjoy	P1	1	3	0	0		0	0	0	0			.000	.000
		98	3669	662	961		122	74	34	139	261		.262	.363

PITCHERS	W	L	PCT	G	GS	CG	SH	SV	IP	H	BB	SO	ERA
Will White	43	22	.662	65	64	64	6	0	577	473	104	141	2.09
Ren Deagle	10	8	.556	18	18	17	1	0	148	136	34	48	2.31
Harry McCormick	8	6	.571	15	15	14	1	0	129	139	27	21	2.87
Bill Mountjoy	0	1	.000	1	1	1	0	0	8	9	2	3	2.25
Joe Sommer	0	0	----	1	0	0	0	0	5	9	1	2	5.40
	61	37	.622	98	98	96	8	0	867	766	168	215	2.26

NEW YORK Metropolitans
54-42   .563   -11   4th   Jim Mutrie

BATTERS	POS/GAMES		GP	AB	R	H	BI	2B	3B	HR	BB	SO	SB	BA	SA
Steve Brady	1B81,OF16		97	432	69	117		12	6	0	11			.271	.326
Sam Crane	2B96,OF1		96	349	57	82		8	5	0	13			.235	.287
Candy Nelson	SS97		97	417	75	127		19	6	0	31			.305	.379
Dude Esterbrook	3B97		97	407	55	103		9	7	0	15			.253	.310
Chief Roseman	OF91,1B2		93	398	48	100		13	6	0	11			.251	.314
John O'Rourke	OF76,1B1		77	315	49	85		19	5	2	21			.270	.381
Ed Kennedy	OF94		94	356	57	78		6	7	2	17			.219	.292
Bill Holbert	C68,OF5,2B1		73	299	26	71		9	1	0	1			.237	.274
Tim Keefe	P68,2B1,OF1		70	259	39	57		6	9	0	14			.220	.313
Charlie Reipschlager	C29,OF8		37	145	8	27		4	2	0	4			.186	.241
Jack Lynch	P29		29	107	9	20		2	1	0	4			.187	.224
Dave Orr	1B13	(1,3-3)	13	50	6	16		4	3	2	0			.320	.640
			97	3534	498	883		111	58	6	142	259		.250	.319

PITCHERS	W	L	PCT	G	GS	CG	SH	SV	IP	H	BB	SO	ERA
Tim Keefe	41	27	.603	68	68	68	5	0	619	486	98	361	2.41
Jack Lynch	13	15	.464	29	29	29	1	0	255	263	25	119	4.09
	54	42	.563	97	97	97	6	0	874	749	123	480	2.90

LOUISVILLE Eclipse
52-45   .536   -13.5   5th   Joe Gerhardt

BATTERS	POS/GAMES		GP	AB	R	H	BI	2B	3B	HR	BB	SO	SB	BA	SA
Juice Latham	1B67,2B14,SS9		88	368	60	92		7	6	0	12			.250	.302
Joe Gerhardt	2B78		78	319	56	84		11	9	0	14			.263	.354
Jack Leary	SS40	(1-2)	40	165	16	31		1	3	3	2			.188	.285
Jack Gleason	3B84,SS1	(2-2)	84	355	69	105		11	4	2	25			.296	.366
Chicken Wolf	OF78,C20,SS5,2B1		98	389	59	102		17	9	1	5			.262	.350
Leech Maskrey	OF96,SS1		96	361	50	73		13	8	1	10			.202	.291
Pete Browning	OF48,SS26,3B10,2B3,1B1		84	358	95	121		15	9	4	23			.338	.464
Ed Whiting	C50,OF6,2B2,1B1,3B1		58	240	35	70		16	4	2	9			.292	.417
Guy Hecker	P55,OF23,1B10		79	322	56	88		6	6	1	10			.273	.339
Sam Weaver	P48,OF6,1B1		55	203	22	39		6	1	0	13			.192	.232
Tom McLaughlin	SS19,OF17,1B5,2B2,3B2		42	146	16	28		1	2	0	5			.192	.226

1883 AMERICAN ASSOCIATION

LOUISVILLE (cont.)
Eclipse

BATTERS	POS/GAMES		GP	AB	R	H	BI	2B	3B	HR	BB	SO	SB	BA	SA
Dan Sullivan	C32,3B2,OF2,SS1		37	147	8	31		5	2	0	3			.211	.272
John Reccius	OF18,P1		18	63	10	9		2	0	0	7			.143	.175
Lewis Brown	1B14,C	(2-2)	14	60	6	11		2	1	0	1			.183	.250
Henry Luff	1B4,OF2		6	23	1	4		0	0	0	0			.174	.174
George Winkelman	OF4		4	13	2	0		0	0	0	1			.000	.000
Walt Prince	1B2,OF2,SS1		4	11	1	2		0	0	0	0			.182	.182
Jack Jones	OF2,SS1		2	7	1	0		0	0	0	0			.000	.000
Phil Reccius	OF1		1	3	1	1		1	0	0	0			.333	.667
			98	3553	564	891		114	64	14	140	305		.251	.331

PITCHERS			W	L	PCT	G	GS	CG	SH	SV	IP	H	BB	SO	ERA
Sam Weaver			26	22	.542	48	48	47	4	0	419	468	38	116	3.70
Guy Hecker			26	23	.531	51	50	49	3	0	451	509	72	153	3.33
John Reccius			0	0	----	1	0	0	0	0	4	10	0	0	2.25
			52	45	.536	98	98	96	7	0	874	987	110	269	3.50

COLUMBUS
Buckeyes

32-65   .330   -33.5   6th   Horace Phillips

BATTERS	POS/GAMES		GP	AB	R	H	BI	2B	3B	HR	BB	SO	SB	BA	SA
Jim Field	1B76		76	295	31	75		10	6	1	7			.254	.339
Pop Smith	2B73,3B24,P3		97	405	82	106		14	17	4	22			.262	.410
John Richmond	SS91,OF2		92	385	63	109		7	8	0	25			.283	.343
Bill Kuehne	3B69,2B18,SS7,OF3		95	374	38	85		8	14	1	2			.227	.332
Tom Brown	OF96,P3		97	420	69	115		12	7	5	20			.274	.371
Fred Mann	OF82,1B9,3B6,SS1		96	394	61	98		18	13	1	18			.249	.368
Harry Wheeler	OF82,P1,2B1		82	371	42	84		6	7	0	6			.226	.280
Rudy Kemmler	C82,OF2		84	318	27	66		6	2	0	13			.208	.239
Frank Mountain	P59,OF12		70	276	36	60		14	5	3	9			.217	.337
Joe Straub	C14,1B12,OF1		27	100	4	13		0	0	0	4			.130	.130
Ed Dundon	P20,OF9,2B1		26	93	8	15		1	0	0	3			.161	.172
John Valentine	P13,OF4		16	60	9	17		4	0	0	2			.283	.350
Gracie Pierce	2B6,OF5	(1-2)	11	41	5	7		0	0	0	0			.171	.171
Peter Fries	P3		3	10	1	3		1	0	0	1			.300	.400
Frank McIntyre	P2	(2-2)	2	7	0	0		0	0	0	2			.000	.000
Pop Schwartz	C1,1B1		2	4	0	1		0	0	0	0			.250	.250
			97	3553	476	854		101	79	15	134	410		.240	.326

PITCHERS			W	L	PCT	G	GS	CG	SH	SV	IP	H	BB	SO	ERA
Frank Mountain			26	33	.441	59	59	57	4	0	503	546	123	159	3.60
Ed Dundon			3	16	.158	20	19	16	0	0	167	213	38	31	4.48
John Valentine			2	10	.167	13	12	11	0	0	102	130	17	13	3.53
Frank McIntyre		(2-2)	1	1	.500	2	2	2	0	0	19	20	7	6	5.21
Tom Brown			0	1	.000	3	1	1	0	0	14	14	10	6	5.79
Harry Wheeler			0	1	.000	1	1	0	0	0	5	13	2	0	7.20
Peter Fries			0	3	.000	3	3	3	0	0	25	34	14	7	6.48
Pop Smith			0	0	----	3	0	0	0	0	6	10	0	0	6.35
			32	65	.330	97	97	90	4	0	840	980	211	222	3.96

PITTSBURGH
Alleghenys

31-67   .316   -35   7th   Pratt - Butler - Battin

BATTERS	POS/GAMES		GP	AB	R	H	BI	2B	3B	HR	BB	SO	SB	BA	SA
Ed Swartwood	1B60,OF37,C3		94	413	86	147		24	8	3	24			.356	.475
George Creamer	2B91		91	369	54	94		7	9	0	20			.255	.322
Denny Mack	SS38,1B25,2B1		60	224	26	44		5	3	0	13			.196	.246
Joe Battin	3B98,P2		98	388	42	83		9	6	1	11			.214	.276
Buttercup Dickerson	OF78,SS8,2B2		85	355	62	88		15	1	0	17			.248	.296
Bill Taylor	OF37,C33,P19,1B9		83	369	43	96		13	7	2	9			.260	.350
Mike Mansell	OF96		96	412	90	106		12	13	3	25			.257	.371
Jack Hayes	C62,OF18,1B5,SS5,2B1		85	351	41	92		23	5	3	15			.262	.382
Denny Driscoll	P41,OF4,3B1		41	148	19	27		2	1	0	4			.182	.209
Bob Barr	P26,OF14,1B4,3B1		37	142	12	35		4	3	0	5			.246	.317
Bill Morgan	SS21,OF6,C5,2B2		32	114	12	18		2	1	0	7			.158	.193
Frank McLaughlin	SS25,OF4,2B2,P2		29	114	15	25		2	0	1	6			.219	.263

PITTSBURGH (cont.)
Alleghenys

BATTERS	POS/GAMES		GP	AB	R	H	BI	2B	3B	HR	BB	SO	SB	BA	SA
John Neagle	P16,OF15	(3-3)	27	101	14	19	0	1	0	5				.188	.208
Wes Blogg	C6,OF3		9	34	0	5	0	0	0	0				.147	.147
John Peters	SS8		8	28	3	3	0	0	0	0				.107	.107
The Only Nolan	P7,OF1		7	26	4	8	1	0	0	1				.308	.346
Norm Baker	P3,OF2		4	12	1	0	0	0	0	0				.000	.000
Henry Oberbeck	1B2	(1-2)	2	9	1	2	1	0	0	0				.222	.333
			98	3609	525	892		120	58	13	162	345		.247	.323

PITCHERS		W	L	PCT	G	GS	CG	SH	SV	IP	H	BB	SO	ERA
Denny Driscoll		18	21	.462	41	40	35	1	0	336	427	39	79	3.99
Bob Barr		6	18	.250	26	23	19	0	1	203	263	28	81	4.38
Bill Taylor		4	7	.364	19	9	8	0	0	127	166	34	41	5.39
John Neagle	(3-3)	3	12	.200	16	16	12	0	0	114	156	25	41	5.84
Norm Baker		0	2	.000	3	3	2	0	0	19	24	11	5	3.32
The Only Nolan		0	7	.000	7	7	6	0	0	55	81	10	23	4.25
Frank McLaughlin		0	0	----	2	0	0	0	0	9	14	3	1	13.00
Joe Battin		0	0	----	2	0	0	0	0	4	9	1	0	2.25
		31	67	.316	98	98	82	1	1	868	1140	151	271	4.62

BALTIMORE
Orioles

28-68 .292 -37 8th Billy Barnie

BATTERS	POS/GAMES		GP	AB	R	H	BI	2B	3B	HR	BB	SO	SB	BA	SA
Dan Stearns	1B92,OF1		93	382	54	94		10	9	1	34			.246	.327
Tim Manning	2B35		35	121	23	26		5	0	0	14			.215	.256
Louis Say	SS74		74	324	52	83		13	2	1	10			.256	.318
Jerry McCormick	3B93		93	389	40	102		16	6	0	2			.262	.334
Dave Rowe	OF50,SS7,1B3,P1		59	256	40	80		11	6	0	2			.313	.402
Dave Eggler	OF53	(1-2)	53	202	15	38		2	0	0	1			.188	.198
Jim Clinton	OF92,2B2		94	399	69	125		16	8	0	27			.313	.393
John Kelly	C38,OF13	(1-2)	48	202	18	46		9	2	0	3			.228	.292
Hardie Henderson	P44,OF11,SS2,3B1	(2-2)	51	191	13	31		5	1	1	10			.162	.215
Gid Gardner	OF35,2B4,3B3,P2		42	161	28	44		10	3	1	18			.273	.391
Tom O'Brien	2B29,OF4		33	138	16	37		6	4	0	5			.268	.370
Phil Baker	C19,OF14,SS1		28	121	22	33		2	1	1	8			.273	.331
Bob Emslie	P24,OF5		27	97	14	16		1	2	0	6			.165	.216
Rooney Sweeney	C23,OF3		25	101	13	21		5	2	0	4			.208	.297
William Reid	2B23,SS1		24	97	14	27		3	0	0	4			.278	.309
John Fox	P20,OF4,1B1		23	92	12	14		3	0	0	4			.152	.185
Billy Barnie	C13,OF6,SS1		17	55	7	11		0	0	0	2			.200	.200
John Gallagher	OF9,P7,SS4	(1-2)	16	61	9	10		3	1	0	3			.164	.246
John Neagle	P6,OF5	(2-3)	9	35	3	10		4	0	0	2			.286	.400
Cecil Broughton	C8,OF1	(2-2)	9	32	1	6		0	0	0	1			.188	.188
George Baker	SS4,C3,OF1		7	22	0	5		0	0	0	0			.227	.227
Nick Scharf	SS3		3	13	1	2		1	0	0	1			.159	.231
Jack Leary	2B3	(2-2)	3	11	1	2		0	2	0	0			.182	.545
Walt Devine	P2,OF1		2	9	4	2		0	0	0	0			.222	.222
Bill Farrell	SS2		2	7	0	0		0	0	0	1			.000	.000
Bill Laughlin	OF1		1	5	0	2		0	0	0	0			.400	.400
Charles Ingraham	C1		1	4	0	1		0	0	0	0			.250	.250
Dave Oldfield	C1		1	4	0	0		0	0	0	0			.000	.000
Doug Allison	C1,OF1		1	3	2	2		0	0	0	0			.667	.667
			96	3534	471	870		125	49	5	162	331		.246	.314

PITCHERS		W	L	PCT	G	GS	CG	SH	SV	IP	H	BB	SO	ERA
Hardie Henderson		10	32	.238	45	42	38	0	0	358	383	87	145	4.02
Bob Emslie		9	13	.409	24	23	21	1	0	201	188	41	62	3.17
John Fox		6	13	.316	20	19	18	0	0	165	209	32	49	4.03
Gid Gardner		1	0	1.000	2	0	0	0	0	7	9	1	2	5.14
Walt Devine		1	1	.500	2	2	1	0	0	11	15	1	3	7.36
John Neagle	(2-3)	1	4	.200	6	5	4	0	0	46	48	20	9	4.89
John Gallagher		0	5	.000	7	5	4	0	0	52	79	6	19	5.40
Dave Rowe		0	0	----	1	0	0	0	0	4	12	2	1	20.25
		28	68	.292	96	96	86	1	0	845	943	190	290	4.08

1884 NATIONAL LEAGUE

Old Hoss

In July 1884, the picture for Frank Bancroft and his Providence Grays looked grim. On the 16th, their best pitcher, Charley Radbourn, was suspended for indifferent play. On the 22nd, their other pitcher, Charlie Sweeney, was booted off the team for drunkenness. All this happened while the team was in the thick of a pennant race with Boston.

Providence had fielded a team in the National League since 1878 and had done well. They finished first in 1879, second 1880 through 1882, and a close third in 1883. Charley Radbourn had joined the club in 1881 and had quickly become their best pitcher, culminating with a 48 win season in 1883.

On July 23, Radbourn was reinstated. Vowing to pitch the team to the pennant, he quickly took command. By the end of the month, with Radbourn pitching in nearly every game, Providence had caught Boston and taken the lead. During the month of August, they ripped off a 20-game winning streak, of which Radbourn won 18. By season's end, Providence had indeed won the pennant by a comfortable ten and one-half game margin over Boston.

Radbourn's performance in 1884 was simply astounding. When suspended, his record stood at 24-8. After reinstatement, he pitched 40 more complete games, of which he won 35. For more than a month in August and September he pitched every inning of every game. His final record is mind-boggling. Radbourn won 59 games and lost 12. He pitched 73 complete games finishing with 679 innings pitched. And he topped it off by finishing with a puny 1.38 earned run average. For these exploits, Charley Radbourn was known from here on out as "Old Hoss."

It was fortunate that Providence had good pitching in 1884, because they certainly would not have won the pennant with their hitting. While Old Hoss paved the way for the team's second best of all time earned run average (1.61), the batters finished with the lowest average for any nineteenth century pennant winner (.241). Only Paul Hines (.302) finished over .300, but pitcher Charlie Sweeney, before his expulsion, finished second in the league's earned run average race at 1.55.

During most years, Charles Buffinton's 48-win season would have easily garnered him best of the year accolades. But in 1884, he could only finish second, just like his team, Boston. The team's other star this year was third baseman Ezra Sutton who batted .346.

Buffalo finished with their finest season during their National League tenure, finishing in third place, with 64 wins. Pitcher Pud Galvin ended up with 46 of the wins, while the Big Four had their best combined season. Dan Brouthers (.327), Hardy Richardson (.301), Deacon White (.325), and Jack Rowe (.315) all hit well. They were joined by a fifth, Jim O'Rourke, who outhit them all at .347.

Chicago slid to fourth despite the batting championship won by King Kelly (.354) and by Cap Anson's fine year (.335, 102 RBI). However, the startling anomaly about this team comes in the area of home runs. In 1883, the Chicago White Stockings hit 13 home runs as a team. The next year, they clubbed 142, with four of their players swatting at least 20 each. It was a simple change of their home ballpark rules which turned them into the long ball terrors of the National League. The White Stockings played in tiny Lakeside Park which had a left field fence less than 200 feet from home plate. In 1883, balls hit over certain portions of this fence counted as ground rule doubles. In 1884, the rule was changed to count any ball hit over the fence as a home run. Although they moved to a new park the next year, Ned Williamson's 27 homer barrage remained in the record book for another 35 years.

New York, Philadelphia, Cleveland, and Detroit finished in the bottom four slots. The only .300 hitter among the four, was Roger Connor of New York who finished at .317. Detroit, in particular, finished with a dismal year with three of their regulars hitting under .180.

Following the season, the Providence Grays and Old Hoss Radbourn smoothly dispatched the American Association champs, the New York Metropolitans, in what is now called the first World Series. With all three games being played in New York, Radbourn whipped the Metropolitans in three straight, 6-0, 3-1, and 11-2. More games had been planned, but when only 300 attended the third game, the rest of the series was called off.

Old Hoss Radbourn's career continued in steady, if not spectacular fashion until the early 1890s. Although he had five more 20-victory seasons, Radbourn never again reached the heights he achieved in 1884. He will always be remembered for single-handedly pitching his team to the pennant, while setting records that will never be equaled. More likely it was this one season of glory, rather than his 300 career wins, that helped his election to the Hall of Fame in 1939.

1884 NATIONAL LEAGUE

PROVIDENCE Grays   84-28   .750   1st   Frank Bancroft

BATTERS	POS/GAMES		GP	AB	R	H	BI	2B	3B	HR	BB	SO	SB	BA	SA
Joe Start	1B93		93	381	80	105	32	10	5	2	35	25		.276	.344
Jack Farrell	2B106,3B3		111	469	70	102	37	13	6	1	35	44		.217	.277
Art Irwin	SS102,P1		102	404	73	97	44	14	3	2	28	52		.240	.340
Jerry Denny	3B99,1B9,2B3,C1		110	439	57	109	59	22	9	6	14	58		.248	.380
Paul Hines	OF108,1B6,P1		114	490	94	148	41	36	10	3	44	28		.302	.435
Cliff Carroll	OF113		113	452	90	118	54	16	4	3	29	39		.261	.334
Paul Radford	OF96,P2		97	355	56	70	29	11	2	1	25	43		.197	.244
Barney Gilligan	C81,3B1,1B1		82	294	47	72	38	13	2	1	35	41		.245	.313
Old Hoss Radbourn	P75,1B5,OF4,3B3,SS2,2B1		87	361	48	83	37	7	1	1	26	42		.230	.263
Charlie Sweeney	P27,OF15,1B1	(1-2)	41	168	24	50	19	9	0	1	11	17		.298	.369
Sandy Nava	C27,SS6,2B1		34	116	10	11	6	0	0	0	11	35		.095	.095
Charley Bassett	3B13,SS7,OF2,2B1		27	79	10	11	6	2	1	0	4	15		.139	.190
Miah Murray	C7,1B1,OF1		8	27	1	5	1	0	0	0	1	8		.185	.185
Ed Conley	P8		8	28	0	4		0	0	0	0	9		.143	.143
Cyclone Miller	P6,OF3	(2-3)	6	23	3	1		0	0	0	1	10		.043	.043
John Cattanach	P1,OF1	(1-2)	1	4	0	0	0	0	0	0	0	2		.000	.000
Harry Arundel	P1		1	3	2	1		0	0	0	1	1		.333	.333
			114	4093	665	987	403	153	43	21	300	469		.241	.315

PITCHERS			W	L	PCT	G	GS	CG	SH	SV	IP	H	BB	SO	ERA
Old Hoss Radbourn			59	12	.881	75	73	73	11	1	679	528	98	441	1.38
Charlie Sweeney		(1-2)	17	8	.680	27	24	22	4	1	221	153	29	145	1.55
Ed Conley			4	4	.500	8	8	8	1	0	71	63	22	33	2.15
Cyclone Miller		(2-3)	3	2	.600	6	5	2	0	0	35	36	11	12	2.08
Harry Arundel			1	0	1.000	1	1	1	0	0	9	8	4	4	1.00
Paul Radford			0	2	.000	2	2	1	0	0	13	27	3	2	7.62
John Cattanach		(1-2)	0	0	----	1	1	0	0	0	5	2	4	2	9.00
Art Irwin			0	0	----	1	0	0	0	0	3	5	1	0	3.00
Paul Hines			0	0	----	1	0	0	0	0	1	3	0	0	0.00
			84	28	.750	114	114	107	16	2	1036	825	172	639	1.61

BOSTON Beaneaters   73-38   .658   -10.5   2nd   John Morrill

BATTERS	POS/GAMES		GP	AB	R	H	BI	2B	3B	HR	BB	SO	SB	BA	SA
John Morrill	1B91,2B17,P7,3B2,OF1		111	438	80	114	61	19	7	3	30	87		.260	.356
Jack Burdock	2B87,3B1		87	361	65	97	49	14	4	6	15	52		.269	.380
Sam Wise	SS107,2B7		114	426	60	91	41	15	9	4	25	104		.214	.319
Ezra Sutton	3B110		110	468	102	162	61	28	7	3	29	22		.346	.455
Bill Crowley	OF108		108	407	50	110	61	14	6	6	33	74		.270	.378
Jim Manning	OF73,2B9,SS9,3B3		89	345	52	83	35	8	6	2	19	47		.241	.316
Joe Hornung	OF110,1B6		115	518	119	139	51	27	10	7	17	80		.268	.400
Mert Hackett	C71,3B1		72	268	28	55	20	13	2	1	2	66		.205	.280
Charles Buffinton	P67,OF13,1B11		87	352	48	94	39	18	3	1	16	12		.267	.344
Jim Whitney	P38,1B15,OF15,3B1		66	270	41	70	40	17	5	3	16	38		.259	.393
Mike Hines	C35		35	132	16	23	3	3	0	0	3	24		.174	.197
Bill Annis	OF27		27	96	17	17	3	2	0	0	0	8		.177	.198
Tom Gunning	C12		12	45	4	5	2	1	1	0	1	12		.111	.178
John Connor	P7		7	25	1	2		0	0	0	1	13		.080	.080
Gene Moriarity	OF4	(1-2)	4	16	1	1	0	0	0	0	0	8		.063	.063
Daisy Davis	P4,OF1	(1-2)	4	16	0	0		0	0	0	0	9		.000	.000
Marty Barrett	C3	(1-2)	3	6	0	0	0	0	0	0	0	4		.000	.000
			116	4189	684	1063	466	179	60	36	207	660		.254	.351

PITCHERS			W	L	PCT	G	GS	CG	SH	SV	IP	H	BB	SO	ERA
Charles Buffinton			48	16	.750	67	67	63	8	0	587	506	76	417	2.15
Jim Whitney			23	14	.622	38	37	35	6	0	336	272	27	270	2.09
Daisy Davis		(2-2)	1	3	.250	4	4	3	0	0	31	50	8	13	7.84
John Connor			1	4	.200	7	7	7	0	0	60	70	18	29	3.15
John Morrill			0	1	.000	7	1	1	0	2	23	34	6	13	7.43
			73	38	.658	116	116	109	14	2	1037	932	135	742	2.47

1884 NATIONAL LEAGUE

BUFFALO Bisons   64-47   .577   -19.5   3rd   Jim O'Rourke

BATTERS	POS/GAMES		GP	AB	R	H	BI	2B	3B	HR	BB	SO	SB	BA	SA
Dan Brouthers	1B93,3B1		94	398	82	130	79	22	15	14	33	20		.327	.563
Hardy Richardson	2B71,OF24,3B5,1B3		102	439	85	132	60	27	9	6	22	41		.301	.444
Davy Force	SS105,2B1		106	403	47	83	36	13	3	0	27	41		.206	.253
Deacon White	3B108,C3		110	452	82	147	74	16	11	5	32	13		.325	.442
Jim Lillie	OF114,P2		114	471	68	105	53	12	5	3	5	71		.223	.289
Dave Eggler	OF63		63	241	25	47	20	3	1	0	6	54		.195	.216
Jim O'Rourke	OF86,1B18,C10,P4,3B1		108	467	119	162	63	33	7	5	35	17		.347	.480
Jack Rowe	C65,OF30,SS6		93	400	85	126	61	14	14	4	23	14		.315	.450
George Myers	C49,OF34		78	325	34	59	32	9	2	2	13	33		.182	.240
Pud Galvin	P72,OF1		72	274	34	49		6	1	0	2	80		.179	.208
Chub Collins	2B42,SS3	(1-2)	45	169	24	30	20	6	0	0	14	36		.178	.213
Billy Serad	P37,OF3		37	137	12	24		2	1	0	3	33		.175	.204
Art Hagan	P3		3	13	3	4	0	0	0	0	0	1		.308	.308
Ed Coughlin	P1,OF1		1	4	0	1	1	0	0	0	0	2		.250	.250
Bones Ely	P1,OF1		1	4	0	0	0	0	0	0	0	2		.000	.000
			115	4197	700	1099	499	163	69	39	215	458		.262	.361

PITCHERS		W	L	PCT	G	GS	CG	SH	SV	IP	H	BB	SO	ERA
Pud Galvin		46	22	.676	72	72	71	12	0	636	566	63	369	1.99
Billy Serad		16	20	.444	37	37	34	2	0	308	373	111	150	4.27
Art Hagan		1	2	.333	3	3	3	0	0	26	53	4	4	5.88
Jim O'Rourke		0	1	.000	4	0	0	0	1	13	7	1	3	2.84
Jim Lillie		0	1	.000	2	1	0	0	0	13	22	5	4	6.23
Bones Ely		0	1	.000	1	1	0	0	0	5	17	5	4	14.40
Ed Coughlin		0	0	----	1	0	0	0	0	0	3	0	0	inf.
		64	47	.577	115	114	108	14	1	1001	1041	189	534	2.95

CHICAGO White Stockings   62-50   .554   -22   4th (tie)   Cap Anson

BATTERS	POS/GAMES		GP	AB	R	H	BI	2B	3B	HR	BB	SO	SB	BA	SA
Cap Anson	1B112,C3,P1,SS1		112	475	108	159	102	30	3	21	29	13		.335	.543
Fred Pfeffer	2B112,P1		112	467	105	135	101	10	10	25	25	47		.289	.514
Tom Burns	SS80,3B3		83	343	54	84	44	14	2	7	13	50		.245	.359
Ned Williamson	3B99,C10,P2		107	417	84	116	84	18	8	27	42	56		.278	.554
King Kelly	OF63,C28,SS12,3B10,1B2,P2		108	452	120	160	95	28	5	13	46	24		.354	.524
George Gore	OF103		103	422	104	134	34	18	4	5	61	26		.318	.415
Abner Dalrymple	OF111		111	521	111	161	69	18	9	22	14	39		.309	.505
Silver Flint	C73		73	279	35	57	45	5	2	9	7	57		.204	.333
Larry Corcoran	P60,OF4,SS2		64	251	43	61	19	3	4	1	10	33		.243	.299
Billy Sunday	OF43		43	176	25	39	28	4	1	4	4	36		.222	.324
Fred Goldsmith	P21,OF2	(1-2)	22	81	11	11	6	2	0	2	7	26		.136	.235
John Clarkson	P14,OF8,3B2,1B1		21	84	16	22		6	2	3	2	16		.262	.488
Walt Kinzie	SS17,2B2	(1-2)	19	82	4	13	8	3	0	2	0	13		.159	.268
Joe Brown	OF9,P7,1B1,C1		15	61	6	13	3	1	0	0	0	15		.213	.230
Tom Lee	P5,3B1,SS1	(1-2)	6	24	0	3		1	0	0	0	6		.125	.200
Sy Sutcliffe	C4		4	15	4	3	2	1	0	0	2	4		.200	.267
George Crosby	P3		3	13	1	4		0	0	1	0	1		.308	.538
John Hibbard	P2		2	7	0	0		0	0	0	0	4		.000	.000
Fred Andrus	P1		1	5	3	1	0	0	0	0	1	0		.200	.200
Thomas Lynch	P1,1B1		1	4	0	0		0	0	0	0	2		.000	.000
Mike Corcoran	P1		1	3	0	0		0	0	0	1	1		.000	.000
			113	4182	834	1176	640	162	50	142	264	469		.281	.446

PITCHERS		W	L	PCT	G	GS	CG	SH	SV	IP	H	BB	SO	ERA
Larry Corcoran		35	23	.603	60	59	57	7	0	517	473	116	272	2.40
John Clarkson		10	3	.769	14	13	12	0	0	118	94	25	102	2.14
Fred Goldsmith		9	11	.450	21	21	20	1	0	188	245	29	34	4.26
Joe Brown		4	2	.667	7	6	5	0	0	50	56	7	27	4.68
Fred Andrus		1	0	1.000	1	1	1	0	0	9	11	2	2	2.00
John Hibbard		1	1	.500	2	2	2	1	0	17	18	9	4	2.65
George Crosby		1	2	.333	3	3	3	0	0	28	27	12	11	3.54
Tom Lee	(1-2)	1	4	.200	5	5	5	0	0	45	55	15	14	3.77
Mike Corcoran		0	1	.000	1	1	1	0	0	9	16	7	2	4.00
King Kelly		0	1	.000	2	0	0	0	0	5	12	2	1	8.44
Cap Anson		0	1	.000	1	0	0	0	0	1	3	1	1	18.00
Thomas Lynch		0	0	----	1	1	0	0	0	7	7	3	2	2.57

1884 NATIONAL LEAGUE

CHICAGO (cont.)
White Stockings

PITCHERS		W	L	PCT	G	GS	CG	SH	SV	IP	H	BB	SO	ERA
Ned Williamson		0	0	----	2	0	0	0	0	2	8	2	0	18.00
Fred Pfeffer		0	0	----	1	0	0	0	0	1	3	1	0	9.00
		62	50	.554	113	113	106	9	0	997	1028	231	472	3.03

NEW YORK
Gothams

62-50 .554 -22 4th (tie) Price - Ward

BATTERS	POS/GAMES		GP	AB	R	H	BI	2B	3B	HR	BB	SO	SB	BA	SA
Alex McKinnon	1B116		116	470	66	128	73	21	12	4	8	62		.272	.394
Roger Connor	2B67,OF37,3B12		116	477	98	151	82	28	4	4	38	32		.317	.417
Ed Caskin	SS96,C6		100	351	49	81	40	11	1	1	34	55		.231	.276
Frank Hankinson	3B105,OF1		105	389	44	90	43	16	7	2	23	59		.231	.324
Mike Dorgan	OF64,P14,C6,2B3		83	341	61	94	48	11	6	1	13	27		.276	.352
Monte Ward	OF59,2B47,P9		113	482	98	122	51	11	8	2	28	47		.253	.322
Pete Gillespie	OF101		101	413	75	109	44	7	4	2	19	35		.264	.315
Buck Ewing	C80,OF12,SS3,3B1,P1		94	382	90	106	41	15	20	3	28	22		.277	.445
Danny Richardson	OF55,SS19		74	277	36	70	27	8	1	1	16	17		.253	.300
Mickey Welch	P65,OF7		71	249	47	60		14	3	3	16	49		.241	.357
Ed Begley	P31,OF2		33	121	12	22		4	0	0	8	31		.182	.215
John Humphries	C20	(2-2)	20	64	6	6	2	0	0	0	9	19		.094	.094
Sandy Griffin	OF16		16	62	7	11	6	2	0	0	1	19		.177	.210
----- Loughran	C9,OF1		9	29	4	3	3	1	1	0	7	11		.103	.207
Charles Manlove	C3,OF1	(2-2)	3	10	0	0	0	0	0	0	0	4		.000	.000
Henry Oxley	C3	(1-2)	3	4	0	0	0	0	0	0	1	2		.000	.000
James Brown	P1	(2-3)	1	3	0	0	0	0	0	0	0	1		.000	.000
			116	4124	693	1053	460	149	67	23	249	492		.255	.341

PITCHERS		W	L	PCT	G	GS	CG	SH	SV	IP	H	BB	SO	ERA
Mickey Welch		39	21	.650	65	65	62	4	0	557	528	146	345	2.50
Ed Begley		12	18	.400	31	30	30	0	0	266	296	99	104	4.16
Mike Dorgan		8	6	.571	14	14	12	0	0	113	98	51	90	3.50
Monte Ward		3	3	.500	9	5	5	0	0	61	72	18	23	3.41
James Brown	(2-3)	0	1	.000	1	1	1	0	0	9	10	8	2	5.00
Buck Ewing		0	1	.000	1	1	1	0	0	8	7	4	3	1.13
		62	50	.554	116	116	111	4	0	1014	1011	326	567	3.12

PHILADELPHIA
Quakers

39-73 .348 -45 6th Harry Wright

BATTERS	POS/GAMES		GP	AB	R	H	BI	2B	3B	HR	BB	SO	SB	BA	SA
Sid Farrar	1B111		111	428	62	105	45	16	6	1	9	25		.245	.318
Ed Andrews	2B109		109	420	74	93	23	21	2	0	9	42		.221	.281
Bill McClellan	SS111,OF1		111	450	71	116	33	13	2	3	28	43		.258	.316
Joe Mulvey	3B100		100	401	47	92	32	11	2	2	4	49		.229	.282
Jack Manning	OF104		104	424	71	115	52	29	4	5	40	67		.271	.394
Jim Fogarty	OF78,3B14,2B4,SS3,P1		97	378	42	80	37	12	6	1	20	54		.212	.283
Blondie Purcell	OF103,P1		103	428	67	108	31	11	7	1	29	30		.252	.318
John Crowley	C48		48	168	26	41	19	7	3	0	15	21		.244	.321
Charlie Ferguson	P50,OF5		52	203	26	50		6	3	0	19	54		.246	.305
Jack Coleman	OF27,P21,1B2	(1-2)	43	171	16	42	22	7	2	0	8	20		.246	.310
Frank Ringo	C26	(1-2)	26	91	4	12	6	2	0	0	3	19		.132	.154
Bill Vinton	P21,OF1		21	78	9	9		1	0	0	3	21		.115	.128
James McElroy	P13,OF3	(1-2)	14	48	3	7		0	0	0	1	12		.146	.146
Thomas Lynch	OF7,C7	(2-2)	13	48	7	15	3	4	2	0	4	5		.313	.479
Jack Remsen	OF12	(1-2)	12	43	9	9	3	2	0	0	6	9		.209	.256
Buster Hoover	OF10	(2-2)	10	42	6	8	4	1	0	1	4	9		.190	.286
Jack Clements	C9	(2-2)	9	30	3	7	0	0	0	0	4	8		.233	.233
Tony Cusick	C9	(2-2)	9	29	2	4	1	0	0	0	0	3		.138	.138
Joe Knight	P6		6	24	2	6	2	3	0	0	0	0		.250	.375
Joe Koppel	C4		4	15	1	1	0	0	0	0	0	2		.067	.067
E. Vadeboncoeur	C4		4	14	1	3	3	0	0	0	1	2		.214	.214
Mike DePangher	C4		4	10	0	2	0	0	0	0	1	3		.200	.200
Paul Cook	C3		3	12	0	1	0	0	0	0	0	2		.083	.083
Con Murphy	P3		3	10	0	0		0	0	0	1	1		.000	.000
Lew Hardie	C3		3	8	0	3	0	2	0	0	0	2		.375	.625
Sparrow Morton	P2		2	8	0	3		1	0	0	0	3		.375	.500
Shadow Pyle	P1		1	4	0	0		0	0	0	0	0		.000	.000
Cyclone Miller	P1	(1-3)	1	4	0	0		0	0	0	0	3		.000	.000

PHILADELPHIA (cont.)
Quakers

BATTERS	POS/GAMES		GP	AB	R	H	BI	2B	3B	HR	BB	SO	SB	BA	SA
Bill Conway	C1		1	4	0	0	0	0	0	0	0	1		.000	.000
Hezekiah Allen	C1		1	3	0	2	0	0	0	0	0	0		.667	.667
Ed Sixsmith	C1		1	2	0	0	0	0	0	0	0	0		.000	.000
			113	3998	549	934	316	149	39	14	209	512		.234	.301

PITCHERS			W	L	PCT	G	GS	CG	SH	SV	IP	H	BB	SO	ERA
Charlie Ferguson			21	25	.457	50	47	46	2	1	417	443	93	194	3.54
Bill Vinton			10	10	.500	21	21	20	0	0	182	166	35	105	2.23
Jack Coleman			5	15	.250	21	19	14	1	0	154	216	22	37	4.90
Joe Knight			2	4	.333	6	6	6	0	0	51	66	21	8	5.47
James McElroy			1	12	.077	13	13	13	0	0	111	115	54	45	4.86
Shadow Pyle			0	1	.000	1	1	1	0	0	9	9	6	4	4.00
Cyclone Miller		(3-3)	0	1	.000	1	1	1	0	0	9	17	6	1	10.00
Sparrow Morton			0	2	.000	2	2	2	0	0	17	16	11	5	5.29
Con Murphy			0	3	.000	3	3	3	0	0	26	37	6	10	6.58
Blondie Purcell			0	0	----	1	0	0	0	0	4	3	0	1	2.25
Jim Fogarty			0	0	----	1	0	0	0	0	1	2	0	1	0.00
			39	73	.348	113	113	106	3	1	981	1090	254	411	3.93

CLEVELAND
Blues

35-77   .313   -49   7th   Charlie Hackett

BATTERS	POS/GAMES		GP	AB	R	H	BI	2B	3B	HR	BB	SO	SB	BA	SA
Bill Phillips	1B111		111	464	58	128	46	25	12	3	18	80		.276	.401
Germany Smith	2B42,SS30	(2-2)	72	291	31	74	26	14	4	4	2	45		.254	.371
Jack Glasscock	SS68,2B4,P2	(1-2)	72	281	45	70	22	4	4	1	25	16		.249	.302
Mike Muldoon	3B109,2B1,OF1		110	422	46	101	38	16	6	2	18	67		.239	.320
Jake Evans	OF76,2B4,SS2		80	313	32	81	39	18	3	1	15	49		.259	.345
Pete Hotaling	OF102,2B1		102	408	69	99	27	16	6	3	28	50		.243	.333
Willie Murphy	OF42	(1-2)	42	168	18	38	9	3	3	1	1	23		.226	.298
Doc Bushong	C62,OF1		62	203	24	48	10	6	1	0	17	11		.236	.276
Sam Moffett	OF42,P24,1B2,2B1,3B1		67	256	26	47	14	12	2	0	8	56		.184	.246
John Harkins	P46,OF17,3B1,SS1		61	229	24	47	20	4	2	0	7	45		.205	.240
Jim McCormick	P42,OF8	(1-2)	49	190	15	50		5	4	0	1	11		.263	.332
Fatty Briody	C42,OF1	(1-2)	43	148	17	25	12	6	0	1	6	19		.169	.230
George Pinkney	2B25,SS11		36	144	18	45	16	9	0	0	10	7		.313	.375
Ernie Burch	OF32		32	124	9	26	7	4	0	0	5	24		.210	.242
Joe Ardner	2B25,3B1		26	92	6	16	4	1	1	0	1	24		.174	.207
Mike Moynahan	2B6,SS3,OF3	(2-2)	12	45	9	13	6	2	1	0	7	11		.289	.378
Jerry Moore	C9	(2-2)	9	30	1	6	10	0	0	0	0	5		.200	.200
John Henry	P5,OF4		9	26	2	4	0	0	0	0	0	12		.154	.154
Gurd Whitely	OF8		8	34	4	5	0	0	0	0	1	8		.147	.147
George Strief	OF6,3B2	(4-4)	8	29	2	7	0	2	0	0	0	5		.241	.310
George Fisher	2B6,C1	(2-3)	6	24	2	3	0	0	0	0	0	3		.125	.125
Pit Gilman	OF2		2	10	0	1	0	0	0	0	0	3		.100	.100
Bill Smith	OF1		1	3	0	0	0	0	0	0	0	2		.000	.000
			113	3934	458	934	306	147	49	16	170	576		.237	.312

PITCHERS			W	L	PCT	G	GS	CG	SH	SV	IP	H	BB	SO	ERA
Jim McCormick		(1-2)	19	22	.463	42	41	39	3	0	359	357	75	182	2.86
John Harkins			12	32	.273	46	45	42	3	0	391	399	108	192	3.68
Sam Moffett			3	19	.136	24	22	21	0	0	198	236	58	84	3.87
John Henry			1	4	.200	5	5	5	1	0	42	46	26	23	3.64
Jack Glasscock			0	0	----	2	0	0	0	0	5	8	2	1	5.40
			35	77	.313	113	113	107	7	0	995	1046	269	482	3.43

DETROIT
Wolverines

28-84   .250   -56   8th   Jack Chapman

BATTERS	POS/GAMES	GP	AB	R	H	BI	2B	3B	HR	BB	SO	SB	BA	SA
Milt Scott	1B110	110	438	29	108	50	17	5	3	9	62		.247	.329
Bill Geiss	2B73,1B1,OF1,P1	75	283	23	50	16	11	4	2	6	60		.177	.265
Frank Meinke	SS51,P35,OF4,2B3,3B3	92	341	28	56	24	5	7	6	6	89		.164	.273
Joe Farrell	3B110,OF1	110	461	59	104	41	10	5	3	14	66		.226	.289
Stump Weidman	OF56,P26,SS1,2B1	81	300	24	49	26	6	0	0	13	41		.163	.183
Ned Hanlon	OF114	114	450	86	119	39	18	6	5	40	52		.264	.364

DETROIT (cont.)
Wolverines

BATTERS	POS/GAMES		GP	AB	R	H	RBI	2B	3B	HR	BB	SO	SB	BA	SA
George Wood	OF114,3B1		114	473	79	119	29	16	10	8	39	75		.252	.378
Charlie Bennett	C79,OF5,SS4,1B1,2B1,3B1		90	341	37	90	40	18	6	3	36	40		.264	.378
Dupee Shaw	P28,OF10	(1-2)	36	136	15	26		4	1	1	4	21		.191	.257
Henry Jones	2B16,OF12,SS8		34	127	24	28	3	3	1	0	16	18		.220	.260
Harry Buker	SS19,OF11		30	111	5	15	3	1	0	0	4	15		.135	.144
Frank Cox	SS27		27	102	6	13	4	3	1	0	2	36		.127	.176
Ed Gastfield	C19,1B2,OF2		23	82	6	6	2	1	0	0	2	34		.073	.085
Tom Kearns	2B21		21	79	9	16	7	0	1	0	2	10		.203	.228
Pretzels Getzien	P17		17	55	4	6		0	0	0	5	20		.109	.109
Frank Brill	P12,OF1		13	44	5	6		0	0	0	1	13		.136	.136
Fred Wood	C7,OF6,SS1		12	42	4	2	1	0	0	0	3	18		.048	.048
Chief Zimmer	C6,OF2		8	29	0	2	0	1	0	0	1	14		.069	.103
Walt Prince	OF7	(1-3)	7	21	0	3	1	0	0	0	3	4		.143	.143
Ed Santry	SS5,2B1		6	22	1	4	0	0	0	0	1	2		.182	.182
Frank Jones	SS1,OF1		2	8	0	1	0	0	0	0	0	1		.125	.125
Harry Weber	OF2		2	8	0	0	0	0	0	0	0	2		.000	.000
Ben Guiney	C2		2	7	0	0	0	0	0	0	0	3		.000	.000
Wallie Walker	C1		1	4	1	1	0	0	0	0	0	0		.250	.250
Dickie Lowe	C1		1	3	0	1	0	0	0	0	0	1		.333	.333
Dave Beatle	OF1		1	3	0	0	0	0	0	0	0	2		.000	.000
			114	3970	445	825	286	114	47	31	207	699		.208	.284

PITCHERS			W	L	PCT	G	GS	CG	SH	SV	IP	H	BB	SO	ERA
Dupee Shaw		(1-2)	9	18	.333	28	28	25	0	0	228	219	72	142	3.04
Frank Meinke			8	23	.258	35	31	31	1	0	289	341	63	124	3.18
Pretzels Getzien			5	12	.294	17	17	17	1	0	147	118	25	107	1.95
Stump Weidman			4	21	.160	26	26	24	0	0	213	257	57	96	3.72
Frank Brill			2	10	.167	12	12	12	1	0	103	148	26	18	5.50
Bill Geiss			0	0	----	1	0	0	0	0	5	14	2	1	14.40
			28	84	.250	114	114	109	3	0	985	1097	245	488	3.38

1884 AMERICAN ASSOCIATION

Equality

Moses Fleetwood (Fleet) Walker was a ball player — a catcher — for Oberlin College and the University of Michigan. His pro career began in 1883 for Toledo of the minor Northwest League. When Toledo jumped to the major league American Association in 1884, Fleet and his brother Welday jumped with them. These two are not remembered for their playing record, which, though adequate, was not stellar. They are notable because Fleet and Welday Walker were the first African-Americans to play major league baseball.

African-Americans, though not encouraged, were not forbidden to play in organized baseball. There were no specific laws preventing this activity. And generally, African-Americans were supported by the fans of the teams on which they played. Their real enemies were the other players and teammates. Many ball players could not tolerate African-Americans on theirs or any other team. For instance, a teammate of the Walkers in Toledo, pitcher Tony Mullane, was reported to have said the following about his catcher, Fleet Walker. "Walker was the best catcher I have worked with — but since he was a Negro, I disregarded his signals and pitched what I wanted." This behavior was an ominous sign that African-Americans would not long be tolerated in organized baseball. This grim forecast would come true before the decade was out.

To keep the outlaw Union Association in check, the American Association expanded to an unwieldy 12 teams in 1884. The four new teams added were the aforementioned Toledo, Washington, Indianapolis, and Brooklyn clubs. With two other major leagues operating this year with more than 30 teams, it would have been a miracle for the stretched thin American Association to finish the season intact. The miracle did not happen, and Washington shut up shop in early August. On August 5, a team from Richmond was admitted in its stead.

The New York Metropolitans cruised to the pennant and finished six and one-half games ahead of second place Columbus. Batting champion, Dave Orr (.354), sparked the offense for New York, while pitchers Jack Lynch and Tim Keefe won 37 games each. Columbus's strength was pitching, as demonstrated by Ed Morris with his 34 wins and leading .723 winning percentage.

Louisville and St. Louis finished third and fourth respectively. Louisville was paced by Pete Browning (.336) and the remarkable Guy Hecker who finished with 52 wins, and a 1.80 earned average. St. Louis was led by Fred Lewis (.323).

Cincinnati, Baltimore, and Philadelphia all finished above .500 as well in fifth, sixth and seventh places. The two best players on these teams were Cincinnati's Long John Reilly who won the home run title at eleven while batting .339, and Philadelphia's Harry Stovey who finished second in the home run race with ten, first in the triple race with 23, and hit .326 as well.

Toledo, Brooklyn, and fill-in Richmond finished next in eighth, ninth, and tenth. Toledo's Sam Barkely (.306) and Richmond's Mike Mansell (.301) were the only good hitters on the triad of teams. Toledo pitcher, Tony Mullane, won 36 of his team's 46 victories.

The three tailenders, Pittsburgh, Indianapolis, and Washington, used almost 100 players among the three of them in a vain attempt to improve their lot. Washington's group was particularly inept as five of their regulars batted under .200.

The Walkers and a handful of African-Americans played in the high minor leagues through the decade of the 1880s. The high point would come in 1887 when seven played in organized ball. Fleet Walker teamed with one of the seven, pitcher George Stovey, on the Newark team of the International League. In July 1887, Cap Anson, of the White Stockings, refused to take the field against Newark in an exhibition game, unless Walker and Stovey were barred from playing. This proved to be the beginning of the end for African-Americans in organized baseball. In 1888, the International League passed the following motion: " ... no contracts of colored players except the two now in the league (Walker of Syracuse and Grant of Buffalo) should be approved." By 1889, Fleet Walker was the last African-American left in professional baseball as he ended his career with Syracuse. If Walker had stayed one more year with the team, he would have been back in the major leagues, when the Syracuse Stars moved to the American Association in 1890.

The insensitivity of American society would mean a lengthy wait for the next arrival of an African-American in the major leagues. A wait that was at least 60 years too long.

1884 AMERICAN ASSOCIATION

NEW YORK Metropolitans   75-32   .701   1st   Jim Mutrie

BATTERS	POS/GAMES		GP	AB	R	H	BI	2B	3B	HR	BB	SO	SB	BA	SA
Dave Orr	1B110,OF3		110	458	82	162		32	13	9	5			.354	.539
Dasher Troy	2B107		107	421	80	111		22	10	2	19			.264	.378
Candy Nelson	SS110,2B1		111	432	114	110		15	3	1	74			.255	.310
Dude Esterbrook	3B112		112	477	110	150		29	11	1	12			.314	.428
Steve Brady	OF110,1B5,2B1		112	485	102	122		11	3	1	21			.252	.293
Ed Kennedy	OF100,SS1,2B1,C1		103	378	49	72		6	2	1	16			.190	.225
Chief Roseman	OF107		107	436	97	130		16	11	4	21			.298	.413
Bill Holbert	C59,OF5,SS1		65	255	28	53		5	0	0	7			.208	.227
Tim Keefe	P58,OF5		63	213	27	50		3	6	3	18			.235	.347
Charlie Reipschlager	C51,OF8		59	233	21	56		13	2	0	1			.240	.313
Jack Lynch	P54		54	195	21	30		2	3	0	9			.187	.224
Gracie Pierce	2B3,OF3		5	20	2	5		1	0	0	0			.250	.300
Tony Murphy	C1		1	3	1	1		0	0	0	0			.333	.333
Jim Becannon	P1		1	3	0	0		0	0	0	0			.000	.000
Henry Oxley	C1	(2-2)	1	3	0	0		0	0	0	0			.000	.000
			112	4012	734	1052		155	64	22	203	315		.262	.349

PITCHERS	W	L	PCT	G	GS	CG	SH	SV	IP	H	BB	SO	ERA
Jack Lynch	37	15	.712	54	53	53	5	0	487	410	42	286	2.64
Tim Keefe	37	17	.685	58	58	57	4	0	492	388	75	323	2.29
Jim Becannon	1	0	1.000	1	1	1	0	0	6	2	2	2	1.50
	75	32	.701	112	112	111	9	0	985	800	119	611	2.46

COLUMBUS Buckeyes   69-39   .639   -6.5   2nd   Gus Schmelz

BATTERS	POS/GAMES		GP	AB	R	H	BI	2B	3B	HR	BB	SO	SB	BA	SA
Jim Field	1B105		105	417	74	97		9	7	4	23			.233	.317
Pop Smith	2B108		108	445	78	106		18	10	6	20			.238	.364
John Richmond	SS105		105	398	57	100		13	7	3	35			.251	.342
Bill Kuehne	3B109,OF1		110	415	48	98		13	16	5	9			.236	.381
Tom Brown	OF107,P4		107	451	93	123		9	11	5	24			.273	.375
Fred Mann	OF97,2B2		99	366	70	101		12	18	7	25			.276	.464
John Cahill	OF54,SS5,P2		59	210	28	46		3	3	0	6			.219	.262
Rudy Kemmler	C58,1B2,OF1		61	211	28	42		3	3	0	15			.199	.242
Fred Carroll	C54,OF15		69	252	46	70		13	5	6	13			.278	.440
Frank Mountain	P42,OF17		58	210	26	50		7	3	4	9			.238	.357
Ed Morris	P52,OF10		57	199	19	37		4	8	0	5			.186	.286
Ed Dundon	OF16,P11,1B3		26	86	6	12		2	2	0	5			.140	.209
Tom Mansell	OF23	(2-2)	23	77	9	15		1	3	0	6			.195	.286
Tom Sullivan	P4		4	11	1	1		0	0	0	1			.091	.091
Al Bauers	P3		3	11	2	3		0	0	0	0			.273	.273
			110	3759	585	901		107	96	40	196	404		.240	.351

PITCHERS	W	L	PCT	G	GS	CG	SH	SV	IP	H	BB	SO	ERA
Ed Morris	34	13	.723	52	52	47	3	0	430	335	51	302	2.18
Frank Mountain	23	17	.575	42	41	40	5	1	361	209	70	156	2.45
Ed Dundon	6	4	.600	11	9	7	0	0	81	85	15	37	3.78
Tom Brown	2	1	.667	4	0	0	0	0	19	27	7	5	7.11
Tom Sullivan	2	2	.500	4	4	4	0	0	31	42	3	12	4.06
John Cahill	1	0	1.000	2	1	1	0	0	16	15	4	1	5.06
Al Bauers	1	2	.333	3	3	3	0	0	25	22	14	13	4.68
	69	39	.639	110	110	102	8	1	962	815	172	526	2.68

LOUISVILLE Eclipse   68-40   .630   -7.5   3rd   Mike Walsh

BATTERS	POS/GAMES	GP	AB	R	H	BI	2B	3B	HR	BB	SO	SB	BA	SA
Juice Latham	1B76,3B1	77	308	31	52		3	3	0	8			.169	.198
Joe Gerhardt	2B105,SS1	106	404	39	89		7	8	0	13			.220	.277
Tom McLaughlin	SS93,3B4,2B2	98	335	41	67		11	6	0	22			.200	.269
Pete Browning	3B52,OF24,1B23,2B4,P1	103	447	101	150		33	8	4	13			.336	.472
Chicken Wolf	OF101,C11,1B1,3B1,SS1	110	486	79	146		24	11	3	4			.300	.414
Monk Cline	OF90,SS6	94	396	91	115		16	7	2	27			.290	.381

1884 AMERICAN ASSOCIATION

LOUISVILLE (cont.)
Eclipse

BATTERS	POS/GAMES		GP	AB	R	H	BI	2B	3B	HR	BB	SO	SB	BA	SA
Leech Maskrey	OF103,3B3,SS1		105	412	48	103		13	4	0	17			.250	.301
Dan Sullivan	C63,OF1		63	247	27	59		8	6	0	9			.239	.320
Guy Hecker	P76,OF5		78	316	53	94		14	8	4	10			.297	.430
Phil Reccius	3B51,P18,SS10		73	263	23	63		9	2	3	5			.240	.323
Ed Whiting	C40,1B2,OF2		42	157	16	35		7	3	0	9			.223	.306
Wally Andrews	1B9,3B3,OF1,SS1		14	49	10	10		5	1	0	4			.204	.347
Denny Driscoll	P13,OF2		13	48	5	9		1	0	0	2			.188	.208
Ren Deagle	P12,OF3	(2-2)	12	45	2	6		1	0	0	0			.133	.156
Buttercup Dickerson	OF8	(3-3)	8	28	6	4		0	2	1	3			.143	.393
Leonard Stockwell	OF2,C1		2	9	0	1		0	0	0	0			.111	.111
Bill Hunter	C2		2	7	1	1		0	0	0	0			.143	.143
			110	3957	573	1004		152	69	17	146	408		.254	.340

PITCHERS			W	L	PCT	G	GS	CG	SH	SV	IP	H	BB	SO	ERA
Guy Hecker			52	20	.722	75	73	72	6	0	671	526	56	385	1.80
Denny Driscoll			6	6	.500	13	13	10	0	0	102	110	7	16	3.44
Phil Reccius			6	7	.462	18	11	11	0	0	129	118	19	46	2.71
Ren Deagle		(2-2)	4	6	.400	12	12	8	0	0	87	80	13	23	2.58
Pete Browning			0	1	.000	1	1	0	0	0	0.3	2	2	0	54.00
			68	40	.630	110	110	101	6	0	990	836	97	470	2.17

ST. LOUIS
Browns

67-40 .626 -8 4th Williams - Comiskey

BATTERS	POS/GAMES		GP	AB	R	H	BI	2B	3B	HR	BB	SO	SB	BA	SA
Charlie Comiskey	1B108,2B1,P1		108	460	76	110		17	6	2	5			.239	.315
Joe Quest	2B81	(1-2)	81	310	46	64		9	5	0	19			.206	.268
Bill Gleason	SS110,3B1		110	472	97	127		21	7	1	28			.269	.350
Arlie Latham	3B110,C1		110	474	115	130		17	12	1	19			.274	.367
Hugh Nicol	OF87,2B23,3B1,SS1		110	442	79	115		14	5	0	22			.260	.314
Fred Lewis	OF73	(1-2)	73	300	59	97		25	3	0	16			.323	.427
Tip O'Neill	OF64,P17,1B1		78	297	49	82		13	11	3	12			.276	.424
Pat Deasley	C75,OF2,1B1		75	254	27	52		5	4	0	7			.205	.256
George Strief	OF43,2B4,1B1	(1-4)	48	184	22	37		5	2	2	13			.201	.283
Jumbo McGinnis	P40		40	146	16	34		9	1	0	4			.233	.308
Tom Dolan	C33,OF2	(1-2)	35	137	19	36		6	2	0	6			.263	.336
Dave Foutz	P25,OF14		33	119	17	27		4	0	0	8			.227	.261
Daisy Davis	P25,OF5	(2-2)	25	87	5	15		0	1	0	5			.172	.195
Bob Caruthers	OF16,P13		23	82	15	21		2	0	2	4			.256	.354
Charles Krehmeyer	OF15,C7,1B1		21	70	3	16		0	1	0	2			.229	.257
John Lavin	OF16		16	52	9	11		2	0	0	3			.212	.250
Walt Goldsby	OF5	(1-3)	5	20	2	4		0	0	0	0			.200	.200
Harry Wheeler	OF5	(1-5)	5	19	0	5		2	0	0	1			.263	.368
Walt Kinzie	2B2	(2-2)	2	9	0	1		0	0	0	0			.111	.111
Al Struve	OF1,C1		2	7	2	2		0	0	0	0			.286	.286
Chick Fulmer	2B1	(2-2)	1	5	0	0		0	0	0	0			.000	.000
Nin Alexander	C1	(2-2)	1	4	0	0		0	0	0	0			.000	.000
Jim McCauley	C1		1	2	0	0		0	0	0	0			.000	.000
			110	3952	658	986		151	60	11	174	339		.249	.326

PITCHERS			W	L	PCT	G	GS	CG	SH	SV	IP	H	BB	SO	ERA
Jumbo McGinnis			24	16	.600	40	40	39	5	0	354	331	35	141	2.84
Dave Foutz			15	6	.714	25	25	19	2	0	207	167	36	95	2.18
Tip O'Neill			11	4	.733	17	14	14	0	0	141	125	51	36	2.68
Daisy Davis		(1-2)	10	12	.455	25	24	20	1	0	198	196	35	143	2.90
Bob Caruthers			7	2	.778	13	7	7	0	0	83	61	15	58	2.61
Charlie Comiskey			0	0	----	1	0	0	0	0	4	1	0	4	2.25
			67	40	.626	110	110	99	8	0	987	881	172	477	2.67

CINCINNATI
Red Stockings

68-41 .624 -8 5th White - Snyder

BATTERS	POS/GAMES	GP	AB	R	H	BI	2B	3B	HR	BB	SO	SB	BA	SA
Long John Reilly	1B103,OF3,SS1	105	448	114	152		24	19	11	5			.339	.551
Bid McPhee	2B112	112	450	107	125		8	7	5	27			.278	.360
Jim Peoples	SS47,C14,OF10,1B1,3B1	69	267	28	45		2	2	1	6			.169	.202

CINCINNATI (cont.)
Red Stockings

BATTERS	POS/GAMES		GP	AB	R	H	BI	2B	3B	HR	BB	SO	SB	BA	SA
Hick Carpenter	3B108,OF1		108	474	80	121		16	2	4	6			.255	.323
Pop Corkhill	OF92,SS11,1B6,3B3,P1		110	452	85	124		13	11	4	6			.274	.378
Tom Mansell	OF65	(1-2)	65	266	49	66		4	6	0	15			.248	.308
Charlie Jones	OF112		112	472	117	148		19	17	7	37			.314	.470
Pop Snyder	C65,1B2,OF1		67	268	32	69		9	9	0	7			.257	.358
Will White	P52		52	184	28	35		1	2	1	10			.190	.234
Phil Powers	C31,1B2,OF2		34	130	10	18		1	0	0	5			.138	.146
Bill Mountjoy	P33,OF2,3B1		34	119	13	18		2	1	0	9			.151	.185
Buck West	OF33		33	131	20	32		2	8	1	2			.244	.405
Chick Fulmer	SS29,OF2	(1-2)	31	114	13	20		2	1	0	1			.175	.211
Frank Fennelly	SS28	(2-2)	28	122	42	43		5	8	2	11			.352	.574
Gus Shallix	P23		23	84	3	3		0	0	0	4			.036	.036
Jim Woulfe	OF7,3B1	(1-2)	8	34	3	5		0	1	0	1			.147	.206
Frank Berkelbach	OF6		6	25	3	6		0	1	0	0			.240	.320
George Miller	C6		6	20	6	5		1	1	0	1			.250	.400
Ren Deagle	P4	(1-2)	4	13	1	0		0	0	0	1			.000	.000
Icicle Reeder	OF3	(1-2)	3	14	0	2		0	0	0	0			.143	.143
John Parsons	OF1		1	3	0	0		0	0	0	0			.000	.000
			112	4090	754	1037		109	96	36	154	404		.254	.353

PITCHERS		W	L	PCT	G	GS	CG	SH	SV	IP	H	BB	SO	ERA
Will White		34	18	.654	52	52	52	7	0	456	479	74	118	3.32
Bill Mountjoy		19	12	.613	33	33	32	3	0	289	274	43	96	2.93
Gus Shallix		11	10	.524	23	23	23	0	0	200	163	53	78	3.70
Ren Deagle		3	1	.750	4	4	4	1	0	34	39	9	12	5.03
Pop Corkhill		1	0	1.000	1	0	0	0	0	5	1	2	4	1.80
		68	41	.624	112	112	111	11	0	984	956	181	308	3.33

BALTIMORE
Orioles

63-43 .594 -11.5 6th Billy Barnie

BATTERS	POS/GAMES		GP	AB	R	H	BI	2B	3B	HR	BB	SO	SB	BA	SA
Dan Stearns	1B100,2B1		100	396	61	94		12	3	3	28			.237	.306
Tim Manning	2B91		91	341	49	70		14	5	2	26			.205	.293
Jimmy Macullar	SS107		107	360	73	73		16	6	4	36			.203	.314
Joe Sommer	3B97,OF9,2B1		107	479	96	129		11	10	4	8			.269	.359
Gid Gardner	OF40,1B2	(1-4)	41	173	32	37		6	8	2	14			.214	.376
Jim Clinton	OF103,2B1		103	437	82	118		12	6	4	29			.270	.352
Tom York	OF83		83	314	64	70		14	7	1	34			.223	.322
Sam Trott	C60,2B6,OF5		71	284	36	73		17	9	3	4			.257	.401
Bill Traffley	C47,OF6,1B1		53	210	25	37		4	6	0	3			.176	.252
Hardie Henderson	P52,OF3		53	203	24	46		7	7	0	5			.227	.330
Bob Emslie	P50,OF1		51	195	21	37		6	3	0	2			.190	.251
Dennis Casey	OF37	(2-2)	37	149	20	37		7	4	3	5			.248	.409
Oyster Burns	OF24,2B10,P2,3B1	(2-2)	35	131	34	39		2	6	6	7			.298	.542
Buttercup Dickerson	OF10,3B3	(2-3)	13	56	9	12		2	1	0	4			.214	.286
John Ake	3B9,OF3,SS1		13	52	1	10		0	1	0	0			.192	.231
Pat Burns	1B6	(1-2)	6	25	3	5		2	1	0	3			.200	.360
Jim McLaughlin	P3,OF3		5	22	3	5		1	1	0	0			.227	.364
Fred Goldsmith	P4	(2-2)	4	14	2	2		0	0	0	2			.143	.143
Jim Roxburgh	C2		2	4	1	2		0	0	0	1			.500	.500
			108	3845	636	896		133	84	32	211			.233	.336

PITCHERS		W	L	PCT	G	GS	CG	SH	SV	IP	H	BB	SO	ERA
Bob Emslie		32	17	.653	50	50	50	4	0	455	419	88	264	2.75
Hardie Henderson		27	23	.540	52	52	50	4	0	439	382	116	346	2.62
Fred Goldsmith		3	1	.750	4	4	3	0	0	30	29	2	11	2.70
Jim McLaughlin		1	2	.333	3	2	2	0	0	22	27	11	8	3.68
Oyster Burns		0	0	----	2	0	0	0	1	9	12	2	6	3.00
		63	43	.594	108	108	105	8	1	956	869	219	635	2.71

1884 AMERICAN ASSOCIATION

PHILADELPHIA 61-46 .570 -14 7th Lon Knight
Athletics

BATTERS	POS/GAMES		GP	AB	R	H	BI	2B	3B	HR	BB	SO	SB	BA	SA
Harry Stovey	1B104		104	448	124	146		22	23	10	26			.326	.545
Cub Stricker	2B107,C1,OF1,P1		107	399	59	92		16	11	1	19			.231	.333
Sadie Houck	SS108,2B1		108	472	93	140		19	14	0	7			.297	.396
Fred Corey	3B104		104	439	64	121		17	16	5	17			.276	.421
Lon Knight	OF108,P2,1B1		108	484	94	131		18	12	1	10			.271	.364
Henry Larkin	OF85,2B2		85	326	59	90		21	9	3	15			.276	.423
Jud Birchall	OF52,3B2		54	221	36	57		2	2	0	4			.258	.285
Jocko Milligan	C65,OF1		66	268	39	77		20	3	3	8			.287	.418
Bobby Mathews	P49,OF1		49	184	26	34		5	1	0	7			.185	.223
Jack O'Brien	C30,OF5,1B1		36	138	25	39		6	1	1	9			.283	.362
Bob Blakiston	OF28,1B,3B2,2B1,SS1	(1-2)	32	128	21	33		6	0	0	11			.258	.305
Bill Taylor	P30	(2-2)	30	111	8	28		6	2	0	2			.252	.342
Jack Coleman	OF24,P3,1B2	(2-2)	28	107	16	22		2	3	2	5			.206	.336
Al Atkinson	P22,OF2	(1-4)	22	83	13	16		3	1	0	4			.193	.253
Mike Mansell	OF20	(2-3)	20	70	6	14		1	1	0	5			.200	.243
Frank Siffel	C7		7	17	3	3		1	0	0	0			.176	.235
Charles Hilsey	P3,OF3		6	24	5	5		1	1	0	0			.208	.333
Ed Rowen	C4		4	15	4	6		1	0	0	1			.400	.467
Elmer Foster	C4,OF1	(1-2)	4	11	4	2		0	0	0	3			.182	.182
Frank Ringo	C2	(2-2)	2	6	0	0		0	0	0	0			.000	.000
Phenomenal Smith	P1	(2-3)	1	4	1	1		0	0	0	0			.250	.250
Mike Moynahan	SS1	(1-2)	1	4	0	0		0	0	0	0			.000	.000
			108	3959	700	1057		167	100	26	153	425		.267	.379

PITCHERS			W	L	PCT	G	GS	CG	SH	SV	IP	H	BB	SO	ERA
Bobby Mathews			30	18	.625	49	49	48	3	0	431	401	49	286	3.32
Bill Taylor		(2-2)	18	12	.600	30	30	30	1	0	260	232	44	130	2.53
Al Atkinson		(1-4)	11	11	.500	22	22	20	1	0	184	186	21	93	4.21
Charles Hilsey			2	1	.667	3	3	3	0	0	27	29	5	10	4.67
Lon Knight			0	1	.000	2	1	1	0	0	14	24	4	2	9.00
Phenomenal Smith		(2-3)	0	1	.000	1	1	1	0	0	9	14	1	3	4.00
Jack Coleman		(2-2)	0	2	.000	3	2	2	0	0	21	28	2	5	3.43
Cub Stricker			0	0	----	1	0	0	0	0	3	6	1	1	6.00
			61	46	.570	108	108	105	5	0	949	920	127	530	3.42

TOLEDO 46-58 .442 -27.5 8th Charlie Morton
Blue Stockings

BATTERS	POS/GAMES		GP	AB	R	H	BI	2B	3B	HR	BB	SO	SB	BA	SA
Chappy Lane	1B46,OF9,3B2,C1		57	215	26	49		9	5	1	2			.228	.330
Sam Barkley	2B103,C2		104	435	71	133		39	9	1	22			.306	.444
Joe Miller	SS105		105	423	46	101		12	8	1	26			.239	.312
Ed Brown	3B39,OF2,C1,P1,2B1		42	153	13	27		3	0	0	2			.176	.196
Tom Poorman	OF93,P1		94	382	56	89		8	7	0	10			.233	.291
Curt Welch	OF106,2B2,C2,1B1		109	425	61	95		24	5	0	10			.224	.304
Frank Olin	OF26	(3-3)	26	86	16	22		0	1	1	5			.256	.314
Fleet Walker	C41,OF1		42	152	23	40		2	3	0	8			.263	.316
Tony Mullane	P67,OF18,1B7,3B6,2B1,SS1		95	352	49	97		19	3	3	33			.276	.372
Hank O'Day	P39,OF24,3B3,1B3		64	242	23	51		9	1	0	10			.211	.256
Joe Moffett	1B38,3B12,2B3,OF3		56	204	17	41		5	3	0	2			.201	.255
Deacon McGuire	C41,OF4,SS3		45	151	12	28		7	0	1	5			.185	.252
George Meister	3B34		34	119	9	23		6	0	0	3			.193	.244
Charlie Morton	3B16,OF15,P3,2B1		32	111	11	18		6	2	0	7			.162	.252
Trick McSorley	1B16,OF5,3B1,P1		21	68	12	17		1	0	0	3			.250	.265
John Tilley	OF17	(1-2)	17	56	5	10		2	0	0	4			.179	.214
Tug Arundel	C15		15	47	6	4		0	0	0	3			.085	.085
Sim Bullas	C12,OF2		13	45	4	4		0	1	0	1			.089	.133
Ed Miller	OF8		8	24	2	6		0	0	0	1			.250	.250
Welday Walker	OF5		5	18	1	4		1	0	0	0			.222	.278
Ed Kent	P1		1	4	0	0		0	0	0	0			.000	.000
			110	3712	463	859		153	48	8	157	541		.231	.305

PITCHERS		W	L	PCT	G	GS	CG	SH	SV	IP	H	BB	SO	ERA
Tony Mullane		36	26	.581	67	65	64	7	0	567	481	89	325	2.52
Hank O'Day		9	28	.243	41	40	35	2	1	327	335	66	163	3.75
Charles Morton		0	1	.000	3	1	1	0	0	23	18	5	7	3.09
Tom Poorman		0	1	.000	1	1	1	0	0	9	13	2	0	3.00
Ed Kent		0	1	.000	1	1	1	0	0	9	14	3	4	6.00

TOLEDO (cont.)
Blue Stockings

PITCHERS	W	L	PCT	G	GS	CG	SH	SV	IP	H	BB	SO	ERA
Ed Brown	0	1	.000	1	1	1	0	0	9	19	4	1	9.00
Trick McSorley	0	0	----	1	0	0	0	0	2	5	0	1	4.50
	46	58	.442	110	109	103	9	1	946	885	169	501	3.06

BROOKLYN
Trolley Dodgers

40-64 .385 -33.5 9th George Taylor

BATTERS	POS/GAMES		GP	AB	R	H	BI	2B	3B	HR	BB	SO	SB	BA	SA
Charles Householder	1B40,C31,OF6,2B1		76	273	28	66		15	3	3	12			.242	.352
Bill Greenwood	2B92,SS1		92	385	52	83		8	3	3	10			.216	.275
Billy Geer	SS106,2B2,P2,1B1	(2-2)	107	391	68	82		15	7	0	38			.210	.284
Fred Warner	3B83,OF1		84	352	40	78		4	0	1	17			.222	.241
John Cassidy	OF100,3B5,SS1		106	433	57	109		11	6	2	19			.252	.319
Jack Remsen	OF81	(2-2)	81	301	45	67		6	6	3	23			.223	.312
Oscar Walker	OF59,1B36		95	382	59	103		12	8	2	9			.270	.359
John Corcoran	C38,OF9,2B4,SS2,P1		52	185	17	39		4	3	0	8			.211	.265
Adonis Terry	P56,OF13		68	240	16	56		10	3	0	8			.233	.300
Ike Benners	OF49	(1-2)	49	189	25	38		11	5	1	7			.201	.328
Tim Knowles	1B29,3B11,SS1	(2-2)	41	153	19	36		5	1	1	3			.235	.301
Sam Kimber	P41		41	138	13	20		1	2	0	9			.145	.181
Charles Jones	2B13,3B11,OF2		25	90	10	16		1	0	0	5			.178	.189
Hickie Wilson	OF12,C10,1B3,2B1		24	82	13	19		4	0	0	5			.232	.280
John Farrar	C16		16	58	7	11		2	0	0	3			.190	.224
Jack Hayes	C14,OF2	(2-2)	16	51	4	12		3	0	0	3			.235	.294
Jim Conway	P13,OF2,SS2		14	47	1	6		0	0	0	0			.128	.128
Jerry Dorgan	C4	(2-2)	4	13	2	4		0	0	0	0			.308	.308
			109	3763	476	845		112	47	16	179	417		.225	.292

PITCHERS	W	L	PCT	G	GS	CG	SH	SV	IP	H	BB	SO	ERA
Adonis Terry	19	35	.352	56	55	54	2	0	476	486	72	230	3.55
Sam Kimber	18	20	.474	41	41	41	4	0	361	364	72	122	3.81
Jim Conway	3	9	.250	13	13	10	0	0	105	132	15	25	4.44
Billy Geer	0	0	----	2	0	0	0	0	5	14	3	1	12.60
John Corcoran	0	0	----	1	0	0	0	0	1	0	1	0	0.00
	40	64	.385	109	109	105	6	0	949	996	163	378	3.79

RICHMOND
Virginians

12-30 .286 -30.5 10th Felix Moses

BATTERS	POS/GAMES		GP	AB	R	H	BI	2B	3B	HR	BB	SO	SB	BA	SA
Jim Powell	1B41		41	151	23	37		8	4	0	7			.245	.351
Terry Larkin	2B40	(2-2)	40	139	17	28		1	4	0	9			.201	.266
Bill Schenck	SS40,2B2		42	151	14	31		4	0	3	1			.205	.291
Billy Nash	3B45		45	166	31	33		8	8	1	12			.199	.361
Mike Mansell	OF29	(3-3)	29	113	21	34		2	5	0	8			.301	.407
Dick Johnston	OF37,SS2		39	146	23	41		5	5	2	2			.281	.425
Ed Glenn	OF43		43	175	26	43		2	4	1	5			.246	.320
John Hanna	C21,SS1	(2-2)	22	67	6	13		2	1	0	0			.194	.254
Marsh Quinton	C14,OF10,SS2		26	94	12	22		5	0	0	0			.234	.287
Peter Meegan	P22,OF1		23	75	6	12		1	2	0	2			.160	.227
Ed Dugan	P20,2B2		22	70	4	8		0	0	0	5			.114	.114
Walt Goldsby	OF11	(3-3)	11	40	4	9		1	0	0	1			.225	.250
Bill Dugan	C9	(1-2)	9	28	4	2		1	0	0	0			.071	.107
Bill Morgan	C3,OF2,2B1	(1-2)	6	20	0	2		0	0	0	1			.100	.100
Andy Swan	1B3	(2-2)	3	10	2	5		0	0	0	0			.500	.500
Wes Curry	P2		2	8	1	2		0	0	0	0			.250	.250
Wash Williams	OF2		2	8	0	2		0	0	0	0			.250	.250
Ed Ford	1B1,SS1		2	5	0	0		0	0	0	0			.000	.000
Ted Firth	P1		1	3	0	1		0	0	0	0			.333	.333
			46	1469	194	325		40	33	7	53	284		.221	.308

PITCHERS	W	L	PCT	G	GS	CG	SH	SV	IP	H	BB	SO	ERA
Peter Meegan	7	12	.368	22	22	22	1	0	179	177	29	106	4.32
Ed Dugan	5	14	.263	20	20	20	0	0	166	196	15	60	4.49

1884 AMERICAN ASSOCIATION

RICHMOND (cont.)
Virginians

PITCHERS		W	L	PCT	G	GS	CG	SH	SV	IP	H	BB	SO	ERA
Ted Firth		0	1	.000	1	1	1	0	0	9	14	5	0	8.00
Wes Curry		0	2	.000	2	2	2	0	0	16	15	3	1	5.06
		12	30	.286	46	45	45	1	0	370	402	52	167	4.52

PITTSBURGH
Alleghenys

30-78 .278 -45.5 11th McKnight - Ferguson
Battin - Creamer - Phillips

BATTERS	POS/GAMES		GP	AB	R	H	BI	2B	3B	HR	BB	SO	SB	BA	SA
Jim Knowles	1B46	(1-2)	46	182	19	42		5	7	0	5			.231	.335
George Creamer	2B98		98	339	38	62		8	5	0	16			.183	.236
Bill White	SS60,3B10,OF4		74	291	25	66		7	10	0	13			.227	.320
Joe Battin	3B43	(1-3)	43	158	10	28		1	2	0	3			.177	.209
Ed Swartwood	OF79,1B22,3B1,P1		102	399	74	115		19	6	0	33			.288	.366
Oak Taylor	OF41		41	152	22	32		4	1	0	6			.211	.250
Doggie Miller	OF49,C36,3B3,2B1		89	347	46	78		10	2	0	13			.225	.265
Bill Colgan	C44,OF4		48	161	10	25		4	1	0	3			.155	.193
Fleury Sullivan	P51,OF3		54	189	14	29		2	1	0	5			.153	.175
John Neagle	P38,OF6		43	148	13	22		6	0	0	6			.149	.189
Jim McDonald	3B22,OF15,2B1	(1-2)	38	145	11	23		3	0	0	2			.159	.179
Tom Forster	SS28,3B6,2B1		35	126	10	28		5	0	0	7			.222	.262
Jack Hayes	C24,1B5,OF3,2B1	(1-2)	33	124	11	28		6	1	0	4			.226	.290
Charles Eden	OF31,P2		32	122	12	33		7	4	1	7			.270	.418
Jay Faatz	1B29		29	112	18	27		2	3	0	1			.241	.313
Mike Mansell	OF27	(1-3)	27	100	15	14		0	3	1	7			.140	.230
Art Whitney	3B21,OF1,SS1		23	94	10	28		4	0	0	1			.298	.340
William Reid	OF17,1B1,2B1,3B1		19	70	11	17		2	0	0	4			.243	.271
Conny Doyle	OF14,SS1		15	58	8	17		3	2	0	2			.293	.414
Jim Woulfe	OF15	(2-2)	15	53	7	6		1	0	0	0			.113	.132
Chuck Lauer	OF10,P3,1B1		13	44	5	5		0	0	0	0			.114	.114
Joe Quest	2B6,SS5	(2-2)	12	43	2	9		3	0	0	0			.209	.279
Jim Dee	SS12		12	40	0	5		0	0	0	1			.125	.125
Bob Ferguson	OF6,1B3,3B1		10	41	2	6		0	0	0	0			.146	.146
Frank Smith	C7,OF3		10	36	3	9		0	1	0	0			.250	.306
John Gorman	P3,OF3,3B2	(2-2)	8	27	3	4		0	1	0	1			.148	.222
John Fox	P7,SS1		8	25	4	6		2	0	0	0			.240	.320
Charles Hautz	1B5,OF2		5	24	0	5		0	0	0	3			.208	.208
Frank Beck	P3	(1-2)	3	12	1	4		1	0	0	0			.333	.417
Bill Nelson	P3		3	12	1	2		0	0	0	0			.167	.167
Gus Alberts	SS2	(1-2)	2	5	1	1		0	0	0	0			.200	.200
John Peters	SS1		1	4	0	0		0	0	0	0			.000	.000
Phenomenal Smith	P1	(3-3)	1	4	0	0		0	0	0	0			.000	.000
Jim Gray	3B1		1	2	0	1		0	0	0	0			.500	.500
			110	3689	406	777		105	50	2	143	411		.211	.268

PITCHERS		W	L	PCT	G	GS	CG	SH	SV	IP	H	BB	SO	ERA
Fleury Sullivan		16	35	.314	51	51	51	2	0	441	496	96	189	4.20
John Neagle		11	26	.297	38	38	37	2	0	326	354	70	85	3.73
Bill Nelson		1	2	.333	3	3	3	0	0	26	26	8	6	4.50
John Gorman		1	2	.333	3	3	3	0	0	25	22	5	10	4.68
John Fox		1	6	.143	7	7	7	0	0	59	76	16	22	5.64
Charles Eden		0	1	.000	2	1	1	0	0	12	12	3	3	6.00
Phenomenal Smith	(3-3)	0	1	.000	1	1	1	0	0	8	11	2	4	9.00
Chuck Lauer		0	2	.000	3	3	2	0	0	19	23	9	8	7.58
Frank Beck	(1-2)	0	3	.000	3	3	3	0	0	25	33	6	11	6.12
Ed Swartwood		0	0	----	1	0	0	0	0	2	6	1	0	11.57
		30	78	.278	110	110	108	4	0	943	1059	216	338	4.35

INDIANAPOLIS
Hoosiers

29-78 .271 -46 12th Gifford - Watkins

BATTERS	POS/GAMES		GP	AB	R	H	BI	2B	3B	HR	BB	SO	SB	BA	SA
John Kerins	1B87,C5,OF4,3B1		94	364	58	78		10	3	6	6			.214	.308
Ed Merrill	2B55		55	196	14	35		3	1	0	6			.179	.204
Marr Phillips	SS97		97	413	41	111		18	8	0	5			.269	.351
Pat Callahan	3B61		61	258	38	67		8	5	2	8			.260	.353
Podgie Weihe	OF58,2B4,1B3		63	256	29	65		13	2	4	9			.254	.367
John Morrison	OF44		44	182	26	48		6	8	1	7			.264	.401

INDIANAPOLIS (cont.)
Hoosiers

BATTERS	POS/GAMES		GP	AB	R	H	BI	2B	3B	HR	BB	SO	SB	BA	SA
John Peltz	OF106		106	393	40	86		13	17	3	7			.219	.361
Jim Keenan	C59,1B6,OF2,P1		68	249	36	73		14	4	3	16			.293	.418
Larry McKeon	P61,1B5,2B3,OF1		69	250	29	53		8	1	0	1			.212	.252
Jim Donnelly	3B24,SS8,OF6,2B2	(2-2)	40	134	22	34		2	2	0	5			.254	.299
Chub Collins	2B38	(2-2)	38	138	18	31		3	1	0	9			.225	.261
Jerry Dorgan	OF29,C5	(1-2)	34	141	22	42		6	1	0	2			.298	.355
Bill Watkins	3B23,2B9,SS2		34	127	16	26		4	0	0	5			.205	.236
John Sneed	OF27		27	102	14	22		4	0	1	6			.216	.284
Tug Thompson	OF12,C12		24	97	10	20		3	0	0	2			.206	.237
Charlie Robinson	C17,SS3,OF1		20	80	11	23		2	0	0	3			.288	.313
Bob Barr	P16,1B2	(2-2)	18	65	6	12		3	2	0	3			.185	.292
Allen McCauley	P10,1B5,OF3		17	53	7	10		0	1	0	12			.189	.226
Jake Aydelotte	P12,OF1		12	44	1	5		1	0	0	2			.114	.136
Gene Moriarity	OF7,P2,3B1	(2-2)	10	37	4	8		0	2	0	0			.216	.324
Bill Butler	OF9		9	31	7	7		3	2	0	1			.226	.452
Marsh Locke	OF7		7	29	5	7		0	1	0	0			.241	.310
Tommy Bond	P5,OF2	(2-2)	7	23	0	3		1	1	0	0			.130	.261
Jim Tray	C4,1B2		6	21	2	6		0	0	0	2			.286	.286
Mal MacArthur	P6		6	21	1	2		0	0	0	1			.095	.095
Bob Blakiston	1B5,OF1	(2-2)	6	18	0	4		1	0	0	1			.222	.278
Jim Holdsworth	OF5		5	18	1	2		0	0	0	2			.111	.111
Frank Bahret	C4,OF1	(1-2)	5	13	1	1		1	0	0	1			.077	.154
Harry Decker	C4	(1-2)	4	15	1	4		1	0	0	1			.267	.333
Charles Levis	1B3	(3-3)	3	10	0	2		0	0	0	0			.200	.200
George Mundinger	C3		3	8	1	2		0	0	0	0			.250	.250
Harry Weber	C3		3	8	0	0		0	0	0	0			.000	.000
Charlie Reising	OF2		2	8	0	0		0	0	0	1			.000	.000
Frank Monroe	OF1,C1		2	8	1	0		0	0	0	0			.000	.000
Peter Fries	OF1		1	3	0	1		1	0	0	1			.333	.667
			110	3813	462	890		129	62	20	125	560		.233	.315

PITCHERS			W	L	PCT	G	GS	CG	SH	SV	IP	H	BB	SO	ERA
Larry McKeon			18	41	.305	61	60	59	2	0	512	488	94	308	3.50
Jake Aydelotte			5	7	.417	12	12	11	0	0	106	129	29	30	4.92
Bob Barr		(2-2)	3	11	.214	16	16	15	0	0	132	160	19	69	4.98
Allen McCauley			2	7	.222	10	9	9	0	0	76	87	25	34	5.09
Mal MacArthur			1	5	.167	6	6	6	0	0	52	57	21	19	5.02
Gene Moriarity			0	2	.000	2	2	2	0	0	14	16	7	4	5.27
Tommy Bond		(2-2)	0	5	.000	5	5	5	0	0	43	62	4	15	5.65
Jim Keenan			0	0	----	1	0	0	0	0	3	2	0	0	3.00
			29	78	.271	110	110	107	2	0	938	1001	199	479	4.20

WASHINGTON
Nationals

12-51   .190   -41   13th   Hollingshead - Bickerson

BATTERS	POS/GAMES		GP	AB	R	H	BI	2B	3B	HR	BB	SO	SB	BA	SA
Walt Prince	1B43	(2-3)	43	166	22	36		3	2	1	13			.217	.277
Thorny Hawkes	2B38,OF2		38	151	16	42		4	2	0	4			.278	.331
Frank Fennelly	SS60,2B4	(1-2)	62	257	52	75		17	7	2	20			.292	.436
Buck Gladman	3B53,OF2,SS1		56	224	17	35		5	3	1	3			.156	.219
Bill Morgan	OF31,2B14,SS2		45	162	8	28		1	1	0	8			.173	.191
Henry Mullin	OF34,3B1	(1-2)	34	120	13	17		3	1	0	8			.142	.183
Ed Trumbull	OF15,P10		25	86	5	10		2	0	0	2			.116	.140
John Humphries	C35,OF12,1B4	(1-2)	49	193	23	34		2	0	0	9			.176	.187
Bob Barr	P32,OF7	(1-2)	39	135	15	20		3	1	2	5			.148	.185
Ed Yewell	2B11,3B7,OF7,SS2	(1-2)	27	93	14	23		3	1	0	1			.247	.301
John Hanna	C18,OF2	(1-2)	23	76	8	5		0	0	0	6			.066	.066
Frank Olin	2B12,OF11	(1-3)	21	83	12	32		4	1	0	8			.386	.458
John Hamill	P19,OF3		21	71	5	7		0	2	0	6			.099	.155
Edgar Smith	OF12,P3		14	57	5	5		0	1	0	1			.088	.123
John Kiley	OF14		14	56	9	12		2	2	0	3			.214	.321
Tom Farley	OF14		14	52	5	11		4	0	0	1			.212	.288
Sam King	1B12		12	45	3	8		2	0	0	1			.178	.222
Jack Beach	OF8		8	31	3	3		2	0	0	0			.097	.161
Walt Goldsby	OF6	(2-3)	6	24	4	9		0	0	0	1			.375	.375
Willie Murphy	OF4,2B1	(2-2)	5	21	3	10		0	0	0	1			.476	.476
Andy Swan	1B3,3B2	(1-2)	5	21	3	3		1	0	0	0			.143	.190
----- Jones	OF4		4	17	2	5		0	0	0	1			.294	.294
----- Wills	OF4	(1-2)	4	15	1	2		2	0	0	0			.133	.267

WASHINGTON (cont.)
Nationals

BATTERS	POS/GAMES		GP	AB	R	H	BI	2B	3B	HR	BB	SO	SB	BA	SA
Lyman Drake	OF2		2	7	0	2		1	0	0	0			.286	.429
Alex Gardner	C1		1	3	0	0		0	0	0	0			.000	.000
			63	2166	248	434		61	24	6	102	377		.200	.259

PITCHERS			W	L	PCT	G	GS	CG	SH	SV	IP	H	BB	SO	ERA
Bob Barr		(1-2)	9	23	.281	32	32	32	2	0	281	311	31	138	3.46
John Hamill			2	17	.105	19	19	18	1	0	157	197	43	50	4.48
Ed Trumbull			1	9	.100	10	10	10	0	0	84	108	31	43	4.71
Edgar Smith			0	2	.000	3	2	2	0	0	22	27	5	4	4.91
			12	51	.190	63	63	62	3	0	544	643	110	235	4.01

1884 UNION ASSOCIATION

One Man's Dream

Wealthy St. Louis businessman, Henry V. Lucas, was by all accounts an avid baseball fan—so much so, that he had a baseball field built at his country estate "Normandy" on which he and his guests played. His dream was to place a National League team in St. Louis—a formidable task considering the presence of the popular St. Louis Browns of the American Association. To accomplish this goal, Lucas turned toward the fledgling Union Association.

The Union Association was formed in Pittsburgh in September 1883 by promoter James Jackson. Its stated objective was to be a league in direct competition with organized baseball. At first glance, the Union constitution appeared to be a near copy of the existing Major League constitutions. There was, however, one glaring exception. The Union publicly stated that they would not honor the reserve clause, the veritable cornerstone of professional baseball. This difference alone would place the Union at loggerheads with the established leagues.

Several strong financial backers were found to bankroll the Union. The biggest financial mentor proved to be Henry Lucas himself who would sponsor and manage the St. Louis club. Shortly, Lucas would come to dominate the whole league, becoming its president and most outspoken promoter. To flesh out the league, teams were formed in Washington, Philadelphia, Boston, Baltimore, Chicago, Altoona, and Cincinnati—making a total of eight. All but Altoona would face major league competition in their own cities.

The Union went after any and all ball players. With no allegiance to the reserve clause, no qualms were felt in approaching already reserved ball players and luring them away with enticing contracts. In all, about 30 players from the major leagues ended up on Union rosters. The clubs were then filled out by using minor leaguers and amateurs.

Lucas's St. Louis Maroons looked to be a strong club with several experienced major leaguers, including Fred Dunlap and Orator Shaffer, on the roster. They quickly lived up to expectations by reeling off 20 wins in a row to start the season. St. Louis continued to win games at a rate never before seen. On June 1, the Maroons were 22-1; by July 6 they 41-6; by August 24 they were 59-9; and by September 14 they were 73-10. At no point was any other team close to catching them.

While St. Louis was well stocked and financed, other teams were not. Altoona (consisting of mostly locals and amateurs) announced it was ceasing operations at the end of May. On June 7, a team from Kansas City was admitted in its place. As the summer progressed, more franchises folded. On August 7, the Keystone club of Philadelphia ceased operations. Shortly thereafter, the Wilmington club of the Eastern (minor) League jumped to the Union. After winning two of 18 games they went under on September 12. Much the same happened to the Chicago club; after transferring to Pittsburgh on August 25, eighteen games later, on September 18, they too folded. In late September, with all of the clubs traveling in the West, two new clubs were added from the Northwestern (minor) League. The schedule was revised, and play continued until October 19 with St. Paul and Milwaukee taking the places of Pittsburgh and Wilmington.

At season's close, St. Louis was the runaway winner finishing with a 94-19 record and a superb .832 win percentage, the second best of all time. Cincinnati, winners of 30 of their last 35 games, finished a distant 21 games out with a record of 69-36. Milwaukee, Baltimore, and Boston also won more than they lost. Kansas City finished on the bottom, managing only 16 wins in 79 games.

The juggernaut Maroons were indeed in a class by themselves. This was a team that averaged over eight runs a game and led the league in all major offensive categories but most triples. This was also a team that led the league in all major pitching (except most strikeouts) and fielding categories (among teams that played a full season). This was a direct result of outstanding individual performances, none better than Maroon second baseman Fred Dunlap whose .412 average and 13 home runs led the league. The pitching staff was also impressive. All five of the primary starters posted winning percentages over .774, and ERAs under 2.02. In all, a truly impressive amalgamation.

Other players, on other teams, also had fine years. Philadelphia's Buster Hoover finished second in the batting race at .364, while pitcher Jim McCormick of Cincinnati won the winning percentage and ERA titles (21-3, 1.54). Finally, it should be noted that Chicago pitcher One Arm Daily stunned Boston on July 7 by striking out 19 batters; a mark that would last more than a century.

However, as one can imagine, the overall legacy of the Union Association was red ink — a veritable sea. Only two of the teams (Kansas City and Washington) claimed to earn a profit, while Boston, Cincinnati, and Chicago all lost at least $5,000 each. Henry Lucas lost upwards of $100,000 of his own money, much of which was used to keep the league afloat.

Plans for a second year of the Union Association were well under way by December 1884. Both Milwaukee and Kansas City were especially eager for the new season to start. Players were signed and rosters filled when a disquieting rumor put a stop to all of the activity. Henry Lucas himself was negotiating for a National League franchise, while two other club owners were negotiating with the American Association. Without the financial support of Lucas, the Union could not continue. So in January 1885, they voted to disband.

On April 18, 1885, the St. Louis Maroons were admitted to the National League. Henry Lucas had his wish at last. Only the tattered remains of the Union Association and its players were testimony to the price he paid.

1884 UNION ASSOCIATION

ST. LOUIS Maroons — 94-19 .832 1st Henry Lucas

BATTERS	POS/GAMES		GP	AB	R	H	BI	2B	3B	HR	BB	SO	SB	BA	SA
Joe Quinn	1B100,OF3,SS1		103	429	74	116		21	1	0	9			.270	.324
Fred Dunlap	2B100,OF1,P1		101	449	160	185		39	8	13	29			.412	.621
Milt Whitehead	SS94,OF2,3B1,2B1,P1	(1-2)	99	393	61	83		15	1	1	8			.211	.262
Jack Gleason	3B92		92	395	90	128		30	2	4	23			.324	.441
Orator Shaffer	OF100,2B7,1B1		106	467	130	168		40	10	2	30			.360	.501
Dave Rowe	OF92,SS14,2B2,1B2,P1		109	485	95	142		32	11	4	10			.293	.429
Buttercup Dickerson	OF44,3B2	(1-2)	46	211	49	77		15	1	0	8			.365	.445
George Baker	C68,OF5,2B4,3B3,SS2		80	317	39	52		6	0	0	5			.164	.183
Henry Boyle	OF43,P19,3B4,2B1,SS1,1B1		65	262	41	68		10	3	4	9			.260	.366
James Brennan	C33,OF16,3B7,SS1		56	231	38	50		6	1	0	12			.216	.251
Charlie Sweeney	P33,OF12	(2-2)	45	171	31	54		14	2	1	10			.316	.439
Bill Taylor	P33,1B10,OF3	(1-2)	43	186	44	68		23	1	3	7			.366	.548
Tom Dolan	C15,3B3,OF2	(2-2)	19	69	9	13		3	0	0	4			.188	.232
Perry Werden	P16,OF6		18	76	7	18		2	0	0	2			.237	.263
Charles Hodnett	P14		14	58	9	12		1	0	0	10			.207	.224
Fred Lewis	OF8	(2-2)	8	30	6	9		1	0	0	3			.300	.333
Tom Ryder	OF8		8	28	4	7		1	0	0	2			.250	.286
Tom Sullivan	C1,OF1,P1		2	9	0	1		0	0	0	0			.111	.111
John Cattanach	P2	(2-2)	2	7	0	0		0	0	0	0			.000	.000
Dan Cronin	OF1	(2-2)	1	5	0	0		0	0	0	0			.000	.000
C.V. Matterson	P1		1	4	0	0		0	0	0	0			.000	.000
Ed Callahan	OF1	(1-2)	1	3	0	0		0	0	0	0			.000	.000
			114	4285	887	1251		259	41	32	181	542		.292	.393

PITCHERS		W	L	PCT	G	GS	CG	SH	SV	IP	H	BB	SO	ERA
Bill Taylor	(1-2)	25	4	.862	33	29	29	2	4	263	222	40	154	1.68
Charlie Sweeney	(2-2)	24	7	.774	33	32	31	2	0	271	207	13	192	1.83
Henry Boyle		15	3	.833	19	16	16	2	1	150	118	10	88	1.74
Perry Werden		12	1	.923	16	16	12	1	0	141	113	22	51	1.97
Charles Hodnett		12	2	.857	14	14	12	1	0	121	121	16	41	2.01
Dave Rowe		1	0	1.000	1	1	1	0	0	9	10	0	2	2.00
C.V. Matterson		1	0	1.000	1	1	0	0	0	6	9	3	3	9.00
Tom Sullivan		1	0	1.000	1	1	0	0	0	6	10	0	3	4.50
John Cattanach	(2-2)	1	1	.500	2	2	2	0	0	17	12	4	13	2.12
Milt Whitehead	(1-2)	0	1	.000	1	1	1	0	0	8	14	2	2	9.00
Fred Dunlap		0	1	.000	1	0	0	0	1	1	2	0	1	13.50
		94	19	.832	114	113	104	8	6	993	838	110	550	1.96

MILWAUKEE Cream Citys — 8-4 .667 -35.5 2nd Tom Loftus

BATTERS	POS/GAMES	GP	AB	R	H	BI	2B	3B	HR	BB	SO	SB	BA	SA
Thomas Griffin	1B11	11	41	5	9		2	0	0	3			.220	.268
Al Myers	2B12	12	46	6	15		6	0	0	0			.326	.457
Tom Sexton	SS12	12	47	9	11		2	0	0	4			.234	.277
Tom Morrissey	3B12	12	47	3	8		2	0	0	0			.170	.213
Eddie Hogan	OF11	11	37	6	3		1	0	0	7			.081	.108
Lady Baldwin	OF5,P2	7	27	6	6		3	0	0	0			.222	.333
Steve Behel	OF9	9	33	5	8		1	0	0	3			.242	.273
Cecil Broughton	C7,OF5	11	39	5	12		5	0	0	0			.308	.436
Henry Porter	P6,OF3,1B1	10	40	3	11		3	0	0	0			.275	.350
Anton Falch	OF3,C2	5	18	0	2		0	0	0	0			.111	.111
Ed Cushman	P4	4	11	1	1		0	0	0	2			.091	.091
George Bignal	C4	4	9	4	2		0	0	0	1			.222	.222
		12	395	53	88		25	0	0	20	70		.223	.286

PITCHERS	W	L	PCT	G	GS	CG	SH	SV	IP	H	BB	SO	ERA
Ed Cushman	4	0	1.000	4	4	4	2	0	36	10	3	47	1.00
Henry Porter	3	3	.500	6	6	6	1	0	51	32	9	71	3.00
Lady Baldwin	1	1	.500	2	2	2	0	0	17	7	1	21	2.65
	8	4	.667	12	12	12	3	0	104	49	13	139	2.25

1884 UNION ASSOCIATION

CINCINNATI Outlaw Reds — 69-36 .657 -21 3rd O'Leary - Crane

BATTERS	POS/GAMES		GP	AB	R	H	BI	2B	3B	HR	BB	SO	SB	BA	SA
Martin Powell	1B43		43	185	46	59		4	2	1	13			.319	.378
Sam Crane	2B80		80	309	56	72		9	3	1	11			.233	.291
Jack Jones	SS41,2B19,3B10		69	272	36	71		5	1	2	12			.261	.309
Charlie Barber	3B55		55	204	38	41		1	4	0	11			.201	.245
Bill Hawes	OF58,1B21		79	349	80	97		7	4	4	5			.278	.355
Bill Harbridge	OF80,SS3,1B2		82	341	59	95		12	5	2	25			.279	.361
Lou Sylvester	OF81,P6,SS2		82	333	67	89		13	8	2	18			.267	.372
John Kelly	C38,OF1	(1-2)	38	142	23	40		5	1	1	6			.282	.352
Dick Burns	OF44,P40,SS2		79	350	84	107		17	12	4	5			.306	.457
George Bradley	P41,OF16,SS5,1B2		58	226	31	43		4	7	0	7			.190	.270
Jack Glasscock	SS37,2B1	(2-2)	38	172	48	72		9	5	2	8			.419	.564
Mox McQuery	1B35		35	132	31	37		5	0	2	8			.280	.364
Dan O'Leary	OF32		32	132	14	34		0	2	1	5			.258	.311
Elmer Cleveland	3B29		29	115	24	37		9	1	1	4			.322	.443
Pop Schwartz	C25,OF3,3B1		29	106	14	25		4	0	1	3			.236	.302
Jim McCormick	P24,OF3	(2-2)	27	110	12	27		3	1	0	0			.245	.292
Fatty Briody	C22	(2-2)	22	89	11	30		2	2	0	1			.337	.404
Joe Crotty	C21		21	84	11	22		4	2	1	1			.262	.393
Frank McLaughlin	SS16	(1-2)	16	67	10	16		4	1	2	2			.239	.418
Charles Kennedy	3B8,SS4,OF1		13	48	6	10		1	1	0	1			.208	.271
Fred Robinson	2B3		3	13	1	3		0	0	0	0			.231	.231
Lewis Myers	C2,OF1		2	3	1	0		0	0	0	1			.000	.000
John Ewing	OF1		1	4	0	0		0	0	0	0			.000	.000
			105	3786	703	1027		118	62	27	147	482		.271	.357

PITCHERS		W	L	PCT	G	GS	CG	SH	SV	IP	H	BB	SO	ERA
George Bradley		25	15	.625	41	38	36	3	0	342	350	23	168	2.71
Dick Burns		23	15	.605	40	40	34	1	0	330	298	47	167	2.45
Jim McCormick	(2-2)	21	3	.875	24	24	24	7	0	210	151	14	161	1.54
Lou Sylvester		0	1	.000	6	1	1	0	1	33	32	6	7	3.55
		69	36	.657	105	103	95	11	1	915	831	90	503	2.38

BALTIMORE Monumentals — 58-47 .552 -32 4th Levis - Henderson

BATTERS	POS/GAMES		GP	AB	R	H	BI	2B	3B	HR	BB	SO	SB	BA	SA
Charles Levis	1B87	(1-3)	87	373	59	85		11	4	6	3			.228	.327
James Phelan	2B100,3B5,OF1		101	402	63	99		13	3	3	12			.246	.316
Louis Say	SS78	(1-2)	78	339	65	81		14	2	2	11			.239	.310
Yank Robinson	3B71,SS14,C11,P11,2B3		102	415	101	111		24	4	2	37			.267	.359
Bernard Graham	OF41,1B1	(2-2)	42	167	21	45		11	0	0	2			.269	.335
Ned Cuthbert	OF44		44	168	29	34		5	0	0	10			.202	.232
Emmett Seery	OF105,C3,3B1	(1-2)	105	463	113	144		25	7	2	20			.311	.408
Ed Fusselback	C54,3B6,SS5,OF4		68	303	60	86		16	3	1	3			.284	.366
Bill Sweeney	P62,OF11,2B6,SS1,1B1		74	296	35	71		7	0	0	9			.240	.264
Rooney Sweeney	C33,OF16,3B1		48	186	37	42		7	1	0	15			.226	.274
Henry Oberbeck	OF27,3B9,P1	(1-2)	33	125	19	23		4	0	0	3			.184	.216
Tom Lee	P15,OF6,3B2,SS1	(2-2)	21	82	11	23		1	0	0	5			.280	.293
John O'Brien	OF18		18	77	7	19		1	1	0	2			.247	.286
Harry Wheeler	OF17	(5-5)	17	69	3	18		2	0	0	0			.261	.290
Joe Battin	3B17	(2-2)	17	59	3	6		1	0	0	0			.102	.119
Jumbo Schoeneck	1B16	(3-3)	16	60	5	15		2	0	0	0			.250	.283
----- Scott	OF13,3B1		13	53	10	12		1	1	1	2			.226	.340
Phenomenal Smith	P9,OF2	(3-3)	9	35	3	5		0	0	0	2			.143	.143
Albert Atkinson	P8	(4-4)	8	29	3	4		1	0	0	1			.138	.172
Joe Ellick	SS6,OF1		7	27	2	4		0	0	0	2			.148	.148
John Ryan	P6,OF1		6	25	2	2		0	0	0	2			.080	.080
Joe Stanley	OF6		6	21	3	5		1	0	0	0			.238	.286
Frank Beck	OF4,P2	(2-2)	5	20	1	2		1	0	0	0			.100	.150
Claude McFarland	OF3,P1		3	14	2	3		1	0	0	0			.214	.286
Frank Shaffer	OF3	(3-3)	3	13	1	1		0	0	0	0			.077	.077
John Cuff	C3		3	11	1	1		1	0	0	1			.091	.182
Tony Suck	C3	(3-3)	3	10	2	3		0	0	0	0			.300	.300
Bill Morgan	C1,OF1,2B1	(2-2)	2	9	1	2		0	0	0	1			.222	.222
Frank Bahret	OF2		2	8	0	0		0	0	0	0			.000	.000
Jeremiah Dorsey	OF2,P1		2	3	0	0		0	0	0	0			.000	.000
----- Smith	P1		1	4	0	1		0	0	0	0			.250	.250
Pat Burns	1B1		1	4	0	2		0	0	0	0			.500	.500
Gid Gardner	SS1	(4-4)	1	4	0	1		0	0	0	0			.250	.250
William Tierney	OF1		1	3	0	1		0	0	0	1			.333	.333

BALTIMORE (cont.)
Monumentals

BATTERS	POS/GAMES		GP	AB	R	H	BI	2B	3B	HR	BB	SO	SB	BA	SA
Al Skinner	OF1		1	3	0	1		0	0	0	0			.333	.333
E. Morris	OF1,P1		1	3	0	0		0	0	0	0			.000	.000
			106	3883	662	952		150	26	17	144	652		.245	.310

PITCHERS			W	L	PCT	G	GS	CG	SH	SV	IP	H	BB	SO	ERA
Bill Sweeney			40	21	.656	62	60	58	4	0	538	522	74	374	2.59
Tom Lee			5	8	.385	15	14	12	0	0	122	121	29	81	3.39
John Ryan			3	2	.600	6	6	5	0	0	51	61	16	33	3.35
Yank Robinson			3	3	.500	11	3	3	0	0	75	96	18	61	3.48
Phenomenal Smith		(1-3)	3	3	.500	9	8	4	0	0	59	83	16	10	3.35
Al Atkinson		(4-4)	3	5	.375	8	8	8	0	0	70	60	12	50	2.33
----- Smith			0	1	.000	1	1	1	0	0	9	15	3	5	1.00
Jeremiah Dorsey			0	1	.000	1	1	0	0	0	4	7	0	3	9.00
Claude McFarland			0	1	.000	1	1	0	0	0	3	9	1	3	15.00
Frank Beck		(2-2)	0	2	.000	2	2	1	0	0	9	17	4	7	8.00
Henry Oberbeck		(2-2)	0	0	----	2	1	0	0	0	6	9	2	1	3.00
E. Morris			0	0	----	1	0	0	0	0	1	2	2	0	9.00
			58	47	.552	106	105	92	4	0	946	1002	177	628	3.20

BOSTON
Reds

58-51   .532   -34   5th   Murnane - Furniss Morse

BATTERS	POS/GAMES		GP	AB	R	H	BI	2B	3B	HR	BB	SO	SB	BA	SA
Tim Murnane	1B63,OF16		76	311	55	73		5	2	0	22			.235	.264
Tom O'Brien	2B99,OF3,1B2,C1		103	449	80	118		31	8	4	12			.263	.394
Walter Hackett	SS103		103	415	71	101		19	0	1	7			.243	.296
John Irwin	3B105		105	432	81	101		22	6	1	15			.234	.319
Cannonball Crane	OF57,C42,1B5,P4		101	428	83	122		23	6	12	14			.285	.451
Mike Slattery	OF96,1B11		106	413	60	86		6	2	0	4			.208	.232
Frank Butler	OF53,2B12,SS6,3B2		71	255	36	43		15	0	0	12			.169	.227
Lewis Brown	C54,1B33,OF2,P1		85	325	50	75		18	3	1	13			.231	.314
Tommy McCarthy	OF48,P7		53	209	37	45		2	2	0	6			.215	.249
Walter Burke	P38,OF13		45	184	21	41		8	3	0	6			.223	.299
Dupee Shaw	P39,OF9	(2-2)	44	153	13	37		8	0	0	5			.242	.353
Tommy Bond	P23,OF13,3B1	(1-2)	37	162	21	48		8	0	0	4			.296	.346
Jim McKeever	C12,OF4		16	66	13	9		0	0	0	0			.136	.136
Joe Flynn	C6,OF3	(2-2)	9	31	4	7		2	0	0	2			.226	.290
John Scannell	OF6		6	24	2	7		1	0	0	0			.292	.333
Fred Tenney	P4	(2-3)	4	17	1	2		0	0	0	0			.118	.118
Ed Callahan	OF4	(3-3)	4	13	2	5		0	0	0	1			.385	.385
Charlie Daniels	P2,OF1		3	11	1	3		0	0	0	2			.273	.273
Joe Reilly	OF2,2B1		3	11	1	0		0	0	0	1			.000	.000
Henry Mullin	OF2	(2-2)	2	8	1	0		0	0	0	0			.000	.000
Art Sladen	OF2		2	7	0	0		0	0	0	0			.000	.000
Clarence Dow	OF1		1	6	1	2		0	0	0	0			.333	.333
John Rudderham	OF1		1	4	0	1		0	0	0	0			.250	.250
Elias Peak	OF1	(1-2)	1	3	2	2		0	0	0	1			.667	.667
----- Murphy	OF1,C1		1	3	0	0		0	0	0	1			.000	.000
			109	3940	636	928		168	32	19	128	787		.236	.309

PITCHERS			W	L	PCT	G	GS	CG	SH	SV	IP	H	BB	SO	ERA
Dupee Shaw		(2-2)	21	15	.583	39	38	35	5	0	316	227	37	309	1.77
Walter Burke			19	15	.559	38	36	34	0	0	322	326	31	255	2.85
Tommy Bond		(1-2)	13	9	.591	23	21	19	0	0	189	185	14	128	3.00
Fred Tenney		(1-3)	3	1	.750	4	4	4	0	0	35	31	5	18	2.31
Cannonball Crane			0	2	.000	4	2	1	0	0	18	17	6	13	4.00
Charlie Daniels			0	2	.000	2	2	2	0	0	17	20	2	12	4.24
Tommy McCarthy			0	7	.000	7	6	5	0	0	56	73	14	18	4.82
Lewis Brown			0	0	----	1	0	0	0	1	1	6	1	0	36.00
			58	51	.532	109	109	100	5	1	954	885	110	753	2.70

1884 UNION ASSOCIATION

CHICAGO Browns   34-39   .465   -40   6th   Edward Hengle

BATTERS	POS/GAMES		GP	AB	R	H	BI	2B	3B	HR	BB	SO	SB	BA	SA
Jumbo Schoeneck	1B72	(1-3)	72	289	47	94		19	2	2	7			.325	.426
Emery Hengle	2B19	(1-2)	19	74	9	15		2	1	0	3			.203	.257
Steve Matthias	SS36,OF2		37	142	24	39		7	1	0	5			.275	.338
Charles Householder	3B41,OF23,SS3,P2	(1-2)	66	244	28	57		8	3	1	11			.233	.303
Joe Ellick	OF57,SS15,2B4	(1-4)	74	314	58	80		8	0	0	13			.254	.280
Charlie Briggs	OF37,2B12,SS2		49	182	29	31		8	2	1	11			.170	.253
Harry Wheeler	OF20	(3-5)	20	85	14	19		4	2	1	0			.223	.353
Bill Krieg	C43,OF19,SS1,1B1	(1-2)	61	240	27	55		10	3	0	10			.229	.296
One Arm Daily	P46,2B2,OF2,SS1	(1-3)	46	160	19	39		5	0	0	8			.244	.275
Tony Suck	C18,SS15,OF12,3B1	(1-3)	43	153	15	22		2	0	0	12			.144	.157
Emil Gross	C15,OF8		23	95	13	34		6	2	4	6			.358	.589
Gid Gardner	OF14,3B8,P1	(2-4)	22	85	14	21		7	0	0	5			.247	.329
John Horan	P13,OF10		20	68	3	6		0	0	0	1			.088	.088
Will Foley	3B19		19	71	15	20		1	1	0	5			.282	.324
Chippy McGarr	2B13,OF6		19	70	10	11		2	0	0	0			.157	.186
Frank McLaughlin	2B14,OF1,SS1	(2-2)	15	67	11	16		4	1	0	1			.239	.328
Charlie Baker	OF8,SS3,2B1	(1-2)	12	45	5	7		1	0	1	0			.155	.244
Jack Leary	2B4,OF3,3B2,P2,2B1	(2-2)	10	40	0	7		1	0	0	0			.175	.200
Al Atkinson	P8,OF2	(2-4)	10	35	3	10		0	0	0	0			.286	.286
Charles Cady	P4,OF2	(2-2)	6	20	4	2		1	1	0	1			.100	.250
Charlie Berry	2B5	(3-4)	5	17	3	2		2	0	0	0			.117	.235
Frank Bishop	3B3,SS1		4	16	1	3		1	0	0	0			.188	.250
Frank Foreman	P3,OF1	(1-2)	3	11	0	1		0	0	0	0			.091	.091
Frank Wyman	1B2	(2-2)	2	8	1	3		0	0	0	0			.375	.375
Phillip Corridan	2B2,OF1		2	7	1	1		0	0	0	0			.143	.143
Bernard Graham	OF1	(1-2)	1	5	2	1		0	0	0	0			.200	.200
Daniel Cronin	2B1	(1-2)	1	4	1	1		0	0	0	1			.250	.250
Cyclone Miller	P1	(1-2)	1	4	1	1		0	0	0	0			.250	.250
Art Richardson	2B1		1	4	0	0		0	0	0	0			.000	.000
Charles Fisher	3B1	(2-2)	1	3	1	2		0	0	0	1			.667	.667
Al Skinner	SS1	(2-2)	1	3	1	1		0	0	0	0			.333	.333
Harry Koons	3B1	(2-2)	1	3	0	0		0	0	0	0			.000	.000
			74	2564	360	601		99	19	10	101			.234	.300

PITCHERS			W	L	PCT	G	GS	CG	SH	SV	IP	H	BB	SO	ERA
One Arm Daily		(1-3)	22	23	.485	46	46	44	3	0	397	353	58	403	2.43
Al Atkinson		(2-4)	4	4	.500	8	8	8	1	0	71	65	8	51	2.66
Charles Cady		(2-2)	3	1	.750	4	4	4	0	0	35	37	13	15	2.83
John Horan			3	6	.333	13	10	9	0	0	98	94	24	55	3.49
Cyclone Miller		(1-2)	1	0	1.000	1	1	1	0	0	9	4	0	13	1.00
Frank Foreman		(1-2)	1	2	.333	3	3	1	0	0	18	23	2	10	4.00
Gid Gardner		(2-4)	0	1	.000	1	1	0	0	0	6	10	1	4	6.00
Jack Leary		(2-2)	0	2	.000	2	1	1	0	0	10	14	5	6	5.40
Charles Householder			0	0	----	2	0	0	0	0	3	4	0	3	3.00
			34	39	.465	74	74	68	4	0	647	604	111	560	2.74

WASHINGTON Nationals   47-65   .420   -46.5   7th   Michael Scanlon

BATTERS	POS/GAMES		GP	AB	R	H	BI	2B	3B	HR	BB	SO	SB	BA	SA
Phil Baker	1B39,OF32,C27		86	371	75	107		12	5	1	11			.288	.356
Tom Evers	2B109		109	427	54	99		6	1	0	7			.232	.251
Jim Halpin	SS39,3B7		46	168	24	31		3	0	0	2			.185	.202
Jerry McCormick	3B38,SS4	(2-2)	42	157	23	34		8	2	0	1			.217	.293
Bill Wise	OF43,P50,3B8,SS2,1B1		85	339	51	79		17	1	2	12			.233	.307
Abner Powell	OF30,P18,3B2,SS1,2B1		48	191	36	54		10	5	0	3			.283	.387
Harry Moore	OF105,SS8		111	461	77	155		23	5	1	19			.336	.414
Chris Fulmer	C34,OF16,1B5		48	181	39	50		9	0	0	11			.276	.326
Alex Voss	P26,3B16,1B15,OF13,SS1	(1-2)	63	245	33	47		9	0	0	5			.192	.229
Joe Gunson	C33,OF18		45	166	15	23		2	0	0	3			.139	.151
Charlie Gagus	P23,OF21,SS3		42	154	14	38		7	1	0	4			.247	.305
Pop Joy	1B36		36	130	12	28		0	0	0	2			.215	.215
Fred Tenney	OF27,1B5	(1-3)	32	119	17	28		3	1	0	6			.235	.277
Ed McKenna	C23,OF10,3B7		32	117	19	22		1	0	0	4			.188	.197
Jim Deasley	SS31	(1-2)	31	134	20	29		1	1	0	3			.216	.239
Milo Lockwood	P11,OF11,3B3		20	67	9	14		1	0	0	8			.209	.224
Terry Larkin	3B17	(1-2)	17	70	11	17		0	0	0	4			.243	.243
Bill Hughes	1B9,OF6		14	49	5	6		0	0	0	2			.122	.122
David Drew	SS9,1B5,OF1	(2-2)	13	53	8	16		1	2	0	1			.302	.396
Jim McLaughlin	SS9,3B1		10	37	3	7		3	0	0	0			.189	.270

1884 UNION ASSOCIATION

WASHINGTON (cont.)
Nationals

BATTERS	POS/GAMES		GP	AB	R	H	BI	2B	3B	HR	BB	SO	SB	BA	SA
Jim Green	3B9,OF1		10	36	4	5		1	0	0	0			.139	.167
Marty Creegan	OF6,C3,3B2,1B1		9	33	4	5		0	0	0	1			.152	.152
John Ryan	OF7,3B1	(1-2)	7	28	2	4		0	1	0	1			.143	.214
William White	SS2,3B1,2B1		4	18	2	1		0	0	0	0			.056	.056
August Alberts	SS4	(2-2)	4	16	4	4		0	0	0	4			.250	.250
Chick Carroll	OF4		4	16	1	4		0	0	0	0			.250	.250
John Kelly	C3,OF1	(2-2)	4	14	1	5		1	0	0	0			.357	.429
----- McKee	OF2,3B2		3	13	2	3		0	0	0	1			.231	.231
Mike Lehane	SS3,OF1,3B1		3	12	1	4		2	0	0	0			.333	.500
Icicle Reeder	OF3		3	12	0	2		0	0	0	0			.167	.167
Maury Pierce	3B2		2	7	0	1		0	0	0	0			.143	.143
Mike Lawlor	C2		2	7	0	0		0	0	0	0			.000	.000
Jim McDonald	C1,OF1	(1-1)	2	6	0	1		0	0	0	0			.167	.167
One Arm Daily	P2	(3-3)	2	5	0	0		0	0	0	1			.000	.000
John Ewing	OF1	(2-2)	1	5	1	1		0	1	0	0			.200	.600
Charlie Kalbfuss	OF1		1	5	1	1		0	0	0	0			.200	.200
John Shoupe	OF1		1	4	1	3		0	0	0	0			.750	.750
John Ward	OF1		1	4	0	1		0	0	0	0			.250	.250
Walt Prince	1B1		1	4	0	1		0	0	0	0			.250	.250
----- Mulligan	3B1		1	4	2	1		0	0	0	0			.250	.250
----- Wiley	3B1		1	4	0	0		0	0	0	0			.000	.000
Ed Yewell	3B1	(2-2)	1	4	0	0		0	0	0	0			.000	.000
F. McGee	3B1,C1		1	4	0	0		0	0	0	0			.000	.000
Emory Nusz	OF1		1	4	1	0		0	0	0	0			.000	.000
Frank Olin	OF1	(2-2)	1	4	0	0		0	0	0	0			.000	.000
Nick Bradley	OF1		1	3	0	0		0	0	0	2			.000	.000
----- Franklin	OF1		1	3	0	0		0	0	0	0			.000	.000
Charles Levis	1B1	(2-3)	1	3	0	0		0	0	0	0			.000	.000
Art Thompson	P1		1	3	0	0		0	0	0	0			.000	.000
P. Morris	SS1		1	3	0	0		0	0	0	0			.000	.000
----- McRemer	OF1		1	3	0	0		0	0	0	0			.000	.000
----- Rollinson	C1		1	3	0	0		0	0	0	0			.000	.000
			114	3926	572	931		120	26	4	118	558		.237	.284

PITCHERS		W	L	PCT	G	GS	CG	SH	SV	IP	H	BB	SO	ERA
Bill Wise		23	18	.561	50	41	34	4	0	364	383	60	268	3.04
Charlie Gagus		10	9	.526	23	21	19	0	0	177	143	38	156	2.54
Abner Powell		6	12	.333	18	17	14	1	0	134	135	19	78	3.43
Alex Voss	(1-2)	5	14	.263	27	20	18	0	0	186	206	32	112	3.58
Milo Lockwood		1	9	.100	11	10	6	0	0	68	99	15	48	7.41
One Arm Daily	(3-3)	1	1	.500	2	2	2	0	0	16	16	1	14	2.25
Art Thompson		0	1	.000	1	1	1	0	0	8	10	3	8	6.75
		47	65	.420	114	112	94	5	0	953	992	168	684	3.43

PITTSBURGH
Stogies

7-11 .389 -39.5 8th Battin - Ellick

BATTERS	POS/GAMES		GP	AB	R	H	BI	2B	3B	HR	BB	SO	SB	BA	SA
Jumbo Schoeneck	1B18	(2-3)	18	77	9	22		3	0	0	1			.286	.325
George Strief	2B15	(3-4)	15	55	6	11		5	0	0	3			.200	.002
Joe Ellick	SS18	(2-4)	18	80	13	13		3	0	0	3			.163	.200
Joe Battin	3B18	(2-2)	17	69	8	13		2	0	0	0			.188	.217
Gid Gardner	OF15,2B1	(3-4)	16	64	8	17		3	2	0	5			.266	.375
Harry Wheeler	OF17	(4-5)	17	73	15	17		1	1	0	4			.233	.274
Charles Householder	OF17	(2-2)	17	66	4	17		4	2	0	1			.258	.379
Tony Suck	C10	(2-3)	10	35	3	6		0	0	0	1			.171	.171
Bill Krieg	C9,OF1	(2-2)	10	39	8	14		5	1	0	1			.359	.538
One Arm Daily	P10	(2-3)	10	36	2	4		1	1	0	0			.111	.194
Al Atkinson	P8,OF1	(3-4)	9	33	1	4		0	0	0	0			.121	.121
Charlie Baker	OF3	(2-2)	3	12	0	1		1	0	0	0			.083	.167
Charlie Berry	2B2	(4-4)	2	10	1	1		0	0	0	0			.100	.100
Kid Baldwin	C1	(2-2)	1	1	0	1		0	0	0	0			1.000	1.000
			18	648	78	141		28	7	0	19			.218	.282

PITCHERS		W	L	PCT	G	GS	CG	SH	SV	IP	H	BB	SO	ERA
One Arm Daily	(2-3)	5	4	.556	10	10	10	1	0	88	77	13	66	2.45
Al Atkinson	(3-4)	2	6	.250	8	8	8	0	0	69	62	13	53	2.88
		7	11	.389	18	18	18	1	0	157	139	26	119	2.64

1884 UNION ASSOCIATION

PHILADELPHIA Keystones

21-46 .313 -50 9th Malone - Pratt

BATTERS	POS/GAMES		GP	AB	R	H	BI	2B	3B	HR	BB	SO	SB	BA	SA
John McGuiness	1B48,2B5,SS1		53	220	25	52		8	1	0	5			.236	.282
Elias Peak	2B47,OF5,SS2	(2-2)	54	215	35	42		6	4	0	7			.195	.221
Henry Easterday	SS28		28	115	12	28		5	0	0	5			.243	.287
Jerry McCormick	3B53,OF5,2B5,SS3,P1	(1-2)	67	295	41	84		12	2	0	4			.285	.339
Joe Flynn	OF42,C10,SS1,1B1	(1-2)	52	209	38	52		9	4	4	11			.249	,388
Bill Keinzle	OF67		67	299	76	76		13	8	0	21			.254	.351
Buster Hoover	OF37,SS15,1B6,2B6,3B1	(1-2)	63	275	76	100		20	8	0	12			.364	.495
Tom Gillen	C27,OF3		29	116	5	18		2	0	0	1			.155	.172
Jersey Bakely	P39,OF3,1B2,SS1	(1-3)	43	167	21	22		4	2	0	11			.132	.180
Jack Clements	OF22,C20,SS1	(1-2)	41	177	37	50		13	2	3	9			.282	.429
Henry Luff	OF12,1B6,3B5,2B3	(1-2)	26	111	9	30		4	2	0	4			.270	.342
Sam Weaver	P17,OF6		17	84	11	18		2	0	0	2			.214	.238
George Fisher	P8,1B2	(1-2)	10	36	7	8		2	0	0	3			.222	.278
Billy Geer	SS9	(1-2)	9	36	7	9		2	1	0	4			.250	.361
John Siegel	3B8		8	31	4	7		2	0	0	1			.226	.290
Chris Rickley	SS6		6	25	5	5		2	0	0	2			.200	.280
Pat Carroll	C5	(2-2)	5	19	1	3		1	0	0	0			.158	.211
Bill Jones	C4,OF1		4	14	2	2		0	0	0	1			.143	.143
Levi Meyerle	1B2,OF1		3	11	0	1		1	0	0	0			.091	.182
Bill Gallagher	P3		3	11	1	1		0	0	0	0			.091	.091
David Drew	P1,SS1,2B1	(1-2)	2	9	1	4		0	0	0	0			.444	.444
Clarence Cross	SS2	(2-2)	2	9	0	2		0	0	0	0			.222	.222
Con Daily	C2		2	8	0	0		0	0	0	0			.000	.000
George Pattison	OF2		2	7	0	1		0	0	0	0			.143	.143
----- O'Donnell	C1		1	4	0	1		0	0	0	0			.250	.250
Fergy Malone	C1		1	4	0	1		0	0	0	0			.250	.250
Al Maul	P1		1	4	0	0		0	0	0	0			.000	.000
Bill Johnson	OF1		1	4	0	0		0	0	0	0			.000	.000
Elmer Foster	C1	(2-2)	1	3	0	1		0	1	0	0			.333	1.000
			67	2518	414	618		108	35	7	103	405		.245	.324

PITCHERS			W	L	PCT	G	GS	CG	SH	SV	IP	H	BB	SO	ERA
Jersey Bakely		(1-3)	14	25	.359	39	38	38	1	0	345	390	76	204	4.49
Sam Weaver			5	10	.333	17	17	14	0	0	136	206	11	40	5.76
Bill Gallagher			1	2	.333	3	3	3	0	0	25	32	4	12	3.24
George Fisher		(1-2)	1	7	.125	8	8	8	0	0	71	76	13	42	3.55
Al Maul			0	1	.000	1	1	1	0	0	8	10	1	7	4.50
David Drew		(1-2)	0	1	.000	1	0	0	0	0	7	7	0	2	3.86
Jerry McCormick		(1-2)	0	0	----	1	0	0	0	0	2	5	0	3	9.00
			21	46	.313	67	67	64	1	0	594	726	105	310	4.63

ST. PAUL White Caps

2-6 .250 -39.5 10th A. M. Thompson

BATTERS	POS/GAMES		GP	AB	R	H	BI	2B	3B	HR	BB	SO	SB	BA	SA
Stephen Dunn	1B9,3B1		9	32	2	8		2	0	0	0			.250	.313
Emery Hengle	2B9	(2-2)	9	33	2	5		1	1	0	0			.152	.242
Joe Werrick	SS9		9	27	3	2		0	0	0	1			.074	.074
Billy O'Brien	3B8,P2	(1-2)	8	30	1	7		3	0	0	0			.233	.333
Scrappy Carroll	OF8,3B4		9	31	3	3		1	0	0	2			.097	.129
Bill Barnes	OF8		8	30	2	6		1	0	0	0			.200	.233
John Tilley	OF9	(2-2)	9	26	2	4		1	0	0	3			.154	.192
Charles Ganzel	C6,OF1		7	23	2	5		0	0	0	0			.217	.217
James Brown	P6,OF1,1B1	(3-3)	6	16	5	5		4	0	0	1			.313	.583
Pat Dealey	C4,OF1		5	15	2	2		0	0	0	0			.133	.133
Louis Galvin	P3		3	9	0	2		0	0	0	0			.222	.222
			9	272	24	49		13	1	0	7	47		.180	.235

PITCHERS			W	L	PCT	G	GS	CG	SH	SV	IP	H	BB	SO	ERA
Billy O'Brien			1	0	1.000	2	0	0	0	0	10	8	3	7	1.80
James Brown		(3-3)	1	4	.200	6	6	4	1	0	36	43	14	20	3.75
Louis Galvin			0	2	.000	3	3	3	0	0	25	21	10	17	2.88
			2	6	.250	9	9	7	1	0	71	72	27	44	3.17

1884 UNION ASSOCIATION

ALTOONA Mountain Citys   6-19   .240   -44   11th   Ed Curtis

BATTERS	POS/GAMES		GP	AB	R	H	BI	2B	3B	HR	BB	SO	SB	BA	SA
Frank Harris	1B17,OF8		24	95	10	25		2	1	0	3			.263	.305
Charles Daugherty	2B16,OF8,SS1		23	85	6	22		5	0	0	2			.259	.318
Germany Smith	SS25,P1		25	108	9	34		8	1	0	1			.315	.407
Harry Koons	3B21	(1-2)	21	78	8	18		2	1	0	2			.231	.282
Frank Shaffer	OF17,C2,3B1	(1-3)	19	74	11	21		2	0	0	3			.284	.311
John Murphy	OF11,P14,2B2	(1-2)	25	94	10	14		1	0	0	4			.149	.159
James Brown	OF14,P11	(1-3)	21	88	12	22		2	2	1	1			.250	.352
Jerry Moore	C12,OF9	(1-2)	20	80	10	25		3	1	1	0			.313	.412
Pat Carroll	C8,OF3	(1-2)	11	49	4	13		1	0	0	1			.265	.280
John Grady	1B8,OF1		9	36	5	11		3	0	0	2			.306	.389
Jack Leary	OF7,P3,3B1	(1-2)	8	33	1	3		0	0	0	1			.091	.091
George Noftsker	OF5,C3,SS1		7	25	0	1		0	0	0	0			.040	.040
Charlie Berry	2B7	(1-4)	7	25	2	6		0	0	0	0			.240	.240
Joe Connors	P1,3B1,OF1	(1-2)	3	11	0	1		0	0	0	0			.091	.091
Clarence Cross	3B2		2	7	1	4		1	0	0	2			.571	.714
Charles Manlove	C1,OF1		2	7	1	3		0	0	0	0			.429	.429
George Daisey	OF1	(1-2)	1	4	0	0		0	0	0	0			.000	.000
			25	899	90	223		30	6	2	22	130		.248	.301

PITCHERS			W	L	PCT	G	GS	CG	SH	SV	IP	H	BB	SO	ERA
John Murphy		(1-2)	5	6	.455	14	10	10	0	0	112	141	9	46	3.86
James Brown		(1-3)	1	9	.100	11	11	7	0	0	74	99	36	39	5.35
Joe Connors		(1-2)	0	1	.000	1	1	1	0	0	9	18	5	0	7.00
Jack Leary		(1-2)	0	3	.000	3	3	2	0	0	24	31	2	7	5.25
Germany Smith		(1-2)	0	0	----	1	0	0	0	0	1	3	0	1	9.00
			6	19	.240	25	25	20	0	0	220	292	52	93	4.67

KANSAS CITY Unions   16-63   .203   -61   12th   Ted Sullivan

BATTERS	POS/GAMES		GP	AB	R	H	BI	2B	3B	HR	BB	SO	SB	BA	SA
Jerry Sweeney	1B31		31	129	16	34		3	0	0	4			.264	.287
Charlie Berry	2B21,OF9,3B1	(2-4)	29	118	15	29		6	1	1	1			.246	.339
Clarence Cross	SS25,3B1	(3-3)	25	93	13	20		1	0	0	6			.215	.226
Pat Sullivan	3B21,OF9,C1,P1		31	114	15	22		2	1	1	4			.193	.254
Frank Shaffer	OF40,3B1,2B1,C1,SS1	(2-3)	44	164	18	28		3	2	0	15			.171	.213
Frank Wyman	OF25,P3,1B3,3B3	(1-2)	30	124	16	27		4	0	0	3			.218	.250
Barney McLaughlin	OF24,2B12,P7,SS2		42	162	15	37		7	3	0	9			.228	.309
Kid Baldwin	C44,OF10,2B1,3B1	(1-3)	50	191	19	37		5	3	1	4			.194	.266
Bob Black	OF19,P16,2B6,SS1		38	146	25	36		14	2	1	10			.247	.390
John Gorman	1B24,OF5,3B4	(3-3)	33	137	25	38		5	2	0	4			.277	.343
Frank McLaughlin	2B10,OF10,3B6,SS6,P4	(3-3)	32	123	17	28		11	0	1	9			.228	.341
James Cudworth	1B19,OF12,P2		32	116	7	17		3	1	0	2			.147	.190
Henry Oberbeck	3B16,OF6,P4,1B2	(2-2)	27	90	7	17		3	0	0	7			.189	.222
Peek A Boo Veach	OF14,P12,2B1,1B1		27	82	9	11		1	0	1	9			.134	.183
Harry Decker	OF17,C11	(2-2)	23	75	8	10		2	0	0	5			.133	.160
Nin Alexander	C17,SS2,OF1	(1-2)	19	65	2	9		0	0	0	1			.138	.138
Ernest Hickman	P17,OF3,3B1		17	72	4	12		1	0	0	1			.167	.181
Louis Say	SS16,2B1	(2-2)	17	70	6	14		?	0	1	?			.200	.271
Joseph Strauss	OF10,C3,2B2,3B1		16	60	4	12		3	0	0	1			.200	.250
George Strief	2B15	(2-4)	15	56	5	6		5	0	0	4			.107	.196
Harry Wheeler	OF13,P1	(2-5)	14	62	11	16		1	0	0	3			.258	.274
Alex Voss	P8,OF8	(2-2)	14	45	1	4		0	0	0	0			.089	.089
Jeremiah Turbidy	SS13		13	49	5	11		4	0	0	3			.224	.306
Jim Deasley	SS13	(2-2)	13	40	3	7		2	0	0	2			.175	.225
Al Dwight	C11,OF6		12	43	8	10		2	0	0	2			.233	.279
Charlie Bastian	2B11	(2-2)	11	46	6	9		3	0	1	4			.196	.326
Charles Fisher	3B8,SS2	(1-2)	10	40	3	8		2	0	0	0			.200	.250
Jumbo Davis	3B7		7	29	3	6		0	0	0	0			.207	.207
Jim Donnelly	3B5,C1	(1-2)	6	23	2	3		1	0	0	1			.130	.174
Jersey Bakely	P5,OF3	(3-3)	6	20	3	3		1	0	0	1			.150	.200
Milt Whitehead	2B3,SS2,3B1	(2-2)	5	22	2	3		0	0	0	0			.136	.136
---- Wills	OF5	(2-2)	5	21	2	3		1	0	0	0			.143	.190
Henry Luff	3B4,OF4	(2-2)	5	19	0	1		0	0	0	1			.053	.053
Billy O'Brien	3B3,1B1	(2-2)	4	17	2	4		0	0	0	0			.235	.235
Howard Blaisdell	P3,OF1		4	16	1	5		1	0	0	0			.313	.375
James Chatterton	OF2,1B2,P1		4	15	4	2		1	0	0	2			.133	.200
Doug Crothers	P3,OF1		3	15	2	2		0	0	0	0			.133	.133
Matt Porter	OF3		3	12	1	1		1	0	0	0			.083	.167
Joe Connors	OF2,P2	(2-2)	3	11	2	1		0	0	0	1			.091	.091

1884 UNION ASSOCIATION

KANSAS CITY (cont.)
Unions

BATTERS	POS/GAMES		GP	AB	R	H	BI	2B	3B	HR	BB	SO	SB	BA	SA
Ed Callahan	SS3		3	11	0	4	0	0	0	0	0			.364	.364
Ted Sullivan	OF2,SS1	(2-2)	3	9	0	3	0	0	0	0	1			.333	.333
Bill Dugan	OF3		3	6	0	0	0	0	0	0	0			.000	.000
Bill Hutchinson	P2	(2-2)	2	8	1	2	0	0	0	0	0			.250	.250
Jim Say	3B2		2	8	0	2	0	0	0	0	0			.250	.250
Joe Ellick	2B1,OF1	(2-2)	2	8	0	0	0	0	0	0	0			.000	.000
John Kirby	P2,OF1	(2-2)	2	7	1	1	0	0	0	0	0			.143	.143
Charles Cady	2B1,C1	(2-2)	2	3	0	0	0	0	0	0	0			.000	.000
Emmett Seery	OF1	(2-2)	1	4	2	2	1	0	0	0	1			.500	.750
----- Krieger	P1,OF1		1	3	0	0	0	0	0	0	0			.000	.000
Frank Foreman	P1	(2-2)	1	3	0	0	0	0	0	0	0			.000	.000
			82	2802	311	557		102	15	8	123	529		.199	.254

PITCHERS		W	L	PCT	G	GS	CG	SH	SV	IP	H	BB	SO	ERA
Bob Black		4	9	.308	16	15	13	0	0	123	127	17	93	3.22
Ernest Hickman		4	13	.235	17	17	15	0	0	137	172	36	68	4.53
Peek A Boo Veach		3	9	.250	12	12	12	0	0	104	95	10	62	2.42
Jersey Bakely	(3-3)	2	3	.400	5	5	3	0	0	33	29	4	13	2.45
Bill Hutchinson		1	1	.500	2	2	2	0	0	17	14	1	5	2.65
Doug Crothers		1	2	.333	3	3	3	0	0	25	26	6	11	1.80
Barney McLaughlin		1	3	.250	7	4	4	0	0	49	62	15	14	5.51
Frank Wyman	(1-2)	0	1	.000	3	1	1	0	0	21	37	3	9	6.86
Joe Connors	(2-2)	0	1	.000	2	1	1	0	0	12	24	0	1	4.50
John Kirby		0	1	.000	2	2	1	0	0	11	13	2	1	4.09
Harry Wheeler	(2-5)	0	1	.000	1	1	1	0	0	8	7	0	6	1.13
Frank Foreman	(2-2)	0	1	.000	1	1	1	0	0	8	17	2	5	5.63
----- Krieger		0	1	.000	1	1	0	0	0	7	9	5	3	0.00
Pat Sullivan		0	1	.000	1	1	0	0	0	7	15	5	1	11.57
James Chatterton		0	1	.000	1	1	0	0	0	5	11	2	2	3.60
Howard Blaisdell		0	3	.000	3	3	3	0	0	26	49	4	8	8.65
Henry Oberbeck	(2-2)	0	5	.000	6	4	3	0	0	30	47	3	6	6.00
Alex Voss	(2-2)	0	6	.000	7	6	6	0	0	53	74	7	17	4.25
James Cudworth		0	0	----	2	1	1	0	0	17	19	3	6	4.24
Frank McLaughlin	(3-3)	0	0	----	2	1	0	0	0	10	15	2	3	5.40
		16	63	.203	82	82	70	0	0	703	862	127	334	4.07

WILMINGTON
Quicksteps

2-16   .111   -44.5   13th   Joe Simmons

BATTERS	POS/GAMES		GP	AB	R	H	BI	2B	3B	HR	BB	SO	SB	BA	SA
Redleg Snyder	1B16,OF1		17	52	4	10	0	0	0	0	1			.192	.192
Charlie Bastian	2B16,P1,SS1	(1-2)	17	60	6	12	1	3	2	0	3			.200	.417
Henry Myers	SS6		6	24	3	3	0	0	0	0	0			.125	.125
Jim Say	3B16	(1-2)	16	59	3	13	1	2	0	0	1			.220	.305
John Munce	OF7		7	21	1	4	0	0	0	0	1			.190	.190
George Fisher	OF6,SS2	(2-2)	8	29	0	2	0	0	0	0	0			.069	.069
Tom Lynch	OF8,C8,1B1	(1-2)	16	58	6	16	3	1	0	0	5			.276	.362
Tony Cusick	C6,OF3,SS3,3B1,2B1	(1-2)	11	34	0	5	0	0	0	0	1			.147	.147
John Murphy	P7,OF2,SS2,2B1,3B1	(2-2)	10	31	4	2	0	0	0	0	3			.065	.065
The Only Nolan	P5,OF4		9	33	5	9	2	1	0	0	2			.273	.394
John Cullen	OF6,SS3		9	31	2	6	0	0	0	0	1			.194	.194
Bill McCloskey	OF5,C5		9	30	0	3	0	0	0	0	0			.100	.100
Ike Benners	OF6	(2-2)	6	22	0	1	0	0	0	0	1			.045	.045
Dennis Casey	OF2	(1-2)	2	8	1	2	1	0	0	0	0			.250	.375
Oyster Burns	SS2	(1-2)	2	7	0	1	0	1	0	0	1			.143	.429
Dan Casey	P2		2	6	0	1	0	0	0	0	0			.167	.167
John Ryan	OF2	(2-2)	2	6	0	1	0	0	0	0	1			.167	.167
Jersey Bakely	P2	(2-3)	2	5	0	0	0	0	0	0	1			.000	.000
Fred Tenney	P1	(3-3)	1	3	0	0	0	0	0	0	0			.000	.000
James McElroy	P1	(1-2)	1	2	0	0	0	0	0	0	0			.000	.000
			17	521	35	91		8	8	2	22	123		.175	.232

PITCHERS		W	L	PCT	G	GS	CG	SH	SV	IP	H	BB	SO	ERA
Dan Casey		1	1	.500	2	2	2	0	0	18	23	4	10	1.00
The Only Nolan		1	4	.200	5	5	5	0	0	40	44	7	52	2.93
Fred Tenney	(3-3)	0	1	.000	1	1	1	0	0	8	6	4	10	1.13
James McElroy	(2-2)	0	1	.000	1	1	0	0	0	5	10	0	3	10.80
Jersey Bakely	(2-3)	0	2	.000	2	2	2	0	0	17	24	1	9	4.24
John Murphy	(2-2)	0	6	.000	7	6	5	0	0	48	52	2	27	3.00
Charlie Bastian	(1-2)	0	0	----	1	0	0	0	0	6	6	0	2	3.00
		2	16	.111	17	17	15	0	0	142	165	18	113	3.04

1885 NATIONAL LEAGUE

The Best Second

New York had a fine year in 1885. They finished the season with 85 wins, good for a winning percentage of .759, which was better than all but seven teams in major league history. However, from one perspective, their mark was the best. New York's winning percentage of .759 was the best ever for a second place team.

New York and Chicago fought bitterly for first place all during the summer of 1885. Save for a few days in mid-June, Chicago managed to hold on to a narrow lead through the course of the race. In late September, the two teams met for a crucial series in New York that would determine the final victor. New York was confident of victory, for they had bested Chicago in nine of the 12 meetings between the two. But the tables got turned. The visitors captured three of the four games to all but assure them the pennant. Chicago's final margin of victory was two games.

When two league members play over .700 ball, the rest of the league takes up the slack. In 1885, Philadelphia finished a respectable third. But their mark was barely over the .500 mark, and a whopping 30 games out of first, the furthest back of any third place team.

The team that nosed out New York was a powerhouse. Climbing back to the top after a three-year absence, Cap Anson's White Stockings were led offensively by the manager himself who hit .310, while leading the league in runs batted in (114), and doubles (35). King Kelly's average dropped to .288, but he scored a league best 124 runs. Fellow outfielder, Abner Dalrymple, poled 11 home runs to top the circuit. These performances were all bested by one member of the pitching staff. John Clarkson won an incredible 53 games, while striking out 308 in 623 innings. Needless to say, all three totals led the league.

Though finishing second, New York had the league's best hitting and pitching. First baseman Roger Connor won the batting title with a figure of .371, while pitcher Tim Keefe won the earned run average title with a mark of 1.58. Helping these two were Mike Dorgan (.326), Buck Ewing (.304), Jim O'Rourke (.300), as well as pitcher Mickey Welch's 44 wins and 1.66 earned run average.

Philadelphia and Providence finished third and fourth. Charlie Ferguson proved to be the best hitter and pitcher for Philadelphia by winning 26 while batting .326. Providence's Old Hoss Radbourn won less than half of his 1884 total, but less than half still totaled 28. Neither team prospered, because neither could hit. Both finished with averages under .230.

Boston and Detroit finished next in fifth and sixth. Boston's best was Ezra Sutton at .313, while Detroit had two over the .300 mark. One of them was Ned Hanlon, while the other was a young slugger named Sam Thompson who popped seven home runs in half a season to accompany his .303 average.

Buffalo slumped to seventh during their final year in the National League. During their seven-year tenure, the team never finished higher than third, but they did develop and acquire players that caught everyone's attention. One of them was Dan Brouthers who clubbed the ball at a .359 clip also finishing with a league-leading .543 slugging average.

Based upon their showing the previous year in the Union Association, the St. Louis Maroons were predicted to win the 1885 pennant. Taking the place of Cleveland, the team stumbled badly out of the gate and never did get on track, finishing in the cellar. They learned the hard lesson of the differences between a league with one good team, versus a league with several.

New York lost a memorable battle in 1885, but in doing so, became the best second place team in baseball history. It would be a few years before they approached this mark again. When they did, the team actually had a better year. That was the year they finished second to none.

1885 NATIONAL LEAGUE

CHICAGO White Stockings — 87-25 — .777 — 1st — Cap Anson

BATTERS	POS/GAMES		GP	AB	R	H	BI	2B	3B	HR	BB	SO	SB	BA	SA
Cap Anson	1B112,C1		112	464	100	144	114	35	7	7	34	13		.310	.461
Fred Pfeffer	2B109,P5,OF1		112	469	90	113	71	12	7	5	26	47		.241	.328
Tom Burns	SS111,2B1		111	445	82	121	70	23	9	7	16	48		.272	.411
Ned Williamson	3B113,P2,C1		113	407	87	97	64	16	5	3	75	60		.238	.324
King Kelly	OF69,C37,2B6,1B2,3B2		107	438	124	126	74	24	7	9	46	24		.288	.436
George Gore	OF109		109	441	115	138	51	21	13	5	68	25		.313	.454
Abner Dalrymple	OF113		113	492	109	135	58	27	12	11	46	42		.274	.445
Silver Flint	C68,OF1		68	249	27	52	19	8	2	1	2	52		.209	.269
John Clarkson	P70,OF3,3B1		72	283	34	61	31	11	5	4	3	44		.216	.332
Billy Sunday	OF46		46	172	36	44	20	3	3	2	12	33		.256	.343
Jim McCormick	P24,OF1	(2-2)	25	103	13	23		1	4	0	1	18		.223	.311
Sy Sutcliffe	C11,OF1	(1-2)	11	43	5	8	4	1	1	0	2	5		.186	.256
Ted Kennedy	P9,3B1		9	36	3	3	0	0	0	0	0	10		.083	.083
Larry Corcoran	P7,SS1	(1-2)	7	22	6	6	4	1	0	0	6	1		.273	.318
Jimmy Ryan	SS2,OF1		3	13	2	6	2	1	0	0	1	1		.462	.538
Jim McCauley	C2,OF1	(2-2)	3	6	1	1	0	0	0	0	2	3		.167	.167
Wash Williams	P1,OF1		1	4	0	1	0	0	0	0	0	0		.250	.250
Ed Gastfield	C1	(2-2)	1	3	0	0	0	0	0	0	0	1		.000	.000
Bill Krieg	OF1	(1-2)	1	3	0	0	0	0	0	0	0	2		.000	.000
			113	4093	834	1079	582	184	75	54	340	429		.264	.385

PITCHERS		W	L	PCT	G	GS	CG	SH	SV	IP	H	BB	SO	ERA
John Clarkson		53	16	.768	70	70	68	10	0	623	497	97	308	1.85
Jim McCormick	(2-2)	20	4	.833	24	24	24	3	0	215	187	40	88	2.43
Ted Kennedy		7	2	.778	9	9	8	0	0	79	91	28	36	3.43
Larry Corcoran	(1-2)	5	2	.714	7	7	6	1	0	59	63	24	10	3.64
Fred Pfeffer		2	1	.667	5	2	2	0	2	32	26	8	13	2.56
Ned Williamson		0	0	----	2	0	0	0	2	6	2	0	3	0.00
Wash Williams		0	0	----	1	1	0	0	0	2	2	5	0	13.50
		87	25	.777	113	113	108	14	4	1016	868	202	458	2.23

NEW YORK Giants — 85-27 — .759 — -2 — 2nd — Jim Mutrie

BATTERS	POS/GAMES		GP	AB	R	H	BI	2B	3B	HR	BB	SO	SB	BA	SA
Roger Connor	1B110		110	455	102	169	65	23	15	1	51	8		.371	.495
Joe Gerhardt	2B112		112	399	43	62	33	12	2	0	24	47		.155	.195
Monte Ward	SS111		111	446	72	101	37	8	9	0	17	39		.226	.285
Dude Esterbrook	3B84,OF4		88	359	48	92	44	14	5	2	4	28		.256	.340
Mike Dorgan	OF88,1B1		89	347	60	113	46	17	8	0	11	24		.326	.421
Jim O'Rourke	OF112,C8		112	477	119	143	42	21	16	5	40	21		.300	.442
Pete Gillespie	OF102		102	420	67	123	52	17	6	0	15	32		.293	.362
Buck Ewing	C63,OF14,3B8,1B1,SS1,P1		81	342	81	104	63	15	12	6	13	17		.304	.471
Mickey Welch	P56		56	199	28	41		8	0	2	14	39		.206	.276
Pat Deasley	C54,OF2,SS1		54	207	22	53	24	5	1	0	9	20		.256	.290
Danny Richardson	OF22,3B21,P9		49	198	26	52	25	9	3	0	10	14		.263	.338
Tim Keefe	P46,OF2		47	166	20	27		1	5	0	13	22		.163	.229
Larry Corcoran	P3	(2-2)	3	14	3	5	2	0	0	0	0	1		.357	.357
			112	4029	691	1085	433	150	82	16	221	312		.269	.359

PITCHERS		W	L	PCT	G	GS	CG	SH	SV	IP	H	BB	SO	ERA
Mickey Welch		44	11	.800	56	55	55	7	1	492	372	131	258	1.66
Tim Keefe		32	13	.711	46	46	45	7	0	400	300	102	227	1.58
Danny Richardson		7	1	.875	9	8	7	1	0	75	58	18	21	2.40
Larry Corcoran	(2-2)	2	1	.667	3	3	2	0	0	25	24	11	10	2.88
Buck Ewing		0	1	.000	1	0	0	0	0	2	4	3	0	4.50
		85	27	.759	112	112	109	16	1	994	758	265	516	1.72

PHILADELPHIA Quakers — 56-54 — .509 — -30 — 3rd — Harry Wright

BATTERS	POS/GAMES	GP	AB	R	H	BI	2B	3B	HR	BB	SO	SB	BA	SA
Sid Farrar	1B111	111	420	49	103	36	20	3	3	28	34		.245	.329
Al Myers	2B93	93	357	25	73	28	13	2	1	11	41		.204	.261
Charlie Bastian	SS103	103	389	63	65	29	11	5	4	35	82		.167	.252

1885 NATIONAL LEAGUE

PHILADELPHIA (cont.)
Quakers

BATTERS	POS/GAMES		GP	AB	R	H	BI	2B	3B	HR	BB	SO	SB	BA	SA
Joe Mulvey	3B107		107	443	74	119	64	25	6	6	3	18		.269	.393
Jack Manning	OF107		107	445	61	114	40	24	4	3	37	27		.256	.348
Jim Fogarty	OF88,2B10,SS8,3B5		111	427	49	99	39	13	3	0	30	37		.232	.276
Ed Andrews	OF99,2B5		103	421	77	112	23	15	3	0	32	25		.266	.316
Jack Clements	C41,OF11		52	188	14	36	14	11	3	1	2	30		.191	.298
Charlie Ferguson	P48,OF15		61	235	42	72		8	3	1	23	18		.306	.379
Ed Daily	P50		50	184	22	38	13	8	2	1	0	25		.207	.288
Tony Cusick	C38,OF1		39	141	12	25	5	1	0	0	1	24		.177	.184
Charles Ganzel	C33,OF1		34	125	15	21	6	3	1	0	4	13		.168	.208
Tom Lynch	OF13		13	53	7	10	1	3	0	0	10	3		.189	.245
Bill Vinton	P9,OF1	(1-2)	9	30	2	2		0	0	0	1	12		.067	.067
The Only Nolan	P7,OF1		7	26	1	2		1	0	0	3	8		.077	.115
John Hiland	2B3		3	9	0	0	0	0	0	0	0	4		.000	.000
			111	3893	513	891	298	156	35	20	220	401		.229	.302

PITCHERS			W	L	PCT	G	GS	CG	SH	SV	IP	H	BB	SO	ERA
Charlie Ferguson			26	20	.565	48	45	45	5	0	405	345	81	197	2.22
Ed Daily			26	23	.531	50	50	49	4	0	440	370	90	140	2.21
Bill Vinton		(1-2)	3	6	.333	9	9	8	0	0	77	90	23	21	3.09
The Only Nolan			1	5	.167	7	7	6	0	0	54	55	24	20	4.17
			56	54	.509	111	111	108	10	0	976	860	218	378	2.39

PROVIDENCE
Grays

53-57   .482   -33   4th   Frank Bancroft

BATTERS	POS/GAMES		GP	AB	R	H	BI	2B	3B	HR	BB	SO	SB	BA	SA
Joe Start	1B101		101	374	47	103	41	11	4	0	39	10		.275	.326
Jack Farrell	2B68		68	257	27	53	19	7	1	1	10	25		.206	.253
Art Irwin	SS58,2B1,3B1		59	218	16	39	14	2	1	0	14	29		.179	.197
Jerry Denny	3B83		83	318	40	71	25	14	4	3	12	53		.223	.321
Paul Radford	OF88,SS16,P3,2B1		105	371	55	90	32	12	5	0	33	43		.243	.302
Paul Hines	OF92,1B4,2B1,3B1,SS1		98	411	63	111	35	20	4	1	19	18		.270	.345
Cliff Carroll	OF104		104	426	62	99	40	12	3	1	29	29		.232	.282
Barney Gilligan	C65,SS5,2B1,OF1		71	252	23	54	12	7	3	0	23	33		.214	.266
Charley Bassett	2B39,SS23,3B20,C1		82	285	21	41	16	8	2	0	19	60		.144	.186
Old Hoss Radbourn	P49,OF16,2B2		66	249	34	58	22	9	2	0	36	27		.233	.285
Con Daily	C48,1B7,OF6		60	223	20	58	19	6	1	0	12	20		.260	.296
Dupee Shaw	P49,OF2		49	165	17	22	9	2	0	0	4	38		.133	.145
Lon Knight	OF25,P1	(2-2)	25	81	8	13	8	1	0	0	11	17		.160	.173
Tim Manning	SS10	(2-2)	10	35	3	2	0	1	0	0	0	11		.057	.086
Denny Lyons	3B4		4	16	3	2	1	1	0	0	0	3		.125	.188
Jim McCormick	P4	(1-2)	4	14	2	3		1	0	0	1	0		.214	.286
Edgar Smith	P1		1	4	0	1	0	0	0	0	0	0		.250	.250
Charles Hallstrom	P1		1	4	1	0	0	0	0	0	0	2		.000	.000
Wyman Andrus	3B1		1	4	0	0	0	0	0	0	0	1		.000	.000
Bill Stalberger	P1		1	4	0	0	0	0	0	0	0	2		.000	.000
Mike Hines	C1	(3-3)	1	3	0	0	0	0	0	0	0	2		.000	.000
Sam Kimber	P1		1	3	0	0	0	0	0	0	0	2		.000	.000
Ed Seward	P1		1	3	0	0	0	0	0	0	0	2		.000	.000
John Ward	P1		1	3	0	0	0	0	0	0	0	2		.000	.000
Cannonball Crane	OF1	(2-2)	1	2	0	0	0	0	0	0	1	1		.000	.000
John Foley	P1		1	2	0	0	0	0	0	0	1	0		.000	.000
			110	3727	442	820	293	114	30	6	264	430		.220	.272

PITCHERS			W	L	PCT	G	GS	CG	SH	SV	IP	H	BB	SO	ERA
Old Hoss Radbourn			28	21	.571	49	49	49	2	0	446	423	83	154	2.20
Dupee Shaw			23	26	.469	49	49	47	6	0	400	343	99	194	2.57
Edgar Smith			1	0	1.000	1	1	1	0	0	9	9	0	1	1.00
Jim McCormick		(1-2)	1	3	.250	4	4	4	0	0	37	34	20	8	2.43
Charles Hallstrom			0	1	.000	1	1	1	0	0	9	18	6	0	11.00
John Foley			0	1	.000	1	1	1	0	0	8	6	5	2	4.50
Sam Kimber			0	1	.000	1	1	1	0	0	8	15	5	4	11.25
Bill Stalberger			0	1	.000	1	1	1	0	0	8	14	4	0	7.88
John Ward			0	1	.000	1	1	1	0	0	8	10	1	3	4.50
Paul Radford			0	2	.000	3	2	2	0	0	18	34	8	3	7.85
Ed Seward			0	0	----	1	0	0	0	0	6	2	0	1	0.00
Lon Knight		(2-2)	0	0	----	1	0	0	0	0	4	4	4	1	6.75
			53	57	.482	110	110	108	8	0	961	912	235	371	2.71

1885 NATIONAL LEAGUE

BOSTON 46-66 .411 -41 5th John Morrill
Beaneaters

BATTERS	POS/GAMES		GP	AB	R	H	BI	2B	3B	HR	BB	SO	SB	BA	SA
John Morrill	1B92,2B17,3B2		111	394	74	89	44	20	7	4	64	78		.226	.343
Jack Burdock	2B45		45	169	18	24	7	5	0	0	8	18		.142	.172
Sam Wise	SS79,2B22,OF6		107	424	71	120	46	20	10	4	25	61		.283	.406
Ezra Sutton	3B91,SS16,2B2,1B1		110	457	78	143	47	23	8	4	17	25		.313	.425
Tom Poorman	OF56		56	227	44	54	25	5	3	3	7	32		.238	.326
Jim Manning	OF83,SS1	(1-2)	84	306	34	63	27	8	9	2	19	36		.206	.310
Tommy McCarthy	OF40		40	148	16	27	11	2	0	0	5	25		.182	.196
Tom Gunning	C48		48	174	17	32	15	3	0	0	5	29		.184	.201
Charles Buffinton	P51,OF18,1B15		82	338	26	81	33	12	3	1	3	26		.240	.302
Jim Whitney	P51,OF17,1B5		72	290	35	68	36	8	4	0	17	24		.234	.290
Pat Dealy	C29,3B3,OF2,SS2,1B1		35	130	18	29	9	4	1	1	2	14		.223	.292
Walt Hackett	2B20,SS15		35	125	8	23	9	3	0	0	3	22		.184	.208
Mert Hackett	C34		34	115	9	21	4	7	1	0	2	28		.183	.261
Gurd Whiteley	OF32,C1		33	135	14	25	7	2	2	1	1	25		.185	.252
Dick Johnston	OF26		26	111	17	26	23	6	3	1	0	15		.234	.369
Billy Nash	3B19,2B8		26	94	9	24	11	4	0	0	2	9		.255	.298
Joe Hornung	OF25		25	109	14	22	7	4	1	1	1	20		.202	.284
Blondie Purcell	OF21	(2-2)	21	87	9	19	3	1	1	0	3	15		.218	.253
Mike Hines	OF14	(1-3)	14	56	11	13	4	4	0	0	4	5		.232	.304
Daisy Davis	P11		11	37	4	7	3	2	0	0	1	11		.189	.243
Pop Tate	C4		4	13	1	2	2	0	0	0	1	3		.154	.154
Bill Stemmeyer	P2		2	7	1	3	2	1	0	0	0	0		.429	.571
Bill Colliver	OF1		1	4	0	0	0	0	0	0	0	1		.000	.000
			113	3950	528	915	375	144	53	22	190	522		.232	.312

PITCHERS		W	L	PCT	G	GS	CG	SH	SV	IP	H	BB	SO	ERA
Charles Buffinton		22	27	.449	51	50	49	6	0	434	425	112	242	2.88
Jim Whitney		18	32	.360	51	50	50	2	0	441	503	37	200	2.98
Daisy Davis		5	6	.455	11	11	10	1	0	94	110	28	30	4.29
Bill Stemmeyer		1	1	.500	2	2	2	1	0	11	7	11	8	0.00
		46	66	.411	113	113	111	10	0	981	1045	188	480	3.03

DETROIT 41-67 .380 -44 6th Morton - Watkins
Wolverines

BATTERS	POS/GAMES		GP	AB	R	H	BI	2B	3B	HR	BB	SO	SB	BA	SA
Mox McQuery	1B69,OF1		70	278	34	76	30	15	4	3	8	29		.273	.388
Sam Crane	2B68		68	245	23	47	20	4	6	1	13	45		.192	.269
Marr Phillips	SS33	(1-2)	33	139	13	29	17	5	0	0	0	13		.209	.245
Jim Donnelly	3B55,1B1		56	211	24	49	22	4	3	1	10	29		.232	.294
Sam Thompson	OF62,3B1		63	254	58	77	44	11	9	7	16	22		.303	.500
Ned Hanlon	OF105		105	424	93	128	29	18	8	1	47	18		.302	.389
George Wood	OF70,3B12,P1,SS1		82	362	62	105	28	19	8	5	13	19		.290	.428
Charlie Bennett	C62,OF19,3B10		91	349	49	94	60	24	13	5	47	37		.269	.456
Joe Quest	2B39,SS15,OF1		55	200	24	39	21	8	2	0	14	25		.195	.255
Stump Weidman	P38,OF8,2B1		44	153	7	24	14	2	1	1	8	32		.157	.203
Pretzels Getzien	P37,OF3		40	137	9	29	16	3	0	0	4	27		.212	.234
Jerry Dorgan	OF39		39	161	23	46	24	6	2	0	8	10		.286	.348
Milt Scott	1B38	(1-2)	38	148	14	39	12	7	0	0	4	16		.264	.311
Deacon McGuire	C31,OF3		34	121	11	23	9	4	2	0	5	23		.190	.256
Lady Baldwin	P21,OF12		31	124	12	30	18	6	3	0	6	22		.242	.339
Charlie Morton	3B18,SS4		22	79	9	14	3	1	2	0	5	10		.177	.241
Jim Manning	SS20	(2-2)	20	78	15	21	9	4	0	1	4	10		.269	.359
Frank Ringo	C8,3B8,OF1	(1-2)	17	65	12	16	2	3	0	0	0	7		.246	.292
Jim Halpin	SS15		15	54	3	7	1	2	0	0	1	12		.130	.167
Chub Collins	SS14		14	55	8	10	6	0	2	0	0	11		.182	.255
Dan Casey	P12		12	43	3	5	1	0	1	0	1	11		.116	.163
Gene Moriarity	OF6,3B4,P1,SS1		11	39	1	1	0	1	0	0	0	10		.026	.051
Jerry Moore	C6		6	23	2	4	0	1	0	0	1	3		.174	.219
Nat Kellogg	SS5		5	17	4	2	0	1	0	0	1	5		.118	.176
Frank Olin	3B1		1	4	1	2	0	0	0	0	0	0		.500	.500
George Bryant	2B1		1	4	0	0	1	0	0	0	0	2		.000	.000
Ed Gastfield	C1	(1-2)	1	3	0	0	0	0	0	0	0	2		.000	.000
Frank Meinke	P1,OF1		1	3	0	0	0	0	0	0	0	1		.000	.000
			108	3773	514	917	387	149	66	25	216	451		.243	.337

PITCHERS		W	L	PCT	G	GS	CG	SH	SV	IP	H	BB	SO	ERA
Stump Weidman		14	24	.368	38	38	37	3	0	330	343	63	149	3.14
Pretzels Getzien		12	25	.324	37	37	37	1	0	330	360	92	110	3.03

1885 NATIONAL LEAGUE

DETROIT (cont.)
Wolverines

PITCHERS		W	L	PCT	G	GS	CG	SH	SV	IP	H	BB	SO	ERA
Lady Baldwin		11	9	.550	21	20	19	1	1	179	137	28	135	1.86
Dan Casey		4	8	.333	12	12	12	1	0	104	105	35	79	3.29
Frank Meinke		0	1	.000	1	1	0	0	0	5	13	4	0	3.60
George Wood		0	0	----	1	0	0	0	0	4	5	1	1	0.00
Gene Moriarity		0	0	----	1	0	0	0	0	2	3	1	1	9.00
		41	67	.380	108	108	105	6	1	954	966	224	475	2.88

BUFFALO
Bisons

38-74 .339 -49 7th Galvin - Chapman

BATTERS	POS/GAMES		GP	AB	R	H	BI	2B	3B	HR	BB	SO	SB	BA	SA
Dan Brouthers	1B98		98	407	87	146	60	32	11	7	34	10		.359	.543
Davy Force	2B42,SS24,3B6		71	253	20	57	17	6	1	0	13	19		.225	.257
Jack Rowe	SS65,C23,OF12		98	421	62	122	51	28	8	2	13	19		.290	.409
Deacon White	3B98		98	404	54	118	57	6	6	0	12	11		.292	.337
Jim Lillie	OF112,SS3,1B1		112	430	49	107	30	13	3	2	6	39		.249	.307
Hardy Richardson	OF48,2B50,SS1,P1		96	426	90	136	44	19	11	6	20	22		.319	.458
Bill Crowley	OF92		92	344	29	83	36	14	1	1	21	32		.241	.297
George Myers	C69,OF23		89	326	40	67	19	7	2	0	23	40		.206	.239
Pud Galvin	P33,OF1	(1-2)	33	122	14	23	10	4	2	1	1	27		.189	.279
Dan Stearns	SS19,1B12,C2	(2-2)	30	105	7	21	9	6	1	0	8	23		.200	.276
Bill Serad	P30		30	104	8	16	3	3	0	0	1	19		.154	.183
Peter Conway	P27,OF2,SS1,1B1		29	90	7	10	7	5	0	1	5	28		.111	.200
Peter Wood	P24,OF4,1B2		28	104	10	23	5	3	1	0	0	18		.221	.269
Jim McCauley	C24,OF5	(1-2)	24	84	4	15	7	2	1	0	11	12		.179	.226
Cannonball Crane	OF13	(2-2)	13	51	5	14	9	0	1	2	3	8		.275	.431
Scrappy Carroll	OF13		13	40	1	3	1	0	0	0	2	8		.075	.075
Gil Hatfield	3B8,2B3		11	30	1	4	0	0	1	0	0	11		.133	.200
Emery Hengle	2B5,OF3		7	26	2	4	0	0	0	0	1	2		.154	.154
Joe Staples	OF6,2B1		7	22	0	1	0	0	0	0	0	9		.045	.045
Denny Driscoll	2B7		7	19	2	3	0	0	0	0	2	5		.158	.158
Dave Eggler	OF6		6	24	0	2	0	0	0	0	2	4		.083	.083
Buttercup Dickerson	OF5		5	21	1	1	0	1	0	0	1	4		.048	.095
Jim McDonald	SS4,OF1		5	14	0	0	0	0	0	0	0	4		.000	.000
James Phelan	2B4	(1-2)	4	16	2	2	3	0	0	1	0	3		.125	.313
Charles Ritter	2B2		2	6	0	1	0	0	0	0	0	2		.167	.167
Fred Wood	C1		1	4	0	1	0	0	0	0	0	0		.250	.250
George Fisher	P1		1	4	0	0	0	0	0	0	0	0		.000	.000
John Connor	P1	(1-2)	1	3	0	0	0	0	0	0	0	1		.000	.000
			112	3900	495	980	368	149	50	23	179	380		.251	.333

PITCHERS		W	L	PCT	G	GS	CG	SH	SV	IP	H	BB	SO	ERA
Pud Galvin	(1-2)	13	19	.406	33	32	31	3	1	284	356	37	93	4.09
Peter Conway		10	17	.370	27	27	26	1	0	210	256	44	94	4.67
Peter Wood		8	15	.348	24	22	21	0	0	199	235	66	38	4.44
Bill Serad		7	21	.250	30	29	27	0	0	241	299	80	90	4.10
George Fisher		0	1	.000	1	1	1	0	0	9	10	2	4	5.00
John Connor	(1-2)	0	1	.000	1	1	1	0	0	9	14	2	0	4.00
Hardy Richardson		0	0	----	1	0	0	0	0	4	5	3	1	2.25
		38	74	.339	112	112	107	4	1	956	1175	234	320	4.29

ST. LOUIS
Maroons

36-72 .333 -49 8th Dunlap - McKinnon

BATTERS	POS/GAMES		GP	AB	R	H	BI	2B	3B	HR	BB	SO	SB	BA	SA
Alex McKinnon	1B100		100	411	42	121	44	21	6	1	8	31		.294	.382
Fred Dunlap	2B106		106	423	70	114	25	11	5	2	41	24		.270	.333
Jack Glasscock	SS110,2B1		111	446	66	125	40	18	3	1	29	10		.280	.341
Ed Caskin	3B69,C2,SS1		71	262	31	47	12	3	0	0	12	22		.179	.191
Orator Shaffer	OF69	(1-2)	69	257	30	50	18	11	2	0	19	31		.195	.253
Joe Quinn	OF57,3B31,1B11		97	343	27	73	15	8	2	0	9	38		.213	.248
Emmett Seery	OF59,3B1		59	216	20	35	14	7	0	1	16	37		.162	.208
Fatty Briody	C60,2B1,3B1,OF1		62	215	14	42	17	9	0	1	12	23		.195	.251
Henry Boyle	P42,OF31,2B2		72	258	24	52	21	9	1	0	13	38		.202	.256
Charlie Sweeney	OF39,P35		71	267	27	55	24	7	1	0	12	33		.206	.240
Fred Lewis	OF45		45	181	12	53	27	9	0	1	9	10		.293	.359

ST. LOUIS (cont.)
Maroons

BATTERS	POS/GAMES		GP	AB	R	H	BI	2B	3B	HR	BB	SO	SB	BA	SA
George Baker	C32,3B3,OF2,2B1		38	131	5	16	5	0	0	0	9	28		.122	.122
Dave Rowe	OF16		16	62	8	10	3	3	0	0	5	8		.161	.210
Sy Sutcliffe	C14,OF2	(2-2)	16	49	2	6	4	1	0	0	5	10		.122	.143
Dick Burns	OF14,P1		14	54	2	12	4	2	1	0	3	8		.222	.296
John Kirby	P14		14	50	2	3	0	0	0	0	1	17		.060	.060
One Arm Daily	P11		11	35	1	3	1	0	0	0	2	10		.086	.086
Egyptian Healy	P8		8	24	0	1	0	0	0	0	0	12		.042	.042
---- Palmer	P4		4	11	1	1	1	0	0	0	3	7		.091	.091
Rooney Sweeney	OF3,C1		3	11	1	1	0	0	0	0	0	4		.091	.091
James Brennan	OF2,3B1		3	10	0	1	1	0	0	0	1	1		.100	.100
Tom Dolan	C3		3	9	1	2	0	0	0	0	2	1		.222	.222
Joe Fogarty	OF2		2	8	1	1	0	0	0	0	0	1		.125	.125
Jack Gleason	3B2		2	7	0	1	0	0	0	0	0	1		.143	.143
Trick McSorley	3B2		2	6	2	3	1	1	0	0	2	1		.500	.667
Bill Alvord	3B2		2	5	0	0	0	0	0	0	1	2		.000	.000
James Phelan	3B2	(2-2)	2	4	1	1	1	1	0	0	0	2		.250	.500
Charles Krehmeyer	OF1	(2-2)	1	3	0	0	0	0	0	0	0	2		.000	.000
			111	3758	390	829	278	121	21	8	214	412		.221	.270

PITCHERS	W	L	PCT	G	GS	CG	SH	SV	IP	H	BB	SO	ERA
Henry Boyle	16	24	.400	42	39	39	1	0	367	346	100	133	2.75
Charlie Sweeney	11	21	.344	35	35	32	2	0	275	276	50	84	3.93
John Kirby	5	8	.385	14	14	14	0	0	129	118	44	46	3.55
One Arm Daily	3	8	.273	11	11	10	1	0	91	92	44	31	3.94
Egyptian Healy	1	7	.125	8	8	8	0	0	66	54	20	32	3.00
---- Palmer	0	4	.000	4	4	4	0	0	34	46	20	9	3.44
Dick Burns	0	0	----	1	0	0	0	0	3	3	0	2	9.00
	36	72	.333	111	111	107	4	0	965	935	278	337	3.37

1885 AMERICAN ASSOCIATION

The World Series

Since the start of the American Association in 1882 as a rival to the National League, baseball enthusiasts were looking for a way to pit each league's winners against its rivals to determine the very best team. The owners thought of this idea as well, but for different reasons. They were thinking of all the fans that would pay dearly to see such a series of contests, and all of the resulting lucre that would flow into their coffers.

In 1882, an aborted attempt at a post-season series was staged, but it was called off by American Association officials after two games. The two leagues agreed again in 1884 to have their champions square off in a "World Series." The series proved to be anticlimactic as the National League's Providence polished off the Association's New York in three straight in front of disappointingly small crowds.

The leagues felt that the idea of the World Series was sound. What it needed was expansion — a longer series of games played in several locations. The planned World Series for 1885 was lengthened and included games to be played at neutral sites. The two participants were to be the Association's St. Louis Browns facing the League's Chicago White Stockings.

St. Louis, a charter member of the American Association, won their first pennant in 1885. Playing in a wisely cut down eight-team league, the Browns no longer had to face Indianapolis, Washington, Toledo, Richmond, or Columbus as the five were dropped from the 13-team league of 1884. As in the National League, pitching dominated the circuit, best evidenced by St. Louis's Bob Caruthers who won a league best forty, while also winning the earned run average race (2.07). The team's best hitter was newcomer Tip O'Neill who hit .350.

Cincinnati finished a distant second, while Pittsburgh finished a more distant third, as neither team could come within fifteen games of the front runners. Cincinnati's best player was veteran Charlie Jones (.322), while Tom Brown (.307) paced Pittsburgh. Pitcher Ed Morris won more than 60 percent of Pittsburgh's games and compiled a league best 298 strikeouts to boot.

Both Philadelphia, who finished fourth, and Brooklyn, who tied for fifth, were led by their first basemen. Harry Stovey, of Philadelphia, paced the league with 13 home runs to go with his .315 average. Bill Phillips, of Brooklyn, batted .302. Brooklyn's partner in fifth place, Louisville, boasted the league's best hitter, Pete Browning, who won his second batting title with a mark of .362.

New York and Baltimore brought up the rear. New York, experiencing a 30-win drop from the previous year, still managed to have the second leading hitter in the league. First baseman, Dave Orr hit .342 and also led the circuit with 21 triples. Baltimore's first baseman, even after adding his catcher's batting average to his own, could not equal Orr's total.

The upstart American Association was given little chance in the World Series against the established National League. The first game, played in Chicago, ended in a tie, while the second was stopped at midpoint because of unruly fans, with St. Louis legally ahead. The Browns took the next two games played in St. Louis, 7-4 and 3-2. Traveling to Pittsburgh and Cincinnati, Chicago took the two played at these neutral sites by 9-2 scores. At the following game, still at Cincinnati, St. Louis prevailed again, thus apparently winning the World Series, four games to two.

Chicago later claimed that the series should be declared a three all draw. Their argument went back to the shortened second game. The game had been stopped in the sixth inning just after Chicago had scored three runs to take a 5-4 lead. Because the stoppage in play did not allow the inning to be completed, St. Louis claimed the score should revert back to the last full inning played after which they had a 4-2 lead. The history books today uphold Chicago's claim, and the World Series of 1885 is officially listed as a three to three tie.

Despite this dispute, the World Series proved to be a popular and lucrative post-season vehicle. This guaranteed the series would continue for several years to come as a money-making venture for the lucky participating owners, and as a crucial factor in determining the world's best team.

1885 AMERICAN ASSOCIATION

ST. LOUIS Browns
79-33 .705 1st Charlie Comiskey

BATTERS	POS/GAMES		GP	AB	R	H	BI	2B	3B	HR	BB	SO	SB	BA	SA
Charlie Comiskey	1B83		83	340	68	87		15	7	2	14			.256	.359
Sam Barkley	2B96,1B11		106	418	67	112		18	10	3	25			.268	.380
Bill Gleason	SS112		112	472	79	119		9	5	3	29			.252	.311
Arlie Latham	3B109,C2		110	485	84	100		15	3	1	18			.206	.256
Hugh Nicol	OF111,3B1		112	425	59	88		11	1	0	34			.207	.238
Curt Welch	OF112		112	432	84	117		18	8	3	23			.271	.370
Tip O'Neill	OF52		52	206	44	72		7	4	3	13			.350	.466
Doc Bushong	C85,3B1		85	300	42	80		13	5	0	11			.267	.343
Yank Robinson	OF52,2B19,C5,3B2,1B1		78	287	63	75		8	8	0	29			.261	.345
Dave Foutz	P47,1B15,OF4		65	238	42	59		6	4	0	11			.248	.307
Bob Caruthers	P53,OF7		60	222	37	50		10	2	1	20			.225	.302
Dan Sullivan	C13,1B4	(2-2)	17	60	4	7		2	0	0	6			.117	.150
Jumbo McGinnis	P13,OF1		13	50	3	11		0	0	1	1			.220	.280
Mike Drissel	C6		6	20	0	1		0	0	0	0			.050	.050
Cecil Broughton	C4	(1-2)	4	17	1	1		0	0	0	0			.059	.059
			112	3972	677	979		132	57	17	234	282		.246	.321

PITCHERS		W	L	PCT	G	GS	CG	SH	SV	IP	H	BB	SO	ERA
Bob Caruthers		40	13	.755	53	53	53	6	0	482	430	57	190	2.07
Dave Foutz		33	14	.702	47	46	46	2	0	408	351	92	147	2.63
Jumbo McGinnis		6	6	.500	13	13	12	3	0	112	98	19	41	3.38
		79	33	.705	112	112	111	11	0	1002	879	168	378	2.44

CINCINNATI Red Stockings
63-49 .563 -16 2nd Ollie Caylor

BATTERS	POS/GAMES		GP	AB	R	H	BI	2B	3B	HR	BB	SO	SB	BA	SA
Long John Reilly	1B107,OF7		111	482	92	143		18	11	5	11			.297	.411
Bid McPhee	2B110		110	431	78	114		12	4	0	19			.265	.311
Frank Fennelly	SS112		112	454	82	124		14	17	10	38			.273	.445
Hick Carpenter	3B112		112	473	89	131		12	8	2	9			.277	.349
Pop Corkhill	OF110,P8,1B3		112	440	64	111		10	8	1	7			.252	.318
Jim Clinton	OF105		105	408	48	97		5	5	0	15			.238	.275
Charlie Jones	OF112		112	487	108	157		19	17	5	21			.322	.462
Pop Snyder	C38,1B1		39	152	13	36		4	3	1	6			.237	.322
Jim Keenan	C33,1B4,P1		36	132	16	35		2	2	1	8			.265	.333
Kid Baldwin	C25,OF6,2B2,P2,3B1		34	126	9	17		1	0	1	3			.135	.167
Will White	P34		34	118	9	20		5	0	0	4			.169	.212
Larry McKeon	P33,OF1		33	121	14	20		3	1	0	0			.165	.207
Bill Mountjoy	P17	(2-2)	17	60	7	10		0	0	0	8			.167	.167
Phil Powers	C15	(1-2)	15	60	6	16		2	0	0	0			.267	.300
Gus Shallix	P13,OF3		13	39	3	5		0	0	0	3			.128	.128
George Pechiney	P11		11	40	3	6		1	1	0	0			.150	.225
Jim Peoples	C5,P2,OF1	(1-2)	7	22	1	4		0	0	0	1			.182	.182
Harry McCaffrey	P1		1	5	0	0		0	0	0	0			.000	.000
			112	4050	642	1046		108	77	26	153	420		.258	.342

PITCHERS		W	L	PCT	G	GS	CG	SH	SV	IP	H	BB	SO	ERA
Larry McKeon		20	13	.606	33	33	32	2	0	290	273	50	117	2.86
Will White		18	15	.545	34	34	33	2	0	293	295	64	80	3.53
Bill Mountjoy	(1-2)	10	7	.588	17	17	17	1	0	154	149	52	50	3.16
George Pechiney		7	4	.636	11	11	11	1	0	98	95	30	49	2.02
Gus Shallix		6	4	.600	13	12	7	0	0	91	95	33	15	3.25
Harry McCaffrey		1	0	1.000	1	1	1	0	0	9	13	2	2	6.00
Pop Corkhill		1	4	.200	8	1	0	0	1	37	36	10	12	3.65
Jim Peoples		0	2	.000	2	2	1	0	0	15	30	2	4	12.00
Jim Keenan		0	0	----	1	0	0	0	0	8	7	1	0	1.13
Kid Baldwin		0	0	----	2	1	0	0	0	4	5	6	1	9.00
		63	49	.563	112	112	102	7	1	999	998	250	330	3.26

PITTSBURGH Alleghenys
56-55 .505 -22.5 3rd Horace Phillips

BATTERS	POS/GAMES		GP	AB	R	H	BI	2B	3B	HR	BB	SO	SB	BA	SA
Jim Field	1B56	(1-2)	56	209	28	50		9	1	1	13			.239	.306
Pop Smith	2B106		106	453	85	113		11	13	0	25			.249	.331

1885 AMERICAN ASSOCIATION

PITTSBURGH (cont.)
Alleghenys

BATTERS	POS/GAMES		GP	AB	R	H	BI	2B	3B	HR	BB	SO	SB	BA	SA
Art Whitney	SS75,3B8,2B4,OF3		90	373	53	87		10	4	0	16			.233	.282
Bill Kuehne	3B97,SS7		104	411	54	93		9	19	0	15			.226	.341
Tom Brown	OF108,P2		108	437	81	134		16	12	4	34			.307	.426
Fred Mann	OF97,3B3		99	391	60	99		17	6	0	31			.253	.327
Charles Eden	OF96,P4,3B2		98	405	57	103		18	6	0	17			.254	.328
Fred Carroll	C60,OF12		71	280	45	75		13	8	0	7			.268	.371
Ed Morris	P63,OF1		64	237	19	44		3	3	0	5			.186	.224
Milt Scott	1B55	(2-2)	55	210	15	52		7	1	0	5			.248	.290
Doggie Miller	C33,OF6,3B2,SS2		42	166	19	27		3	1	0	4			.163	.193
John Richmond	SS23,OF11		34	131	11	27		2	2	0	8			.206	.252
Peter Meegan	P18,OF3,2B1		19	67	3	13		1	0	0	3			.194	.209
Rudy Kemmler	C18		18	64	2	13		2	1	0	2			.203	.266
Hank O'Day	P12,OF3		13	49	7	12		2	1	0	1			.245	.327
Pud Galvin	P11	(2-2)	11	38	2	4		0	0	0	0			.105	.105
Frank Mountain	P5		5	20	1	2		0	1	0	1			.100	.200
Marr Phillips	SS4	(2-2)	4	15	1	4		0	0	0	2			.267	.267
Frank Ringo	C3	(2-2)	3	11	0	2		0	0	0	0			.182	.182
John Hofford	P3		3	8	1	1		0	0	0	0			.125	.125
			111	3975	547	955		123	79	5	189	537		.240	.315

PITCHERS			W	L	PCT	G	GS	CG	SH	SV	IP	H	BB	SO	ERA
Ed Morris			39	24	.619	63	63	63	7	0	581	459	101	298	2.35
Peter Meegan			7	8	.467	18	16	14	1	0	146	146	38	58	3.39
Hank O'Day			5	7	.417	12	12	10	0	0	103	110	16	36	3.67
Pud Galvin		(2-2)	3	7	.300	11	11	9	0	0	88	97	7	27	3.67
Charles Eden			1	2	.333	4	1	0	0	0	16	22	3	5	5.17
Frank Mountain			1	4	.200	5	5	5	0	0	46	56	24	7	4.30
John Hofford			0	3	.000	3	3	3	0	0	25	28	9	21	3.60
Tom Brown			0	0	----	2	0	0	0	0	6	0	3	2	3.00
			56	55	.505	111	111	104	8	0	1011	918	201	454	2.92

PHILADELPHIA
Athletics

55-57   .491   -24   4th   Harry Stovey

BATTERS	POS/GAMES		GP	AB	R	H	BI	2B	3B	HR	BB	SO	SB	BA	SA
Harry Stovey	1B82,OF30		112	486	130	153		27	9	13	39			.315	.488
Cub Stricker	2B106		106	398	71	93		9	3	1	21			.234	.279
Sadie Houck	SS93		93	388	74	99		10	9	0	10			.255	.327
Fred Corey	3B92,P1,SS1		94	384	61	94		14	8	1	17			.245	.331
Jack Coleman	OF93,P8		96	398	71	119		15	11	3	25			.299	.415
Henry Larkin	OF108		108	453	114	149		37	14	8	26			.329	.525
Blondie Purcell	OF66,P1	(1-2)	66	304	71	90		15	5	0	16			.296	.378
Jocko Milligan	C61,1B6,OF2		67	265	35	71		15	4	2	7			.268	.377
Jack O'Brien	C43,SS9,1B7,OF3,3B2		62	225	35	60		9	1	2	20			.267	.342
Bobby Mathews	P48,OF1		48	179	22	30		3	0	0	10			.168	.184
George Strief	3B19,SS10,OF8,2B7		44	175	19	48		8	5	0	9			.274	.377
Lon Knight	OF29,P1		29	119	17	25		1	1	0	9			.210	.235
Martin Powell	1B19		19	75	5	12		0	3	0	1			.160	.240
Tom Lovett	P16,OF1		16	58	9	13		0	1	0	3			.224	.259
Ed Knouff	P14,OF1		14	48	5	9		0	0	0	2			.188	.188
Ed Cushman	P10	(2-2)	10	37	5	7		1	0	0	1			.189	.216
Marsh Quinton	C7		7	29	6	6		1	0	0	1			.207	.241
Bill Vinton	P7,OF1	(2-2)	7	26	5	4		2	0	0	3			.154	.231
Bill Taylor	P6		6	21	0	4		0	0	0	0			.190	.190
Ed Fusselbach	C5		5	19	2	6		1	0	0	0			.316	.368
Bill Hughes	P2,OF2		4	16	3	3		1	1	0	1			.188	.375
Bob Emslie	P4	(2-2)	4	12	1	1		0	0	0	0			.083	.083
Frank Siffel	C2,OF1		3	10	0	1		0	0	0	0			.100	.100
Orator Shaffer	OF2		2	9	1	2		0	1	0	1			.222	.444
Jim Conway	P2,OF1		2	6	2	0		0	0	0	1			.000	.000
Phenomenal Smith	P1	(2-2)	1	2	0	0		0	0	0	0			.000	.000
			113	4142	764	1099		169	76	30	223	410		.265	.365

PITCHERS			W	L	PCT	G	GS	CG	SH	SV	IP	H	BB	SO	ERA
Bobby Mathews			30	17	.638	48	48	46	2	0	422	394	57	286	2.43
Ed Knouff			7	6	.538	14	13	12	0	0	106	103	44	43	3.65
Tom Lovett			7	8	.467	16	16	15	1	0	139	130	38	56	3.70
Bill Vinton		(2-2)	4	3	.571	7	7	6	2	0	55	46	15	34	2.45
Ed Cushman		(2-2)	3	7	.300	10	10	10	0	0	87	101	17	37	3.52

PHILADELPHIA (cont.)
Athletics

PITCHERS			W	L	PCT	G	GS	CG	SH	SV	IP	H	BB	SO	ERA
Jack Coleman			2	2	.500	8	3	3	0	0	60	82	5	12	3.43
Fred Corey			1	0	1.000	1	1	1	0	0	9	18	1	3	7.00
Bill Taylor			1	5	.167	6	6	6	0	0	52	68	9	11	3.27
Jim Conway			0	1	.000	2	2	1	0	0	12	19	2	0	7.30
Blondie Purcell			0	1	.000	1	0	0	0	0	6	11	2	3	6.00
Phenomenal Smith		(2-2)	0	1	.000	1	1	0	0	0	4	7	4	7	9.00
Bill Hughes			0	2	.000	2	2	2	0	0	17	18	10	4	4.86
Bob Emslie		(2-2)	0	4	.000	4	4	3	0	0	29	37	6	9	6.28
Lon Knight		(1-2)	0	0	----	1	0	0	0	0	5	4	2	1	1.80
			55	57	.491	113	113	105	5	0	1003	1038	212	506	3.23

BROOKLYN
Trolley Dodgers

53-59 .473 -26 5th (tie) Hackett - Byrne

BATTERS	POS/GAMES		GP	AB	R	H	BI	2B	3B	HR	BB	SO	SB	BA	SA
Bill Phillips	1B99		99	391	65	118		16	11	3	27			.302	.422
George Pinckney	2B57,3B51,SS3		110	447	77	124		16	5	0	27			.277	.336
Germany Smith	SS108		108	419	63	108		17	11	4	10			.258	.379
Bill McClellan	3B57,2B55		112	464	85	124		22	7	0	28			.267	.345
John Cassidy	OF54		54	221	36	47		6	2	1	8			.213	.271
Pete Hotaling	OF94		94	370	73	95		9	5	1	49			.257	.316
Ed Swartwood	OF95,1B4,C1,SS1		99	399	80	106		8	9	0	36			.266	.331
Jack Hayes	C42		42	137	10	18		3	0	0	5			.131	.153
Adonis Terry	OF47,P25,3B1		71	264	23	45		1	3	1	10			.170	.208
Henry Porter	P54		54	195	28	40		1	4	0	5			.205	.251
John Harkins	P34,OF9,3B1		43	159	20	42		4	2	1	9			.264	.333
Jim Peoples	C37,SS2,1B1,3B1,OF1	(2-2)	41	151	21	30		4	1	1	5			.199	.258
Jim McTamany	OF35		35	131	21	36		7	2	1	9			.275	.382
Charlie Robinson	C11		11	40	5	6		2	1	0	3			.150	.250
Bill Krieg	C12,OF5	(2-2)	17	60	7	9		4	0	1	2			.150	.267
Frank Bell	C5,OF4,3B2		10	29	5	5		0	1	0	0			.172	.241
Dave Oldfield	C9,OF2		10	25	2	8		1	0	0	3			.320	.360
George McVey	C3,1B3		6	21	2	3		0	0	0	2			.143	.143
Mike Hines	C3	(2-3)	3	13	1	1		0	1	0	0			.077	.231
Bill Schenk	3B1		1	4	0	0		0	0	0	0			.000	.000
Phenomenal Smith	P1	(1-2)	1	3	0	1		0	0	0	0			.333	.333
			112	3943	624	966		121	65	14	238	324		.245	.319

PITCHERS			W	L	PCT	G	GS	CG	SH	SV	IP	H	BB	SO	ERA
Henry Porter			33	21	.611	54	54	53	2	0	482	427	107	197	2.78
John Harkins			14	20	.412	34	34	33	1	0	293	303	56	141	3.75
Adonis Terry			6	17	.261	25	23	23	0	1	209	213	42	96	4.26
Phenomenal Smith		(1-2)	0	1	.000	1	1	1	0	0	8	12	6	2	12.38
			53	59	.473	112	112	110	3	1	992	955	211	436	3.46

LOUISVILLE
Colonels

53-59 .473 -26 5th (tie) Jim Hart

BATTERS	POS/GAMES		GP	AB	R	H	BI	2B	3B	HR	BB	SO	SB	BA	SA
John Kerins	1B96,C19,OF3,3B1		112	456	65	111		9	16	3	20			.243	.353
Tom McLaughlin	2B93,SS19		112	411	49	87		13	9	2	15			.212	.302
Joe Miller	SS79,3B11,2B8		98	339	44	62		9	5	0	28			.183	.239
Phil Reccius	3B97,P7		102	402	57	97		8	10	1	13			.241	.318
Chicken Wolf	OF111,C2,3B1,P1		112	483	79	141		23	17	1	11			.292	.416
Pete Browning	OF112		112	481	98	174		34	10	9	25			.362	.530
Leech Maskrey	OF108,3B3		109	423	54	97		8	11	1	19			.229	.307
Joe Crotty	C38,1B1		39	129	14	20		2	0	0	3			.155	.171
Guy Hecker	P54,1B17,OF3		72	297	48	81		9	2	2	5			.273	.337
Amos Cross	C35		35	130	11	37		2	1	0	0			.285	.315
Norm Baker	P25		25	87	15	18		2	0	0	2			.207	.230
Al Mays	P17		17	61	8	13		1	1	0	2			.213	.262
Billy Geer	SS14		14	51	2	6		2	0	0	2			.118	.157
Dan Sullivan	C13	(1-2)	13	44	3	8		1	0	0	2			.182	.205
Miah Murray	C12,1B2		12	43	4	8		0	0	0	2			.186	.186
Reddy Mack	2B11		11	41	7	10		1	0	0	2			.244	.268
Toad Ramsey	P9		9	31	2	4		0	0	0	0			.129	.129
Charles Krehmeyer	C4,OF2,1B1	(1-2)	7	31	4	7		1	1	0	1			.226	.323

LOUISVILLE (cont.)
Colonels

BATTERS	POS/GAMES		GP	AB	R	H	BI	2B	3B	HR	BB	SO	SB	BA	SA
John Connor	P4	(2-2)	4	14	0	2		0	0	0	0			.143	.143
Monk Cline	OF1,3B1		2	9	0	2		1	0	0	0			.222	.333
Joseph Strauss	C1,OF1		2	6	0	1		0	0	0	0			.167	.167
			112	3969	564	986		126	83	19	152	448		.248	.336

PITCHERS			W	L	PCT	G	GS	CG	SH	SV	IP	H	BB	SO	ERA
Guy Hecker			30	23	.566	53	53	51	2	0	480	454	54	209	2.18
Norm Baker			13	12	.520	25	24	24	1	0	217	210	69	79	3.40
Al Mays			6	11	.353	17	17	17	0	0	150	129	43	61	2.76
Toad Ramsey			3	6	.333	9	9	9	0	0	79	44	28	83	1.94
John Connor		(2-2)	1	3	.250	4	4	4	0	0	35	43	12	19	4.89
Phil Reccius			0	4	.000	7	5	4	0	1	40	46	11	10	3.82
Chicken Wolf			0	0	----	1	0	0	0	0	1	1	0	1	9.00
			53	59	4.73	112	112	109	3	1	1002	927	217	462	2.68

NEW YORK
Metropolitans

44-64 .407 -33 7th Jim Gifford

BATTERS	POS/GAMES		GP	AB	R	H	BI	2B	3B	HR	BB	SO	SB	BA	SA
Dave Orr	1B107,P3		107	444	76	152		29	21	6	8			.342	.543
Tom Forster	2B52,OF5		57	213	28	47		7	2	0	17			.221	.272
Candy Nelson	SS107,3B1		107	420	98	107		12	4	1	61			.255	.310
Frank Hankinson	3B94,P1		94	362	43	81		12	2	2	12			.224	.285
Steve Brady	OF105,1B4,2B2,3B1		108	434	60	128		14	5	3	25			.295	.371
Chief Roseman	OF101,P1		101	410	72	114		13	14	4	25			.278	.407
Ed Kennedy	OF96		96	349	35	71		8	4	2	12			.203	.266
Charlie Reipschlager	C59,3B6,OF6,2B1,SS1		72	268	29	65		11	1	0	9			.243	.291
Bill Holbert	C39,OF13,3B5		56	202	13	35		3	0	0	8			.173	.188
Dasher Troy	2B42,OF2,SS1		45	177	24	39		3	3	2	5			.220	.305
Jack Lynch	P44		44	153	16	30		5	1	0	11			.196	.242
Ed Cushman	P22	(1-2)	22	69	5	10		1	0	0	9			.145	.159
Doug Crothers	P18		18	51	11	8		0	0	0	8			.157	.157
Ed Begley	P15,OF4		15	52	5	9		1	0	1	1			.173	.250
Cecil Broughton	C11	(2-2)	11	41	1	6		1	0	0	1			.146	.171
Joe Reilly	2B8,3B2		10	40	6	7		3	0	0	2			.175	.250
Jim Becannon	P10		10	33	3	10		0	0	0	1			.303	.303
Dick Pierson	2B3		3	9	1	1		0	0	0	2			.111	.111
Charlie Jones	3B1		1	4	0	1		0	0	0	0			.250	.250
			108	3731	526	921		123	57	21	217	428		.247	.327

PITCHERS			W	L	PCT	G	GS	CG	SH	SV	IP	H	BB	SO	ERA
Jack Lynch			23	21	.523	44	43	43	1	0	379	410	42	177	3.61
Ed Cushman		(2-2)	8	14	.364	22	22	22	0	0	191	158	33	133	2.78
Doug Crothers			7	11	.389	18	18	18	1	0	154	192	49	40	5.08
Ed Begley			4	9	.308	15	14	10	0	0	115	131	48	44	4.93
Jim Becannon			1	8	.200	10	10	10	0	0	85	108	24	13	6.25
Chief Roseman			0	1	.000	1	1	0	0	0	1	3	2	0	27.00
Dave Orr			0	0	----	3	0	0	0	0	10	11	5	1	7.20
Frank Hankinson			0	0	----	1	0	0	0	0	2	2	1	0	4.50
			44	64	.407	108	108	103	2	0	937	1015	204	408	4.15

BALTIMORE
Orioles

41-68 .376 -36.5 8th Billy Barnie

BATTERS	POS/GAMES		GP	AB	R	H	BI	2B	3B	HR	BB	SO	SB	BA	SA
Dan Stearns	1B63,OF3,C2	(1-2)	67	253	40	47		3	8	1	38			.186	.273
Tim Manning	2B41,3B3	(1-2)	43	157	17	32		8	1	0	10			.204	.268
Jimmy Macullar	SS98,OF2		100	320	52	61		7	6	3	49			.191	.278
Mike Muldoon	3B101,2B1		102	410	47	103		20	6	2	20			.251	.344
Ed Greer	OF47,C12		56	211	32	42		7	0	0	8			.199	.232
Dennis Casey	OF63		63	264	50	76		10	5	3	21			.288	.398
Joe Sommer	OF107,3B2,P2,SS2,1B1		110	471	84	118		23	6	1	24			.251	.331
Bill Traffley	C61,OF10,2B3		69	254	27	39		4	5	1	17			.154	.220
Oyster Burns	OF45,P15,SS10,2B6,3B6,1B1		78	321	47	74		11	6	5	16			.231	.349
Hardie Henderson	P61,OF1,2B1		61	229	23	51		5	2	1	12			.223	.275

BALTIMORE (cont.)
Orioles

BATTERS	POS/GAMES		GP	AB	R	H	BI	2B	3B	HR	BB	SO	SB	BA	SA
Gid Gardner	2B39,OF5,1B1,P1		44	170	22	37		5	4	0	12			.218	.294
Jim Field	1B38	(2-2)	38	144	16	30		3	2	0	13			.208	.257
Tom York	OF22		22	87	6	23		4	2	0	8			.264	.356
Sam Trott	C17,OF4,2B2,SS1		21	88	12	24		2	2	0	5			.273	.341
Jake Evans	OF20		20	77	18	17		1	1	0	7			.221	.260
Bob Emslie	P13	(1-2)	13	51	6	12		1	1	0	0			.235	.294
Harry Jacoby	2B11		11	43	4	6		2	0	0	2			.140	.186
John Henry	P9,OF1		10	34	4	9		3	0	0	1			.265	.353
Gene Derby	C9,OF1		10	31	4	4		0	0	0	1			.129	.129
Phil Powers	C8,OF1	(2-2)	9	34	6	4		1	0	0	1			.118	.147
Tom O'Brien	1B6,2B2		8	33	4	7		3	0	0	2			.212	.303
Sandy Nava	C8		8	27	2	5		1	0	0	1			.185	.222
Bill Mountjoy	P6,OF1	(1-2)	7	18	5	1		0	0	0	7			.056	.056
George Mappes	2B6		6	19	2	4		0	1	0	1			.211	.316
Joe Brown	P4,2B1		5	19	2	3		0	0	0	0			.158	.158
Joe Visner	OF4		4	13	2	3		0	0	0	2			.231	.231
Walt Walker	OF4		4	13	1	0		0	0	0	0			.000	.000
Frank Foreman	P3,OF1		3	14	4	4		0	1	0	0			.286	.429
George Wetzel	P2		2	7	0	0		0	0	0	1			.000	.000
Charles Levis	1B1		1	4	2	1		0	0	0	0			.250	.250
John Tener	OF1		1	4	0	0		0	0	0	0			.000	.000
			110	3820	541	837		124	59	17	279	529		.219	.296

PITCHERS		W	L	PCT	G	GS	CG	SH	SV	IP	H	BB	SO	ERA
Hardie Henderson		25	35	.417	61	61	59	0	0	539	539	117	263	3.19
Oyster Burns		7	4	.636	15	11	10	1	3	106	112	21	30	3.58
Bob Emslie	(1-2)	3	10	.231	13	13	11	0	0	107	131	30	27	4.29
Frank Foreman		2	1	.667	3	3	2	0	0	27	33	9	11	6.00
Bill Mountjoy	(2-2)	2	4	.333	6	6	6	1	0	53	72	13	15	5.43
John Henry		2	7	.222	9	9	9	0	0	71	71	13	31	4.31
Gid Gardner		0	1	.000	1	1	1	0	0	9	16	6	3	10.00
George Wetzel		0	2	.000	2	2	1	0	0	17	27	9	6	8.47
Joe Brown		0	4	.000	4	4	4	0	0	38	52	4	9	5.68
Joe Sommer		0	0	----	2	0	0	0	1	3	6	0	0	9.00
		41	68	.376	110	110	103	2	4	971	1059	222	395	3.90

1886 NATIONAL LEAGUE

The King

Baseball in the 1880s featured flamboyant, larger than life stars whose every action was watched closely. These stars lived well, played hard, and were generally major nuisances to their unfortunate managers. No player fit this description better than Michael Joseph Kelly, who was known simply as King Kelly.

Kelly was born in Troy, New York, on the last day of 1857. He started his career with Cincinnati in 1878, moving to the Chicago White Sox in 1880. It was here that his career began to blossom. By 1881, his average had risen to .323 — and in 1884 he won the National League batting title with a mark of .354. In the field, Kelly did not play any one position exclusively, although most of the time he caught or played in the outfield.

Off the field, Kelly lived life to the utmost. He dressed well, drank too much, and generally could not say no to anything. He went on the stage reciting poetry ("Casey at the Bat"), demanded and received endorsement money for use of his picture, and was driven in his own personal carriage to the ballpark.

On the field, there was not anything Kelly would not try. As a base runner he would take a shortcut across the diamond behind the umpire's back. His daring base stealing antics even inspired a hit song "Slide, Kelly, Slide." And while on the bench one day, when a pop foul drifted his way, Kelly brazenly announced himself into the game, catching the ball and retiring the batter. It was even said by some, that any rule change made by the league during these years was to counteract some ploy of Kelly's.

In 1886, Kelly had his best year. With a league-leading .388 average, and 155 runs scored, he led the White Stockings to their second straight pennant, while typically playing six different positions. Cap Anson finished a strong second in the batting race (.371) and first in the runs batted in contest (147).

Detroit jumped several notches to second place. This was due to the acquisition of Dan Brouthers (.370), and Hardy Richardson (.351) who also hit eleven league-leading homers each. Pitcher Lady Baldwin also excelled by winning the most games (42), while striking out the most batters (323).

New York finished third, while Philadelphia finished fourth. New York was led by Roger Connor's .355 average and league best 20 triples. Philadelphia featured the circuit's best pitching (2.45) anchored by Charlie Ferguson with his 30 wins and 1.98 earned run average.

Boston and St. Louis finished next. The two best players from this duo both played on St. Louis. Jack Glasscock (.325) finished with a fine average, while pitcher Henry Boyle won the earned run average title with a mark of 1.76.

The last two teams, Kansas City and Washington, took the places of the moribund Buffalo and Providence franchises. Neither team could win a quarter of their games, and only Washington's Paul Hines (.312) could crack the .300 barrier.

Following the 1886 season, Chicago sold King Kelly to Boston for the outrageously large sum of $10,000, of which Kelly pocketed half. He enjoyed several more good seasons for Boston and other clubs before calling it quits in the early 1890s. A little more than a year later, Kelly fell ill while visiting Boston, and died at the age of 36.

It was true that King Kelly disregarded any rule he thought inconvenient. It was also true, that he was a talented ball player who could improve any team, or excite any crowd that had the pleasure of watching him perform. It was the latter that got King Kelly elected to the Hall of Fame in 1945.

1886 NATIONAL LEAGUE

CHICAGO White Stockings — 90-34 .726 1st Cap Anson

BATTERS	POS/GAMES	GP	AB	R	H	BI	2B	3B	HR	BB	SO	SB	BA	SA
Cap Anson	1B125,C12	125	504	117	187	147	35	11	10	55	19	29	.371	.544
Fred Pfeffer	2B118,1B1	118	474	88	125	95	17	8	7	36	46	30	.264	.378
Ned Williamson	SS121,C4,P2	121	430	69	93	58	17	8	6	80	71	13	.216	.335
Tom Burns	3B112	112	445	64	123	65	18	10	3	14	40	15	.276	.382
George Gore	OF118	118	444	150	135	63	20	12	6	102	30	23	.304	.444
Abner Dalrymple	OF82	82	331	62	77	26	7	12	3	33	44	16	.233	.353
Jimmy Ryan	OF70,3B6,SS6,2B5,P5	84	327	58	100	53	17	6	4	12	28	10	.306	.431
Silver Flint	C54,1B3	54	173	30	35	13	6	2	1	12	36	1	.202	.277
King Kelly	OF54,C53,1B9,3B8,2B6,SS5	118	451	155	175	79	32	11	4	83	33	53	.388	.534
John Flynn	P32,OF24	57	205	40	41	19	6	2	4	18	45	9	.200	.307
John Clarkson	P53,OF5	55	210	21	49	23	9	1	3	0	38	2	.233	.329
Jim McCormick	P42,OF4	42	174	17	41	21	9	2	2	2	30	1	.236	.345
Billy Sunday	OF28	28	103	16	25	6	2	2	0	7	26	10	.243	.301
George Moolic	C16	16	56	9	8	2	3	0	0	2	17	0	.143	.196
Lew Hardie	C16	16	51	4	9	3	0	0	0	4	10	1	.176	.176
		126	4378	900	1223	673	198	87	53	460	513	213	.279	.401

PITCHERS		W	L	PCT	G	GS	CG	SH	SV	IP	H	BB	SO	ERA
John Clarkson		36	17	.679	55	55	50	3	0	467	419	86	313	2.41
Jim McCormick		31	11	.738	42	42	38	2	0	348	341	100	172	2.82
John Flynn		23	6	.793	32	29	28	2	1	257	207	63	146	2.24
Jimmy Ryan		0	0	----	5	0	0	0	1	23	19	13	15	4.63
Ned Williamson		0	0	----	2	0	0	0	1	3	2	0	1	0.00
		90	34	.726	126	126	116	8	3	1098	988	262	647	2.54

DETROIT Wolverines — 87-36 .707 -2.5 2nd Bill Watkins

BATTERS	POS/GAMES		GP	AB	R	H	BI	2B	3B	HR	BB	SO	SB	BA	SA
Dan Brouthers	1B121		121	489	139	181	72	40	15	11	66	16	21	.370	.581
Fred Dunlap	2B51	(2-2)	51	196	32	56	37	8	3	4	16	21	13	.286	.418
Jack Rowe	SS110,C3		111	468	97	142	87	21	9	6	26	27	12	.303	.425
Deacon White	3B124		124	491	65	142	76	19	5	1	31	35	9	.289	.354
Sam Thompson	OF122		122	503	101	156	89	18	13	8	35	31	13	.310	.445
Ned Hanlon	OF126,2B1		126	494	105	116	60	6	6	4	57	39	50	.235	.296
Hardy Richardson	OF80,2B42,P4,SS3,3B2		125	538	125	189	61	27	11	11	46	27	42	.351	.504
Charlie Bennett	C69,OF4,SS1		72	235	37	57	34	13	5	4	48	29	4	.243	.391
Charles Ganzel	C45,OF7,1B5	(2-2)	57	213	28	58	31	7	2	1	7	22	5	.272	.338
Lady Baldwin	P56,OF2		57	204	25	41	25	6	3	0	18	44	3	.201	.260
Sam Crane	2B38,SS8,OF4	(1-2)	47	185	24	26	12	2	2	1	8	34	3	.141	.189
Pretzels Getzien	P43,OF1		43	165	14	29	19	3	3	0	6	46	3	.176	.230
Jim Manning	OF26,SS1		26	97	14	18	7	2	3	0	6	10	7	.186	.268
Harry Decker	C14,OF1	(1-2)	14	54	2	12	5	1	0	0	2	9	0	.222	.241
Peter Conway	P11,OF1	(2-2)	12	43	10	8	3	1	0	2	1	8	0	.186	.349
Bill Smith	P9,OF1		10	38	2	7	4	2	0	0	1	14		.184	.237
Bill Shindle	SS7		7	26	4	7	4	0	0	0	0	5	2	.269	.269
Jack McGeachey	OF6	(1-2)	6	27	3	9	4	0	1	0	0	3	2	.333	.407
Larry Twitchell	P4,OF2		4	16	0	1	0	0	0	0	0	2	0	.063	.063
Phenomenal Smith	P3		3	9	0	1	1	0	0	0	0	3		.111	.111
Tom Gillen	C2		2	10	2	4	4	0	0	0	0	1	0	.400	.400
			126	4501	829	1260	635	176	81	53	374	426	194	.280	.391

PITCHERS		W	L	PCT	G	GS	CG	SH	SV	IP	H	BB	SO	ERA
Lady Baldwin		42	13	.764	56	56	55	7	0	487	371	100	323	2.24
Pretzels Getzien		30	11	.732	43	43	42	1	0	387	388	85	172	3.03
Peter Conway	(2-2)	6	5	.545	11	11	11	0	0	91	93	25	35	3.36
Bill Smith		5	4	.556	9	9	9	0	0	77	81	30	36	4.09
Hardy Richardson		3	0	1.000	4	0	0	0	0	12	11	10	5	4.50
Phenomenal Smith		1	1	.500	3	3	3	0	0	25	16	8	15	2.16
Larry Twitchell		0	2	.000	4	4	2	0	0	25	35	12	6	6.48
		87	36	.707	126	126	122	8	0	1104	995	270	592	2.85

1886 NATIONAL LEAGUE

NEW YORK Giants
75-44 .630 -12.5 3rd Jim Mutrie

BATTERS	POS/GAMES		GP	AB	R	H	BI	2B	3B	HR	BB	SO	SB	BA	SA
Roger Connor	1B118		118	485	105	172	71	29	20	7	41	15	17	.355	.540
Joe Gerhardt	2B123		123	426	44	81	40	11	7	0	22	63	8	.190	.249
Monte Ward	SS122		122	491	82	134	81	17	5	2	19	46	36	.273	.340
Dude Esterbrook	3B123		123	473	62	125	43	20	6	3	8	43	13	.264	.351
Mike Dorgan	OF116,1B3		118	442	61	129	79	19	4	2	29	37	9	.292	.367
Jim O'Rourke	OF63,C47,1B2		105	440	106	136	34	26	6	1	39	21	14	.309	.402
Pete Gillespie	OF97		97	396	65	108	58	13	8	0	16	30	17	.273	.346
Buck Ewing	C50,OF23.1B2		73	275	59	85	31	11	7	4	16	17	18	.309	.444
Danny Richardson	OF64,P5,2B1,SS1,3B1		68	237	43	55	27	9	1	1	17	21	12	.232	.291
Tim Keefe	P64,OF1		64	205	26	35	20	10	1	1	17	42	3	.171	.244
Mickey Welch	P59,OF3		59	213	17	46	18	4	2	0	7	47	3	.216	.254
Pat Deasley	C30,OF15		41	143	18	38	17	6	1	0	4	12	2	.266	.322
Bill Finley	C8,OF8		13	44	2	8	5	0	0	0	1	8	2	.182	.182
Gene Begley	C3,OF2		5	16	1	2	1	0	0	0	1	3	1	.125	.125
Ed Caskin	SS1		1	4	1	2	1	0	0	0	0	1	0	.500	.500
Larry Corcoran	OF1	(1-2)	1	4	0	0	0	0	0	0	0	2	0	.000	.000
Jim Devine	OF1		1	3	0	0	0	0	0	0	0	1	0	.000	.000
James Devlin	P1		1	1	0	0	1	0	0	0	0	1	0	.000	.000
			124	4298	692	1156	527	175	68	21	237	410	155	.269	.356

PITCHERS	W	L	PCT	G	GS	CG	SH	SV	IP	H	BB	SO	ERA
Tim Keefe	42	20	.677	64	64	62	2	0	535	479	102	297	2.56
Mickey Welch	33	22	.600	59	59	56	1	0	500	514	163	272	2.99
Danny Richardson	0	2	.000	5	1	1	0	0	25	33	11	17	5.76
James Devlin	0	0	----	1	0	0	0	1	2	3	4	2	18.00
	75	44	.630	124	124	119	3	1	1062	1029	280	588	2.86

PHILADELPHIA Quakers
71-43 .623 -14 4th Harry Wright

BATTERS	POS/GAMES		GP	AB	R	H	BI	2B	3B	HR	BB	SO	SB	BA	SA
Sid Farrar	1B118		118	439	55	109	50	19	7	5	16	47	10	.248	.358
Charlie Bastian	2B87,SS10,3B8		105	373	46	81	38	9	11	2	33	73	29	.217	.316
Art Irwin	SS100,3B1		101	373	51	87	34	6	6	0	35	39	24	.233	.282
Joe Mulvey	3B107,OF1		107	430	71	115	53	16	10	2	15	31	27	.267	.365
Jim Fogarty	OF60,2B13,3B3,SS3,P1		77	280	54	82	47	13	5	3	42	16	30	.293	.407
Ed Andrews	OF104,2B3		107	437	93	109	28	15	4	2	31	35	56	.249	.316
George Wood	OF97,SS6,3B3		106	450	81	123	50	18	15	4	23	75	9	.273	.407
Deacon McGuire	C49,OF1		50	167	25	33	18	7	1	2	19	25	2	.198	.287
Ed Daily	OF56,P27		79	309	40	70	50	17	1	4	7	34	23	.227	.327
Charlie Ferguson	P48,OF27		72	261	56	66	25	9	1	2	37	28	9	.253	.318
Jack Clements	C47,OF7		54	185	15	38	11	5	1	0	7	34	4	.205	.243
Dan Casey	P44,OF5		44	151	11	23	9	4	1	0	9	41	0	.152	.192
Tony Cusick	C25,OF3,1B1		29	104	10	23	4	5	1	0	3	14	1	.221	.288
Jack Farrell	2B17	(1-2)	17	60	7	11	3	0	1	0	3	11	1	.183	.217
Tommy McCarthy	OF8,P1		8	27	6	5	3	2	1	0	2	3	1	.185	.333
Ledell Titcomb	P5		5	16	0	1	1	0	0	0	0	5	0	.063	.063
John Strike	P2,OF1		2	7	0	0	0	0	0	0	0	4	0	.000	.000
Charles Ganzel	C1	(1-2)	1	3	0	0	0	0	0	0	0	1	0	.000	.000
			119	4072	621	976	424	145	66	26	282	516	226	.240	.327

PITCHERS	W	L	PCT	G	GS	CG	SH	SV	IP	H	BB	SO	ERA
Charlie Ferguson	30	9	.769	48	45	43	4	2	396	317	69	212	1.98
Dan Casey	24	18	.571	44	44	39	4	0	369	326	104	193	2.41
Ed Daily	16	9	.640	27	23	22	1	0	218	211	59	95	3.06
John Strike	1	1	.500	2	2	1	0	0	15	19	7	11	4.80
Jim Fogarty	0	0	.000	1	0	0	0	0	6	7	0	4	0.00
Ledell Titcomb	0	5	.000	5	5	5	0	0	41	43	24	24	3.73
Tommy McCarthy	0	0	----	1	0	0	0	0	1	0	1	1	0.00
	71	43	.623	119	119	110	10	2	1046	923	264	540	2.45

BOSTON Beaneaters
56-61 .479 -30.5 5th John Morrill

BATTERS	POS/GAMES	GP	AB	R	H	BI	2B	3B	HR	BB	SO	SB	BA	SA
Sam Wise	1B57,2B20,SS18	96	387	71	112	72	19	12	4	33	61	31	.289	.432
Jack Burdock	2B59	59	221	26	48	25	6	1	0	11	27	3	.217	.253

BOSTON (cont.)
Beaneaters

BATTERS	POS/GAMES	GP	AB	R	H	BI	2B	3B	HR	BB	SO	SB	BA	SA
John Morrill	SS55,1B42,2B20,P1	117	430	86	106	69	25	6	7	56	81	9	.247	.381
Billy Nash	3B90,SS17	109	417	61	117	45	11	8	1	24	28	16	.281	.353
Tom Poorman	OF96	96	371	72	97	41	16	6	3	19	52	31	.261	.361
Dick Johnston	OF109	109	413	48	99	57	18	9	1	3	70	11	.240	.334
Joe Hornung	OF94	94	424	49	109	40	12	2	2	10	62	16	.257	.309
Con Daily	C49	50	180	25	43	21	4	2	0	19	29	2	.239	.283
Ezra Sutton	OF43,3B28,SS28,2B18	116	499	83	138	48	21	6	3	26	21	18	.277	.361
Old Hoss Radbourn	P58,OF9	66	253	30	60	22	5	1	2	17	36	5	.237	.289
Charles Buffinton	1B19,P18	44	176	27	51	30	4	1	1	6	12	3	.290	.341
Bill Stemmeyer	P41	41	148	24	41	20	3	2	0	12	17	3	.277	.324
Pop Tate	C31	31	106	13	24	3	3	1	0	7	17	0	.226	.274
Tom Gunning	C27	27	98	15	22	7	2	1	0	3	19	3	.224	.265
Pat Dealy	C14,OF1	15	46	9	15	3	1	1	0	4	4	5	.326	.391
Charles Parsons	P2	2	8	0	3	0	1	0	0	0	0	0	.375	.375
Myron Allen	2B1	1	3	0	0	0	0	0	0	0	1	0	.000	.000
		118	4180	657	1085	503	151	59	24	250	537	156	.260	.341

PITCHERS		W	L	PCT	G	GS	CG	SH	SV	IP	H	BB	SO	ERA
Old Hoss Radbourn		27	31	.466	58	58	57	3	0	509	521	111	218	3.00
Bill Stemmeyer		22	18	.550	41	41	41	0	0	349	300	144	239	3.02
Charles Buffinton		7	10	.412	18	17	16	0	0	151	203	39	47	4.59
Charles Parsons		0	2	.000	2	2	2	0	0	16	20	4	5	3.94
John Morrill		0	0	----	1	0	0	0	0	4	5	0	2	0.00
		56	61	.479	118	118	116	3	0	1029	1049	298	511	3.24

ST. LOUIS
Maroons

43-79   .352   -46   6th   Gus Schmelz

BATTERS	POS/GAMES		GP	AB	R	H	BI	2B	3B	HR	BB	SO	SB	BA	SA
Alex McKinnon	1B119,OF3		122	491	75	148	72	24	7	8	21	23	10	.301	.428
Fred Dunlap	2B71,OF1	(1-2)	71	285	53	76	32	15	2	3	28	30	7	.267	.365
Jack Glasscock	SS120,OF1		121	486	96	158	40	29	7	3	38	13	38	.325	.432
Jerry Denny	3B117,SS3		119	475	58	122	62	24	6	9	14	68	16	.257	.389
John Cahill	OF124,P2,3B1,SS1		125	463	43	92	32	17	6	1	9	79	16	.199	.268
Joe Quinn	OF48,2B15,1B7,3B4,SS2		75	271	33	63	21	11	3	1	8	31	12	.232	.306
Emmett Seery	OF126,P2		126	453	73	108	48	22	6	2	57	82	24	.238	.327
George Myers	C72,OF6,3B1		79	295	26	56	27	7	3	0	18	42	6	.190	.234
Jack McGeachey	OF55,2B2,3B2	(2-2)	59	226	31	46	24	12	3	2	1	37	8	.204	.310
Egyptian Healy	P42,OF1		43	145	10	14	5	5	0	0	2	67	0	.097	.131
Frank Graves	C41,OF3,P1		43	138	7	21	9	2	0	0	7	48	11	.152	.167
John Kirby	P41,OF3		42	136	10	15	5	4	0	0	3	47	0	.110	.110
Sam Crane	2B39	(2-2)	39	116	10	20	7	3	1	0	13	27	6	.172	.216
Henry Boyle	P25,OF6		30	108	8	27	13	2	2	1	5	19	0	.250	.333
Charlie Sweeney	P11,OF4,SS2		17	64	4	16	7	2	0	0	3	10	0	.250	.281
Tom Dolan	C15	(1-2)	15	44	8	11	1	3	0	0	7	9	2	.250	.318
George Mappes	C3,3B2,2B1		6	14	1	2	0	0	0	0	1	5	0	.143	.143
Joe Murphy	P4	(2-3)	4	14	0	3	1	1	0	0	0	8	0	.214	.214
Al Bauers	P4		4	12	1	2	0	0	0	0	0	4	0	.167	.167
Red Connally	OF2		2	7	0	0	0	0	0	0	0	3	0	.000	.000
Jim Reardon	P1	(1-2)	1	4	0	1	0	0	0	0	0	1	0	.250	.500
Bill Pelouze	OF1		1	3	0	0	0	0	0	0	0	0	0	.000	.000
			126	4250	547	1001	406	183	46	30	235	656	156	.236	.321

PITCHERS		W	L	PCT	G	GS	CG	SH	SV	IP	H	BB	SO	ERA
Egyptian Healy		17	23	.425	43	41	39	3	0	354	315	118	213	2.88
John Kirby		11	26	.297	41	41	38	1	0	325	329	134	129	3.30
Henry Boyle		9	15	.375	25	24	23	2	0	210	183	46	101	1.76
Charlie Sweeney		5	6	.455	11	11	11	0	0	93	108	39	28	4.16
John Cahill		1	0	1.000	2	0	0	0	0	12	11	3	2	3.00
Jim Reardon	(1-2)	0	1	.000	1	1	1	0	0	8	10	5	0	6.75
Joe Murphy	(2-3)	0	4	.000	4	4	3	0	0	33	45	16	11	8.18
Al Bauers		0	4	.000	4	4	3	0	0	29	31	27	13	5.97
Emmett Seery		0	0	----	2	0	0	0	0	7	8	3	2	7.71
Frank Graves		0	0	----	1	0	0	0	0	7	10	1	2	9.00
		43	79	.352	126	126	118	6	0	1077	1050	392	501	3.24

1886 NATIONAL LEAGUE 143

KANSAS CITY Cowboys   30-91   .248   -58.5   7th   Dave Rowe

BATTERS	POS/GAMES		GP	AB	R	H	BI	2B	3B	HR	BB	SO	SB	BA	SA
Mox McQuery	1B122		122	449	62	111	38	27	4	4	36	44	4	.247	.352
Al Myers	2B118		118	473	69	131	51	22	9	4	22	42	3	.277	.387
Charley Bassett	SS82,3B8		90	342	41	89	32	19	8	2	36	43	6	.260	.380
Jim Donnelly	3B113		113	438	51	88	38	11	3	0	36	57	16	.201	.240
Paul Radford	OF92,SS30,2B1		122	493	78	113	20	17	5	0	58	48	39	.229	.284
Dave Rowe	OF90,SS11,2B4		105	429	53	103	57	24	8	3	15	43	2	.240	.354
Jim Lillie	OF114,P1		114	416	37	73	22	9	0	0	11	80	13	.175	.197
Fatty Briody	C54,OF2,1B1		56	215	14	51	29	10	3	0	3	35	0	.237	.312
Jim Whitney	P46,OF22,3B1		67	247	25	59	23	13	3	2	29	39	5	.239	.340
Mert Hackett	C52,OF13		62	230	18	50	25	8	3	3	4	59	1	.217	.317
Peter Conway	OF31,P23	(1-2)	51	194	22	47	18	8	2	1	5	34	3	.242	.320
Stump Weidman	P51,OF3		51	179	13	30	7	2	0	0	5	46	3	.168	.179
Frank Ringo	C13,OF2,3B1	(2-2)	16	56	6	13	7	7	0	0	5	10	0	.232	.357
Dan Dugdale	C7,OF6		12	40	4	7	2	0	0	0	2	13	1	.175	.175
Silver King	P5,OF2		7	22	0	1	1	0	0	0	2	12	0	.045	.045
Larry McKeon	P3	(2-2)	3	9	0	0	0	0	0	0	0	2	0	.000	.000
George Baker	C1		1	4	1	1	0	0	0	0	0	1	0	.250	.250
			126	4236	494	967	370	177	48	19	269	608	96	.228	.306

PITCHERS			W	L	PCT	G	GS	CG	SH	SV	IP	H	BB	SO	ERA
Jim Whitney			12	32	.273	46	44	42	3	0	393	465	55	167	4.49
Stump Weidman			12	36	.250	51	51	48	1	0	428	549	112	168	4.50
Peter Conway		(1-2)	5	15	.250	23	20	19	0	0	180	236	61	81	5.75
Silver King			1	3	.250	5	5	5	0	0	39	43	9	23	4.85
Larry McKeon		(2-2)	0	2	.000	3	3	3	0	0	21	44	8	3	10.71
Jim Lillie			0	0	----	1	0	0	0	0	6	8	1	0	4.50
			30	91	.248	126	126	117	4	0	1067	1345	246	442	4.84

WASHINGTON Statesmen   28-92   .233   -60   8th   Scanlon - Gaffney

BATTERS	POS/GAMES		GP	AB	R	H	BI	2B	3B	HR	BB	SO	SB	BA	SA
Phil Baker	1B56,OF21,C16		81	325	37	72	34	6	5	1	20	32	16	.222	.280
Jimmy Knowles	2B62,3B53		115	443	43	94	35	16	11	3	15	73	20	.212	.318
Davy Force	SS56,2B8,3B4		68	242	26	44	16	5	1	0	17	26	9	.182	.211
Buck Gladman	3B44		44	152	17	21	15	5	3	1	12	30	5	.138	.230
Cannonball Crane	OF68,P10,C4		80	292	20	50	20	11	3	0	13	54	8	.171	.229
Paul Hines	OF92,1B4,SS1,3B1,2B1		121	487	80	152	56	30	8	9	35	21	21	.312	.462
Cliff Carroll	OF111		111	433	73	99	22	11	6	2	44	26	31	.229	.296
Barney Gilligan	C71,OF14,3B1,SS1		81	273	23	52	17	9	2	0	39	35	6	.190	.238
Sadie Houck	SS51,2B1	(2-2)	52	195	14	42	14	3	0	0	2	28	4	.215	.231
Jack Farrell	2B47	(2-2)	47	171	24	41	18	11	4	2	15	12	12	.240	.386
Dupee Shaw	P45,OF1		45	148	13	13	6	2	0	0	14	44	0	.088	.101
Joe Start	1B31		31	122	10	27	17	4	1	0	5	13	4	.221	.270
Bill Krieg	1B27		27	98	11	25	15	6	3	1	3	12	2	.255	.408
George Shoch	OF25,SS1		26	95	11	28	18	2	1	1	2	13	2	.295	.368
Jack Hayes	C14,OF12,2B1		26	89	8	17	9	3	0	3	4	23	0	.191	.326
Bob Barr	P22		22	79	6	13	2	2	0	0	4	23	0	.165	.190
Larry Corcoran	OF11,SS9,P2	(2-2)	21	81	9	15	3	2	1	0	7	14	3	.185	.235
Dave Oldfield	C12,OF9	(2-2)	21	71	2	10	2	2	0	0	5	15	0	.141	.169
Pony Madigan	P14,OF1		14	48	2	4	2	1	0	0	1	20	0	.083	.104
Connie Mack	C10		10	36	4	13	5	2	1	0	0	2	0	.361	.472
Frank Gilmore	P9		9	29	2	0	0	0	0	0	2	12	0	.000	.000
Harry Decker	C4,3B2,SS1	(2-2)	7	23	0	5	2	1	1	0	1	5	0	.217	.348
Ed Whiting	C6		6	21	0	0	0	0	0	0	1	12	0	.000	.000
Hank O'Day	P6		6	19	0	1	0	0	0	0	0	9	0	.053	.053
Walt Goldsby	OF6		6	18	0	4	1	1	0	0	2	3	0	.222	.278
One Arm Daily	P6		6	16	2	2	1	0	0	0	2	5	0	.125	.125
John McGlone	3B4		4	15	2	1	1	0	0	0	0	3	0	.067	.067
John Henry	P4		4	14	3	5	0	0	0	0	0	3	0	.357	.357
George Keefe	P4		4	14	1	0	0	0	0	0	0	5	0	.000	.000
Tom Kinslow	C3		3	8	1	2	1	0	0	0	0	1	0	.250	.250
Ed Fuller	P2,OF1		2	7	0	1	0	0	0	0	0	3	0	.143	.143
Jim Gallagher	SS1		1	5	1	1	0	0	0	0	0	2	0	.200	.200
George Winkelman	P1,OF1		1	5	0	1	0	0	0	0	0	1	0	.200	.200
John Fox	P1		1	3	0	1	0	0	0	0	0	0	0	.333	.333
Bill Wise	P1		1	3	0	0	0	0	0	0	0	1	0	.000	.000
Joe Yingling	P1		1	2	0	0	0	0	0	0	0	1	0	.000	.000
			125	4082	445	856	332	135	51	23	265	582	143	.210	.285

WASHINGTON (cont.)
Statesmen

PITCHERS		W	L	PCT	G	GS	CG	SH	SV	IP	H	BB	SO	ERA
Dupee Shaw		13	31	.295	45	44	43	1	0	386	384	91	177	3.34
Frank Gilmore		4	4	.500	9	9	9	1	0	75	57	22	75	2.52
Bob Barr		3	18	.143	22	22	21	1	0	191	216	54	80	4.30
Hank O'Day		2	2	.500	6	6	6	0	0	49	41	17	47	1.65
John Henry		1	3	.250	4	4	4	0	0	28	35	15	19	4.23
Cannonball Crane		1	7	.125	10	8	7	1	0	70	91	53	39	7.20
Pony Madigan		1	13	.071	14	14	13	0	0	116	159	44	29	5.06
Larry Corcoran	(2-2)	0	1	.000	2	1	1	0	0	14	16	4	3	5.71
Ed Fuller		0	1	.000	2	1	1	0	0	13	15	5	3	6.92
John Fox		0	1	.000	1	1	1	0	0	8	11	11	3	9.00
George Winkelman		0	1	.000	1	1	0	0	0	6	12	5	4	10.50
Bill Wise		0	1	.000	1	1	0	0	0	3	6	2	0	9.00
George Keefe		0	3	.000	4	4	4	0	0	31	28	15	5	5.17
One Arm Daily		0	6	.000	6	6	6	0	0	49	69	40	15	7.35
Joe Yingling		0	0	----	1	0	0	0	0	3	7	1	1	12.00
		28	92	.233	125	122	116	4	0	1041	1147	379	500	4.30

1886 AMERICAN ASSOCIATION

The $15,000 Slide

In 1886, once more, Chicago and St. Louis squared off in the World Series. And this time the outcome would be just as dramatic. But this World Series had more at stake for it was to be a winner-take-all affair. The winner would get all the money from the gate receipts, and the loser would get nothing.

The two team presidents, Von der Ahe of the Browns and Spalding of the White Stockings agreed to play a six-game series, with a seventh game added if the two teams were tied at that point. They also agreed that the first three games were to be played in Chicago, with the next three to be in St. Louis. The first game was won by Chicago 6-0. St. Louis doubled that (12-0) in the second game and evened the series. Chicago won the third, 11-4, while St. Louis won the next two, 8-5 and 10-3 to take a commanding three games to two lead. The sixth game remained tied until the bottom of the tenth, when in dramatic fashion, so the story goes, Curt Welch of the Browns slid home with the winning run. As the series was well attended, the money that St. Louis divvied up was in the neighborhood of $15,000. Thus Welch's dash home was immortalized as "the $15,000 slide."

To get to the World Series, St. Louis once more breezed to the pennant. Finishing twelve games up, the Browns featured a balanced attack led by Arlie Latham (.301, 152 runs), Tip O'Neill (.328), and by pitcher Dave Foutz (41-16). Latham's runs total and Foutz's wins and winning percentage were league-leading efforts. As a team, St. Louis led the league in seven major hitting and pitching categories, including the stolen bases category which was being compiled again after an 11-year hiatus.

Pittsburgh and Brooklyn finished away back in second and third. Pittsburgh was a strong pitching club which showcased Ed Morris, whose 41 wins tied him with the league lead in wins. Brooklyn had no regular over .280, yet they finished 15 games over .500.

Fourth place Louisville's pitcher Guy Hecker slumped to 26 wins, half of his all-time best for one year. But he made up for that relapse by winning the batting title with a mark of .341. (He also played at first base and in the outfield.) Teammate Pete Browning finished a close second at .340. Hecker's pitching alternate, Toad Ramsey, pitched a staggering 588 innings, striking out 499 batters.

Cincinnati and Philadelphia finished in fifth and sixth. Cincinnati's best was home run champ Bid McPhee (8), while Henry Larkin proved to be the best for Philadelphia at .319.

New York finished seventh even with the powerful bat of Dave Orr in the lineup. Orr finished with a solid .338 batting average, and a league best 31 triples. Dave Orr was one of the hardest hitters of the American Association while being the slowest runner. In the era of the distant fences, many of his triples would have been inside the park home runs for anyone else.

Last place Baltimore featured an ironman pitching performance. With little support (the team hit .204) Matt Kilroy somehow managed to win 29 games, while pitching 583 innings and striking out 513 batters. No other pitcher has struck out more in one season.

Although making an exciting tale, the story of Curt Welch's slide may be apocryphal at best. Contemporary accounts indicate that Welch scored the winning run easily, on a wild pitch, while standing up.

1886 AMERICAN ASSOCIATION

ST. LOUIS Browns
93-46 .669 1st Charlie Comiskey

BATTERS	POS/GAMES		GP	AB	R	H	BI	2B	3B	HR	BB	SO	SB	BA	SA
Charlie Comiskey	1B122,2B9,OF2		131	578	95	147		15	9	3	10		41	.254	.327
Yank Robinson	2B123,3B6,OF1,P1,SS1		133	481	89	132		26	9	3	64		51	.274	.385
Bill Gleason	SS125		125	524	97	141		18	5	0	43		19	.269	.323
Arlie Latham	3B133,2B1		134	578	152	174		23	8	1	55		60	.301	.374
Tip O'Neill	OF138		138	579	106	190		28	14	3	47		9	.328	.440
Curt Welch	OF138,2B2		138	563	114	158		31	13	2	29		59	.281	.393
Hugh Nicol	OF57,SS8,2B4		67	253	44	52		6	3	0	26		38	.206	.253
Doc Bushong	C106,1B1		107	386	56	86		8	0	1	31		12	.223	.251
Dave Foutz	P59,OF34,1B11		102	414	66	116		18	9	3	9		17	.280	.389
Bob Caruthers	P44,OF43,2B2		87	317	91	106		21	14	4	64		26	.334	.527
Nat Hudson	P29,OF12,2B2		43	150	16	35		4	1	0	11		2	.233	.273
Rudy Kemmler	C32,1B3		35	123	13	17		2	0	0	8		0	.138	.154
Jumbo McGinnis	P10	(2-2)	10	37	4	7		2	0	0	3		1	.189	.243
Trick McSorley	SS5		5	20	1	3		3	0	0	0		0	.150	.300
Louis Harding	C1		1	3	0	1		1	0	0	0		0	.333	.667
Joe Murphy	P1	(3-3)	1	3	0	0		0	0	0	0		1	.000	.000
			139	5009	944	1365		206	85	20	400	425	336	.273	.360

PITCHERS			W	L	PCT	G	GS	CG	SH	SV	IP	H	BB	SO	ERA
Dave Foutz			41	16	.719	59	57	55	11	1	504	418	144	283	2.11
Bob Caruthers			30	14	.682	44	43	42	2	0	387	323	86	166	2.32
Nat Hudson			16	10	.615	29	27	25	0	1	234	224	62	100	3.03
Jumbo McGinnis		(2-2)	5	5	.500	10	10	10	1	0	88	107	27	30	3.80
Joe Murphy		(3-3)	1	0	1.000	1	1	1	0	0	7	5	3	3	5.00
Yank Robinson			0	1	.000	1	1	1	0	0	9	10	7	1	3.00
			93	46	.669	139	139	134	14	2	1229	1087	329	583	2.49

PITTSBURGH Alleghenys
80-57 .584 -12 2nd Horace Phillips

BATTERS	POS/GAMES		GP	AB	R	H	BI	2B	3B	HR	BB	SO	SB	BA	SA
Otto Schomberg	1B72		72	246	53	67		6	6	1	57		7	.272	.358
Sam Barkley	2B112,OF8,1B2		122	478	77	127		31	8	1	58		22	.266	.370
Pop Smith	SS98,2B28,C1		126	483	75	105		20	9	2	42		38	.217	.308
Art Whitney	3B95,SS42,P1		136	511	70	122		13	4	0	51		15	.239	.280
Tom Brown	OF115,P1		115	460	106	131		11	11	1	56		30	.285	.363
Fred Mann	OF116		116	440	85	110		16	14	2	45		26	.250	.384
Ed Glenn	OF71		71	277	32	53		6	5	0	17		19	.191	.249
Fred Carroll	C70,OF27,1B25,SS1		122	486	92	140		28	11	5	52		20	.288	.422
Bill Kuehne	OF54,3B47,1B18		117	481	73	98		16	17	1	19		26	.204	.314
Doggie Miller	C61,OF23,2B1		83	317	70	80		15	1	2	43		35	.252	.325
Ed Morris	P64		64	227	26	38		8	3	1	10		6	.198	.214
Pud Galvin	P50		50	194	24	49		7	2	0	3		8	.253	.309
Frank Mountain	1B16,P2		18	55	6	8		1	1	0	13		3	.145	.200
Frank Ringo	C9,1B6	(1-2)	15	56	3	12		2	2	0	1		0	.214	.321
Jim Handiboe	P14,OF2		14	44	10	5		1	0	0	6		1	.114	.136
Jack Coleman	OF11	(2-2)	11	43	3	15		2	1	0	2		1	.349	.442
John Hofford	P9		9	34	4	10		3	1	0	3		2	.294	.441
Tom Quinn	C3		3	11	1	0		0	0	0	0		1	.000	.000
Bill Bishop	P2		2	7	0	1		0	0	0	0		0	.143	.143
Dan Sullivan	C1		1	4	0	0		0	0	0	0		0	.000	.000
			140	4854	810	1171		186	96	16	478	713	260	.241	.329

PITCHERS			W	L	PCT	G	GS	CG	SH	SV	IP	H	BB	SO	ERA
Ed Morris			41	20	.672	64	63	63	12	1	555	455	118	326	2.45
Pud Galvin			29	21	.580	50	50	49	2	0	435	457	75	72	2.67
Jim Handiboe			7	7	.500	14	14	12	1	0	114	82	33	83	3.32
John Hofford			3	6	.333	9	9	9	0	0	81	88	40	25	4.33
Bill Bishop			0	1	.000	2	2	2	0	0	17	17	11	4	3.18
Frank Mountain			0	2	.000	2	2	2	0	0	16	22	14	2	7.88
Art Whitney			0	0	----	1	0	0	0	0	6	7	3	2	3.00
Tom Brown			0	0	----	1	0	0	0	0	2	2	5	1	9.00
			80	57	.584	140	140	137	15	1	1226	1130	299	515	2.83

BROOKLYN Trolley Dodgers   76-61   .555   -16   3rd   Charlie Byrne

BATTERS	POS/GAMES		GP	AB	R	H	BI	2B	3B	HR	BB	SO	SB	BA	SA
Bill Phillips	1B141		141	585	68	160		26	15	0	33		13	.274	.369
Bill McClellan	2B141		141	595	131	152		33	9	1	56		43	.255	.346
Germany Smith	SS105,C1,OF1		105	426	66	105		17	6	2	19		22	.246	.329
George Pinkney	3B141,C1,P1		141	597	119	156		22	7	0	70		32	.261	.322
Ed Swartwood	OF122		122	471	95	132		13	10	3	70		37	.280	.369
Jim McTamany	OF111		111	418	86	106		23	10	2	54		18	.254	.371
Ernie Burch	OF113		113	456	78	119		22	6	2	39		16	.261	.349
Jim Peoples	C76,SS14,OF8,3B1		93	340	43	74		7	3	3	20		20	.218	.282
Adonis Terry	P34,OF32,SS13		75	299	34	71		8	9	2	10		17	.237	.344
Bob Clark	C44,OF17,SS12		71	269	37	58		8	2	0	17		14	.216	.260
Henry Porter	P48		48	184	20	33		4	0	0	4		7	.179	.201
John Harkins	P34,OF8		41	142	18	32		4	2	1	17		2	.225	.303
Steve Toole	P13,OF3		14	57	7	20		4	0	0	1		0	.351	.421
Dave Oldfield	C13,SS1,OF1	(1-2)	14	55	7	13		1	0	0	2		1	.236	.255
Hardie Henderson	P14	(2-2)	14	50	9	9		2	0	0	5		0	.180	.220
Jim McCauley	C11		11	30	5	7		1	0	0	11		1	.236	.255
Joseph Strauss	OF7,C2	(2-2)	9	36	6	9		1	1	0	1		4	.250	.333
Pop Schriver	OF5,C3		8	21	2	1		0	0	0	2		0	.048	.048
Ed Kennedy	OF6		6	22	1	4		0	0	0	2		1	.182	.182
			141	5053	832	1261		196	80	16	433	523	248	.250	.330

PITCHERS			W	L	PCT	G	GS	CG	SH	SV	IP	H	BB	SO	ERA
Henry Porter			27	19	.587	48	48	48	1	0	424	439	120	163	3.42
Adonis Terry			18	16	.529	34	34	32	5	0	288	263	115	162	3.09
John Harkins			15	16	.484	34	33	33	0	0	292	286	114	118	3.60
Hardie Henderson		(2-2)	10	4	.714	14	14	14	0	0	124	112	51	49	2.90
Steve Toole			6	6	.500	13	12	11	0	0	104	100	64	48	4.41
George Pinkney			0	0	----	1	0	0	0	0	2	2	0	0	4.50
			76	61	.555	141	141	138	6	0	1235	1202	464	540	3.42

LOUISVILLE Colonels   66-70   .485   -25.5   4th   Jim Hart

BATTERS	POS/GAMES		GP	AB	R	H	BI	2B	3B	HR	BB	SO	SB	BA	SA
Paul Cook	1B43,C21,OF2		66	262	28	54		5	2	0	10		6	.206	.240
Reddy Mack	2B137		137	483	82	118		23	11	1	68		13	.244	.344
Bill White	SS135,P1		135	557	96	143		17	10	1	37		14	.257	.329
Joe Werrick	3B136		136	561	75	140		20	14	3	33		19	.250	.351
Chicken Wolf	OF122,1B8,C3,2B1,P1		130	545	93	148		17	12	3	27		23	.272	.363
Pete Browning	OF112		112	467	86	159		29	6	2	30		26	.340	.441
Joseph Strauss	OF73,P2,C1	(1-2)	74	297	36	64		5	6	1	8		25	.215	.283
John Kerins	C65,1B47,OF7,SS1		120	487	113	131		19	9	4	66		26	.269	.370
Guy Hecker	P52,1B22,OF17		84	343	76	117		14	5	4	32		25	.341	.446
Amos Cross	C51,1B20,SS2,OF1		74	283	51	78		14	6	1	44		13	.276	.378
Toad Ramsey	P67		67	241	29	58		8	1	0	6		1	.241	.282
Lou Sylvester	OF45		45	154	41	35		5	3	0	29		3	.227	.299
Hub Collins	OF24,3B2,1B1,2B1,SS1		27	101	12	29		3	2	0	5		7	.287	.356
Bones Ely	P6,OF5		10	32	5	5		0	0	0	2		1	.156	.156
Tom Sullivan	P9,OF1		9	27	1	3		0	0	0	4		0	.111	.111
Icebox Chamberlain	P4,OF2		6	19	2	3		0	0	0	4		0	.158	.158
Leech Maskrey	OF5	(1-2)	5	19	1	3		1	0	0	1		0	.158	.211
Phil Reccius	OF5,P1		5	13	4	4		1	1	0	3		0	.308	.538
Ted Kennedy	P4	(2-2)	4	13	1	1		1	0	0	1		0	.077	.154
Joe Neale	OF2,P1		2	5	0	0		0	0	0	0		0	.000	.000
John Heintzman	1B1		1	5	1	0		0	0	0	0		0	.000	.000
Tom Terrell	C1,OF1		1	4	0	1		0	0	0	0		0	.250	.250
Clarence Murphy	OF1		1	3	0	0		0	0	0	0		0	.000	.000
			138	4921	833	1294		182	88	20	410	558	202	.263	.348

PITCHERS			W	L	PCT	G	GS	CG	SH	SV	IP	H	BB	SO	ERA
Toad Ramsey			38	27	.585	67	67	66	3	0	588	447	207	499	2.45
Guy Hecker			26	23	.531	49	48	45	2	0	421	390	118	133	2.87
Tom Sullivan			2	7	.222	9	9	8	0	0	75	94	33	27	3.96
Joe Neale			0	1	.000	1	1	0	0	0	7	11	7	0	7.71
Phil Reccius			0	1	.000	1	1	0	0	0	3	7	3	0	9.00
Icebox Chamberlain			0	3	.000	4	4	4	0	0	31	39	17	18	6.61
Bones Ely			0	4	.000	6	4	4	0	1	44	53	26	28	5.32
Ted Kennedy		(2-2)	0	4	.000	4	4	4	0	0	32	53	16	14	5.34

1886 AMERICAN ASSOCIATION 149

LOUISVILLE (cont.)
Colonels

PITCHERS		W	L	PCT	G	GS	CG	SH	SV	IP	H	BB	SO	ERA
Joseph Strauss		0	0	----	2	0	0	0	1	4	6	3	0	9.00
Chicken Wolf		0	0	----	1	0	0	0	0	3	7	0	0	15.00
Bill White		0	0	----	1	0	0	0	0	1	2	2	1	9.00
		66	70	.485	138	138	131	5	2	1210	1109	432	720	3.07

CINCINNATI
Red Stockings

65-73 .471 -27.5 5th Ollie Caylor

BATTERS	POS/GAMES		GP	AB	R	H	BI	2B	3B	HR	BB	SO	SB	BA	SA
Long John Reilly	1B110,OF6		115	441	92	117		12	11	6	31		19	.265	.383
Bid McPhee	2B140		140	560	139	149		23	12	8	59		40	.266	.395
Frank Fennelly	SS132		132	497	113	124		13	17	6	60		32	.249	.380
Hick Carpenter	3B111		111	458	67	101		8	5	2	18		8	.221	.273
Pop Corkhill	OF112,3B12,1B7,SS3,P1		129	540	81	143		9	7	5	23		24	.265	.335
Fred Lewis	OF76,3B1		77	324	72	103		14	6	2	20		8	.318	.417
Charlie Jones	OF127		127	500	87	135		22	10	6	61		3	.270	.390
Kid Baldwin	C71,3B13,OF6		87	315	41	72		8	7	3	8		12	.229	.327
Tony Mullane	P63,OF27,1B4,3B2,2B1,SS1		91	324	59	73		12	5	0	25		20	.225	.293
Pop Snyder	C41,1B19,OF1		60	220	33	41		8	3	0	13		11	.186	.250
Jim Keenan	C30,OF7,3B5,1B4,P2		44	148	31	40		4	3	3	18		0	.270	.399
George Pechiney	P40,OF4		41	144	14	30		4	2	1	6		1	.208	.285
Leech Maskrey	OF26,3B2	(2-2)	27	98	7	19		3	1	0	5		4	.194	.245
Larry McKeon	P19,1B2,2B1	(1-2)	19	75	9	19		2	3	0	0		0	.253	.360
Abner Powell	SS6,OF,P4	(2-2)	19	74	13	17		1	1	0	4		0	.230	.270
Lou Sylvester	OF17	(2-2)	17	55	10	10		0	0	3	7		2	.182	.345
Elmer Smith	P9,OF1		9	28	6	8		1	1	0	9		0	.286	.393
Lee Richmond	OF7,P3		8	29	3	8		0	0	0	3		0	.276	.276
Lefty Marr	OF8		8	29	2	8		1	1	0	1		1	.276	.379
Joe Murphy	P5	(1-3)	5	18	0	0		0	0	0	0		0	.000	.000
Will White	P3		3	9	1	1		0	0	0	1		0	.111	.111
Bill Irwin	P2		2	6	0	0		0	0	0	1		0	.000	.000
Clarence Stephens	P1		1	5	0	3		0	0	0	0		0	.600	.600
Jack Boyle	C1		1	5	0	1		0	0	0	0		0	.200	.200
Dan Bickham	P1		1	3	2	1		0	0	0	1		0	.333	.333
Jim Reardon	P1,OF1	(2-2)	1	3	0	0		0	0	0	0		0	.000	.000
----- Smith	P1		1	4	1	1		0	0	0	0		0	.250	.250
Farmer Vaughn	C1		1	3	0	0		0	0	0	0		0	.000	.000
			141	4915	883	1224		145	95	45	374	633	185	.249	.345

PITCHERS		W	L	PCT	G	GS	CG	SH	SV	IP	H	BB	SO	ERA
Tony Mullane		33	27	.550	63	56	55	1	0	530	501	166	250	3.70
George Pechiney		15	21	.417	40	40	35	2	0	330	355	133	110	4.10
Larry McKeon	(1-2)	8	8	.500	19	19	16	0	0	156	174	54	46	5.08
Elmer Smith		4	4	.444	9	9	8	0	0	73	57	44	40	3.72
Joe Murphy	(1-3)	2	3	.400	5	5	5	0	0	46	50	21	11	4.89
Dan Bickham		1	0	1.000	1	1	1	0	0	9	13	3	6	3.00
Clarence Stephens		1	0	1.000	1	1	1	0	0	8	9	5	6	5.63
Will White		1	2	.333	3	3	3	0	0	26	28	10	6	4.15
Abner Powell	(2-2)	0	1	.000	4	1	1	0	0	15	16	9	4	4.70
Jim Keenan		0	1	.000	2	0	0	0	0	8	8	3	2	3.38
Jim Reardon	(1-2)	0	1	.000	1	1	0	0	0	2	5	4	0	18.00
Lee Richmond		0	2	.000	3	2	1	0	0	18	24	11	6	8.00
Bill Irwin		0	2	.000	2	2	2	0	0	17	18	8	6	5.82
----- Smith		0	1	.000	1	1	1	0	0	9	8	10	1	4.00
Pop Corkhill		0	0	----	1	0	0	0	0	1	1	0	1	13.50
		65	73	.471	141	141	129	3	0	1248	1267	481	495	4.18

PHILADELPHIA
Athletics

63-72 .467 -28 6th Simmons - Sharsig

BATTERS	POS/GAMES		GP	AB	R	H	BI	2B	3B	HR	BB	SO	SB	BA	SA
Harry Stovey	1B62,OF63,P1		123	489	115	144		28	11	7	64		68	.294	.440
Lou Bierbauer	2B133,C4,P2,SS2		137	522	56	118		17	5	2	21		19	.226	.289
Chippy McGarr	SS71		71	267	41	71		9	3	2	9		17	.266	.345
Jack Gleason	3B77		77	299	39	56		8	7	1	16		8	.187	.271
Jack Coleman	OF115,1B6,P3,2B1	(1-2)	121	492	67	121		18	16	0	33		28	.246	.348
Ed Greer	OF70,C1	(2-2)	71	264	33	51		5	3	1	8		12	.193	.246

1886 AMERICAN ASSOCIATION

PHILADELPHIA (cont.)
Athletics

BATTERS	POS/GAMES		GP	AB	R	H	BI	2B	3B	HR	BB	SO	SB	BA	SA
Henry Larkin	OF139		139	565	133	180		36	16	2	59		32	.319	.450
Wilbert Robinson	C61,1B22,OF5		87	342	57	69		11	3	1	21		33	.202	.260
Jack O'Brien	C36,3B27,1B24,SS10,2B7,OF3		105	423	65	107		25	7	0	38		23	.253	.345
Jocko Milligan	C40,1B29,OF5,3B2		75	301	52	76		17	3	5	21		18	.252	.379
Al Atkinson	P45		45	148	27	18		1	1	0	26		4	.122	.142
Joe Quest	SS41,2B2		42	150	14	31		4	1	0	20		5	.207	.247
Denny Lyons	3B32		32	123	22	26		3	1	0	8		7	.211	.252
Bobby Mathews	P24,OF1		24	88	16	21		3	0	0	3		1	.239	.273
Bill Hart	P22		22	73	3	10		1	1	0	3		1	.137	.178
Orator Shaffer	OF21		21	82	15	22		3	3	0	8		3	.268	.378
Cyclone Miller	P19,OF1,3B1		21	66	8	9		2	0	0	14		3	.136	.167
Ted Kennedy	P20	(1-2)	20	68	3	3		0	0	0	3		0	.044	.044
George Bradley	SS13		13	48	1	4		0	1	0	1		2	.083	.125
John Irwin	SS2,3B1		3	13	4	3		1	0	0	0		0	.231	.308
Sam Weaver	P2,OF1		2	7	0	1		0	0	0	0		0	.143	.143
Jake Aydelotte	P2		2	6	0	0		0	0	0	1		0	.000	.000
Charlie Gessner	P1		1	4	1	1		0	0	0	0		0	.250	.250
Jim Hyndman	P1,OF1		1	4	0	0		0	0	0	0		0	.000	.000
Reggie Smith	P1		1	4	0	0		0	0	0	0		0	.000	.000
Charles Kelly	SS1		1	3	0	0		0	0	0	0		0	.000	.000
James Brown	P1		1	3	0	0		0	0	0	0		0	.000	.000
Ed Clark	P1		1	2	0	0		0	0	0	1		0	.000	.000
			139	4856	772	1142		192	82	21	378	697	284	.235	.321

PITCHERS		W	L	PCT	G	GS	CG	SH	SV	IP	H	BB	SO	ERA
Al Atkinson		25	17	.595	45	45	44	1	0	397	414	101	154	3.95
Bobby Mathews		13	9	.591	24	24	22	0	0	198	226	53	93	3.96
Cyclone Miller		10	8	.556	19	19	19	1	0	170	158	59	99	2.97
Bill Hart		9	13	.409	22	22	22	2	0	186	183	66	78	3.19
Ted Kennedy	(1-2)	5	15	.250	20	19	19	0	0	173	196	65	68	4.53
Jack Coleman		1	1	.500	3	1	1	0	0	21	18	5	2	2.61
Reggie Smith		0	1	.000	1	1	1	0	0	9	15	5	4	9.00
Jim Brown		0	1	.000	1	1	1	0	0	8	9	3	4	3.24
Ed Clark		0	1	.000	1	1	1	0	0	8	10	2	2	6.75
Charlie Gessner		0	1	.000	1	1	1	0	0	8	13	5	0	9.00
Jim Hyndman		0	1	.000	1	1	0	0	0	2	5	5	1	27.00
Jake Aydelotte		0	2	.000	2	2	2	0	0	18	21	12	5	4.00
Sam Weaver		0	2	.000	2	2	1	0	0	11	30	2	2	14.73
Lou Bierbauer		0	0	----	2	0	0	0	0	11	8	5	1	4.22
Harry Stovey		0	0	----	1	0	0	0	0	0	2	0	0	27.00
		63	72	.467	139	139	134	4	0	1219	1308	388	513	3.97

NEW YORK
Metropolitans

53-82 .393 -38 7th Gifford - Ferguson

BATTERS	POS/GAMES	GP	AB	R	H	BI	2B	3B	HR	BB	SO	SB	BA	SA
Dave Orr	1B136	136	571	93	193		25	31	7	17		16	.338	.527
Tom Forster	2B62,OF4,SS1	67	251	33	49		3	2	1	20		9	.195	.235
Candy Nelson	SS73,OF36	109	413	89	93		7	2	0	64		14	.225	.252
Frank Hankinson	3B136	136	522	66	126		14	5	2	49		10	.241	.299
Steve Brady	OF123,1B1	124	466	56	112		8	5	0	35		16	.240	.279
Steve Behel	OF59	59	224	32	46		5	2	0	22		16	.205	.246
Chief Roseman	OF134,P1	134	559	90	127		19	10	5	24		6	.227	.324
Charlie Reipschlager	C57,OF9	65	232	21	49		4	6	0	9		2	.211	.280
Tom McLaughlin	SS63,2B10,OF1	74	250	27	34		3	1	0	26		13	.136	.156
Jack Lynch	P51	51	169	17	27		5	0	0	15		4	.160	.189
Jim Donahue	OF32,C19	49	186	14	37		0	0	0	10		1	.199	.199
Bill Holbert	C45,OF3,SS1	48	171	8	35		4	2	0	6		4	.205	.251
John Meister	2B45	45	186	35	44		7	3	2	4		1	.237	.339
Al Mays	P41	41	135	11	16		3	1	1	4		2	.119	.178
Ed Cushman	P38	38	126	10	19		1	0	0	9		0	.151	.159
Elmer Foster	2B21,OF14	35	125	16	23		0	1	0	7		3	.184	.200
Joe Crotty	C14	14	47	6	8		0	1	0	4		3	.170	.213
John Schafer	P8	8	25	3	6		0	0	0	4		0	.240	.240
Chief Zimmer	C6	6	19	1	3		0	0	0	1		0	.158	.158
Pete Cannell	3B1	1	5	0	0		0	0	0	0		0	.000	.000
Harry Brooks	P1,OF1	1	1	0	0		0	0	0	0		0	.000	.000
		137	4683	628	1047		108	72	18	330	578	120	.224	.289

NEW YORK (cont.)
Metropolitans

PITCHERS	W	L	PCT	G	GS	CG	SH	SV	IP	H	BB	SO	ERA
Jack Lynch	20	30	.400	51	50	50	1	0	433	485	116	193	3.95
Ed Cushman	17	20	.459	38	37	37	2	0	326	278	99	167	3.12
Al Mays	11	28	.282	41	41	39	1	0	350	330	140	163	3.39
John Schafer	5	3	.625	8	8	8	1	0	69	40	29	36	1.96
Harry Brooks	0	1	.000	1	1	0	0	0	2	9	2	0	36.00
Chief Roseman	0	0	----	1	0	0	0	0	7	6	0	0	5.14
	53	82	.393	137	137	134	5	0	1186	1148	386	559	3.50

BALTIMORE
Orioles

48-83   .366   -41   8th   Billy Barnie

BATTERS	POS/GAMES		GP	AB	R	H	BI	2B	3B	HR	BB	SO	SB	BA	SA
Milt Scott	1B131,P1		137	484	48	92		11	4	2	22		11	.190	.242
Mike Muldoon	2B57,3B44		101	381	57	76		13	8	0	34		12	.199	.276
Jimmy Macullar	SS82,OF2,2B1,P1		85	268	49	55		7	1	0	49		23	.205	.239
Jumbo Davis	3B60		60	216	23	42		5	2	1	11		12	.194	.250
Jack Manning	OF137		137	556	78	124		18	7	1	50		24	.223	.286
Pat O'Connell	OF41,1B1,P1		42	166	20	30		3	2	0	11		10	.181	.223
Joe Sommer	OF95,2B32,3B11,SS3,P1		139	560	79	117		18	4	1	24		31	.209	.261
Chris Fulmer	C68,OF12,P1		80	270	54	66		9	3	1	48		29	.244	.311
Joe Farrell	2B45,3B27,OF1		73	301	36	63		8	3	1	12		5	.209	.266
Matt Kilroy	P68,OF2		68	218	33	38		3	1	0	21		25	.174	.197
Sadie Houck	SS55,2B5,OF1	(1-2)	61	260	29	50		8	1	0	4		25	.192	.231
Buster Hoover	OF40		40	157	25	34		2	6	0	16		15	.217	.306
Tom Dolan	C35,OF3	(2-2)	38	125	13	19		3	2	0	8		8	.152	.208
Blondie Purcell	OF26,P1,SS1		26	85	17	19		0	1	0	17		13	.224	.247
Jumbo McGinnis	P26,OF2	(2-2)	26	85	7	16		5	0	1	4		3	.188	.282
Bill Traffley	C25		25	85	15	18		0	1	0	10		8	.212	.235
Jim Clinton	OF23		23	83	8	15		1	0	0	4		3	.181	.193
Len Sowders	OF23,1B1		23	76	10	20		3	1	0	12		6	.263	.329
Hardie Henderson	P19	(1-2)	19	68	5	16		2	2	0	6		0	.235	.324
Abner Powell	P7,OF4	(1-2)	11	39	4	7		2	1	0	1		4	.179	.282
Ed Greer	C11	(1-2)	11	38	2	5		1	0	0	2		4	.132	.158
Bill Taylor	P8,1B1,C1		10	39	4	12		0	1	0	1		1	.308	.359
Dick Conway	P9,OF1		9	34	5	7		2	0	0	3		1	.206	.265
Bill Conway	C7		7	14	4	2		0	0	0	7		0	.143	.143
Ned Bligh	C3		3	9	0	0		0	0	0	1		0	.000	.000
Bill Barnie	C1,OF1		2	6	0	0		0	0	0	1		0	.000	.000
Sandy Nava	C1,SS1		2	5	0	1		0	0	0	0		0	.200	.200
Frank Houseman	P1		1	4	0	1		0	0	0	0		0	.250	.250
Tony Hellman	C1		1	3	0	0		0	0	0	0		0	.000	.000
Ed Knouff	P1		1	3	0	0		0	0	0	0		0	.000	.000
----- Zay	OF1,P1		1	1	0	0		0	0	0	0		0	.000	.000
			139	4639	625	945		124	51	8	379	603	269	.204	.258

PITCHERS		W	L	PCT	G	GS	CG	SH	SV	IP	H	BB	SO	ERA
Matt Kilroy		29	34	.460	68	68	66	5	0	583	476	182	513	3.37
Jumbo McGinnis	(2-2)	11	13	.458	26	25	24	0	0	209	235	48	70	3.48
Hardie Henderson	(1-2)	3	15	.167	19	19	19	0	0	171	188	66	88	4.62
Abner Powell		2	5	.286	7	7	7	0	0	60	66	26	15	5.10
Dick Conway		2	7	.222	9	9	8	0	0	77	106	43	64	6.81
Bill Taylor		1	6	.143	8	8	8	0	0	72	87	20	37	5.72
Ed Knouff		0	1	.000	1	1	1	0	0	9	2	5	8	2.00
Frank Houseman		0	1	.000	1	1	1	0	0	8	6	1	5	3.38
----- Zay		0	1	.000	1	1	0	0	0	2	4	4	2	9.00
Joe Sommer		0	0	----	1	0	0	0	0	4	14	3	1	18.00
Milt Scott		0	0	----	1	0	0	0	0	3	2	2	0	3.00
Pat O'Connell		0	0	----	1	0	0	0	0	3	4	2	1	6.00
Chris Fulmer		0	0	----	1	0	0	0	0	2	2	1	0	4.50
Jimmy Macullar		0	0	----	1	0	0	0	0	2	4	0	1	4.50
Blondie Purcell		0	0	----	1	0	0	0	0	1	1	0	0	9.00
		48	83	.366	139	139	134	5	0	1207	1197	403	805	4.08

1887 NATIONAL LEAGUE

A Walk Is as Good as a Hit

During the first few years of organized baseball, the playing rules of baseball were in a constant state of flux. The search was always for the perfect balance between the batter and the pitcher. Thus, when the batters hit too well, a rule was changed which gave the pitcher an extra edge. And contrarily, when pitchers dominated, some way was found to give batters an edge for the next campaign. One of the specific ways to control the batter-pitcher relationship was through the ball and strike counts.

The year 1886 was the third consecutive season that pitching dominated the game. The National League as a whole had batted less than .250 for the three-year period. To spice up the hitting, the rules needed to be changed. In 1876, a batter needed nine balls to receive a walk. In 1880, this number was reduced to eight; in 1882 to seven, and in 1884 to six. In 1887, baseball decided to reduce the number needed to five. In addition, it was decided to give the batters a fourth strike, when three had always been the total. But the most interesting change of all was the new rule which gave a batter credit for a hit each time he walked.

The other major story of 1887 came out of Detroit. This franchise got its start in 1881 when it joined the league as a replacement for the Cincinnati team. The Detroit Wolverines suffered through several undistinguished campaigns, culminating with a rock bottom 28-84 finish in 1884. But soon, things would look up. Late in 1885, Detroit bought the entire Buffalo team for $7,000. The Wolverines were after the Big Four (Dan Brouthers, Hardy Richardson, Jack Rowe, and Deacon White) so they bought the entire team to obtain them. These men were considered to be four of the premier players in the game; Brouthers and White had won three batting titles between them. With this quartet, Detroit turned into an instant contender. Without them, in 1885, they finished in sixth place, 44 games out of first. With them, in 1886, they finished in second, two and one-half games behind.

There were two franchise changes before the 1887 season. The first was the move of St. Louis to Indianapolis. The second was the defection of the Pittsburgh club from the American Association to the National League. They took the place of the defunct Kansas City franchise.

No one was surprised when Detroit blasted out of the gate in 1887, winning 20 of their first 25 games. Chicago and New York briefly contended, but were soon left behind, as Detroit marched to the flag. The Wolverines finished three and one-half games ahead of a hard-charging Philadelphia team who beat out Chicago for second. Detroit's success continued in the post-season as they whipped the American Association's St. Louis Browns ten games to five in the World Series.

The rule changes had their desired results as batting averages soared in 1887. Counting the walk-hits, the league batted .321 as a whole, with six of the eight teams reaching the .300 mark. Without counting the walk-hits, the league's average still jumped nearly 20 points, no doubt due to the fourth strike.

Organized baseball noticed that all this hitting was too much of a good thing. So they ruled that in 1888, walks would no longer be considered a hit. The one-year experiment was over. In 1968, the Special Baseball Records Committee decided to normalize the batting records of 1887 (and 1876 where walks counted as at bats) by throwing out (over the protestation of many) all of the walk-hits.

Two of the best hitters appeared in the Detroit lineup. Both Dan Brouthers (.338) and league leader Sam Thompson (.372) had stellar years. In addition to their gaudy averages, both led the circuit in other categories. Brouthers scored the most runs (153) and most doubles (36), while Thompson had the most runs batted in (166) and the most hits (203).

Philadelphia's best performers were pitchers — certain an anomaly for this year. Hurlers Dan Casey, Charles Ferguson, and Charles Buffinton each won over 20 games, while Casey led the league with the best earned run average (2.86). As good as this trio was, they could not match the exploits of Chicago's John Clarkson. He singlehandedly pitched the team into third; his 38 wins accounting for nearly 60 percent of the team's total. He did have help, though, as team captain Cap Anson (.347) hit well. Fourth place New York rode the arm of Tim Keefe (35-19), the bat of Roger Connor and his 17 home runs, and Monte Ward (.338) to a first division finish.

In the second division, several players had good years. The peerless King Kelly played well for his new Boston team by hitting a robust .322. Pud Galvin managed to win 28 for sixth place Pittsburgh, and Billy O'Brien of seventh place Washington led the league in home runs with 19.

Opponents to the "normalization" of the 1887 batting records argue that the rules governing baseball during that year stated clearly that a walk should count as a hit. Also, they claimed, in other years when the rules were different, the records have not been altered to catch up with modern rules.

So far, the arguments have fallen on deaf ears. Original batting leader Cap Anson (.421) will have to wait a little longer to regain his title.

1887 NATIONAL LEAGUE

DETROIT Wolverines

79-45 .639 1st Bill Watkins

BATTERS	POS/GAMES		GP	AB	R	H	BI	2B	3B	HR	BB	SO	SB	BA	SA
Dan Brouthers	1B123		123	500	153	169	101	36	20	12	71	9	34	.338	.562
Fred Dunlap	2B65,P1		65	272	60	72	45	13	10	5	25	12	15	.265	.441
Jack Rowe	SS124		124	537	135	171	96	30	10	6	39	11	22	.318	.445
Deacon White	3B106,OF3,1B2		111	449	71	136	75	20	11	3	26	15	20	.303	.416
Sam Thompson	OF127		127	545	118	203	166	29	23	11	32	19	22	.372	.571
Ned Hanlon	OF118		118	471	79	129	69	13	7	4	30	24	69	.274	.357
Larry Twitchell	OF53,P15		65	264	44	88	51	14	6	0	8	19	12	.333	.432
Charles Ganzel	C51,OF4,1B2,3B1		57	227	40	59	20	6	5	0	8	2	3	.260	.330
Hardy Richardson	2B64,OF59		120	543	131	178	94	25	18	8	31	40	29	.328	.484
Charlie Bennett	C45,OF1,1B1		46	160	26	39	20	6	5	3	30	22	7	.244	.400
Pretzels Getzien	P43,OF1		43	156	19	29	14	4	5	1	10	32	2	.186	.295
Fatty Briody	C33		33	128	24	29	26	6	1	1	9	10	6	.227	.313
Peter Conway	P17,OF8		24	95	16	22	7	5	1	1	2	9	0	.232	.337
Lady Baldwin	P24		24	85	15	23	7	0	1	0	10	6	4	.271	.294
Bill Shindle	3B21,OF1		22	84	17	24	12	3	2	0	7	10	13	.286	.369
Stump Weidman	P21	(1-3)	21	82	12	17		2	0	0	3	3	6	.207	.232
Jim Manning	OF10,SS3		13	52	5	10	3	1	0	0	5	4	3	.192	.212
Henry Gruber	P7		7	24	3	4	0	0	1	0	6	6	0	.167	.250
Walter Burke	P2,OF1		2	8	1	2	1	0	0	0	0	1	0	.250	.250
Eb Beatin	P2		2	7	0	0	0	0	0	0	0	4	0	.000	.000
			127	4689	969	1404	818	213	126	55	352	258	267	.299	.434

PITCHERS			W	L	PCT	G	GS	CG	SH	SV	IP	H	BB	SO	ERA
Pretzels Getzien			29	13	.690	43	42	41	2	0	367	373	106	135	3.73
Stump Weidman		(1-3)	13	7	.650	21	20	20	0	0	183	221	60	56	5.36
Lady Baldwin			13	10	.565	24	24	24	1	0	211	225	61	60	3.84
Larry Twitchell			11	1	.917	15	12	11	0	1	112	120	36	24	4.33
Peter Conway			8	9	.471	17	17	16	0	0	146	132	47	40	2.90
Henry Gruber			4	3	.571	7	7	7	0	0	62	63	21	12	2.74
Eb Beatin			1	1	.500	2	2	2	0	0	18	13	8	6	4.00
Walter Burke			0	1	.000	2	2	1	0	0	15	21	5	3	6.00
Fred Dunlap			0	0	----	1	0	0	0	0	2	4	0	1	4.50
			79	45	.639	127	126	122	3	1	1116	1172	344	337	3.77

PHILADELPHIA Quakers

75-48 .610 -3.5 2nd Harry Wright

BATTERS	POS/GAMES		GP	AB	R	H	BI	2B	3B	HR	BB	SO	SB	BA	SA
Sid Farrar	1B116		116	443	83	125	72	20	9	4	42	29	24	.282	.395
Barney McLaughlin	2B50		50	205	26	45	26	8	3	1	11	27	2	.220	.302
Art Irwin	SS100		100	374	65	95	56	14	8	2	48	26	19	.254	.350
Joe Mulvey	3B11		111	474	93	136	78	21	6	2	21	14	43	.287	.369
Jim Fogarty	OF123,SS2,3B2,P1		126	495	113	129	50	26	12	8	82	44	102	.261	.410
George Wood	OF104,SS3,3B3,2B3		113	491	118	142	66	22	19	14	40	51	19	.289	.497
Ed Andrews	OF99,2B4,1B1		104	464	110	151	67	19	7	4	21	21	57	.325	.422
Jack Clements	C59,3B4,SS3		66	246	48	69	47	13	7	1	9	24	7	.280	.402
Charlie Ferguson	P37,2B27,OF6,3B5		72	264	67	89	85	14	6	3	34	19	13	.337	.470
Charles Buffinton	P40,OF22,1B10		66	269	34	72	46	12	1	1	11	3	8	.268	.331
Charlie Bastian	2B39,SS18,3B4		60	221	33	47	21	11	1	1	19	29	11	.213	.285
Dan Casey	P45,OF1		45	164	22	27	17	3	0	1	6	20	1	.165	.201
Deacon McGuire	C41		41	150	22	46	23	6	6	2	11	8	3	.307	.467
Tom Gunning	C28		28	104	22	27	16	6	1	1	5	6	18	.260	.365
Ed Daily	OF21,P6	(1-2)	26	106	18	30	17	11	1	1	3	9	8	.283	.334
Tommy McCarthy	OF8,2B5,SS3,3B2		18	70	7	13	6	4	0	0	2	5	15	.186	.243
Al Maul	OF8,P7,1B2		16	56	15	17	4	2	2	1	15	10	5	.304	.464
Tony Cusick	C4,1B3,2B1		7	24	3	7	5	1	0	0	3	1	0	.292	.333
James Devlin	P2		2	6	2	2	0	0	0	0	1	0	0	.333	.333
Harry Lyons	OF1	(1-2)	1	4	0	0	0	0	0	0	1	0	0	.000	.000
			128	4630	901	1269	702	213	89	47	385	346	355	.274	.389

PITCHERS			W	L	PCT	G	GS	CG	SH	SV	IP	H	BB	SO	ERA
Dan Casey			28	13	.683	45	45	43	4	0	390	377	115	119	2.86
Charlie Ferguson			22	10	.688	37	33	31	2	1	297	297	47	125	3.00
Charles Buffinton			21	17	.553	40	38	35	1	0	332	352	92	160	3.66
Al Maul			4	2	.667	7	5	4	0	0	50	72	15	18	5.58
James Devlin			0	2	.000	2	2	2	0	0	18	20	10	6	6.00
Ed Daily		(1-2)	0	4	.000	6	5	4	0	0	41	52	25	7	7.24
Jim Fogarty			0	0	----	1	0	0	0	0	3	3	1	0	9.00
			75	48	.610	128	128	119	7	1	1131	1173	305	435	3.47

1887 NATIONAL LEAGUE

CHICAGO White Stockings — 71-50 .587 -6.5 3rd Cap Anson

BATTERS	POS/GAMES	GP	AB	R	H	BI	2B	3B	HR	BB	SO	SB	BA	SA
Cap Anson	1B122,C1	122	472	107	164	102	33	13	7	60	18	27	.347	.517
Fred Pfeffer	2B123,OF2	123	479	95	133	89	21	6	16	34	20	57	.278	.447
Ned Williamson	SS127,P1	127	439	77	117	78	20	14	9	73	57	45	.267	.437
Tom Burns	3B107,OF8	115	424	57	112	60	20	10	3	34	32	32	.264	.380
Billy Sunday	OF50	50	199	41	58	32	6	6	3	21	20	34	.291	.427
Jimmy Ryan	OF122,P8,2B3	126	508	117	145	74	23	10	11	53	19	50	.285	.435
Marty Sullivan	OF115,P1	115	472	98	134	77	13	16	7	36	53	35	.284	.424
Tom Daly	C64,OF8,SS2,2B2,1B2	74	256	45	53	17	10	4	2	22	25	29	.207	.301
John Clarkson	P60,OF5	63	215	40	52	25	5	5	6	11	25	6	.242	.395
Silver Flint	C47,1B2	49	187	22	50	21	8	6	3	4	28	7	.267	.422
George Van Haltren	OF27,P20	45	172	30	35	17	4	0	3	15	15	12	.203	.279
Mark Baldwin	P40,OF5,1B1	40	139	18	26	17	1	1	4	10	42	4	.187	.295
Dell Darling	C20,OF20	38	141	28	45	20	7	4	3	22	18	19	.319	.489
Bob Pettit	OF32,C1,P1	32	138	29	36	12	3	3	2	8	15	16	.261	.370
Patsy Tebeau	3B20	20	68	8	11	10	3	0	0	4	4	8	.162	.206
Shadow Pyle	P4,OF1	4	16	1	3	4	1	0	1	0	0	1	.188	.438
Charles Sprague	P3,OF1	3	13	0	2	0	0	0	0	0	2	0	.154	.154
Emil Geis	P1,1B1,2B1	3	12	0	1	0	0	0	0	0	7	0	.083	.083
John Flynn	OF1	1	0	0	0	0	0	0	0	0	0	0	----	----
		127	4350	813	1177	655	178	98	80	407	400	382	.271	.412

PITCHERS	W	L	PCT	G	GS	CG	SH	SV	IP	H	BB	SO	ERA
John Clarkson	38	21	.644	60	59	56	2	0	523	513	92	237	3.08
Mark Baldwin	18	17	.514	40	39	35	1	1	334	329	122	164	3.40
George Van Haltren	11	7	.611	20	18	18	1	1	161	177	66	76	3.86
Jimmy Ryan	2	1	.667	8	3	2	0	0	45	53	17	14	4.20
Charles Sprague	1	0	1.000	3	3	2	0	0	22	24	13	9	4.91
Shadow Pyle	1	3	.250	4	4	3	0	0	27	32	21	5	5.00
Emil Geis	0	1	.000	1	1	1	0	0	9	17	3	4	8.00
Ned Williamson	0	0	----	1	0	0	0	0	2	2	1	0	9.00
Marty Sullivan	0	0	----	1	0	0	0	0	2	6	1	1	9.00
Bob Pettit	0	0	----	1	0	0	0	1	1	3	2	0	0.00
	71	50	.587	127	127	117	4	3	1126	1156	338	510	3.46

NEW YORK Giants — 68-55 .553 -10.5 4th Jim Mutrie

BATTERS	POS/GAMES		GP	AB	R	H	BI	2B	3B	HR	BB	SO	SB	BA	SA
Roger Connor	1B127		127	471	113	134	104	26	22	17	75	50	43	.285	.541
Danny Richardson	2B108,3B14,P1		122	450	79	125	62	19	10	3	36	25	41	.278	.384
Monte Ward	SS129		129	545	114	184	53	16	5	1	29	12	111	.338	.391
Buck Ewing	3B51,2B19,C8		77	318	83	97	44	17	13	6	30	33	26	.305	.497
Pete Gillespie	OF76,3B1		76	295	40	78	37	9	3	3	12	21	37	.264	.346
George Gore	OF111		111	459	95	133	49	16	5	1	42	18	39	.290	.353
Mike Tiernan	OF103,P5		103	407	82	117	62	13	12	10	32	31	28	.287	.452
Willard Brown	C46,3B3,OF2		49	170	17	37	25	3	2	0	10	15	10	.218	.259
Jim O'Rourke	C40,3B38,OF28,2B2		103	397	73	113	88	15	13	3	36	11	46	.285	.411
Mike Dorgan	OF69,1B2		71	283	41	73	34	10	0	0	15	20	22	.258	.293
Tim Keefe	P56,OF1		56	191	27	42	23	7	6	2	20	41	2	.243	.338
Mickey Welch	P40,OF1		40	148	16	36	15	4	2	2	6	1	2	.243	.338
Pat Deasley	C24,3B7,SS1		30	118	12	37	23	5	0	0	9	7	3	.314	.356
John Rainey	3B17		17	58	6	17	12	3	0	0	5	6	0	.293	.345
Pat Murphy	C17		17	56	4	12	4	2	0	0	2	4	1	.214	.250
William George	P13,OF1		13	53	6	9	5	0	0	0	1	6	2	.170	.170
Ledell Titcomb	P9	(1-2)	9	29	1	2	1	0	0	0	1	9	1	.069	.069
Mike Mattimore	P7,OF2		8	32	5	8	4	1	0	0	0	6	1	.250	.281
William Swabach	P2		2	7	0	0	0	0	0	0	0	4	0	.000	.000
Gil Hatfield	3B2		2	7	2	3	3	1	0	0	0	1	0	.429	.571
Jim Becannon	3B1		1	5	0	0	0	0	0	0	0	2	0	.000	.000
John Roach	P1		1	4	0	1	1	0	0	0	0	1	0	.250	.250
Joe Gerhardt	3B1	(1-2)	1	4	0	0	0	0	0	0	0	0	0	.000	.000
Dennis Casey	2B1		1	4	0	0	2	0	0	0	0	1	0	.000	.000
Stump Weidman	P1	(2-3)	1	3	0	1	0	0	0	0	0	0	0	.333	.333
Candy Nelson	3B1	(2-2)	1	2	0	0	0	0	0	0	0	1	0	.000	.000
			129	4516	816	1259	651	167	93	48	361	326	415	.279	.389

PITCHERS	W	L	PCT	G	GS	CG	SH	SV	IP	H	BB	SO	ERA
Tim Keefe	35	19	.648	56	56	54	2	0	479	447	108	186	3.10
Mickey Welch	22	15	.595	40	40	39	2	0	346	339	91	115	3.36

NEW YORK (cont.)
Giants

PITCHERS			W	L	PCT	G	GS	CG	SH	SV	IP	H	BB	SO	ERA
Ledell Titcomb		(1-2)	4	3	.571	9	9	9	0	0	72	68	37	34	4.13
Mike Mattimore			3	3	.500	7	7	6	1	0	57	47	28	12	2.37
William George			3	9	.250	13	13	11	0	0	108	126	89	49	5.25
Mike Tiernan			1	2	.333	5	0	0	0	1	20	33	7	3	9.00
Stump Weidman		(2-3)	0	1	.000	1	1	1	0	0	8	10	2	4	1.13
John Roach			0	1	.000	1	1	1	0	0	8	18	4	3	11.25
William Swabach			0	2	.000	2	2	2	0	0	16	27	6	6	5.06
Danny Richardson			0	0	----	1	0	0	0	0	0	0	1	0	0.00
			68	55	.553	129	129	123	5	1	1114	1115	373	412	3.60

BOSTON 61-60 .504 -16.5 5th John Morrill
Beaneaters

BATTERS	POS/GAMES		GP	AB	R	H	BI	2B	3B	HR	BB	SO	SB	BA	SA
John Morrill	1B127		127	504	79	141	81	32	6	12	37	86	19	.280	.438
Jack Burdock	2B65		65	237	36	61	29	6	0	0	18	22	19	.257	.283
Sam Wise	SS72,OF27,2B16		113	467	103	156	92	27	17	9	36	44	43	.334	.522
Billy Nash	3B117,OF5		121	475	100	140	94	24	12	6	60	30	43	.295	.434
King Kelly	OF61,2B30,C24,P3,SS2,3B2		116	484	120	156	63	34	11	8	55	40	84	.322	.488
Dick Johnston	OF127		127	507	87	131	77	13	20	5	16	35	52	.258	.393
Joe Hornung	OF98		98	437	85	118	49	10	6	5	17	28	41	.270	.355
Pop Tate	C53,OF8		60	231	34	60	27	5	3	0	8	9	7	.260	.307
Ezra Sutton	SS37,OF18,2B13,3B11		77	326	58	99	46	14	9	3	13	6	17	.304	.429
Old Hoss Radbourn	P50,OF2		51	175	25	40	24	2	2	1	18	21	6	.229	.280
Bobby Wheelock	OF28,SS20,2B4		48	166	32	42	15	4	2	2	15	15	20	.253	.337
Dick Conway	P26,OF16	(2-2)	42	145	20	36	10	4	1	0	16	16	5	.248	.290
Kid Madden	P37,OF1		37	132	23	32	10	2	3	1	12	17	6	.242	.326
Con Daily	C36		36	120	12	19	13	5	0	0	9	8	7	.158	.200
Tom O'Rourke	C21,OF1,3B1		22	78	12	12	10	3	0	0	7	6	4	.154	.192
Bill Stemmeyer	P15		15	47	5	12	9	0	2	1	3	9	0	.255	.404
			127	4531	831	1255	649	185	94	53	340	392	373	.277	.394

PITCHERS			W	L	PCT	G	GS	CG	SH	SV	IP	H	BB	SO	ERA
Old Hoss Radbourn			24	23	.511	50	50	48	1	0	425	505	133	87	4.55
Kid Madden			21	14	.600	37	37	36	3	0	321	317	122	81	3.79
Dick Conway		(2-2)	9	15	.375	26	26	25	0	0	222	249	86	45	4.66
Bill Stemmeyer			6	8	.429	15	14	14	0	1	119	138	41	41	5.22
King Kelly			1	0	1.000	3	0	0	0	0	13	17	14	0	3.46
			61	60	.504	127	127	123	4	1	1100	1226	396	254	4.41

PITTSBURGH 55-69 .444 -24 6th Horace Phillips
Alleghenys

BATTERS	POS/GAMES		GP	AB	R	H	BI	2B	3B	HR	BB	SO	SB	BA	SA
Sam Barkley	1B53,2B36		89	340	44	76	35	10	4	1	30	24	6	.224	.285
Pop Smith	2B89,SS33		122	456	69	98	54	12	7	2	30	48	30	.215	.285
Bill Kuehne	SS91,3B4,1B4,OF3		102	402	68	120	41	18	15	1	14	39	17	.299	.425
Art Whitney	3B119		119	431	57	112	51	11	4	0	55	18	10	.260	.304
Jack Coleman	OF115,1B2		115	475	75	139	54	21	11	2	31	40	25	.293	.396
Tom Brown	OF47	(1-2)	47	192	30	47	6	3	4	0	11	40	12	.245	.302
Abner Dalrymple	OF92		92	358	45	76	31	18	5	2	45	43	29	.212	.307
Doggie Miller	C73,OF14,3B1		87	342	58	83	34	17	2	1	35	13	33	.243	.325
Fred Carroll	OF46,C40,1B17,SS1		102	421	71	138	54	24	15	6	36	21	23	.328	.499
Pud Galvin	P49,OF1		49	193	10	41	22	7	3	2	2	47	5	.212	.311
Alex McKinnon	1B48		48	200	26	68	30	16	4	1	8	9	6	.340	.475
Jocko Fields	OF27,C14,1B3,3B1,P1		43	164	26	44	17	9	2	0	7	13	7	.268	.348
Ed Beecher	OF41		41	169	15	41	22	8	0	2	7	8	8	.243	.325
Ed Morris	P38		38	126	15	25	10	2	0	0	5	16	1	.198	.214
Jim McCormick	P36		36	136	12	33	18	7	0	0	2	0	9	.243	.294
Bill Bishop	P3		3	9	0	0	0	0	0	0	1	2	0	.000	.000
			125	4414	621	1141	479	183	68	20	319	381	221	.258	.349

PITCHERS			W	L	PCT	G	GS	CG	SH	SV	IP	H	BB	SO	ERA
Pud Galvin			28	21	.571	49	48	47	3	0	441	490	67	76	3.29
Ed Morris			14	22	.389	38	38	37	1	0	318	375	71	91	4.31

1887 NATIONAL LEAGUE

PITTSBURGH (cont.)
Alleghenys

PITCHERS	W	L	PCT	G	GS	CG	SH	SV	IP	H	BB	SO	ERA
Jim McCormick	13	23	.361	36	36	36	0	0	322	377	84	77	4.30
Bill Bishop	0	3	.000	3	3	3	0	0	27	45	22	4	13.33
Jocko Fields	0	0	----	1	0	0	0	0	1	0	2	0	0.00
	55	69	.444	125	125	123	4	0	1109	1287	246	248	4.12

WASHINGTON
Statesmen

46-76 .377 -32 7th Walter Dennis

BATTERS	POS/GAMES		GP	AB	R	H	BI	2B	3B	HR	BB	SO	SB	BA	SA
Billy O'Brien	1B104,OF4,3B4,2B2		113	453	71	126	73	16	12	19	21	17	11	.278	.492
Al Myers	2B78,SS27		105	362	45	84	36	9	5	2	40	26	18	.232	.301
Jack Farrell	SS48,2B40		87	339	40	75	41	14	9	0	20	12	31	.221	.316
Jim Donnelly	3B115,SS2		117	425	51	85	46	9	6	1	16	26	42	.200	.256
Ed Daily	OF77,P1	(2-2)	78	311	39	78	36	6	10	2	14	27	26	.251	.354
Paul Hines	OF109,1B7,2B5,SS4		123	478	83	147	72	32	5	10	48	24	46	.308	.458
Cliff Carroll	OF103		103	420	79	104	37	17	4	4	17	30	40	.248	.336
Connie Mack	C76,OF5,2B2		82	314	35	63	20	6	1	0	8	17	26	.201	.226
George Shoch	OF63,SS6,2B1		70	264	47	63	18	9	1	1	21	16	29	.239	.292
Pat Dealy	C28,SS23,OF5,3B5		58	312	33	85	18	8	2	2	8	8	36	.272	.321
Jim Whitney	P47,OF7		54	201	29	53	22	9	6	2	18	24	10	.264	.398
Hank O'Day	P30,SS6,OF2		36	116	10	23	7	3	0	0	7	15	1	.198	.224
Frank Gilmore	P28		28	93	4	6	1	0	0	0	7	46	2	.065	.065
Barney Gilligan	C26,SS3,OF1		28	90	7	18	6	2	0	1	5	18	2	.200	.256
Bill Krieg	1B16,OF9		25	95	9	24	17	4	1	2	7	5	2	.253	.379
Dupee Shaw	P21		21	70	7	13	3	2	0	0	8	14	1	.186	.214
John Irwin	SS5,3B4		8	31	6	11	3	2	0	2	3	6	6	.355	.613
Sam Crane	SS7		7	30	6	9	1	1	1	0	1	6	5	.300	.400
Jerry O'Brien	2B1		1	4	0	0	0	0	0	0	0	2	0	.000	.000
George Keefe	P1		1	3	0	0	0	0	0	0	0	0	0	.000	.000
William Wright	C1		1	3	0	2	0	0	0	0	0	0	0	.667	.667
			126	4414	601	1069	457	149	63	47	269	339	334	.242	.336

PITCHERS		W	L	PCT	G	GS	CG	SH	SV	IP	H	BB	SO	ERA
Jim Whitney		24	21	.533	47	47	46	3	0	405	430	42	146	3.22
Hank O'Day		8	20	.286	30	30	29	0	0	255	255	109	86	4.16
Dupee Shaw		7	13	.350	21	20	20	0	0	181	263	46	47	6.46
Frank Gilmore		7	20	.259	28	27	27	1	0	235	247	92	114	3.87
George Keefe		0	1	.000	1	1	1	0	0	8	16	4	0	9.00
Ed Daily	(2-2)	0	1	.000	1	1	1	0	0	7	5	6	3	7.71
		46	76	.377	126	126	124	4	0	1091	1216	299	396	4.19

INDIANAPOLIS
Hoosiers

37-89 .294 -43 8th Fogel - Burnham - Thomas

BATTERS	POS/GAMES		GP	AB	R	H	BI	2B	3B	HR	BB	SO	SB	BA	SA
Otto Schomberg	1B112,OF1		112	419	91	129	83	18	16	5	56	32	21	.308	.463
Charley Bassett	2B119		119	452	41	104	47	14	6	1	25	31	25	.230	.294
Jack Glasscock	SS122,P1		122	483	91	142	40	18	7	0	41	8	62	.294	.360
Jerry Denny	3B116,SS4,OF1,2B1		122	510	86	165	97	34	12	11	13	22	29	.324	.502
John Cahill	OF56,3B9,P6,SS1		68	263	22	54	26	4	3	0	9	5	34	.205	.243
Jack McGeachey	OF98,3B1,P1		99	405	49	109	56	17	3	1	5	16	27	.269	.333
Emmett Seery	OF122,SS1		122	465	104	104	28	18	15	4	71	68	48	.224	.353
George Myers	C50,OF15,1B6,3B1		69	235	25	51	20	8	1	1	22	7	26	.217	.272
John Arundel	C42,OF2,1B1		43	157	13	31	13	4	0	0	8	12	8	.197	.223
Mert Hackett	C40,OF2,1B1		42	147	12	35	10	6	3	2	7	24	4	.238	.361
Henry Boyle	P38,OF4		41	141	17	27	13	9	1	2	9	18	2	.191	.312
Egyptian Healy	P41		41	138	14	24	14	4	2	3	4	42	7	.174	.243
Tom Brown	OF36	(2-2)	36	140	20	25	9	3	0	2	8	25	13	.179	.243
Mark Polhemus	OF20		20	75	6	18	8	1	0	0	2	9	4	.240	.253
Gid Gardner	OF11,2B7		18	63	8	11	8	1	0	1	12	11	7	.175	.238
Ledell Shreve	P14	(2-2)	14	49	6	13		1	0	0	3	4	2	.265	.286
Bill Johnson	OF11		11	42	3	8	3	0	0	0	0	6	5	.190	.190
Sam Moffett	P6,OF5		11	41	6	5	1	1	0	0	1	6	2	.122	.146
Henry Jackson	1B10		10	38	1	10	3	1	0	0	0	12	2	.263	.289
John Kirby	P8	(1-2)	8	29	3	4	2	0	1	0	0	7	0	.138	.207
Doc Leitner	P8		8	27	3	4	0	0	0	0	0	5	1	.148	.148

1887 NATIONAL LEAGUE

INDIANAPOLIS (cont.)
Hoosiers

BATTERS	POS/GAMES		GP	AB	R	H	RBI	2B	3B	HR	BB	SO	SB	BA	SA
Hank Morrison	P7		7	26	4	3	3	0	0	0	2	4	2	.115	.115
----- Fast	P4		4	11	1	2	0	0	0	0	0	3	1	.182	.182
Larry Corcoran	P2,OF2		3	10	2	2	0	0	0	0	2	1	2	.200	.200
John Sowders	P1		1	2	0	0	0	0	0	0	0	1	0	.000	.000
			127	4368	628	1080	488	162	70	33	300	379	334	.247	.339

PITCHERS			W	L	PCT	G	GS	CG	SH	SV	IP	H	BB	SO	ERA
Henry Boyle			13	24	.351	38	37	37	0	0	328	356	69	85	3.65
Egyptian Healy			12	29	.293	41	41	40	3	0	341	415	108	75	5.17
Ledell Shreve		(2-2)	5	9	.357	14	14	14	1	0	122	141	65	22	4.72
Hank Morrison			3	4	.429	7	7	5	0	0	57	79	27	13	7.58
Doc Leitner			2	6	.250	8	8	8	0	0	65	69	41	27	5.68
Sam Moffett			1	5	.167	6	6	6	0	0	50	47	23	3	3.78
John Kirby		(1-2)	1	6	.143	8	8	5	0	0	62	70	43	7	6.10
----- Fast			0	1	.000	4	2	1	0	1	16	25	8	0	10.69
Jack McGeachey			0	1	.000	1	0	0	0	0	6	13	4	3	12.00
John Cahill			0	2	.000	6	1	1	0	0	22	40	19	5	14.32
Larry Corcoran			0	2	.000	2	2	1	0	0	15	23	19	4	12.60
John Sowders			0	0	----	1	0	0	0	0	3	11	5	0	21.00
Jack Glasscock			0	0	----	1	0	0	0	0	1	0	0	1	0.00
			37	89	.294	127	126	118	4	1	1088	1289	431	245	5.25

TOP TWENTY-FIVE ORIGINAL QUALIFIERS FOR BATTING CHAMPIONSHIP   (Min. 90 Games Played)

BATTERS	TEAMS	BA
Cap Anson	Chicago	.421
Dan Brouthers	Detroit	.420
Sam Thompson	Detroit	.407
King Kelly	Boston	.391
Otto Schomberg	Indianapolis	.389
Roger Connor	New York	.383
Sam Wise	Boston	.382
Fred Carroll	Pittsburgh	.381
Billy Nash	Boston	.374
Paul Hines	Washington	.371
Ned Williamson	Chicago	.371
Jim Fogarty	Philadelphia	.366
Jack Rowe	Detroit	.365
Hardy Richardson	Detroit	.364
George Andrews	Philadelphia	.355
Monte Ward	New York	.354
Jimmy Ryan	Chicago	.353
Jack Glasscock	Indianapolis	.349
George Gore	New York	.349
Art Whitney	Pittsburgh	.344
Jim O'Rourke	New York	.344
Sid Farrar	Philadelphia	.344
George Wood	Philadelphia	.343
Deacon White	Detroit	.341
Jerry Denny	Indianapolis	.340

1887 AMERICAN ASSOCIATION

The St. Louis Browns

The St. Louis Browns, one of the charter members of the American Association, were the property of one of the league's most colorful owners, Chris Von der Ahe. Originally a saloon owner, he purchased a controlling interest in the new St. Louis club in 1882. Von der Ahe soon assembled a fine nucleus of players, captained by Charlie Comiskey, and including Arlie Latham, Tip O'Neill, Dave Foutz, and Bob Caruthers. By 1885, this nucleus jelled and the team won the first of its four pennants in a row — a feat making the Browns the class of the American Association.

The 1887 version was easily the best of the four. This team galloped home 14 lengths ahead of the pack, finishing with 95 wins, the most ever in the American Association. Other all-time bests included: most runs (1131), most stolen bases (581) (also the all-time record), and highest batting average (.307). The bulwark of this club was outfielder Tip O'Neill. He had a mammoth year by hitting .435, swatting fourteen home runs, and scoring 167 runs. (If you include his walk-hits, his average jumps to an astronomical .485.) Pitchers Bob Caruthers and Dave Foutz won 54 games between them, each batting .357 as well. Other .300 hitters on the club included Charlie Comiskey (.335), and Arlie Latham (.316).

Second place Cincinnati featured stolen base king Hugh Nicol who swiped 138, the all time major league best. (This record is tempered by the fact that until 1897, rules defining a stolen base were not as strict.) This feat is remarkable considering Nicol only batted .215. Cincinnati's good hitters included Long John Reilly (.309), and Pop Corkhill (.311).

Baltimore's jump to third featured the hitting of Oyster Burns (.341) and the pitching of Matt Kilroy, who won 17 more than the previous year, finishing with a league-leading 46.

Fourth place Louisville also featured a strong duo. Pete Browning finished with his best year (.402), yet still finished second in the batting race. Pitcher Toad Ramsey won 37 and struck out a league best 355 batters. This feat is made all the more remarkable by the fact that batters were entitled to four strikes in 1887.

Philadelphia, in fifth, featured the bat of third baseman Denny Lyons who finished at .367. Notable about Lyons's year, is that from June 24 to August 27, he was credited with a base hit in 52 straight games, the second leading streak of all time. It should be noted that twice during the streak he benefited from the rule change that counted a walk as a hit.

Brooklyn finished sixth, while New York finished seventh. Brooklyn's forte was mediocrity as all of their regulars (save one) finished between .253 and .267. For New York, Dave Orr once more had a robust year finishing with a .368 average.

Last place Cleveland was a new entrant to the American Association in 1887. They took the place of the Pittsburgh club who jumped lock, stock, and barrel to the National League. This action did little to strengthen the fragile peace between the two leagues.

After winning four pennants in a row, Von der Ahe's Browns remained competitive for the remaining years of the association. After moving to the National League, Von der Ahe was forced to sell many of his players to meet rising costs. He also turned his ballpark into a flamboyant amusement center featuring amusement park rides, fountains, and horse racing. These activities tarnished Von der Ahe's reputation, and thereafter the public considered him a buffoon. Finally, late in the 1890s, he was forced out as the team's owner.

In retrospect, the good outweighed the bad for Chris Von der Ahe. It was true that he turned his ballpark into a three-ring circus, trivializing the baseball played there. But Von der Ahe was the off the field brains behind the most powerful team in the American Association's history. His feat of four straight pennants would not be duplicated for another 30 years.

ST. LOUIS Browns   95-40   .704   1st   Charlie Comiskey

BATTERS	POS/GAMES		GP	AB	R	H	BI	2B	3B	HR	BB	SO	SB	BA	SA
Charlie Comiskey	1B116,2B9,OF3		125	538	139	180		22	5	4	27		117	.335	.416
Yank Robinson	2B117,3B6,OF2,SS2,C1,P1		125	430	102	131		32	4	1	92		75	.305	.405
Bill Gleason	SS135		135	598	135	172		19	1	0	41		23	.288	.323
Arlie Latham	3B132,2B5,C2		136	627	163	198		35	10	2	45		129	.316	.413
Bob Caruthers	OF54,P39,1B7		98	364	102	130		23	11	8	66		49	.357	.547
Curt Welch	OF123,2B8,1B1		131	544	98	151		32	7	3	25		89	.278	.379
Tip O'Neill	OF124		124	517	167	225		52	19	14	50		30	.435	.691
Jack Boyle	C86,1B2,OF2,3B1		88	350	48	66		3	1	2	20		7	.189	.220
Dave Foutz	OF50,P40,1B15		102	423	79	151		26	13	4	23		22	.357	.508
Silver King	P46,OF17		62	222	28	46		6	1	0	24		10	.207	.243
Doc Bushong	C52,OF2,3B2		53	201	35	51		4	0	0	11		14	.254	.274
Lou Sylvester	OF29,2B1		29	112	20	25		4	3	1	13		13	.223	.339
Ed Knouff	OF9,P6	(2-2)	15	56	4	10		1	2	0	1		1	.179	.268
Nat Hudson	P9,OF6		13	48	7	12		2	1	0	4		0	.250	.333
Harry Lyons	2B1,OF1	(2-2)	2	8	2	1		0	0	0	0		2	.125	.125
Joe Murphy	P1		1	6	2	1		0	0	0	0		0	.167	.167
Mike Goodfellow	C1		1	4	0	0		0	0	0	0		0	.000	.000
			138	5048	1131	1550		261	78	39	442	340	581	.307	.413

PITCHERS		W	L	PCT	G	GS	CG	SH	SV	IP	H	BB	SO	ERA
Silver King		32	12	.727	46	44	43	2	1	390	401	109	128	3.78
Bob Caruthers		29	9	.763	39	39	39	2	0	341	337	61	74	3.30
Dave Foutz		25	12	.676	40	38	36	1	0	339	369	90	94	3.87
Ed Knouff	(2-2)	4	2	.667	6	6	6	1	0	50	40	36	18	4.50
Nat Hudson		4	4	.500	9	9	7	0	0	67	91	20	15	4.97
Joe Murphy		1	0	1.000	1	1	1	0	0	9	13	4	5	5.00
Yank Robinson		0	0	----	1	0	0	0	1	3	3	3	0	3.00
		95	40	.704	138	137	132	7	2	1199	1254	323	334	3.77

CINCINNATI Red Stockings   81-54   .600   -14   2nd   Gus Schmelz

BATTERS	POS/GAMES		GP	AB	R	H	BI	2B	3B	HR	BB	SO	SB	BA	SA
Long John Reilly	1B127,OF9		134	551	106	170		35	14	10	22		50	.309	.477
Bid McPhee	2B129		129	540	137	156		20	19	2	55		95	.289	.407
Frank Fennelly	SS134		134	526	133	140		15	16	8	82		74	.266	.401
Hick Carpenter	3B127		127	498	70	124		12	6	1	19		44	.249	.303
Hugh Nicol	OF125		125	475	122	102		18	2	1	86		138	.215	.267
Pop Corkhill	OF128,P5		128	541	79	168		19	11	5	14		30	.311	.414
White Wings Tebeau	OF84,P1		85	318	57	94		12	5	4	31		37	.296	.403
Kid Baldwin	C96,OF2		96	388	46	98		15	10	1	6		13	.253	.351
Tony Mullane	P48,OF9		56	199	35	44		6	3	3	16		20	.221	.327
Elmer Smith	P52,OF2		52	186	26	47		10	6	0	11		5	.253	.371
Jim Keenan	C38,1B11		47	174	19	44		4	1	0	11		7	.253	.287
Charlie Jones	OF41	(1-2)	41	153	28	48		7	4	2	19		7	.314	.451
Heinie Kappel	3B9,OF7,2B6,SS1		23	78	11	22		3	2	0	2		3	.282	.372
Bill Serad	P22,OF1		22	79	9	14		1	2	0	3		0	.177	.241
Jack O'Connor	OF7,C5		12	40	4	4		0	0	0	2		3	.100	.100
Jumbo McGinnis	P8		8	31	8	6		2	1	0	1		1	.194	.323
Mike Shea	P2		2	8	1	2		0	0	0	1		0	.250	.250
Mother Watson	P2,OF1		2	8	1	1		0	0	0	1		0	.125	.125
Wild Bill Widner	P1		1	4	0	1		0	0	0	0		0	.250	.250
			136	4797	892	1285		179	102	37	382	366	527	.268	.371

PITCHERS		W	L	PCT	G	GS	CG	SH	SV	IP	H	BB	SO	ERA
Elmer Smith		34	17	.667	52	52	49	3	0	447	400	126	176	2.94
Tony Mullane		31	17	.646	48	48	47	6	0	416	414	121	97	3.24
Bill Serad		10	11	.476	22	21	20	2	1	187	201	80	34	4.08
Jumbo McGinnis		3	5	.375	8	8	8	0	0	69	85	43	18	5.45
Pop Corkhill		1	0	1.000	5	0	0	0	0	15	22	5	3	5.52
Wild Bill Widner		1	0	1.000	1	1	1	0	0	9	11	2	0	5.00
Mike Shea		1	1	.500	2	2	2	0	0	17	26	10	0	7.02
Mother Watson		0	1	.000	2	2	1	0	0	14	22	6	1	5.79
White Wings Tebeau		0	1	.000	1	1	1	0	0	8	21	3	1	13.50
		81	54	.600	136	135	129	11	1	1183	1202	396	330	3.58

1887 AMERICAN ASSOCIATION

BALTIMORE
Orioles
77-58   .570   -18   3rd   Billy Barnie

BATTERS	POS/GAMES		GP	AB	R	H	BI	2B	3B	HR	BB	SO	SB	BA	SA
Tommy Tucker	1B136		136	524	114	144		15	9	6	29		85	.275	.372
Bill Greenwood	2B117,OF1		118	495	114	130		16	6	0	54	71		.263	.319
Oyster Burns	SS98,3B42,P3,2B1		140	551	122	188		33	19	9	63	58		.341	.519
Jumbo Davis	3B87,SS43		130	485	81	150		23	19	8	28	49		.309	.485
Blondie Purcell	OF140,P1		140	567	101	142		25	8	4	46	88		.250	.344
Mike Griffin	OF136		136	532	142	160		32	13	3	55	94		.301	.427
Joe Sommer	OF110,2B13,3B10,SS2,P1		131	463	88	123		11	5	0	63	29		.266	.311
Sam Trott	C69,2B11,OF3,1B2,SS1		85	300	44	77		16	3	0	27		8	.257	.330
Matt Kilroy	P69,OF4,SS1		72	239	46	59		5	6	0	31		12	.247	.318
Phenomenal Smith	P58,OF7		64	205	37	48		7	6	1	26		7	.234	.341
Chris Fulmer	C48,OF8		56	201	52	54		11	4	0	36		35	.269	.363
Law Daniels	C26,OF15,1B4,2B2,3B1,SS1		48	165	23	41		5	1	0	8		7	.248	.291
Ed Knouff	P9,OF3	(1-2)	9	31	4	9		0	0	0	1		1	.290	.290
Jack Hayes	OF4,3B3,C1		8	28	2	4		3	0	0	0		0	.143	.250
Ledell Shreve	P5,OF2	(2-2)	6	24	3	4		0	1	0	1		1	.167	.250
Fred Gardner	P3,SS1,3B1		4	11	2	3		0	0	0	1		0	.273	.273
Ed Keating	P1		1	4	0	1		0	0	0	0		0	.250	.250
			141	4825	975	1337		202	100	31	469	334	545	.277	.380

PITCHERS			W	L	PCT	G	GS	CG	SH	SV	IP	H	BB	SO	ERA
Matt Kilroy			46	19	.708	69	69	66	6	0	589	585	157	217	3.07
Phenomenal Smith			25	30	.455	58	55	54	1	0	491	526	176	206	3.79
Ledell Shreve		(2-2)	3	1	.750	5	5	4	1	0	38	33	19	13	3.79
Ed Knouff		(1-2)	2	6	.250	9	9	6	0	0	63	79	41	27	7.57
Oyster Burns			1	0	1.000	3	0	0	0	0	11	16	4	2	9.53
Fred Gardner			0	1	.000	3	2	1	0	0	13	23	10	3	11.08
Ed Keating			0	1	.000	1	1	1	0	0	9	16	6	0	11.00
Blondie Purcell			0	0	----	1	0	0	0	0	4	8	4	2	15.75
Joe Sommer			0	0	----	1	0	0	0	0	1	2	1	0	9.00
			77	58	.570	141	141	132	8	0	1220	1288	418	470	3.87

LOUISVILLE
Colonels
76-60   .559   -19.5   4th   John Kelly

BATTERS	POS/GAMES		GP	AB	R	H	BI	2B	3B	HR	BB	SO	SB	BA	SA
John Kerins	1B74,C35,OF5		112	476	101	140		18	19	5	38		49	.294	.443
Reddy Mack	2B128		128	478	117	147		23	8	1	83		22	.308	.395
Bill White	SS132		132	512	85	129		7	9	2	47		41	.252	.313
Joe Werrick	3B136		136	533	90	152		21	13	7	38		49	.285	.413
Chicken Wolf	OF128,1B11		137	569	103	160		27	13	2	34		45	.281	.385
Pete Browning	OF134		134	547	137	220		35	16	4	55		103	.402	.547
Hub Collins	OF109,2B10,1B8,SS4,3B1		130	559	122	162		22	8	1	39		71	.290	.363
Paul Cook	C55,1B6		61	223	34	55		4	?	0	11		15	.247	.283
Guy Hecker	1B43,P34,OF16		91	370	89	118		21	6	4	31		48	.319	.441
Toad Ramsey	P65		65	225	19	43		4	0	0	19		2	.191	.209
Lave Cross	C44,OF10		54	203	32	54		8	3	0	15		15	.266	.335
Icebox Chamberlain	P36,OF2		37	131	14	26		1	1	1	12		2	.198	.244
Phil Reccius	OF10,SS1	(1-2)	11	37	9	9		2	0	0	8		3	.243	.297
Amos Cross	C5,1B2,OF1		8	28	0	3		0	0	0	1		0	.107	.107
Joe Neale	P5		5	19	3	1		0	0	0	3		1	.067	.067
Ducky Hemp	OF1		1	3	1	1		1	0	0	1		0	.333	.667
Peek A Boo Veach	P1		1	3	0	0		0	0	0	1		0	.000	.000
			139	4916	956	1420		194	98	27	436	356	466	.289	.385

PITCHERS			W	L	PCT	G	GS	CG	SH	SV	IP	H	BB	SO	ERA
Toad Ramsey			37	27	.578	65	64	61	0	0	561	544	167	355	3.43
Guy Hecker			18	12	.600	34	32	32	2	1	285	325	50	58	4.16
Icebox Chamberlain			18	16	.529	36	36	35	1	0	309	340	117	118	3.79
Joe Neale			1	4	.200	5	4	4	0	0	41	60	15	11	6.97
Peek A Boo Veach			0	1	.000	1	1	1	0	0	9	5	8	2	4.00
			76	60	.559	139	137	133	3	1	1206	1274	357	544	3.82

1887 AMERICAN ASSOCIATION

PHILADELPHIA
Athletics 64-69 .481 -30 5th Mason - Bancroft

BATTERS	POS/GAMES		GP	AB	R	H	BI	2B	3B	HR	BB	SO	SB	BA	SA
Jocko Milligan	1B50,C47,OF1		95	377	54	114		27	4	2	21		8	.302	.411
Lou Bierbauer	2B126,P1		126	530	74	144		19	7	1	13		40	.272	.340
Chippy McGarr	SS137		137	536	93	158		23	6	1	23		84	.295	.366
Denny Lyons	3B137		137	570	128	209		43	14	6	47		73	.367	.523
Tom Poorman	OF135,2B2,P1		135	585	140	155		18	19	4	35		88	.265	.381
Harry Stovey	OF80,1B46		124	497	125	142		31	12	4	56		74	.286	.421
Henry Larkin	OF93,1B23,2B10		126	497	105	154		22	12	3	48		37	.310	.421
Wilbert Robinson	C67,1B3,OF1		68	264	28	60		6	2	1	14		15	.227	.277
Ed Seward	P55,OF21		74	266	31	50		10	0	5	16		14	.188	.282
Gus Weyhing	P55,OF3		57	209	19	42		6	1	0	6		8	.201	.239
Fred Mann	OF55	(2-2)	55	229	42	63		14	6	0	15		16	.275	.389
George Townshend	C28,OF3		31	109	12	21		3	0	0	3		8	.193	.220
Chief Roseman	OF21	(1-3)	21	73	16	16		2	1	0	10		3	.219	.274
Ed Flanagan	1B19		19	80	12	20		5	0	1	3		3	.250	.350
Al Atkinson	P15,OF4		16	59	8	12		2	0	1	5		3	.203	.288
Bobby Mathews	P7		7	25	5	5		0	0	0	4		0	.200	.200
Bill Hart	P3		3	13	0	1		0	0	0	0		0	.077	.077
Ed Greer	OF3	(1-2)	3	11	1	2		0	0	0	0		2	.182	.182
Ledell Titcomb	P3	(2-2)	3	10	0	0		0	0	0	2		0	.000	.000
Jim Roxburgh	C2,2B1		2	8	0	1		0	0	0	0		0	.125	.125
Bill Taylor	P1		1	4	0	1		0	0	0	0		0	.250	.250
Fred Chapman	P1		1	2	0	0		0	0	0	0		0	.000	.000
Bill Casey	P1		1	0	0	0		0	0	0	0		0	----	----
			137	4954	893	1370		231	84	29	321	388	476	.277	.375

PITCHERS		W	L	PCT	G	GS	CG	SH	SV	IP	H	BB	SO	ERA
Gus Weyhing		26	28	.481	55	55	53	2	0	466	465	167	193	4.27
Ed Seward		25	25	.500	55	52	52	3	0	471	445	140	155	4.13
Al Atkinson		6	8	.429	15	15	11	0	0	125	156	54	34	5.92
Bobby Mathews		3	4	.429	7	7	7	0	0	58	75	25	9	6.67
Bill Taylor		1	0	1.000	1	1	1	0	0	9	10	7	0	3.00
Bill Hart		1	2	.333	3	3	3	0	0	26	28	17	4	4.50
Ledell Titcomb		1	2	.333	3	3	3	0	0	24	31	19	16	6.75
Fred Chapman		0	0	----	1	1	1	0	0	5	8	2	4	7.20
Bill Casey		0	0	----	1	0	0	0	0	0	4	1	0	18.00
Lou Bierbauer		0	0	----	1	0	0	0	1	1	0	0	1	0.00
Tom Poorman		0	0	----	1	0	0	0	0	1	5	1	1	40.50
		64	69	.481	137	137	131	5	1	1186	1227	433	417	4.59

BROOKLYN
Trolley Dodgers 60-74 .448 -34.5 6th Charlie Byrne

BATTERS	POS/GAMES		GP	AB	R	H	BI	2B	3B	HR	BB	SO	SB	BA	SA
Bill Phillips	1B132		132	533	82	142		34	11	2	45		16	.266	.383
Bill McClellan	2B136		136	548	109	144		24	6	1	80		70	.263	.334
Germany Smith	SS101,3B2		103	435	79	128		19	16	4	13		26	.294	.439
George Pinkney	3B136,SS2		138	580	133	155		26	6	3	61		59	.267	.348
Ed Swartwood	OF91		91	363	72	92		14	8	1	46		29	.253	.344
Jim McTamany	OF134		134	520	123	134		22	10	1	76		66	.258	.344
Ed Greer	OF76,C16	(2-2)	91	327	49	83		13	2	2	25		33	.254	.352
Jim Peoples	C57,OF8,1B4,SS4,2B1		73	268	36	68		14	2	1	16		22	.254	.332
Adonis Terry	OF49,P40,SS2		86	352	56	103		6	10	3	16		27	.293	.392
Ernie Burch	OF49		49	188	47	55		4	4	2	29		15	.293	.388
Bob Clark	C45,OF3		48	177	24	47		3	1	0	7		15	.266	.294
Henry Porter	P40,OF1		40	146	16	29		2	4	1	10		6	.199	.288
Jack O'Brien	C25,OF4,2B1		30	123	18	28		4	1	1	6		8	.228	.301
Bill Ottarson	SS30		30	100	16	20		4	1	2	8		8	.200	.320
John Harkins	P24,OF4,2B1		27	98	10	23		5	0	0	7		4	.235	.286
Steve Toole	P24,1B3		26	103	19	24		6	0	1	3		4	.233	.320
Hardie Henderson	P13		13	41	10	5		0	0	0	6		1	.122	.122
Bert Cunningham	P3		3	8	3	0		0	0	0	2		0	.000	.000
Chief Roseman	OF1	(3-3)	1	3	2	1		0	0	0	0		0	.333	.333
			138	4913	904	1281		200	82	25	456	365	409	.261	.350

PITCHERS		W	L	PCT	G	GS	CG	SH	SV	IP	H	BB	SO	ERA
Adonis Terry		16	16	.500	40	35	35	1	3	318	331	99	138	4.02
Henry Porter		15	24	.385	40	40	38	1	0	340	416	96	74	4.21
Steve Toole		14	10	.583	24	24	22	1	0	194	186	106	48	4.31

BROOKLYN (cont.)
Trolley Dodgers

PITCHERS	W	L	PCT	G	GS	CG	SH	SV	IP	H	BB	SO	ERA
John Harkins	10	14	.417	24	24	22	0	0	199	262	77	36	6.02
Hardie Henderson	5	8	.385	13	12	12	0	0	112	127	63	28	3.95
Elmer Cunningham	0	2	.000	3	3	3	0	0	23	26	13	8	5.09
	60	74	.448	138	138	132	3	3	1185	1348	454	332	4.47

NEW YORK
Metropolitans

44-89 .331 -50 7th Ferguson - Orr - Caylor

BATTERS	POS/GAMES		GP	AB	R	H	BI	2B	3B	HR	BB	SO	SB	BA	SA
Dave Orr	1B81,OF3		84	345	63	127		25	10	2	22		17	.368	.516
Joe Gerhardt	2B84,3B1	(2-2)	85	307	40	68		13	2	0	24		15	.221	.277
Paul Radford	SS76,OF37,2B18,P2		128	486	127	129		15	5	4	106		73	.265	.342
Frank Hankinson	3B127		127	512	79	137		29	11	1	38		19	.268	.373
Chief Roseman	OF59,1B3,P2	(2-3)	60	241	30	55		10	1	1	9		3	.228	.290
Charlie Jones	OF62,P2,1B1	(2-2)	62	247	30	63		11	3	3	12		8	.255	.360
Darby O'Brien	OF121,1B10,SS2,3B1,P1		127	522	97	157		30	13	5	40		49	.301	.437
Bill Holbert	C60,1B8,SS2,2B1		69	255	20	58		4	3	0	7		12	.227	.267
Candy Nelson	OF37,SS32,2B1	(1-2)	68	257	61	63		5	1	0	48		29	.245	.272
Al Mays	P52,OF11,1B1		62	221	23	45		15	4	2	10		7	.204	.335
Jim Donahue	C51,OF5,1B4,2B1,3B1		60	220	33	62		4	1	1	21		6	.282	.323
John Meister	OF22,2B14,3B3,SS1		39	157	24	35		6	2	1	16		9	.223	.306
Pete Sommers	C31,OF1,1B1		33	116	9	21		3	0	1	7		6	.181	.233
Eddie Hogan	OF29,SS4,3B1		32	120	22	24		6	1	0	30		12	.200	.267
Tom O'Brien	1B20,OF8,2B2,3B2,P1		31	129	13	25		3	2	0	2		10	.194	.248
Dude Esterbrook	1B9,OF7,2B5,SS5		26	101	11	17		1	0	0	6		8	.168	.178
Ed Cushman	P26,OF1		26	93	14	23		4	2	0	10		2	.247	.333
Jack Lynch	P21,1B2		23	83	4	14		1	0	0	7		3	.169	.181
Jimmy Knowles	2B16,3B1		16	60	12	15		1	1	0	1		6	.250	.300
Clarence Cross	SS13,3B4		16	55	9	11		2	1	0	2		0	.200	.273
Stump Weidman	P12,OF4	(2-3)	14	46	5	7		1	1	0	4		2	.152	.217
John Schafer	P13		13	48	4	8		1	1	0	1		1	.167	.229
Sadie Houck	SS10,2B1		10	33	3	5		1	0	0	3		2	.152	.182
John Morrison	OF9		9	34	7	4		0	0	0	6		0	.118	.118
Cyclone Ryan	1B8,P2		8	32	4	7		1	0	0	3		1	.219	.250
Fred O'Neill	OF6		6	26	4	8		1	1	0	1		3	.308	.423
Bill Fagan	P6		6	21	0	3		0	0	0	0		0	.143	.143
Charles Parsons	P4		4	15	3	3		0	0	0	1		1	.200	.200
George McMullen	P3,OF1		3	12	2	1		0	0	0	0		0	.083	.083
Charlie Hall	OF3		3	12	1	1		0	0	0	2		1	.083	.083
Tom Kinslow	C2		2	6	0	0		0	0	0	0		0	.000	.000
Hugh Collins	C1		1	4	0	1		0	0	0	0		0	.250	.250
Lip Pike	OF1		1	4	0	0		0	0	0	0		0	.000	.000
			138	4820	754	1197		193	66	21	439	463	305	.248	.329

PITCHERS		W	L	PCT	G	GS	CG	SH	SV	IP	H	BB	SO	ERA
Al Mays		17	34	.333	52	52	50	0	0	441	551	136	124	4.73
Ed Cushman		10	15	.400	26	26	25	0	0	220	310	83	64	5.97
Jack Lynch		7	14	.333	21	21	21	0	0	187	245	36	45	5.10
Stump Weidman	(2-3)	4	8	.333	12	12	11	1	0	97	122	25	37	4.64
George McMullen		2	1	.667	3	3	2	0	0	21	25	19	2	7.71
John Schafer		2	11	.154	13	13	13	0	0	112	148	53	22	6.19
Charles Parsons		1	1	.500	4	4	4	0	0	34	51	6	5	4.50
Bill Fagan		1	4	.200	6	6	6	0	0	45	55	24	12	4.00
Cyclone Ryan		0	1	.000	2	2	1	0	0	2	5	6	0	23.14
Chief Roseman	(2-3)	0	0	----	2	0	0	0	0	8	11	5	1	7.88
Paul Radford		0	0	----	2	0	0	0	0	5	15	3	4	18.00
Charlie Jones	(2-2)	0	0	----	2	0	0	0	0	3	2	4	0	3.00
Tom O'Brien		0	0	----	1	0	0	0	0	4	4	5	0	7.36
Darby O'Brien		0	0	----	1	0	0	0	0	1	1	1	0	0.00
		44	89	.331	138	138	132	1	0	1180	1545	406	316	5.28

CLEVELAND
Blues

39-92 .298 -54 8th Jimmy Williams

BATTERS	POS/GAMES		GP	AB	R	H	BI	2B	3B	HR	BB	SO	SB	BA	SA
Jim Toy	1B82,OF11,C10,3B8,SS3		109	423	56	94		20	5	1	17		8	.222	.300
Cub Stricker	2B126,SS6,P3		131	534	122	141		19	4	2	53		86	.264	.326
Ed McKean	SS123,2B8,OF4		132	539	97	154		16	13	2	60		76	.286	.375
Phil Reccius	3B62,P1	(2-2)	62	229	23	47		6	3	0	24		9	.205	.258

CLEVELAND (cont.)
Blues

BATTERS	POS/GAMES		GP	AB	R	H	BI	2B	3B	HR	BB	SO	SB	BA	SA
Fred Mann	OF64	(1-2)	64	259	45	80		15	7	2	23		25	.309	.444
Pete Hotaling	OF126		126	505	108	151		28	13	3	53		43	.299	.424
Myron Allen	OF115,3B3,P2,SS2		117	463	66	128		22	10	4	36		26	.276	.393
Pop Snyder	C63,1B13		74	282	33	72		12	6	0	9		5	.255	.340
Charlie Reipschlager	C48,1B16		63	231	20	49		8	3	0	11		7	.212	.273
Scrappy Carroll	OF54,3B3,2B1		57	216	30	43		5	1	0	15		19	.199	.231
Bill Crowell	P45		45	156	15	22		1	0	0	10		5	.141	.147
Mike Morrison	P40,OF4,3B1,2B1		41	141	23	27		3	2	0	11		5	.191	.241
Charlie Sweeney	1B20,OF10,P3,3B2,SS2		36	133	22	30		4	4	0	21		11	.226	.316
Bob Gilks	P13,1B6,OF3,2B1		22	83	12	26		2	0	0	3		5	.313	.337
John McGlone	3B21		21	79	14	20		2	1	0	7		15	.253	.304
Jim Say	3B16		16	64	9	24		5	3	0	1		0	.375	.547
John Munyan	OF12,C3,3B2		16	58	9	14		1	1	0	3		4	.241	.293
One Arm Daily	P16		16	58	1	4		0	0	0	3		0	.069	.069
Chief Zimmer	C12,1B2		14	52	9	12		5	0	0	4		1	.231	.327
Ed Herr	3B11		11	44	6	12		2	0	0	6		2	.273	.318
George Pechiney	P10		10	36	6	9		1	0	0	2		0	.250	.278
Ed Flynn	3B6,OF1		7	27	0	5		1	0	0	1		3	.185	.222
John Kirby	P5	(2-2)	5	18	0	3		0	1	0	0		0	.167	.278
Henry Simon	OF3		3	10	1	1		0	0	0	0		0	.100	.100
Frank Scheibeck	P1,3B1,SS1		3	9	2	2		0	0	0	2		0	.222	.222
			133	4649	729	1170		178	77	14	375	463	355	.252	.332

PITCHERS			W	L	PCT	G	GS	CG	SH	SV	IP	H	BB	SO	ERA
Bill Crowell			14	31	.311	45	45	45	1	0	389	541	138	72	4.88
Mike Morrison			12	25	.324	40	40	35	0	0	317	385	205	158	4.92
Bob Gilks			7	5	.583	13	13	12	1	0	108	104	42	28	3.08
One Arm Daily			4	12	.250	16	16	16	0	0	140	181	44	30	3.67
Myron Allen			1	0	1.000	2	0	0	0	0	10	9	3	1	0.93
George Pechiney			1	9	.100	10	10	10	0	0	86	118	44	24	7.12
Frank Scheibeck			0	1	.000	1	1	1	0	0	9	17	4	3	12.00
Charlie Sweeney			0	3	.000	3	3	3	0	0	24	42	13	8	8.25
John Kirby		(2-2)	0	5	.000	5	5	5	0	0	41	62	28	6	9.00
Cub Stricker			0	0	----	3	0	0	0	1	6	5	7	2	3.18
Phil Reccius			0	0	----	1	0	0	0	0	7	8	5	0	7.71
			39	92	.298	133	133	127	2	1	1136	1472	533	332	4.99

TOP TWENTY-FIVE ORIGINAL QUALIFIERS FOR BATTING CHAMPIONSHIP (Min. 100 Games Played)

BATTERS	TEAMS	BA
Tip O'Neill	St. Louis	.485
Pete Browning	Louisville	.457
Yank Robinson	St. Louis	.427
Denny Lyons	Philadelphia	.415
Reddy Mack	Louisville	.410
Oyster Burns	Baltimore	.409
Paul Radford	New York	.397
Dave Foutz	St. Louis	.390
Henry Larkin	Philadelphia	.371
Pete Hotaling	Cleveland	.366
Mike Griffin	Baltimore	.366
Charlie Comiskey	St. Louis	.366
Frank Fennelly	Cincinnati	.365
Arlie Latham	St. Louis	.362
Harry Stovey	Philadelphia	.358
Bill McClellan	Brooklyn	.357
Ed McKean	Cleveland	.357
Bid McPhee	Cincinnati	.355
Joe Sommer	Baltimore	.354
Jim McTamany	Brooklyn	.352
Darby O'Brien	New York	.351
Jumbo Davis	Baltimore	.347
John Kerins	Louisville	.346
Bill Phillips	Brooklyn	.341
George Pinckney	Brooklyn	.337

1888 NATIONAL LEAGUE

The Giants

The city of New York had a rich baseball heritage dating back to the dawn of the sport. It began with the Knickerbockers in the era of the amateurs, and continued with the Mutuals through the National Association. In 1876, the Mutuals were one of the founding members of the National League. The team's involvement lasted only a short while as they were unceremoniously booted out later that same year for not finishing their schedule. New York would not field another team in the National League until 1883.

In 1885, the owner of the National League franchise in New York acquired three new players (pitchers Tim Keefe, Mickey Welch, and outfielder Dude Esterbrook) from the New York Metropolitans of the American Association. This was easily accomplished because the same man, John Day, owned both teams. The immediate result was the Metropolitans dropped from first to seventh, while their National League counterparts rose from fourth to second. When the American Association squawked about this tampering, Day thumbed his nose at the group and shifted the Metropolitan's manager to his National League franchise as well. The manager's name was Jim Mutrie, and he would lead the National League New Yorkers to their greatest nineteenth century seasons.

During a crucial moment of an exhibition game in 1885, Mutrie was said to have uttered "come on, you giants" in order to spur his team on. The term "giants" stuck as the moniker for this team for many years to come.

Mutrie led the Giants to a second, and two thirds in 1885, 1886, and 1887 before taking them to the top of the National League in 1888. Offensively, the team hit only .242 — Roger Connor (.291, 14 HR) and Buck Ewing (.306) possessed the two big bats. However, the pitching was superb. Tim Keefe led the league in wins (35), earned run average (1.74) and strikeouts (333) to capture the pitching Triple Crown. Overall, the team led the league with an earned run average of 1.96.

Second place Chicago finished nine games off the pace. They were bolstered by Cap Anson who won his final batting title at .344, and by Jimmy Ryan who hit .332, and paced the circuit with 16 home runs.

In general, hitting plummeted leaguewide in 1888. This was certainly true in Philadelphia, where no regular hit over .245, yet with their .225 batting average, the team finished in third. Good pitching got them there thanks to Charlie Buffinton (1.91) and Ben Sanders (1.90).

Boston and Detroit also finished over .500. King Kelly (.318), and John Clarkson (33 wins) continued to play well for Boston, while Dan Brouthers (.307) played skillfully for Detroit who sank from first to fifth.

Pittsburgh, Indianapolis, and Washington finished in the last three slots. There were few individuals who played with distinction for this trio of teams. One exception was Pittsburgh pitcher Ed Morris, who won 29 with an earned run average of 2.31. Another exception was Dummy Hoy, an outfielder for Washington who stole the league's most bases, 82.

Following the season, the New York Giants took on the association's St. Louis Browns in the World Series. The best of ten game series started in New York and finished in St. Louis, with the outcome being a six game to four decision for the Giants.

Also following the season, Al Spalding led another goodwill baseball tour overseas. This venture was an ambitious, around the world venture featuring stops in Asia, Africa, and Australia. The tour started in Chicago in November 1888, and ended there in March 1889 after a 53-game schedule played on four continents.

New York continued to be successful under Jim Mutrie until the early 1890s, when new ownership let him go. History should remember him for the fact that his teams won 60 percent of their games. But, history will remember Jim Mutrie through his nickname for his team — a nickname that has spanned a century and a continent to be with us today.

1888 NATIONAL LEAGUE

NEW YORK Giants   84-47   .641   1st   Jim Mutrie

BATTERS	POS/GAMES		GP	AB	R	H	BI	2B	3B	HR	BB	SO	SB	BA	SA
Roger Connor	1B133,2B1		134	481	98	140	71	15	17	14	73	44	27	.291	.480
Danny Richardson	2B135		135	561	82	127	61	16	7	8	15	35	35	.226	.323
Art Whitney	3B90		90	328	28	72	28	1	4	1	8	22	7	.220	.256
Monte Ward	SS122		122	510	70	128	49	14	5	2	9	13	38	.251	.310
Mike Tiernan	OF113		113	443	75	130	52	16	8	9	42	42	52	.293	.427
Mike Slattery	OF103		103	391	50	96	35	12	6	1	13	28	26	.246	.315
Jim O'Rourke	OF87,C15,1B4,3B2		107	409	50	112	50	16	6	4	24	30	25	.274	.372
Buck Ewing	C78,SS4,3B2,P2		103	415	83	127	58	18	15	6	24	28	53	.306	.465
George Gore	OF64		64	254	37	56	17	4	4	2	30	31	11	.220	.291
Tim Keefe	P51,OF1		51	181	10	23	8	3	0	2	4	56	3	.127	.177
Mickey Welch	P47		47	169	16	32	10	5	0	2	1	33	4	.189	.254
Elmer Foster	OF37,3B1		37	136	15	20	10	3	2	0	9	20	13	.147	.199
Pat Murphy	C28		28	106	11	18	4	1	0	0	6	11	3	.170	.179
Gil Hatfield	3B14,SS13,OF1,2B1		28	105	7	19	9	1	0	0	2	18	8	.181	.190
Ledell Titcomb	P23,3B1		23	82	6	10	5	1	0	0	1	22	5	.122	.134
Willard Brown	C20		20	59	4	16	6	1	0	0	1	8	1	.271	.288
Cannonball Crane	P12		12	37	3	6	2	2	0	1	3	11	1	.162	.297
William George	OF6,P4		9	39	7	9	6	1	0	1	0	2	1	.231	.333
Elmer Cleveland	3B9	(1-2)	9	34	6	8	5	0	2	2	3	1	1	.235	.529
Stump Weidman	P2		2	7	1	0	1	0	0	0	2	1	0	.000	.000
			138	4747	659	1149	487	130	76	55	270	456	314	.242	.336

PITCHERS		W	L	PCT	G	GS	CG	SH	SV	IP	H	BB	SO	ERA
Tim Keefe		35	12	.745	51	51	48	8	0	434	317	90	335	1.74
Mickey Welch		26	19	.578	47	47	47	5	0	425	328	108	167	1.93
Ledell Titcomb		14	8	.636	23	23	22	4	0	197	149	46	129	2.24
Cannonball Crane		5	6	.455	12	12	11	1	1	93	70	40	58	2.42
William George		2	1	.667	4	3	3	1	0	34	18	11	26	1.32
Stump Weidman		1	1	.500	2	2	2	0	0	18	17	8	5	3.50
Buck Ewing		0	0	----	2	0	0	0	0	7	8	4	6	2.57
		84	47	.641	138	138	133	20	1	1208	907	307	726	1.96

CHICAGO White Stockings   77-58   .570   -9   2nd   Cap Anson

BATTERS	POS/GAMES	GP	AB	R	H	BI	2B	3B	HR	BB	SO	SB	BA	SA
Cap Anson	1B134	134	515	101	177	84	20	12	12	47	24	28	.344	.499
Fred Pfeffer	2B135	135	517	90	129	57	22	10	8	32	38	64	.250	.377
Ned Williamson	SS132	132	452	75	113	73	9	14	8	65	71	25	.250	.385
Tom Burns	3B134	134	483	60	115	70	12	6	3	26	49	34	.238	.306
Hugh Duffy	OF67,SS3,3B1	71	298	60	84	41	10	4	7	9	32	13	.282	.413
Jimmy Ryan	OF128,P8	129	549	115	182	64	33	10	16	35	50	60	.332	.515
Marty Sullivan	OF75	75	314	40	74	39	12	6	7	15	32	9	.236	.379
Tom Daly	C62,OF4	65	219	34	42	29	2	6	0	10	26	10	.192	.256
George Van Haltren	OF57,P30	81	318	46	90	34	9	14	4	22	34	21	.283	.437
Duke Farrell	C33,OF31,1B1	64	241	34	56	19	6	3	3	4	41	8	.232	.320
Bob Pettit	OF43	43	169	23	43	23	1	4	4	7	9	7	.254	.379
Gus Krock	P39	39	134	9	22	11	0	0	1	5	34	1	.164	.187
Mark Baldwin	P30,OF3	30	106	11	16	5	1	2	1	5	47	4	.151	.226
Silver Flint	C22	22	77	6	14	3	3	0	0	1	21	1	.182	.221
Dell Darling	C20	20	75	12	16	7	3	1	2	3	12	0	.213	.360
John Tener	P12,OF1	12	46	4	9	1	1	0	0	1	15	1	.196	.217
George Borchers	P10,OF3	10	33	3	2	2	2	0	0	1	13	1	.061	.121
Ad Gumbert	P6,OF2	7	24	3	8	2	0	1	0	0	2	0	.333	.417
Frank Dwyer	P5	5	21	2	4	2	1	0	0	0	5	0	.190	.238
Tod Brynan	P3,OF1	3	11	1	2	1	0	1	0	0	3	0	.182	.364
Dad Clarke	P2,OF1	2	7	4	2	2	0	1	1	1	2	0	.286	1.000
Willard Mains	P2,OF1	2	7	1	1	0	0	0	0	1	3	0	.143	.143
		136	4616	734	1201	569	147	95	77	290	563	287	.260	.383

PITCHERS	W	L	PCT	G	GS	CG	SH	SV	IP	H	BB	SO	ERA
Gus Krock	25	14	.641	39	39	39	4	0	340	295	45	161	2.44
George Van Haltren	13	13	.500	30	24	24	4	1	246	263	60	139	3.52
Mark Baldwin	13	15	.464	30	30	27	2	0	251	241	99	157	2.76
John Tener	7	5	.583	12	12	11	1	0	102	90	25	39	2.74
Jimmy Ryan	4	0	1.000	8	2	1	0	0	38	47	12	11	3.05
Frank Dwyer	4	1	.800	5	5	5	1	0	42	32	9	17	1.07
George Borchers	4	4	.500	10	10	7	1	0	67	67	29	26	3.49

CHICAGO (cont.)
White Stockings

PITCHERS	W	L	PCT	G	GS	CG	SH	SV	IP	H	BB	SO	ERA
Ad Gumbert	3	3	.500	6	6	5	0	0	49	44	10	16	3.14
Tod Brynan	2	1	.667	3	3	2	0	0	25	29	7	11	6.48
Dad Clarke	1	0	1.000	2	2	1	0	0	16	23	6	6	5.06
Willard Mains	1	1	.500	2	2	1	0	0	11	8	6	5	4.91
	77	58	.570	136	135	123	13	1	1186	1139	308	588	2.96

PHILADELPHIA
Quakers

69-61 .531 -14.5 3rd Harry Wright

BATTERS	POS/GAMES		GP	AB	R	H	BI	2B	3B	HR	BB	SO	SB	BA	SA
Sid Farrar	1B131		131	508	53	124	53	24	7	1	31	38	21	.244	.325
Charlie Bastian	2B65,3B14,SS1		80	275	30	53	17	4	1	1	27	41	12	.193	.225
Art Irwin	SS122,2B3		125	448	51	98	28	12	4	0	33	56	19	.219	.263
Joe Mulvey	3B100		100	398	37	86	39	12	3	0	9	33	18	.216	.261
Jim Fogarty	OF117,3B5,SS1		121	454	72	107	35	14	6	1	53	66	58	.236	.300
Ed Andrews	OF124		124	528	75	126	44	14	4	3	21	41	35	.239	.297
George Wood	OF104,3B2,P2		106	433	67	99	15	19	6	6	39	44	20	.229	.342
Jack Clements	C85,OF1		86	326	26	80	32	8	4	1	10	36	3	.245	.304
Ed Delahanty	2B56,OF17		74	290	40	66	31	12	2	1	12	26	38	.228	.293
Ben Sanders	P31,OF25,3B1		57	236	26	58	25	11	2	1	8	12	13	.246	.322
Charles Buffinton	P46,OF1		46	160	14	29	12	4	1	0	7	5	1	.181	.219
Pop Schriver	C27,3B6,SS6,OF1		40	134	15	26	23	5	2	1	7	21	2	.194	.284
Dan Casey	P33		33	118	11	18	5	2	1	0	3	28	2	.153	.186
Kid Gleason	P24,OF1		24	83	4	17	5	2	0	0	3	16	3	.205	.229
Bill Hallman	C10,2B4,OF3,3B1,SS1		18	63	5	13	6	4	1	0	1	12	1	.206	.302
Deacon McGuire	C10,3B2	(1-3)	12	51	7	17	11	4	2	0	4	9	0	.333	.490
Woodie Wagenhurst	3B2		2	8	2	1	0	0	0	0	0	1	0	.125	.125
John Grim	2B1,OF1		2	7	0	1	0	0	0	0	0	0	0	.143	.143
Cupid Childs	2B2		2	4	0	0	0	0	0	0	0	0	0	.000	.000
Gid Gardner	2B1	(2-3)	1	3	0	2	1	0	0	0	0	0	0	.667	.667
Jim Tyng	P1		1	1	0	0	0	0	0	0	0	0	0	.000	.000
			132	4528	535	1021	382	151	46	16	268	485	246	.225	.290

PITCHERS	W	L	PCT	G	GS	CG	SH	SV	IP	H	BB	SO	ERA
Charles Buffinton	28	17	.622	46	46	43	6	0	400	324	59	199	1.91
Ben Sanders	19	10	.655	31	29	28	8	0	275	240	33	121	1.90
Dan Casey	14	18	.438	33	33	31	2	0	286	298	48	108	3.15
Kid Gleason	7	16	.304	24	23	23	0	0	200	199	53	89	2.84
George Wood	0	0	----	2	0	0	0	2	2	3	1	0	4.50
Jim Tyng	0	0	----	1	0	0	0	1	4	8	2	2	4.50
	69	61	.531	132	131	125	16	3	1167	1072	196	519	2.38

BOSTON
Beaneaters

70-64 .522 -15.5 4th John Morrill

BATTERS	POS/GAMES		GP	AB	R	H	BI	2B	3B	HR	BB	SO	SB	BA	SA
John Morrill	1B133,2B2		135	486	60	96	39	18	7	4	55	68	21	.198	.288
Joe Quinn	2B38		38	156	19	47	29	8	3	4	2	5	12	.301	.468
Sam Wise	SS89,3B6,1B5		105	417	66	100	40	19	12	4	34	66	33	.240	.372
Billy Nash	3B105,2B31		135	526	71	149	75	18	15	4	50	46	20	.283	.397
Tom Brown	OF107		107	420	62	104	49	10	7	9	30	68	46	.248	.369
Dick Johnston	OF135		135	585	102	173	68	31	18	12	15	33	35	.296	.472
Joe Hornung	OF107		107	431	61	103	53	11	7	3	16	39	29	.239	.318
King Kelly	C76,OF34		107	440	85	140	71	22	11	9	31	39	56	.318	.480
John Clarkson	P54,OF1		55	205	20	40	17	9	1	1	7	48	5	.195	.263
Irv Ray	SS48,2B3		50	206	26	51	26	2	3	2	6	11	7	.248	.316
Pop Tate	C41,OF1		41	148	18	34	6	7	1	1	8	7	3	.230	.311
Bill Sowders	P36		36	122	14	18	6	2	0	0	3	24	1	.148	.164
Ezra Sutton	3B27,SS1		28	110	16	24	16	3	1	1	7	3	10	.218	.291
Billy Clusman	2B28		28	107	9	18	11	4	0	2	5	13	3	.168	.262
Old Hoss Radbourn	P24		24	79	6	17	6	1	0	0	3	14	4	.215	.228
Jack Burdock	2B22	(1-2)	22	79	5	16	4	0	0	0	2	5	1	.203	.203
Tom O'Rourke	C20,OF4,2B2,OF1		20	74	3	13	4	0	0	0	1	9	2	.176	.176
Kid Madden	P20		20	67	7	11	5	0	0	0	1	6	4	.164	.164
Ed Glenn	OF19,3B1	(2-2)	20	65	8	10	3	0	2	0	2	8	0	.154	.215
Bill Higgins	2B14		14	54	5	10	4	1	0	0	1	3	1	.185	.204
Dick Conway	P6,OF1		7	25	2	4	1	0	0	0	1	6	0	.160	.160

1888 NATIONAL LEAGUE

BOSTON (cont.)
Beaneaters

BATTERS	POS/GAMES	GP	AB	R	H	BI	2B	3B	HR	BB	SO	SB	BA	SA
Mike Hines	OF3,C1	4	16	3	2	2	0	1	0	2	0	0	.125	.250
Pete Sommers	C4	4	13	1	3	0	1	0	0	0	3	0	.231	.308
Nick Wise	C1,OF1	1	3	0	0	0	0	0	0	0	0	0	.000	.000
		137	4834	669	1183	535	167	89	56	282	524	293	.245	.351

PITCHERS		W	L	PCT	G	GS	CG	SH	SV	IP	H	BB	SO	ERA
John Clarkson		33	20	.623	54	54	53	3	0	483	448	119	223	2.76
Bill Sowders		19	15	.559	36	35	34	2	0	317	278	73	132	2.07
Kid Madden		7	11	.389	20	18	17	1	0	165	142	24	53	2.95
Old Hoss Radbourn		7	16	.304	24	24	24	1	0	207	187	45	64	2.87
Dick Conway		4	2	.667	6	6	6	0	0	53	49	8	12	2.38
		70	64	.522	137	137	134	7	0	1225	1104	269	484	2.61

DETROIT
Wolverines

68-63   .519   -16   5th   Watkins - Leadley

BATTERS	POS/GAMES	GP	AB	R	H	BI	2B	3B	HR	BB	SO	SB	BA	SA
Dan Brouthers	1B129	129	522	118	160	66	33	11	9	68	13	34	.307	.464
Hardy Richardson	2B58	58	266	60	77	32	18	2	6	17	23	13	.289	.440
Jack Rowe	SS105	105	451	62	125	74	19	8	2	19	28	10	.277	.368
Deacon White	3B125	125	527	75	157	71	22	5	4	21	24	12	.298	.381
Count Campau	OF70	70	251	28	51	18	5	3	1	19	36	27	.203	.259
Ned Hanlon	OF109	109	459	64	122	39	6	8	5	15	32	38	.266	.346
Larry Twitchell	OF131,P2	131	524	71	128	67	19	4	5	28	45	14	.244	.324
Charlie Bennett	C73,1B1	74	258	32	68	29	12	4	5	31	40	4	.264	.399
Charles Ganzel	2B49,C28,3B9,OF5,SS3,1B1	95	386	45	96	46	13	5	1	14	15	12	.249	.299
Sam Thompson	OF56	56	238	51	67	40	10	8	6	23	10	5	.282	.466
Sy Sutcliffe	SS24,C14,1B5,OF4,2B2	49	191	17	49	23	5	3	0	5	14	6	.257	.314
Pretzels Getzien	P46	46	167	14	41	10	2	2	1	12	30	6	.249	.299
Peter Conway	P45,OF1	45	167	28	46	23	4	2	3	8	25	1	.275	.377
Ted Scheffler	OF27	27	94	17	19	4	3	1	0	9	9	4	.202	.255
Henry Gruber	P27	27	92	8	13	4	2	1	0	6	23	0	.141	.185
Parson Nicholson	2B24	24	85	11	22	9	2	3	1	2	7	6	.259	.388
Jake Wells	C16	16	57	5	9	2	1	0	0	0	5	0	.158	.175
Eb Beatin	P12,OF2,SS2	16	56	8	14	9	1	2	2	6	8	1	.250	.446
Lady Baldwin	P6,OF1	6	23	5	6	3	0	0	0	3	3	0	.261	.261
Deacon McGuire	C3 (2-3)	3	13	0	0	0	0	0	0	0	4	0	.000	.000
Sam LaRoque	2B2	2	9	1	4	2	0	0	0	1	1	0	.444	.444
Barney Gilligan	C1	1	5	1	1	0	0	0	0	0	1	0	.200	.200
Cecil Broughton	C1	1	4	0	0	0	0	0	0	0	0	0	.000	.000
Frank Scheibeck	SS1	1	4	0	0	0	0	0	0	0	0	0	.000	.000
		134	4849	721	1275	571	177	72	51	307	396	193	.263	.361

PITCHERS		W	L	PCT	G	GS	CG	SH	SV	IP	H	BB	SO	ERA
Peter Conway		30	14	.682	45	45	43	4	0	391	315	57	176	2.26
Pretzels Getzien		19	25	.432	46	46	45	2	0	404	411	54	202	3.05
Henry Gruber		11	14	.440	27	25	25	3	0	240	196	41	71	2.29
Eb Beatin		5	7	.417	12	12	12	1	0	107	111	16	44	2.86
Lady Baldwin		3	3	.500	6	6	5	0	0	53	76	15	26	5.43
Larry Twitchell		0	0	----	2	0	0	0	1	4	6	0	3	6.75
		68	63	.519	134	134	130	10	1	1199	1115	183	522	2.74

PITTSBURGH
Alleghenys

66-68   .493   -19.5   6th   Horace Phillips

BATTERS	POS/GAMES	GP	AB	R	H	BI	2B	3B	HR	BB	SO	SB	BA	SA
Jake Beckley	1B71	71	283	35	97	27	15	3	0	7	22	20	.343	.417
Fred Dunlap	2B82	82	321	41	84	36	12	4	1	16	30	24	.262	.333
Pop Smith	SS75,2B56	131	481	61	99	52	15	2	4	22	78	37	.206	.270
Bill Kuehne	3B75,SS63	138	524	60	123	62	22	11	3	9	68	34	.235	.336
Jack Coleman	OF91,1B25	116	438	49	101	26	11	4	0	29	52	15	.231	.274
Billy Sunday	OF120	120	505	69	119	15	14	3	0	12	36	71	.236	.275
Abner Dalrymple	OF57	57	227	19	50	14	9	2	0	6	28	7	.220	.278
Doggie Miller	C68,OF32,3B4	103	404	50	112	36	17	5	0	18	16	27	.277	.344

1888 NATIONAL LEAGUE

PITTSBURGH (cont.)
Alleghenys

BATTERS	POS/GAMES		GP	AB	R	H	BI	2B	3B	HR	BB	SO	SB	BA	SA
Fred Carroll	C54,OF38,1B5,3B1		97	366	62	91	48	14	5	2	32	31	18	.249	.331
Al Maul	1B38,OF34,P3		74	259	21	54	31	9	4	0	21	45	9	.208	.274
Ed Morris	P55		55	189	12	19	6	0	2	0	3	44	2	.101	.122
Pud Galvin	P50,OF1		50	175	6	25	3	1	1	1	1	51	4	.143	.177
Jocko Fields	OF29,C14,3B3		45	169	22	33	15	7	2	1	8	19	9	.195	.278
Elmer Cleveland	3B30	(2-2)	30	108	10	24	11	2	1	2	5	23	3	.222	.315
Pete McShannic	3B26		26	98	5	19	5	1	0	0	1	9	3	.194	.204
Harry Staley	P25		25	85	6	11	1	1	0	0	1	18	2	.129	.141
Sam Nichol	OF8		8	22	3	1	0	0	0	0	2	2	0	.045	.045
Cliff Carroll	OF5		5	20	1	0	0	0	0	0	0	8	2	.000	.000
Hardie Henderson	P5,OF1		5	18	2	5	3	0	0	0	0	2	0	.278	.278
Phil Knell	P3		3	11	0	1	0	0	0	0	0	0	0	.091	.091
Henry Yaik	C1,OF1		2	6	0	2	1	0	0	0	1	0	0	.333	.333
Bill Farmer	C1,OF1	(1-2)	2	4	0	0	0	0	0	0	0	1	0	.000	.000
			139	4713	534	1070	392	150	49	14	194	583	287	.227	.289

PITCHERS	W	L	PCT	G	GS	CG	SH	SV	IP	H	BB	SO	ERA
Ed Morris	29	23	.558	55	55	54	5	0	480	470	74	135	2.31
Pud Galvin	23	25	.479	50	50	49	6	0	437	446	53	107	2.63
Harry Staley	12	12	.500	25	24	24	2	0	207	185	53	89	2.69
Phil Knell	1	2	.333	3	3	3	0	0	26	20	18	15	3.76
Hardie Henderson	1	3	.250	5	5	4	0	0	35	43	20	9	5.35
Al Maul	0	2	.000	3	1	1	0	0	17	26	5	12	6.35
	66	68	.493	139	138	135	13	0	1203	1190	223	367	2.67

INDIANAPOLIS   50-85   .370   -36   7th   Harry Spence
Hoosiers

BATTERS	POS/GAMES		GP	AB	R	H	BI	2B	3B	HR	BB	SO	SB	BA	SA
Dude Esterbrook	1B61,3B3	(1-2)	64	246	21	54	17	8	0	0	2	20	11	.220	.252
Charley Bassett	2B128		128	481	58	116	60	20	3	2	32	41	24	.241	.308
Jack Glasscock	SS110,2B3,P1		113	442	63	119	45	17	3	1	14	17	48	.269	.328
Jerry Denny	3B96,SS25,2B5,OF1,P1		126	524	92	137	63	27	7	12	9	79	32	.261	.408
Jack McGeachey	OF117,P1,SS1		118	452	45	99	30	15	2	0	5	21	49	.219	.261
Paul Hines	OF125,1B6,SS2		133	513	84	144	58	26	3	4	41	45	31	.281	.366
Emmett Seery	OF133,SS1		133	500	87	110	50	20	10	5	64	73	80	.220	.330
Dick Buckley	C51,3B22,OF1,1B1		71	260	28	71	22	9	3	5	6	24	4	.273	.388
George Myers	C47,3B14,OF10,1B1		66	248	36	59	16	9	0	2	16	14	28	.238	.298
Con Daily	C42,1B5,3B5,OF5,2B1		57	202	14	44	14	6	1	0	10	28	15	.218	.257
Jumbo Schoeneck	1B48,P2		48	169	15	40	20	4	0	0	9	24	11	.237	.260
Egyptian Healy	P37,OF1		37	131	14	30	13	9	0	0	1	39	5	.229	.289
Henry Boyle	P37,1B1		37	125	13	18	6	2	0	1	6	31	1	.144	.184
Ledell Shreve	P35,OF1		36	115	10	21	2	3	0	0	4	9	5	.183	.209
Otto Schomberg	1B15,OF15		30	112	11	24	10	5	1	1	10	12	6	.214	.304
Bill Burdick	P20,OF1		21	68	6	10	1	0	0	0	2	11	0	.147	.147
Sam Moffett	P7,OF3		10	35	6	4	0	0	0	0	5	4	0	.114	.114
			136	4623	603	1100	427	180	33	33	236	492	350	.238	.313

PITCHERS	W	L	PCT	G	GS	CG	SH	SV	IP	H	BB	SO	ERA
Henry Boyle	15	22	.405	37	37	36	3	0	323	315	58	98	3.26
Egyptian Healy	12	24	.333	37	37	36	1	0	321	347	87	124	3.89
Ledell Shreve	11	24	.314	35	35	34	1	0	298	352	93	101	4.63
Bill Burdick	10	10	.500	20	20	20	0	0	176	168	43	55	2.81
Sam Moffett	2	5	.286	7	7	6	1	0	56	62	17	7	4.66
Jumbo Schoeneck	0	0	----	2	0	0	0	0	4	5	1	1	0.00
Jack McGeachey	0	0	----	1	0	0	0	0	5	5	3	0	7.20
Jerry Denny	0	0	----	1	0	0	0	0	4	5	4	1	9.00
Jack Glasscock	0	0	----	1	0	0	0	0	0	1	2	1	54.00
	50	85	.370	136	136	132	6	0	1188	1260	308	388	3.81

WASHINGTON   48-86   .358   -37.5   8th   Hewett - Sullivan
Statesmen

BATTERS	POS/GAMES	GP	AB	R	H	BI	2B	3B	HR	BB	SO	SB	BA	SA
Billy O'Brien	1B132,3B1	133	528	42	119	66	15	2	9	9	70	10	.225	.313
Al Myers	2B132	132	502	46	104	46	12	7	2	37	46	20	.207	.271

WASHINGTON (cont.)
Statesmen

BATTERS	POS/GAMES		GP	AB	R	H	BI	2B	3B	HR	BB	SO	SB	BA	SA
George Shoch	SS52,OF35,2B1,P1		90	317	46	58	24	6	3	2	25	22	23	.183	.240
Jim Donnelly	3B117,SS5		122	428	43	86	23	9	4	0	20	16	44	.201	.241
Ed Daily	OF100,P9,1B1		110	453	56	102	39	8	4	7	7	42	44	.225	.307
Dummy Hoy	OF136		136	503	77	138	29	10	8	2	69	48	82	.274	.338
Walt Wilmot	OF119		119	473	61	106	43	16	9	4	23	55	46	.224	.321
Connie Mack	C79,OF4,1B1,SS1		85	300	49	56	29	5	6	3	17	18	31	.187	.273
Shorty Fuller	SS47,2B2		49	170	11	31	12	5	2	0	10	14	6	.182	.235
Hank O'Day	P46,SS2		47	166	6	23	6	2	0	0	4	41	3	.139	.151
Jim Whitney	P39,OF3,1B1		42	141	13	24	17	0	0	1	7	20	3	.170	.191
John Irwin	SS27,3B10		37	126	14	28	8	5	2	0	5	18	15	.222	.294
Pat Deasley	C31,2B1,OF1,SS1		34	127	6	20	4	1	0	0	2	18	2	.157	.165
Tug Arundel	C17		17	51	2	10	3	0	1	0	5	10	1	.196	.235
Wild Bill Widner	P13,OF2		15	60	4	12	6	0	0	0	0	8	1	.200	.200
George Keefe	P13		13	42	2	9	6	3	0	0	2	10	0	.214	.286
Frank Gilmore	P12,OF1,C1		13	41	0	1	2	0	0	0	0	20	0	.024	.024
Miah Murray	C10,1B2		12	42	1	4	3	1	0	0	1	7	0	.095	.119
Peter Sweeney	3B8,OF3		11	44	3	8	5	0	1	0	0	4	0	.182	.227
Perry Werden	OF3		3	10	0	3	2	0	0	0	1	4	0	.300	.300
Dupee Shaw	P3		3	10	0	0	0	0	0	0	0	3	0	.000	.000
George Haddock	P2		2	5	0	1	0	0	0	0	1	2	0	.200	.200
Gid Gardner	SS1,2B1	(1,3-3)	2	4	0	1	0	0	0	0	1	1	0	.250	.250
John Greening	P1		1	3	0	0	0	0	0	0	0	2	0	.000	.000
Jim Banning	C1		1	0	0	0	0	0	0	0	0	0	0	----	----
			136	4546	482	944	373	98	49	30	246	499	331	.208	.271

PITCHERS		W	L	PCT	G	GS	CG	SH	SV	IP	H	BB	SO	ERA
Jim Whitney		18	21	.462	39	39	37	2	0	325	317	54	79	3.05
Hank O'Day		16	29	.356	46	46	46	3	0	403	359	117	186	3.10
George Keefe		6	7	.462	13	13	13	1	0	114	87	43	52	2.84
Wild Bill Widner		5	7	.417	13	13	13	0	0	115	111	22	33	2.82
Ed Daily		2	7	.222	9	8	8	0	0	74	88	19	20	4.89
Frank Gilmore		1	9	.100	12	11	10	0	0	96	131	29	23	6.59
John Greening		0	1	.000	1	1	1	0	0	9	17	4	2	11.00
George Haddock		0	2	.000	2	2	2	0	0	16	9	2	3	2.25
Dupee Shaw		0	3	.000	3	3	3	0	0	25	36	7	8	6.48
George Shoch		0	0	----	1	0	0	0	0	3	2	1	0	0.00
		48	86	.358	136	136	133	6	0	1179	1157	298	406	3.54

1888 AMERICAN ASSOCIATION

Giving Away the Store

Picture this. After winning three pennants in a row by a large margin, a team owner takes pity on his fellow owners and sends five of his best players to their teams to help make them more competitive. Impossible? This scenario actually happened at the end of the 1887 season in the American Association.

After winning their third pennant in a row, the St. Louis Browns sold their two best pitchers, Dave Foutz, and Bob Caruthers, as well as their catcher Doc Bushong to Brooklyn. Then, outfielder Curt Welch and shortstop Bill Gleason were sold to Philadelphia.

At first glance, this appears to have been a strictly altruistic event. But on further reflection, St. Louis owner Chris Von der Ahe's motive becomes clear. The Browns had won the past three pennants by an average of 14 games. Such one-sided races do not generate much fan interest. Since any profit to be made in 1880's era baseball came through the turnstile, it made sense that a close pennant race would generate more money than a rout. By evening up the competition, Von der Ahe was striving to make the pennant race more profitable for all, including himself. This turned out to be a shrewd strategy.

The tricky part of the strategy was to not give away the store, and turn your team into an unprofitable cellar dweller. The cushion that Von der Ahe had against that possibility were the funds he received from the sale of his five players. He did not give them away, he sold them. The transactions themselves were for between $3,000 and $8,000 each, certainly enough to warrant the risk of mediocrity.

Bereft of their two best pitchers, center fielder, catcher, and shortstop, the Browns won ten fewer games in 1888. However, that was still good enough to win the pennant for the fourth straight year. Their beneficiaries, Brooklyn and Philadelphia, finished in second and third.

The St. Louis Browns may have sold five good players, but they wisely kept their best player. Tip O'Neill won his second straight batting mark in 1888 at .335, a full 100 points lower than his record-breaking average of the year before. Pitcher Silver King proved to be the stingiest of the league with his 1.64 earned run average to accompany his circuit topping 45 wins.

Second place Brooklyn came closer than any other American Association team in unseating the Browns. Dave Orr (.305) and pitcher Bob Caruthers (29-15) carried Brooklyn to within six and one-half games of the top.

Philadelphia and Cincinnati finished third and fourth. Philadelphia won the team batting title without a single regular over .300. Harry Stovey with 20 triples, and Ed Seward (35-19) and a league-leading 272 strikeouts paved the way. Cincinnati's Long John Reilly (.321, 13 HR, 103 RBI) had a strong year — his home run and runs batted in totals led the league.

Baltimore, Cleveland, and Louisville finished in fifth, sixth and seventh places. Players of note for these three included Pete Browning (.313) of Louisville, and Cleveland's Jersey Bakely who won half of his team's games.

Last place Kansas City was a newcomer to the American Association. The moribund New York Metropolitans had been purchased by Brooklyn (thus explaining their acquisition of hard-hitting Dave Orr, and Kansas City had been admitted to fill the vacancy.

This strategy by the Browns would be unheard of in today's world of baseball. But back in the pre-television dollars era, the fan was an owner's meal ticket. And to keep the fan interested in spending his money at the ballpark, the games needed to be interesting, and the pennant race close and exciting.

1888 AMERICAN ASSOCIATION

ST. LOUIS
Browns

92-43   .681   1st   Charlie Comiskey

BATTERS	POS/GAMES		GP	AB	R	H	BI	2B	3B	HR	BB	SO	SB	BA	SA
Charlie Comiskey	1B133,OF5,2B3		137	576	102	157	83	22	5	6	12		72	.273	.359
Yank Robinson	2B102,SS34		134	455	111	105	53	17	6	3	116		56	.231	.314
Bill White	SS74,2B2	(2-2)	76	275	31	48	30	2	3	2	21		6	.175	.225
Arlie Latham	3B133,SS1		133	570	119	151	31	19	5	2	43		109	.265	.326
Tommy McCarthy	OF131,P2		131	511	107	140	68	20	3	1	38		93	.274	.331
Harry Lyons	OF122,3B2,2B1,SS1		123	499	66	97	63	10	5	4	20		36	.194	.259
Tip O'Neill	OF130		130	529	96	177	98	24	10	5	44		26	.335	.446
Jack Boyle	C70,OF1		71	257	33	62	23	8	1	1	13		11	.241	.292
Silver King	P66,OF2		66	207	25	43	14	4	6	1	40		6	.208	.300
Jocko Milligan	C58,1B5		63	219	19	55	37	6	2	5	17		3	.251	.365
Nat Hudson	P39,OF16,1B3,SS1		56	196	27	50	28	7	0	2	18		9	.255	.321
Ed Herr	SS28,OF11,3B4		43	172	21	46	43	7	1	3	11		9	.267	.372
Chippy McGarr	2B33,SS1		34	132	17	31	13	1	0	0	6		25	.235	.242
Icebox Chamberlain	P14	(2-2)	14	50	6	5	2	0	0	1	3		3	.100	.160
James Devlin	P11		11	37	7	11	3	1	0	0	4		2	.297	.324
Tom Dolan	C11		11	36	1	7	1	1	0	0	1		1	.194	.222
Ed Knouff	P9		9	31	1	3	1	0	0	0	3		1	.097	.097
Julie Freeman	P1		1	3	0	1	0	0	0	0	0		0	.333	.333
			137	4755	789	1189	591	149	47	36	410	521	468	.250	.324

PITCHERS			W	L	PCT	G	GS	CG	SH	SV	IP	H	BB	SO	ERA
Silver King			45	21	.682	66	65	64	6	0	586	437	76	258	1.64
Nat Hudson			25	10	.714	39	37	36	5	0	333	283	59	130	2.54
Icebox Chamberlain		(2-2)	11	2	.846	14	14	13	1	0	112	61	27	57	1.61
James Devlin			6	5	.545	11	11	10	0	0	90	82	20	45	3.19
Ed Knouff		(1-2)	5	4	.556	9	9	9	0	0	81	66	37	25	2.67
Julie Freeman			0	1	.000	1	1	0	0	0	6	7	4	1	4.26
Tommy McCarthy			0	0	----	2	0	0	0	0	4	3	2	1	4.15
			92	43	.681	137	137	132	12	0	1213	939	225	517	2.09

BROOKLYN
Trolley Dodgers

88-52   .629   -6.5   2nd   Bill McGunnigle

BATTERS	POS/GAMES		GP	AB	R	H	BI	2B	3B	HR	BB	SO	SB	BA	SA
Dave Orr	1B99		99	394	57	120	59	20	5	1	7		11	.305	.388
Jack Burdock	2B70	(2-2)	70	246	15	30	8	1	2	1	8		9	.122	.154
Germany Smith	SS103,2B1		103	402	47	86	61	10	7	3	22		27	.214	.296
George Pinkney	3B143		143	575	134	156	52	18	8	4	66		51	.271	.351
Dave Foutz	OF78,1B42,P23		140	563	91	156	99	20	13	3	28		35	.277	.375
Paul Radford	OF88,2B2		90	308	48	67	29	9	3	2	35		33	.218	.286
Darby O'Brien	OF136		136	532	105	149	65	27	6	2	30		55	.280	.365
Doc Bushong	C69		69	253	23	53	16	5	1	0	5		9	.209	.237
Bob Caruthers	OF51,P44		94	335	58	77	53	10	5	5	45		23	.230	.334
Bill McClellan	2B56,OF18	(1-2)	74	278	33	57	21	7	3	0	40		13	.205	.252
Oyster Burns	SS36,OF14,2B3	(2-2)	52	204	40	58	25	9	6	2	14		21	.284	.417
Bob Clark	C36,OF8,1B1		45	150	23	36	20	5	3	1	9		11	.240	.333
Mickey Hughes	P40		40	139	10	19	10	5	0	0	7		1	.137	.173
Jim Peoples	C25,SS5,OF2		32	103	15	20	17	5	3	0	8		10	.194	.301
Adonis Terry	P23,OF7		30	115	13	29	8	6	0	0	5		7	.252	.304
Pop Corkhill	OF19	(2-2)	19	71	17	27	19	4	3	1	4		3	.380	.563
Al Mays	P18,OF1		18	63	4	5	5	1	1	0	5		2	.079	.127
Bill Holbert	C15		15	50	4	6	1	1	0	0	2		0	.120	.140
Ed Silch	OF14		14	48	5	13	3	4	0	0	4		4	.271	.354
Hub Collins	2B12	(2-2)	12	42	16	13	3	5	1	0	9		9	.310	.476
			143	4871	758	1177	574	172	70	25	353	439	334	.242	.321

PITCHERS			W	L	PCT	G	GS	CG	SH	SV	IP	H	BB	SO	ERA
Bob Caruthers			29	15	.659	44	43	42	4	0	392	337	53	140	2.39
Mickey Hughes			25	13	.658	40	40	40	2	0	363	281	98	159	2.13
Adonis Terry			13	8	.619	23	23	20	2	0	195	145	67	138	2.03
Dave Foutz			12	7	.632	23	19	19	0	0	176	146	35	73	2.51
Al Mays			9	9	.500	18	18	17	1	0	161	150	32	67	2.80
			88	52	.629	143	143	138	9	0	1286	1059	285	577	2.33

1888 AMERICAN ASSOCIATION

PHILADELPHIA Athletics

81-52 .609 -10 3rd Bill Sharsig

BATTERS	POS/GAMES		GP	AB	R	H	BI	2B	3B	HR	BB	SO	SB	BA	SA
Henry Larkin	1B122,2B14		135	546	92	147	101	28	12	7	33		20	.269	.406
Lou Bierbauer	2B121,3B13,P1		134	535	83	143	80	20	9	0	25		34	.267	.338
Bill Gleason	SS121,1B1,3B1		123	499	55	112	61	10	2	0	12		27	.224	.253
Denny Lyons	3B111		111	456	93	135	83	22	5	4	41		39	.296	.406
Tom Poorman	OF97		97	383	76	87	44	16	6	2	31		46	.227	.316
Curt Welch	OF135,2B3		136	549	125	155	61	22	8	1	33		95	.282	.357
Harry Stovey	OF118,1B13		130	530	127	152	65	25	20	9	62		87	.287	.460
Wilbert Robinson	C65,1B1		66	254	32	62	31	7	2	1	9		11	.244	.299
Ed Seward	P57,OF7		64	225	27	32	14	3	3	2	18		12	.142	.209
Gus Weyhing	P47,OF2		48	184	19	40	14	6	8	1	1		5	.217	.353
George Townshend	C42		42	161	13	25	12	6	0	0	4		2	.155	.193
Mike Mattimore	P26,OF16		41	142	22	38	12	6	5	0	12		16	.268	.380
Mike Sullivan	OF18,3B10		28	112	20	31	19	5	6	1	3		10	.277	.455
Tom Gunning	C23		23	92	18	18	5	0	0	0	2		14	.196	.196
Blondie Purcell	OF17,3B1	(2-2)	18	66	10	11	6	3	1	0	5		10	.167	.242
Frank Fennelly	SS15	(2-2)	15	47	13	11	12	2	2	1	9		5	.234	.426
Bill Blair	P4,OF1		4	13	1	4	1	1	0	0	1		0	.308	.385
Bill Farmer	C3	(2-2)	3	12	0	2	1	0	0	0	0		0	.167	.167
Phenomenal Smith	P3	(2-2)	3	9	1	3	2	1	0	0	1		1	.333	.444
Frank Zinn	C2		2	7	0	0	0	0	0	0	1		0	.000	.000
Robert Gamble	P1		1	3	0	1	0	0	0	0	0		0	.333	.333
Whitey Gibson	C1		1	3	0	0	0	0	0	0	0		0	.000	.000
			136	4828	827	1209	624	183	89	31	303	473	434	.250	.344

PITCHERS	W	L	PCT	G	GS	CG	SH	SV	IP	H	BB	SO	ERA
Ed Seward	35	19	.648	57	57	57	6	0	519	388	127	272	2.01
Gus Weyhing	28	18	.609	47	47	45	3	0	404	314	111	204	2.25
Mike Mattimore	15	10	.600	26	24	24	4	0	221	221	65	80	3.38
Phenomenal Smith	2	1	.667	3	3	3	0	0	22	21	10	19	2.86
Bill Blair	1	3	.250	4	4	3	0	0	31	29	8	16	2.61
Robert Gamble	0	1	.000	1	1	1	0	0	9	10	3	2	8.00
Lou Bierbauer	0	0	----	1	0	0	0	0	3	5	0	3	0.00
	81	52	.609	136	136	133	13	0	1209	988	324	596	2.41

CINCINNATI Red Stockings

80-54 .597 -11.5 4th Gus Schmelz

BATTERS	POS/GAMES		GP	AB	R	H	BI	2B	3B	HR	BB	SO	SB	BA	SA
Long John Reilly	1B117,OF10		127	527	112	169	103	28	14	13	17		82	.321	.501
Bid McPhee	2B109,3B1,OF1		111	458	88	110	51	12	10	4	43		54	.240	.336
Frank Fennelly	SS112,2B4,OF4	(1-2)	120	448	64	88	56	8	7	2	63		43	.196	.259
Hick Carpenter	3B136		136	551	68	147	67	14	5	3	5		59	.267	.327
Hugh Nicol	OF125,2B12,SS1		135	548	112	131	35	10	2	1	67		103	.239	.270
Pop Corkhill	OF116,P2,1B1,2B1	(1-2)	118	490	68	133	74	11	9	1	15		27	.271	.337
White Wings Tebeau	OF121		121	411	72	94	51	12	3	0	61		37	.229	.338
Jim Keenan	C69,1B16		85	313	38	73	40	9	8	1	22		9	.233	.323
Kid Baldwin	C65,OF2,1B1		67	271	27	59	25	11	3	1	3		4	.218	.292
Tony Mullane	P44,1B4,OF3,2B2		51	175	27	44	16	4	4	1	8		12	.251	.337
Leon Viau	P42,OF1		43	149	16	13	8	1	2	0	11		5	.087	.121
Elmer Smith	P40,OF2		40	129	15	29	9	4	1	0	20		2	.225	.271
Heinie Kappel	SS25,2B10,3B1		36	143	18	37	15	4	4	1	2		20	.259	.364
Jack O'Connor	OF34,C2		36	137	14	28	17	3	1	1	6		12	.204	.263
John Weyhing	P8		8	23	2	3	0	0	0	0	1		0	.130	.130
Billy Serad	P6		6	23	4	3	4	1	0	0	1		0	.130	.174
Ned Bligh	C2,OF1		3	5	0	0	0	0	0	0	0		0	.000	.000
			137	4801	745	1161	571	132	82	32	345	555	469	.242	.323

PITCHERS	W	L	PCT	G	GS	CG	SH	SV	IP	H	BB	SO	ERA
Leon Viau	27	14	.659	42	42	42	1	0	389	331	110	164	2.65
Tony Mullane	26	16	.619	44	42	41	4	1	380	341	75	186	2.84
Elmer Smith	22	17	.564	40	40	37	5	0	348	309	89	154	2.74
John Weyhing	3	4	.429	8	8	7	0	0	66	52	17	30	1.23
Billy Serad	2	3	.400	6	5	5	0	0	51	62	19	4	3.55
Pop Corkhill	0	0	----	2	0	0	0	1	5	8	0	1	10.80
	80	54	.597	137	137	132	10	2	1238	1103	310	539	2.73

1888 AMERICAN ASSOCIATION

BALTIMORE Orioles   57-80   .416   -36   5th   Billy Barnie

BATTERS	POS/GAMES		GP	AB	R	H	BI	2B	3B	HR	BB	SO	SB	BA	SA
Tommy Tucker	1B129,OF7,P1		136	520	74	149	61	17	12	6	16		43	.287	.400
Bill Greenwood	2B86,SS28,OF1		115	409	69	78	29	13	1	0	30		46	.191	.227
Jack Farrell	SS54,2B52		103	398	72	81	36	19	5	3	26		29	.204	.299
Bill Shindle	3B135		135	514	61	107	53	14	8	1	20		52	.208	.272
Blondie Purcell	OF100,SS2,1B1	(1-2)	101	406	53	96	39	9	4	2	27		16	.236	.293
Mike Griffin	OF137		137	542	103	139	46	21	11	0	55		46	.256	.336
Oyster Burns	OF56,SS23,P5,3B2,2B1	(1-2)	79	325	54	97	42	18	9	4	24		23	.298	.446
Chris Fulmer	C45,OF47		52	166	20	31	10	5	1	0	21		10	.187	.229
Joe Sommer	OF44,SS34,2B2,1B1		79	297	31	65	35	10	0	0	18		13	.219	.253
Jack O'Brien	C37,OF13,1B7		57	196	25	44	18	11	5	0	17		14	.224	.332
Bert Cunningham	P51,OF1		51	177	17	33	9	3	2	1	5		2	.186	.243
Walt Goldsby	OF45		45	165	13	39	14	1	1	0	8		17	.236	.255
Matt Kilroy	P40,OF7		43	145	13	26	19	5	2	0	11		10	.179	.241
Bart Cantz	C33,OF4		37	126	7	21	9	2	1	0	2		0	.167	.198
Phenomenal Smith	P35,OF1	(1-2)	35	109	16	27	12	3	4	1	12		2	.248	.376
Sam Trott	C27,OF3,1B1,2B1		31	108	19	30	22	11	4	0	4		1	.278	.454
Sam Shaw	P6		6	20	3	3	0	0	0	0	2		1	.150	.150
George Walker	P4		4	13	1	1	1	0	0	0	0		0	.077	.077
Bill Whitaker	P2		2	6	0	0	0	0	0	0	0		0	.000	.000
John Peltz	OF1		1	4	1	1	0	0	0	0	0		1	.250	.250
Mike Kilroy	P1		1	4	0	0	0	0	0	0	0		0	.000	.000
John Harkins	P1		1	4	1	0	0	0	0	0	0		0	.000	.000
George Bradley	SS1		1	3	0	0	0	0	0	0	0		0	.000	.000
			137	4657	653	1068	455	162	70	19	298	479	326	.229	.306

PITCHERS		W	L	PCT	G	GS	CG	SH	SV	IP	H	BB	SO	ERA
Bert Cunningham		22	29	.431	51	51	50	0	0	453	412	157	186	3.39
Matt Kilroy		17	21	.447	40	40	35	2	0	321	347	79	135	4.04
Phenomenal Smith	(1-2)	14	19	.424	35	32	31	0	0	292	249	137	152	3.61
Sam Shaw		2	4	.333	6	6	6	0	0	53	65	15	22	3.40
Bill Whitaker		1	1	.500	2	2	2	0	0	14	13	6	5	5.14
George Walker		1	3	.250	4	4	4	1	0	35	36	14	18	5.91
Oyster Burns	(1-2)	0	1	.000	5	0	0	0	0	13	12	3	2	4.26
Mike Kilroy		0	1	.000	1	1	1	0	0	9	12	5	1	8.00
John Harkins		0	1	.000	1	1	1	0	0	8	12	3	2	6.75
Tommy Tucker		0	0	----	1	0	0	0	0	2	4	0	2	3.86
		57	80	.416	137	137	130	3	0	1200	1162	419	525	3.78

CLEVELAND Blues   50-82   .379   -40.5   6th   Williams - Loftus

BATTERS	POS/GAMES		GP	AB	R	H	BI	2B	3B	HR	BB	SO	SB	BA	SA
Jay Faatz	1B120		120	470	73	124	51	10	2	0	12		64	.264	.294
Cub Stricker	2B122,OF6,P2		127	493	80	115	33	13	6	1	50		60	.233	.290
Ed McKean	SS78,OF48,2B9,3B1		131	548	94	164	68	21	15	6	28		52	.299	.425
Gus Alberts	3B49,SS53		102	364	51	75	48	10	6	1	41		26	.206	.275
Eddie Hogan	OF78		78	269	60	61	24	16	6	0	50		30	.227	.331
Pete Hotaling	OF98		98	403	67	101	55	7	6	0	26		35	.251	.298
Bob Gilks	OF87,3B28,P4,SS4,2B1		119	484	59	111	63	14	4	1	7		16	.229	.281
Chief Zimmer	C59,1B3,OF3,SS1		65	212	27	51	22	11	4	0	18		15	.241	.330
Mike Goodfellow	OF62,C4,1B3,SS1		68	269	24	66	29	7	0	0	11		7	.245	.271
Pop Snyder	C58,1B4,OF3		64	237	22	51	14	7	3	0	6		9	.215	.270
Jersey Bakely	P61,SS1		61	194	19	26	9	0	1	1	26		1	.134	.160
John McGlone	3B48,OF7		55	203	22	37	22	1	3	1	16		26	.182	.232
John O'Brien	P30,OF2		32	109	13	20	9	1	0	0	4		2	.183	.193
Deacon McGuire	C17,1B6,OF3	(3-3)	26	94	15	24	13	1	3	1	7		2	.255	.362
Bill McClellan	OF15,2B5,SS2	(2-2)	22	72	6	16	5	0	0	0	6		6	.222	.222
Bill Crowell	P18,OF1	(1-2)	18	58	5	5	3	2	0	0	3		2	.086	.121
Dick Van Zant	3B10		10	31	1	8	1	1	0	0	1		1	.258	.290
George Proeser	P7		7	23	5	7	1	2	0	0	1		0	.304	.391
Ed Keas	P6		6	23	1	2	0	0	0	0	0		0	.087	.087
Mike Morrison	P4		4	17	2	4	0	0	0	0	0		0	.235	.235
Hart Oberlander	P3		3	14	3	3	4	2	0	0	0		0	.214	.357
Bill Stemmeyer	P2,1B1		3	10	2	4	1	1	0	0	1		0	.400	.500
Ed Knouff	P2	(1-2)	2	6	0	1	0	1	0	0	1		0	.167	.333
			135	4603	651	1076	475	128	59	12	315	559	353	.234	.295

CLEVELAND (cont.)
Blues

PITCHERS		W	L	PCT	G	GS	CG	SH	SV	IP	H	BB	SO	ERA
Jersey Bakely		25	33	.431	61	61	60	4	0	533	518	128	212	2.97
John O'Brien		11	19	.367	30	30	30	1	0	259	245	99	135	3.30
Bill Crowell	(1-2)	5	13	.278	18	18	16	0	0	151	212	61	61	5.79
Ed Keas		3	3	.500	6	6	6	0	0	51	53	12	18	2.29
George Proeser		3	4	.429	7	7	7	1	0	59	53	30	20	3.81
Cub Stricker		1	0	1.000	2	0	0	0	0	12	16	2	5	4.50
Hart Oberlander		1	2	.333	3	3	3	0	0	26	27	18	23	5.26
Mike Morrison		1	3	.250	4	4	4	0	0	35	40	19	14	5.40
Ed Knouff	(2-2)	0	1	.000	2	2	1	0	0	9	8	3	2	1.00
Bob Gilks		0	2	.000	4	2	2	0	1	21	26	8	3	8.14
Bill Stemmeyer		0	2	.000	2	2	2	0	0	16	37	9	7	9.00
		50	82	.379	135	135	131	6	1	1171	1235	389	500	3.72

LOUISVILLE
Colonels

48-87 .356 -44 7th Kelly - Kerins - Davidson

BATTERS	POS/GAMES		GP	AB	R	H	BI	2B	3B	HR	BB	SO	SB	BA	SA
Skyrocket Smith	1B58		58	206	27	49	31	9	4	1	24		5	.238	.335
Reddy Mack	2B112		112	446	77	97	34	13	5	3	52		18	.217	.289
Bill White	SS38,3B11	(1-2)	49	198	35	55	30	6	5	1	7		15	.278	.374
Joe Werrick	3B89,SS11,2B8,OF3		111	413	49	89	51	12	7	0	30		15	.215	.278
Chicken Wolf	OF85,SS39,3B4,C3,1B1		128	538	80	154	67	28	11	0	25		41	.286	.379
Pete Browning	OF99		99	383	58	120	72	22	8	3	37		36	.313	.436
Hub Collins	OF82,2B19,SS15	(1-2)	116	485	117	149	50	*26	11	2	41		62	.307	.419
Paul Cook	C53,OF4,SS1		57	185	20	34	13	2	0	0	5		9	.184	.195
John Kerins	OF47,C33,1B4,3B2,2B1		83	319	38	75	41	11	4	2	25		16	.235	.313
Scott Stratton	OF38,P33		67	249	35	64	29	8	1	1	12		10	.257	.309
Guy Hecker	1B30,P28,OF1		56	211	32	48	29	9	2	0	11		20	.227	.289
Farmer Vaughn	OF28,C25		51	189	15	37	21	4	2	1	4		4	.196	.254
Lave Cross	C37,OF12,SS2		47	181	20	41	15	3	0	0	2		10	.227	.243
Toad Ramsey	P40,OF4		42	142	12	17	9	6	0	0	9		0	.120	.162
Phil Tomney	SS34		34	120	15	18	4	3	0	0	7		11	.150	.175
Harry Raymond	3B31,OF1		32	123	8	26	13	2	0	0	1		7	.211	.228
Icebox Chamberlain	P24		26	94	11	18	3	4	2	0	6		8	.191	.277
Farmer Weaver	OF26		26	112	12	28	8	1	1	0	3		12	.250	.277
Wally Andrews	1B26		26	93	12	18	6	6	3	0	13		5	.194	.323
Dude Esterbrook	1B23	(2-2)	23	93	9	21	7	6	0	0	3		5	.226	.290
John Ewing	P21		21	79	6	16	5	1	1	0	1		7	.203	.241
Phil Reccius	3B2		2	9	0	2	4	1	0	0	1		0	.222	.333
Ed Fusselbach	OF1		1	4	0	1	1	0	0	0	0		0	.250	.250
Hercules Burnett	OF1		1	4	1	0	0	0	0	0	1		1	.000	.000
Bill Crowell	P1	(2-2)	1	3	0	0	0	0	0	0	1		1	.000	.000
Harry Long	OF1		1	2	0	0	0	0	0	0	1		0	.000	.000
			139	4881	689	1177	543	183	67	14	322	604	318	.241	.315

PITCHERS		W	L	PCT	G	GS	CG	SH	SV	IP	H	BB	SO	ERA
Icebox Chamberlain	(1-2)	14	9	.609	24	24	21	1	0	196	177	59	119	2.53
Scott Stratton		10	17	.370	33	28	28	2	0	270	287	53	97	3.64
John Ewing		8	13	.381	21	21	21	2	0	191	175	34	87	2.83
Guy Hecker		8	17	.320	26	25	25	0	0	223	251	43	63	3.39
Toad Ramsey		8	30	.211	40	40	37	1	0	342	362	86	228	3.42
Bill Crowell	(2-2)	0	1	.000	1	1	1	0	0	9	12	6	5	6.00
		48	87	.356	139	139	133	6	0	1231	1264	281	599	3.25

KANSAS CITY
Cowboys

43-89 .326 -47.5 8th Rowe - Barkley - Watkins

BATTERS	POS/GAMES	GP	AB	R	H	BI	2B	3B	HR	BB	SO	SB	BA	SA
Bill Phillips	1B129	129	509	57	120	56	20	10	1	27		10	.236	.320
Sam Barkley	2B116	116	482	67	104	51	21	6	4	26		15	.216	.309
Henry Easterday	SS115	115	401	42	76	37	7	6	3	31		23	.190	.259
Jumbo Davis	3B113,SS8	121	491	70	131	61	22	8	3	20		42	.267	.363
Monk Cline	OF70,2B3,3B1	73	293	45	69	19	13	2	0	20		29	.235	.294
Jim McTamany	OF130	130	516	94	127	41	12	10	4	67		55	.246	.331
Myron Allen	OF35,P2	37	136	23	29	10	6	4	0	9		4	.213	.316
Jim Donahue	C67,OF18,3B5,2B1	88	337	29	79	28	11	3	1	21		12	.234	.294

KANSAS CITY (cont.)
Cowboys

BATTERS	POS/GAMES		GP	AB	R	H	BI	2B	3B	HR	BB	SO	SB	BA	SA
Law Daniels	OF30,C29,3B2,SS1		61	218	32	45	28	2	0	2	14		20	.206	.243
Henry Porter	P55,OF2		55	195	12	28	10	3	0	0	8		1	.144	.159
Frank Hankinson	2B13,SS9,3B7,OF7,1B2		37	155	20	27	20	4	1	1	11		2	.174	.232
Billy Hamilton	OF35		35	129	21	34	11	4	4	0	4		19	.264	.357
James Brennan	C25,3B5,OF5		34	118	5	20	6	2	0	0	3		3	.169	.186
Dave Rowe	OF32		32	122	14	21	13	3	4	0	6		2	.172	.262
Tom Sullivan	P24,OF4		28	92	10	10	5	1	0	0	9		7	.109	.120
Bill Fagan	P17,OF2		18	65	5	14	4	3	0	0	2		0	.215	.262
Red Ehret	OF10,P7,1B1,2B1		17	63	4	12	4	4	0	0	1		1	.190	.254
Jim Burns	OF15		15	66	13	20	4	0	0	0	1		6	.303	.303
Steve Toole	P12,OF2		13	48	6	10	7	2	2	0	1		2	.208	.333
Fatty Briody	C13		13	48	1	10	8	1	0	0	1		0	.208	.229
Frank Hoffman	P12		12	39	6	6	2	1	0	0	4		2	.154	.179
Charlie Jones	OF6		6	25	2	4	5	0	1	0	1		1	.160	.240
John Kirby	P5		5	16	1	1	0	0	0	0	0		0	.063	.063
Charlie Hoover	C3		3	10	0	3	1	0	0	0	0		0	.300	.300
Ed Glenn	OF3	(1-2)	3	8	0	0	0	0	0	0	0		1	.000	.000
Bill Haffner	P2		2	6	0	0	0	0	0	0	1		0	.000	.000
			132	4588	579	1000	431	142	61	19	288	604	257	.218	.288

PITCHERS	W	L	PCT	G	GS	CG	SH	SV	IP	H	BB	SO	ERA
Henry Porter	18	37	.327	55	54	53	4	0	474	527	120	145	4.16
Tom Sullivan	8	16	.333	24	24	24	0	0	215	227	68	84	3.40
Steve Toole	5	6	.455	12	10	10	0	0	92	124	50	35	6.68
Bill Fagan	5	11	.313	17	17	15	0	0	142	179	75	49	5.69
Red Ehret	3	2	.600	7	6	5	0	0	52	58	22	12	3.98
Frank Hoffman	3	9	.250	12	12	12	0	0	104	102	42	38	2.77
John Kirby	1	4	.200	5	5	5	0	0	43	48	7	11	4.19
Myron Allen	0	2	.000	2	2	2	0	0	18	17	1	2	2.50
Bill Haffner	0	2	.000	2	2	2	0	0	18	24	16	5	7.00
	43	89	.326	132	132	128	4	0	1158	1306	401	381	4.29

1889 NATIONAL LEAGUE

The Very Last Day

From the inception of the National League in 1876, the pennant races as a rule had not been very exciting. Of course there were exceptions. Chicago had bested Providence by only three games in 1882, and Chicago had prevailed by only two over New York in 1885. But by and large the margin had been great — the average distance between first and second so far was over six games. This was all to change in 1889. For the first time in league history, the first place team played its final game knowing that a win would clinch the pennant.

The two teams in contention were Boston and New York. The Giants had won the flag the previous year, while Boston had not won since 1883. In 1889, Boston got off to a fast start and pulled away from the field. On the other hand, New York started off slowly and languished in the middle of the pack through the early part of the summer. Then the Giants caught fire. A hot August got them within reach of Boston, and by the first of September, they were only a game and one-half behind. The two teams sprinted neck and neck through the campaign's final month with nary more than two games separating them at any time. Before the season's final game on October 5, the two teams stood in a virtual tie, with New York holding only a .656 to .654 percentage point lead. New York's record read 82-43, while Boston's read 83-44. A win for the Giants would clinch the flag, while a Boston win coupled with a New York loss would give the pennant to Boston. If both won or lost, New York would take the championship by two percentage points.

Both teams were on the road for their final game. New York was at Cleveland, while Boston was at Pittsburgh. The Giants' game started first, and they soon took the lead against Cleveland. When the results were telegraphed to Pittsburgh, Boston became demoralized. The Giants kept their lead and prevailed, 5-3, thus clinching the pennant. Boston, playing out the string, lost to Pittsburgh 6-1, and finished in second, a slim one game back.

New York's narrow win was led by a battery of stars. Five of their regulars batted over .300, and the team bested the league with a .282 batting average. The best of the quintet were Roger Connor (.317, 13 HR) and Mike Tiernan (.335, 11 HR).

Boston was nosed out at the end, but their first baseman, Dan Brouthers, finished head and shoulders above the pack winning his third batting title (.373) accompanied by 118 runs batted in. Pitcher John Clarkson led the league in wins (49), winning percentage (.721), and earned run average (2.73).

Hovering around the .500 mark were Chicago and Philadelphia in third and fourth. Chicago was paced by Cap Anson (.311, 117 RBI) and by Jimmy Ryan (.307, 17 HR), and by a quartet of pitchers who each won 15 or 16 games. Sam Thompson of Philadelphia won the home run title with 20.

Pittsburgh, Cleveland, Indianapolis, and Washington finished on the four bottom rungs. Their players of note included Pittsburgh's Fred Carroll (.330), Cleveland's Ed McKean (.318), and Jack Glasscock of Indianapolis who finished second (.352) in the batting race, but first (205) in the hits race.

Cleveland was a new entry in 1889, but they did not have to start from scratch. Like Pittsburgh the previous year, they jumped intact from the American Association. Cleveland took the place of Detroit, who ceased operations.

Following the season, the Giants took on their nearby rivals from Brooklyn in the World Series. From the outset, it was determined that the series would go to the team who first won six games. After Brooklyn and New York split the first six games, the Giants ripped off three wins in a row (11-7, 16-7, and 3-2) to take the series six games to three, and their second straight World Series.

The pennant race was easily the most exciting the National League had seen to date. During the final frantic month, neither Boston or New York showed any sign of letting up. The two teams stared each other down the entire stretch, and unfortunately for Boston, they were the first to blink.

1889 NATIONAL LEAGUE

NEW YORK Giants — 83-43 .659 1st Jim Mutrie

BATTERS	POS/GAMES		GP	AB	R	H	BI	2B	3B	HR	BB	SO	SB	BA	SA
Roger Connor	1B131,3B1		131	496	117	157	130	32	17	13	93	46	21	.317	.528
Danny Richardson	2B125		125	497	88	139	100	22	8	7	46	37	32	.280	.398
Monte Ward	SS108,2B7		114	479	87	143	67	13	4	1	27	7	62	.299	.349
Art Whitney	3B129,P1		129	473	71	103	59	12	2	1	56	39	19	.218	.258
Mike Tiernan	OF122		122	499	147	167	73	23	14	10	96	32	33	.335	.497
George Gore	OF120		120	488	132	149	54	21	7	7	84	28	28	.305	.420
Jim O'Rourke	OF128,C1		128	502	89	161	81	36	7	3	40	34	33	.321	.438
Buck Ewing	C97,P3,OF1		99	407	91	133	87	23	13	4	37	32	34	.327	.477
Tim Keefe	P47		47	149	17	23	8	5	2	0	8	40	2	.154	.215
Mickey Welch	P45		45	156	20	30	12	5	1	0	5	27	0	.192	.237
Willard Brown	C37,OF3		40	139	16	36	29	10	0	1	9	9	6	.259	.353
Gil Hatfield	SS24,P6,3B2		32	125	21	23	12	2	0	1	9	15	9	.184	.224
Cannonball Crane	P29,1B1		29	103	16	21	11	1	0	2	13	21	6	.204	.272
Mike Slattery	OF12		12	48	7	14	12	2	0	1	4	3	2	.292	.396
Hank O'Day	P10	(2-2)	10	31	5	3		0	0	0	4	10	2	.097	.097
Pat Murphy	C9		9	28	5	10	4	1	1	1	2	0	0	.357	.571
Harry Lyons	OF5		5	20	1	2	2	0	1	0	2	0	0	.100	.200
William George	OF3	(1-2)	3	15	1	4	0	0	0	0	0	3	1	.267	.267
Ledell Titcomb	P3		3	12	2	1	0	0	0	0	0	2	0	.083	.083
Elmer Foster	OF2		2	4	2	0	0	0	0	0	3	1	2	.000	.000
			131	4671	935	1319	741	208	77	52	538	386	292	.282	.393

PITCHERS			W	L	PCT	G	GS	CG	SH	SV	IP	H	BB	SO	ERA
Tim Keefe			28	13	.683	47	45	39	3	1	364	319	151	225	3.31
Mickey Welch			27	12	.692	45	41	39	3	2	375	340	149	125	3.02
Cannonball Crane			14	10	.583	29	25	23	0	0	230	221	136	130	3.68
Hank O'Day		(2-2)	9	1	.900	10	10	8	0	0	78	83	35	28	4.27
Buck Ewing			2	0	1.000	3	2	2	0	0	20	23	8	12	4.05
Gil Hatfield			2	4	.333	6	5	5	0	0	52	53	25	28	3.98
Ledell Titcomb			1	2	.333	3	3	3	0	0	26	27	16	7	6.58
Art Whitney			0	1	.000	1	0	0	0	0	6	7	3	3	3.00
			83	43	.659	131	131	119	6	3	1151	1073	523	558	3.47

BOSTON Beaneaters — 83-45 .648 -1 2nd Jim Hart

BATTERS	POS/GAMES		GP	AB	R	H	BI	2B	3B	HR	BB	SO	SB	BA	SA
Dan Brouthers	1B126		126	485	105	181	118	26	9	7	66	6	22	.373	.507
Hardy Richardson	2B86,OF46		132	536	122	163	79	33	10	6	48	44	47	.304	.437
Joe Quinn	SS63,2B47,3B2		112	444	57	116	69	13	5	2	25	21	24	.261	.327
Billy Nash	3B128,P1		128	481	84	132	76	20	2	3	79	44	26	.274	.343
King Kelly	OF113,C23		125	507	120	149	78	41	5	9	65	40	68	.294	.448
Dick Johnston	OF132		132	539	80	123	67	16	4	5	41	60	34	.228	.301
Tom Brown	OF90		90	362	93	84	24	10	5	2	59	56	63	.232	.304
Charlie Bennett	C82		82	247	42	57	28	8	2	4	21	43	7	.231	.328
Charles Ganzel	C39,OF26,1B7,SS6,3B1		73	275	30	73	43	3	5	1	15	11	13	.265	.324
John Clarkson	P73,OF2,3B1		73	262	36	54	23	9	3	2	11	59	8	.206	.286
Pop Smith	SS59	(2-2)	59	208	21	54	32	13	4	0	23	*30	11	.260	.361
Old Hoss Radbourn	P33,OF2,3B1		35	122	17	23	13	1	0	1	9	19	3	.189	.221
Kid Madden	P22,OF2		24	86	7	25	14	1	0	0	3	7	4	.291	.302
Irv Ray	SS5,3B4	(1-2)	9	33	8	10	2	1	0	0	4	0	1	.303	.333
Bill Daley	P9		9	20	2	3	0	1	0	0	1	8	0	.150	.200
Bill Sowders	P7	(1-2)	7	17	2	4	0	0	0	0	1	2	0	.235	.235
Jerry Hurley	C1,OF1		1	4	0	0	0	0	0	0	0	0	0	.000	.000
			133	4628	826	1251	666	196	54	42	471	450	331	.270	.363

PITCHERS			W	L	PCT	G	GS	CG	SH	SV	IP	H	BB	SO	ERA
John Clarkson			49	19	.721	73	72	68	8	1	620	589	203	284	2.73
Old Hoss Radbourn			20	11	.645	33	31	28	1	0	277	282	72	99	3.67
Kid Madden			10	10	.500	22	19	18	1	1	178	194	71	64	4.40
Bill Daley			3	3	.500	9	7	4	0	0	48	34	43	40	4.31
Bill Sowders		(1-2)	1	2	.333	7	4	3	0	*2	42	53	23	10	5.14
Billy Nash			0	0	----	1	0	0	0	0	1	0	1	0	0.00
			83	45	.648	133	133	121	10	4	1166	1152	413	497	3.36

1889 NATIONAL LEAGUE

CHICAGO
White Stockings   67-65   .508   -19   3rd   Cap Anson

BATTERS	POS/GAMES		GP	AB	R	H	BI	2B	3B	HR	BB	SO	SB	BA	SA
Cap Anson	1B134		134	518	100	161	117	32	7	7	86	19	27	.311	.440
Fred Pfeffer	2B134		134	531	85	121	77	15	7	7	53	51	45	.228	.322
Ned Williamson	SS47		47	173	16	41	30	3	1	1	23	22	2	.237	.283
Tom Burns	3B136		136	525	64	127	66	27	6	4	32	57	18	.242	.339
Hugh Duffy	OF126,SS10		136	584	144	172	89	21	7	12	46	30	52	.295	.416
Jimmy Ryan	OF106,SS29		135	576	140	177	72	31	14	17	70	62	45	.307	.498
George Van Haltren	OF130,SS3,2B1		134	543	126	168	81	20	10	9	82	41	28	.309	.433
Duke Farrell	C76,OF25		101	407	66	101	75	19	7	11	41	21	13	.248	.410
Charlie Bastian	SS45,2B1		46	155	19	21	10	0	0	0	25	46	1	.135	.135
John Tener	P35,OF6,1B2		42	150	18	41	19	4	2	1	7	22	2	.273	.347
Ad Gumbert	P31,OF13		41	153	30	44	29	3	2	7	11	36	2	.288	.471
Bill Hutchinson	P37,OF1		37	133	14	21	7	1	1	1	7	40	2	.158	.203
Frank Dwyer	P32,OF3,SS2		36	135	14	27	6	1	1	1	4	8	0	.200	.244
Dell Darling	C36		36	120	14	23	7	1	1	0	25	22	5	.192	.217
Silver Flint	C15		15	56	6	13	9	1	0	1	3	18	1	.232	.304
Pete Sommers	C11,OF1	(1-2)	12	45	5	10	8	5	0	0	2	8	0	.222	.333
Gus Krock	P7	(1-3)	7	24	4	4		0	0	0	0	0	0	.167	.167
Egyptian Healy	P5	(1-2)	5	20	2	2		0	0	0	0		0	.100	.100
Bill Bishop	P2		2	1	0	0	0	0	0	0	1	1	0	.000	.000
			136	4849	867	1274	702	184	66	79	518	516	243	.263	.377

PITCHERS			W	L	PCT	G	GS	CG	SH	SV	IP	H	BB	SO	ERA
Frank Dwyer			16	13	.552	32	30	27	0	0	276	307	72	63	3.59
Ad Gumbert			16	13	.552	31	28	25	2	0	246	258	76	91	3.62
Bill Hutchinson			16	17	.485	37	36	33	3	0	318	306	117	136	3.54
John Tener			15	15	.500	35	30	28	1	0	287	302	105	105	3.64
Gus Krock		(1-3)	3	3	.500	7	7	5	0	0	61	86	14	16	4.90
Egyptian Healy		(2-2)	1	4	.200	5	5	5	0	0	46	48	18	22	4.50
Bill Bishop			0	0	----	2	0	0	0	2	3	6	6	1	18.00
			67	65	.508	136	136	123	6	2	1237	1313	408	434	3.73

PHILADELPHIA
Quakers   63-64   .496   -20.5   4th   Harry Wright

BATTERS	POS/GAMES		GP	AB	R	H	BI	2B	3B	HR	BB	SO	SB	BA	SA
Sid Farrar	1B130		130	477	70	128	58	22	2	3	52	36	28	.268	.342
Al Myers	2B75	(2-2)	75	305	52	82	28	14	2	0	36	9	8	.269	.328
Bill Hallman	SS106,2B13,C1		119	462	67	117	60	21	8	2	36	54	20	.253	.346
Joe Mulvey	3B129		129	544	77	157	77	21	9	6	23	25	23	.289	.393
Sam Thompson	OF128		128	533	103	158	111	36	4	20	36	22	24	.296	.492
Jim Fogarty	OF128,P4		128	499	107	129	54	15	17	3	65	60	99	.259	.375
George Wood	OF92,SS6,P1	(1-2)	97	422	77	106	53	21	4	5	53	33	17	.251	.355
Jack Clements	C78		78	310	51	88	35	17	1	4	29	21	3	.284	.384
Ed Delahanty	OF31,2B24,SS1		56	246	37	72	27	13	3	0	14	17	19	.293	.370
Pop Schriver	C48,2B6,3B1		55	211	24	56	19	10	0	1	16	8	5	.265	.327
Charles Buffinton	P47,OF1		47	154	16	32	21	2	0	0	9	5	0	.208	.221
Ben Sanders	P44,OF3		44	169	21	47	21	8	2	0	6	11	4	.278	.349
Kid Gleason	P29,OF3,2B2		30	99	11	25	8	5	0	0	8	12	4	.253	.303
Dan Casey	P20		20	68	5	15	8	2	0	0	0	12	0	.221	.250
Art Irwin	SS18	(1-2)	18	73	9	16	10	5	0	0	6	6	6	.219	.288
Harry Decker	2B7,C3,OF1		11	30	4	3	2	0	0	0	2	5	1	.100	.100
Ed Andrews	OF9,2B1	(1-2)	10	39	10	11	7	1	0	0	2	4	7	.282	.308
Piggy Ward	2B6,OF1		7	25	0	4	4	1	0	0	0	7	1	.160	.200
Dave Anderson	P5		5	11	1	2	0	1	0	0	0	2	0	.182	.273
Bill Day	P4		4	10	0	0	0	0	0	0	0	3	0	.000	.000
Peter Wood	P3		3	8	0	0	2	0	0	0	0	1	0	.000	.000
			130	4695	742	1248	605	215	52	44	393	353	269	.266	.362

PITCHERS		W	L	PCT	G	GS	CG	SH	SV	IP	H	BB	SO	ERA
Charles Buffinton		28	16	.636	47	43	37	2	0	380	390	121	153	3.24
Ben Sanders		19	18	.514	44	39	34	1	1	350	406	96	123	3.55
Kid Gleason		9	15	.375	29	21	15	0	1	205	242	97	64	5.58
Dan Casey		6	10	.375	20	20	15	1	0	153	170	72	65	3.77
Peter Wood		1	1	.500	3	2	2	0	0	19	28	3	8	5.21
Dave Anderson		0	1	.000	5	2	1	0	0	23	30	14	8	7.43
Bill Day		0	3	.000	4	3	2	0	0	19	16	23	20	5.21
Jim Fogarty		0	0	----	4	0	0	0	0	4	4	2	0	9.00
George Wood		0	0	----	1	0	0	0	0	1	2	0	2	18.00
		63	64	.496	130	130	106	4	2	1153	1288	428	443	4.00

1889 NATIONAL LEAGUE

PITTSBURGH Alleghenys 61-71 .462 -25 5th Phillips - Dunlap - Hanlon

BATTERS	POS/GAMES		GP	AB	R	H	BI	2B	3B	HR	BB	SO	SB	BA	SA
Jake Beckley	1B122,OF1		123	522	91	157	97	24	10	9	29	29	11	.301	.437
Fred Dunlap	2B121		121	451	59	106	65	19	0	2	46	33	21	.235	.290
Jack Rowe	SS75		75	317	57	82	32	14	3	2	22	16	5	.259	.341
Bill Kuehne	3B75,OF13,2B5,1B2,SS2		97	390	43	96	57	20	5	5	9	36	15	.246	.362
Billy Sunday	OF81		81	321	62	77	25	10	6	2	27	33	47	.240	.327
Ned Hanlon	OF116		116	461	81	110	37	14	10	2	58	25	53	.239	.325
Al Maul	OF64,P6		68	257	37	71	44	6	6	4	29	41	18	.276	.393
Doggie Miller	C76,OF27,3B3		104	422	77	113	56	25	3	6	31	11	16	.268	.384
Fred Carroll	C43,OF41,1B7,3B1		91	318	80	105	51	21	11	2	85	26	19	.330	.484
Jocko Fields	OF60,C16		75	289	41	90	43	22	5	2	29	30	7	.311	.443
Pop Smith	SS58,2B9,3B3,OF3	(1-2)	72	258	26	54	27	10	2	5	24	*38	12	.209	.322
Deacon White	3B52,1B3		55	225	35	57	26	10	1	0	16	18	2	.253	.307
Harry Staley	P49,OF2		51	186	11	30	8	3	1	0	4	40	1	.161	.188
Pud Galvin	P41		41	150	15	28	16	7	2	0	3	46	2	.187	.260
Ed Morris	P21		21	72	2	7	4	1	0	0	4	17	1	.097	.111
Bill Sowders	P13,OF2	(2-2)	15	48	4	13		1	0	0	3	10	0	.271	.286
Chuck Lauer	C3,OF1		4	16	2	3	1	0	0	0	0	5	0	.188	.188
Bill Garfield	P4		4	13	0	0	0	0	0	0	0	4	0	.000	.000
Peter Conway	P3,OF1		3	10	2	1	2	0	0	1	1	3	1	.100	.400
Andy Dunning	P2		2	7	0	0	0	0	0	0	0	2	0	.000	.000
Alex Beam	P2		2	6	0	1	0	1	0	0	0	2	0	.167	.333
Alex Jones	P1		1	5	1	1	1	1	0	0	0	0	0	.200	.200
Al Krumm	P1		1	4	0	0	0	0	0	0	0	2	0	.000	.000
			134	4748	726	1202	592	209	65	42	420	467	231	.253	.351

PITCHERS		W	L	PCT	G	GS	CG	SH	SV	IP	H	BB	SO	ERA
Pud Galvin		23	16	.590	41	40	38	4	0	341	392	78	77	4.17
Harry Staley		21	26	.447	49	47	46	1	1	420	433	116	159	3.51
Bill Sowders	(2-2)	6	5	.545	13	11	9	0	*0	53	94	29	33	7.35
Ed Morris		6	13	.316	21	21	18	0	0	170	196	48	40	4.13
Peter Conway		2	1	.667	3	3	2	0	0	22	26	16	2	4.91
Alex Jones		1	0	1.000	1	1	1	0	0	9	7	1	10	3.00
Alex Beam		1	1	.500	2	2	2	0	0	18	11	15	1	6.50
Al Maul		1	4	.200	6	4	4	0	0	42	64	28	11	9.86
Al Krumm		0	1	.000	1	1	1	0	0	9	8	10	4	10.00
Bill Garfield		0	2	.000	4	2	2	0	0	29	45	17	4	7.76
Andy Dunning		0	2	.000	2	2	2	0	0	18	20	16	4	7.00
		61	71	.462	134	134	125	5	1	1131	1296	374	345	4.51

CLEVELAND Spiders 61-72 .459 -25.5 6th Tom Loftus

BATTERS	POS/GAMES	GP	AB	R	H	BI	2B	3B	HR	BB	SO	SB	BA	SA
Jay Faatz	1B117	117	442	50	102	38	12	5	2	17	28	27	.231	.294
Cub Stricker	2B135,SS1	136	566	83	142	47	10	4	1	58	18	32	.251	.288
Ed McKean	SS122,2B1	123	500	88	159	75	22	8	4	42	25	35	.318	.418
Patsy Tebeau	3B136	136	521	72	147	76	20	6	8	37	41	26	.282	.390
Paul Radford	OF136,3B1	136	487	94	116	46	21	5	1	91	37	30	.238	.308
Jimmy McAleer	OF110	110	447	66	105	35	6	6	1	30	49	37	.235	.282
Larry Twitchell	OF134,P1	134	549	73	151	95	16	11	4	29	37	17	.275	.366
Chief Zimmer	C81,1B3	84	259	47	67	21	9	9	1	44	35	14	.259	.375
Bob Gilks	OF29,SS13,1B10,2B1	53	210	17	50	18	5	2	0	7	20	6	.238	.281
Sy Sutcliffe	C37,1B8,OF1	46	161	17	40	21	3	2	1	14	6	5	.248	.311
John O'Brien	P41	41	140	13	35	18	1	0	0	12	18	2	.250	.257
Eb Beatin	P36,OF1	37	121	13	14	8	0	0	1	14	33	0	.116	.140
Jersey Bakely	P36,OF1	36	111	9	15	8	1	1	1	17	40	1	.135	.189
Henry Gruber	P25	25	69	7	7	4	2	0	0	14	18	0	.101	.130
Pop Snyder	C22	22	83	5	16	12	3	0	0	2	12	4	.193	.229
Charles Sprague	P2	2	7	2	1	1	0	0	0	1	0	1	.143	.143
		136	4673	656	1167	523	131	59	25	429	417	237	.250	.317

PITCHERS	W	L	PCT	G	GS	CG	SH	SV	IP	H	BB	SO	ERA
John O'Brien	22	17	.564	41	41	39	1	0	347	345	167	122	4.15
Eb Beatin	20	15	.571	36	36	35	3	0	318	316	141	126	3.57
Jersey Bakely	12	22	.353	36	34	33	2	0	304	296	106	105	2.96
Henry Gruber	7	16	.304	25	23	23	0	1	205	198	94	74	3.64
Charles Sprague	0	2	.000	2	2	2	0	0	17	27	10	8	8.47
Larry Twitchell	0	0	----	1	0	0	0	0	1	0	1	0	0.00
	61	72	.459	136	136	132	6	1	1192	1182	519	435	3.66

1889 NATIONAL LEAGUE

INDIANAPOLIS
Hoosiers

59-75   .440   -28   7th   Bancroft - Glasscock

BATTERS	POS/GAMES		GP	AB	R	H	BI	2B	3B	HR	BB	SO	SB	BA	SA
Paul Hines	1B109,OF12		121	486	77	148	72	27	1	6	49	22	34	.305	.401
Charley Bassett	2B127		127	477	64	117	68	12	5	4	37	38	15	.245	.317
Jack Glasscock	SS132,2B2,P1		134	582	128	205	85	40	3	7	31	10	57	.352	.467
Jerry Denny	3B123,2B7,SS5		133	578	96	163	112	24	0	18	27	63	22	.282	.417
Jack McGeachey	OF131,P3		131	532	83	142	63	32	1	2	9	39	37	.267	.342
Marty Sullivan	OF64,1B5		69	256	45	73	35	11	3	4	50	31	15	.285	.398
Emmett Seery	OF127		127	526	123	165	59	26	12	8	67	59	19	.314	.454
Dick Buckley	C55,3B12,1B1,OF1		68	260	35	67	41	11	0	8	15	32	5	.258	.392
Con Daily	C51,1B6,OF6,3B1		62	219	35	55	26	6	2	0	28	21	14	.251	.297
Henry Boyle	P46,3B1		46	155	17	38	17	10	0	1	9	23	4	.245	.329
Pretzels Getzien	P45		45	139	20	25	14	4	2	2	15	38	2	.180	.281
George Myers	OF23,C18,1B1		43	149	22	29	12	3	0	0	17	13	12	.195	.215
Ed Andrews	OF40,2B1	(2-2)	40	173	32	53	22	11	0	0	5	10	7	.306	.370
Amos Rusie	P33		33	103	15	18	4	3	1	0	2	19	3	.175	.223
Pete Sommers	C21,OF2	(2-2)	23	84	12	21	14	2	2	2	1	16	2	.250	.393
Jumbo Schoeneck	1B16		16	62	3	15	8	2	2	0	3	3	1	.242	.339
Jim Whitney	P9,OF1		10	32	6	12	4	4	1	0	5	6	2	.375	.563
Bill Burdick	P10		10	17	1	2	1	0	0	0	4	1	0	.118	.118
John Fee	P7		7	21	2	3	0	0	0	0	0	1	0	.143	.143
Gus Krock	P4	(2-3)	4	14	2	5		0	0	0	2	1	1	.357	.357
Ledell Shreve	P3		3	7	1	0	0	0	0	0	1	1	0	.000	.000
Varney Anderson	P2		2	5	0	0	0	0	0	0	0	0	0	.000	.000
John Fanning	P1		1	1	0	0	0	0	0	0	0	0	0	.000	.000
Pete Weckbecker	C1		1	1	0	0	2	0	0	0	0	0	0	.000	.000
			135	4879	819	1356	659	228	35	62	377	447	252	.278	.377

PITCHERS		W	L	PCT	G	GS	CG	SH	SV	IP	H	BB	SO	ERA
Henry Boyle		21	23	.477	46	45	38	2	0	379	422	95	97	3.92
Pretzels Getzien		18	22	.450	45	44	36	0	1	349	395	100	139	4.54
Amos Rusie		12	10	.545	33	22	19	1	0	225	246	116	109	5.32
John Fee		2	2	.500	7	3	2	0	0	40	39	31	10	4.27
Gus Krock		2	2	.500	4	4	3	0	0	32	48	14	10	7.31
Bill Burdick		2	4	.333	10	4	2	0	1	46	58	13	16	4.53
Jim Whitney		2	7	.222	9	8	7	0	0	70	106	19	16	6.81
Varney Anderson		0	1	.000	2	1	1	0	0	12	13	9	3	4.50
John Fanning		0	1	.000	1	1	0	0	0	1	3	2	0	18.00
Ledell Shreve		0	3	.000	3	3	1	0	0	16	25	12	5	13.79
Jack McGeachey		0	0	----	3	0	0	0	0	5	7	6	3	11.57
Jack Glasscock		0	0	----	1	0	0	0	0	1	3	3	0	0.00
		59	75	.440	135	135	109	3	2	1174	1365	420	408	4.85

WASHINGTON
Statesmen

41-83   .331   -41   8th   Morrill - Irwin

BATTERS	POS/GAMES		GP	AB	R	H	BI	2B	3B	HR	BB	SO	SB	BA	SA
John Carney	1B53,OF16		69	273	25	63	29	7	0	1	14	14	12	.231	.267
Sam Wise	2B72,SS26,3B13,OF10		121	472	79	118	62	15	8	4	61	62	24	.250	.341
Art Irwin	SS85,P1,2B1	(2-2)	85	313	49	73	32	10	5	0	42	37	9	.233	.297
John Irwin	3B58		58	228	42	66	25	11	4	0	25	14	10	.289	.373
Ed Beecher	OF39,1B3		42	179	20	53	30	9	0	0	5	4	3	.296	.346
Dummy Hoy	OF127		127	507	98	139	39	11	6	0	75	30	35	.274	.320
Walt Wilmot	OF108		108	432	88	125	57	19	19	9	51	32	40	.289	.484
Tom Daly	C57,1B8,2B4,OF3,SS1		71	250	39	75	40	13	5	1	38	28	18	.300	.404
Connie Mack	C45,OF34,1B22		98	386	51	113	42	16	1	0	15	12	26	.293	.339
Peter Sweeney	3B47,OF1,2B1	(1-2)	49	193	13	44	23	7	3	1	11	26	8	.228	.311
Al Myers	2B46	(1-2)	46	176	24	46	20	3	0	0	22	7	10	.261	.278
John Morrill	1B40,3B3,2B1,P1		44	146	20	27	16	5	0	2	30	23	12	.185	.260
Spider Clark	C14,SS13,OF9,2B2,3B2		38	145	19	37	22	7	2	3	6	18	8	.255	.393
Alex Ferson	P36		36	114	6	13	3	3	1	0	10	47	1	.114	.158
George Haddock	P33,OF3		34	112	13	25	14	3	0	2	19	27	3	.223	.304
George Shoch	OF29,SS1		30	109	12	26	11	2	0	0	20	5	9	.239	.257
George Keefe	P30,OF1		30	98	7	16	1	2	1	0	8	29	2	.163	.204
Buck Ebright	C9,OF4,SS3		16	59	7	15	6	2	2	1	3	8	1	.254	.407
Egyptian Healy	P13	(1-2)	13	45	7	10		2	0	1	0		0	.222	.333
Hank O'Day	P13	(1-2)	13	44	1	8		1	0	0	3	7	0	.182	.205
John Riddle	C9,OF2		11	37	3	8	3	3	0	0	2	8	0	.216	.297
Mike Sullivan	P9		9	19	2	1	0	0	0	0	1	2	0	.053	.053
Gus Krock	P6	(3-3)	6	23	3	2	0	0	0	0	0	0	0	.087	.087
Jim Donnelly	3B4		4	13	3	2	0	0	0	0	2	0	1	.154	.154
Billy O'Brien	1B2		2	8	1	0	0	0	0	0	1	1	0	.000	.000

WASHINGTON (cont.)
Statesmen

BATTERS	POS/GAMES		GP	AB	R	H	BI	2B	3B	HR	BB	SO	SB	BA	SA
Art McCoy	2B2		2	6	0	0	0	0	0	0	2	1	0	.000	.000
Jim Banning	C2		2	1	0	0	0	0	0	0	0	0	0	.000	.000
John Thornton	P1		1	4	0	0	1	0	0	0	0	1	0	.000	.000
Harry Clarke	OF1		1	3	0	0	0	0	0	0	0	1	0	.000	.000
			127	4395	632	1105	<u>475</u>	151	57	25	466	456	232	.251	.329

PITCHERS			W	L	PCT	G	GS	CG	SH	SV	IP	H	BB	SO	ERA
Alex Ferson			17	17	.500	36	34	28	1	0	288	319	105	85	3.90
George Haddock			11	19	.367	33	31	30	0	0	276	299	123	106	4.20
George Keefe			8	18	.308	30	27	24	0	0	230	266	143	90	5.13
Gus Krock		(3-3)	2	4	.333	6	6	6	0	0	48	65	22	17	5.25
Hank O'Day		(1-2)	2	10	.167	13	13	11	0	0	108	117	57	23	4.33
Egyptian Healy		(1-2)	1	11	.083	13	12	10	0	0	101	139	38	49	6.24
John Thornton			0	1	.000	1	1	1	0	0	9	8	7	3	5.00
Mike Sullivan			0	3	.000	9	3	3	0	0	41	47	32	15	7.24
Art Irwin			0	0	----	1	0	0	0	0	1	1	0	0	0.00
John Morrill			0	0	----	1	0	0	0	0	0	0	0	0	0.00
			41	83	.331	127	127	113	1	0	1103	1261	527	388	4.68

1889 AMERICAN ASSOCIATION

A New Champion

For four years, the St. Louis Browns had held a stranglehold on the American Association. From 1885 to 1888, they had won the pennant each year by an average of 12 games per year. However, in 1889 a different story was to be told.

Brooklyn had joined the American Association in 1884. They rose from obscurity to respectability during their first five years, culminating in a close second place finish in 1888. In putting the pieces together for their success, Brooklyn relied on a couple of sources. The first was the acquisition of the New York franchise in 1888 which brought them several key players. The most notable of this group was Dave Orr, one of the best hitters of the American Association. The second source were their rivals, the St. Louis Browns, who also in 1888, sold them Bob Caruthers, Dave Foutz and Doc Bushong. This move did not harm the Browns in 1888, but they paid the price the next year.

Following their near miss in 1888, Brooklyn was ready in 1889. Christened the Bridegrooms (several members of Brooklyn had recently wed), Brooklyn fought a tough battle with St. Louis the whole summer before prevailing in the end by a narrow two-game margin.

Brooklyn's close win was accomplished by a compact fifteen man roster. Of that 15, only two, Oyster Burns (.300) and Darby O'Brien (.304) hit .300 or better. But five of the 15 scored more than 100 runs each. Their main cog was pitcher Bob Caruthers, who won 40 games.

St. Louis as a team, out hit and out pitched Brooklyn, but still failed to win their fifth straight pennant. Offensively, Tip O'Neill duplicated his .335 average of the year before. The pitching staff boasted a pair of 30-game winners (Silver King and Icebox Chamberlain) as well as the earned run average champion, Jack Stivetts, who finished with a mark of 2.25.

Third place Philadelphia had the league's best hitting, with five of their regulars batting over .300. The five were topped by Denny Lyons who checked in at .329, while his teammate, Harry Stovey, led the circuit in home runs (19) and runs batted in (119).

Cincinnati finished next in fourth place. They featured Bug Holliday who finished tied with Stovey in the home run race at 19, and by pitcher Jesse Duryea, who finished with 32 wins, as well as placing second in the earned run average race (2.56).

Baltimore and Columbus finished fifth and sixth. Baltimore could claim the batting champion, Tommy Tucker, who slammed out a .372 average. Columbus, which replaced the recently departed Cleveland franchise, featured Dave Orr (.327) and pitcher Mark Baldwin, who struck out a league best 368.

Kansas City finished in seventh, while Louisville finished eighth. Kansas City was led by Billy Hamilton, who stole a league-leading 117 bases. Louisville, on the other hand, was not led by anybody. This franchise suffered through a dismal season which featured a players strike, and numerous managerial changes. They ended up winning only 27 of 138 games to finish with the worst record in the league's history, and the fifth worst of all time.

After four years, the champions had lost. The Browns battled the Bridegrooms all year before succumbing in the end. Brooklyn proved to be the tougher down the stretch, and ended up with the best wedding present of all, the pennant.

1889 AMERICAN ASSOCIATION

BROOKLYN Bridegrooms

93-44 .679 1st Bill McGunnigle

BATTERS

BATTERS	POS/GAMES		GP	AB	R	H	BI	2B	3B	HR	BB	SO	SB	BA	SA
Dave Foutz	1B134,P12		138	553	118	152	113	19	8	6	64	23	43	.275	.371
Hub Collins	2B138		138	560	139	149	73	18	3	2	80	41	65	.266	.320
Germany Smith	SS120,OF1		121	446	89	103	53	22	3	3	40	42	35	.231	.314
George Pinkney	3B138		138	545	103	134	82	25	7	4	59	43	47	.246	.339
Oyster Burns	OF113,SS19		131	504	105	153	100	19	13	5	68	26	32	.304	.423
Pop Corkhill	OF138,1B1,SS1		138	537	91	134	78	21	9	8	42	24	22	.250	.367
Darby O'Brien	OF136		136	567	146	170	80	30	11	5	61	76	91	.300	.418
Bob Clark	C53		53	182	32	50	22	5	2	0	26	7	18	.275	.324
Joe Visner	C53,OF29		80	295	56	76	68	12	10	8	36	36	13	.258	.447
Bob Caruthers	P56,OF3,1B2		59	172	45	43	31	8	3	2	44	17	9	.250	.366
Adonis Terry	P41,1B10		49	160	29	48	26	6	6	2	14	14	8	.300	.450
Tom Lovett	P29		29	100	18	19	19	1	3	2	2	24	2	.190	.320
Doc Bushong	C25		25	84	15	13	8	1	0	0	9	7	2	.155	.167
Mickey Hughes	P20,OF1		20	68	4	12	5	0	0	0	4	15	0	.176	.176
Charles Reynolds	C12	(2-2)	12	42	5	9	3	1	1	0	1	6	2	.214	.286
			140	4815	995	1265	761	188	79	47	550	401	389	.263	.364

PITCHERS

PITCHERS		W	L	PCT	G	GS	CG	SH	SV	IP	H	BB	SO	ERA
Bob Caruthers		40	11	.784	56	50	46	7	1	445	444	104	118	3.13
Adonis Terry		22	15	.595	41	39	35	2	0	326	285	126	186	3.29
Tom Lovett		17	10	.630	29	28	23	1	0	229	234	65	92	4.32
Mickey Hughes		9	8	.529	20	17	13	0	0	153	172	86	54	4.35
Dave Foutz		3	0	1.000	12	4	3	0	0	60	70	19	21	4.37
		93	44	.679	140	138	120	10	1	1213	1205	400	471	3.61

ST. LOUIS Browns

90-45 .667 -2 2nd Charlie Comiskey

BATTERS

BATTERS	POS/GAMES		GP	AB	R	H	BI	2B	3B	HR	BB	SO	SB	BA	SA
Charlie Comiskey	1B134,2B3,OF3,P1		137	587	105	168	102	28	10	3	19	19	65	.286	.383
Yank Robinson	2B132		132	452	97	94	70	17	3	5	118	55	39	.208	.292
Shorty Fuller	SS140		140	517	91	117	51	18	6	0	52	56	38	.226	.284
Arlie Latham	3B116,2B3		118	512	110	126	49	13	3	4	42	30	69	.246	.307
Tommy McCarthy	OF140,2B2,P1		140	604	136	176	63	24	7	2	46	26	57	.291	.364
Charlie Duffee	OF132,3B5,2B2		137	509	93	124	86	15	12	15	60	81	21	.244	.409
Tip O'Neill	OF134		134	534	123	179	110	33	8	9	72	37	28	.335	.478
Jack Boyle	C80,3B12,OF5,1B4,2B1		99	347	54	85	42	11	4	4	21	42	5	.245	.334
Jocko Milligan	C66,1B9		72	273	53	100	76	30	2	12	16	19	2	.366	.623
Silver King	P56,1B2,OF1		56	189	37	43	30	7	3	0	22	40	3	.228	.296
Icebox Chamberlain	P53,2B1		53	171	18	34	31	8	3	2	12	32	3	.199	.316
Jack Stivetts	P26,OF1		27	79	12	18	7	2	2	0	3	13	0	.228	.304
Nat Hudson	P9,OF6,1B3		13	52	6	13	10	1	1	1	2	11	1	.250	.365
Peter Sweeney	3B8,OF1	(1-2)	9	38	8	14	8	2	0	0	1	5	2	.368	.421
James Devlin	P9		9	26	4	5	0	0	0	0	1	4	1	.192	.192
Toad Ramsey	P5	(2-2)	5	17	2	5	4	1	0	0	1	3	0	.294	.253
Tom Gettinger	OF4		4	16	2	7	2	0	0	1	2	1	0	.438	.625
Jim Gill	OF1,2B1		2	8	2	2	1	1	0	0	1	2	1	.250	.375
Jumbo Davis	SS1,OF1	(2-2)	2	4	1	0	0	0	0	0	1	1	0	.000	.000
Dad Meek	C2		2	2	2	1	1	0	0	0	0	0	1	.500	.500
John Bellman	C1		1	2	0	1	0	0	0	0	1	0	0	.500	.500
			141	4939	957	1312	743	211	64	58	493	477	336	.266	.370

PITCHERS

PITCHERS		W	L	PCT	G	GS	CG	SH	SV	IP	H	BB	SO	ERA
Silver King		35	16	.686	56	53	47	2	1	458	462	125	188	3.14
Icebox Chamberlain		32	15	.681	53	51	44	3	1	422	376	165	202	2.97
Jack Stivetts		12	7	.632	26	20	18	2	1	192	153	68	143	2.25
James Devlin		5	3	.625	9	8	5	0	0	60	56	24	37	2.40
Toad Ramsey		3	1	.750	5	3	3	0	0	41	44	10	33	3.95
Nat Hudson		3	2	.600	9	5	4	0	0	60	71	15	13	4.20
Tommy McCarthy		0	0	----	1	0	0	0	0	5	4	6	1	7.20
Charlie Comiskey		0	0	----	1	0	0	0	0	0	0	0	0	0.00
		90	45	.667	141	140	121	7	3	1238	1166	413	617	3.00

1889 AMERICAN ASSOCIATION

PHILADELPHIA Athletics   75-58   .564   -16   3rd   Bill Sharsig

BATTERS	POS/GAMES		GP	AB	R	H	BI	2B	3B	HR	BB	SO	SB	BA	SA
Henry Larkin	1B131,3B1,2B1		133	516	105	164	74	23	12	3	83	41	11	.318	.426
Lou Bierbauer	2B130,C1		130	549	80	167	105	27	7	7	29	30	17	.304	.417
Frank Fennelly	SS138		138	513	70	132	64	20	5	1	65	78	15	.257	.322
Denny Lyons	3B130,1B1		131	510	135	168	82	36	4	9	79	44	10	.329	.469
Blondie Purcell	OF129		129	507	72	160	85	19	7	0	50	27	22	.316	.381
Curt Welch	OF125		125	516	134	140	39	39	6	0	67	30	66	.271	.370
Harry Stovey	OF137,1B1		137	556	152	171	119	38	13	19	77	68	63	.308	.525
Wilbert Robinson	C69		69	264	31	61	28	13	2	0	6	34	9	.231	.295
Lave Cross	C55		55	199	22	44	23	8	2	0	14	9	11	.221	.281
Gus Weyhing	P54,OF1		54	191	16	25	12	2	0	0	9	59	4	.131	.141
Ed Seward	P39,OF8,2B1		46	143	22	31	17	5	3	2	22	19	6	.217	.336
James Brennan	C13,2B7,OF7,3B4		31	113	12	25	15	4	0	0	10	15	1	.221	.257
Sadie McMahon	P28,OF2		30	104	9	16	4	2	1	0	4	16	3	.154	.192
Mike Mattimore	OF12,1B7,P5	(1-2)	23	73	10	17	8	1	2	1	9	7	6	.233	.342
Tom Gunning	C8		8	24	3	6	1	0	1	1	0	4	3	.250	.458
George Bausewine	P7		7	21	1	1	0	0	0	0	4	8	2	.048	.048
Jack Coleman	P5,OF1		6	19	1	1	1	0	0	0	1	3	1	.053	.053
Phenomenal Smith	P5		5	16	3	3	0	1	0	0	3	3	0	.188	.250
Barney Graham	3B4		4	18	0	3	0	0	0	0	0	0	0	.167	.167
Ed Knouff	P3		3	12	2	3	2	1	0	0	1	1	1	.250	.250
Bill Collins	C1		1	4	0	1	1	0	0	0	1	0	1	.250	.250
			138	4868	880	1339	680	239	65	43	534	496	252	.275	.377

PITCHERS			W	L	PCT	G	GS	CG	SH	SV	IP	H	BB	SO	ERA
Gus Weyhing			30	21	.588	54	53	50	4	0	449	382	212	213	2.95
Ed Seward			21	15	.583	39	38	35	3	0	320	353	101	102	3.97
Sadie McMahon			14	12	.571	28	27	27	2	0	242	230	102	117	3.35
Jack Coleman			3	2	.600	5	5	4	0	0	34	38	14	6	2.91
Ed Knouff			2	0	1.000	3	3	2	0	0	25	37	9	5	3.96
Mike Mattimore		(1-2)	2	1	.667	5	1	1	0	1	31	43	13	6	5.81
Phenomenal Smith			2	3	.400	5	5	5	0	0	43	53	25	12	4.40
George Bausewine			1	4	.200	7	6	6	0	0	55	64	33	18	3.90
			75	58	.564	138	138	130	9	1	1199	1200	509	479	3.53

CINCINNATI Red Stockings   76-63   .547   -18   4th   Gus Schmelz

BATTERS	POS/GAMES	GP	AB	R	H	BI	2B	3B	HR	BB	SO	SB	BA	SA
Long John Reilly	1B109,OF2	111	427	84	111	66	24	13	5	34	37	43	.260	.412
Bid McPhee	2B135,3B1	135	540	109	145	57	25	7	5	60	29	63	.269	.368
Oliver Beard	SS141	141	558	96	159	77	13	14	1	35	39	36	.285	.364
Hick Carpenter	3B121,1B2	123	486	67	127	63	23	6	0	18	41	47	.261	.333
Hugh Nicol	OF115,2B7,3B3	122	474	82	121	58	7	8	2	54	35	80	.255	.316
Bug Holliday	OF135	135	563	107	181	104	28	7	19	43	59	46	.321	.497
White Wings Tebeau	OF134,1B1	135	496	110	125	70	21	11	7	69	62	61	.252	.381
Jim Keenan	C66,1B21,3B1	87	300	52	86	60	10	11	6	48	35	18	.287	.453
Tony Mullane	P33,3B18,OF12,1B4	63	196	53	58	29	16	4	0	27	21	24	.296	.418
Kid Baldwin	C55,OF4,1B3,3B1	60	223	34	55	34	14	2	1	5	32	7	.247	.341
Jesse Duryea	P53,OF3	54	162	37	44	17	6	3	0	11	30	5	.272	.346
Billy Earle	OF26,C23,1B5	53	169	37	45	31	4	7	4	30	24	26	.266	.444
Leon Viau	P47,OF1	47	147	14	21	9	2	1	0	11	47	4	.143	.170
Elmer Smith	P29	29	83	12	23	17	3	1	2	7	18	1	.277	.410
Charlie Petty	P5	5	20	3	6	4	1	1	0	0	2	1	.300	.450
Ted Conover	P1	1	0	0	0	0	0	0	0	0	0	0	----	----
		141	4844	897	1307	696	197	96	52	452	511	462	.270	.382

PITCHERS		W	L	PCT	G	GS	CG	SH	SV	IP	H	BB	SO	ERA
Jesse Duryea		32	19	.627	53	48	38	2	1	401	372	127	183	2.56
Leon Viau		22	20	.524	47	42	38	1	1	373	379	136	152	3.79
Tony Mullane		11	9	.550	33	24	17	0	5	220	218	89	112	2.99
Elmer Smith		9	12	.429	29	22	16	0	0	203	253	101	104	4.88
Charlie Petty		2	3	.400	5	5	5	0	0	44	44	20	10	5.52
Ted Conover		0	0	----	1	0	0	0	1	2	4	2	1	13.50
		76	63	.547	141	141	114	3	8	1243	1270	475	562	3.50

1889 AMERICAN ASSOCIATION

BALTIMORE Orioles   70-65   .519   -22   5th   Billy Barnie

BATTERS	POS/GAMES		GP	AB	R	H	BI	2B	3B	HR	BB	SO	SB	BA	SA
Tommy Tucker	1B123,OF12		134	527	103	196	99	22	11	5	42	26	63	.372	.484
Reddy Mack	2B135,OF1		136	519	84	125	87	24	7	1	60	69	23	.241	.320
Jack Farrell	SS42		42	157	25	33	26	3	0	1	15	15	14	.210	.248
Bill Shindle	3B138		138	567	122	178	64	24	7	3	42	37	56	.314	.397
Joe Sommer	OF105,SS1		106	386	51	85	36	13	2	1	42	49	18	.220	.272
Mike Griffin	OF109,SS25,2B5		137	531	152	148	48	21	14	4	91	29	39	.279	.394
Joe Hornung	OF134,3B1		135	533	73	122	78	13	9	1	22	72	34	.229	.293
Pop Tate	C62,1B10		72	253	28	46	27	6	3	1	13	37	4	.182	.241
Matt Kilroy	P59,OF8		65	208	32	57	26	3	6	1	23	26	13	.274	.361
Tom Quinn	C55		55	194	18	34	15	2	1	1	19	22	6	.175	.211
Frank Foreman	P51,OF3		54	181	18	26	11	2	1	1	12	35	7	.144	.182
Bert Cunningham	P39,OF2,SS1		41	131	10	27	18	4	2	0	4	25	3	.206	.267
Will Holland	SS39,OF1		40	143	13	27	16	1	2	0	9	28	4	.189	.224
Irv Ray	SS20,OF6	(2-2)	26	106	20	36	17	4	1	0	7	6	12	.340	.396
Joe Dowie	OF20		20	75	12	17	8	5	0	0	2	10	5	.227	.293
Bart Cantz	C18,OF2		20	69	6	12	8	2	0	0	4	14	2	.174	.203
Chris Fulmer	OF14,C2		16	58	11	15	13	3	1	0	6	12	2	.259	.345
John Kerins	1B9,C4,OF3,SS1	(2-2)	16	53	7	15	12	2	0	0	2	4	2	.283	.321
Dusty Miller	SS8,OF3		11	40	4	6	6	1	1	0	2	11	3	.150	.225
George Wood	OF3	(2-2)	3	10	1	2	1	0	0	0	0	2	1	.200	.200
Chippy McGarr	SS3	(2-2)	3	7	1	1	0	0	0	0	1	1	0	.143	.143
Bill Whitaker	P1		1	4	0	1	2	0	0	0	0	2	0	.250	.250
George Goetz	P1		1	4	0	0	0	0	0	0	0	4	0	.000	.000
			139	4756	791	1209	618	155	68	20	418	536	311	.254	.328

PITCHERS		W	L	PCT	G	GS	CG	SH	SV	IP	H	BB	SO	ERA
Matt Kilroy		29	25	.537	59	56	55	5	0	481	476	142	217	2.85
Frank Foreman		23	21	.523	51	48	43	5	0	414	364	137	180	3.52
Bert Cunningham		16	19	.457	39	33	29	0	1	279	306	141	140	4.87
Bill Whitaker		1	0	1.000	1	1	1	0	0	9	10	4	1	2.00
George Goetz		1	0	1.000	1	1	0	0	0	9	12	0	2	4.00
		70	65	.519	139	139	128	10	1	1192	1168	424	540	3.56

COLUMBUS Buckeyes   60-78   .435   -33.5   6th   Al Buckenberger

BATTERS	POS/GAMES		GP	AB	R	H	BI	2B	3B	HR	BB	SO	SB	BA	SA
Dave Orr	1B134		134	560	70	183	87	31	12	4	9	38	12	.327	.446
Bill Greenwood	2B118		118	414	62	93	49	7	10	3	58	71	37	.225	.312
Henry Easterday	SS89,2B5,3B1		95	324	43	56	34	5	8	4	41	57	10	.173	.275
Lefty Marr	3B66,OF47,SS26,1B1,C1		139	546	110	167	75	26	15	1	87	32	29	.306	.414
Spud Johnson	OF69,3B14,1B2,SS1		116	459	91	130	79	14	10	2	39	47	34	.283	.370
Jim McTamany	OF139		139	529	113	146	52	21	7	4	116	66	40	.276	.365
Ed Daily	OF136,P2		136	578	105	148	70	22	8	3	38	65	60	.256	.337
Jack O'Connor	C84,OF19,2B4,1B3		107	398	69	107	60	17	7	4	33	37	26	.269	.377
Mark Baldwin	P63,OF1		64	208	19	39	25	6	5	2	16	63	2	.188	.293
Heinie Kappel	3B23,SS23		46	173	25	47	21	7	5	3	21	28	10	.272	.422
Wild Bill Widner	P41,OF1,1B1		41	133	16	28	10	3	0	2	2	31	5	.211	.278
Hank Gastright	P32		32	94	5	17	11	0	1	0	3	24	2	.181	.202
Jim Peoples	C22,OF5,2B2,SS1		29	100	13	23	16	6	2	1	6	8	3	.230	.360
Ned Bligh	C28		28	93	6	13	5	1	1	0	4	14	2	.140	.172
Al Mays	P21,OF2		21	54	4	7	4	1	0	0	11	10	1	.130	.148
Jack Crooks	2B12		12	43	13	14	7	2	3	0	10	4	10	.326	.512
Jack Doyle	C7,OF3,2B2		11	36	6	10	3	1	1	0	6	6	9	.278	.361
Rudy Kemmler	C8		8	26	2	3	0	0	0	0	3	3	0	.115	.115
Charlie Reilly	3B6		6	23	5	11	6	1	0	3	2	2	9	.478	.913
William George	OF4,P2	(2-2)	5	17	1	4	3	0	0	0	1	1	1	.235	.235
John Easton	P4		4	7	0	0	0	0	0	0	0	2	0	.000	.000
Sparrow McCaffrey	C2		2	1	1	1	0	0	0	0	1	0	0	1.000	1.000
John Weyhing	P1		1	0	0	0	0	0	0	0	0	0	0	----	----
			140	4816	779	1247	617	171	95	36	507	609	304	.259	.356

PITCHERS		W	L	PCT	G	GS	CG	SH	SV	IP	H	BB	SO	ERA
Mark Baldwin		27	34	.443	63	59	54	6	1	514	458	274	368	3.61
Wild Bill Widner		12	20	.375	41	34	25	2	1	294	368	85	63	5.20
Al Mays		10	7	.588	21	19	13	1	0	140	167	56	52	4.87
Hank Gastright		10	16	.385	32	26	21	0	0	223	255	104	115	4.57
John Easton		1	0	1.000	4	1	1	0	1	18	13	21	7	3.50

1889 AMERICAN ASSOCIATION

COLUMBUS (cont.)
Buckeyes

PITCHERS		W	L	PCT	G	GS	CG	SH	SV	IP	H	BB	SO	ERA
William George		0	0	----	2	0	0	0	0	8	11	3	3	7.88
Ed Daily		0	0	----	2	0	0	0	1	2	1	4	2	21.60
John Weyhing		0	0	----	1	0	0	0	0	1	1	4	0	27.00
		60	78	.435	140	139	114	9	4	1199	1274	551	610	4.39

KANSAS CITY
Cowboys

55-82 .401 -44 7th Bill Watkins

BATTERS	POS/GAMES		GP	AB	R	H	BI	2B	3B	HR	BB	SO	SB	BA	SA
Dan Stearns	1B135,3B4		139	560	96	160	87	24	12	3	56	69	67	.286	.387
Sam Barkley	2B41,1B4		45	176	36	50	23	6	2	0	15	20	8	.284	.341
Germany Long	SS128,2B8,OF1		136	574	137	158	60	32	6	3	64	63	89	.275	.368
Jumbo Davis	3B62	(1-2)	62	241	40	64	30	4	3	0	17	35	25	.266	.307
Billy Hamilton	OF137		137	534	144	161	77	17	12	3	87	41	111	.301	.395
Jim Burns	OF134,3B1		134	579	103	176	97	23	11	5	20	68	56	.304	.408
Jim Manning	OF69,2B63,3B1,SS1		132	506	68	103	68	16	7	3	54	61	58	.204	.281
Charlie Hoover	C66,3B4,OF3		71	258	44	64	25	2	5	1	29	38	9	.248	.306
Jim Donahue	C46,OF14,3B10		67	252	30	59	32	5	4	0	21	20	12	.234	.286
John Pickett	OF28,3B14,2B11		53	201	20	45	12	7	0	0	11	21	7	.224	.259
Parke Swartzel	P48,OF4		51	174	19	25	20	4	0	0	18	33	7	.144	.167
Bill Alvord	3B34,2B8,SS8		50	186	23	43	18	8	9	0	10	35	3	.231	.371
Jim Conway	P41		41	149	14	31	12	2	2	0	2	26	1	.208	.248
Joe Gunson	C32,3B1,OF1		34	122	15	24	12	3	1	0	3	17	2	.197	.238
John Sowders	P25,OF3		28	87	11	19	6	3	0	0	4	20	1	.218	.253
Chippy McGarr	3B11,OF6,2B5,SS3	(1-2)	25	108	22	31	16	3	0	0	6	11	12	.287	.315
John McCarty	P15,OF6		20	79	12	18	12	0	1	0	1	9	3	.228	.253
Mike Mattimore	OF19,P1	(2-2)	19	75	6	12	5	1	1	0	3	16	0	.160	.200
Tom Sullivan	P10		10	33	8	5	1	1	0	0	5	8	0	.152	.182
Henry Bittman	2B4		4	14	2	4	2	0	0	0	1	1	1	.286	.286
Henry Porter	P4		4	10	0	1	1	0	0	0	1	3	0	.100	.100
Frank Pears	P3,OF1		3	11	0	1	1	0	0	0	0	3	0	.091	.091
Charlie Bell	P1,OF1		2	6	1	1	3	1	0	0	2	2	0	.167	.333
Steve LaDew	P1,OF1		2	4	0	0	0	0	0	0	0	3	0	.000	.000
Charles Reynolds	C1	(1-2)	1	4	1	1	1	0	0	0	0	1	0	.250	.250
Bush Bates	P1		1	4	0	0	0	0	0	0	0	2	0	.000	.000
			139	4947	852	1256	621	162	76	18	430	626	472	.254	.328

PITCHERS		W	L	PCT	G	GS	CG	SH	SV	IP	H	BB	SO	ERA
Jim Conway		19	19	.500	41	37	33	0	0	335	334	90	115	3.25
Parke Swartzel		19	27	.413	48	47	45	0	1	410	481	117	147	4.32
John McCarty		8	6	.571	15	14	13	0	0	120	147	61	36	3.91
John Sowders		6	16	.273	25	23	20	0	1	185	204	105	104	4.82
Tom Sullivan		2	8	.200	10	10	10	0	0	87	111	48	24	5.67
Charlie Bell		1	0	1.000	1	1	1	0	0	9	4	3	3	1.00
Bush Bates		0	1	.000	1	1	1	0	0	8	15	5	3	13.50
Frank Pears		0	2	.000	3	2	2	0	0	22	21	9	5	4.91
Henry Porter		0	3	.000	4	4	3	0	0	23	52	14	9	12.52
Mike Mattimore	(2-2)	0	0	----	1	0	0	0	0	3	3	2	1	3.00
Steve LaDew		0	0	----	1	0	0	0	0	2	1	3	0	4.50
		55	82	.401	139	139	128	0	2	1204	1373	457	447	4.36

LOUISVILLE
Colonels

27-111 .196 -66.5 8th Esterbrook - Wolf - Shannon - Chapman

BATTERS	POS/GAMES	GP	AB	R	H	BI	2B	3B	HR	BB	SO	SB	BA	SA
Guy Hecker	1B65,P19,OF1	82	327	42	93	36	17	5	1	18	27	17	.284	.376
Dan Shannon	2B121	121	498	90	128	48	22	12	4	42	52	26	.257	.373
Phil Tomney	SS112	12	376	61	80	38	8	5	4	46	47	26	.213	.293
Harry Raymond	3B129,P1,OF1	130	515	58	123	47	12	9	0	19	45	19	.239	.297
Chicken Wolf	OF88,1B16,2B13,SS10,3B7	130	546	72	159	57	20	9	3	29	34	18	.291	.377
Farmer Weaver	OF123,C2,1B1,3B1	124	499	62	145	60	17	6	0	40	22	21	.291	.349
Pete Browning	OF83	83	324	39	83	32	19	5	2	34	30	21	.256	.364
Paul Cook	C74,OF7,1B1,SS1	81	286	34	65	15	10	1	0	15	48	11	.227	.269
Farmer Vaughn	C54,OF20,1B18,3B3	90	360	39	86	45	11	5	3	7	41	13	.239	.322
Red Ehret	P45,OF22,2B1,SS1,3B1	67	258	27	65	31	6	6	1	4	23	4	.252	.333
Scott Stratton	OF29,P19,1B17	62	229	30	66	34	7	5	4	13	36	10	.288	.415
John Ewing	P40,1B1	41	134	12	23	6	2	0	0	9	30	5	.172	.187

LOUISVILLE (cont.)
Colonels

BATTERS	POS/GAMES		GP	AB	R	H	BI	2B	3B	HR	BB	SO	SB	BA	SA
John Galligan	OF31		31	120	6	20	7	0	2	0	6	17	1	.167	.200
Fred Carl	OF18,2B6,3B1		25	99	13	20	13	2	2	0	16	22	0	.202	.263
Ed Flanagan	1B23		23	88	11	22	8	7	3	0	7	11	1	.250	.398
Jack Ryan	C15,OF4,3B2		21	79	8	14	2	1	0	0	3	17	2	.177	.190
Toad Ramsey	P18	(2-2)	18	57	3	15	3	1	0	0	1	8	1	.263	.283
Bill Gleason	SS16		16	58	6	14	5	2	0	0	4	1	1	.241	.276
Dude Esterbrook	1B8,OF2,SS1		11	44	8	14	9	3	0	0	5	2	6	.318	.386
Mike McDermott	P9		9	33	7	6	3	2	0	0	2	3	0	.182	.242
John Kerins	OF1,C1	(1-2)	2	9	2	3	3	1	0	0	0	1	0	.333	.444
Bill Anderson	P1		1	3	2	1	0	0	0	0	0	1	0	.333	.333
Harry Scherer	OF1		1	3	0	1	0	0	0	0	0	0	0	.333	.333
---- Fisher	OF1		1	2	0	1	0	0	0	0	0	0	0	.500	.500
Harry Smith	C1,OF1		1	2	0	1	1	0	0	0	0	1	0	.500	.500
John Traffley	OF1		1	2	0	1	0	0	0	0	0	0	0	.500	.500
Ed Springer	P1		1	2	0	0	0	0	0	0	0	1	0	.000	.000
Mike Gaule	OF1		1	2	0	0	0	0	0	0	0	1	0	.000	.000
			140	4955	632	1249	503	170	75	22	320	521	203	.252	.330

PITCHERS		W	L	PCT	G	GS	CG	SH	SV	IP	H	BB	SO	ERA
Red Ehret		10	29	.256	45	38	35	1	0	364	441	115	135	4.80
John Ewing		6	30	.167	40	39	37	1	0	331	407	147	155	4.87
Guy Hecker		5	13	.278	19	16	15	0	0	151	215	47	33	5.59
Scott Stratton		3	13	.188	19	17	13	0	1	134	157	42	42	3.23
Harry Raymond		1	0	1.000	1	1	1	0	0	9	8	11	1	1.00
Mike McDermott		1	8	.111	9	9	9	0	0	84	108	34	22	4.16
Toad Ramsey	(1-2)	1	16	.059	18	18	15	0	0	140	175	71	60	5.59
Bill Anderson		0	1	.000	1	1	1	0	0	8	10	6	2	10.13
Ed Springer		0	1	.000	1	1	1	0	0	5	8	2	1	9.00
		27	111	.196	140	140	127	2	1	1226	1529	475	451	4.81

1890 PLAYERS' LEAGUE

The Brotherhood

In 1889, the Players' National League was formed to compete with the National League and American Association at the major league level. This new league was the logical next step for the "Brotherhood of Professional Base Ball Players," a players union formed in 1885 to help alleviate the pressures put on the players by the owners.

Baseball in the mid 1880s was a game dominated by the owners. Players had little say in their own careers. The Brotherhood was formed to give players a forum to help air their grievances. When baseball put a defacto salary cap in place after the 1888 season, the Brotherhood thought it time to act. Led by their founder, John Montgomery Ward, the Brotherhood approached several wealthy businessmen during the summer of 1889 about the idea of a third major league circuit. Several of the businessmen, including Albert Johnson of Cleveland, were convinced of the soundness of the idea. Plans were drawn, and an eight-team league was ready to launch by 1890. Teams were placed in the following cities: Boston, Brooklyn, Buffalo, Chicago, Cleveland, New York, Philadelphia, and Pittsburgh.

The Players' League contained some novel ideas including: 1) abolishment of the reserve clause, 2) multi-year contracts, 3) a rule stating that no player could be released before the end of the season, and 4) a clause claiming that most of the profits be shared by players and backers on a leaguewide basis.

The defections from organized baseball were numerous. Over 100 players fled the National League, while another twenty jumped from the American Association. Such stars as Dan Brouthers, Pete Browning, and Roger Connor all found homes in the new league. The cream of the baseball world in 1890 was to be found in the Players' League.

The Players' League schedule was deliberately designed to conflict with the established leagues. Quite often games were scheduled for the same city at the same time. In New York, where the National League and Players' League ballparks abutted one another, it was possible to see both games at once. The first few games were well attended, but by June all three leagues had low attendance. The Players' League managed to stay afloat through the summer, despite mounting losses, and was able to complete the campaign.

Boston won the inaugural pennant by six and one-half games. They were paced by Dan Brouthers (.330) and Hardy Richardson (.321) who also led the league with 146 runs batted in.

Brooklyn finished a strong second. They were led by Dave Orr who finished second in both the batting race (.373) and the runs batted in race (124), and by league founder Monte Ward who hit .337. Pitcher Gus Weyhing also had a fine year, finishing with 30 wins.

New York, in third, was led by their bats, while Chicago, in fourth, was led by their hurlers. Jim O'Rourke (.360) and Roger Connor (.349) and a league best 14 home runs, paved the way for New York, while Mark Baldwin's 34 wins and Silver King's 2.69 earned run average (both league best marks) did the same for Chicago.

Philadelphia, Pittsburgh, Cleveland, and Buffalo finished in the last four spots. The four best hitters out of this group were batting champion Pete Browning (.373) and Harry Larkin (.332) from Cleveland, Jake Beckley (.324) from Pittsburgh, and Bill Shindle (.323) from Philadelphia.

After the dust cleared, the Players' League proved not to be a profitable venture as their total losses exceeded $125,000. So, when the first peace offerings were made by the National League in October, the Players' League jumped at the chance. Wary of further losses, the new league quickly capitulated. But in hindsight, it was revealed that perhaps the Players' League had acted in haste. The National League had lost almost $500,000—one more push and it might have gone under. One can only speculate.

The Boston, Brooklyn, Pittsburgh, and New York franchises merged with their National League counterparts. The Chicago club was sold to National League magnate Al Spalding, while the backers of the Philadelphia team bought the Philadelphia American Association franchise. The Buffalo and Cleveland clubs were left to twist in the wind.

With the demise of the Players' League, the Brotherhood was broken, and any semblance of player power was lost. The powerful owners were free to have their way with the ball players, setting salaries and the like to suit their own needs. In other words, business as usual.

1890 PLAYERS' LEAGUE

BOSTON Reds
81-48 .628 1st King Kelly

BATTERS	POS/GAMES		GP	AB	R	H	BI	2B	3B	HR	BB	SO	SB	BA	SA
Dan Brouthers	1B123		123	460	117	152	97	36	9	1	99	17	28	.330	.454
Joe Quinn	2B130		130	509	87	153	82	19	8	7	44	24	29	.301	.411
Art Irwin	SS96		96	354	60	92	45	17	1	0	57	29	16	.260	.314
Billy Nash	3B129		129	488	103	130	90	28	6	5	88	43	26	.266	.379
Harry Stovey	OF117,1B1		118	481	142	143	85	25	11	12	81	38	97	.297	.470
Tom Brown	OF128		128	543	146	150	61	23	14	4	86	84	79	.276	.392
Hardy Richardson	OF124,SS6,1B1		130	555	126	181	146	26	14	13	52	46	42	.326	.494
Morg Murphy	C67,SS2,3B1,OF1		68	246	38	56	32	10	2	2	24	31	16	.228	.309
King Kelly	C56,SS27,OF6,1B4,3B2,P1		89	340	83	111	66	18	6	4	52	22	51	.326	.450
Old Hoss Radbourn	P41,OF4,1B1		45	154	20	39	16	6	0	0	9	20	7	.253	.292
Ad Gumbert	P39,OF7		44	145	23	35	20	7	1	3	18	26	5	.241	.366
Bill Daley	P34,OF3		37	110	14	17	7	1	0	2	9	15	1	.155	.218
Pop Swett	C34,OF3		37	94	16	18	12	4	3	1	16	26	4	.191	.330
Matt Kilroy	P30,OF2,SS1,3B1		31	93	11	20	8	1	1	0	12	9	11	.215	.247
Kid Madden	P10,OF2,SS1		13	38	5	7	4	2	0	0	3	3	0	.184	.237
Dick Johnston	OF2	(1-2)	2	9	0	1	0	0	0	0	0	1	0	.111	.111
John Morrill	1B1,SS1		2	7	1	1	2	0	0	0	2	1	0	.143	.143
			130	4626	992	1306	773	223	76	54	652	435	412	.282	.398

PITCHERS			W	L	PCT	G	GS	CG	SH	SV	IP	H	BB	SO	ERA
Old Hoss Radbourn			27	12	.692	41	38	36	1	0	343	352	100	80	3.31
Ad Gumbert			23	12	.657	39	33	27	1	0	277	338	86	81	3.96
Bill Daley			18	7	.720	34	25	19	2	2	235	246	167	110	3.60
Matt Kilroy			9	15	.375	30	27	18	0	0	218	268	87	48	4.29
Kid Madden			3	2	.600	10	7	5	1	0	62	85	25	24	4.79
King Kelly			1	0	1.000	1	0	0	0	0	2	1	2	2	4.50
Billy Nash			0	0	----	1	0	0	0	0	0	1	0	0	0.00
			81	48	.628	130	130	105	6	2	1137	1291	467	345	3.80

BROOKLYN Wonders
76-56 .576 -6.5 2nd Monte Ward

BATTERS	POS/GAMES		GP	AB	R	H	BI	2B	3B	HR	BB	SO	SB	BA	SA
Dave Orr	1B107		107	464	89	173	124	32	13	6	30	11	10	.373	.537
Lou Bierbauer	2B133		133	589	128	180	99	31	11	7	40	15	16	.306	.431
Monte Ward	SS128		128	561	134	189	60	15	12	4	51	22	63	.337	.428
Bill Joyce	3B133		133	489	121	123	78	18	18	1	123	77	43	.252	.368
Jack McGeachey	OF104		104	443	84	108	65	24	4	1	19	12	21	.244	.323
Ed Andrews	OF94		94	395	84	100	38	14	2	3	40	32	21	.253	.322
Emmett Seery	OF104		104	394	78	88	50	12	7	1	70	36	44	.223	.297
Tom Kinslow	C64		64	242	30	64	46	11	6	4	10	22	2	.264	.409
George Van Haltren	OF67,P28,SS3		92	376	84	126	54	8	9	5	41	23	35	.335	.444
Paul Cook	C36,1B21,OF1		58	218	32	55	31	3	3	0	14	18	7	.252	.294
Gus Weyhing	P49		49	165	21	27	15	2	3	1	16	44	2	.164	.230
Con Daily	C40,1B6,OF1		46	168	20	42	35	6	3	0	15	14	6	.250	.321
John Sowders	P39,OF3		40	132	14	25	20	3	0	1	10	12	0	.189	.235
Art Sunday	OF24		24	83	26	22	13	5	1	0	15	9	0	.265	.349
Con Murphy	P20,OF3	(1-2)	23	69	11	15	7	2	0	0	5	7	1	.217	.246
George Hemming	P19,OF	(2-2)	19	57	5	9	8	0	1	0	1	11	1	.158	.193
Jack Hayes	OF6,SS3,C2,2B1		12	42	3	8	5	0	0	0	2	4	0	.190	.190
			133	4887	964	1354	748	186	93	34	502	369	272	.277	.374

PITCHERS			W	L	PCT	G	GS	CG	SH	SV	IP	H	BB	SO	ERA
Gus Weyhing			30	16	.652	49	46	38	3	0	390	419	179	177	3.60
John Sowders			19	16	.543	39	37	28	1	0	309	358	161	91	3.82
George Van Haltren			15	10	.600	28	25	23	0	2	223	272	89	48	4.28
George Hemming		(2-2)	8	4	.667	19	11	11	0	3	123	117	59	32	3.80
Con Murphy		(1-2)	4	10	.286	20	14	11	0	2	139	168	82	29	4.79
			76	56	.576	133	133	111	4	7	1184	1334	570	377	3.95

NEW YORK Giants
74-57 .567 -8 3rd Buck Ewing

BATTERS	POS/GAMES		GP	AB	R	H	BI	2B	3B	HR	BB	SO	SB	BA	SA
Roger Connor	1B123		123	484	133	169	103	24	15	14	88	32	22	.349	.548
Dan Shannon	2B77,SS6	(2-2)	83	324	59	70	44	7	8	3	25	34	21	.216	.315

1890 PLAYERS' LEAGUE

NEW YORK (cont.)
Giants

BATTERS	POS/GAMES		GP	AB	R	H	BI	2B	3B	HR	BB	SO	SB	BA	SA
Danny Richardson	SS68,2B56		123	528	102	135	80	12	9	4	37	19	37	.256	.335
Art Whitney	3B88,SS31		119	442	71	97	45	12	3	0	64	19	8	.219	.260
Jim O'Rourke	OF111		111	478	112	172	115	37	5	9	33	20	23	.360	.515
George Gore	OF93		93	399	132	127	55	26	8	10	77	23	28	.318	.499
Mike Slattery	OF97		97	411	80	126	67	20	11	5	27	25	18	.307	.445
Buck Ewing	C81,2B1,P1		83	352	98	119	72	19	15	8	39	12	36	.338	.545
Dick Johnston	OF76,SS2	(2-2)	77	306	37	74	43	9	7	1	18	25	7	.242	.327
Gil Hatfield	3B42,SS27,P3,OF1		71	287	32	80	37	13	6	2	17	19	12	.279	.387
Willard Brown	C34,OF13,1B9,3B3,2B2		60	230	47	64	43	8	4	4	13	13	5	.278	.400
Farmer Vaughn	C30,OF12,2B1,3B1		44	166	27	44	22	7	0	1	10	9	6	.265	.325
Hank O'Day	P43		43	150	24	34	23	2	1	1	10	27	1	.227	.273
Cannonball Crane	P43		43	146	27	46	16	5	4	0	10	26	5	.315	.404
John Ewing	P35		35	114	18	24	17	2	1	2	5	35	2	.211	.298
Tim Keefe	P30		30	92	18	10	11	1	0	2	13	26	0	.109	.185
Fred Dunlap	2B1	(2-2)	1	4	1	2	0	0	0	0	0	0	0	.500	.500
			132	4913	1018	1393	793	204	97	66	486	364	231	.284	.405

PITCHERS			W	L	PCT	G	GS	CG	SH	SV	IP	H	BB	SO	ERA
Hank O'Day			22	13	.629	43	35	32	1	3	329	356	163	94	4.21
John Ewing			18	12	.600	35	31	27	1	2	267	293	104	145	4.25
Tim Keefe			17	11	.607	30	30	23	1	0	229	228	85	88	3.38
Cannonball Crane			16	19	.457	43	35	28	0	0	330	323	210	117	4.64
Gil Hatfield			1	1	.500	3	0	0	0	1	8	8	4	3	3.38
Buck Ewing			0	1	.000	1	1	1	0	0	9	11	3	2	4.00
			74	57	.565	132	132	111	3	6	1172	1219	569	449	4.17

CHICAGO
Pirates

75-62 .547 -10 4th Charlie Comiskey

BATTERS	POS/GAMES		GP	AB	R	H	BI	2B	3B	HR	BB	SO	SB	BA	SA
Charlie Comiskey	1B88		88	377	53	92	59	11	3	0	14	17	34	.244	.289
Fred Pfeffer	2B124		124	499	86	128	80	21	8	5	44	23	27	.257	.361
Charlie Bastian	SS64,2B12,3B4		80	283	38	54	29	10	5	0	33	37	4	.191	.261
Ned Williamson	3B52,SS21		73	261	34	51	26	7	3	2	36	35	3	.195	.268
Hugh Duffy	OF138		138	596	161	191	82	36	16	7	59	20	78	.320	.470
Jimmy Ryan	OF118		118	486	99	165	89	32	5	6	60	36	30	.340	.463
Tip O'Neill	OF137		137	577	112	174	75	20	16	3	65	36	29	.302	.407
Duke Farrell	C90,1B22,OF10		117	451	79	131	84	21	12	2	42	28	8	.290	.404
Jack Boyle	C50,3B30,SS16,1B7,OF2		100	369	56	96	49	9	5	1	44	29	11	.260	.320
Mark Baldwin	P59		59	215	27	45	25	4	6	1	15	51	4	.209	.298
Dell Darling	1B29,SS15,C9,OF7,2B3,3B2		58	221	45	57	39	12	4	2	29	28	5	.258	.376
Silver King	P56,OF1,1B1		58	185	24	31	16	2	5	1	13	22	3	.168	.249
Arlie Latham	3B52	(1-2)	52	214	47	49	20	7	2	1	22	22	32	.229	.294
Frank Shugart	SS25,OF5		29	106	8	20	15	5	5	0	5	13	5	.189	.330
Charles Bartson	P25		25	75	7	13	6	1	0	0	11	11	2	.173	.187
Frank Dwyer	P12,OF4		16	53	10	14	11	2	0	0	0	2	1	.264	.302
			138	4968	886	1311	705	200	95	31	492	410	276	.264	.361

PITCHERS			W	L	PCT	G	GS	CG	SH	SV	IP	H	BB	SO	ERA
Mark Baldwin			34	24	.586	59	57	54	1	0	501	498	249	211	3.31
Silver King			30	22	.577	56	56	48	4	0	461	420	163	185	2.69
Charles Bartson			8	10	.444	25	19	16	0	1	188	222	66	47	4.26
Frank Dwyer			3	6	.333	12	6	6	0	1	69	98	25	17	6.23
			75	62	.547	138	138	124	5	2	1219	1238	503	460	3.39

PHILADELPHIA
Quakers

68-63 .519 -14 5th Fogarty - Buffinton

BATTERS	POS/GAMES	GP	AB	R	H	BI	2B	3B	HR	BB	SO	SB	BA	SA
Sid Farrar	1B127	127	481	84	122	69	17	11	1	51	23	9	.254	.341
John Pickett	2B100	100	407	82	114	64	7	9	4	40	17	12	.280	.371
Bill Shindle	SS130,3B2	132	584	127	188	90	21	21	10	40	30	51	.322	.481
Joe Mulvey	3B120	120	519	96	149	87	26	15	6	27	36	20	.287	.430
Jim Fogarty	OF91,3B1	91	347	71	83	58	17	6	4	59	50	36	.239	.357
Mike Griffin	OF115	115	489	127	140	54	29	6	6	64	19	30	.286	.407

1890 PLAYERS' LEAGUE

PHILADELPHIA (cont.)
Quakers

BATTERS	POS/GAMES		GP	AB	R	H	BI	2B	3B	HR	BB	SO	SB	BA	SA
George Wood	OF132,3B1		132	539	115	156	102	20	14	9	51	35	20	.289	.429
Jocko Milligan	C59,1B3		62	234	38	69	57	9	3	3	19	19	2	.295	.397
Bill Hallman	OF34,C26,2B14,3B10,SS2		84	356	59	95	37	16	7	1	33	24	6	.267	.360
Lave Cross	C49,OF15		63	245	42	73	47	7	8	3	12	6	5	.298	.429
Ben Sanders	P43,OF10		52	189	31	59	30	6	6	0	10	10	2	.312	.407
Charles Buffinton	P36,OF5,1B3		42	150	24	41	24	3	2	1	9	3	1	.273	.340
Phil Knell	P35,OF2		36	132	19	29	18	3	3	0	7	17	3	.220	.288
Dan Shannon	2B19	(2-2)	19	75	15	18	16	5	1	1	4	12	4	.240	.373
Bill Husted	P18		18	56	5	6	5	0	0	0	3	9	1	.107	.107
Bert Cunningham	P14,OF1	(1-2)	15	52	6	6	3	1	1	0	2	11	1	.115	.203
			132	4855	942	1348	762	187	113	49	431	321	203	.278	.393

PITCHERS		W	L	PCT	G	GS	CG	SH	SV	IP	H	BB	SO	ERA
Phil Knell		22	11	.667	35	31	30	2	0	287	287	166	99	3.83
Charles Buffinton		19	15	.559	36	33	28	0	1	283	312	126	89	3.81
Ben Sanders		19	18	.514	43	40	37	2	1	347	412	69	107	3.76
Bill Husted		5	10	.333	18	17	12	0	0	129	148	67	33	4.88
Bert Cunningham	(1-2)	3	9	.250	14	11	11	0	0	109	133	67	33	5.22
		68	63	.519	132	132	118	4	2	1154	1292	495	361	4.05

PITTSBURGH
Burghers

60-68   .469   -20.5   6th   Ned Hanlon

BATTERS	POS/GAMES		GP	AB	R	H	BI	2B	3B	HR	BB	SO	SB	BA	SA
Jake Beckley	1B121		121	516	109	167	120	38	22	19	42	32	18	.324	.535
Yank Robinson	2B98		98	306	59	70	38	10	3	0	101	33	17	.229	.281
Tom Corcoran	SS123		123	503	80	117	61	14	13	1	38	45	43	.233	.318
Bill Kuehne	3B126		126	528	66	126	73	21	12	5	28	37	21	.239	.352
Joe Visner	OF127		127	521	110	138	71	15	22	3	76	44	18	.265	.395
Ned Hanlon	OF118		118	472	106	131	44	16	6	1	80	24	65	.278	.343
Jocko Fields	OF80,2B30,C15,SS4		126	526	101	149	86	18	20	9	57	52	24	.283	.445
Fred Carroll	C56,OF49,1B7		111	416	95	124	71	20	7	2	75	22	35	.298	.394
Tom Quinn	C55		55	207	23	44	15	4	3	1	17	8	1	.213	.275
Harry Staley	P46,OF1		47	164	25	34	25	3	2	1	13	16	0	.207	.268
Al Maul	P30,OF15,SS1		45	162	31	42	21	6	2	0	22	12	5	.259	.321
Pud Galvin	P26		26	97	8	20	12	2	1	0	6	20	1	.206	.247
John Tener	P14,OF2,3B2		18	63	7	12	5	0	0	2	7	10	1	.190	.286
Ed Morris	P18		18	63	7	9	5	0	0	0	5	13	0	.143	.143
Jerry Hurley	C7,OF1		8	22	5	6	2	1	0	0	2	5	0	.273	.318
Reddy Gray	2B2	(1-2)	2	9	3	2	3	0	0	1	0	2	0	.222	.222
Al Doe	P1	(2-2)	1	2	0	1	0	0	0	0	0	0	0	.500	.500
			128	4577	835	1192	652	168	113	35	569	375	249	.260	.369

PITCHERS		W	L	PCT	G	GS	CG	SH	SV	IP	H	BB	SO	ERA
Harry Staley		21	25	.457	46	46	44	3	0	388	392	74	145	3.23
Al Maul		16	12	.571	30	28	26	2	0	247	258	104	81	3.79
Pud Galvin		12	13	.480	26	25	23	1	0	217	275	49	35	4.35
Ed Morris		8	7	.533	18	15	15	1	0	144	178	35	25	4.86
John Tener		3	11	.214	14	14	13	0	0	117	160	70	30	7.31
Al Doe	(2-2)	0	0	----	1	0	0	0	0	4	4	2	2	4.50
		60	68	.469	128	128	121	7	0	1117	1267	334	318	4.22

CLEVELAND
Infants

55-75   .423   -26.5   7th   Larkin - Tebeau

BATTERS	POS/GAMES	GP	AB	R	H	BI	2B	3B	HR	BB	SO	SB	BA	SA
Henry Larkin	1B125,OF1	125	506	93	168	112	32	15	5	65	18	5	.332	.484
Cub Stricker	2B109,SS20	127	544	93	133	65	19	8	2	54	16	24	.244	.320
Ed Delahanty	SS76,2B20,OF18,3B3,1B1	115	517	107	154	64	26	13	3	24	30	25	.298	.416
Patsy Tebeau	3B110	110	450	86	135	74	26	6	5	34	20	14	.300	.418
Paul Radford	OF80,SS36,3B7,2B4,P1	122	466	98	136	62	24	12	2	82	28	25	.292	.408
Jimmy McAleer	OF86	86	341	58	91	42	8	7	1	37	33	21	.267	.340
Pete Browning	OF118	118	493	112	184	93	40	8	5	75	36	35	.373	.517
Sy Sutcliffe	C84,OF15,SS4,3B2	99	386	62	127	60	14	8	2	33	16	10	.329	.422

1890 PLAYERS' LEAGUE

CLEVELAND (cont.)
Infants

BATTERS	POS/GAMES		GP	AB	R	H	BI	2B	3B	HR	BB	SO	SB	BA	SA
James Brennan	C42,3B14,OF6		59	233	32	59	26	3	7	0	13	29	8	.253	.326
Larry Twitchell	OF56	(1-2)	56	233	33	52	36	6	3	2	17	17	4	.223	.300
Henry Gruber	P48,OF3,3B1		50	163	21	36	9	3	3	0	26	29	0	.221	.276
Jersey Bakely	P43,OF1		43	138	10	28	9	3	0	0	11	28	0	.203	.225
John O'Brien	P25,OF1		26	96	12	15	6	1	1	0	2	6	0	.156	.188
John Carney	OF19,1B6	(2-2)	25	89	15	31	21	5	3	0	14	5	6	.348	.472
Willie McGill	P24,OF1		24	68	10	10	6	2	0	0	21	16	0	.147	.176
Pop Snyder	C13		13	48	5	9	12	1	0	0	1	9	1	.188	.208
George Hemming	P3	(1-2)	3	11	1	2	1	0	0	0	0	3	2	.182	.192
Charles Dewald	P2		2	8	1	3	3	0	0	0	0	2	0	.375	.375
Neil Stynes	C2		2	8	0	0	0	0	0	0	0	0	0	.000	.000
----- Budd	OF1		1	4	0	0	0	0	0	0	0	3	0	.000	.000
Bill Gleason	P1		1	2	0	0	0	0	0	0	0	1	0	.000	.000
			131	4804	849	1373	701	213	94	27	509	345	180	.286	.386

PITCHERS			W	L	PCT	G	GS	CG	SH	SV	IP	H	BB	SO	ERA
Henry Gruber			22	23	.489	48	44	39	1	0	383	464	204	110	4.27
Jersey Bakely			12	25	.324	43	38	32	0	0	326	412	147	67	4.47
Willie McGill			11	9	.550	24	20	19	0	0	184	222	96	82	4.12
John O'Brien			8	16	.333	25	25	22	0	0	206	229	93	54	3.40
Charles Dewald			2	0	1.000	2	2	2	0	0	14	13	5	6	0.64
George Hemming		(1-2)	0	1	.000	3	1	1	0	*0	21	25	19	3	6.86
Bill Gleason			0	1	.000	1	1	0	0	0	4	14	6	0	27.00
Paul Radford			0	0	----	1	0	0	0	0	5	7	1	3	3.60
			55	75	.423	131	131	115	1	0	1144	1386	571	325	4.23

BUFFALO
Bisons

36-96   .273   -46.5   8th   Rowe - Faatz

BATTERS	POS/GAMES		GP	AB	R	H	BI	2B	3B	HR	BB	SO	SB	BA	SA
Deacon White	1B57,3B64,SS1,P1		122	439	62	114	47	13	4	0	67	30	3	.260	.308
Sam Wise	2B119		119	505	95	148	102	29	11	6	46	45	19	.293	.430
Jack Rowe	SS125		125	504	77	126	76	22	7	2	48	18	10	.250	.333
John Irwin	3B64,1B12,2B1		77	308	62	72	34	11	4	0	43	19	18	.234	.295
Jocko Halligan	OF43,C16		57	211	28	53	33	9	2	3	20	19	7	.251	.355
Dummy Hoy	OF122,2B1		122	493	107	147	53	17	8	1	94	36	39	.298	.371
Ed Beecher	OF126,P1		126	536	69	159	90	22	10	3	29	23	14	.297	.392
Connie Mack	C112,OF9,1B5		123	503	95	134	53	15	12	0	47	13	16	.266	.344
Spider Clark	OF34,C14,2B13,1B6,3B3,SS1,P1		69	260	45	69	25	11	1	1	20	16	8	.265	.327
Larry Twitchell	OF32,P13,1B3	(2-2)	44	172	24	38	17	3	1	2	23	12	4	.221	.285
John Rainey	OF28,SS7,3B6,2B2		42	166	29	39	20	5	1	1	24	15	12	.235	.295
George Haddock	P35,OF7		42	146	21	36	24	11	0	0	24	32	3	.247	.322
Jay Faatz	1B32		32	111	18	21	16	0	2	1	9	5	2	.189	.252
John Carney	1B24,OF4	(1-2)	28	107	11	29	13	3	0	0	7	14	2	.271	.299
Bert Cunningham	P25,OF3	(2-2)	28	101	11	23	11	5	1	0	6	23	0	.228	.297
George Keefe	P25		25	79	15	16	7	1	0	0	13	14	0	.203	.215
General Stafford	P12,OF4		15	49	11	7	3	1	0	0	7	8	2	.143	.163
Alex Ferson	P10,OF1		11	32	4	7	2	0	0	0	6	7	1	.219	.219
Lady Baldwin	P7	(2-2)	7	28	4	8	2	1	0	0	2	1	0	.286	.321
John Buckley	P4		4	15	1	0	0	0	0	0	2	10	0	.000	.000
Gus Krock	P4		4	12	1	1	1	0	0	0	1	4	0	.083	.083
Bill Duzen	P2		2	4	2	1	1	1	0	0	3	0	0	.250	.500
----- Lewis	P1,OF1		1	5	1	1	0	0	0	0	0	0	0	.200	.200
Dan Cotter	P1		1	4	0	0	0	0	0	0	0	0	0	.000	.000
Jim Gillespie	OF1		1	3	0	0	0	0	0	0	0	2	0	.000	.000
Al Doe	P1	(1-2)	1	2	0	0	0	0	0	0	0	0	0	.000	.000
			134	4795	793	1249	630	180	64	20	541	367	160	.260	.337

PITCHERS			W	L	PCT	G	GS	CG	SH	SV	IP	H	BB	SO	ERA
Bert Cunningham		(2-2)	9	15	.375	25	25	24	2	0	211	251	134	78	5.11
George Haddock			9	26	.257	35	34	31	0	0	291	366	149	123	5.76
George Keefe			6	16	.273	25	22	22	0	0	196	280	138	55	6.52
Larry Twitchell		(2-2)	5	7	.417	13	12	12	0	0	104	112	72	29	4.57
General Stafford			3	9	.250	12	12	11	0	0	98	123	43	21	5.14
Lady Baldwin		(2-2)	2	5	.286	7	7	7	0	0	62	90	24	13	4.50
John Buckley			1	3	.250	4	4	4	0	0	34	49	16	4	7.68
Alex Ferson			1	7	.125	10	10	7	0	0	71	88	40	13	5.45
Dan Cotter			0	1	.000	1	1	1	0	0	9	18	7	0	14.00
Al Doe		(1-2)	0	1	.000	1	1	1	0	0	6	10	7	2	12.00

BUFFALO (cont.)
Bisons

PITCHERS	W	L	PCT	G	GS	CG	SH	SV	IP	H	BB	SO	ERA
----- Lewis	0	1	.000	1	1	0	0	0	3	13	7	1	60.00
Bill Duzen	0	2	.000	2	2	2	0	0	13	20	14	5	13.85
Gus Krock	0	3	.000	4	3	3	0	0	25	43	15	5	6.12
Deacon White	0	0	----	1	0	0	0	0	8	18	2	0	9.00
Ed Beecher	0	0	----	1	0	0	0	0	6	10	3	0	12.00
Spider Clark	0	0	----	1	0	0	0	0	4	8	2	2	6.75
	36	96	.273	134	134	125	2	0	1141	1499	673	351	6.11

1890 NATIONAL LEAGUE

The Remnants

The National League of 1890 was hurt badly by the Players' League raids. Every team lost players to the new league, none more than the defending champion New York Giants. Virtually the entire starting lineup from 1889 appeared intact as the 1890 Players' League entry from New York.

Somehow the National League kept going. Cobbled together teams kept the franchises intact, and many players were called to play for the first and last time in 1890. A prime case in point was the Pittsburgh team. Over the course of the season, their bloated roster contained 46 members, 22 of whom pitched. None of the 46 distinguished themselves. Pittsburgh wobbled to the end of the season posting only 23 wins out of 136 decisions. The resulting .169 winning percentage was the worst to date in the National League.

The competition was so diluted, that none of the established National League teams could win their own pennant. That honor fell to the Brooklyn American Association franchise which jumped to the National League in 1890. Brooklyn, the 1889 Association pennant winners, thus gained the distinction of winning successive pennants in two different leagues. They were joined in their defection by Cincinnati, who also made the move from the American Association to the National League. The League's two weakest franchises, Indianapolis and Washington, were dropped to make room for them.

Brooklyn used a balanced attack to win their first National League pennant. Manager and first baseman Dave Foutz (.303), George Pinkney (.309), and Darby O'Brien (.314) were the three regulars who hit well, while teammate Oyster Burns won the runs batted in title with 128.

Chicago finished second behind Cap Anson (.312) who was the most visible star not to jump to the Players' camp, a decision that would come back to haunt him. Chicago pitcher, Bill Hutchinson, single-handedly kept the team only six games back by winning half of the team's 84 victories. He also logged over 600 innings, the last pitcher to accomplish the feat.

Philadelphia and Cincinnati finished third and fourth, about ten games off the pace. The star of the Philadelphia squad was Billy Hamilton, who stole 102 bases to accompany his .325 average. Three .300 hitters helped Cincinnati, led by Long John Reilly, who also hit 26 triples. Their pitcher, Bill Rhines, was the league's earned run average leader (1.95).

Boston, New York, Cleveland and Pittsburgh brought up the rear. Although decimated, and doomed to a sixth place finish, New York managed to pluck two of the defunct Indianapolis team's finest players. Shortstop Jack Glasscock won the batting title (.336), while fire balling pitcher Amos Rusie led the league with 341 strikeouts.

Many predicted financial ruin for the National League in 1890, a prediction that nearly came to pass. But the league persevered by putting together teams that, even if not very prettily, managed to get the job done. This proved the point that survival of the league was more important than who did or did not play for them.

1890 NATIONAL LEAGUE

BROOKLYN Bridegrooms 86-43 .667 1st Bill McGunnigle

BATTERS	POS/GAMES		GP	AB	R	H	BI	2B	3B	HR	BB	SO	SB	BA	SA
Dave Foutz	1B113,OF13,P5		129	509	106	154	98	25	13	5	52	25	42	.303	.432
Hub Collins	2B129		129	510	148	142	69	32	7	3	85	47	85	.278	.386
Germany Smith	SS129		129	481	76	92	47	6	5	1	42	23	24	.191	.231
George Pinkney	3B126		126	485	115	150	83	20	9	7	80	19	47	.309	.431
Oyster Burns	OF116,3B3		119	472	102	134	128	22	12	13	51	42	21	.284	.464
Darby O'Brien	OF85		85	350	78	110	63	28	6	2	32	43	38	.314	.446
Adonis Terry	OF54,P46,1B1		99	363	63	101	59	17	9	4	40	34	32	.278	.408
Tom Daly	C69,1B12,OF1		82	292	55	71	43	9	4	5	32	43	20	.243	.353
Bob Caruthers	OF39,P37		71	238	46	63	29	7	4	1	47	18	13	.265	.340
Pop Corkhill	OF48,1B6		51	204	23	46	21	4	2	1	15	11	6	.225	.279
Tom Lovett	P44,OF1		44	164	22	33	20	4	0	1	12	29	6	.201	.244
Bob Clark	C42,OF1		43	151	24	33	15	3	3	0	15	8	10	.219	.278
Patsy Donovan	OF28	(2-2)	28	105	17	23	8	5	1	0	5	5	3	.219	.286
Doc Bushong	C15,OF1		16	55	5	13	7	2	0	0	6	4	2	.236	.273
Mickey Hughes	P9,OF1	(1-2)	9	26	2	1	1	0	0	0	1	6	0	.038	.038
George Stallings	C4		4	11	1	0	0	0	0	0	1	3	0	.000	.000
Lady Baldwin	P2	(1-2)	2	3	1	0	0	0	0	0	1	1	0	.000	.000
			129	4419	884	1166	691	184	75	43	517	361	349	.264	.369

PITCHERS			W	L	PCT	G	GS	CG	SH	SV	IP	H	BB	SO	ERA
Tom Lovett			30	11	.732	44	41	39	4	0	372	327	141	124	2.78
Adonis Terry			26	16	.619	46	44	38	1	0	370	362	133	185	2.94
Bob Caruthers			23	11	.676	37	33	30	1	0	300	292	87	64	3.09
Mickey Hughes		(1-2)	4	4	.500	9	8	6	0	0	66	77	30	22	5.16
Dave Foutz			2	1	.667	5	2	2	0	2	29	29	6	4	1.86
Lady Baldwin		(1-2)	1	0	1.000	2	1	0	0	0	8	15	4	4	7.04
			86	43	.667	129	129	115	6	2	1145	1102	401	403	3.06

CHICAGO White Stockings 84-53 .613 -6 2nd Cap Anson

BATTERS	POS/GAMES		GP	AB	R	H	BI	2B	3B	HR	BB	SO	SB	BA	SA
Cap Anson	1B135,C3,2B2		139	504	95	157	107	14	5	7	113	23	29	.312	.401
Bob Glenalvin	2B66		66	250	43	67	26	10	3	4	19	31	30	.268	.380
Jim Cooney	SS135,C1		135	574	114	156	52	19	10	4	73	23	45	.272	.361
Tom Burns	3B139		139	538	86	149	86	17	6	5	57	45	44	.277	.359
Jim Andrews	OF53		53	202	32	38	17	4	2	3	23	41	11	.188	.272
Walt Wilmot	OF139		139	571	114	159	99	15	12	13	64	44	76	.278	.415
Cliff Carroll	OF136		136	582	134	166	65	16	6	7	53	34	34	.285	.369
Mal Kittredge	C96		96	333	46	67	35	8	3	3	39	53	7	.201	.270
Howard Earl	OF49,2B39,SS4,1B3		92	384	57	95	51	10	3	7	18	47	17	.247	.344
Bill Hutchinson	P71		71	261	28	53	27	7	2	2	13	63	6	.203	.268
Tom Nagle	C33,OF6		38	144	21	39	11	5	1	1	7	24	4	.271	.340
John Luby	P34,1B2		36	116	27	31	17	5	3	3	9	6	3	.267	.440
Peter O'Brien	2B27		27	106	15	30	16	7	0	3	5	10	4	.283	.434
Elmer Foster	OF27		27	105	20	26	23	4	2	5	9	21	18	.248	.467
Ed Stein	P20		20	59	4	9	7	1	0	0	7	20	1	.153	.169
Mike Sullivan	P12		12	40	1	5	7	1	0	0	2	12	0	.125	.150
Jake Stenzel	OF6,C6		11	41	3	11	3	1	0	0	1	0	0	.268	.293
Roscoe Coughlin	P11		11	39	5	10	1	1	1	0	2	12	0	.256	.333
Ed Hutchinson	2B4		4	17	0	1	0	1	0	0	0	0	0	.059	.118
Chuck Lauer	C2		2	8	1	2	2	1	0	0	0	0	0	.250	.250
Dad Lytle	OF1	(1-2)	1	4	1	0	0	0	0	0	0	1	0	.000	.000
Bob Gibson	P1	(1-2)	1	4	0	0		0	0	0	1	0	0	.000	.000
Marty Honan	C1		1	3	0	0	1	0	0	0	0	2	0	.000	.000
Pat Wright	2B1		1	2	0	0	0	0	0	0	1	0	0	.000	.000
Fred De Marais	P1		1	2	0	0	0	0	0	0	0	1	0	.000	.000
Ed Eiteljorg	P1		1	1	0	0	0	0	0	0	0	1	0	.000	.000
Ossie France	P1		1	1	0	0	0	0	0	0	0	0	0	.000	.000
			139	4891	847	1271	653	147	59	67	516	514	329	.260	.355

PITCHERS			W	L	PCT	G	GS	CG	SH	SV	IP	H	BB	SO	ERA
Bill Hutchinson			42	25	.627	71	66	65	5	2	603	505	199	289	2.70
John Luby			20	9	.690	34	31	26	0	1	268	226	95	85	3.19
Ed Stein			12	6	.667	20	18	14	1	0	161	147	83	65	3.81
Mike Sullivan			5	6	.455	12	12	10	0	0	96	108	58	33	4.59
Roscoe Coughlin			4	6	.400	11	10	10	0	0	95	102	40	29	4.26
Bob Gibson		(1-2)	1	0	1.000	1	1	1	0	0	9	6	2	1	0.00

CHICAGO (cont.)
White Stockings

PITCHERS		W	L	PCT	G	GS	CG	SH	SV	IP	H	BB	SO	ERA
Ed Eiteljorg		0	1	.000	1	1	0	0	0	2	5	1	1	22.50
Fred DeMarais		0	0	----	1	0	0	0	0	2	1	1	1	0.00
Ossie France		0	0	----	1	0	0	0	0	2	3	2	0	13.50
		84	53	.613	139	139	126	6	3	1237	1103	481	504	3.24

PHILADELPHIA
Phillies

78-54   .591   -9.5   3rd   Wright - Reach - Allen - Clements

BATTERS	POS/GAMES		GP	AB	R	H	BI	2B	3B	HR	BB	SO	SB	BA	SA
Allen McCauley	1B112		112	418	64	102	45	25	7	1	57	38	8	.244	.346
Al Myers	2B117		117	487	95	135	81	29	7	2	57	46	44	.277	.378
Bob Allen	SS133		133	456	69	103	57	15	11	2	87	54	13	.226	.320
Ed Mayer	3B117		117	484	50	117	70	25	5	1	22	36	20	.242	.320
Sam Thompson	OF132		132	549	117	172	103	41	9	4	42	29	25	.313	.443
Ed Burke	OF96,2B4	(1-2)	100	430	85	113	50	16	11	4	49	40	38	.263	.379
Billy Hamilton	OF123		123	496	133	161	49	13	9	2	83	37	102	.325	.399
Jack Clements	C91,1B5		97	381	65	120	74	23	8	7	45	30	10	.315	.472
Kid Gleason	P60,2B2		63	224	22	47	17	3	0	0	12	21	10	.210	.223
Pop Schriver	C34,1B10,3B8,2B3,OF2		57	223	37	61	35	9	6	0	22	15	9	.274	.368
Tom Vickery	P46		46	159	15	33	11	4	0	0	7	25	12	.208	.233
Bill Grey	OF10,3B8,2B8,C7,1B1		34	128	20	31	21	8	4	0	6	3	5	.242	.367
Billy Sunday	OF31	(2-2)	31	119	26	31	6	3	1	0	18	7	28	.261	.303
Phenomenal Smith	P24,OF3	(1-2)	26	86	15	24		4	0	0			6	.279	.326
Harry Decker	1B2,OF2,C1	(1-2)	5	19	5	7	2	1	0	0	4	1	4	.368	.421
Duke Esper	P5	(3-3)	5	19	2	3		1	0	0	0		0	.158	.211
Bill Day	P4	(1-2)	4	10	2	1	0	0	0	0	0		0	.100	.100
Dave Anderson	P3	(1-2)	3	9	0	1		0	0	0			0	.111	.111
Sumner Bowman	P1	(1-2)	1	4	0	2	0	0	0	0			0	.500	.500
John McFetridge	P1		1	4	0	3	1	0	0	0	0	1	0	.750	.750
Frank Motz	1B1		1	2	1	0	3	0	0	0	1	1	1	.000	.000
John Coleman	P1		1	0	0	0	0	0	0	0	0	0	0	----	----
			133	4707	823	1267	625	220	78	23	522	403	335	.269	.364

PITCHERS		W	L	PCT	G	GS	CG	SH	SV	IP	H	BB	SO	ERA
Kid Gleason		38	17	.691	60	55	54	6	2	506	479	167	222	2.63
Tom Vickery		24	22	.522	46	46	41	1	0	382	405	184	162	3.44
Phenomenal Smith	(1-2)	8	12	.400	24	20	19	1	0	204	209	89	81	4.28
Duke Esper	(3-3)	5	0	1.000	5	5	4	0	0	41	40	16	18	3.07
John McFetridge		1	0	1.000	1	1	1	0	0	9	5	2	4	1.00
Bill Day	(1-2)	1	1	.500	4	2	2	0	0	24	26	12	9	3.00
Dave Anderson	(1-2)	1	1	.500	3	2	1	0	0	19	31	11	7	7.58
John Coleman		0	1	.000	1	1	0	0	0	2	4	3	2	27.00
Sumner Bowman	(1-2)	0	0	----	1	1	0	0	0	8	11	2	2	7.88
		78	54	.591	133	133	122	9	2	1195	1210	486	507	3.32

CINCINNATI
Reds

77-55   .583   -10.5   4th   Tom Loftus

BATTERS	POS/GAMES		GP	AB	R	H	BI	2B	3B	HR	BB	SO	SB	BA	SA
Long John Reilly	1B132,OF1		133	553	114	166	86	25	26	6	16	41	29	.300	.472
Bid McPhee	2B132		132	528	125	135	39	16	22	3	82	26	55	.256	.386
Oliver Beard	SS113,3B9		122	492	64	132	72	17	15	3	44	13	30	.268	.382
Arlie Latham	3B41,OF1	(2-2)	41	164	35	41	15	6	2	0	23	18	20	.250	.311
Lefty Marr	OF64,3B63,SS3		130	527	91	158	73	17	12	1	46	29	44	.300	.383
Bug Holliday	OF131		131	518	93	140	75	18	14	4	49	36	50	.270	.382
Joe Knight	OF127		127	481	67	150	67	26	8	4	38	31	17	.312	.424
Jerry Harrington	C65		65	236	25	58	23	7	1	1	15	29	4	.246	.297
Tony Mullane	OF28,P25,3B21,SS10,1B1		81	286	41	79	34	9	8	0	39	30	19	.276	.364
Jim Keenan	C50,1B2,OF1,3B1		54	202	21	28	19	4	2	3	19	36	5	.139	.223
Hugh Nicol	OF46,SS3,2B1		50	186	28	39	19	1	4	0	19	12	24	.210	.258
Bill Rhines	P46		46	154	14	29	11	1	2	0	7	26	2	.188	.221
Jesse Duryea	P33,OF1		33	99	13	15	6	1	1	1	19	21	9	.152	.212
Frank Foreman	P25,OF1		25	75	13	10	7	1	3	1	10	13	0	.133	.267
Kid Baldwin	C20,OF2	(1-2)	22	72	5	11	10	0	0	0	3	6	2	.153	.153
Leon Viau	P13	(1-2)	13	36	2	5		0	0	0	3	7	2	.139	.139
Bill Clingman	SS6,2B1		7	27	2	7	5	1	0	0	1	0	0	.259	.296
John Dolan	P2		2	8	0	1	1	0	0	0	0	3	0	.125	.125
			134	4644	753	1204	562	150	120	27	433	377	312	.259	.361

1890 NATIONAL LEAGUE

CINCINNATI (cont.)
Reds

PITCHERS		W	L	PCT	G	GS	CG	SH	SV	IP	H	BB	SO	ERA
Bill Rhines		28	17	.622	46	45	45	6	0	401	337	113	182	1.95
Jesse Duryea		16	12	.571	33	32	29	2	0	274	270	60	108	2.92
Frank Foreman		13	10	.565	25	24	20	0	0	198	201	89	57	3.95
Tony Mullane		12	10	.545	25	21	21	0	1	209	175	96	91	2.24
Leon Viau	(1-2)	7	5	.583	13	10	7	1	0	90	97	39	41	4.50
John Dolan		1	1	.500	2	2	2	0	0	18	17	10	9	4.50
		77	55	.583	134	134	124	9	1	1191	1097	407	488	2.79

BOSTON
Beaneaters

76-57 .571 -12 5th Frank Selee

BATTERS	POS/GAMES		GP	AB	R	H	BI	2B	3B	HR	BB	SO	SB	BA	SA
Tommy Tucker	1B132		132	539	104	159	62	17	8	1	56	22	43	.295	.362
Pop Smith	2B134,SS1		134	463	82	106	53	16	12	1	80	81	39	.229	.322
Germany Long	SS101		101	431	95	108	52	15	3	8	40	34	49	.251	.355
Chippy McGarr	3B115,SS5,OF1		121	487	68	115	51	12	7	1	34	38	39	.236	.296
Steve Brodie	OF132		132	514	77	152	67	19	9	0	66	20	29	.296	.368
Paul Hines	OF69,1B1	(2-2)	69	273	41	72	48	12	3	2	32	20	9	.264	.352
Marty Sullivan	OF120,3B1		121	505	82	144	61	19	7	6	56	48	33	.285	.386
Charlie Bennett	C85		85	281	59	60	40	17	2	3	72	56	6	.214	.320
Bobby Lowe	SS24,OF15,3B12		52	207	35	58	21	13	2	2	26	32	15	.280	.391
Kid Nichols	P48,OF2		49	174	18	43	23	5	1	0	11	36	2	.247	.287
Lew Hardie	C25,OF15,3B7,SS1,1B1		47	185	17	42	17	8	0	3	18	36	4	.227	.319
John Clarkson	P44,OF1		45	173	18	43	26	6	3	2	8	31	2	.249	.353
Pretzels Getzien	P40,OF1		41	147	27	34	25	9	2	2	16	25	4	.231	.361
Charles Ganzel	C22,OF15,SS3,2B1		38	163	21	44	24	7	3	0	5	6	1	.270	.350
Patsy Donovan	OF32	(2-2)	32	140	17	36	9	0	0	0	8	17	10	.257	.257
Al Schellhasse	OF5,C2,SS1,3B1		9	29	1	4	1	0	0	0	1	10	0	.138	.138
John Taber	P2		2	6	1	0	0	0	0	0	0	1	0	.000	.000
Hon Fricken	P1		1	3	0	0	0	0	0	0	0	1	0	.000	.000
Al Lawson	P1	(1-2)	1	2	0	0	0	0	0	0	1	1	0	.000	.000
			134	4722	763	1220	580	175	62	31	530	515	285	.258	.341

PITCHERS		W	L	PCT	G	GS	CG	SH	SV	IP	H	BB	SO	ERA
Kid Nichols		27	19	.587	48	47	47	7	0	424	374	112	222	2.23
John Clarkson		26	18	.591	44	44	43	2	0	383	370	140	138	3.27
Pretzels Getzien		23	17	.575	40	40	39	4	0	350	342	82	140	3.19
John Taber		0	1	.000	2	1	1	0	1	13	11	8	3	4.15
Al Lawson	(1-2)	0	1	.000	1	1	1	0	0	9	12	4	1	4.00
Hon Fricken		0	1	.000	1	1	1	0	0	8	23	8	2	10.13
		76	57	.571	134	134	132	13	1	1187	1132	354	506	2.93

NEW YORK
Giants

63-68 .481 -24 6th Jim Mutrie

BATTERS	POS/GAMES		GP	AB	R	H	BI	2B	3B	HR	BB	SO	SB	BA	SA
Dude Esterbrook	1B45		45	197	29	57	29	14	1	0	10	8	12	.289	.371
Charley Bassett	2B100		100	410	52	98	54	13	8	0	29	25	14	.239	.310
Jack Glasscock	SS124		124	512	91	172	66	32	9	1	41	8	54	.336	.439
Jerry Denny	3B106,SS7,2B1		114	437	50	93	42	18	7	3	28	62	11	.213	.307
Jesse Burkett	OF90,P21		101	401	67	124	60	23	13	4	33	52	14	.309	.461
Mike Tiernan	OF133		133	553	132	168	59	25	21	13	68	53	56	.304	.495
Joe Hornung	OF77,1B36,3B5,SS2		120	513	62	122	65	18	5	0	12	37	39	.238	.292
Dick Buckley	C62,3B8		70	266	39	68	26	11	0	2	23	35	3	.256	.320
Archie Clarke	C36,OF33,3B16,2B15,SS1		101	395	55	89	49	12	8	0	32	38	44	.225	.296
Amos Rusie	P67,OF14		73	284	31	79	28	13	6	0	7	26	6	.278	.366
Lew Whistler	1B45		45	170	27	49	29	9	7	2	20	37	8	.288	.459
John Henry	OF37		37	144	19	35	16	6	0	0	7	12	12	.243	.285
Mickey Welch	P37		37	123	15	22	10	4	0	0	9	25	1	.179	.211
Pat Murphy	C29,OF3,SS1		32	119	14	28	9	5	1	0	14	13	3	.235	.294
John Sharrott	P25,OF9		32	109	16	22	14	3	2	0	0	14	6	.202	.266
Shorty Howe	2B18,3B1		19	64	4	11	4	0	0	0	3	2	3	.172	.172
Pete Sommers	C11,1B5,OF2	(1-2)	17	47	4	5	1	1	1	0	4	13	0	.106	.170
Reddy McMillan	OF10		10	35	4	5	1	0	0	0	7	4	1	.143	.143
Ed Daily	OF3,P2	(2-3)	4	15	1	2	1	1	0	0	0	4	0	.133	.200
Sam Crane	2B2,1B1,OF1	(1,3-3)	4	12	0	0	0	0	0	0	0	2	1	.000	.000
Mort Scanlon	1B3		3	10	0	0	0	0	0	0	2	5	0	.000	.000

NEW YORK (cont.)
Giants

BATTERS	POS/GAMES		GP	AB	R	H	RBI	2B	3B	HR	BB	SO	SB	BA	SA
Bob Murphy	P3		3	9	0	1	0	0	0	0	0	4	0	.111	.111
Tom O'Rourke	C2	(1-2)	2	7	1	0	0	0	0	0	1	0	0	.000	.000
			135	4832	713	1250	563	208	89	25	350	479	288	.259	.354

PITCHERS		W	L	PCT	G	GS	CG	SH	SV	IP	H	BB	SO	ERA
Amos Rusie		29	34	.460	67	63	56	4	1	549	436	289	341	2.56
Mickey Welch		17	14	.548	37	37	33	2	0	292	268	122	97	2.99
John Sharrott		11	10	.524	25	20	18	0	0	184	162	88	84	2.89
Jesse Burkett		3	10	.231	21	12	6	0	0	118	134	92	82	5.57
Ed Daily		2	0	1.000	2	1	1	0	0	16	6	6	0	2.25
Bob Murphy		1	0	1.000	3	2	1	0	0	18	23	10	8	5.50
		63	68	.481	135	135	115	6	1	1177	1029	607	612	3.06

CLEVELAND
Spiders

44-88 .333 -43.5 7th Schmelz - Leadley

BATTERS	POS/GAMES		GP	AB	R	H	BI	2B	3B	HR	BB	SO	SB	BA	SA
Peek A Boo Veach	1B64	(1-2)	64	238	24	56	32	10	5	0	33	28	9	.235	.319
Joe Ardner	2B84		84	323	28	72	35	13	1	0	17	40	9	.223	.269
Ed McKean	SS134,2B3		136	530	95	157	61	15	14	7	87	25	23	.296	.417
Will Smalley	3B136		136	502	62	107	42	11	1	0	60	44	10	.213	.239
Vince Dailey	OF64,P2		64	246	41	71	32	5	7	0	33	23	17	.289	.366
George Davis	OF133,2B2,SS1		136	526	98	139	73	22	9	6	53	34	22	.264	.375
Bob Gilks	OF123,P4,SS3,2B2		130	544	65	116	41	10	3	0	32	38	17	.213	.243
Chief Zimmer	C125		125	444	54	95	57	16	6	2	46	54	15	.214	.291
Jake Virtue	1B62		62	223	39	68	25	6	5	2	49	15	9	.305	.404
Eb Beatin	P54		54	191	25	27	21	4	3	1	12	43	2	.141	.209
Tom Dowse	OF26,1B10,C3,P1		40	159	20	33	9	2	1	0	12	22	3	.208	.233
Buck West	OF37		37	151	20	37	29	6	1	2	7	11	4	.245	.338
Bill Delancy	2B36		36	116	16	22	7	1	1	1	21	19	5	.190	.241
Jack Wadsworth	P20		20	68	6	12	7	2	0	0	2	18	1	.176	.206
Cy Young	P17		17	65	6	8	4	2	0	0	0	8	1	.123	.154
Ezra Lincoln	P15	(1-2)	15	51	4	8		1	0	0	2	15	0	.157	.176
Rasty Wright	OF13	(2-2)	13	45	7	5	2	1	0	0	12	4	3	.111	.133
Leon Viau	P13	(2-2)	13	43	6	7		1	0	0	4	8	2	.163	.167
Pat Lyons	2B11		11	38	2	2	1	1	0	0	4	4	0	.053	.079
Joe Sommer	OF9,P1	(1-2)	9	35	4	8	0	1	0	0	2	2	0	.229	.257
Pete Sommers	C8,OF1	(2-2)	9	34	4	7	1	1	1	0	2	3	0	.206	.294
Bill Garfield	P9		9	26	0	4	2	0	0	0	3	12	0	.154	.154
Edgar Smith	P6,OF2		8	24	2	7	4	0	1	0	4	1	0	.292	.375
Leonard Stockwell	OF1,1B1		2	7	2	2	0	1	0	0	0	3	0	.286	.429
Charles Parsons	P2		2	4	0	3	2	0	0	0	0	0	0	.750	.750
			136	4633	630	1073	487	132	59	21	497	474	152	.232	.299

PITCHERS		W	L	PCT	G	GS	CG	SH	SV	IP	H	BB	SO	ERA
Eb Beatin		22	30	.423	54	54	53	1	0	474	518	186	155	3.83
Cy Young		9	7	.563	17	16	16	0	0	148	145	32	36	3.47
Leon Viau	(2-2)	4	9	.308	13	13	13	1	0	107	101	42	30	3.36
Ezra Lincoln	(1-2)	3	11	.214	15	15	13	0	0	118	157	53	22	4.42
Bob Gilks		2	2	.500	4	3	3	0	0	32	34	9	5	4.26
Jack Wadsworth		2	16	.111	20	19	19	0	0	170	202	81	26	5.20
Edgar Smith		1	4	.200	6	6	5	0	0	44	42	10	11	4.30
Bill Garfield		1	7	.125	9	8	7	0	0	70	91	35	16	4.89
Charles Parsons		0	1	.000	2	1	0	0	0	9	12	6	2	6.00
Vince Dailey		0	1	.000	2	1	0	0	0	7	12	7	0	7.71
Tom Dowse		0	0	----	1	0	0	0	0	5	6	1	0	5.40
Joe Sommer		0	0	----	1	0	0	0	0	1	2	2	0	0.00
		44	88	.333	136	136	129	2	0	1184	1322	464	303	4.13

PITTSBURGH
Alleghenys

23-113 .169 -66.5 8th Guy Hecker

BATTERS	POS/GAMES	GP	AB	R	H	BI	2B	3B	HR	BB	SO	SB	BA	SA
Guy Hecker	1B69,P14,OF7	86	340	43	77	38	13	9	0	19	17	13	.226	.318
Sam LaRoque	2B78,SS31,1B2,OF1	111	434	59	105	40	20	4	1	35	29	27	.242	.313
Ed Sales	SS51	51	189	19	43	23	7	3	1	16	15	3	.228	.312

1890 NATIONAL LEAGUE

PITTSBURGH (cont.)
Alleghenys

BATTERS	POS/GAMES		GP	AB	R	H	BI	2B	3B	HR	BB	SO	SB	BA	SA
Doggie Miller	3B88,OF25,SS13,C10,2B6		138	549	85	150	66	24	3	4	68	11	32	.273	.350
Billy Sunday	OF86,P1	(1-2)	86	358	58	92	33	9	2	1	32	20	56	.257	.302
Tun Berger	OF41,SS33,C21,2B6,3B1		104	391	64	104	40	18	4	0	35	23	11	.266	.332
John Kelty	OF59		59	207	24	49	27	10	2	1	22	42	10	.237	.319
Harry Decker	C70,1B16,OF5,2B1,SS1	(2-2)	92	354	52	97	38	14	3	5	26	36	8	.274	.373
Bill Wilson	C38,OF25,1B18,SS1		83	304	30	65	21	11	3	0	22	50	5	.214	.270
Fred Roat	3B44,1B9,OF4		57	215	18	48	17	2	0	2	16	22	7	.223	.260
Fred Osborne	OF35,P8		41	168	24	40	14	8	3	1	6	18	0	.238	.339
Mike Jordan	OF37		37	125	8	12	6	1	0	0	15	19	5	.096	.104
Ed Burke	OF31	(2-2)	31	124	17	26	7	5	2	1	14	9	6	.210	.306
Paul Hines	1B17,OF14	(1-2)	31	121	11	22	9	1	0	0	11	7	6	.182	.190
Kirtley Baker	P26		26	68	6	10	0	0	0	0	10	6	1	.147	.147
Sam Crane	2B15,SS7,OF1	(2-3)	22	82	3	16	3	3	0	0	0	5	5	.195	.232
Ducky Hemp	OF21	(1-2)	21	81	9	19	4	0	2	0	8	12	3	.235	.284
Fred Dunlap	2B17	(1-2)	17	64	9	11	3	1	1	0	7	6	2	.172	.219
Bill Sowders	P15,OF2		17	50	3	9	4	0	0	0	2	7	1	.180	.180
Dad Lytle	2B8,OF7	(2-2)	15	55	2	8	0	1	0	0	8	9	0	.145	.164
Bill Phillips	P10,OF4		14	46	6	11	2	2	0	0	3	13	0	.239	.283
Henry Youngman	3B7,2B6		13	47	6	6	4	1	1	0	6	9	1	.128	.191
Dave Anderson	P13	(2-2)	13	42	5	3		0	0	0			0	.071	.071
Charlie Heard	P6,OF6		12	43	2	8	0	2	0	0	1	15	0	.186	.233
Crazy Schmit	P11		11	33	4	2	0	0	0	0	5	8	2	.061	.061
Bill Gumbert	P10,1B1		10	37	8	9	7	3	0	1	2	5	1	.243	.405
Sumner Bowman	P9,OF1	(2-2)	10	36	7	10		1	0	0			0	.278	.306
Peek A Boo Veach	1B8	(2-2)	8	30	6	9	5	1	1	2	8	3	0	.300	.600
Bill Day	P6	(2-2)	6	23	0	1		0	0	0	0		0	.043	.043
Phenomenal Smith	P5	(2-2)	5	17	3	7		0	0	0			0	.412	.412
Charlie Gray	P5		5	15	1	3	3	1	0	0	0	5	0	.200	.267
Henry Jones	P5		5	9	0	2	0	0	0	0	0	0	1	.222	.222
Peter Daniels	P4		4	12	1	4	2	1	0	0	1	2	0	.333	.417
Jack Coleman	P2,OF2		3	11	1	2	0	0	0	0	3	0	1	.182	.182
Bob Gibson	P3	(2-2)	3	13	1	3		0	0	0	0	3	0	.231	.231
Al Lawson	P2	(2-2)	2	4	0	0	0	0	0	0	0	2	0	.000	.000
Harry Gilbert	2B2		2	8	1	2	0	0	0	0	0	3	0	.250	.250
John Gilbert	SS2		2	8	0	0	0	0	0	0	0	2	0	.000	.000
Duke Esper	P2	(2-3)	2	7	0	1		0	0	0	0		0	.143	.143
Philip Routcliffe	OF1		1	4	1	1	1	0	0	0	0	0	1	.250	.250
Frank McGinn	OF1		1	4	0	0	0	0	0	0	0	2	0	.000	.000
Reddy Gray	SS1	(2-2)	1	3	0	0	0	0	0	0	0	1	0	.000	.000
Fred Truax	OF1		1	3	0	1	1	0	0	0	1	1	0	.333	.333
John Heyner	P1		1	2	0	0	0	0	0	0	0	0	0	.000	.000
George Ziegler	P1		1	2	0	0	0	0	0	0	0	0	0	.000	.000
Ed Clements	SS1		1	1	0	0	0	0	0	0	0	0	0	.000	.000
			138	4739	597	1088	418	160	43	20	408	458	208	.230	.294

PITCHERS			W	L	PCT	G	GS	CG	SH	SV	IP	H	BB	SO	ERA
Ad Gumbert			4	6	.400	10	10	8	0	0	79	96	31	18	5.22
Bill Sowders			3	8	.273	15	11	9	0	0	106	117	24	30	4.42
Kirtley Baker			3	19	.136	25	21	19	2	0	178	209	86	76	5.60
Henry Jones			2	1	.667	5	4	2	0	0	31	35	14	13	3.48
Sumner Bowman		(2-2)	2	5	.286	9	7	6	0	0	71	100	50	22	6.59
Dave Anderson		(2-2)	2	11	.154	13	13	13	0	0	108	116	49	41	4.67
Guy Hecker			2	12	.143	14	12	11	0	0	119	160	44	32	5.11
Peter Daniels			1	2	.333	4	4	3	0	0	28	40	12	8	7.07
Phenomenal Smith		(2-2)	1	3	.250	5	5	5	0	0	44	39	13	15	3.07
Charlie Gray			1	4	.200	5	4	3	0	0	31	48	24	10	7.55
Crazy Schmit			1	9	.100	11	10	9	1	0	83	108	42	35	5.83
Bill Phillips			1	9	.100	10	10	9	0	0	82	123	29	25	7.57
George Ziegler			0	1	.000	1	1	0	0	0	6	12	0	1	10.50
Al Lawson		(2-2)	0	2	.000	2	2	1	0	0	10	15	10	2	9.00
Duke Esper		(2-3)	0	2	.000	2	2	2	0	0	17	18	10	9	5.29
Jack Coleman			0	2	.000	2	2	1	0	0	14	28	6	3	9.64
Bob Gibson		(2-2)	0	3	.000	3	3	2	0	0	12	24	23	3	17.25
Fred Osborne			0	5	.000	8	5	5	0	0	58	82	45	14	8.38
Bill Day		(2-2)	0	6	.000	6	6	6	0	0	50	66	24	10	5.22
Charlie Heard			0	6	.000	6	6	5	0	0	44	75	32	13	8.39
John Heyner			0	0	----	1	0	0	0	0	4	7	5	1	13.50
Billy Sunday			0	0	----	1	0	0	0	0	0	2	0	0	inf.
			23	113	.169	138	138	119	3	0	1176	1520	573	381	5.97

1890 AMERICAN ASSOCIATION

The Last Shall Be First

In 1889, Louisville finished in last place. Not an ordinary last place, but a purely awful last place with the worst record in the American Association's history. It was then a great surprise to all that the Louisville Colonels, with the same core of players, won the pennant handily in 1890.

The Players' League stripped the National League clean in 1890, but they also took over 30 players from the rosters of the association. Almost every team lost several players, but Louisville lost only Pete Browning. In addition, the 1889 pennant winners, Brooklyn, left the league to join the National League. So it was not the case of Louisville being suddenly blessed with an influx of new stars. It was rather the case that the rest of the league was bereft of talent, coupled with departed teams. Thus comparatively, Louisville emerged as one of the stronger teams.

The National League convinced the Cincinnati American Association franchise to join their ranks. In addition, the Baltimore and Kansas City franchises folded. At the last minute, the American Association was forced to add four new clubs to keep the league afloat. Teams from Toledo, Rochester, Syracuse, and a new team from Brooklyn were pasted onto the league structure. Louisville was one of only four teams to survive intact in the American Association from the previous year.

The American Association was the weakest of the three leagues, so it was no surprise that it failed to get through the season intact. The Brooklyn franchise, competing with two other major league teams and in last place, folded on August 25. A new team from Baltimore was added to fill out the schedule.

Louisville won the pennant by ten games with both the best hitting and pitching in the league. They were led in each department by career years from two veterans. Outfielder Chicken Wolf led the circuit with a .363 average and 197 hits. Pitcher Scott Stratton set a personal record with 34 wins, leading the league with a 2.36 earned run average.

Second place Columbus was led by one-year wonder Spud Johnson (.346), helped by teammate Jim McTamany's 140 runs (20 more than his hits). Hank Gastright also pitched in by winning 30.

St. Louis dropped to third with almost a whole new team, as no starters remained from their glory years. Part time outfielder Count Campau won the home run crown with nine, part time first baseman Ed Cartwright (.300) hit well, and full time outfielder Tommy McCarthy helped with his .350 average.

Two new teams, Toledo four games over .500, and Rochester right at .500, finished in fourth and fifth. Ed Swartwood of Toledo (.327), and Sandy Griffin (.307) of Rochester were their best players.

Baltimore, Syracuse, Philadelphia, and Brooklyn finished next. The best players from this group were Cupid Childs (.345) from Syracuse, and pitcher Sadie McMahon who won a league best 36 while splitting time between Philadelphia and Baltimore.

Following their surprising pennant, Louisville squared off against Brooklyn in what would prove to be the last, and quite possibly the best, World Series of the nineteenth century. The first four games were played in Louisville, of which Brooklyn won two and Louisville one (one finished in a tie). Brooklyn won the next game in their home park to take a commanding three games to one lead. But Louisville rallied to take the next two games, 9-8, and 6-2, to knot the series at three. And that is where it remained, as cold weather canceled the rest of the games.

Louisville's pennant-winning turnaround, although accomplished with much help, was remarkable. They improved by 59 wins and 469 percentage points over the space of only one year. Other teams have gone from last to first, but never to this degree.

1890 AMERICAN ASSOCIATION

LOUISVILLE Colonels   88-44   .667   1st   Jack Chapman

BATTERS	POS/GAMES		GP	AB	R	H	BI	2B	3B	HR	BB	SO	SB	BA	SA
Harry Taylor	1B118,SS12,2B4,C1		134	553	115	169		7	7	0	68		45	.306	.382
Tim Shinnick	2B130,3B3		133	493	87	126		16	11	1	62		62	.256	.339
Phil Tomney	SS108		108	386	72	107		21	7	1	43		27	.277	.376
Harry Raymond	3B119,SS4		123	521	91	135		7	4	2	22		18	.259	.299
Chicken Wolf	OF123,3B12		134	543	100	197		29	11	4	43		46	.363	.479
Farmer Weaver	OF127,SS2,3B1		130	557	101	161		27	9	3	29		45	.289	.386
Charlie Hamburg	OF133		133	485	93	132		22	2	3	69		46	.272	.344
Jack Ryan	C89,OF3,SS1,1B1		93	337	43	73		16	4	0	12		6	.217	.288
Scott Stratton	P50,OF5		55	189	29	61		3	5	0	16		8	.323	.392
Red Ehret	P43		43	146	11	31		2	1	0	1		1	.212	.240
Pete Weckbecker	C32		32	101	17	24		1	0	0	8		7	.238	.248
George Meakim	P28,OF1		29	72	6	11		0	0	0	8		8	.153	.153
Ned Bligh	C24	(2-2)	24	73	9	15		0	0	1	9		1	.205	.293
Ed Daily	OF13,P10	(3-3)	23	80	24	20		0	2	0	13		13	.250	.355
Herb Goodall	P18,OF1		19	45	10	19		2	0	0	1		0	.422	.467
Dan Phelan	1B8		8	32	4	8		1	1	0	0		1	.250	.344
Henry Easterday	SS6,3B1	(3-3)	7	24	2	2		0	0	0	2		1	.083	.083
Dan O'Connor	1B6		6	26	3	12		1	1	0	1		5	.462	.577
Mike Jones	P3		3	9	1	4		0	0	0	2		0	.444	.444
Chief Roseman	1B2	(2-2)	2	8	0	2		0	0	0	0		0	.250	.250
Peter Sweeney	SS2	(2-2)	2	7	1	1		1	0	0	1		1	.143	.286
			136	4687	819	1310		156	65	15	410	460	341	.279	.350

PITCHERS			W	L	PCT	G	GS	CG	SH	SV	IP	H	BB	SO	ERA
Scott Stratton			34	14	.708	50	49	44	4	0	431	398	61	207	2.36
Red Ehret			25	14	.641	43	38	35	4	2	359	351	79	174	2.53
George Meakim			12	7	.632	28	21	16	3	1	192	173	63	123	2.91
Herb Goodall			8	5	.615	18	13	8	1	4	109	94	51	46	3.39
Ed Daily		(3-3)	6	3	.667	12	10	9	1	0	93	83	30	31	1.94
Mike Jones			2	0	1.000	3	3	2	0	0	22	21	9	6	3.27
			88	44	.667	136	134	114	13	7	1206	1120	293	587	2.57

COLUMBUS Buckeyes   79-55   .590   -10   2nd   Buckenberger - Schmelz - Sullivan

BATTERS	POS/GAMES		GP	AB	R	H	BI	2B	3B	HR	BB	SO	SB	BA	SA
Mike Lehane	1B140		140	512	54	108		19	5	0	43		13	.211	.275
Jack Crooks	2B133,3B2,OF1		135	485	86	107		5	4	1	96		57	.221	.254
Henry Easterday	SS58	(1-3)	58	197	25	31		5	1	1	23		5	.157	.208
Charlie Reilly	3B136,2B1		137	530	75	141		23	3	4	35		43	.266	.343
John Sneed	OF126,SS2	(2-2)	128	484	114	141		13	15	2	63		39	.291	.393
Jim McTamany	OF125		125	466	140	120		27	7	1	112		43	.258	.352
Spud Johnson	OF135		135	538	106	186		23	18	1	48		43	.346	.461
Jack O'Connor	C106,OF9,SS8,2B2,3B1		121	457	89	148		14	10	2	38		29	.324	.411
Jack Doyle	C38,SS25,OF9,2B6,3B3		77	298	47	80		17	7	2	13		27	.268	.393
Bobby Wheelock	SS52		52	190	24	45		6	1	1	25		34	.237	.295
Hank Gastright	P48		48	169	18	36		2	2	0	13		1	.213	.249
John Easton	P37,OF2,SS2,2B1		41	107	14	19		0	2	0	10		6	.178	.215
Frank Knauss	P37		37	106	18	24		0	2	1	12		6	.226	.292
Icebox Chamberlain	P25	(2-2)	25	65	8	15		3	0	0	7		2	.231	.277
Sam Nichol	OF14		14	56	7	9		0	0	0	2		3	.161	.161
Wild Bill Widner	P13		13	41	3	8		0	0	0	2		2	.195	.195
Ned Bligh	C8	(1-2)	8	29	2	6		2	0	0	2		0	.207	.276
John Munyan	OF2	(2-2)	2	7	1	1		0	0	0	0		0	.143	.143
Al Mays	P1		1	3	0	0		0	0	0	1		0	.000	.000
Tom Ford	P1	(1-2)	1	1	0	0		0	0	0	0		0	.000	.000
			140	4741	831	1225		159	77	16	545	557	353	.258	.335

PITCHERS			W	L	PCT	G	GS	CG	SH	SV	IP	H	BB	SO	ERA
Hank Gastright			30	14	.682	48	45	41	4	0	401	312	135	199	2.94
Frank Knauss			17	12	.586	37	34	28	3	2	276	206	106	148	2.80
John Easton			15	14	.517	37	29	23	0	1	256	213	125	147	3.52
Icebox Chamberlain		(2-2)	12	6	.667	25	21	19	6	0	175	128	70	114	2.21
Wild Bill Widner			4	8	.333	13	10	8	1	0	96	103	24	14	3.28
Al Mays			0	1	.000	1	1	1	0	0	9	14	8	2	8.00
Tom Ford		(1-2)	0	0	----	1	1	0	0	0	2	0	3	0	0.00
			79	55	.590	140	140	120	14	3	1215	976	471	624	2.99

1890 AMERICAN ASSOCIATION

ST. LOUIS 78-58 .574 -12 3rd McCarthy - Kerins - Rose-
Browns man - Campau - Gerhardt

BATTERS	POS/GAMES		GP	AB	R	H	BI	2B	3B	HR	BB	SO	SB	BA	SA
Ed Cartwright	1B75		75	300	70	90		12	4	8	29		26	.300	.447
Bill Higgins	2B67	(1-2)	67	258	39	65		6	2	0	24		7	.252	.291
Shorty Fuller	SS130		130	526	118	146		9	9	1	73		60	.278	.335
Peter Sweeney	2B23,3B21,1B3,OF2	(1-2)	49	190	23	34		3	2	0	17		8	.179	.216
Tommy McCarthy	OF102,3B32,2B1		133	548	137	192		28	9	6	66		83	.350	.467
Charlie Duffee	OF66,3B33,SS1		98	378	68	104		11	7	3	37		20	.275	.365
Count Campau	OF74,3B1,1B1		75	314	68	101		9	12	9	26		36	.322	.513
John Munyan	C83,OF7,2B5,3B3,SS1	(2-2)	96	342	61	91		15	7	4	32		11	.266	.386
Chief Roseman	OF58,1B22	(1-2)	80	302	47	103		26	0	2	30		7	.341	.447
Jack Stivetts	P54,OF10,1B3		67	226	36	65		15	6	7	16		2	.288	.500
Tom Gettinger	OF58		58	227	31	54		7	5	3	20		8	.238	.352
Toad Ramsey	P44		44	145	17	33		6	1	0	5		0	.228	.283
Joe Gerhardt	2B20,3B17	(2-2)	37	125	15	32		0	0	1	9		5	.256	.280
Jake Wells	C28,OF3		30	105	17	25		3	0	0	10		1	.238	.267
Bill Hart	P26,OF1		27	78	7	15		1	0	1	9		1	.192	.244
Dusty Miller	OF24,SS3		26	96	17	21		5	3	1	8		4	.219	.365
Billy Earle	C18,OF3,SS1,3B1,1B1		22	73	16	17		3	1	0	7		6	.233	.301
Jumbo Davis	3B21	(1-2)	21	71	8	18		3	1	0	9		5	.254	.324
John Kerins	1B17,C1		18	63	8	8		2	0	0	8		2	.127	.159
Mike Trost	C13,OF4		17	51	10	13		2	0	1	6		4	.255	.353
Bill Whitrock	P16,OF1		16	48	7	7		3	0	0	2		0	.146	.208
Billy Klusman	2B15		15	65	9	18		4	1	1	1		1	.277	.415
Pat Hartnett	1B14		14	53	6	10		2	1	0	6		1	.189	.264
Ed Herr	2B7,OF4,3B1		12	41	5	9		2	1	0	5		2	.220	.317
Jim Donnelly	3B11		11	42	11	14		0	0	0	8		5	.333	.333
Joe Neale	P10,OF1		11	30	4	2		0	0	0	3		0	.067	.067
Jerry Kane	1B5,C4		8	25	3	5		0	0	0	2		0	.200	.200
Icebox Chamberlain	P5	(1-2)	5	15	1	2		0	0	0	0		0	.133	.133
Dad Meek	C4		4	16	3	5		0	0	0	0		1	.313	.313
Gus Creely	SS4		4	15	0	0		0	0	0	0		1	.000	.000
Ed Pabst	OF4	(2-2)	4	14	1	2		0	1	0	0		0	.143	.286
George Nicol	P3		3	7	4	2		1	0	0	4		0	.286	.429
Joe Burke	3B2		2	6	3	4		0	0	0	1		0	.667	.667
Jim Adams	C1		1	4	0	1		0	0	0	0		0	.250	.250
Frank Millard	2B1		1	1	0	0		0	0	0	1		0	.000	.000
			139	4800	870	1308		178	73	48	474	490	307	.273	.370

PITCHERS			W	L	PCT	G	GS	CG	SH	SV	IP	H	BB	SO	ERA
Jack Stivetts			27	21	.563	54	46	41	3	0	419	399	179	289	3.52
Toad Ramsey			24	17	.585	44	40	34	1	0	349	325	102	257	3.69
Bill Hart			12	8	.600	26	24	20	0	0	201	188	66	95	3.67
Joe Neale			5	3	.625	10	9	8	0	0	69	53	15	23	3.39
Bill Whitrock			5	6	.455	16	11	10	0	0	105	104	40	39	3.51
Icebox Chamberlain		(1-2)	3	1	.750	5	5	3	0	0	35	47	26	14	5.91
George Nicol			2	1	.667	3	3	2	0	0	17	11	19	16	4.76
			78	58	.574	139	138	118	4	1	1195	1127	447	733	3.67

TOLEDO 68-64 .515 -20 4th Charlie Morton
Maumees

BATTERS	POS/GAMES		GP	AB	R	H	BI	2B	3B	HR	BB	SO	SB	BA	SA
Perry Werden	1B124,OF5		128	498	113	147		22	20	6	78		59	.295	.456
Parson Nicholson	2B134,C1		134	523	78	140		16	11	4	42		46	.268	.363
Frank Scheibeck	SS134		134	485	72	117		13	5	1	76		57	.241	.295
Bill Alvord	3B116		116	495	69	135		13	16	2	22		21	.273	.376
Ed Swartwood	OF126,P1		126	462	106	151		23	11	3	80		53	.327	.444
White Wings Tebeau	OF94,P1		94	381	71	102		16	10	1	51		55	.268	.370
Bill Van Dyke	OF110,3B18,2B2,C1		129	502	74	129		14	11	2	25		73	.257	.341
Henry Sage	C80,OF1		81	275	40	41		8	4	2	29		10	.149	.229
Charles Sprague	OF40,P19		55	199	25	47		5	6	1	16		10	.236	.337
Egyptian Healy	P46,1B2		48	156	27	34		7	4	1	15		7	.218	.333
Ed Cushman	P40		40	130	9	13		0	2	0	10		4	.100	.131
Fred Smith	P35,OF3		38	126	11	21		7	1	0	8		4	.167	.238
Emmett Rogers	C34,OF1		35	110	18	19		3	3	0	14		2	.173	.255
Tub Welch	C25,1B10		35	108	15	31		3	1	1	8		7	.287	.361
John Peltz	OF20	(3-3)	20	73	8	18		2	2	0	3		7	.247	.329
John Sneed	OF9	(1-2)	9	30	3	6		0	0	0	8		5	.200	.200
Dan Abbott	P3		3	7	0	1		0	1	0	0		1	.143	.429
Ed O'Neil	P2	(2-2)	2	9	0	0		0	0	0	0		0	.000	.000

TOLEDO (cont.)
Maumees

BATTERS	POS/GAMES		GP	AB	R	H	BI	2B	3B	HR	BB	SO	SB	BA	SA
Babe Doty	P1		1	3	0	0		0	0	0	1		0	.000	.000
Floyd Ritter	C1		1	3	0	0		0	0	0	0		0	.000	.000
			134	4575	739	1152		152	108	24	486	558	421	.252	.348

PITCHERS		W	L	PCT	G	GS	CG	SH	SV	IP	H	BB	SO	ERA
Egyptian Healy		22	21	.512	46	46	44	2	0	389	326	127	225	2.89
Fred Smith		19	13	.594	35	34	31	2	0	286	273	90	116	3.27
Ed Cushman		17	21	.447	40	38	34	0	1	316	346	107	125	4.19
Charles Sprague		9	5	.643	19	12	9	0	0	123	111	78	59	3.89
Babe Doty		1	0	1.000	1	1	1	0	0	9	9	1	4	1.00
Ed O'Neil	(1-2)	0	2	.000	2	2	2	0	0	16	27	13	2	7.88
Dan Abbott		0	2	.000	3	1	1	0	1	13	19	8	1	6.23
White Wings Tebeau		0	0	----	1	0	0	0	0	5	9	5	0	9.00
Ed Swartwood		0	0	----	1	0	0	0	0	3	2	0	1	11.57
		68	64	.515	134	134	122	4	2	1159	1122	429	533	3.56

ROCHESTER
Hop Bitters

63-63 .500 -22 5th Pat Powers

BATTERS	POS/GAMES		GP	AB	R	H	BI	2B	3B	HR	BB	SO	SB	BA	SA
Tom O'Brien	1B68,2B8		73	273	36	52		6	5	0	30		6	.190	.249
Bill Greenwood	2B123,SS1		124	437	76	97		11	6	2	48		40	.222	.288
Marr Phillips	SS64		64	257	18	53		8	0	0	16		10	.206	.237
Jimmy Knowles	3B123		123	491	83	138		12	8	5	59		55	.281	.369
Ted Scheffler	OF119,C1		119	445	111	109		12	6	3	78		77	.245	.319
Sandy Griffin	OF107,2B1		107	407	85	125		28	4	5	50		21	.307	.432
Harry Lyons	OF132,3B2,C1,P1		133	584	83	152		11	11	3	27		47	.260	.332
Deacon McGuire	C71,1B15,OF3,P1		87	331	46	99		16	4	4	21		8	.299	.408
Dave McKeough	C47,SS13,2B2,3B1		62	218	38	49		5	0	0	29		14	.225	.248
Bob Barr	P57		57	201	22	36		2	0	2	13		1	.179	.219
Jim Field	1B51,P2		52	188	30	38		7	5	4	21		8	.202	.356
John Grim	SS21,C15,3B8,2B4,OF3,1B2,P1		50	192	30	51		6	9	2	7		14	.266	.422
Will Calihan	P37,OF13		48	159	16	23		4	2	1	8		2	.145	.214
Leo Smith	SS35		35	112	11	21		1	3	0	14		1	.188	.250
Dan Burke	OF29,C4,1B2	(1-2)	32	102	14	22		1	0	0	17		2	.216	.225
Ledell Titcomb	P20,3B1,2B1		21	75	3	8		0	1	0	3		0	.107	.133
Bob Miller	P13,OF3		15	40	3	6		1	0	0	3		0	.150	.175
John Fitzgerald	P11		11	31	1	6		0	0	0	2		1	.194	.194
Henry Blauvelt	P2		2	6	3	3		0	0	0	0		3	.500	.500
Phil Reccius	OF1		1	4	0	0		0	0	0	0		0	.000	.000
			133	4553	709	1088		131	64	31	446	538	310	.239	.316

PITCHERS		W	L	PCT	G	GS	CG	SH	SV	IP	H	BB	SO	ERA
Bob Barr		28	24	.538	57	54	52	3	0	493	458	219	209	3.25
Will Calihan		18	15	.545	37	36	31	0	0	296	276	125	127	3.28
Ledell Titcomb		10	9	.526	20	19	19	1	0	169	168	97	73	3.74
Bob Miller		3	7	.300	13	12	11	0	1	92	89	26	20	4.29
John Fitzgerald		3	8	.273	11	11	8	1	0	78	77	45	35	4.40
Jim Field		1	0	1.000	2	1	1	0	1	10	7	4	2	2.79
Henry Blauvelt		0	0	----	2	0	0	0	0	12	19	8	5	10.22
Deacon McGuire		0	0	----	1	0	0	0	0	4	10	1	1	6.75
Harry Lyons		0	0	----	1	0	0	0	0	4	8	1	2	12.27
John Grim		0	0	----	1	0	0	0	0	3	3	4	3	0.00
		63	63	.500	133	133	122	5	2	1162	1115	530	477	3.56

BALTIMORE
Orioles

15-19 .441 -24 6th Billy Barnie

BATTERS	POS/GAMES		GP	AB	R	H	BI	2B	3B	HR	BB	SO	SB	BA	SA
Tom Power	1B26,OF12		38	125	11	26		3	1	0	13		6	.208	.248
Reddy Mack	2B26		26	95	14	27		3	5	0	10		7	.284	.421
Irv Ray	SS38		38	139	28	50		6	2	1	15		11	.360	.453
Pete Gilbert	3B29		29	100	25	28		2	1	1	10		12	.280	.350
Bill Johnson	OF24		24	95	15	28		2	3	0	7		8	.295	.379
Dan Long	OF21		21	77	19	12		0	0	0	14		16	.156	.156
Joe Sommer	OF38	(2-2)	38	129	13	33		4	2	0	13		10	.256	.318
George Townshend	C18		18	67	6	16		4	1	0	4		3	.239	.328

1890 AMERICAN ASSOCIATION

BALTIMORE (cont.)
Orioles

BATTERS	POS/GAMES		GP	AB	R	H	BI	2B	3B	HR	BB	SO	SB	BA	SA
Pop Tate	C11,1B8		19	71	7	13		1	1	0	4		3	.183	.225
Curt Welch	OF17,1B2	(2-2)	19	68	16	9		4	0	0	9		8	.132	.191
Les German	P17		17	51	7	6		1	0	0	8		5	.118	.137
Wilbert Robinson	C11,1B3	(2-2)	14	48	7	13		1	0	0	3		1	.271	.292
Sadie McMahon	P12	(2-2)	12	39	4	4		0	0	0	1		2	.103	.103
Joe McGuckin	OF11		11	37	2	4		0	0	0	6		3	.108	.108
Belden Hill	3B9		9	30	3	5		2	0	0	3		6	.167	.233
Mike O'Rourke	P5,OF3		8	26	5	3		1	0	0	5		0	.115	.154
Mike Morrison	P4	(2-2)	4	9	0	1		0	0	0	0		0	.111	.111
Norman Baker	P2		2	7	0	0		0	0	0	0		0	.000	.000
			38	1213	182	278		34	16	2	125	152	101	.229	.289

PITCHERS		W	L	PCT	G	GS	CG	SH	SV	IP	H	BB	SO	ERA
Sadie McMahon	(2-2)	7	3	.700	12	11	11	1	0	99	84	33	66	3.00
Les German		5	11	.313	17	16	15	0	0	132	147	54	37	4.83
Norman Baker		1	1	.500	2	2	2	0	0	17	16	6	10	3.71
Mike O'Rourke		1	2	.333	5	5	5	0	0	41	45	10	8	3.95
Mike Morrison	(2-2)	1	2	.333	4	4	3	0	0	26	15	20	13	3.81
		15	19	.441	38	38	36	1	0	315	307	123	134	4.00

SYRACUSE
Stars

55-72   .433   -30.5   7th   Frazer - Fessenden

BATTERS	POS/GAMES		GP	AB	R	H	BI	2B	3B	HR	BB	SO	SB	BA	SA
Mox McQuery	1B122		122	461	64	142		17	6	2	53		26	.308	.384
Cupid Childs	2B125,SS1		126	493	109	170		33	14	2	72		56	.345	.481
Barney McLaughlin	SS86		86	329	43	87		8	1	2	47		13	.264	.313
Tim O'Rourke	3B87		87	332	48	94		13	6	1	36		22	.283	.367
Pat Friel	OF62		62	261	51	65		8	2	3	17		34	.249	.330
Rasty Wright	OF88	(1-2)	88	348	82	106		10	6	0	69		30	.305	.368
Bones Ely	OF78,SS36,1B4,2B2,3B1,P1		119	496	72	130		16	6	0	31		44	.262	.319
Grant Briggs	C46,OF33,3B5,SS4		86	316	44	57		6	5	0	16		7	.180	.231
Dan Casey	P45,OF1		46	160	11	26		5	2	0	6		3	.163	.219
John Keefe	P43		43	157	10	30		0	0	0	3		0	.191	.191
Tom O'Rourke	C40,1B1	(2-2)	41	153	16	33		8	0	0	12		2	.216	.268
Henry Simon	OF38	(2-2)	38	156	33	47		5	3	2	17		12	.301	.410
Mike Morrison	P17,OF16,SS1	(1-2)	34	120	17	29		3	4	1	6		3	.242	.358
Mike Dorgan	OF33		33	139	19	30		8	0	0	16		8	.216	.273
Joe Battin	3B29		29	119	15	25		2	1	0	8		8	.210	.244
Herm Pitz	C27,SS1,OF1	(2-2)	29	95	17	21		0	0	0	13		14	.221	.221
Pat Dealey	C10,3B6,OF2		18	66	9	12		1	0	0	5		4	.182	.197
Ed Mars	P16		16	51	9	14		1	1	0	5		0	.275	.333
George Proeser	OF13		13	53	11	13		1	1	1	10		1	.245	.358
Ducky Hemp	OF9	(2-2)	9	33	1	5		1	0	0	0		1	.152	.182
Dan Burke	C9	(2-2)	9	20	1	0		0	0	0	5		0	.000	.000
John Leighton	OF7		7	27	6	8		2	0	0	3		2	.296	.370
Bill Sullivan	P6,OF1		6	22	2	2		0	0	0	1		0	.091	.091
John Peltz	OF5	(2-3)	5	17	2	3		1	1	0	3		0	.176	.353
Toby Lyons	P3		3	12	3	4		0	0	0	0		0	.333	.333
Charles McCullough	P3	(2-2)	3	9	1	1		0	0	0	3		2	.111	.111
Ezra Lincoln	P3	(2-2)	3	8	0	0		0	0	0	0		0	.000	.000
Frank Keffer	P2		2	7	1	1		0	0	0	0		0	.143	.143
Louis Graff	C1		1	5	0	2		1	0	0	0		0	.400	.400
Bill Higgins	2B1	(2-2)	1	4	1	1		1	0	0	0		0	.250	.500
			128	4469	698	1158		151	59	14	457	482	292	.259	.329

PITCHERS		W	L	PCT	G	GS	CG	SH	SV	IP	H	BB	SO	ERA
Dan Casey		19	22	.463	45	42	40	2	0	361	365	165	169	4.14
John Keefe		17	24	.415	43	41	36	2	0	352	355	148	120	4.32
Ed Mars		9	5	.643	16	14	14	0	0	121	132	49	59	4.67
Mike Morrison	(1-2)	6	9	.400	17	14	13	1	0	127	131	81	69	5.88
Frank Keffer		1	1	.500	2	1	1	0	0	16	15	9	4	5.63
Charles McCullough	(2-2)	1	2	.333	3	3	3	0	0	26	29	14	8	7.27
Bill Sullivan		1	4	.200	6	6	4	0	0	42	51	27	13	7.93
Toby Lyons		0	3	.000	3	3	2	0	0	22	40	21	6	10.48
Ezra Lincoln	(2-2)	0	3	.000	3	3	2	0	0	20	33	4	6	10.35
Bones Ely		0	0	----	1	0	0	0	0	2	7	0	0	22.50
		55	72	.433	128	127	115	5	0	1090	1158	518	454	4.98

1890 AMERICAN ASSOCIATION

PHILADELPHIA Athletics — 54-78 .409 -34 8th Bill Sharsig

BATTERS	POS/GAMES		GP	AB	R	H	BI	2B	3B	HR	BB	SO	SB	BA	SA
Jack O'Brien	1B109,OF1,C1		109	433	80	113		24	14	4	52		31	.261	.409
Taylor Shaffer	2B69		69	261	28	45		3	4	0	28		19	.172	.215
Ben Conroy	SS74,2B42,OF1		117	404	45	69		13	1	0	45		17	.171	.208
Denny Lyons	3B88		88	339	79	120		29	5	7	57		21	.354	.531
Orator Shaffer	OF98,1B3		100	390	55	110		15	5	1	47		29	.282	.354
Curt Welch	OF103,P1	(1-2)	103	396	100	106		21	4	2	49		64	.268	.356
Blondie Purcell	OF110		110	463	110	128		28	3	2	43		48	.276	.363
Wilbert Robinson	C82	(1-2)	82	329	32	78		13	4	4	16		20	.237	.337
Joe Kappel	OF23,SS18,3B11,C3,2B2		56	208	29	50		8	1	1	20		12	.240	.303
Sadie McMahon	P48,OF1	(1-2)	49	175	27	40		5	1	2	7		2	.229	.303
Ed Green	P25,3B10,SS3,2B2		39	126	15	15		1	1	0	13		7	.119	.143
George Carmen	SS15,OF10,2B2,3B1		28	97	9	17		2	0	0	8		5	.175	.196
John Riddle	C13,OF12,2B2,3B1		27	85	7	7		0	1	0	17		4	.082	.106
Ed Seward	P21,OF6		26	72	7	10		4	0	0	8		3	.139	.194
Kid Baldwin	C19,3B5	(2-2)	24	90	5	21		1	2	0	4		2	.233	.289
Joe Daly	OF14,C9		21	75	8	21		4	1	0	3		1	.280	.360
Andrew Knox	1B21		21	75	6	19		3	0	0	9		5	.253	.293
Henry Easterday	SS19	(2-3)	19	68	17	10		1	0	1	10		4	.147	.206
Duke Esper	P18	(1-3)	18	61	11	18		2	2	0	2		1	.295	.393
Peter Sweeney	2B9,OF4,3B2	(3-3)	14	49	5	8		1	1	0	7		0	.163	.224
Al Sauters	3B11,OF2,2B2		14	41	1	4		0	0	0	11		0	.098	.098
Charlie Stecher	P10,3B1		10	29	3	7		0	1	0	1		0	.241	.310
Ed O'Neil	P6,OF3,3B1	(1-2)	10	31	0	5		0	0	0	3		0	.161	.161
Charlie Snyder	OF5,C5		9	33	5	9		1	0	0	2		0	.273	.303
Ed Pabst	OF8	(1-2)	8	25	7	10		2	0	0	5		3	.400	.480
Jim Whitney	P6,OF1		7	21	3	5		0	0	0	1		0	.238	.238
Mickey Hughes	P6	(2-2)	6	16	2	2		0	0	0	2		2	.125	.125
Bart Cantz	C5		5	22	1	1		0	0	0	0		0	.045	.045
Henry Meyers	3B5		5	19	2	3		0	0	0	1		2	.158	.158
George Crawford	OF4,SS1		5	17	1	2		0	0	0	0		1	.118	.118
Dennis Fitzgerald	SS2		2	8	0	2		0	0	0	0		0	.250	.250
Peter Haynes	OF2		2	7	1	1		0	0	0	1		0	.143	.143
Sam Campbell	2B2		2	5	0	0		0	0	0	1		0	.000	.000
Bill Price	P1		1	4	0	1		0	0	0	0		0	.250	.250
Horace Helmbold	P1		1	3	1	0		0	0	0	0		0	.000	.000
Harry Stine	P1		1	3	0	0		0	0	0	1		0	.000	.000
Bob Stafford	OF1		1	2	0	0		0	0	0	0		0	.000	.000
John Sterling	P1		1	2	0	0		0	0	0	0		0	.000	.000
John McBride	OF1		1	2	0	0		0	0	0	0		0	.000	.000
Bill Collins	SS1		1	1	0	0		0	0	0	0		0	.000	.000
Ham Sweigert	OF1		1	1	0	0		0	0	0	1		1	.000	.000
Howard Luckey	P1		1	1	0	0		0	0	0	0		0	.000	.000
----- Macey	C1		1	1	0	0		0	0	0	0		0	.000	.000
			132	4490	702	1057		181	51	24	475	540	305	.235	.314

PITCHERS		W	L	PCT	G	GS	CG	SH	SV	IP	H	BB	SO	ERA
Sadie McMahon		29	18	.617	48	46	44	0	1	410	414	133	225	3.34
Ed Green		7	15	.318	25	22	20	1	1	191	267	94	56	5.80
Duke Esper	(1-3)	8	9	.471	18	16	14	1	0	144	176	67	61	4.89
Ed Seward		6	12	.333	21	19	15	1	0	154	165	72	55	4.73
Jim Whitney		2	2	.500	6	4	3	0	0	40	61	11	6	5.17
Bill Price		1	0	1.000	1	1	1	0	0	9	6	7	1	2.00
Mickey Hughes	(2-2)	1	3	.250	6	5	4	0	0	41	64	21	15	5.44
Harry Stine		0	1	.000	1	1	1	0	0	8	17	4	1	9.00
Horace Helmbold		0	1	.000	1	1	1	0	0	7	17	6	3	14.14
John Sterling		0	1	.000	1	1	1	0	0	5	16	4	1	21.60
Ed O'Neil	(2-2)	0	6	.000	6	6	6	0	0	52	84	32	17	9.69
Charlie Stecher		0	10	.000	10	10	9	0	0	68	111	60	18	10.32
Howard Luckey		0	0	----	1	0	0	0	0	2	1	3	1	9.00
Curt Welch		0	0	----	1	0	0	0	0	1	6	0	1	54.00
		54	78	.409	132	132	119	3	2	1132	1405	514	461	5.22

BROOKLYN Gladiators — 26-73 .263 -45.5 9th Jim Kennedy

BATTERS	POS/GAMES		GP	AB	R	H	BI	2B	3B	HR	BB	SO	SB	BA	SA
Billy O'Brien	1B96		96	388	47	108		25	8	4	28		5	.278	.415
Joe Gerhardt	2B99	(1-2)	99	369	34	75		10	4	2	30		9	.203	.268
Candy Nelson	SS57,OF4		60	223	44	56		3	2	0	35		12	.251	.283
Jumbo Davis	3B38	(2-2)	38	142	33	43		9	2	2	15		10	.303	.437
Ed Daily	OF64,P27	(1-3)	91	394	68	94		15	7	1	24		49	.239	.320

1890 AMERICAN ASSOCIATION

BROOKLYN (cont.)
Gladiators

BATTERS	POS/GAMES		GP	AB	R	H	BI	2B	3B	HR	BB	SO	SB	BA	SA
John Peltz	OF98	(1-3)	98	384	55	87		9	6	1	32		10	.227	.289
Henry Simon	OF89	(1-2)	89	373	66	96		17	11	0	34		23	.257	.362
Jim Toy	C44		44	160	11	29		3	0	0	11		2	.181	.200
Frank Bowes	C25,OF19,3B13,1B3,SS2		61	232	28	51		5	2	0	7		11	.220	.259
Herm Pitz	C34,3B16,OF9,SS2,2B1	(1-2)	61	189	26	26		0	0	0	45		25	.138	.138
Frank Fennelly	SS38,3B7		45	178	40	44		8	3	2	30		6	.247	.360
Mike Mattimore	P19,OF14		33	129	14	17		1	1	0	16		11	.132	.155
Charles McCullough	P26	(1-2)	26	86	2	2		0	0	0	3		1	.023	.023
Fred Siefke	3B16		16	58	1	8		2	0	0	5		2	.138	.172
Con Murphy	P12,OF4	(2-2)	16	50	4	9		2	0	1	3		0	.180	.280
Pat O'Connell	3B10,1B1		11	40	7	9		2	1	0	7		3	.225	.325
Tom Ford	P7,SS4		10	30	1	1		0	0	0	1		1	.033	.033
Steve Toole	P6		6	20	2	6		3	0	0	0		0	.300	.450
Jim Powers	P4		4	13	5	2		0	0	0	1		1	.154	.154
Hi Church	OF3		3	9	1	1		0	0	0	0		0	.111	.111
Gus Williams	P2		2	4	1	2		0	0	0	0		1	.500	.500
Jack Lynch	P1		1	4	2	3		2	0	0	1		0	.750	1.250
			100	3475	492	769		116	47	13	328	456	182	.221	.293

PITCHERS			W	L	PCT	G	GS	CG	SH	SV	IP	H	BB	SO	ERA
Ed Daily		(1-3)	10	15	.400	27	27	27	0	0	236	252	93	82	4.05
Mike Mattimore			6	13	.316	19	19	19	0	0	178	201	76	33	4.54
Charles McCullough		(1-2)	4	21	.160	26	25	24	0	0	216	247	102	61	4.59
Con Murphy		(2-2)	3	9	.250	12	12	10	0	0	96	121	46	26	5.72
Steve Toole			2	4	.333	6	6	6	0	0	53	47	39	10	4.05
Jim Powers			1	2	.333	4	2	2	0	0	30	38	16	3	5.70
Gus Williams			0	1	.000	2	2	1	0	0	12	13	12	2	7.50
Jack Lynch			0	1	.000	1	1	1	0	0	9	22	5	1	12.00
Tom Ford		(2-2)	0	6	.000	7	6	6	0	0	49	70	32	12	5.14
			26	73	.263	100	100	96	0	0	879	1011	421	230	4.71

1891 NATIONAL LEAGUE

Payback

The cream of the National League crop jumped to the Players' League in 1890. Established stars like Buck Ewing, Monte Ward, Dan Brouthers, and Pete Browning supported the Brotherhood and played in the new league. One notable exception was Cap Anson of Chicago. Anson felt a loyalty to his team (the White Stockings) of which he owned part and managed fully, and to his mentor Al Spalding. But most of his league brethren felt betrayed by Anson's actions. He had let the Brotherhood down.

As the 1891 season unfolded, Anson's White Stockings became pennant contenders for the first time in four years. By mid–September, their lead was five games over second place Boston. However, Boston then commenced to reel off an 18-game winning streak, while Chicago lost eight of 14, to win the pennant by three and one-half games.

It was during this winning streak that something smelt fishy to Chicago. Particularly questioned was a block of five games which Boston played against New York in late September. During a portion of that group of games, four of which were played in Boston, New York had been without the services of their two best pitchers, and their best hitter, Roger Connor, who were left behind in New York. President Hart of the White Stockings sent a telegram to National League President Young protesting the five games on the grounds that 1) two of the games were makeup games and should not have been scheduled all at the same time, and 2) New York deliberately played a second string team against Boston. In short, Hart was complaining that the league (or at least New York) was conspiring to give the pennant to Boston in retaliation for Anson's desertion of the Brotherhood.

Boston's dash to the pennant was fueled by a strong pitching staff led by 30 game winners John Clarkson and Kid Nichols. In addition, the entire staff led the league with an earned run average of 2.76. Hitting leaguewide dropped a notch, and the pennant winners were not immune. No regular batted over .282, though Harry Stovey led the circuit in triples (20) and finished first in home runs (16).

Chicago's second place finish was fueled by pitcher Bill Hutchinson and his 44 wins, 66 games, and 561 innings. Offensively, Cap Anson led the way with a .291 average and a league-leading 120 runs batted in.

New York and Philadelphia also finished in the first division. New York was paced by Mike Tiernan who batted .306 and led with 16 home runs, and by flame-throwing pitcher Amos Rusie who struck out 337, while winning 33. His pitching teammate, John Ewing, had the best winning percentage (.724) and earned run average 2.27. Philadelphia was paced by speedster Billy Hamilton who won the batting (.340) and stolen base (111) crowns.

Cleveland, Brooklyn, and Cincinnati finished on the next three rungs. Their outstanding players included Cleveland's Cy Young with 27 victories and Cincinnati's Bug Holliday (.319)

Pittsburgh finished with 32 more wins and 238 more percentage points than their 1890 counterparts, yet they still finished in last place, two percentage points out of seventh. Their strength was their pitching staff which finished second (2.89) in the earned run average race.

Both the New York team and the National League investigated the charges of collusion thrown their way by the Chicago club. And, both New York and Boston were "officially" cleared of any violation. What the real story was — one may never know. What is certain is that Boston had help in winning the pennant. The question remaining is how much.

1891 NATIONAL LEAGUE

BOSTON Beaneaters
87-51   .630   1st   Frank Selee

BATTERS	POS/GAMES		GP	AB	R	H	BI	2B	3B	HR	BB	SO	SB	BA	SA
Tommy Tucker	1B140,P1		140	548	103	148	69	16	5	2	37	30	26	.270	.328
Joe Quinn	2B124		124	508	70	122	63	8	10	3	28	28	24	.240	.313
Germany Long	SS139		139	577	129	163	76	21	111	10	80	51	60	.282	.409
Billy Nash	3B140		140	537	92	148	95	24	9	5	74	50	28	.276	.382
Harry Stovey	OF135,1B1		135	544	118	152	95	31	20	16	78	69	57	.279	.498
Steve Brodie	OF133		133	523	84	136	78	13	6	2	63	39	25	.260	.319
Bobby Lowe	OF107,2B17,SS2,3B1,P1		125	497	92	129	74	19	5	6	53	54	43	.260	.354
Charlie Bennett	C75		75	256	35	55	39	9	3	5	42	61	3	.215	.332
Charles Ganzel	C59,OF13		70	263	33	68	29	18	5	1	12	13	7	.259	.376
John Clarkson	P55,OF1		55	187	28	42	26	7	4	0	18	51	2	.225	.305
Kid Nichols	P52		52	183	21	36	27	6	0	0	12	31	1	.197	.230
Harry Staley	P31	(2-2)	31	102	7	17	16	4	0	1	8	17	0	.167	.225
Marty Sullivan	OF17	(1-2)	17	67	15	15	7	1	0	2	5	3	7	.224	.328
King Kelly	C11,OF6	(3-3)	16	52	7	12	5	1	0	0	6	10	6	.231	.250
Pretzels Getzien	P11,OF3	(1-2)	14	41	4	7	6	2	1	1	7	18	0	.171	.341
Joe Kelley	OF12		12	45	7	11	3	1	1	0	2	7	0	.244	.311
George Rooks	OF5		5	16	1	2	0	0	0	0	4	1	0	.125	.125
Fred Lake	C4,OF1		5	7	1	1	0	0	0	0	2	4	0	.143	.143
John Kiley	P1		1	2	0	0	0	0	0	0	1	1	0	.000	.000
Cyclone Ryan	P1		1	1	0	0	0	0	0	0	0	0	0	.000	.000
Jim Sullivan	P1		1	0	0	0	0	0	0	0	0	0	0	----	----
Tod Brynan	P1		1	0	0	0	0	0	0	0	0	0	0	----	----
			140	4956	847	1264	708	181	80	54	532	538	289	.255	.357

PITCHERS			W	L	PCT	G	GS	CG	SH	SV	IP	H	BB	SO	ERA
John Clarkson			33	19	.635	55	51	47	3	3	461	435	154	141	2.79
Kid Nichols			30	17	.638	52	48	45	5	3	425	413	103	240	2.39
Harry Staley		(2-2)	20	8	.714	31	30	26	1	0	252	236	69	114	2.50
Pretzels Getzien		(1-2)	4	5	.444	11	9	7	0	0	89	112	23	29	3.84
John Kiley			0	1	.000	1	1	1	0	0	8	13	5	1	6.75
Tod Brynan			0	1	.000	1	1	0	0	0	1	4	3	0	54.00
Cyclone Ryan			0	0	----	1	0	0	0	0	3	2	1	0	0.00
Tommy Tucker			0	0	----	1	0	0	0	0	1	3	0	0	9.00
Bobby Lowe			0	0	----	1	0	0	0	0	1	3	1	0	9.00
Jim Sullivan		(1-2)	0	0	----	1	0	0	0	0	0	2	5	0	81.00
			87	51	.630	140	140	126	9	6	1242	1223	364	525	2.76

CHICAGO White Stockings
82-53   .607   -3.5   2nd   Cap Anson

BATTERS	POS/GAMES	GP	AB	R	H	BI	2B	3B	HR	BB	SO	SB	BA	SA
Cap Anson	1B136,C2	136	540	81	157	120	24	8	8	75	29	17	.291	.409
Fred Pfeffer	2B137	137	498	93	123	77	12	9	7	79	60	40	.247	.349
Jim Cooney	SS118	118	465	84	114	42	15	3	0	48	17	21	.245	.290
Bill Dahlen	3B84,OF37,SS15	135	549	114	143	76	18	13	9	67	60	21	.260	.390
Cliff Carroll	OF130	130	515	87	132	80	20	8	7	50	42	31	.256	.367
Jimmy Ryan	OF117,SS2,P2	118	505	110	140	66	22	15	9	53	38	27	.277	.434
Walt Wilmot	OF121	121	498	102	139	71	14	10	11	55	21	42	.279	.414
Mal Kittredge	C79	79	296	26	62	27	8	5	2	17	28	4	.209	.291
Bill Hutchinson	P66,OF1	67	243	27	45	25	4	2	2	17	62	5	.185	.243
Tom Burns	3B53,SS4,OF2	59	243	36	55	17	8	1	1	21	21	18	.226	.280
Ad Gumbert	P32,OF1,1B1	34	105	18	32	16	7	4	0	13	14	4	.305	.448
John Luby	P30,OF2,1B1	32	98	19	24	24	2	4	2	8	16	3	.245	.408
Pop Schriver	C27,1B2	27	90	15	30	21	1	4	1	10	9	1	.333	.467
Bill Bowman	C15	15	45	2	4	5	1	0	0	5	9	0	.089	.111
Ed Stein	P14	14	43	4	7	4	1	0	0	3	10	0	.163	.186
Tom Vickery	P14,SS1	14	39	3	7	1	1	0	0	0	10	3	.179	.205
Bill Merritt	C11,1B1	11	42	4	9	4	1	0	0	2	2	0	.214	.238
Tom Nagle	C7,OF1	8	25	3	3	1	0	0	0	1	3	0	.120	.120
Marty Honan	C5	5	12	1	2	3	0	1	0	1	3	0	.167	.333
Elmer Foster	OF4	4	16	3	3	1	0	0	1	1	2	1	.188	.375
George Nicol	P3	3	6	0	2	3	0	1	0	0	1	0	.333	.667
		137	4873	832	1233	684	159	88	60	526	457	238	.253	.359

PITCHERS	W	L	PCT	G	GS	CG	SH	SV	IP	H	BB	SO	ERA
Bill Hutchinson	44	19	.698	66	58	56	4	1	561	508	178	261	2.81
Ad Gumbert	17	11	.607	32	31	24	1	0	256	282	90	73	3.58
John Luby	8	11	.421	30	24	18	0	1	206	221	94	52	4.76

1891 NATIONAL LEAGUE 219

CHICAGO (cont.)
White Stockings

PITCHERS	W	L	PCT	G	GS	CG	SH	SV	IP	H	BB	SO	ERA
Ed Stein	7	6	.538	14	10	9	1	0	101	99	57	38	3.74
Tom Vickery	6	5	.545	14	12	7	0	0	80	72	44	39	4.07
George Nicol	0	1	.000	3	2	0	0	0	11	14	10	12	4.91
Jimmy Ryan	0	0	----	2	0	0	0	1	6	11	2	2	1.59
	82	53	.607	137	137	114	6	3	1221	1207	475	477	3.47

NEW YORK
Giants

71-61 .538 -13 3rd Jim Mutrie

BATTERS	POS/GAMES		GP	AB	R	H	BI	2B	3B	HR	BB	SO	SB	BA	SA
Roger Connor	1B129		129	479	112	139	94	29	13	6	83	39	27	.290	.443
Danny Richardson	2B114,SS9		123	516	85	139	51	18	5	5	33	27	28	.269	.353
Jack Glasscock	SS97		97	369	46	89	55	12	6	0	36	11	29	.241	.306
Charley Bassett	3B121,2B9		130	524	60	136	68	19	8	4	36	29	16	.260	.349
Mike Tiernan	OF134		134	542	111	166	73	30	12	16	69	32	53	.306	.494
George Gore	OF130		130	528	103	150	48	22	7	2	74	34	19	.284	.364
Jim O'Rourke	OF126,C14		136	555	92	164	95	28	7	5	26	29	19	.295	.398
Dick Buckley	C74,3B1		75	253	23	55	31	9	1	4	11	30	3	.217	.308
Lew Whistler	SS33,OF22,1B7,2B6,3B5		72	265	39	65	38	8	7	3	24	45	4	.245	.362
Amos Rusie	P61,OF1		62	220	30	54	15	5	2	0	3	25	2	.245	.286
Archie Clarke	C42,3B5,OF2		48	174	17	33	21	2	2	0	15	16	5	.190	.224
John Ewing	P33		33	113	10	23	8	1	0	0	3	14	4	.204	.212
Mickey Welch	P22		22	71	4	10	4	0	0	0	3	13	0	.141	.141
Buster Burrell	C15,OF1		15	53	1	5	1	0	0	0	3	12	2	.094	.094
Buck Ewing	2B8,C6		14	49	8	17	18	2	1	0	5	5	5	.347	.429
John Sharrott	P10		10	30	5	10	7	2	0	1	1	2	3	.333	.500
Roscoe Coughlin	P8		8	23	3	3	1	1	1	0	5	9	1	.130	.261
Tim Keefe	P8	(1-2)	8	21	2	2	1	0	0	0	3	13	1	.095	.095
Bob Barr	P5		5	11	0	1	0	0	0	0	2	3	0	.091	.091
Dad Clarkson	P5		5	9	0	4	0	0	0	0	2	2	0	.444	.444
Jerry Denny	3B4	(1-3)	4	16	0	4	1	1	0	0	0	3	2	.250	.313
Mike Sullivan	P3	(1-2)	3	10	3	2	0	0	0	0	0	0	1	.200	.200
Jack Taylor	P1		1	2	0	0	0	0	0	0	1	1	0	.000	.000
Andy Dunning	P1		1	0	0	0	0	0	0	0	0	0	0	----	----
			136	4833	754	1271	630	189	72	48	438	394	224	.263	.360

PITCHERS		W	L	PCT	G	GS	CG	SH	SV	IP	H	BB	SO	ERA
Amos Rusie		33	20	.623	61	57	52	6	1	500	391	262	337	2.55
John Ewing		21	8	.724	33	30	28	5	0	269	237	105	138	2.27
John Sharrott		5	5	.500	10	9	6	0	1	69	47	35	41	2.60
Mickey Welch		5	9	.357	22	15	14	0	0	160	176	97	46	4.27
Roscoe Coughlin		3	4	.429	8	7	6	0	0	61	74	23	22	3.84
Tim Keefe	(1-2)	2	5	.286	8	7	4	0	0	55	71	27	29	5.24
Dad Clarkson		1	2	.333	5	2	1	0	0	28	24	18	11	2.89
Mike Sullivan	(2-2)	1	2	.333	3	3	3	0	0	24	24	8	11	3.38
Jack Taylor		0	1	.000	1	1	1	0	0	8	4	3	1	1.13
Andy Dunning		0	1	.000	1	1	0	0	0	2	3	3	2	4.50
Bob Barr		0	4	.000	5	4	2	0	0	27	47	12	11	5.33
		71	61	.538	136	136	117	11	3	1204	1098	593	651	2.99

PHILADELPHIA
Phillies

68-69 .496 -18.5 4th Harry Wright

BATTERS	POS/GAMES	GP	AB	R	H	BI	2B	3B	HR	BB	SO	SB	BA	SA
Willard Brown	1B97,C19,OF2	115	441	62	107	50	20	4	0	34	35	7	.243	.306
Al Myers	2B135	135	514	67	118	69	27	2	2	69	46	8	.230	.302
Bob Allen	SS118	118	438	46	97	51	7	4	1	43	44	12	.221	.263
Bill Shindle	3B100,SS3	103	415	68	87	38	13	1	0	33	39	17	.210	.246
Sam Thompson	OF133	133	554	108	163	90	23	10	8	52	20	29	.294	.415
Ed Delahanty	OF99,1B27,2B3	128	543	92	132	86	19	9	4	33	50	25	.243	.333
Billy Hamilton	OF133	133	527	141	179	60	23	7	2	102	28	111	.340	.421
Jack Clements	C107,1B2	107	423	58	131	75	29	4	4	43	19	3	.310	.426
Ed Mayer	3B31,OF29,SS7,2B1	68	268	24	50	31	2	4	0	14	29	7	.187	.224
Kid Gleason	P53,OF9,SS4	65	214	31	53	17	5	2	0	20	17	6	.248	.290
Duke Esper	P39	39	123	18	27	9	4	1	0	7	19	1	.220	.268
John Thornton	P37,OF3	39	123	7	17	6	3	0	0	2	10	1	.138	.163
Bill Grey	C11,OF10,SS3,3B1	23	75	11	18	7	0	0	0	3	10	3	.240	.240

PHILADELPHIA (cont.)
Phillies

BATTERS	POS/GAMES		GP	AB	R	H	BI	2B	3B	HR	BB	SO	SB	BA	SA
Jerry Denny	1B12,3B7	(3-3)	19	73	5	21	11	1	1	0	4	6	1	.288	.329
Bill Kling	P12,OF1		13	31	3	6	2	0	0	0	7	3	0	.194	.194
Tim Keefe	P11	(2-2)	11	29	0	5	1	0	1	0	4	16	0	.172	.241
Jocko Fields	C8	(2-2)	8	30	4	7	5	2	1	0	4	2	0	.233	.367
Lew Graulich	C4,1B3		7	26	2	8	3	0	0	0	1	2	0	.308	.308
Joe Donohue	OF4,SS2		6	22	2	7	2	1	0	0	1	3	0	.318	.364
Ed Cassian	P6	(1-2)	6	17	0	2	1	0	0	0	0	4	0	.118	.118
John Schultze	P6		6	6	3	1	0	1	0	0	0	2	0	.167	.333
Harry Morelock	SS4		4	14	1	1	0	0	0	0	3	3	0	.071	.071
Phenomenal Smith	P3		3	8	0	3	2	0	0	0	2	0	1	.375	.375
Mike Kilroy	P3		3	5	1	2	1	0	0	0	1	1	0	.400	.400
Walt Plock	OF2		2	5	2	2	0	0	0	0	0	1	0	.400	.400
Ed Gormley	P1		1	4	0	0	0	0	0	0	0	3	0	.000	.000
Lefty Saylor	P1		1	1	0	0	0	0	0	0	0	0	0	.000	.000
Charlie Bastian	SS1	(2-2)	1	0	0	0	0	0	0	0	0	0	0	----	----
			138	4929	756	1244	617	180	51	21	482	412	232	.252	.322

PITCHERS			W	L	PCT	G	GS	CG	SH	SV	IP	H	BB	SO	ERA
Kid Gleason			24	22	.522	53	44	40	1	0	418	431	165	100	3.51
Duke Esper			20	15	.571	39	36	25	1	1	296	302	121	108	3.56
John Thornton			15	16	.484	37	32	23	1	2	269	268	115	52	3.68
Bill Kling			4	2	.667	12	7	4	0	0	75	90	32	26	4.32
Tim Keefe		(2-2)	3	6	.333	11	10	9	0	1	78	84	28	35	3.91
Phenomenal Smith			1	1	.500	3	2	0	0	0	19	20	8	3	4.26
Ed Cassian		(1-2)	1	3	.250	6	4	3	0	0	38	40	16	10	2.84
John Schultze			0	1	.000	6	1	0	0	0	15	18	11	4	6.60
Ed Gormley			0	1	.000	1	1	1	0	0	8	10	5	2	5.63
Mike Kilroy			0	2	.000	3	3	1	0	0	10	15	4	3	9.90
Lefty Saylor			0	0	----	1	0	0	0	0	3	2	0	0	6.00
			68	69	.496	138	138	105	3	5	1229	1280	505	343	3.73

CLEVELAND
Spiders

65-74 .468 -22.5 5th Leadley - Tebeau

BATTERS	POS/GAMES		GP	AB	R	H	BI	2B	3B	HR	BB	SO	SB	BA	SA
Jake Virtue	1B139		139	517	82	135	72	19	14	2	75	40	15	.261	.364
Cupid Childs	2B141		141	551	120	155	83	21	12	2	97	32	39	.281	.374
Ed McKean	SS141		141	603	115	170	69	13	12	6	64	19	14	.282	.373
Patsy Tebeau	3B61,OF1		61	249	38	65	41	8	3	1	16	13	12	.261	.329
Spud Johnson	OF79,1B1		80	327	49	84	46	8	3	1	22	23	16	.257	.309
George Davis	OF116,3B22,P3		136	570	115	165	89	35	12	3	53	29	42	.289	.409
Jimmy McAleer	OF136		136	565	97	134	61	16	11	1	49	47	51	.237	.310
Chief Zimmer	C116,3B1		116	440	55	112	69	21	4	3	33	49	15	.255	.341
Jack Doyle	C29,OF21,3B20,SS1		69	250	43	69	43	14	4	0	26	44	24	.276	.364
Cy Young	P55		55	174	23	29	18	5	2	1	11	30	2	.167	.236
Henry Gruber	P44,OF2		46	141	17	23	20	3	2	1	21	35	0	.163	.234
Leon Viau	P45,OF1		45	144	15	23	6	3	2	0	12	28	2	.160	.208
Jesse Burkett	OF40		40	167	29	45	13	7	4	0	23	19	1	.269	.359
Jerry Denny	3B29,OF7	(1-3)	36	138	17	31	21	5	0	0	12	23	3	.225	.261
John Shearon	OF28,P6		30	124	10	30	13	1	1	0	1	15	6	.242	.266
Bill Alvord	3B13	(1-2)	13	59	7	17	7	2	2	1	0	7	0	.288	.441
Ed Seward	P3,OF3,1B1		7	19	2	4	1	2	0	0	3	4	0	.211	.316
Eb Beatin	P5		5	13	0	1	0	0	0	0	0	2	0	.077	.077
Frank Knauss	P3		3	6	1	1	0	0	0	0	1	0	0	.167	.167
Bill Collins	OF1,C1		2	3	0	0	0	0	0	0	0	0	0	.000	.000
Marty Sullivan	OF1	(2-2)	1	4	0	1	1	0	0	0	0	1	0	.250	.250
Pretzels Getzien	P1	(2-2)	1	4	0	0	0	0	0	0	0	1	0	.000	.000
Henry Killeen	P1		1	3	0	0	0	0	0	0	1	0	0	.000	.000
Joe Daly	OF1		1	3	0	0	0	0	0	0	0	2	0	.000	.000
			141	5074	835	1294	673	183	88	22	519	464	242	.255	.339

PITCHERS			W	L	PCT	G	GS	CG	SH	SV	IP	H	BB	SO	ERA
Cy Young			27	22	.551	55	46	43	0	2	424	431	140	147	2.85
Leon Viau			18	17	.514	45	38	31	0	0	344	367	138	130	3.01
Henry Gruber			17	22	.436	44	40	35	1	0	349	407	119	79	4.13
Ed Seward			2	1	.667	3	3	0	0	0	16	16	7	4	3.86
John Shearon			1	3	.250	6	5	4	0	0	46	57	24	19	3.52
Henry Killeen			0	1	.000	1	1	1	0	0	9	11	8	3	6.23
Pretzels Getzien		(2-2)	0	1	.000	1	1	1	0	0	9	12	4	4	8.00

1891 NATIONAL LEAGUE 221

CLEVELAND (cont.)
Spiders

PITCHERS		W	L	PCT	G	GS	CG	SH	SV	IP	H	BB	SO	ERA
George Davis		0	1	.000	3	0	0	0	1	4	8	3	4	15.75
Eb Beatin		0	3	.000	5	4	2	0	0	29	39	21	4	5.28
Frank Knauss		0	3	.000	3	3	1	0	0	15	23	8	6	7.20
		65	74	.468	141	141	118	1	3	1244	1371	466	400	3.50

BROOKLYN
Bridegrooms

61-76 .445 -25.5 6th Monte Ward

BATTERS	POS/GAMES		GP	AB	R	H	BI	2B	3B	HR	BB	SO	SB	BA	SA
Dave Foutz	1B124,P6,SS1		130	521	87	134	73	26	8	2	40	25	48	.257	.349
Hub Collins	2B72,OF35		107	435	82	120	31	16	5	3	59	63	32	.276	.356
Monte Ward	SS87,2B18		105	441	85	122	39	13	5	0	36	10	57	.277	.329
George Pinkney	3B130,SS5		135	501	80	137	71	19	6	2	66	32	44	.273	.347
Oyster Burns	OF113,SS6,3B5		123	470	75	134	83	24	13	4	53	30	21	.285	.417
Mike Griffin	OF134		134	519	106	139	65	36	9	3	57	31	65	.267	.388
Darby O'Brien	OF103		103	395	79	100	57	18	6	5	39	53	31	.253	.367
Tom Kinslow	C61		61	228	22	54	33	6	0	0	9	22	3	.237	.263
Con Daily	C55,OF3,SS2,1B1		60	206	25	66	30	10	1	0	15	13	7	.320	.379
Tom Daly	C26,1B15,SS11,OF7		58	200	29	50	27	11	5	2	21	34	7	.250	.385
Bob Caruthers	P38,OF17,2B1		56	171	24	48	23	5	3	2	25	13	4	.281	.380
Tom Lovett	P44		44	153	14	25	17	1	2	0	7	29	4	.163	.196
John O'Brien	2B43		43	167	22	41	26	4	2	0	12	17	4	.246	.293
Bones Ely	SS28,3B2,2B1		31	111	9	17	11	0	1	0	7	9	4	.153	.171
Adonis Terry	P25,OF5		30	91	10	19	6	7	1	0	9	26	4	.209	.308
George Hemming	P27		27	82	11	13	10	3	2	0	6	21	2	.159	.244
Bert Inks	P13		13	35	3	10	0	1	0	0	2	5	0	.286	.314
Jack Burdock	2B3		3	12	1	1	1	0	0	0	1	1	0	.083	.083
Dude Esterbrook	OF2,2B1		3	8	1	3	0	0	0	0	0	1	0	.375	.375
			137	4748	765	1233	603	200	69	23	464	435	337	.260	.345

PITCHERS		W	L	PCT	G	GS	CG	SH	SV	IP	H	BB	SO	ERA
Tom Lovett		23	19	.548	44	43	39	3	0	366	361	129	129	3.69
Bob Caruthers		18	14	.563	38	32	29	2	1	297	323	107	69	3.12
George Hemming		8	15	.348	27	22	19	1	1	200	231	84	83	4.96
Adonis Terry		6	16	.273	25	22	18	1	1	194	207	80	65	4.22
Dave Foutz		3	2	.600	6	5	5	0	0	52	51	16	14	3.29
Bert Inks		3	10	.231	13	13	11	1	0	96	99	43	47	4.02
		61	76	.445	137	137	121	8	3	1205	1272	459	407	3.86

CINCINNATI
Reds

56-81 .409 -30.5 7th Tom Loftus

BATTERS	POS/GAMES		GP	AB	R	H	BI	2B	3B	HR	BB	SO	SB	BA	SA
Long John Reilly	1B100,OF36		135	546	60	132	64	20	13	4	9	42	22	.242	.348
Bid McPhee	2B138		138	562	107	144	38	14	16	6	74	35	33	.256	.370
Germany Smith	SS138		138	512	50	103	53	11	5	3	38	32	16	.201	.260
Arlie Latham	3B135		135	533	119	145	53	20	10	7	74	35	87	.272	.386
Lefty Marr	OF72	(1-2)	72	286	32	74	32	9	7	0	25	15	16	.259	.339
Bug Holliday	OF111		111	442	74	141	84	21	10	9	37	28	30	.319	.473
Jocko Halligan	OF61		61	247	43	77	44	13	6	3	24	25	5	.312	.449
Jerry Harrington	C92,3B1		92	333	25	76	41	10	5	2	19	34	4	.228	.306
Jim Keenan	1B41,C34,3B1		75	252	30	51	33	7	5	4	33	39	2	.202	.317
Tony Mullane	P51,OF12,3B3		64	209	16	31	10	1	2	0	18	33	4	.148	.172
Pete Browning	OF55	(2-2)	55	216	29	74	33	10	3	0	24	23	12	.343	.417
Bill Rhines	P48		48	148	10	18	5	3	1	0	7	30	1	.122	.155
Mike Slattery	OF41	(1-2)	41	158	24	33	16	3	2	1	10	10	1	.209	.272
Old Hoss Radbourn	P26,OF2,3B1		29	96	11	17	10	2	2	0	4	11	1	.177	.240
Jim Curtis	OF27	(1-2)	27	108	11	29	13	3	3	1	9	19	3	.269	.380
Bob Clark	C16		16	54	2	6	3	0	0	0	6	9	3	.111	.111
Cannonball Crane	P15	(2-2)	15	46	3	5	2	0	0	0	3	12	3	.109	.109
Jesse Duryea	P10	(1-2)	10	32	0	1	3	0	0	0	0	5	1	.031	.031
Frank Foreman	OF1	(1-2)	1	4	0	1	0	1	0	0	0	0	0	.250	.500
Pop Corkhill	OF1	(2-3)	1	4	0	0	0	0	0	0	1	0	0	.000	.000
Clarence Stephens	P1		1	3	0	0	0	0	0	0	0	1	0	.000	.000
			138	4791	646	1158	537	148	90	40	414	439	244	.242	.335

1891 NATIONAL LEAGUE

CINCINNATI (cont.)
Reds

PITCHERS		W	L	PCT	G	GS	CG	SH	SV	IP	H	BB	SO	ERA
Tony Mullane		23	26	.469	51	47	42	1	0	426	390	187	124	3.23
Bill Rhines		17	24	.415	48	43	40	1	1	373	364	124	138	2.87
Old Hoss Radbourn		11	13	.458	26	24	23	2	0	218	236	62	54	4.25
Cannonball Crane	(2-2)	4	8	.333	15	13	11	1	0	117	134	64	51	4.09
Jesse Duryea	(1-2)	1	9	.100	10	10	8	0	0	77	101	25	23	5.38
Clarence Stephens		0	1	.000	1	1	1	0	0	8	9	3	3	7.88
		56	81	.409	138	138	125	6	1	1219	1234	465	393	3.55

PITTSBURGH Pirates 55-80 .407 -30.5 8th Hanlon - McGunnigle

BATTERS	POS/GAMES		GP	AB	R	H	BI	2B	3B	HR	BB	SO	SB	BA	SA
Jake Beckley	1B133		133	554	94	162	73	20	19	4	44	46	13	.292	.419
Lou Bierbauer	2B121		121	500	60	103	47	13	6	1	28	19	12	.206	.262
Frank Shugart	SS75		75	320	57	88	33	19	8	3	20	26	21	.275	.412
Charlie Reilly	3B99,SS11,OF4		114	415	43	91	44	8	5	3	29	58	20	.219	.284
Fred Carroll	OF91		91	353	55	77	48	13	4	4	48	36	22	.218	.312
Ned Hanlon	OF119,SS1		119	455	87	121	60	12	8	0	48	30	54	.266	.327
Pete Browning	OF50	(1-2)	50	203	35	59	28	14	1	4	27	31	4	.291	.429
Connie Mack	C72,1B3		75	280	43	60	29	10	0	0	19	11	4	.214	.250
Doggie Miller	C41,SS37,3B34,OF24,1B1		135	548	80	156	57	19	6	4	59	26	35	.285	.363
Mark Baldwin	P53		53	177	11	27	12	3	2	1	15	67	1	.153	.209
Silver King	P48,3B1		49	148	12	25	9	2	3	0	14	31	0	.169	.223
Al Maul	OF40,P8		47	149	15	28	14	2	4	0	20	28	4	.188	.255
Tun Berger	C18,2B17,SS6,OF2		43	134	15	32	14	2	1	1	12	10	4	.239	.291
Pop Corkhill	OF41	(3-3)	41	145	16	33	20	1	1	3	7	10	7	.228	.310
Bud Lally	OF41		41	143	24	32	17	6	2	1	16	20	0	.224	.315
Pud Galvin	P33		33	109	11	18	7	0	0	0	3	29	0	.165	.165
Jocko Fields	C15,SS8	(1-2)	23	75	10	18	5	3	0	0	10	13	1	.240	.280
Harry Staley	P9	(1-2)	9	31	4	7	3	0	1	0	0	4	0	.226	.290
Piggy Ward	OF5		6	18	3	6	2	0	0	0	3	3	3	.333	.333
John Newell	3B5		5	18	1	2	2	0	0	0	0	0	0	.111	.111
Ed Spurney	SS3		3	7	2	2	0	1	0	0	2	1	0	.286	.429
Scott Stratton	P2	(1-2)	2	8	1	1	0	0	0	0	0	3	0	.125	.125
Sam LaRoque	3B1	(1-2)	1	4	0	0	0	0	0	0	0	1	0	.000	.000
			137	4794	679	1148	524	148	71	29	427	503	205	.239	.318

PITCHERS		W	L	PCT	G	GS	CG	SH	SV	IP	H	BB	SO	ERA
Mark Baldwin		22	28	.440	53	50	48	2	0	438	385	227	197	2.76
Pud Galvin		14	14	.500	33	31	23	2	0	247	256	62	46	2.88
Silver King		14	29	.326	48	44	40	3	1	384	382	144	160	3.11
Harry Staley	(1-2)	4	5	.444	9	7	6	0	0	72	77	11	25	2.89
Al Maul		1	2	.333	8	3	3	0	1	39	44	16	13	2.31
Scott Stratton	(1-2)	0	2	.000	2	2	2	0	0	18	16	5	5	2.45
		55	80	.407	137	137	122	7	2	1198	1160	465	446	2.89

1891 AMERICAN ASSOCIATION

The Last Gasp

The American Association had been through the wringer. It had survived several acrimonious disputes with the National League and one with the Union Association. The most recent conflict with the Players' League reignited the association's battle with the National League. This encounter proved to be too much.

After the 1890 season, the ball players in the Players' League were to have reverted back to their 1889 teams as outlined by the peace agreement. Two players, Lou Bierbauer and Harry Stovey were on the Philadelphia Association team in 1889, and thus reserved by them. However, the two were in turn signed by Boston and Pittsburgh of the National League. The governing body of baseball, the National Board, upheld these signings on a technicality. Rightly perceiving that their interests were being violated, the American Association withdrew from the National Agreement and decided to go it alone in 1891. (Note: the Pittsburgh National League team that signed Lou Bierbauer, was referred to in the press as a "pirate" for stealing the player in this manner. The nickname has stuck to this day.)

Once again, there was a four-team turnover in the American Association. Philadelphia, Toledo, Rochester, and Syracuse were replaced by the Players' League's Philadelphia and Boston, as well as two new franchises in Cincinnati and Washington. Once again the league could not make it through the year intact. This time the victim was Cincinnati. Competing against a National League club, with a poor location, and with the undisciplined King Kelly as manager, the team struggled into August. On the 17th, the Cincinnati club ceased operations. On the 18th, with four of Cincinnati's players in tow, the Milwaukee club of the minor league Western Association joined the American Association.

Cincinnati's manager, King Kelly, did not accompany the team to Milwaukee. He spent a week with the Boston American Association franchise, and then, to the surprise of all, he jumped to the National League club of the same city. The American Association raised a clamor for his return, but the National League turned a deaf ear to their pleas. To the American Association, this would prove to be the last straw.

Boston won the Players' League title in 1890, so it was no great surprise that much the same team won the American Association title in 1891. Dan Brouthers (.350) won the batting title, while Tom Brown scored an association record 177 runs. George Haddock was an impressive pitcher, winning 34 with a 2.49 earned run average.

Second place St. Louis had three .300 hitters topped by Tip O'Neill (.321). Their workhorse pitcher, Jack Stivetts won 33 while leading the league in walks (232) and strikeouts (259). Third place Milwaukee, playing in only 36 games, finished with a 2.50 team earned run average, better than anyone else.

Baltimore and Philadelphia finished in a virtual tie for fourth. Baltimore's Sadie McMahon won the most games (35) for the second straight year, while Philadelphia had three over .300 topped by George Wood (.309).

Columbus, Cincinnati, Louisville, and Washington brought up the rear. Among their better players were Cincinnati's Cannonball Crane, who won the earned run average title (2.45) and Louisville's Patsy Donovan, who hit .321.

The American Association had proven itself a viable league. During its ten year tenure, many great teams and players graced its fields. But alas, 1891 would be the last year of the league's existence as a separate entity. However, they would not go under without a fight.

1891 AMERICAN ASSOCIATION

BOSTON Reds — 93-42 .689 1st Art Irwin

BATTERS	POS/GAMES		GP	AB	R	H	BI	2B	3B	HR	BB	SO	SB	BA	SA
Dan Brouthers	1B130		130	486	117	170	109	26	19	5	87	20	31	.350	.512
Cub Stricker	2B139		139	514	96	111	46	15	4	0	63	34	54	.216	.261
Paul Radford	SS131,OF4,P1		133	456	102	118	65	11	5	0	96	36	55	.259	.305
Duke Farrell	3B66,C37,OF23,1B4		122	473	108	143	110	19	13	12	59	48	21	.302	.474
Hugh Duffy	OF124,3B3,SS1		127	536	134	180	110	20	8	9	61	29	85	.336	.453
Tom Brown	OF137		137	589	177	189	71	30	21	5	70	96	106	.321	.469
Hardy Richardson	OF60,3B9,SS4,1B3		74	278	45	71	51	9	4	7	40	26	16	.255	.392
Morg Murphy	C104,OF4		106	402	60	87	54	11	4	4	36	58	17	.216	.294
Bill Joyce	3B64,1B1		65	243	76	75	51	9	15	3	63	27	36	.309	.506
George Haddock	P51,OF8		58	185	30	45	23	4	1	3	21	46	3	.243	.324
Charles Buffinton	P48,OF10,1B4		58	181	16	34	16	2	1	1	19	15	0	.188	.227
Jack McGeachey	OF41	(2-2)	41	178	26	45	21	2	1	1	12	8	11	.253	.292
John O'Brien	P40		41	128	19	30	10	1	0	0	8	17	3	.234	.242
Bill Daley	P19,OF2		20	59	5	10	9	0	1	0	1	6	1	.169	.203
John Irwin	OF17,3B2,SS1	(1-2)	19	72	6	16	15	2	2	0	6	9	6	.222	.306
Clark Griffith	P7,OF3	(2-2)	10	23	6	4	3	1	1	1	6	5	1	.174	.435
Art Irwin	SS6		6	17	1	2	0	0	0	0	2	1	0	.118	.118
John Fitzgerald	P6		6	14	0	1	1	1	0	0	0	5	0	.071	.143
Tom Cotter	C5,OF1		6	12	1	3	4	0	0	0	1	2	0	.250	.250
King Kelly	C4	(2-3)	4	15	2	4	4	0	0	1	0	2	1	.267	.467
Tommy Dowd	OF4	(1-2)	4	11	1	1	0	0	0	0	0	1	0	.091	.091
Tim Donahue	C4		4	7	0	0	0	0	0	0	0	5	0	.000	.000
Frank Quinlan	C1,OF1		2	5	0	0	0	0	0	0	0	2	0	.000	.000
Kid Madden	P1	(1-2)	1	3	0	2	1	0	0	0	0	0	0	.667	.667
Mike Flynn	C1		1	2	0	0	0	0	0	0	0	1	0	.000	.000
			139	4889	1028	1341	774	163	100	52	651	499	447	.274	.380

PITCHERS		W	L	PCT	G	GS	CG	SH	SV	IP	H	BB	SO	ERA
George Haddock		34	11	.756	51	47	37	5	1	380	330	137	169	2.49
Charles Buffinton		29	9	.763	48	43	33	2	1	364	303	120	158	2.55
John O'Brien		18	13	.581	40	30	22	0	2	269	300	127	87	3.65
Bill Daley		8	6	.571	19	11	10	0	2	127	119	81	68	2.98
Clark Griffith	(2-2)	3	1	.750	7	4	3	0	0	40	47	15	20	5.62
John Fitzgerald		1	1	.500	6	3	2	0	0	32	49	11	16	5.63
Kid Madden	(1-2)	0	1	.000	1	1	1	0	0	8	10	6	6	6.75
Paul Radford		0	0	----	1	0	0	0	0	1	0	0	0	0.00
		93	42	.689	139	139	108	9	7	1220	1158	497	524	3.03

ST. LOUIS Browns — 86-52 .623 -8.5 2nd Charlie Comiskey

BATTERS	POS/GAMES		GP	AB	R	H	BI	2B	3B	HR	BB	SO	SB	BA	SA
Charlie Comiskey	1B141,OF2		141	580	86	152	93	16	2	3	33	25	41	.262	.312
Bill Eagan	2B83		83	302	49	65	43	11	4	4	44	54	21	.215	.318
Shorty Fuller	SS103,2B39		137	586	107	127	63	15	7	2	67	28	42	.217	.276
Denny Lyons	3B120		120	451	124	142	84	24	3	11	88	58	9	.315	.455
Tommy McCarthy	OF113,2B14,SS12,3B3,P1		136	578	127	179	95	21	6	8	50	19	37	.310	.408
Dummy Hoy	OF141		141	567	136	165	66	14	5	5	119	25	59	.291	.360
Tip O'Neill	OF129		129	521	112	167	95	28	4	10	62	33	25	.321	.447
Jack Boyle	C91,SS26,3B8,OF3,2B3,1B3		123	439	78	123	79	18	8	5	47	36	19	.280	.392
Jack Stivetts	P64,OF24		85	302	45	92	54	10	2	7	10	32	4	.305	.421
John Munyan	C45,OF12,SS5,3B3		62	182	44	42	20	4	3	0	43	39	13	.231	.286
Willie McGill	P35	(2-2)	35	87		14	4	1	1	0	28	25	2	.161	.195
Clark Griffith	P27	(1-2)	27	77	11	12	8	1	0	1	8	15	2	.156	.208
Dell Darling	C17,2B2,SS1		17	53	9	7	9	1	3	0	10	11	0	.132	.264
Joe Neale	P15		15	51	6	6	8	0	1	1	3	11	1	.118	.216
George Rettger	P14,OF1		15	42	5	3	2	2	0	1	5	10	1	.071	.143
John Easton	P7,OF2	(2-3)	9	28		5	2	0	0	0	3	3	2	.179	.179
Harry Burrell	P7,OF2		9	22	2	5	6	2	0	0	1	5	0	.227	.318
Paul Cook	C7	(2-2)	7	25	3	5	1	0	0	0	1	2	0	.200	.200
Joe Visner	OF6	(2-2)	6	27	2	4	1	0	1	0	0	3	0	.148	.222
Ted Breitenstein	P6,OF1		6	12	2	0	0	0	0	0	2	0	1	.000	.000
John Ricks	3B5		5	18	3	3	0	0	0	0	0	2	0	.167	.167
Jim McQuaid	2B3,OF1		4	11	1	4	1	2	0	0	0	1	1	.364	.545
Paul McSweeney	2B3,3B1		3	12	2	3	2	1	0	0	0	0	1	.250	.333
Art Whitney	3B3	(2-2)	3	11	0	0	0	0	0	0	1	2	0	.000	.000
Jesse Duryea	P3	(2-2)	3	11		4	2	0	1	0	0	0	2	.364	.545
Bill Zies	C2		2	3	0	1	0	0	0	0	0	0	0	.333	.333
Yank Robinson	2B1	(2-2)	1	3	0	0	0	0	0	0	0	0	0	.000	.000

ST. LOUIS (cont.)
Browns

BATTERS	POS/GAMES		GP	AB	R	H	BI	2B	3B	HR	BB	SO	SB	BA	SA
John Schultz	C1		1	2	0	0	0	0	0	0	0	0	0	.000	.000
Harry Fuller	3B1		1	2	0	0	0	0	0	0	0	1	0	.000	.000
			141	5005	976	1330	738	169	51	58	625	440	283	.266	.355

PITCHERS		W	L	PCT	G	GS	CG	SH	SV	IP	H	BB	SO	ERA
Jack Stivetts		33	22	.600	64	56	40	3	1	440	357	232	259	2.86
Willie McGill	(2-2)	19	10	.655	35	31	22	1	1	249	225	131	154	2.93
Clark Griffith	(1-2)	11	8	.579	27	17	12	0	0	186	195	58	68	3.33
George Rettger		7	3	.700	14	12	10	1	1	93	85	51	49	3.40
Joe Neale		6	4	.600	15	11	9	1	1	110	109	36	24	4.24
Harry Burrell		4	2	.667	7	4	3	0	0	43	51	21	19	4.81
John Easton	(2-3)	3	2	.600	7	6	4	0	0	48	48	23	22	5.10
Ted Breitenstein		2	0	1.000	6	1	1	1	1	29	15	14	13	2.20
Jesse Duryea	(2-2)	1	1	.500	3	3	2	0	0	24	19	10	13	3.38
Tommy McCarthy		0	0	----	1	0	0	0	0	1	2	0	0	9.00
		86	52	.623	141	141	103	8	5	1223	1106	576	621	3.27

MILWAUKEE
Brewers

21-15 .583 -22.5 3rd Charlie Cushman

BATTERS	POS/GAMES		GP	AB	R	H	BI	2B	3B	HR	BB	SO	SB	BA	SA
John Carney	1B31	(2-2)	31	110	22	33	23	5	2	3	13	8	5	.300	.464
Jimmy Canavan	2B24,SS11	(2-2)	35	142	33	38	21	2	4	3	16	10	7	.268	.401
George Shoch	SS25,3B9		34	127	29	40	16	7	1	1	18	5	12	.315	.409
Gus Alberts	3B12		12	41	6	4	2	0	0	0	7	5	1	.098	.098
Howard Earl	OF30,1B2		31	129	21	32	17	5	2	1	5	13	3	.248	.341
Ed Burke	OF35		35	144	31	34	21	9	0	2	12	19	7	.236	.340
Abner Dalrymple	OF32		32	135	31	42	22	7	5	1	7	18	6	.311	.459
Farmer Vaughn	C20,1B4,OF1	(2-2)	25	99	13	33	9	7	0	0	4	5	1	.333	.404
John Grim	C16,3B10,2B3		29	119	14	28	14	5	1	1	2	5	1	.235	.319
Bob Pettit	2B9,OF7,3B6		21	80	10	14	5	4	0	1	7	7	2	.175	.263
George Davies	P12		12	37	5	9	4	2	0	0	0	6	0	.243	.297
Frank Dwyer	P10	(2-2)	11	40	1	9	2	1	0	0	1	2	1	.225	.225
Frank Killen	P11		11	35	8	8	5	3	0	0	8	7	0	.229	.314
Tom Letcher	OF6		6	21	3	4	2	1	0	0	0	1	1	.190	.238
Jim Hughey	P2		2	7	0	1	1	0	0	0	0	2	0	.143	.143
Willard Mains	P2	(2-2)	2	5	0	3	1	0	0	0	0	1	0	.600	.600
			36	1271	227	332	165	58	15	13	107	114	47	.261	.361

PITCHERS		W	L	PCT	G	GS	CG	SH	SV	IP	H	BB	SO	ERA
Frank Killen		7	4	.636	11	11	11	2	0	97	73	51	38	1.68
George Davies		7	5	.583	12	12	12	1	0	102	94	35	61	2.65
Frank Dwyer	(2-2)	6	4	.600	10	10	10	0	0	86	92	21	27	2.20
Jim Hughey		1	0	1.000	2	2	1	1	0	15	18	3	9	3.00
Willard Mains	(2-2)	0	2	.000	2	2	1	0	0	10	14	10	2	10.80
		21	15	.583	36	36	35	3	0	310	291	120	137	2.50

BALTIMORE
Orioles

71-64 .526 -22 4th Billy Barnie

BATTERS	POS/GAMES		GP	AB	R	H	BI	2B	3B	HR	BB	SO	SB	BA	SA
Perry Werden	1B139		139	552	102	160	104	20	18	6	52	59	46	.290	.424
Sam Wise	2B99,SS4		103	388	70	96	48	14	5	1	62	52	33	.247	.317
Irv Ray	SS40,OF64		103	418	72	116	58	17	5	0	54	18	28	.278	.342
Pete Gilbert	3B139		139	513	81	118	72	15	7	3	37	77	31	.230	.304
Bill Johnson	OF129		129	480	101	130	79	13	14	2	89	55	32	.271	.369
Curt Welch	OF113,2B21,SS2		132	514	122	138	55	22	10	3	77	42	50	.268	.368
George Van Haltren	OF81,SS59,P6,2B2		139	566	136	180	83	14	15	9	71	46	75	.318	.443
Wilbert Robinson	C92,OF1		93	334	25	72	46	8	5	2	16	37	18	.216	.287
Sadie McMahon	P61,OF2		61	210	31	43	15	2	4	1	7	36	6	.205	.267
George Townshend	C58,OF3		61	204	29	39	18	5	4	0	20	21	3	.191	.255
Kid Madden	P32,OF7	(2-2)	38	107	18	29	15	2	2	1	9	10	2	.271	.355
John McGraw	SS21,OF9,2B3		33	115	17	31	14	3	5	0	12	17	4	.270	.383
Bert Cunningham	P30,OF2,SS1		31	100	17	15	11	3	1	1	13	20	4	.150	.230
Joe Walsh	SS13,2B13		26	100	14	21	10	0	1	1	6	18	4	.210	.260

1891 AMERICAN ASSOCIATION

BALTIMORE (cont.)
Orioles

BATTERS	POS/GAMES		GP	AB	R	H	BI	2B	3B	HR	BB	SO	SB	BA	SA
Egyptian Healy	P23		23	64	4	9	6	2	0	0	8	23	1	.141	.172
Lew Hardie	OF15		15	56	7	13	1	0	3	0	8	8	3	.232	.339
John O'Connell	SS3,2B3,OF2		8	29	2	5	7	1	0	0	3	6	2	.172	.207
Jersey Bakely	P8	(1-2)	8	21	2	2	1	1	0	0	7	8	0	.045	.045
			139	4771	850	1217	643	142	99	30	551	553	342	.255	.345

PITCHERS			W	L	PCT	G	GS	CG	SH	SV	IP	H	BB	SO	ERA
Sadie McMahon			35	24	.593	61	58	53	5	1	503	493	149	219	2.81
Kid Madden		(2-2)	13	12	.520	32	27	20	1	1	224	239	88	56	4.10
Bert Cunningham			11	14	.440	30	25	21	0	0	238	241	138	59	4.01
Egyptian Healy			8	10	.444	23	22	19	0	0	170	179	57	54	3.75
Jersey Bakely		(2-2)	4	2	.667	8	6	5	0	0	59	48	30	13	2.29
George Van Haltren			0	1	.000	6	1	0	0	0	23	38	10	7	5.09
			71	64	.526	139	139	118	6	2	1217	1238	472	408	3.43

PHILADELPHIA
Athletics

73-66   .525   -22   5th   Sharsig - Wood

BATTERS	POS/GAMES		GP	AB	R	H	BI	2B	3B	HR	BB	SO	SB	BA	SA
Henry Larkin	1B111,OF23		133	526	94	147	93	27	14	10	66	56	2	.279	.441
Bill Hallman	2B141		141	587	112	166	69	21	13	6	38	56	18	.283	.394
Tom Corcoran	SS133		133	511	84	130	71	11	15	7	29	56	30	.254	.376
Joe Mulvey	3B113		113	453	63	115	66	9	13	5	17	32	11	.254	.364
Jim McTamany	OF58	(2-2)	58	218	57	49	21	6	3	3	43	44	13	.225	.321
Pop Corkhill	OF83	(1-3)	83	349	50	73	31	7	7	0	26	15	12	.209	.269
George Wood	OF122,3B6,SS5		132	528	106	163	63	17	14	4	72	52	22	.309	.417
Jocko Milligan	C87,1B32		118	455	75	138	106	35	12	11	56	51	2	.303	.505
Lave Cross	OF43,C43,3B24,2B1,SS1		110	402	66	121	52	20	14	5	38	23	14	.301	.458
Gus Weyhing	P52,OF2		54	198	11	22	11	5	1	0	7	65	2	.111	.146
Icebox Chamberlain	P49,OF6		54	176	21	33	19	3	5	2	21	33	3	.188	.295
Jack McGeachey	OF50	(1-2)	50	201	24	46	13	4	3	2	6	12	9	.229	.308
Ben Sanders	OF22,P19		40	156	24	39	19	6	4	1	7	12	2	.250	.359
Ed Beecher	OF16	(2-2)	16	71	9	15	7	2	4	0	3	4	7	.211	.352
Will Calihan	P13,SS1,3B1		15	56	6	11	4	1	0	0	5	8	0	.196	.214
David McKeough	C14,SS1		15	54	4	14	3	1	1	0	8	6	0	.259	.315
Sumner Bowman	P8,OF6		14	54	8	13	2	4	0	0	2	12	1	.241	.315
George Meakim	P6		6	15	2	3	1	1	0	0	2	3	0	.200	.267
Bill Clymer	SS3		3	11	0	0	0	0	0	0	1	2	0	.000	.000
Pat Friel	OF2		2	8	2	2	0	1	0	0	0	0	0	.250	.250
Mike Sullivan	P2	(2-2)	2	7	0	0	0	0	0	0	0	5	0	.000	.000
Bobby Mathews	OF1		1	3	1	1	0	0	0	0	0	1	0	.333	.333
			143	5039	817	1301	649	182	123	55	447	548	149	.258	.376

PITCHERS			W	L	PCT	G	GS	CG	SH	SV	IP	H	BB	SO	ERA
Gus Weyhing			31	20	.608	52	51	51	3	0	450	428	161	219	3.18
Icebox Chamberlain			22	23	.489	49	46	44	0	0	406	397	206	204	4.22
Ben Sanders			11	5	.688	19	18	15	0	0	145	157	37	40	3.79
Will Calihan			6	6	.500	13	11	11	0	0	112	151	47	28	6.43
Sumner Bowman			2	5	.286	8	8	8	0	0	68	73	37	22	3.44
George Meakim			1	4	.200	6	6	4	0	0	35	51	22	13	6.94
Mike Sullivan		(1-2)	0	2	.000	2	2	2	0	0	18	17	10	7	3.50
			73	66	.525	143	142	135	3	0	1234	1274	520	533	4.01

COLUMBUS
Buckeyes

61-76   .445   -33   6th   Gus Schmelz

BATTERS	POS/GAMES		GP	AB	R	H	BI	2B	3B	HR	BB	SO	SB	BA	SA
Mike Lehane	1B137		137	511	59	110	52	12	7	1	34	77	16	.215	.272
Jack Crooks	2B138		138	519	110	127	46	19	13	0	103	47	50	.245	.331
Bobby Wheelock	SS136		136	498	82	114	39	15	1	0	78	55	52	.229	.263
Bill Kuehne	3B68	(1-2)	68	261	32	56	22	9	0	2	10	22	21	.215	.272
John Sneed	OF99		99	366	66	94	61	9	6	1	55	29	24	.257	.322
Jim McTamany	OF81	(1-2)	81	304	59	76	35	17	9	3	58	48	20	.250	.395
Charlie Duffee	OF128,3B7,SS2		137	552	86	166	90	28	4	10	42	36	41	.301	.420
Jim Donahue	C75,OF1,1B1		77	280	27	61	35	4	3	0	31	18	2	.218	.254

COLUMBUS (cont.)
Buckeyes

BATTERS	POS/GAMES		GP	AB	R	H	BI	2B	3B	HR	BB	SO	SB	BA	SA
Phil Knell	P58,OF9,2B1		66	215	25	34	19	2	3	0	8	34	4	.158	.195
Larry Twitchell	OF56,P6		57	224	32	62	35	9	4	2	20	28	10	.277	.379
Jack O'Connor	OF40,C21		56	229	28	61	37	12	3	0	11	14	10	.266	.345
Tom Dowse	C51,OF5		55	201	24	45	22	7	0	0	13	22	2	.224	.259
Hank Gastright	P35		35	117	11	23	10	2	4	0	12	20	2	.197	.282
Tim O'Rourke	3B34		34	136	22	38	12	1	3	0	15	7	9	.279	.331
John Dolan	P27,OF1		28	78	6	7	8	3	0	1	8	33	1	.090	.167
John Easton	P20,OF4	(1,3-3)	24	74	11	15	8	4	1	0	3	12	4	.203	.284
Jim Donnelly	3B17		17	54	6	13	9	0	0	0	13	5	7	.241	.241
Elmer Cleveland	3B12		12	41	12	7	4	0	0	0	12	9	4	.171	.171
John Leiper	P6,OF1		6	21	2	3	3	0	0	0	0	6	0	.143	.143
Dad Clarke	P4		4	9	2	1	0	1	0	0	2	5	0	.111	.222
Jim Sullivan	P1	(2-2)	1	4	0	0	0	0	0	0	0	1	0	.000	.000
Bill Lyston	P1		1	2	0	0	0	0	0	0	1	2	1	.000	.000
Ed Clark	P1		1	1	0	0	0	0	0	0	0	0	0	.000	.000
			138	4697	702	1113	547	154	61	20	529	530	280	.237	.308

PITCHERS			W	L	PCT	G	GS	CG	SH	SV	IP	H	BB	SO	ERA
Phil Knell			28	27	.509	58	52	47	5	0	462	363	226	228	2.92
John Dolan			12	11	.522	27	24	19	0	0	203	216	84	68	4.16
Hank Gastright			12	19	.387	35	33	28	1	0	284	280	136	109	3.78
John Easton		(1,3-3)	5	12	.294	20	18	15	0	0	150	160	63	65	4.44
John Leiper			2	2	.500	6	5	4	0	0	45	41	39	19	5.40
Larry Twitchell			1	1	.500	6	1	1	0	0	31	29	13	8	4.06
Dad Clarke			1	2	.333	4	3	2	0	0	21	30	16	2	6.86
Jim Sullivan		(2-2)	0	1	.000	1	1	1	0	0	9	10	5	1	4.00
Bill Lyston			0	1	.000	1	1	1	0	0	6	10	6	1	10.50
Ed Clark			0	0	----	1	0	0	0	0	2	2	0	1	0.00
			61	76	.445	138	138	118	6	0	1213	1141	588	502	3.75

CINCINNATI
Kellys

43-57   .430   -32.5   7th   King Kelly

BATTERS	POS/GAMES		GP	AB	R	H	BI	2B	3B	HR	BB	SO	SB	BA	SA
John Carney	1B99	(1-2)	99	367	47	102	43	10	8	3	35	18	15	.278	.373
Yank Robinson	2B97	(1-2)	97	342	48	61	37	9	4	1	68	51	23	.178	.237
Jimmy Canavan	SS101	(1-2)	101	426	74	97	66	13	4	7	27	44	21	.228	.373
Art Whitney	3B93	(1-2)	93	347	42	69	3	6	1	3	31	20	8	.199	.248
Emmett Seery	OF97		97	372	77	106	36	15	10	4	81	52	19	.285	.411
Dick Johnston	OF99		99	376	59	83	51	11	2	6	38	44	12	.221	.309
Ed Andrews	OF83		83	356	47	75	26	7	4	0	33	35	22	.211	.253
King Kelly	C66,2B6,3B8,OF7,1B8,P3,SS1	(1-3)	82	283	56	84	53	15	7	1	51	28	22	.297	.410
Farmer Vaughn	C44,OF6,3B2,1B2,P1	(1-2)	51	175	21	45	14	7	1	1	14	15	7	.257	.326
Frank Dwyer	P35,OF3,2B2	(1-2)	37	141	24	40	18	4	3	0	5	14	4	.284	.355
Cannonball Crane	P32,OF3		34	110	13	17	7	0	0	1	8	28	4	.155	.182
Willard Mains	P30		30	90	14	22	10	3	2	1	5	8	2	.244	.356
Jerry Hurley	C24,OF1,1B1		24	66	10	14	6	3	2	0	12	13	2	.212	.318
Lefty Marr	OF14	(2-2)	14	57	9	11	4	1	0	0	7	4	2	.193	.211
Matt Kilroy	P7,OF1		8	20	2	3	0	0	0	0	4	2	0	.150	.150
Willie McGill	P8	(1-2)	8	20	4	2	0	0	0	0	9	4	0	.100	.100
Bill Clingman	2B1		1	5	0	1	0	1	0	0	0	0	0	.200	.400
Charlie Bell	P1	(2-2)	1	4	1	2	1	0	0	0	0	0	0	.500	.500
Kid Keenan	P1		1	4	1	2	1	0	0	0	0	1	1	.500	.500
Joe Burke	2B1		1	4	0	1	1	0	0	0	0	2	0	.250	.250
Wild Bill Widner	P1		1	4	0	1	0	0	0	0	0	1	0	.250	.250
Charlie Bastian	2B1	(1-2)	1	4	0	0	0	0	0	0	0	0	0	.000	.000
John Slagle	P1		1	1	0	0	0	0	0	0	0	1	0	.000	.000
			102	3574	549	838	407	105	58	28	428	385	164	.234	.320

PITCHERS			W	L	PCT	G	GS	CG	SH	SV	IP	H	BB	SO	ERA
Cannonball Crane		(1-2)	14	14	.500	32	31	25	1	0	250	216	139	122	2.45
Frank Dwyer		(1-2)	13	19	.406	35	31	29	1	0	289	332	124	101	4.52
Willard Mains		(1-2)	12	12	.500	30	23	19	0	0	204	196	107	76	2.69
Willie McGill		(1-2)	2	5	.286	8	8	6	0	0	65	69	37	19	4.98
Matt Kilroy			1	4	.200	7	6	4	0	0	45	51	19	6	2.98
Charlie Bell		(2-2)	1	0	1.000	1	1	1	0	0	9	2	3	1	0.00
King Kelly		(1-3)	0	1	.000	3	0	0	0	0	15	21	7	0	5.28
Wild Bill Widner			0	1	.000	1	1	1	0	0	8	13	4	0	7.88
Kid Keenan			0	1	.000	1	1	1	0	0	8	6	4	5	0.00

CINCINNATI (cont.)
Kellys

PITCHERS			W	L	PCT	G	GS	CG	SH	SV	IP	H	BB	SO	ERA
Farmer Vaughn		(1-2)	0	0	----	1	0	0	0	0	7	12	1	0	3.86
John Slagle			0	0	----	1	0	0	0	1	1	3	1	1	0.00
			43	57	.430	102	102	86	2	1	902	921	446	331	3.43

LOUISVILLE   55-84   .396   -40   8th   Jack Chapman
Colonels

BATTERS	POS/GAMES		GP	AB	R	H	BI	2B	3B	HR	BB	SO	SB	BA	SA
Harry Taylor	1B92,3B1,2B1,C1		93	356	81	105	37	7	4	2	55	33	15	.295	.354
Tim Shinnick	2B120,3B7,SS1		128	443	79	98	54	10	11	1	54	47	36	.221	.300
Hugh Jennings	SS70,1B17,3B3		90	360	53	105	58	10	8	1	17	36	12	.292	.372
Oliver Beard	3B61,SS7		68	257	35	62	24	4	5	0	33	9	7	.241	.296
Chicken Wolf	OF133,1B5,3B1		138	537	67	136	82	17	8	1	42	36	13	.253	.320
Farmer Weaver	OF132,C4		135	565	76	160	55	25	7	1	33	23	30	.283	.358
Patsy Donovan	OF105	(1-2)	105	439	73	141	53	10	3	2	30	18	27	.321	.371
Tom Cahill	C56,SS49,OF12,2B6,3B2		120	433	70	111	47	18	7	3	41	51	39	.256	.351
Jack Ryan	C56,1B11,3B6,OF4,2B3		75	253	24	57	25	5	4	2	15	40	3	.225	.300
Paul Cook	C35,1B10	(1-2)	45	153	21	35	23	3	1	0	11	17	4	.229	.261
Bill Kuehne	3B41	(2-2)	41	159	28	44	18	3	1	1	8	13	10	.277	.327
Scott Stratton	P20,1B8,OF6	(2-2)	34	115	9	27	8	2	0	0	11	13	8	.235	.252
John Fitzgerald	P33,OF1		34	112	15	19	10	2	2	1	14	38	3	.170	.250
Jouett Meekin	P29,OF3,1B1		33	97	14	21	10	0	3	1	15	19	4	.216	.309
Red Ehret	P26		26	91	9	22	9	2	1	0	5	15	3	.242	.286
Ed Daily	P15,OF7	(1-2)	22	64	10	16	8	2	0	0	8	6	4	.250	.281
Monk Cline	OF21		21	76	13	23	12	3	1	0	19	3	2	.303	.368
John Doran	P15		15	53	5	10	0	2	0	0	1	14	0	.189	.226
Harry Raymond	SS14		14	59	4	12	2	2	0	0	5	6	3	.203	.237
John Irwin	3B14	(2-2)	14	55	7	15	7	1	1	0	5	6	1	.273	.327
Sam LaRoque	2B10,1B1	(2-2)	10	35	6	11	8	2	1	1	5	8	1	.314	.514
Charlie Bell	P10	(1-2)	10	28	3	1	0	0	0	0	6	8	8	.036	.036
Al Schellhasse	C7		7	20	4	3	1	0	0	0	1	2	3	.150	.150
James Long	OF6		6	25	5	6	4	0	0	0	3	6	1	.240	.240
George Fox	3B6		6	19	1	2	2	0	1	0	2	3	0	.105	.211
George Boone	P4		4	6	0	2	0	0	0	0	0	1	0	.333	.333
Joe Gerhardt	2B2		2	6	0	0	0	0	0	0	1	0	0	.000	.000
Pat Petee	2B2		2	5	1	0	0	0	0	0	3	0	0	.000	.000
John Wentz	2B1		1	4	0	1	0	0	0	0	0	0	0	.250	.250
Grant Briggs	C1		1	4	0	1	0	0	0	0	0	0	0	.250	.250
Jack Darragh	1B1		1	2	0	1	0	0	0	0	0	0	0	.500	.500
Nick Reeder	3B1		1	2	0	0	0	0	0	0	0	1	0	.000	.000
			141	4833	713	1247	557	130	69	17	443	473	230	.258	.324

PITCHERS			W	L	PCT	G	GS	CG	SH	SV	IP	H	BB	SO	ERA
John Fitzgerald			14	18	.438	33	32	29	3	0	276	280	95	111	3.59
Red Ehret			13	13	.500	26	24	23	2	0	221	225	70	76	3.47
Jouett Meekin			10	16	.385	29	26	25	2	0	228	227	113	144	4.30
Scott Stratton		(2-2)	6	13	.316	20	20	20	1	0	172	204	34	52	4.08
John Doran			5	10	.333	15	14	12	1	0	126	160	75	55	5.43
Ed Daily		(1-2)	4	8	.333	15	14	11	0	0	111	149	48	27	5.74
Charlie Bell		(1-2)	2	6	.250	10	9	8	0	0	77	93	20	16	4.68
George Boone			0	0	----	4	1	0	0	1	15	15	9	4	7.80
			55	84	.396	141	140	128	9	1	1226	1353	464	485	4.27

WASHINGTON   44-91   .326   -49   9th   Trott - Snyder - Shannon - Griffin
Statesmen

BATTERS	POS/GAMES		GP	AB	R	H	BI	2B	3B	HR	BB	SO	SB	BA	SA
Mox McQuery	1B68		68	261	40	63	37	9	4	2	18	19	3	.241	.330
Tommy Dowd	2B103,OF9	(2-2)	112	464	66	120	44	9	10	1	19	44	39	.259	.328
Gil Hatfield	SS105,3B27,P4,OF3		134	500	83	128	48	11	8	1	50	39	43	.256	.316
Bill Alvord	3B81	(2-2)	81	312	28	73	30	8	3	0	11	38	3	.234	.279
Larry Murphy	OF101		101	400	73	106	35	15	3	1	63	27	29	.265	.325
Paul Hines	OF47,1B8		54	206	25	58	31	7	5	0	21	16	6	.282	.364
Ed Beecher	OF58	(1-2)	58	235	35	57	28	11	3	2	27	9	17	.243	.340
Deacon McGuire	C98,OF18,3B3,1B1		114	413	55	125	66	22	10	3	43	34	10	.303	.426

WASHINGTON (cont.)
Statesmen

BATTERS	POS/GAMES		GP	AB	R	H	BI	2B	3B	HR	BB	SO	SB	BA	SA
Kid Carsey	P54,OF7,SS2		61	187	25	28	15	5	2	0	19	38	2	.150	.198
Allen McCauley	1B59		59	206	36	58	31	5	8	1	30	13	9	.282	.398
Sy Sutcliffe	OF35,C22,SS3,3B1		53	201	29	71	33	8	3	2	17	17	8	.353	.453
Frank Foreman	P43,OF8	(2-2)	50	153	26	34	19	4	5	4	23	35	6	.222	.392
Pete Lohman	C21,OF8,3B4,SS1,2B1		32	109	18	21	11	1	4	1	16	17	1	.193	.303
Jim Curtis	OF29	(2-2)	29	103	17	26	12	3	2	0	13	16	2	.252	.320
Pop Smith	2B19,SS5,3B4		27	90	13	16	13	2	2	0	13	16	2	.178	.244
Ed Daily	OF21	(2-2)	21	79	13	18	6	2	0	0	11	10	8	.228	.253
Jim Burns	OF20,SS1		20	82	15	26	10	6	0	0	6	10	2	.317	.390
Sandy Griffin	OF20		20	69	15	19	10	4	2	0	10	3	2	.275	.391
Dan Shannon	SS14,2B5		19	67	7	9	3	2	0	0	6	9	3	.134	.164
Joe Visner	OF17,3B1,C1	(1-2)	18	68	13	19	7	2	3	1	8	7	2	.279	.441
Pat Donovan	OF17	(2-2)	17	70	9	14	3	1	0	0	4	5	1	.200	.214
Mike Slattery	OF15	(2-2)	15	60	8	17	5	1	0	0	4	5	6	.283	.300
Tom McLaughlin	SS14		14	41	9	11	3	0	1	0	7	6	3	.268	.317
Jersey Bakely	P13	(1-2)	13	45	2	10	4	1	0	0	3	10	0	.222	.244
Jumbo Davis	3B12		12	44	7	14	9	3	2	0	7	5	8	.318	.477
Will Smalley	3B9,2B2		11	38	5	6	3	0	1	0	5	2	0	.158	.211
Pop Snyder	1B4,C3,OF1		8	27	4	5	2	0	1	0	0	3	0	.185	.259
Ed Eiteljorg	P8		8	26	3	5	4	1	0	0	1	6	0	.192	.231
Fred Dunlap	2B8		8	25	4	5	4	1	1	0	5	4	3	.200	.320
Tom Hart	C5,OF3		8	24	1	3	2	0	0	0	2	1	1	.125	.125
Ed Cassian	P7	(2-2)	7	26	4	9	4	1	1	0	0	4	0	.346	.462
Bob Miller	P7		7	18	1	2	2	0	0	0	0	5	0	.111	.111
Buck Freeman	P5		5	18	1	4	1	1	0	0	2	2	0	.222	.278
George Keefe	P5		5	14	1	2	1	0	0	0	3	3	0	.143	.143
Martin Duke	P4		4	9	0	1	0	1	0	0	0	0	0	.111	.222
Bill Quarles	P3		3	11	0	0	0	0	0	0	0	3	0	.000	.000
Harry Mace	P3		3	6	0	0	0	0	0	0	1	3	0	.000	.000
Miah Murray	C2		2	8	0	0	0	0	0	0	0	1	0	.000	.000
			139	4715	691	1183	536	147	84	19	468	485	219	.251	.330

PITCHERS		W	L	PCT	G	GS	CG	SH	SV	IP	H	BB	SO	ERA
Frank Foreman	(2-2)	18	20	.474	43	41	39	1	1	345	381	142	170	3.73
Kid Carsey		14	37	.275	54	53	46	1	0	415	513	161	174	4.99
Buck Freeman		3	2	.600	5	4	4	0	0	44	35	33	28	3.89
Ed Cassian	(2-2)	2	4	.333	7	5	5	0	0	53	73	35	14	5.60
Bob Miller		2	5	.286	7	7	3	0	0	42	53	24	13	4.29
Jersey Bakely	(1-2)	2	10	.167	13	12	11	0	0	104	127	60	32	5.35
Bill Quarles		1	1	.500	3	2	2	0	0	22	32	12	10	8.18
Ed Eiteljorg		1	5	.167	8	7	6	0	0	61	79	41	23	6.16
Harry Mace		0	1	.000	3	1	1	0	0	16	18	8	3	7.31
Martin Duke		0	3	.000	4	3	2	0	0	23	36	19	5	7.43
George Keefe		0	3	.000	5	4	4	0	1	37	44	17	11	2.68
Gil Hatfield		0	0	----	4	0	0	0	0	18	29	14	3	11.00
		44	91	.326	139	139	123	2	2	1181	1420	566	486	4.83

1892 NATIONAL LEAGUE

Monopoly

After the 1891 season, during the aftermath of the Kelly signing, both the National League and the American Association raided each other with glee. No fewer than 30 players jumped leagues to sign lucrative contracts. This policy, left unchecked, would have resulted in bankruptcy for all.

On December 15, 1891, both leagues met separately to draw up plans for a consolidated league. As a result, five of the association teams would be bought out. At this juncture, Milwaukee, Chicago (a new franchise), Boston, Philadelphia, and Columbus ceased to be. The four remaining American Association franchises, St. Louis, Baltimore, Washington, and Louisville joined the National League to form one 12-team circuit. The name of this league was "The National League and American Association of Baseball Clubs." The name notwithstanding, the American Association had been totally absorbed into the National League, with the unpalatable half spit out. Any smaller city (Milwaukee and Columbus) as well as competing teams within any one city (Chicago, Boston, and Philadelphia) were not wanted.

When the 1892 season was being scheduled, a provision was made for a 154-game split-season schedule, the longest season to date. The owners felt that in a 12-team league, as the season progressed, the pennant race for the bottom tier would soon have no meaning. By having a split season, the owners would be assured of two pennant races and a championship series pitting the two winners.

In July, with Boston holding a comfortable lead, that is just what happened. On July 11, with Boston holding a two and one-half game lead over Brooklyn, the first half ended. On July 15, the second half started and when it ended in October, Cleveland had bested Boston by three games. In the post-season Championship Series, Boston blanked Cleveland five games to zero, with one tie.

Both Boston and Cleveland won their season halves with pitching, as Boston's Hugh Duffy (.301) was the only .300 hitter on either team. Boston did brag of two 35-game winners (Kid Nichols and Jack Stivetts), while Cleveland enjoyed the services of Cy Young, who won 36 while having the best earned run average at 1.93.

Brooklyn and Philadelphia, in third and fourth, were the two strongest hitting teams in the National League. Brooklyn's Dan Brouthers (.335) won the batting title while Billy Hamilton (.330) of Philadelphia finished second.

Cincinnati, Pittsburgh, and Chicago finished in the next three spots. None of the three had any regular over .300, but Bug Holliday of Cincinnati (.292) was close. He also led the home run race at 13. Cincinnati pitcher Bumpus Jones made his major league debut a memorable one as he pitched a no-hitter in his first start in October. That victory would equal one-third of his major league wins.

New York, Louisville, Washington, St. Louis, and Baltimore occupied the last five places. Only New York's Buck Ewing (.310) and George Van Haltren of Baltimore (.302) hit well.

The National League finally had their monopoly. Nominally, the two leagues had merged, but the terms had been dictated by the senior circuit. Under no circumstances were the National League magnates going to let the American Association's strongest teams survive. It was no accident then that places nine through twelve in 1892, were taken by the four teams coming in from the association.

1892 NATIONAL LEAGUE

BOSTON Beaneaters 102-48 .680 1st Frank Selee

BATTERS	POS/GAMES		GP	AB	R	H	BI	2B	3B	HR	BB	SO	SB	BA	SA
Tommy Tucker	1B140		140	542	85	153	62	15	7	1	45	35	22	.280	.341
Joe Quinn	2B143		143	532	63	116	59	14	1	1	35	40	17	.218	.254
Germany Long	SS141,OF12,3B1		151	646	115	181	77	33	6	6	44	36	57	.280	.378
Billy Nash	3B135,OF1		135	526	94	137	95	25	5	4	59	41	31	.260	.350
Tommy McCarthy	OF152		152	603	119	146	63	19	5	4	93	29	53	.242	.310
Hugh Duffy	OF146,3B2		147	612	125	184	81	28	12	5	60	37	51	.301	.410
Bobby Lowe	OF90,3B14,SS13,2B10		124	475	79	115	57	16	7	3	37	46	36	.242	.324
King Kelly	C72,OF2,3B2,1B2,P1		78	281	40	53	41	7	0	2	39	31	24	.189	.235
Jack Stivetts	P53,OF18,1B1		70	240	40	71	36	14	2	3	27	28	8	.296	.408
Kid Nichols	P53,OF5		57	197	21	39	21	6	2	2	16	51	3	.198	.279
Charles Ganzel	C51,OF2,1B1		54	198	25	53	25	9	3	0	18	12	7	.268	.343
Harry Stovey	OF38	(1-2)	38	146	21	24	12	8	1	0	14	19	20	.164	.233
Harry Staley	P37,OF1		38	122	9	16	9	2	0	1	9	38	2	.131	.172
Charlie Bennett	C35		35	114	19	23	16	4	0	1	27	23	6	.202	.263
John Clarkson	P16	(1-2)	16	57	7	13	13	3	0	1	3	15	1	.228	.333
Dan Burke	C1		1	4	0	0	0	0	0	0	0	2	0	.000	.000
Leon Viau	P1	(3-3)	1	3	0	0	0	0	0	0	0	2	0	.000	.000
Dad Clarkson	P1		1	3	0	0	0	0	0	0	0	3	0	.000	.000
Joe Daly	C1		1	0	0	0	0	0	0	0	0	0	0	----	----
			152	5301	862	1324	667	203	51	34	526	488	338	.250	.327

PITCHERS			W	L	PCT	G	GS	CG	SH	SV	IP	H	BB	SO	ERA
Kid Nichols			35	16	.686	53	51	49	5	0	453	404	121	187	2.84
Jack Stivetts			35	16	.686	54	48	45	3	1	416	346	171	180	3.03
Harry Staley			22	10	.688	37	35	31	3	0	300	273	97	93	3.03
John Clarkson		(1-2)	8	6	.571	16	16	15	4	0	146	115	60	48	2.35
Leon Viau		(3-3)	1	0	1.000	1	1	1	0	0	9	5	4	1	0.00
Dad Clarkson			1	0	1.000	1	1	1	0	0	7	5	3	0	1.29
King Kelly			0	0	----	1	0	0	0	0	6	8	4	0	1.50
			102	48	.680	152	152	142	15	1	1336	1156	460	509	2.86

CLEVELAND Spiders 93-56 .624 -8.5 2nd Patsy Tebeau

BATTERS	POS/GAMES		GP	AB	R	H	BI	2B	3B	HR	BB	SO	SB	BA	SA
Jake Virtue	1B147		147	557	98	157	89	15	20	2	84	68	14	.282	.391
Cupid Childs	2B145		145	558	136	177	53	14	11	3	117	20	26	.317	.398
Ed McKean	SS128		128	526	76	139	93	14	10	0	49	28	19	.264	.329
George Davis	3B79,OF44,SS20,2B3		144	597	95	144	82	27	12	5	58	51	36	.241	.352
Jack O'Connor	OF106,C34		140	572	71	142	58	22	5	1	25	48	17	.248	.309
Jimmy McAleer	OF149,SS1		150	576	92	136	70	26	7	4	63	54	40	.236	.326
Jesse Burkett	OF145		145	608	119	167	66	15	14	6	67	59	36	.275	.375
Chief Zimmer	C111		111	413	63	108	64	29	13	1	32	47	18	.262	.402
Patsy Tebeau	3B74,2B5,1B4,SS3		86	340	47	83	49	13	3	2	23	34	6	.244	.318
Cy Young	P53		53	196	14	31	15	5	0	1	7	34	3	.158	.199
Nig Cuppy	P47,OF3		50	168	15	36	24	11	0	0	7	40	2	.214	.280
John Clarkson	P29	(2-2)	29	101	8	14	4	0	0	0	8	24	2	.139	.139
George Davies	P26		26	87	3	12	6	1	0	0	3	14	1	.138	.149
Jack Doyle	OF12,C9,1B1,SS1	(1-2)	24	88	17	26	14	4	1	1	6	10	5	.295	.398
George Rettger	P6	(1-2)	6	15	0	2	0	0	0	0	3	3	0	.133	.133
Tom Williams	P2,OF1		3	10	1	1	0	0	0	0	0	2	0	.100	.100
Leon Viau	P1	(1-3)	1	0	0	0	0	0	0	0	0	0	0	----	----
			153	5412	855	1375	687	196	96	26	552	536	225	.254	.340

PITCHERS			W	L	PCT	G	GS	CG	SH	SV	IP	H	BB	SO	ERA
Cy Young			36	12	.750	53	49	48	9	0	453	363	118	168	1.93
Nig Cuppy			28	13	.683	47	42	38	1	1	376	333	121	103	2.51
John Clarkson		(2-2)	17	10	.630	29	28	27	1	1	243	235	72	91	2.55
George Davies			10	16	.385	26	26	23	0	0	216	201	64	95	2.59
Tom Williams			1	0	1.000	2	1	1	0	0	9	9	1	3	3.00
George Rettger		(1-2)	1	3	.250	6	5	3	0	0	38	32	31	12	4.26
Leon Viau		(1-3)	0	1	.000	1	1	0	0	0	1	5	1	0	36.00
			93	56	.624	153	152	140	11	2	1336	1178	413	472	2.41

1892 NATIONAL LEAGUE

BROOKLYN Bridegrooms — 95-49 .617 -9 3rd Monte Ward

BATTERS	POS/GAMES		GP	AB	R	H	BI	2B	3B	HR	BB	SO	SB	BA	SA
Dan Brouthers	1B152		152	588	121	197	124	30	20	5	84	30	31	.335	.480
Monte Ward	2B148		148	614	109	163	47	13	3	1	82	19	88	.265	.301
Tom Corcoran	SS151		151	613	77	145	74	11	6	1	34	51	39	.237	.279
Bill Joyce	3B94,OF3		97	372	89	91	45	15	12	6	82	55	23	.245	.398
Oyster Burns	OF129,3B7,SS5		141	542	88	171	96	27	18	4	65	42	33	.315	.454
Mike Griffin	OF127,SS2		129	452	103	125	66	17	11	3	68	36	49	.277	.383
Darby O'Brien	OF122		122	490	72	119	56	14	5	1	29	52	57	.243	.298
Con Daily	C68,OF13		80	278	38	65	28	10	1	0	38	21	18	.234	.277
Tom Daly	3B57,OF30,C27,2B10		124	446	76	114	51	15	6	4	64	61	34	.256	.343
Tom Kinslow	C66		66	246	37	75	40	6	11	2	13	16	4	.305	.443
Dave Foutz	OF29,P27,1B6		61	220	33	41	26	5	3	1	14	14	19	.186	.250
Ed Stein	P48		48	144	18	31	8	2	1	0	17	33	0	.215	.243
George Haddock	P46,OF1		47	158	23	28	11	6	1	0	12	31	2	.177	.228
Bill Hart	P28,OF12		37	125	14	24	17	3	4	2	7	22	4	.192	.328
Brickyard Kennedy	P26,OF1		26	85	12	14	11	3	2	0	4	8	3	.165	.247
Hub Collins	OF21		21	87	17	26	17	5	1	0	14	13	4	.299	.379
Bert Inks	P9	(1-2)	9	25	8	10	2	1	0	0	2	2	1	.400	.440
			158	5485	935	1439	719	183	105	30	629	506	409	.262	.350

PITCHERS			W	L	PCT	G	GS	CG	SH	SV	IP	H	BB	SO	ERA
George Haddock			29	13	.690	46	44	39	3	1	381	340	163	153	3.14
Ed Stein			27	16	.628	48	42	38	6	1	377	310	150	190	2.84
Dave Foutz			13	8	.619	27	20	17	0	1	203	210	63	56	3.41
Brickyard Kennedy			13	8	.619	26	21	18	0	1	191	189	95	108	3.86
Bill Hart			9	12	.429	28	23	16	2	1	195	188	96	65	3.28
Bert Inks		(1-2)	4	2	.667	9	8	4	1	0	58	48	33	25	3.88
			95	59	.617	158	158	132	12	5	1406	1285	600	597	3.25

PHILADELPHIA Phillies — 87-66 .569 -16.5 4th Harry Wright

BATTERS	POS/GAMES		GP	AB	R	H	BI	2B	3B	HR	BB	SO	SB	BA	SA
Roger Connor	1B155		155	564	123	166	73	37	11	12	116	39	22	.294	.463
Bill Hallman	2B138		138	586	106	171	84	27	10	2	32	52	19	.292	.382
Bob Allen	SS152		152	563	77	128	64	20	14	2	61	60	15	.227	.323
Charlie Reilly	3B70,OF15,2B4		91	331	42	65	24	7	3	1	18	43	13	.196	.245
Sam Thompson	OF153		153	609	109	186	104	28	11	9	59	19	28	.305	.432
Ed Delahanty	OF121,3B4		123	477	79	146	91	30	21	6	31	32	29	.306	.495
Billy Hamilton	OF139		139	554	132	183	53	21	7	3	81	29	57	.330	.410
Jack Clements	C109		109	402	50	106	76	25	6	8	43	40	7	.264	.415
Lave Cross	3B65,C39,OF25,2B14,SS5		140	541	84	149	69	15	10	4	39	16	18	.275	.362
Gus Weyhing	P59,OF7		66	214	14	29	13	5	0	0	11	67	2	.136	.159
Kid Carsey	P43,OF2		44	131	8	20	10	2	1	1	9	24	1	.153	.206
Tim Keefe	P39		39	117	6	10	3	2	0	1	13	47	1	.085	.128
Joe Mulvey	3B25		25	98	9	14	4	1	1	0	6	9	2	.143	.173
Duke Esper	P21	(1-2)	23	70	8	17	11	2	0	1	2	18	1	.243	.314
Tom Dowse	C16	(3-4)	16	54	3	10	6	0	0	0	2	4	1	.185	.185
Phil Knell	P11	(2-2)	11	34	4	3	1	0	0	0	3	13	0	.088	.088
Dummy Stephenson	OF8		8	37	4	10	5	3	0	0	0	2	0	.270	.351
John Thornton	P3,OF2	(1-2)	5	13	1	5	2	0	0	0	0	0	0	.385	.385
Jack Taylor	P3		3	12	1	2	0	0	0	0	1	0	0	.167	.167
Harry Morelock	3B1		1	3	0	0	0	0	0	0	1	0	0	.000	.000
Jerry Connors	OF1		1	3	0	0	0	0	0	0	0	1	0	.000	.000
			155	5413	860	1420	693	225	95	50	528	515	216	.262	.367

PITCHERS			W	L	PCT	G	GS	CG	SH	SV	IP	H	BB	SO	ERA
Gus Weyhing			32	21	.604	59	49	46	6	3	470	411	168	202	2.66
Kid Carsey			19	16	.543	43	36	30	1	1	318	320	104	76	3.12
Tim Keefe			19	16	.543	39	38	31	2	0	313	264	100	127	2.36
Duke Esper		(1-2)	11	6	.647	21	18	14	0	1	160	171	58	45	3.42
Phil Knell		(2-2)	5	5	.500	11	9	7	0	0	80	87	35	43	4.05
Jack Taylor			1	0	1.000	3	3	2	0	0	26	28	10	7	1.38
John Thornton			0	2	.000	3	2	1	0	0	12	16	17	2	12.75
			87	66	.569	155	155	131	10	5	1379	1297	492	502	2.93

1892 NATIONAL LEAGUE

CINCINNATI Reds — 82-68 .547 -20 5th — Charlie Comiskey

BATTERS	POS/GAMES		GP	AB	R	H	BI	2B	3B	HR	BB	SO	SB	BA	SA
Charlie Comiskey	1B141		141	551	61	125	71	14	6	3	32	16	30	.227	.290
Bid McPhee	2B144		144	573	111	157	60	19	12	4	84	48	44	.274	.370
Germany Smith	SS139		139	506	58	121	63	13	6	8	42	52	19	.239	.336
Arlie Latham	3B142,2B9,OF1		152	622	111	148	44	20	4	0	60	54	66	.238	.283
Bug Holliday	OF152,OF1		152	602	114	176	91	23	16	13	57	39	43	.292	.449
Pete Browning	OF82,1B2	(2-2)	83	307	47	93	52	12	5	3	40	25	8	.303	.404
Tip O'Neill	OF109		109	419	63	105	52	14	6	2	53	25	14	.251	.327
Morg Murphy	C74		74	234	29	46	24	8	2	2	25	57	4	.197	.274
Farmer Vaughn	C67,1B15,OF11,3B5		91	346	45	88	50	10	5	2	16	13	10	.254	.329
Icebox Chamberlain	P52,OF1		53	160	13	36	15	3	1	2	7	17	1	.225	.294
Frank Dwyer	P33,OF6	(2-2)	40	129	15	21	6	0	2	0	4	9	2	.163	.194
Tony Mullane	P37,1B2		39	118	14	20	9	3	1	0	9	8	4	.169	.212
Frank Genins	SS17,OF14,3B4	(1-2)	35	110	12	20	7	4	0	0	12	12	7	.182	.218
George Wood	OF30	(2-2)	30	107	10	21	14	2	4	0	10	17	4	.196	.290
Jocko Halligan	OF26	(1-2)	26	101	14	29	12	4	0	2	12	9	3	.287	.386
Curt Welch	OF25	(2-2)	25	94	14	19	7	0	2	1	7	8	7	.202	.277
Jerry Harrington	C22,1B1		22	61	6	13	3	1	0	0	6	1	0	.213	.230
Mike Sullivan	P21		21	74	5	13	5	1	1	0	0	17	0	.176	.216
Ed Burke	OF14,3B1	(1-2)	15	41	6	6	4	1	0	0	9	4	2	.146	.171
Buster Hoover	OF14		14	51	7	9	2	0	0	0	5	4	1	.176	.176
Bill Rhines	P12,OF1		13	30	2	5	4	0	1	1	3	8	0	.167	.333
Jesse Duryea	P9	(1-2)	9	27	3	3	0	1	0	0	5	11	0	.111	.148
Bill Kuehne	3B4,2B2	(3-4)	6	24	3	5	4	1	0	1	1	5	0	.208	.375
Dan Mahoney	C5		5	21	1	4	1	0	1	0	1	4	0	.190	.286
Dan Daub	P4		4	7	0	0	0	0	0	0	0	2	0	.000	.000
Willie McGill	P3		3	7	1	2	1	0	0	0	0	3	1	.286	.286
George Meakim	P3	(2-2)	3	5	0	0	0	0	0	0	0	0	0	.000	.000
George Rettger	P1,OF1	(2-2)	2	8	1	1	3	1	0	0	1	1	0	.125	.250
Tom Dowse	C1	(2-4)	1	4	0	0	0	0	0	0	0	0	0	.000	.000
Frank Knauss	P1		1	3	0	1	0	0	0	0	1	1	0	.333	.333
George Hemming	P1	(1-2)	1	3	0	1	0	0	0	0	0	0	0	.333	.333
Bumpus Jones	P1		1	2	0	0	0	0	0	0	1	2	0	.000	.000
Clarence Stephens	P1		1	2	0	0	0	0	0	0	0	2	0	.000	.000
			155	5349	766	1288	604	155	75	44	503	474	270	.241	.322

PITCHERS		W	L	PCT	G	GS	CG	SH	SV	IP	H	BB	SO	ERA
Tony Mullane		21	13	.618	37	34	30	3	1	295	222	127	109	2.59
Frank Dwyer	(2-2)	19	10	.655	33	27	24	3	1	259	251	49	45	2.33
Icebox Chamberlain		19	23	.452	52	49	43	2	0	406	391	170	169	3.39
Mike Sullivan		12	4	.750	21	16	15	0	0	166	179	74	56	3.08
Bill Rhines		4	7	.364	12	10	7	0	0	83	113	36	12	5.06
Jesse Duryea	(1-2)	2	5	.286	9	7	5	0	0	68	55	26	21	3.57
George Rettger	(2-2)	1	0	1.000	1	1	1	0	0	9	8	10	1	4.00
Bumpus Jones		1	0	1.000	1	1	1	0	0	9	0	4	3	0.00
Willie McGill		1	1	.500	3	3	1	0	0	17	18	5	7	5.29
George Meakim	(2-2)	1	1	.500	3	3	1	0	0	14	19	9	4	8.56
Dan Daub		1	2	.333	4	3	2	0	0	25	23	13	7	2.88
Clarence Stephens		0	1	.000	1	1	0	0	0	7	12	4	1	1.29
George Hemming	(1-2)	0	1	.000	1	0	0	0	0	6	10	2	0	7.50
Frank Knauss		0	0	----	1	0	0	0	0	8	13	5	2	3.38
Bug Holliday		0	0	----	1	0	0	0	0	4	13	1	0	11.25
		82	68	.547	155	155	130	8	2	1377	1327	535	437	3.17

PITTSBURGH Pirates — 80-73 .523 -23.5 6th — Buckenberger - Burns

BATTERS	POS/GAMES		GP	AB	R	H	BI	2B	3B	HR	BB	SO	SB	BA	SA
Jake Beckley	1B151		151	614	102	145	96	21	19	10	31	44	30	.236	.381
Lou Bierbauer	2B152		152	649	81	153	65	20	9	8	25	29	11	.236	.331
Frank Shugart	SS134,C2,OF1		137	554	94	148	62	19	14	0	47	48	28	.267	.352
Duke Farrell	3B133,OF20		152	605	96	130	77	10	13	8	46	53	20	.215	.314
Patsy Donovan	OF90	(2-2)	90	388	77	114	26	15	3	2	20	16	40	.294	.363
Doggie Miller	OF76,C63,SS19,3B2		149	623	103	158	59	15	12	2	69	14	28	.254	.326
Elmer Smith	OF126,P17		138	511	86	140	63	16	14	4	82	43	22	.274	.384
Connie Mack	C92,OF3,1B1		97	346	39	84	31	9	4	1	21	22	11	.243	.301
Pop Corkhill	OF68		68	256	23	47	25	1	4	0	12	19	6	.184	.219
Joe Kelley	OF56	(1-2)	56	205	26	49	28	7	7	0	17	21	8	.239	.341
Mark Baldwin	P56		56	178	18	18	13	2	0	1	13	60	1	.101	.129
Red Ehret	P39		40	132	12	34	19	2	0	0	7	22	1	.258	.273
Adonis Terry	P30,OF1	(2-2)	31	100	10	16	11	0	4	2	10	11	2	.160	.300

1892 NATIONAL LEAGUE

PITTSBURGH (cont.)
Pirates

BATTERS	POS/GAMES		GP	AB	R	H	BI	2B	3B	HR	BB	SO	SB	BA	SA
George Van Haltren	OF13	(2-2)	13	55	10	11	5	2	2	0	6	0	6	.200	.309
Ed Swartwood	OF13		13	42	8	10	4	1	0	0	13	11	1	.238	.262
Harry Raymond	3B12	(1-2)	12	49	4	4	2	0	1	0	4	8	1	.082	.122
Pud Galvin	P12	(1-2)	12	41	4	5	4	1	0	0	2	9	0	.122	.146
Tom Burns	3B8,OF3		12	39	7	8	4	0	0	0	3	8	1	.205	.205
Bill Gumbert	P6,OF1		7	18	2	2	1	0	1	0	0	4	2	.111	.222
Fred Woodcock	P5		5	15	2	3	1	0	1	0	1	3	0	.200	.333
Billy Earle	C5		5	13	5	7	3	2	0	0	4	1	2	.538	.692
Kid Camp	P4		4	11	0	1	0	0	0	0	0	2	0	.091	.091
Jake Stenzel	OF2,C1		3	9	0	0	0	0	0	0	1	3	1	.000	.000
Duke Esper	P3	(2-2)	3	9	0	0	1	0	0	0	0	2	0	.000	.000
Chick Cargo	SS2		2	4	0	1	0	0	0	0	0	0	0	.250	.250
Jock Menefee	P1,OF1		2	3	0	0	0	0	0	0	0	0	0	.000	.000
Will Thompson	P1		1	0	0	0	0	0	0	0	1	0	0	----	----
			155	5469	802	1288	600	143	108	38	435	453	222	.236	.322

PITCHERS			W	L	PCT	G	GS	CG	SH	SV	IP	H	BB	SO	ERA
Mark Baldwin			26	27	.491	56	53	45	0	0	440	447	194	157	3.47
Adonis Terry		(2-2)	18	7	.720	30	26	24	2	1	240	185	106	95	2.51
Red Ehret			16	20	.444	39	36	32	0	0	316	290	83	101	2.65
Elmer Smith			6	7	.462	17	13	12	1	0	134	140	58	51	3.63
Pud Galvin		(1-2)	5	6	.455	12	12	10	0	0	96	104	28	29	2.63
Bill Gumbert			3	2	.600	6	3	2	0	0	40	30	23	3	1.36
Duke Esper		(2-2)	2	0	1.000	3	3	1	0	0	18	18	12	5	5.40
Fred Woodcock			1	2	.333	5	4	3	0	0	33	42	17	8	3.55
Kid Camp			0	1	.000	4	1	1	0	0	23	31	9	6	6.26
Will Thompson			0	1	.000	1	1	0	0	0	3	3	5	0	3.00
Jock Menefee			0	0	----	1	0	0	0	0	4	10	2	0	11.25
			80	73	.523	155	152	130	3	1	1347	1300	537	455	3.10

CHICAGO
White Stockings

70-76   .479   -30   7th   Cap Anson

BATTERS	POS/GAMES		GP	AB	R	H	BI	2B	3B	HR	BB	SO	SB	BA	SA
Cap Anson	1B146		146	559	62	152	74	25	9	1	67	30	13	.272	.354
Jimmy Canavan	2B112,OF4,SS2		118	439	48	73	32	10	11	0	48	48	33	.166	.239
Bill Dahlen	SS72,3B68,OF2,2B1		143	581	114	169	58	23	19	5	45	56	60	.291	.422
Jiggs Parrott	3B78		78	333	38	67	22	8	5	2	8	30	7	.201	.273
Sam Dungan	OF113		113	433	46	123	53	19	7	0	35	19	15	.284	.360
Jimmy Ryan	OF120,SS9		128	505	105	148	65	21	11	10	61	41	27	.293	.438
Walt Wilmot	OF92		92	380	47	82	35	7	7	2	40	20	31	.216	.287
Pop Schriver	C82,OF10		92	326	40	73	34	10	6	1	27	25	4	.224	.301
George Decker	OF62,2B16		78	291	32	66	28	6	7	1	20	49	9	.227	.306
Bill Hutchinson	P75,OF2		77	263	23	57	22	10	5	1	10	60	8	.217	.304
Mal Kittredge	C69		69	229	19	41	10	5	0	0	11	27	2	.179	.201
Jim Cooney	SS65	(1-2)	65	238	18	41	20	1	0	0	23	5	10	.172	.176
Ad Gumbert	P46,OF7		52	178	18	42	8	1	2	1	14	24	5	.236	.281
John Luby	P31,OF16		45	163	14	31	20	3	2	2	12	27	3	.190	.270
Charles Newman	OF16	(2-2)	16	61	4	10	2	0	0	0	1	6	2	.164	.164
Jim Connor	2B9		9	34	0	2	0	0	0	0	1	7	0	.059	.059
Fred Roat	2B8		8	31	4	6	2	0	1	0	2	3	2	.194	.258
Henry Miller	P4		4	10	2	3	5	0	0	0	2	1	2	.300	.300
George Meakim	P1	(1-2)	1	5	1	2	2	0	0	0	0	0	0	.400	.400
John Hollison	P1		1	3	0	0	0	0	0	0	0	3	0	.000	.000
Ed Griffith	P1		1	1	0	0	0	0	0	0	0	1	0	.000	.000
			147	5063	635	1188	492	149	92	26	427	482	233	.235	.316

PITCHERS			W	L	PCT	G	GS	CG	SH	SV	IP	H	BB	SO	ERA
Bill Hutchinson			37	36	.507	75	71	67	5	0	627	572	187	316	2.74
Ad Gumbert			22	19	.537	46	45	39	0	0	383	399	107	118	3.41
John Luby			10	16	.385	31	26	24	1	1	247	247	106	64	3.13
Henry Miller			1	1	.500	4	2	2	0	0	24	29	16	15	6.38
George Meakim		(1-2)	0	1	.000	1	1	1	0	0	9	18	2	0	11.00
Ed Griffith			0	1	.000	1	1	0	0	0	4	3	6	3	11.25
John Hollison			0	0	----	1	0	0	0	0	4	1	0	2	2.25
			70	76	.479	147	146	133	6	1	1298	1269	424	518	3.16

1892 NATIONAL LEAGUE

NEW YORK Giants

71-80 .470 -31.5 8th Pat Powers

BATTERS	POS/GAMES		GP	AB	R	H	BI	2B	3B	HR	BB	SO	SB	BA	SA
Buck Ewing	1B73,C30,2B2		105	393	58	122	76	10	15	8	38	26	42	.310	.473
Ed Burke	2B59,OF30	(2-2)	89	363	81	94	41	10	5	6	46	37	42	.259	.364
Shorty Fuller	SS141		141	508	74	115	48	11	4	1	52	22	37	.226	.270
Denny Lyons	3B108		108	389	71	100	51	16	7	8	59	36	11	.257	.396
Mike Tiernan	OF116		116	450	79	129	66	16	10	5	57	46	20	.287	.400
Harry Lyons	OF96		96	411	67	98	53	5	2	0	33	29	25	.238	.260
Jim O'Rourke	OF111,C4,1B		115	448	62	136	56	28	5	0	30	30	16	.304	.388
Jack Boyle	C79,1B40,OF2,SS2		120	436	52	80	32	8	8	0	36	40	10	.183	.239
Jack Doyle	2B31,C26,OF17,3B13,SS7	(2-2)	90	366	61	109	55	22	1	5	18	30	42	.298	.404
Amos Rusie	P64,OF4		69	252	63	53	26	6	4	1	3	29	4	.210	.278
Hardy Richardson	2B33,OF17,1B9,SS6	(2-2)	64	248	36	53	34	11	5	2	21	26	14	.214	.323
George Gore	OF53	(1-2)	53	193	47	49	11	11	2	0	49	16	20	.254	.332
Silver King	P52		52	167	27	35	23	3	4	2	16	26	1	.210	.311
Cannonball Crane	P47,OF1		48	163	20	40	14	1	1	0	11	30	2	.245	.264
John McMahon	1B36,C5		40	147	21	33	24	5	7	1	10	9	3	.224	.374
Charley Bassett	2B30,3B5	(1-2)	35	130	9	27	16	2	3	0	6	10	0	.208	.269
Jocko Fields	OF11,C10		21	66	8	18	5	4	2	0	9	10	2	.273	.394
Jimmy Knowles	3B15,SS1		16	59	9	9	7	1	0	0	6	8	2	.153	.169
Willie Keeler	3B14		14	53	7	17	6	3	0	0	3	3	5	.321	.377
Dan Murphy	C8		8	26	2	3	0	0	0	0	5	4	0	.115	.115
John Sharrott	OF3,P1		4	8	1	1	0	0	0	0	0	1	0	.125	.125
Charles Newman	OF3	(1-2)	3	12	1	4	1	0	0	0	2	0	3	.333	.333
Mickey Welch	P1		1	3	0	1	0	0	0	0	0	1	0	.333	.333
			153	5291	811	1326	645	173	85	39	510	469	301	.251	.338

PITCHERS		W	L	PCT	G	GS	CG	SH	SV	IP	H	BB	SO	ERA
Amos Rusie		31	31	.500	64	61	58	2	0	532	405	267	288	2.88
Silver King		23	24	.489	52	47	46	1	0	419	397	174	177	3.24
Cannonball Crane		16	24	.400	47	43	35	2	1	364	350	189	174	3.80
Mickey Welch		0	0	----	1	1	0	0	0	5	11	4	1	14.40
John Sharrott		0	0	----	1	0	0	0	0	2	2	1	1	4.50
		71	80	.470	153	152	139	5	1	1323	1165	635	641	3.29

LOUISVILLE Colonels

63-89 .414 -40 9th Chapman - Pfeffer

BATTERS	POS/GAMES		GP	AB	R	H	BI	2B	3B	HR	BB	SO	SB	BA	SA
Lew Whistler	1B72,2B10	(1-2)	80	285	42	67	34	4	7	5	30	45	14	.235	.351
Fred Pfeffer	2B116,1B10,OF1,P1		124	470	78	121	76	14	9	2	67	36	27	.257	.338
Hugh Jennings	SS152		152	594	65	132	61	16	4	2	30	30	28	.222	.273
Bill Kuehne	3B76	(1-4)	76	287	22	48	36	4	5	0	13	36	6	.167	.216
Harry Taylor	OF73,1B34,2B14,3B5,SS2		125	493	66	128	34	7	1	0	58	23	24	.260	.278
Tom Brown	OF153		153	660	105	150	45	16	8	2	47	94	78	.227	.285
Farmer Weaver	OF122,C15,1B10		138	551	58	140	57	15	4	0	40	17	30	.254	.296
John Grim	C69,1B11,2B10,OF8,SS1,3B1		97	370	40	90	36	16	4	1	13	24	18	.243	.316
Charley Bassett	3B73,2B6	(2-2)	79	313	36	67	35	5	5	2	15	19	16	.214	.281
Scott Stratton	P42,OF17,1B6		63	219	22	56	23	2	9	0	17	21	9	.256	.347
Ben Sanders	P31,1B15,OF9		54	198	30	54	18	12	2	3	16	17	6	.273	.399
Bill Merritt	C46		46	168	22	33	13	4	2	1	11	15	3	.196	.262
Emmett Seery	OF42		42	154	18	31	15	6	1	0	24	19	6	.201	.253
Tom Dowse	C29,1B11,OF3,2B1	(1-4)	41	145	10	21	7	2	0	0	2	15	1	.145	.159
Fred Clausen	P24		24	84	4	13	3	1	0	0	5	11	0	.155	.167
Pete Browning	OF21	(1-2)	21	77	10	19	4	4	0	0	12	7	5	.247	.299
Leon Viau	P16,OF5	(2-3)	21	66	5	13	5	2	0	0	7	16	2	.197	.227
Jouett Meekin	P19,OF1	(1-2)	20	64	7	5	3	1	0	0	6	9	1	.078	.094
Alex Jones	P18	(1-2)	18	55	6	8	2	0	0	0	7	26	0	.145	.145
Alex McFarland	OF12,2B2		14	42	2	7	1	0	0	0	8	11	1	.167	.167
John Fitzgerald	P4		4	15	1	2	1	1	0	0	1	8	0	.133	.200
George Hemming	P4	(2-2)	4	13	0	1	0	0	0	0	2	5	0	.077	.077
Egyptian Healy	P2	(2-2)	2	7	0	2	0	1	0	0	1	1	0	.286	.429
Harry Dooms	OF1		1	4	0	0	0	0	0	0	1	3	0	.000	.000
			154	5334	649	1208	509	133	61	18	433	508	275	.226	.284

PITCHERS		W	L	PCT	G	GS	CG	SH	SV	IP	H	BB	SO	ERA
Scott Stratton		21	19	.525	42	40	39	2	0	352	342	70	93	2.92
Ben Sanders		12	19	.387	31	31	30	3	0	268	281	62	77	3.22
Fred Clausen		9	13	.409	24	24	24	2	0	200	181	87	94	3.06
Jouett Meekin	(1-2)	7	10	.412	19	18	17	0	0	156	168	78	67	4.03
Alex Jones	(1-2)	5	11	.313	18	16	13	1	0	147	130	56	44	3.31

1892 NATIONAL LEAGUE

LOUISVILLE (cont.) Colonels

PITCHERS			W	L	PCT	G	GS	CG	SH	SV	IP	H	BB	SO	ERA
Leon Viau		(2-3)	4	11	.267	16	15	14	1	0	131	156	56	36	3.99
George Hemming		(2-2)	2	2	.500	4	4	4	0	0	35	36	17	12	4.63
Egyptian Healy		(2-2)	1	1	.500	2	2	2	0	0	18	15	5	4	1.96
John Fitzgerald			1	3	.250	4	4	4	0	0	34	45	11	3	4.24
Fred Pfeffer			0	0	----	1	0	0	0	0	5	4	5	0	1.80
			63	89	.414	154	154	147	9	0	1346	1358	447	430	3.34

WASHINGTON Senators

58-93 .384 -44.5 10th Barnie - Irwin - Richardson

BATTERS	POS/GAMES		GP	AB	R	H	BI	2B	3B	HR	BB	SO	SB	BA	SA
Henry Larkin	1B117,OF2		119	464	76	130	96	13	7	8	39	21	21	.280	.390
Tommy Dowd	2B98,OF23,3B18,SS6		144	584	94	142	50	9	10	1	34	49	49	.243	.298
Danny Richardson	SS93,2B49,3B1		142	551	48	132	58	13	4	3	25	45	25	.240	.294
Yank Robinson	3B58,SS5,2B4		67	218	26	39	19	4	3	0	38	28	11	.179	.225
Paul Radford	OF64,3B54,SS20		137	510	93	130	37	19	4	1	86	47	35	.255	.314
Dummy Hoy	OF152		152	593	108	166	75	19	8	3	86	23	60	.280	.354
Charlie Duffee	OF125,3B6,1B4		132	492	64	122	51	12	11	6	36	33	28	.248	.354
Deacon McGuire	C89,1B8,OF1		97	315	46	73	43	14	4	4	61	48	7	.232	.340
Jocko Milligan	C59,1B28		88	323	40	89	43	20	9	4	26	24	2	.276	.430
Frank Killen	P60,OF2		65	186	27	37	23	4	4	4	26	61	2	.199	.328
Larry Twitchell	OF48,SS3,3B1		51	192	20	42	20	9	5	0	11	31	8	.219	.318
Patsy Donovan	OF40	(1-2)	40	163	29	39	12	3	3	0	11	13	16	.239	.294
Bert Abbey	P27		27	75	5	9	3	1	0	0	9	27	2	.120	.133
Tun Berger	SS18,C9		26	97	9	14	3	2	1	0	7	9	3	.144	.186
Phil Knell	P22	(1-2)	22	68	8	8	1	0	0	0	3	20	0	.118	.118
Jesse Duryea	P18	(2-2)	18	50	4	6	3	1	0	0	2	17	0	.120	.140
Jouett Meekin	P14	(2-2)	14	45	7	6	7	0	0	2	3	12	0	.133	.267
Hank Gastright	P11		12	29	1	4	2	1	1	0	5	0	0	.138	.241
Frank Foreman	P11	(1-2)	11	28	5	13	3	2	2	1	3	3	0	.464	.786
Hardy Richardson	OF7,3B2,2B1	(1-2)	10	37	2	4	0	0	0	0	5	3	2	.108	.108
Jake Drauby	3B10		10	34	3	7	3	0	1	0	2	12	0	.206	.265
Tom Dowse	OF4,C3	(4-4)	7	27	5	7	2	1	0	0	0	3	0	.259	.296
Jim Cooney	SS6	(2-2)	6	25	5	4	4	0	1	0	4	3	1	.160	.240
George Ulrich	3B3,SS2,C2		6	24	1	7	0	1	0	0	0	4	2	.292	.333
Cozy Dolan	P5		5	13	1	3	1	0	0	0	2	5	0	.231	.231
Harry Raymond	3B4	(2-2)	4	15	2	1	0	0	0	0	3	2	1	.067	.067
Alex Jones	P4	(2-2)	4	11	0	3	1	0	0	0	1	3	1	.273	.273
Matt Kilroy	P4		4	10	0	2	0	0	0	0	1	0	0	.200	.200
Bert Inks	P3	(2-2)	3	10	1	3	0	1	0	0	0	1	0	.300	.400
Frank Shannon	SS1		1	4	0	1	2	0	0	0	0	2	0	.250	.250
Dan Potts	C1		1	4	0	1	0	0	0	0	0	1	0	.250	.250
Hal O'Hagan	C1		1	4	1	1	0	0	0	0	0	2	0	.250	.250
Fred Miller	SS1		1	3	0	0	0	0	0	0	0	1	0	.000	.000
			153	5204	731	1245	562	149	78	37	529	553	276	.239	.319

PITCHERS		W	L	PCT	G	GS	CG	SH	SV	IP	H	BB	SO	ERA
Frank Killen		29	26	.527	60	52	46	2	0	460	448	182	147	3.31
Phil Knell	(1-2)	9	13	.409	22	21	17	1	0	170	156	76	74	3.65
Bert Abbey		5	18	.217	27	23	19	0	1	196	207	76	77	3.45
Hank Gastright		3	3	.500	11	7	6	0	0	80	94	38	32	5.08
Jouett Meekin	(2-2)	3	10	.231	14	14	13	1	0	112	112	48	58	3.46
Jesse Duryea	(2-2)	3	11	.214	18	15	13	1	2	127	102	45	48	2.41
Cozy Dolan		2	2	.500	5	4	3	0	0	37	39	15	8	4.38
Frank Foreman	(1-2)	2	4	.333	11	7	4	0	0	60	53	37	16	3.30
Matt Kilroy		1	1	.500	4	3	2	0	0	26	20	15	1	2.39
Bert Inks	(2-2)	1	2	.333	3	3	3	0	0	21	29	10	11	5.14
Alex Jones	(2-2)	0	3	.000	4	4	3	0	0	27	33	14	7	4.00
		58	93	.384	153	153	129	5	3	1315	1293	556	479	3.46

ST. LOUIS Browns

56-94 .373 -46 11th Glasscock - Stricker - Crooks - Gore - Caruthers

BATTERS	POS/GAMES	GP	AB	R	H	BI	2B	3B	HR	BB	SO	SB	BA	SA
Perry Werden	1B149	149	598	73	154	84	22	6	8	59	52	20	.258	.355
Jack Crooks	2B101,3B25,OF2	128	445	82	95	38	7	4	7	136	52	23	.213	.294
Jack Glasscock	SS139	139	566	83	151	72	27	5	3	44	19	26	.267	.348
George Pinkney	3B78	78	290	31	50	25	3	2	0	36	26	4	.172	.197

1892 NATIONAL LEAGUE

ST. LOUIS (cont.)
Browns

BATTERS	POS/GAMES		GP	AB	R	H	BI	2B	3B	HR	BB	SO	SB	BA	SA
Bob Caruthers	OF122,P16,2B6,1B4		143	513	76	142	69	16	8	3	86	29	24	.277	.357
Steve Brodie	OF137,2B16,3B2		154	602	85	152	60	10	9	4	52	31	28	.252	.319
Cliff Carroll	OF101		101	407	82	111	49	14	8	4	47	22	30	.273	.376
Dick Buckley	C119,1B2		121	410	43	93	52	17	4	5	22	34	7	.227	.334
Kid Gleason	P46,OF10,2B9,1B1,C1		66	233	35	50	25	4	2	3	34	23	7	.215	.288
Gene Moriarity	OF47		47	177	20	31	19	4	1	3	4	37	7	.175	.260
Ted Breitenstein	P39,OF10		47	131	16	16	6	1	1	0	16	20	4	.122	.145
Llewellyn Camp	3B39,OF3		42	145	19	30	13	3	1	2	17	27	12	.207	.283
Cub Stricker	2B26,SS2	(1-2)	28	98	12	20	11	1	0	0	10	7	5	.204	.214
Bill Moran	C22,OF2		24	81	2	11	5	1	0	0	2	12	0	.136	.148
Grant Briggs	C15,OF8		23	55	2	4	1	1	0	0	5	16	2	.073	.091
George Gore	OF20	(2-2)	20	73	9	15	4	0	1	0	18	6	2	.205	.233
Pink Hawley	P20		20	71	3	12	5	1	0	1	1	8	0	.169	.225
Frank Bird	C17		17	50	9	10	1	3	1	1	6	11	2	.200	.360
Frank Genins	SS14,OF1	(2-2)	15	51	5	10	4	1	0	0	1	11	3	.196	.216
Dick Hawke	P14,OF1		15	45	2	4	1	0	0	0	0	6	0	.089	.089
Pretzels Getzien	P13		13	45	3	9	4	0	0	1	3	10	0	.200	.267
Pud Galvin	P12	(2-2)	12	39	2	2	1	0	0	0	1	10	0	.051	.051
Frank Dwyer	P10	(1-2)	10	25	4	2	0	0	0	0	4	2	0	.080	.080
Bill Kuehne	3B6,SS1	(2,4-4)	7	28	1	4	0	1	0	0	0	4	1	.143	.179
John Easton	P5,OF1		5	17	1	3	2	1	0	0	0	3	1	.176	.235
Bill Van Dyke	OF4		4	16	2	2	1	0	0	0	0	1	0	.125	.125
Chicken Wolf	OF3		3	14	1	2	1	0	0	0	0	1	0	.143	.143
Jim McCormick	2B2,3B1		3	11	0	0	0	0	0	0	1	5	0	.000	.000
Ed Haigh	OF1		1	4	0	1	0	0	0	0	0	2	0	.250	.250
Henry DeMiller	3B1		1	4	0	0	0	0	0	0	0	0	0	.000	.000
Hick Carpenter	3B1		1	3	0	1	0	0	0	0	1	1	0	.333	.333
Mark McGrillis	3B1		1	3	0	0	0	0	0	0	0	1	0	.000	.000
Heinie Peitz	C1		1	3	0	0	0	0	0	0	0	0	0	.000	.000
John Thornton	OF1	(2-2)	1	3	0	0	0	0	0	0	0	2	0	.000	.000
----- Collins	OF1		1	2	0	0	0	0	0	0	0	0	0	.000	.000
J. D. Young	P1		1	1	0	0	0	0	0	0	0	0	0	.000	.000
---- Leonard	OF1		1	0	0	0	0	0	0	0	1	0	1	----	----
			155	5259	703	1187	553	138	53	45	607	491	209	.226	.298

PITCHERS			W	L	PCT	G	GS	CG	SH	SV	IP	H	BB	SO	ERA
Kid Gleason			20	24	.455	47	45	43	2	0	400	389	151	133	3.33
Ted Breitenstein			9	19	.321	39	32	28	1	0	282	280	148	126	4.69
Pink Hawley			6	14	.300	20	20	18	0	0	166	160	63	63	3.19
Dick Hawke			5	5	.500	14	11	10	1	0	97	108	45	55	3.70
Pud Galvin		(2-2)	5	6	.455	12	12	10	0	0	92	102	26	27	3.23
Pretzels Getzien			5	8	.385	13	13	12	0	0	108	159	31	32	5.67
John Easton			2	0	1.000	5	2	2	0	0	31	38	26	4	6.39
Frank Dwyer		(1-2)	2	8	.200	10	10	6	0	0	64	90	24	16	5.63
Bob Caruthers			2	10	.167	16	10	10	0	1	102	131	27	21	5.84
J. D. Young			0	0	----	1	0	0	0	0	2	9	2	1	22.50
			56	94	.373	155	155	139	4	1	1345	1466	543	478	4.20

BALTIMORE
Orioles

46-101 .313 -54.5 12th Van Haltren - Waltz - Hanlon

BATTERS	POS/GAMES		GP	AB	R	H	BI	2B	3B	HR	BB	SO	SB	BA	SA
Sy Sutcliffe	1B66		66	276	41	77	27	10	7	1	14	15	12	.279	.377
Cub Stricker	2B75	(2-2)	75	269	45	71	37	5	5	3	32	18	13	.264	.353
Tim O'Rourke	SS58,OF4,3B1		63	239	40	74	35	8	4	0	24	19	12	.310	.377
Bill Shindle	3B134,SS9		143	619	100	156	50	20	18	3	35	34	24	.252	.357
George Van Haltren	OF130,P4,3B3,SS2,1B2	(1-2)	135	556	105	168	57	20	12	7	70	34	49	.302	.419
Curt Welch	OF63	(1-2)	63	237	42	56	22	1	3	1	36	9	14	.236	.278
Harry Stovey	OF64,1B10	(2-2)	74	283	58	77	55	14	11	4	40	32	20	.272	.442
Wilbert Robinson	C87,1B2,OF1		90	330	36	88	57	14	4	2	15	35	5	.267	.352
Joe Gunson	C67,OF20,1B2,2B1		89	314	35	67	32	10	5	0	16	17	2	.213	.277
John McGraw	OF34,2B34,SS8,3B3		79	286	41	77	26	13	2	1	32	21	15	.269	.339
George Shoch	SS57,OF12,3B7		76	308	42	85	50	15	3	1	24	19	14	.276	.354
George Cobb	P53,OF6		57	172	20	36	13	4	5	1	22	37	2	.209	.308
Piggy Ward	OF43,2B7,SS5,C1		56	186	28	54	33	6	5	1	31	18	10	.290	.392
Lew Whistler	1B51,OF1	(1-2)	52	209	32	47	21	6	6	2	18	22	12	.225	.340
Sadie McMahon	P48,1B1		49	177	12	25	18	1	2	0	7	31	0	.141	.169
Jocko Halligan	OF22,1B19,C5	(2-2)	46	178	38	47	43	4	7	2	30	24	8	.264	.399
John Pickett	2B36		36	141	13	30	12	2	3	1	7	10	2	.213	.291

BALTIMORE (cont.)
Orioles

BATTERS	POS/GAMES		GP	AB	R	H	BI	2B	3B	HR	BB	SO	SB	BA	SA
Tom Vickery	P24		24	74	6	18	4	2	1	0	5	16	3	.243	.297
George Wood	OF21	(1-2)	21	76	9	17	10	1	1	0	10	8	1	.224	.263
Monte Cross	SS15		15	50	5	8	2	0	0	0	4	10	2	.160	.160
Sun Daly	OF13		13	48	5	12	7	0	2	0	1	4	0	.250	.333
Charles Buffinton	P13		13	43	7	15	4	1	1	0	3	6	1	.349	.419
Ned Hanlon	OF11		11	43	3	7	2	1	1	0	3	3	0	.163	.233
Joe Kelley	OF10	(2-2)	10	33	3	7	4	0	0	0	4	7	2	.212	.212
Egyptian Healy	P9	(1-2)	9	27	3	6	1	0	1	0	2	3	0	.222	.296
Frank Foreman	P4,OF3	(2-2)	7	23	2	4	1	1	1	0	3	3	1	.174	.304
Crazy Schmit	P6,OF1		7	19	1	2	0	0	0	0	3	5	1	.105	.105
John Godar	OF5		5	14	2	3	1	0	0	0	2	1	1	.214	.214
George Stephens	P5		5	13	2	0	0	0	0	0	2	7	0	.000	.000
Pete Gilbert	3B4		4	15	0	3	0	0	0	0	1	3	1	.200	.200
Bill Johnson	OF4		4	15	2	2	2	0	0	0	2	0	0	.133	.133
Bill Gilbert	P2		2	6	0	2	1	1	0	0	0	3	0	.333	.500
Bill Kling	P2		2	4	1	1	1	0	1	0	1	2	0	.250	.750
Alex Ferson	P2		2	4	0	0	0	0	0	0	0	2	0	.000	.000
Adonis Terry	P1	(1-2)	1	4	0	0	0	0	0	0	0	1	0	.000	.000
Bones Ely	P1		1	3	0	0	0	0	0	0	0	1	0	.000	.000
Tom Hess	C1		1	2	0	0	0	0	0	0	0	0	0	.000	.000
			152	5296	779	1342	628	160	111	30	499	480	227	.253	.343

PITCHERS		W	L	PCT	G	GS	CG	SH	SV	IP	H	BB	SO	ERA
Sadie McMahon		19	25	.432	48	46	44	2	1	397	430	145	118	3.24
George Cobb		10	37	.213	53	47	42	0	0	394	495	140	159	4.86
Tom Vickery		8	10	.444	24	21	17	0	0	176	189	87	49	3.53
Charles Buffinton		4	8	.333	13	13	9	0	0	97	130	46	30	4.92
Egyptian Healy	(1-2)	3	6	.333	9	8	5	0	0	68	82	21	24	4.74
George Stephens		1	1	.500	5	2	2	0	1	29	37	9	7	2.79
Crazy Schmit		1	4	.200	6	6	6	0	0	47	37	26	17	3.23
Bill Gilbert		0	1	.000	2	1	1	0	0	14	14	17	5	5.79
Alex Ferson		0	1	.000	2	1	1	0	0	9	17	6	8	11.00
Adonis Terry	(1-2)	0	1	.000	1	1	1	0	0	9	7	7	3	4.00
Bones Ely		0	1	.000	1	1	1	0	0	7	14	7	0	7.71
Bill Kling		0	2	.000	2	2	0	0	0	11	17	7	7	11.45
Frank Foreman	(2-2)	0	3	.000	4	3	2	0	0	25	40	11	5	6.84
George Van Haltren		0	0	----	4	0	0	0	0	15	28	7	5	9.20
		46	101	.313	152	152	131	2	2	1299	1537	536	437	4.28

1893 NATIONAL LEAGUE

Moving Back

One of the best methods to regulate the batter/pitcher relationship is through the distance between the two. Since the modern game's inception in 1845, there had been two major changes in the pitching distance. From an original distance of 45 feet, the distance had lengthened to 50 feet in 1881. Further changes in 1887 had required pitchers to place their back foot on the back line of the pitching box, thus increasing the distance by two feet. But still the pitcher remained dominant. When the league's batting average had dropped to .245 in 1892, the National League decided to move the pitcher back once more.

Prior to the 1893 season, the league moved the pitching distance back to 60 feet, six inches. The stated objective was to make things easier for the batter, and harder for the pitcher. And that is precisely what happened. The league's batting average jumped to its highest total ever, .280. The league's earned run average did the same, ending at 4.66. While the league had a dozen .300 hitters in 1892, the figure increased fivefold in 1893.

Boston won for the third straight year. Their two best hitters were Hugh Duffy (.363) and Tommy McCarthy (.346). Pitcher Kid Nichols once again helped the team with a good year by winning 34.

Pittsburgh made a large jump to second place thanks to the six .300 batters gracing their lineup. Elmer Smith (.346) and George Van Haltren (.338) had fine years as did pitcher Frank Killen who won a league best of 36.

Third place Cleveland and fourth place Philadelphia became the first teams to crack the .300 barrier in the National League since 1876. Cleveland was paced by Buck Ewing (.344) and Jesse Burkett (.348). Philadelphia was led by their hard-hitting outfield of Sam Thompson (.370), batting champion Billy Hamilton (.380) and home run champion Ed Delahanty (19) who also batted .368, and led with the most runs batted in (146).

New York, Brooklyn, and Cincinnati finished in the next three places. New York was led by George Davis (.355) and by pitcher Amos Rusie who won 33 while striking out a league best 208. Brooklyn's best was Dan Brouthers (.337). And Cincinnati, who finished tied with Brooklyn for sixth, featured the hitting of Bug Holliday (.310).

Baltimore and Chicago finished in eighth and ninth. Baltimore was paced by infielder John McGraw (.321), while Cap Anson did the same for Chicago (.314).

St. Louis, Louisville and Washington finished in the last three spots. St. Louis had the league's best pitcher as Ted Breitenstein won the earned run average crown with a high mark of 3.18. Louisville had Willard Brown (.304) and Pete Browning (.355) in a part time role. Washington had Sam Wise who finished at .311.

The year 1893 proved to be a boon for the batter, conversely pitchers took their lumps. Some pitchers could not make the adjustment to the greater distance. George Haddock of Brooklyn saw his win total drop by 20 from 1892 to 1893, and within a year he was out of the league. Interestingly enough, the pitchers gave up only slightly more walks per game in 1893, though their strikeout totals dropped by a third. It would be the turn of the century before these figures and the earned run average would return to a sense of normalcy.

Pitchers in 1893 had to cope with one of the most drastic rule changes ever to govern the rules of baseball. However, as bad as it was for the pitchers, 1893 would seem tame compared to the hell that awaited around the corner.

1893 NATIONAL LEAGUE 243

BOSTON Beaneaters

86-43 .667 1st Frank Selee

BATTERS	POS/GAMES		GP	AB	R	H	BI	2B	3B	HR	BB	SO	SB	BA	SA
Tommy Tucker	1B121		121	486	83	138	91	13	2	7	27	31	8	.284	.362
Bobby Lowe	2B121,SS5		126	526	130	157	89	19	5	14	55	29	22	.298	.433
Germany Long	SS123,2B5		128	552	149	159	58	22	6	6	73	32	38	.288	.382
Billy Nash	3B128		128	485	115	141	123	27	6	10	85	29	30	.291	.433
Cliff Carroll	OF120		120	438	80	98	54	7	5	2	88	28	29	.224	.276
Hugh Duffy	OF131		131	560	147	203	118	23	7	6	50	13	44	.363	.461
Tommy McCarthy	OF108,2B7,SS3		116	462	107	160	111	28	6	5	64	10	46	.346	.465
Charlie Bennett	C60		60	191	34	40	27	6	0	4	40	36	5	.209	.304
Charles Ganzel	C40,OF23,1B10		73	281	50	75	48	10	2	1	22	9	6	.267	.327
Kid Nichols	P52,OF1		53	177	25	39	26	3	2	2	15	22	4	.220	.294
Jack Stivetts	P37,OF8,3B3		49	172	32	51	25	5	6	3	12	14	6	.297	.448
Bill Merritt	C37,OF2		39	141	30	49	26	6	3	3	13	13	3	.348	.496
Harry Staley	P36		36	113	13	30	21	5	0	2	10	17	1	.265	.363
Hank Gastright	P19,OF1	(2-2)	20	68		13	10	3	0	0	6	5	0	.191	.235
Bill Van Dyke	OF3		3	12	2	3	1	1	0	0	0	1	1	.250	.333
Bill Quarles	P3		3	9	0	2	0	0	0	0	1	2	0	.222	.222
Bill Coyle	P2		2	4	0	0	0	0	0	0	0	1	0	.000	.000
James Garry	P1		1	1	0	0	0	0	0	0	0	0	0	.000	.000
			131	4678	1008	1358	828	178	50	65	561	292	243	.290	.391

PITCHERS		W	L	PCT	G	GS	CG	SH	SV	IP	H	BB	SO	ERA
Kid Nichols		34	14	.708	52	44	43	1	1	425	426	118	94	3.52
Jack Stivetts		20	12	.625	38	34	29	1	1	284	315	115	61	4.41
Harry Staley		18	10	.643	36	31	23	0	0	263	344	81	61	5.13
Hank Gastright	(2-2)	12	4	.750	19	18	16	0	0	156	179	76	27	5.13
Bill Quarles		2	1	.667	3	3	3	0	0	27	31	5	6	4.67
Bill Coyle		0	1	.000	2	1	0	0	0	8	14	3	2	9.00
James Garry		0	1	.000	1	0	0	0	0	1	5	4	2	63.00
		86	43	.667	131	131	114	2	2	1164	1314	402	253	4.43

PITTSBURGH Pirates

81-48 .628 -5 2nd Al Buckenberger

BATTERS	POS/GAMES		GP	AB	R	H	BI	2B	3B	HR	BB	SO	SB	BA	SA
Jake Beckley	1B131		131	542	108	164	106	32	19	5	54	26	15	.303	.459
Lou Bierbauer	2B128		128	528	84	150	94	19	11	4	36	12	11	.284	.384
Jack Glasscock	SS66	(2-2)	66	293	49	100	74	7	11	1	17	4	16	.341	.451
Denny Lyons	3B131		131	490	103	150	105	19	16	3	97	29	19	.306	.429
Patsy Donovan	OF112		113	499	114	158	56	5	8	2	42	8	46	.317	.371
George Van Haltren	OF111,SS12,2B2		124	529	129	179	79	14	11	3	75	25	37	.338	.423
Elmer Smith	OF128		128	518	121	179	103	26	23	7	77	23	26	.346	.525
Doggie Miller	C40		41	154	23	28	17	6	1	0	17	8	3	.182	.234
Jake Stenzel	OF45,C12,SS1,2B1		60	224	57	81	37	13	4	4	24	17	16	.362	.509
Frank Killen	P55		55	171	35	47	30	6	6	4	22	28	1	.275	.450
Frank Shugart	SS52	(1-2)	52	210	37	55	32	7	3	1	19	15	12	.262	.338
Red Ehret	P39		39	136	16	24	17	3	0	1	10	18	1	.176	.221
Connie Mack	C37		37	133	22	38	15	3	1	0	10	9	4	.286	.323
Ad Gumbert	P22,OF7		29	95	17	21	10	3	3	0	10	16	0	.221	.316
Billy Earle	C27		27	95	21	24	15	4	4	2	7	6	1	.253	.442
Joe Sugden	C27		27	92	20	24	12	4	3	0	10	11	1	.261	.370
Adonis Terry	P26		26	71	9	18	11	4	3	0	3	11	1	.254	.394
Hank Gastright	P9	(1-2)	9	24	2	1	0	0	0	0	2	2	0	.042	.042
Tom Colcolough	P8		8	14	3	2	1	0	0	0	5	2	0	.143	.143
Sam Gillen	SS3		3	6	0	0	0	0	0	0	0	1	0	.000	.000
Reddy Gray	SS2		2	9	0	4	2	1	0	0	0	1	0	.444	.556
Mark Baldwin	P1	(1-2)	1	1	0	0	0	0	0	0	0	1	0	.000	.000
			131	4834	970	1447	816	176	127	37	537	273	210	.299	.411

PITCHERS		W	L	PCT	G	GS	CG	SH	SV	IP	H	BB	SO	ERA
Frank Killen		36	14	.720	55	48	38	2	0	415	401	140	99	3.64
Red Ehret		18	18	.500	39	35	32	4	0	314	322	115	70	3.44
Adonis Terry		12	8	.600	26	19	14	0	0	170	177	99	52	4.45
Ad Gumbert		11	7	.611	22	20	16	2	0	163	207	78	40	5.15
Hank Gastright	(1-2)	3	1	.750	9	5	3	0	0	59	74	39	12	6.25
Tom Colcolough		1	0	1.000	8	3	1	0	2	44	45	32	7	4.12
Mark Baldwin	(1-2)	0	0	----	1	1	0	0	0	2	6	1	0	11.57
		81	48	.628	131	131	104	8	2	1167	1232	504	280	4.08

1893 NATIONAL LEAGUE

CLEVELAND Spiders   73-55   .570   -12.5   3rd   Patsy Tebeau

BATTERS	POS/GAMES		GP	AB	R	H	BI	2B	3B	HR	BB	SO	SB	BA	SA
Jake Virtue	1B73,OF13,SS5,3B5,P1		97	378	87	100	60	16	10	1	54	14	11	.265	.368
Cupid Childs	2B124		124	485	145	158	65	19	10	3	120	12	23	.326	.425
Ed McKean	SS125		125	545	103	169	133	29	24	4	50	14	16	.310	.473
Chippy McGarr	3B63		63	249	38	77	28	12	0	0	20	15	24	.309	.357
Buck Ewing	OF112,2B5,1B1,C1		116	500	117	172	122	28	15	6	41	18	47	.344	.496
Jimmy McAleer	OF91		91	350	63	83	41	5	1	2	35	21	32	.237	.274
Jesse Burkett	OF125		125	511	145	178	82	25	15	6	98	23	39	.348	.491
Jack O'Connor	C56,OF44		96	384	72	110	75	23	1	4	29	12	29	.286	.383
Patsy Tebeau	1B57,3B56,2B3		116	486	90	160	102	32	8	2	32	11	19	.329	.440
Chief Zimmer	C56,3B1		57	227	27	70	41	13	7	2	16	15	4	.308	.454
Cy Young	P53		53	187	23	44	27	4	0	1	4	15	2	.235	.273
John Clarkson	P36,OF1		37	131	18	27	17	6	2	1	4	20	2	.206	.305
Nig Cuppy	P31,OF2		32	109	14	27	14	6	2	0	8	15	1	.248	.339
Joe Gunson	C21	(2-2)	21	73	11	19	9	1	0	0	6	0	0	.260	.274
Charles Hastings	P15,OF1		16	39	6	7	1	0	2	0	8	12	1	.179	.282
Ed McFarland	OF5,3B2,C1		8	22	5	9	6	2	1	0	1	2	0	.409	.591
Tom Williams	P5,OF3		8	18	5	5	2	0	0	0	4	4	2	.278	.278
Bill Alvord	3B3		3	12	2	2	2	0	0	0	0	1	0	.167	.167
George Davies	P3	(1-2)	3	6	1	2	1	0	0	0	0	1	0	.333	.333
Chauncey Fisher	P2		2	8	0	2	0	0	0	0	0	0	0	.250	.250
Jim Gilman	3B2		2	7	1	2	1	0	0	0	0	2	0	.286	.286
John Scheible	P2		2	7	0	1	1	0	0	0	1	2	0	.143	.143
Frank Boyd	C2		2	5	3	1	3	1	0	0	1	0	0	.200	.400
John Stafford	P2,OF1		2	4	0	0	0	0	0	0	0	0	0	.000	.000
Pete Allen	C1		1	4	0	0	0	0	0	0	0	0	0	.000	.000
			129	4747	976	1425	833	222	98	32	532	229	252	.300	.408

PITCHERS		W	L	PCT	G	GS	CG	SH	SV	IP	H	BB	SO	ERA
Cy Young		34	16	.680	53	46	42	1	1	423	442	103	102	3.36
Nig Cuppy		17	10	.630	31	30	24	0	0	244	316	75	39	4.47
John Clarkson		16	17	.485	36	35	31	0	0	295	358	95	62	4.45
Charles Hastings		4	5	.444	15	9	6	0	1	92	128	33	14	4.70
Tom Williams		1	1	.500	5	2	2	0	0	24	33	10	6	4.88
John Scheible		1	1	.500	2	2	2	1	0	18	15	11	1	2.00
John Stafford		0	1	.000	2	0	0	0	0	7	12	7	4	14.14
Chauncey Fisher		0	2	.000	2	2	2	0	0	18	26	9	9	5.50
George Davies	(1-2)	0	2	.000	3	3	1	0	0	15	28	10	3	11.40
Jake Virtue		0	0	----	1	0	0	0	0	5	3	3	2	1.80
		73	55	.570	129	129	110	2	2	1140	1361	356	242	4.20

PHILADELPHIA Phillies   72-57   .558   -14   4th   Harry Wright

BATTERS	POS/GAMES		GP	AB	R	H	BI	2B	3B	HR	BB	SO	SB	BA	SA
Jack Boyle	1B112,C6,2B2		116	504	105	144	81	29	9	4	41	30	22	.286	.403
Bill Hallman	2B120,1B12		132	596	119	183	76	28	7	5	51	27	22	.307	.403
Bob Allen	SS124		124	471	86	126	90	19	12	8	71	40	8	.268	.410
Charlie Reilly	3B104		104	416	64	102	56	16	7	4	33	36	13	.245	.346
Sam Thompson	OF131,1B1		131	600	130	222	126	37	13	11	50	17	18	.370	.530
Billy Hamilton	OF82		82	355	110	135	44	22	7	5	63	7	43	.380	.524
Ed Delahanty	OF117,2B15,1B6		132	595	145	219	146	35	18	19	47	20	37	.368	.583
Jack Clements	C92,1B1		94	376	64	107	80	20	3	17	39	29	3	.285	.489
Lave Cross	C40,3B30,OF10,SS10,1B6		96	415	81	124	78	17	6	4	26	7	18	.299	.398
John Sharrott	OF33,P12		50	152	25	38	22	4	3	1	8	14	6	.250	.336
Gus Weyhing	P42,OF1		43	147	14	22	11	3	0	0	14	39	1	.150	.170
Kid Carsey	P39		39	145	12	27	10	1	1	0	5	14	2	.186	.207
Tuck Turner	OF36		36	155	32	50	13	4	3	1	9	19	7	.323	.406
Jack Taylor	P25,OF3		31	93	11	20	18	5	1	0	1	8	1	.215	.290
Tom Vickery	P13,2B1		15	35	1	11	4	1	0	0	1	2	0	.314	.343
Tim Keefe	P22		22	79	10	18	6	4	0	0	9	24	1	.228	.278
Gus McGinnis	P5	(2-2)	5	15		3	1	1	0	0	0	2	0	.200	.267
Frank O'Connor	P3		3	2	1	2	3	0	0	1	0	0	0	1.000	2.500
			133	5151	1011	1553	865	246	90	80	468	335	202	.301	.431

PITCHERS	W	L	PCT	G	GS	CG	SH	SV	IP	H	BB	SO	ERA
Gus Weyhing	23	16	.590	42	40	33	2	0	345	399	145	101	4.74
Kid Carsey	20	15	.571	39	35	30	1	0	318	375	124	50	4.81
Tim Keefe	10	7	.588	22	22	17	0	0	178	202	79	53	4.40

1893 NATIONAL LEAGUE

PHILADELPHIA (cont.)
Phillies

PITCHERS		W	L	PCT	G	GS	CG	SH	SV	IP	H	BB	SO	ERA
Jack Taylor		10	9	.526	25	16	14	0	1	170	189	77	41	4.24
John Sharrott		4	2	.667	12	4	2	0	0	56	53	33	11	4.50
Tom Vickery		4	5	.444	13	11	7	0	0	80	100	37	15	5.40
Gus McGinnis	(2-2)	1	3	.250	5	4	4	1	0	37	39	17	12	4.34
Frank O'Connor		0	0	----	3	1	0	0	1	4	2	9	0	11.25
		72	57	.558	133	133	107	4	2	1189	1359	521	283	4.68

NEW YORK
Giants

68-64   .515   -19.5   5th   Monte Ward

BATTERS	POS/GAMES		GP	AB	R	H	BI	2B	3B	HR	BB	SO	SB	BA	SA
Roger Connor	1B135,3B1		135	511	111	156	105	25	8	11	91	26	24	.305	.450
Monte Ward	2B134		135	588	129	193	77	27	9	2	47	5	46	.328	.415
Shorty Fuller	SS130		130	474	78	112	51	14	8	0	60	21	26	.236	.300
George Davis	3B133,SS1		133	549	112	195	119	22	27	11	42	20	37	.355	.554
Mike Tiernan	OF125		125	511	114	158	102	19	12	14	72	24	26	.309	.476
General Stafford	OF67		67	281	58	79	27	7	4	5	25	31	19	.281	.388
Ed Burke	OF135		135	537	122	150	80	23	10	9	51	32	54	.279	.410
Jack Doyle	C48,OF29,SS4,3B3,1B1		82	318	56	102	51	17	5	1	27	12	40	.321	.415
Amos Rusie	P56		56	212	32	57	27	3	4	3	3	19	0	.269	.363
Harry Lyons	OF47		47	187	27	51	21	5	2	0	14	6	10	.273	.321
Mark Baldwin	P45	(2-2)	45	134	12	17	9	4	2	0	8	38	2	.127	.186
Jocko Milligan	C42	(2-2)	42	147	16	34	25	5	6	1	14	13	2	.231	.367
Parke Wilson	C31		31	114	16	28	21	4	1	2	7	9	5	.246	.351
Les German	P20,OF1,3B1		22	74	10	23	15	0	1	0	5	1	1	.311	.338
King Kelly	C17,OF1		20	67	9	18	15	1	0	0	6	5	3	.269	.284
Cannonball Crane	P10,1B1,OF1	(1-2)	12	26	8	12	3	1	0	0	7	0	0	.462	.500
John McMahon	C11		11	30	5	10	4	2	1	0	2	0	0	.333	.467
Charlie Petty	P9		9	22	5	7	4	0	0	1	4	6	0	.318	.455
Willie Keeler	OF,SS2,2B2,	(1-2)	7	24	5	8	7	2	1	1	5	1	3	.333	.625
Silver King	P7	(1-2)	7	17	8	3	3	0	0	0	7	2	0	.176	.176
George Davies	P5	(2-2)	5	12	4	4	0	1	0	0	5	5	0	.333	.417
Crazy Schmit	P4	(2-2)	4	9	2	4	0	0	0	0	0	1	0	.444	.444
Frank Foreman	P2		2	3	0	0	0	0	0	0	0	0	0	.000	.000
Red Donahue	P2		2	2	0	0	0	0	0	0	0	1	0	.000	.000
Shorty Howe	3B1		1	5	1	3	2	0	0	0	0	0	1	.600	.600
----- Kinsler	OF1		1	3	1	0	0	0	0	0	1	1	0	.000	.000
Seth Sigsby	P1,C1		1	1	0	0	0	0	0	0	0	0	0	.000	.000
Bumpus Jones	P1	(2-2)	1	0	0	0	0	0	0	0	1	0	0	----	----
			136	4858	941	1424	768	182	101	61	504	279	299	.293	.410

PITCHERS		W	L	PCT	G	GS	CG	SH	SV	IP	H	BB	SO	ERA
Amos Rusie		33	21	.611	56	52	50	4	1	482	451	218	208	3.23
Mark Baldwin	(2-2)	16	20	.444	45	39	33	2	2	331	335	141	100	4.10
Les German		8	8	.500	20	18	14	0	0	152	162	70	35	4.14
Charlie Petty		5	2	.714	9	6	4	0	0	54	66	28	12	3.33
Silver King	(1-2)	3	4	.429	7	7	4	0	0	49	69	26	13	8.63
Cannonball Crane	(1-2)	2	4	.333	10	7	4	0	0	68	84	41	11	5.93
George Davies	(2-2)	1	1	.500	5	1	1	0	0	36	41	13	7	6.19
Frank Foreman		0	1	.000	2	1	0	0	0	6	19	10	0	27.00
Bumpus Jones	(2-2)	0	1	.000	1	1	0	0	0	4	5	10	1	11.25
Crazy Schmit	(2-2)	0	2	.000	4	4	1	0	0	21	30	17	5	7.40
Red Donahue		0	0	----	2	0	0	0	1	5	8	3	1	9.00
Seth Sigsby		0	0	----	1	0	0	0	0	3	1	4	2	9.00
		68	64	.515	136	136	111	6	4	1211	1271	581	395	4.29

BROOKLYN
Bridegrooms

65-63   .508   -20.5   6th   Dave Foutz
                                 (tie)

BATTERS	POS/GAMES	GP	AB	R	H	BI	2B	3B	HR	BB	SO	SB	BA	SA
Dan Brouthers	1B77	77	282	57	95	59	21	11	2	52	10	9	.337	.511
Tom Daly	2B82,3B45	126	470	94	136	70	21	14	8	76	65	32	.289	.445
Tom Corcoran	SS115	115	459	61	126	58	11	10	2	27	12	14	.275	.355
George Shoch	3B37,OF46,SS11,2B3	94	327	53	86	54	17	1	2	48	13	9	.263	.339
Oyster Burns	OF108,SS1	109	415	68	112	60	22	8	7	36	16	14	.270	.412
Mike Griffin	OF93,2B2	95	362	85	103	59	21	7	6	59	23	30	.285	.431
Dave Foutz	OF77,1B54,P6	130	557	91	137	67	20	10	7	32	34	39	.246	.355
Tom Kinslow	C76,OF2	78	312	38	76	45	8	4	4	11	13	4	.244	.333

1893 NATIONAL LEAGUE

BROOKLYN (cont.)
Bridegrooms

BATTERS	POS/GAMES		GP	AB	R	H	BI	2B	3B	HR	BB	SO	SB	BA	SA
Con Daily	C51,OF9		61	215	33	57	32	4	2	1	20	12	13	.265	.316
Danny Richardson	2B46,3B5,SS3		54	206	36	46	27	6	2	0	13	18	7	.223	.272
Harry Stovey	OF48	(2-2)	48	175	43	44	29	6	6	1	44	11	22	.251	.371
Brickyard Kennedy	P46		46	157	25	39	16	6	2	0	8	4	4	.248	.312
Ed Stein	P37		37	118	12	25	14	1	0	0	8	15	1	.212	.220
Gil Hatfield	3B34		34	120	24	35	19	3	3	2	17	5	9	.292	.417
George Haddock	P23,OF7		29	85	21	24	7	1	2	1	8	15	2	.282	.376
Willie Keeler	3B12,OF	(2-2)	20	80	14	25	9	1	1	1	4	4	2	.313	.387
Tom Lovett	P14,OF4,1B1		18	50	8	9	5	1	0	0	3	3	0	.180	.200
George Sharrott	P13		13	39	4	9	4	1	0	1	1	4	0	.231	.333
Dan Daub	P12		12	42	6	8	4	0	0	0	4	7	2	.190	.190
Candy LaChance	C6,OF5		11	35	1	6	6	1	0	0	2	12	0	.171	.200
Cannonball Crane	P2,OF1	(2-2)	3	5	1	2	0	1	0	0	0	0	0	.400	.600
			130	4511	775	1200	644	173	83	45	473	296	213	.266	.371

PITCHERS			W	L	PCT	G	GS	CG	SH	SV	IP	H	BB	SO	ERA
Brickyard Kennedy			25	20	.556	46	44	40	2	1	383	376	168	107	3.72
Ed Stein			19	15	.559	37	34	28	1	0	298	294	119	81	3.77
George Haddock			8	9	.471	23	20	12	0	0	151	193	89	37	5.60
Dan Daub			6	6	.500	12	12	12	0	0	103	104	61	25	3.84
George Sharrott			4	6	.400	13	10	10	0	1	95	114	58	24	5.87
Tom Lovett			3	5	.375	14	8	6	0	1	96	134	35	15	6.56
Cannonball Crane		(2-2)	0	2	.000	2	2	1	0	0	10	19	9	5	13.50
Dave Foutz			0	0	----	6	0	0	0	0	18	28	8	3	7.50
			65	63	.508	130	130	109	3	3	1154	1262	547	297	4.55

CINCINNATI
Reds

65-63   .508   -20.5   6th (tie)   Charlie Comiskey

BATTERS	POS/GAMES		GP	AB	R	H	BI	2B	3B	HR	BB	SO	SB	BA	SA
Charlie Comiskey	1B64		64	259	38	57	26	12	1	0	11	2	9	.220	.274
Bid McPhee	2B127		127	491	101	138	68	17	11	3	94	20	25	.281	.379
Germany Smith	SS130		130	500	63	118	56	18	6	4	38	20	14	.236	.320
Arlie Latham	3B127		127	531	101	150	49	18	6	2	62	20	57	.282	.350
John McCarthy	OF47,1B2		49	195	28	55	22	8	3	0	22	7	6	.282	.354
Bug Holliday	OF125,1B1		126	500	108	155	89	24	10	5	73	22	32	.310	.428
Jimmy Canavan	OF117,2B5,3B1		121	461	65	104	64	13	7	5	51	20	31	.226	.317
Farmer Vaughn	C80,OF23,1B21		121	483	68	135	108	17	12	1	35	17	16	.280	.371
Morg Murphy	C56,1B1		57	200	25	47	19	5	1	1	14	35	1	.235	.285
Frank Motz	1B43		43	156	16	40	25	7	1	2	19	10	3	.256	.353
Piggy Ward	OF40,1B1	(2-2)	42	150	44	42	10	4	1	0	37	10	27	.280	.320
Frank Dwyer	P37,OF1,1B1		38	120	22	24	17	1	2	1	9	5	2	.200	.267
Icebox Chamberlain	P34		34	97	9	19	10	4	1	0	5	10	3	.196	.258
Mike Sullivan	P27		27	79	7	16	7	2	0	1	2	9	2	.203	.266
Tom Parrott	P22,OF1	(2-2)	24	68	5	13	9	1	1	1	1	9	0	.191	.279
George Henry	OF21		21	83	11	23	13	3	0	0	11	12	2	.277	.313
Iud Smith	OF9,3B6,SS1	(1-2)	17	43	7	10	5	1	0	1	9	5	1	.233	.326
Silver King	P17	(1-2)	17	37	5	6	1	1	1	0	8	14	0	.162	.243
Tony Mullane	P15,3B1		16	52	11	15	6	0	0	1	5	3	1	.288	.346
Bob Caruthers	OF10	(2-2)	13	48	14	14	8	2	0	1	16	1	1	.292	.396
Connie Murphy	C4		6	17	3	3	2	1	0	0	1	2	0	.176	.235
Bumpus Jones	P6	(1-2)	6	16	3	4	0	1	1	0	1	2	1	.250	.438
Charlie Duffee	OF4		4	12	3	2	0	1	0	0	5	0	0	.167	.250
George Darby	P4		4	10	1	3	1	0	0	0	1	0	0	.300	.300
Lem Cross	P3		3	6	1	2	0	0	0	0	2	1	0	.333	.333
George Ulrich	OF1		1	3	0	0	0	0	0	0	0	0	1	.000	.000
			131	4617	759	1195	615	161	65	29	532	256	238	.259	.341

PITCHERS			W	L	PCT	G	GS	CG	SH	SV	IP	H	BB	SO	ERA
Frank Dwyer			18	15	.545	37	30	28	1	2	287	332	93	53	4.13
Icebox Chamberlain			16	12	.571	34	27	19	1	0	241	248	112	59	3.73
Tom Parrott		(2-2)	10	7	.588	22	17	11	1	0	154	174	70	33	4.09
Mike Sullivan			8	11	.421	27	18	14	0	1	184	200	103	40	5.05
Tony Mullane		(1-2)	6	6	.500	15	13	11	0	*1	122	130	65	24	4.41
Silver King		(2-2)	5	6	.455	17	15	8	1	1	105	119	56	30	4.89
George Darby			1	1	.500	4	3	2	0	0	29	41	18	6	7.76
Bumpus Jones		(1-2)	1	3	.250	6	5	2	0	0	29	37	23	6	10.05
Lem Cross			0	2	.000	3	3	2	0	0	21	24	9	7	5.57
			65	63	.508	131	131	97	4	5	1172	1305	549	258	4.55

1893 NATIONAL LEAGUE

BALTIMORE
Orioles 60-70 .462 -26.5 8th Ned Hanlon

BATTERS	POS/GAMES		GP	AB	R	H	BI	2B	3B	HR	BB	SO	SB	BA	SA
Harry Taylor	1B88		88	360	50	102	54	9	1	1	32	11	24	.283	.322
Heinie Reitz	2B130		130	490	90	140	76	17	13	1	65	32	24	.286	.380
John McGraw	SS117,OF11		127	480	123	154	64	9	10	5	101	11	38	.321	.413
Bill Shindle	3B125		125	521	100	136	75	22	11	1	66	17	17	.261	.351
George Treadway	OF115		115	458	78	119	67	16	17	1	57	50	24	.260	.376
Joe Kelley	OF125		125	502	120	153	76	27	16	9	77	44	33	.305	.476
James Long	OF55		55	226	31	48	25	8	1	2	16	27	23	.212	.283
Wilbert Robinson	C93,1B1		95	359	49	120	57	21	3	3	26	22	17	.334	.435
Boileryard Clarke	C38,OF11		49	183	23	32	24	1	3	1	19	14	2	.175	.230
Sadie McMahon	P43		43	148	13	36	22	3	0	0	4	11	1	.243	.264
Tony Mullane	P34,OF2,1B1	(2-2)	38	114	15	26	15	2	1	0	5	14	5	.228	.263
Tim O'Rourke	OF25,3B5,SS1	(1-2)	31	135	22	49	19	4	1	0	12	4	5	.363	.407
Dick Hawke	P29	(2-2)	29	93	8	16	9	2	0	1	7	20	0	.172	.226
Steve Brodie	OF25	(2-2)	25	97	18	35	19	7	2	0	12	2	8	.361	.474
Jocko Milligan	1B22,C1	(1-2)	24	102	19	25	19	5	2	1	5	7	2	.245	.363
Ed McNabb	P21		21	67	11	13	8	1	1	0	4	9	1	.194	.239
Kirtley Baker	P15,OF3		19	57	9	17	6	1	1	0	8	6	1	.298	.351
Hugh Jennings	SS15,OF1	(2-2)	16	55	6	14	6	0	0	1	4	3	0	.255	.309
Bob Gilks	OF15		15	64	10	17	7	2	0	0	0	3	3	.266	.266
Piggy Ward	OF9,1B2	(1-2)	11	49	11	12	5	1	3	0	5	2	4	.245	.388
Crazy Schmit	P9	(1-2)	9	21	4	5	2	1	0	0	2	6	0	.238	.286
Harry Stovey	OF8	(1-2)	8	26	4	4	5	2	0	0	8	3	1	.154	.231
Willard Brown	1B7	(1-2)	7	32	5	4	5	3	0	0	1	3	0	.125	.219
Bill Wadsworth	P3		3	7	0	3	0	0	0	0	1	1	0	.429	.429
Stub Brown	P2		2	5	1	1	1	0	0	0	0	1	0	.200	.200
			130	4651	820	1281	666	164	86	27	537	323	233	.275	.365

PITCHERS			W	L	PCT	G	GS	CG	SH	SV	IP	H	BB	SO	ERA
Sadie McMahon			23	18	.561	43	40	35	0	1	346	378	156	79	4.37
Tony Mullane		(2-2)	12	16	.429	34	26	23	0	*1	245	277	124	71	4.45
Dick Hawke		(2-2)	11	16	.407	29	29	22	1	0	225	248	108	69	4.76
Ed McNabb			8	7	.533	21	14	12	0	0	142	167	53	18	4.12
Crazy Schmit		(1-2)	3	2	.600	9	6	4	0	0	49	67	22	10	6.61
Kirtley Baker			3	8	.273	15	12	8	0	0	92	138	58	26	8.44
Bill Wadsworth			0	3	.000	3	3	0	0	0	16	37	8	2	11.25
Stub Brown			0	0	----	2	0	0	0	0	9	13	5	0	6.00
			60	70	.462	130	130	104	1	2	1124	1325	534	275	4.97

CHICAGO
White Stockings 56-71 .441 -29 9th Cap Anson

BATTERS	POS/GAMES		GP	AB	R	H	BI	2B	3B	HR	BB	SO	SB	BA	SA
Cap Anson	1B101		103	398	70	125	91	24	2	0	68	12	13	.314	.384
Bill Lange	2B57,OF40,3B8,SS7,C7		117	469	92	132	88	8	7	8	52	20	47	.281	.380
Bill Dahlen	SS88,OF17,2B10,3B3		116	485	113	146	64	28	15	5	58	30	31	.301	.452
Jiggs Parrott	3B99,2B7,OF4		110	455	54	111	65	10	9	1	13	25	25	.244	.312
Sam Dungan	OF107		107	465	86	138	64	23	7	2	29	8	11	.297	.389
Jimmy Ryan	OF73,SS10,P1		83	341	82	102	30	21	7	3	59	25	8	.299	.428
Walt Wilmot	OF93		94	392	69	118	61	14	14	3	40	8	39	.301	.431
Mal Kittredge	C70		70	255	32	59	30	9	5	2	17	15	3	.231	.329
George Decker	OF33,1B27,2B20,SS2		81	328	57	89	48	9	8	2	24	22	22	.271	.366
Pop Schriver	C56,OF5		64	229	49	65	34	8	3	4	14	9	4	.284	.397
Bill Hutchinson	P44,OF2		46	162	14	41	25	7	3	0	7	20	2	.253	.333
Willie McGill	P39		40	124	18	29	13	4	0	0	20	13	5	.234	.266
Llewellyn Camp	3B16,OF11,2B9,SS3		38	156	37	41	17	7	7	2	19	19	30	.263	.436
Al Mauck	P23		23	61	2	9	4	0	0	0	3	9	0	.148	.148
Charlie Irwin	SS21		21	82	14	25	13	6	2	0	10	1	4	.305	.427
Bob Glenalvin	2B16		16	61	11	21	12	3	1	0	7	3	7	.344	.426
Gus McGinnis	P13,OF1	(1-2)	13	25	8	6	7	0	0	0	9	2	0	.240	.240
Fred Clausen	P10	(2-2)	10	33	2	4	0	0	0	0	2	1	0	.121	.121
Tom Parrott	P4,3B2,2B1	(1-2)	7	27	4	7	3	1	0	0	1	2	0	.259	.296
Bert Abbey	P7		7	26	2	6	2	1	0	0	2	3	0	.231	.269
Frank Donnelly	P7		7	18	4	8	3	1	2	0	2	2	0	.444	.722
Bill Eagan	2B6		6	19	3	5	2	0	0	0	5	5	4	.263	.263
John O'Brien	2B4		4	14	3	5	1	0	1	0	2	2	0	.357	.500
Henry Lynch	OF4		4	14	0	3	2	2	0	0	1	1	0	.214	.357
Clark Griffith	P4		4	11	1	2	2	0	0	0	0	1	0	.182	.182
Sam Shaw	P2		2	7	1	2	1	0	0	0	0	2	0	.286	.286
Jim Hughey	P2		2	2	1	0	0	0	0	0	1	1	0	.000	.000
Bob Caruthers	OF1	(1-2)	1	3	0	0	0	0	0	0	0	1	0	.000	.000

CHICAGO (cont.)
White Stockings

BATTERS

BATTERS	POS/GAMES		GP	AB	R	H	BI	2B	3B	HR	BB	SO	SB	BA	SA
Doc Parker	P1		1	1	0	0	0	0	0	0	0	0	0	.000	.000
Gus Yost	P1		1	1	0	0	0	0	0	0	0	0	0	.000	.000
Abe Johnson	P1		1	0	0	0	0	0	0	0	0	0	0	----	----
			128	4664	829	1299	682	186	93	32	465	262	255	.279	.379

PITCHERS

PITCHERS		W	L	PCT	G	GS	CG	SH	SV	IP	H	BB	SO	ERA
Willie McGill		17	18	.486	39	34	26	1	0	303	311	181	91	4.61
Bill Hutchinson		16	24	.400	44	40	38	2	0	348	420	156	80	4.75
Al Mauck		8	10	.444	23	18	12	1	0	143	168	60	23	4.41
Fred Clausen	(2-2)	6	2	.750	10	9	8	0	1	76	71	39	31	3.08
Frank Donnelly		3	1	.750	7	5	3	0	2	42	51	17	6	5.36
Bert Abbey		2	4	.333	7	7	5	0	0	56	74	20	6	5.46
Gus McGinnis	(1-2)	2	5	.286	13	5	3	0	0	67	85	31	13	5.35
Sam Shaw		1	0	1.000	2	2	1	0	0	16	12	13	1	5.63
Clark Griffith		1	2	.333	4	2	2	0	0	20	24	5	9	5.03
Jim Hughey		0	1	.000	2	2	1	0	0	9	14	3	4	11.00
Gus Yost		0	1	.000	1	1	0	0	0	3	3	8	1	13.50
Tom Parrott	(1-2)	0	3	.000	4	3	2	0	0	27	35	17	7	6.67
Jimmy Ryan		0	0	----	1	0	0	0	0	5	3	0	1	0.00
Doc Parker		0	0	----	1	0	0	0	1	2	5	1	0	13.50
Abe Johnson		0	0	----	1	0	0	0	0	1	1	2	2	36.00
		56	71	.441	128	128	101	4	5	1117	1278	553	273	4.81

ST. LOUIS
Browns

57-75   .432   -32.5   10th   Bill Watkins

BATTERS

BATTERS	POS/GAMES		GP	AB	R	H	BI	2B	3B	HR	BB	SO	SB	BA	SA
Perry Werden	1B124,OF1		125	500	73	138	94	22	29	1	49	25	11	.276	.442
Joe Quinn	2B135		135	547	68	126	71	18	6	0	33	7	24	.230	.285
Jack Glasscock	SS48	(1-2)	48	195	32	56	26	8	1	1	25	3	20	.287	.354
Jack Crooks	3B123,SS4,C1		128	448	93	106	48	10	9	1	121	37	31	.237	.306
Tommy Dowd	OF132,2B1		132	581	114	164	54	18	7	1	49	23	59	.282	.343
Steve Brodie	OF107	(1-2)	107	469	71	149	79	16	8	2	33	16	41	.318	.399
Charles Frank	OF40		40	164	29	55	17	6	3	1	18	8	8	.335	.427
Heinie Peitz	C74,SS11,OF10,1B5		96	362	53	92	45	12	9	1	54	20	12	.254	.345
Frank Shugart	OF29,SS22,3B9	(2-2)	59	246	41	69	28	10	4	0	22	10	13	.280	.354
Kid Gleason	P48,OF11,SS1		59	199	25	51	20	6	4	0	19	8	2	.256	.327
Ted Breitenstein	P48,OF2		49	160	20	29	14	1	1	1	18	15	3	.181	.219
Bones Ely	SS44		44	178	25	45	16	1	6	0	17	13	2	.253	.326
Joe Gunson	C34,OF5	(1-2)	40	151	20	41	15	5	0	0	6	6	0	.272	.305
Pink Hawley	P31		31	91	10	26	17	7	3	0	11	16	1	.286	.429
Duff Cooley	OF15,C10,SS5		29	107	20	37	21	2	3	0	8	9	8	.346	.421
Jim Bannon	OF24,SS2,P1		26	107	9	36	15	3	4	0	4	5	8	.336	.439
Dad Clarkson	P24,OF1		25	75	8	10	5	1	0	0	9	16	0	.133	.147
Sandy Griffin	OF23		23	92	9	18	9	1	1	0	16	2	2	.196	.228
Old Hoss Twineham	C14		14	48	8	15	11	2	0	0	1	2	0	.313	.354
Lew Whistler	OF9,1B1	(2-2)	10	38	5	9	2	1	0	0	3	2	0	.237	.263
Bill Goodenough	OF10		10	31	4	5	2	1	0	0	3	4	2	.161	.194
Dick Buckley	C9		9	23	2	4	1	1	0	0	0	0	0	.174	.217
Dennie O'Neil	1B7		7	25	3	3	2	0	0	0	4	0	3	.120	.120
Pat McCauley	C5		5	16	0	1	0	0	0	0	0	1	0	.063	.063
Jud Smith	3B4	(2-2)	4	13	1	1	0	0	0	0	1	2	0	.077	.077
John Dolan	P3		3	7	1	1	3	0	1	0	1	0	0	.143	.571
Kid Sommers	OF1,C1		2	1	1	0	0	0	0	0	0	0	0	.000	.000
Dick Hawke	P1	(1-2)	1	3	0	1	1	0	0	0	0	0	0	.333	.333
Frank Pears	P1		1	2	0	0	0	0	0	0	0	0	0	.000	.000
			135	4879	745	1288	616	152	98	10	524	251	250	.264	.341

PITCHERS

PITCHERS		W	L	PCT	G	GS	CG	SH	SV	IP	H	BB	SO	ERA
Kid Gleason		21	22	.488	48	45	37	1	1	380	436	187	86	4.61
Ted Breitenstein		19	24	.442	48	42	38	1	1	383	359	156	102	3.18
Dad Clarkson		12	9	.571	24	21	17	1	0	186	194	79	37	3.48
Pink Hawley		5	17	.227	31	24	21	0	1	227	249	103	73	4.60
John Dolan		0	1	.000	3	1	1	0	1	17	26	7	1	4.15
Dick Hawke	(1-2)	0	1	.000	1	1	0	0	0	5	9	3	1	5.06
Jim Bannon		0	1	.000	1	1	0	0	0	4	10	5	1	22.50
Frank Pears		0	0	----	1	0	0	0	0	4	9	2	0	13.50
		57	75	.432	135	135	114	3	4	1207	1292	542	301	4.06

1893 NATIONAL LEAGUE 249

LOUISVILLE
Colonels

50-75   .400   -34   11th   Billy Barnie

BATTERS	POS/GAMES		GP	AB	R	H	BI	2B	3B	HR	BB	SO	SB	BA	SA
Willard Brown	1B111,C1	(2-2)	111	461	80	140	85	23	7	1	50	32	9	.304	.390
Fred Pfeffer	2B125		125	508	85	129	75	29	12	3	51	18	32	.254	.376
Tim O'Rourke	SS60,OF26,3B6	(2-2)	92	352	80	99	53	8	4	0	77	15	22	.281	.327
George Pinckney	3B118		118	446	64	105	62	12	6	1	50	8	12	.235	.296
Farmer Weaver	OF85,C21		106	439	79	128	49	17	7	2	27	12	17	.292	.376
Tom Brown	OF122		122	529	104	127	54	15	7	5	56	63	66	.240	.323
Pete Browning	OF57		57	220	38	78	37	11	3	1	44	15	8	.355	.445
John Grim	C92,1B3,2B2,OF1,SS1		99	415	68	111	54	19	8	3	12	10	15	.267	.373
Scott Stratton	P37,OF23,1B1		61	217	34	49	16	8	5	0	25	15	6	.226	.308
Larry Twitchell	OF45		45	187	37	58	31	11	3	2	17	20	7	.310	.433
George Hemming	P41,OF4		45	158	17	32	19	5	2	0	12	20	0	.203	.259
Jerry Denny	SS42,3B2		44	175	22	43	22	5	4	1	9	15	4	.246	.337
Hugh Jennings	SS23	(1-2)	23	88	6	12	9	3	0	0	3	3	0	.136	.170
Jock Menefee	P15,OF7		22	73	10	20	12	2	1	0	13	5	2	.274	.329
Bill Rhodes	P20		20	70	6	9	7	1	2	0	8	26	0	.129	.200
Curt Welch	OF14		14	47	5	8	2	1	0	0	16	4	1	.170	.191
Lew Whistler	1B13	(1-2)	13	47	5	10	9	1	1	0	5	5	1	.213	.277
Bob Clark	C10,OF1,SS1		12	28	3	3	3	1	0	0	5	5	0	.107	.143
Jerry Harrington	C10		10	36	4	4	6	1	0	0	3	9	0	.111	.139
Bill Whitrock	P8,OF1		8	25	5	7	4	0	1	0	1	1	1	.286	.381
Matt Kilroy	P5		5	16	4	7	3	3	0	0	1	3	0	.438	.625
Fred Clausen	P5	(1-2)	5	14	2	3	2	0	0	0	0	1	0	.214	.214
Bill Rhines	P5		5	11	0	1	0	0	0	0	0	0	0	.091	.091
Con Lucid	P2		2	3	1	1	0	0	0	0	0	1	0	.333	.333
Bill Gumbert	P1		1	1	0	1	2	1	0	0	0	0	0	1.000	2.000
			126	4566	759	1185	616	177	73	19	485	306	203	.260	.343

PITCHERS		W	L	PCT	G	GS	CG	SH	SV	IP	H	BB	SO	ERA
George Hemming		18	17	.514	41	32	32	1	1	332	369	176	79	5.10
Scott Stratton		12	23	.343	37	35	34	1	0	315	445	100	43	5.43
Jock Menefee		8	7	.533	15	15	14	1	0	129	150	40	30	4.24
Bill Rhodes		5	12	.294	20	19	17	0	0	152	244	66	22	7.60
Matt Kilroy		3	2	.600	5	5	5	1	0	35	57	23	4	9.00
Bill Whitrock		2	5	.286	8	8	5	0	0	47	64	18	8	8.10
Fred Clausen	(1-2)	1	4	.200	5	5	3	0	0	33	41	22	4	6.00
Bill Rhines		1	4	.200	5	5	3	0	0	31	49	19	0	8.71
Con Lucid		0	1	.000	2	1	0	0	0	6	10	10	0	15.00
Bill Gumbert		0	0	----	1	1	0	0	0	1	2	5	0	27.00
		50	75	.400	126	126	113	4	1	1080	1431	479	190	5.90

WASHINGTON
Senators

40-89   .310   -46   12th   Jim O'Rourke

BATTERS	POS/GAMES	GP	AB	R	H	BI	2B	3B	HR	BB	SO	SB	BA	SA
Henry Larkin	1B81	81	319	54	101	73	20	3	4	50	5	1	.317	.436
Sam Wise	2B91,3B31	122	521	102	162	77	27	17	5	49	27	20	.311	.457
Joe Sullivan	SS128	128	508	72	135	64	16	13	2	36	24	7	.266	.360
Joe Mulvey	3B55	55	226	21	53	19	9	4	0	7	8	2	.235	.310
Paul Radford	OF123,2B1,P1	124	464	87	106	34	18	3	2	105	42	32	.228	.293
Dummy Hoy	OF130	130	564	106	138	45	12	6	0	66	9	48	.245	.337
Jim O'Rourke	OF87,1B33,C9	129	547	75	157	95	22	5	2	49	26	15	.287	.356
Duke Farrell	C81,3B41,1B3	124	511	84	143	75	13	13	4	47	12	11	.280	.380
Deacon McGuire	C50,1B12	63	237	29	62	26	14	3	1	26	12	3	.262	.359
Cub Stricker	2B39,OF12,SS4,3B4	59	218	28	40	20	7	1	0	20	12	4	.183	.225
Al Maul	P37,OF7	44	134	10	34	12	8	4	0	33	14	1	.254	.373
Duke Esper	P42	42	143	15	41	24	6	3	0	14	12	0	.287	.371
Jouett Meekin	P31,OF3	33	113	15	29	20	3	2	3	4	11	0	.257	.398
Charlie Abbey	OF31	31	116	11	30	12	1	4	0	12	6	9	.259	.336
Jesse Duryea	P17	17	47	6	13	6	4	0	0	3	9	0	.277	.362
Otis Stocksdale	P11,OF1,1B1	12	40	7	12	6	0	2	0	2	2	1	.300	.400
George Stephens	P9	9	29	0	3	0	0	0	0	1	5	0	.103	.103
John Graff	P2	2	5	0	1	0	0	0	0	0	1	0	.200	.200
		130	4742	722	1260	608	180	83	23	524	237	154	.266	.354

PITCHERS	W	L	PCT	G	GS	CG	SH	SV	IP	H	BB	SO	ERA
Al Maul	12	21	.364	37	33	29	1	0	297	355	144	72	5.30
Duke Esper	12	28	.300	42	36	34	0	0	334	442	156	78	4.71
Jouett Meekin	10	15	.400	31	28	24	1	0	245	289	140	91	4.96

WASHINGTON (cont.)
Senators

PITCHERS	W	L	PCT	G	GS	CG	SH	SV	IP	H	BB	SO	ERA
Jesse Duryea	4	10	.286	17	15	9	0	0	117	182	56	20	7.54
Otis Stocksdale	2	8	.200	11	11	7	0	0	69	111	32	12	8.22
John Graff	0	1	.000	2	1	1	0	0	12	21	13	4	11.25
George Stephens	0	6	.000	9	6	6	0	0	64	83	31	14	5.80
Paul Radford	0	0	----	1	0	0	0	0	1	2	2	1	18.00
	40	89	.310	130	130	110	2	0	1139	1485	574	292	5.56

1894 NATIONAL LEAGUE

Hotter Than Blazes

By most accounts, Philadelphia outfielder Billy Hamilton had a stellar year at the plate in 1894. Having won the batting title the previous year with a mark of .380, he improved his average significantly to .404, one of the best of all time. However, in the hit happy year of 1894, it was good only for fourth. Not fourth in the league, but fourth on his own team.

In 1894, pitching was still adjusting to the increased distance to home plate. The result was a hitting show in the major leagues like never before. From an all-time high of .280 in 1893, the league's average jumped to an astronomical .309. The league's earned run average jumped as well to an all-time high 5.32.

Leading the way was Philadelphia. Sporting an all-time best team average of .349, the team boasted no less than four .400 hitters. They were, Tuck Turner (.416), Sam Thompson (.407), Ed Delahanty (.407), and the aforementioned fourth place Billy Hamilton at .404.

Batting was not the only thing that was hot during the summer of 1894. On May 15, Boston's ballpark was destroyed by fire. In August, the same happened to both the Chicago and Philadelphia stadiums. All three eventually got new parks, but they were forced to play in substitute venues for much of the season.

Baltimore jumped from eighth to first to claim their first pennant. Their starting eight each hit over .300, led by the trio of outfielders Willie Keeler (.371), Steve Brodie (.366), and Joe Kelley (.393). Each one of the eight batted in at least 90 runs, and six of them scored at least 130 runs. The team ended up hitting .343, the second best of all time.

Second place New York did the impossible as they had two pitchers who finished with earned run averages under four. Amos Rusie led the way with a league best 36 wins and a 2.78 earned run average, more than two and one-half runs below the league average. His teammate, Jouett Meekin, won 33, while finishing second in the earned run average race at 3.70. Offensively, Jack Doyle (.367) and George Davis (.352) were their stalwarts.

The story of third place Boston's season starts and ends with Hugh Duffy who won the Triple Crown in 1894. Duffy hit an eye-popping .440, swatted 18 home runs, and garnered 145 runs batted in. The team scored an all-time best 1221 runs, which averages out to over nine per game. Bobby Lowe made baseball history as he cracked four home runs in one game in May.

In addition to their gaudy averages, fourth place Philadelphia batters posted some other incredible numbers. Billy Hamilton scored an all time best 192 runs during the season, including scoring in a record 24 games in a row. Lave Cross (.386) also had a fine year at the plate.

Brooklyn finished in fifth while Cleveland finished just behind. Brooklyn featured a trifecta of good hitters, Tom Daly (.341), Oyster Burns (.354), and Mike Griffin (.358). Cleveland's included Cupid Childs (.353) and Jesse Burkett (.358).

Pittsburgh and Chicago finished in seventh and eighth. Pittsburgh was led by Jake Beckley (.343), Jake Stenzel (.354), and Elmer Smith (.356). Chicago was paced by the surprising Cap Anson (.388) who hit nearly .400 at the age of 42. Also contributing were Jimmy Ryan (.361) and Bill Dahlen (.357) who in addition, had a 42-game hitting streak.

St. Louis, Cincinnati, Washington, and Louisville finished on the bottom. Notable performances from this group featured Doggie Miller (.339) of St. Louis, Bug Holliday (.372) of Cincinnati, and Bill Joyce (.355, 17 HR) of Washington.

A battery of offensive records fell by the wayside in 1894. In addition to the batting average record of .309, the year saw new highs in runs scored and most triples. The best team totals of all time, for all three categories, were each set during the blazing hot summer of 1894.

1894 NATIONAL LEAGUE

BALTIMORE Orioles   89-39   .695   1st   Ned Hanlon

BATTERS	POS/GAMES		GP	AB	R	H	BI	2B	3B	HR	BB	SO	SB	BA	SA
Dan Brouthers	1B123		123	525	137	182	128	39	23	9	67	9	38	.347	.560
Heinie Reitz	2B97,3B12		108	446	86	135	105	22	31	2	42	24	18	.303	.504
Hugh Jennings	SS128		128	501	134	168	109	28	16	4	37	17	37	.335	.479
John McGraw	3B118,2B6		124	512	156	174	92	18	14	1	91	12	78	.340	.436
Willie Keeler	OF128,2B1		129	590	165	219	94	27	22	5	40	6	32	.371	.517
Steve Brodie	OF129		129	573	134	210	113	25	11	3	18	8	42	.366	.464
Joe Kelley	OF129		129	507	165	199	111	48	20	6	107	36	46	.393	.602
Wilbert Robinson	C109		109	414	69	146	98	21	4	1	46	18	12	.353	.420
Sadie McMahon	P35		35	126	17	36	25	5	1	0	9	12	1	.286	.341
Frank Bonner	2B27,OF4,3B2,SS1		33	118	27	38	24	10	2	0	17	5	12	.322	.441
Dick Hawke	P32		32	92	12	28	16	5	1	1	3	16	1	.304	.413
Boileryard Clarke	C23,1B5		28	100	18	24	19	8	0	1	16	14	2	.240	.350
Kid Gleason	P21,1B	(2-2)	26	86	22	30	17	5	1	0	7	2	1	.349	.430
Bert Inks	P22	(1-2)	23	57	9	18	6	3	0	0	5	6	1	.316	.368
Tony Mullane	P21	(1-2)	21	53	3	21	9	3	0	0	6	3	2	.396	.453
Duke Esper	P16	(2-2)	16	45	9	10	6	3	1	0	4	1	0	.222	.333
Stub Brown	P9		9	23	3	2	1	0	0	0	0	5	1	.087	.087
George Hemming	P6	(2-2)	6	21	4	6	3	1	2	0	1	5	0	.286	.524
Frank Horner	P2		2	6	1	1	0	0	1	0	0	0	0	.167	.500
Kirtley Baker	OF1,P1		2	4	0	0	0	0	0	0	0	1	0	.000	.000
			129	4799	1171	1647	976	271	150	33	516	200	324	.343	.483

PITCHERS			W	L	PCT	G	GS	CG	SH	SV	IP	H	BB	SO	ERA
Sadie McMahon			25	8	.758	35	33	26	0	0	276	317	111	60	4.21
Dick Hawke			16	9	.640	32	25	17	0	3	205	264	78	68	5.84
Kid Gleason		(2-2)	15	5	.750	21	20	19	0	0	172	224	44	35	4.45
Duke Esper		(2-2)	10	2	.833	16	9	8	0	2	102	107	36	25	3.88
Bert Inks		(1-2)	9	4	.692	22	14	10	0	1	133	181	54	30	5.55
Tony Mullane		(1-2)	6	9	.400	21	15	9	0	4	123	155	90	43	6.31
Stub Brown			4	0	1.000	9	6	3	0	0	50	59	24	8	4.89
George Hemming		(2-2)	4	0	1.000	6	6	4	0	0	45	48	26	4	3.57
Frank Horner			0	1	.000	2	1	1	0	1	11	15	7	2	9.00
Kirtley Baker			0	1	.000	1	0	0	0	0	0	1	2	0	inf.
			89	39	.695	129	129	97	1	11	1116	1371	472	275	5.00

NEW YORK Giants   88-44   .667   -3   2nd   Monte Ward

BATTERS	POS/GAMES		GP	AB	R	H	BI	2B	3B	HR	BB	SO	SB	BA	SA
Jack Doyle	1B99,C6		105	422	90	155	100	30	8	3	35	3	42	.367	.498
Monte Ward	2B136		136	540	100	143	77	12	5	0	34	6	39	.265	.306
Shorty Fuller	SS89,OF2,3B2,2B1		93	368	81	104	46	14	4	2	52	16	32	.283	.359
George Davis	3B122		122	477	120	168	91	26	19	8	66	10	40	.352	.537
Mike Tiernan	OF111		112	424	84	117	77	19	13	5	54	21	28	.276	.417
George Van Haltren	OF137		137	519	109	172	104	22	4	7	55	22	43	.331	.430
Ed Burke	OF136		136	566	121	172	77	23	11	4	37	35	34	.304	.405
Duke Farrell	C104,3B5,1B4		114	401	47	114	66	20	12	4	35	15	9	.284	.424
Yale Murphy	SS49,OF20,3B3,2B1,1B1		74	280	64	76	28	6	2	0	51	23	28	.271	.307
Amos Rusie	P54		56	186	20	52	26	5	4	3	5	24	5	.280	.398
Jouett Meekin	P52		52	170	28	48	29	2	7	5	7	16	3	.282	.465
Parke Wilson	C34,1B15		49	175	35	58	32	5	5	1	14	5	8	.331	.434
Les German	P23		23	57	8	17	8	2	0	0	3	5	1	.298	.333
Huyler Westervelt	P23		23	56	9	8	7	1	0	0	6	5	2	.143	.161
Roger Connor	1B21,OF1	(1-2)	22	82	10	24	14	7	0	1	8	0	2	.293	.415
Dad Clarke	P15		16	37	4	8	3	2	1	0	4	4	1	.216	.324
General Stafford	3B6,OF5,2B1,1B1		14	46	10	10	4	1	1	0	10	7	2	.217	.283
			137	4806	940	1446	789	197	96	43	476	217	319	.301	.409

PITCHERS			W	L	PCT	G	GS	CG	SH	SV	IP	H	BB	SO	ERA
Amos Rusie			36	13	.735	54	50	45	3	1	444	426	200	195	2.78
Jouett Meekin			33	9	.786	52	48	40	1	2	409	404	171	133	3.70
Les German			9	8	.529	23	15	10	0	1	134	178	66	17	5.78
Huyler Westervelt			7	10	.412	23	18	11	1	0	141	170	76	35	5.04
Dad Clarke			3	4	.429	15	6	5	0	1	84	114	26	15	4.93
			88	44	.667	137	137	111	5	5	1212	1292	539	395	3.83

1894 NATIONAL LEAGUE

BOSTON Beaneaters — 83-49 .629 -8 3rd Frank Selee

BATTERS	POS/GAMES		GP	AB	R	H	BI	2B	3B	HR	BB	SO	SB	BA	SA
Tommy Tucker	1B123,OF1		123	500	112	165	100	24	6	3	53	21	18	.330	.420
Bobby Lowe	2B130,SS2,3B1		133	613	158	212	115	34	11	17	50	25	23	.346	.520
Germany Long	SS98,OF5,2B3		104	475	137	154	79	28	11	12	35	17	24	.324	.505
Billy Nash	3B132		132	512	132	148	87	23	6	8	91	23	20	.289	.404
Jim Bannon	OF128,P1		128	494	130	166	114	29	10	13	62	42	47	.336	.514
Hugh Duffy	OF124,SS2		125	539	160	237	145	51	16	18	66	15	48	.440	.694
Tommy McCarthy	OF127,SS2,2B1,P1		127	539	118	188	126	21	8	13	59	17	43	.349	.490
Charles Ganzel	C59,1B7,OF3,SS2,2B1		70	266	51	74	56	7	6	3	19	6	1	.278	.383
Jack Stivetts	P45,OF16,1B4		68	244	55	80	64	12	7	8	16	21	3	.328	.533
Jack Ryan	C51,1B2		53	201	39	54	29	12	7	1	13	16	3	.269	.413
Kid Nichols	P50,OF1		51	170	39	50	34	11	2	0	16	24	1	.294	.382
Frank Connaughton	SS33,C7,OF4		46	171	42	59	33	9	2	2	16	8	3	.345	.456
Harry Staley	P27,OF1		28	85	12	20	25	2	1	2	13	9	0	.235	.353
Fred Tenney	C20,OF6,1B1		27	86	23	34	21	7	1	2	12	9	6	.395	.570
Tom Lovett	P15		15	49	4	7	5	1	0	1	2	3	0	.143	.224
George Hodson	P12		12	30	4	3	4	0	0	0	3	4	1	.100	.100
Bill Merritt	C8,OF1	(1-3)	10	26	3	6	6	1	0	0	8	0	0	.231	.269
Tom Smith	P2		2	2	1	0	0	0	0	0	1	1	0	.000	.000
Henry Lampe	P2		2	2	0	0	0	0	0	0	0	0	0	.000	.000
George Stultz	P1		1	3	0	1	0	0	0	0	0	0	0	.333	.333
Scott Hawley	P1		1	3	0	0	0	0	0	0	0	0	0	.000	.000
Frank West	P1		1	1	1	0	0	0	0	0	0	0	0	.000	.000
			133	5011	1221	1658	1043	272	93	103	535	261	241	.331	.484

PITCHERS		W	L	PCT	G	GS	CG	SH	SV	IP	H	BB	SO	ERA
Kid Nichols		32	13	.711	50	46	40	3	0	407	488	121	113	4.75
Jack Stivetts		26	14	.650	45	39	30	0	0	338	429	127	76	4.90
Harry Staley		12	10	.545	27	21	18	0	0	209	305	61	32	6.81
Tom Lovett		8	6	.571	15	13	10	0	0	104	155	36	23	5.97
George Hodson		4	4	.500	12	11	8	0	0	74	103	35	12	5.84
George Stultz		1	0	1.000	1	1	1	0	0	9	4	5	1	0.00
Scott Hawley		0	1	.000	1	1	1	0	0	7	10	7	1	7.71
Henry Lampe		0	1	.000	2	1	0	0	0	5	17	7	1	11.81
Tom Smith		0	0	----	2	0	0	0	1	6	8	6	2	15.00
Frank West		0	0	----	1	0	0	0	0	3	5	2	1	9.00
Jimmy Bannon		0	0	----	1	0	0	0	0	2	4	1	0	0.00
Tommy McCarthy		0	0	----	1	0	0	0	0	2	1	3	0	4.50
		83	49	.629	133	133	108	3	1	1166	1529	411	262	5.41

PHILADELPHIA Phillies — 71-57 .555 -18 4th Art Irwin

BATTERS	POS/GAMES		GP	AB	R	H	BI	2B	3B	HR	BB	SO	SB	BA	SA
Jack Boyle	1B114,3B1,2B1		114	495	98	149	88	21	10	4	45	26	21	.301	.408
Bill Hallman	2B119		119	505	107	156	66	19	7	0	36	15	36	.309	.374
Joe Sullivan	SS75	(2-2)	75	304	63	107	63	10	8	3	23	10	10	.352	.467
Lave Cross	3B100,C16,SS7,2B1		119	529	123	204	125	34	9	7	29	7	21	.386	.524
Sam Thompson	OF99		99	437	108	178	141	29	27	13	40	13	24	.407	.686
Billy Hamilton	OF129		129	544	192	220	87	25	15	4	126	17	98	.404	.528
Ed Delahanty	OF88,1B12,3B9,SS8,2B6		114	489	147	199	131	39	18	4	60	16	21	.407	.585
Jack Clements	C45		45	159	26	55	36	6	5	3	24	7	6	.346	.503
Tuck Turner	OF78,P1		80	339	91	141	82	21	9	1	23	13	11	.416	.540
Mike Grady	C44,1B11,OF2		60	190	45	69	40	13	8	0	14	13	3	.363	.516
Dick Buckley	C42,1B1	(2-2)	43	160	18	47	26	7	3	1	6	13	0	.294	.394
Jack Taylor	P41		41	144	20	48	22	11	2	0	6	13	4	.333	.438
Bob Allen	SS40		40	149	26	38	19	10	3	0	17	11	4	.255	.362
Charlie Reilly	3B28,OF5,2B4,SS1,1B1		39	135	21	40	19	1	2	0	16	10	9	.296	.333
Gus Weyhing	P38		38	115	8	20	10	2	1	0	7	20	2	.174	.209
Kid Carsey	P35		35	125	30	34	18	2	2	0	16	11	3	.272	.320
George Harper	P12		12	40	7	6	3	2	0	0	2	7	0	.150	.200
George Haddock	P10	(1-2)	10	29	2	5	1	0	2	0	3	2	0	.172	.310
Nixey Callahan	P9		9	21	4	5	0	0	0	0	0	7	0	.238	.238
John Fanning	P5		5	13	2	2	0	0	0	0	2	1	0	.154	.154
John Johnson	P4		4	16	4	3	3	0	0	0	1	3	0	.188	.188
Al Lukens	P3		3	8	0	0	0	0	0	0	0	3	0	.000	.000
Alex Jones	P1		1	4	1	1	1	0	0	0	0	3	0	.250	.250
Al Burris	P1		1	4	0	2	0	0	0	0	0	0	0	.500	.500
Joe Yingling	SS1		1	4	0	1	0	0	0	0	0	1	0	.250	.250
Tom Delahanty	2B1		1	4	0	1	0	0	0	0	0	1	0	.250	.250
Frank Figgemeier	P1		1	3	0	1	0	0	0	0	0	0	0	.333	.333

1894 NATIONAL LEAGUE 255

PHILADELPHIA (cont.)
Phillies

BATTERS	POS/GAMES		GP	AB	R	H	BI	2B	3B	HR	BB	SO	SB	BA	SA
Tom Murray	SS1		1	2	0	0	0	0	0	0	0	2	0	.000	.000
Art Irwin	SS1		1	0	0	0	0	0	0	0	0	0	0	----	----
John Scheible	P1		1	0	0	0	0	0	0	0	0	0	0	----	----
			129	4967	1143	1732	981	252	131	40	496	245	273	.349	.476

PITCHERS			W	L	PCT	G	GS	CG	SH	SV	IP	H	BB	SO	ERA
Jack Taylor			23	13	.639	41	34	31	1	1	298	347	96	76	4.08
Kid Carsey			18	12	.600	35	31	26	0	0	277	349	102	41	5.56
Gus Weyhing			16	14	.533	38	34	25	2	1	266	365	116	81	5.81
George Harper			6	6	.500	12	9	7	0	0	86	128	49	24	5.32
George Haddock		(1-2)	4	3	.571	10	7	5	0	0	56	63	34	7	5.79
Alex Jones			1	0	1.000	1	1	1	0	0	9	10	0	2	2.00
John Johnson			1	1	.500	4	3	2	0	0	33	44	15	10	6.06
Nixey Callahan			1	2	.333	9	2	1	0	2	34	64	17	9	9.89
John Fanning			1	3	.250	5	4	2	0	0	32	45	20	7	8.07
Al Lukens			0	1	.000	3	2	1	0	0	15	26	10	0	10.20
Frank Figgemeier			0	1	.000	1	1	1	0	0	8	12	4	2	11.25
John Scheible			0	1	.000	1	1	0	0	0	0	6	2	0	189.00
Tuck Turner			0	0	----	1	0	0	0	0	6	9	2	3	7.50
Al Burris			0	0	----	1	0	0	0	0	5	14	2	0	18.00
			71	57	.555	129	129	102	3	4	1126	1482	469	262	5.63

BROOKLYN
Bridegrooms

70-61   .534   -20.5   5th   Dave Foutz

BATTERS	POS/GAMES		GP	AB	R	H	BI	2B	3B	HR	BB	SO	SB	BA	SA
Dave Foutz	1B72,P1		72	293	40	90	51	12	9	0	14	13	14	.307	.410
Tom Daly	2B123		123	492	135	168	82	22	10	8	77	42	51	.341	.476
Tom Corcoran	SS129		129	576	123	173	92	21	20	5	25	17	33	.300	.432
Bill Shindle	3B116		116	476	94	141	96	22	9	4	29	20	19	.296	.405
Oyster Burns	OF124		124	505	106	179	107	32	14	5	44	18	30	.354	.503
Mike Griffin	OF107		107	402	122	144	75	28	4	5	78	14	39	.358	.485
George Treadway	OF122,1B1		123	479	124	157	102	27	26	4	72	43	27	.328	.518
Tom Kinslow	C61,1B1		62	223	39	68	41	5	6	2	20	11	4	.305	.408
Candy LaChance	1B56,OF10,OF3		68	257	48	83	52	13	8	5	16	32	20	.323	.494
Con Daily	C60,1B7		67	234	40	60	32	14	7	0	31	22	8	.256	.376
George Shoch	OF35,3B14,2B9,SS6		64	239	47	77	37	6	5	1	26	6	16	.322	.402
Brickyard Kennedy	P48		48	161	22	49	23	7	3	0	3	5	2	.304	.385
Ed Stein	P45,OF1		47	150	30	40	30	8	4	2	9	18	4	.267	.413
Dan Daub	P33,OF1		33	92	11	16	15	0	1	0	7	14	1	.174	.196
John Anderson	OF16,3B1		17	63	14	19	19	1	3	1	3	3	7	.302	.460
Hank Gastright	P16		16	41	4	7	2	3	0	0	2	3	1	.171	.244
Bill Earle	C12,2B1	(2-2)	14	50	13	17	6	6	0	0	6	2	4	.340	.460
Con Lucid	P10		10	33	4	7	1	1	0	0	0	4	0	.212	.242
Fred Underwood	P7		7	18	3	7	0	0	1	0	2	4	0	.389	.500
Pete Gilbert	2B3,3B3	(1-2)	6	25	1	2	1	0	0	0	1	3	2	.080	.080
George Sharrott	P2		2	3	0	1	0	0	0	0	0	0	0	.333	.333
Pete Browning	OF1	(2-2)	1	2	1	2	2	0	0	0	1	0	0	1.000	1.000
James Korwan	P1		1	2	0	0	0	0	0	0	0	0	0	.000	.000
Andy Somerville	P1		1	0	0	0	0	0	0	0	0	0	0	----	----
			134	4816	1021	1507	866	228	130	42	466	294	282	.313	.440

PITCHERS			W	L	PCT	G	GS	CG	SH	SV	IP	H	BB	SO	ERA
Ed Stein			27	14	.659	45	41	38	2	1	359	396	171	84	4.54
Brickyard Kennedy			24	20	.545	48	41	34	0	2	361	445	149	107	4.92
Dan Daub			9	12	.429	33	26	14	0	0	215	283	90	45	6.32
Con Lucid			5	3	.625	10	9	7	0	0	71	87	44	15	6.56
Fred Underwood			2	4	.333	7	6	5	0	0	47	80	30	10	7.85
Hank Gastright			2	6	.250	16	8	6	1	2	93	135	55	20	6.39
George Sharrott			0	1	.000	2	2	1	0	0	9	7	5	2	7.00
Andy Somerville			0	1	.000	1	1	0	0	0	0	1	5	0	162.00
Dave Foutz			0	0	----	1	0	0	0	0	2	4	1	0	13.50
James Korwan			0	0	----	1	0	0	0	0	5	9	5	2	14.40
			70	61	.534	134	134	105	3	5	1162	1447	555	285	5.51

1894 NATIONAL LEAGUE

CLEVELAND Spiders
68-61 .527 -21.5 6th Patsy Tebeau

BATTERS	POS/GAMES		GP	AB	R	H	BI	2B	3B	HR	BB	SO	SB	BA	SA
Patsy Tebeau	1B115,2B10,3B2,SS1		125	523	82	158	89	23	7	3	35	35	30	.302	.390
Cupid Childs	2B118		118	479	143	169	52	21	12	2	107	11	17	.353	.459
Ed McKean	SS130		130	554	116	198	128	30	15	8	49	12	33	.357	.509
Chippy McGarr	3B128		128	523	94	144	74	24	6	2	28	29	31	.275	.356
Henry Blake	OF73		73	296	51	78	51	15	4	1	30	22	1	.264	.351
Jimmy McAleer	OF64		64	253	36	73	40	15	1	2	13	17	14	.289	.379
Jesse Burkett	OF125,P1		125	523	138	187	94	27	14	8	84	27	28	.358	.509
Chief Zimmer	C89		90	341	55	97	65	20	5	4	17	31	14	.284	.408
Jack O'Connor	C45,OF33,1B7		86	330	67	104	51	23	7	2	15	7	15	.315	.445
Buck Ewing	OF52,2B1		53	211	32	53	39	12	4	2	24	9	18	.251	.374
Cy Young	P52		52	186	24	40	26	8	4	2	2	20	4	.215	.333
Nig Cuppy	P43,OF1		44	135	28	35	19	6	3	0	15	27	3	.259	.348
White Wings Tebeau	OF27,1B12,3B1	(2-2)	40	150	32	47	25	9	4	0	25	18	9	.313	.427
Jake Virtue	OF21,2B3,1B2,P1		29	89	15	23	10	4	1	0	13	3	1	.258	.326
John Clarkson	P22		22	55	8	11	7	0	0	1	6	9	1	.200	.255
Mike Sullivan	P13	(2-2)	13	44	6	13	8	1	1	0	2	9	0	.295	.364
Frank Griffith	P7,OF1		7	24	4	8	9	2	2	0	1	4	0	.333	.583
Bobby Wallace	P4		4	13	0	2	1	1	0	0	0	1	0	.154	.231
Tony Mullane	P4	(2-2)	4	13	0	1	0	0	0	0	4	2	1	.077	.077
Charlie Petty	P4	(2-2)	4	12	0	1	0	0	0	0	0	2	0	.083	.083
Chauncey Fisher	P3	(1-2)	3	4	0	0	1	0	0	0	0	4	0	.000	.000
Frank Knauss	P2		2	4	1	0	1	0	0	0	1	0	0	.000	.000
Bill Lyston	P1		1	2	0	0	0	0	0	0	0	2	0	.000	.000
			130	4764	932	1442	790	241	90	37	471	301	220	.303	.414

PITCHERS			W	L	PCT	G	GS	CG	SH	SV	IP	H	BB	SO	ERA
Cy Young			26	21	.553	52	47	44	2	1	409	488	106	108	3.94
Nig Cuppy			24	15	.615	43	33	29	3	0	316	381	128	65	4.56
John Clarkson			8	10	.444	22	18	13	1	0	151	173	46	28	4.42
Mike Sullivan		(2-2)	6	5	.545	13	11	9	0	0	91	128	47	19	6.35
Bobby Wallace			2	1	.667	4	3	2	0	0	26	28	20	10	5.19
Frank Griffith			1	2	.333	7	6	3	0	0	42	64	37	15	9.99
Tony Mullane		(2-2)	1	2	.333	4	4	3	0	0	33	46	10	3	7.64
Frank Knauss			0	1	.000	2	2	1	0	0	11	7	14	2	5.73
Charlie Petty		(2-2)	0	2	.000	4	3	2	0	0	27	42	14	4	8.67
Chauncey Fisher		(1-2)	0	2	.000	3	2	0	0	0	11	22	5	0	11.45
Bill Lyston			0	0	----	1	1	0	0	0	4	5	4	0	9.82
Jesse Burkett			0	0	----	1	0	0	0	0	4	6	1	0	4.50
Jake Virtue			0	0	----	1	0	0	0	0	0	0	1	0	----
			68	61	.527	130	130	106	6	1	1124	1390	433	254	4.97

PITTSBURGH Pirates
65-65 .500 -25 7th Buckenberger - Mack

BATTERS	POS/GAMES		GP	AB	R	H	BI	2B	3B	HR	BB	SO	SB	BA	SA
Jake Beckley	1B131		131	533	121	183	120	36	18	7	43	16	21	.343	.518
Lou Bierbauer	2B130		130	525	86	159	107	19	13	3	26	9	19	.303	.406
Jack Glasscock	SS85		86	332	46	93	63	10	7	1	31	4	18	.280	.361
Denny Lyons	3B71		71	254	51	82	50	14	4	4	42	12	14	.323	.457
Patsy Donovan	OF132		132	576	145	174	76	21	10	4	33	12	41	.302	.394
Jake Stenzel	OF131		131	522	148	185	121	39	20	13	75	13	61	.354	.580
Elmer Smith	OF125,P1		125	489	128	174	72	33	19	6	65	12	33	.356	.538
Connie Mack	C69		69	228	32	57	21	7	1	1	20	14	8	.250	.303
Fred Hartman	3B49		49	182	41	58	20	4	7	2	16	11	12	.319	.451
Red Ehret	P46		46	135	6	23	11	4	1	0	8	22	0	.170	.215
Joe Sugden	C31,3B4,SS3,OF1		39	139	23	46	23	13	2	2	14	2	3	.331	.496
Ad Gumbert	P37		38	113	18	33	19	4	5	1	6	20	1	.292	.442
Bill Merritt	C28,1B4,OF2	(2-3)	36	109	18	30	18	1	2	1	15	7	2	.275	.349
Farmer Weaver	C14,SS12,3B5,OF1	(2-2)	30	115	16	40	24	7	2	0	6	1	4	.348	.443
Frank Scheibeck	SS11,OF9,3B3,2B2	(1-2)	28	102	20	36	10	2	3	1	11	9	7	.353	.461
Frank Killen	P28		28	80	13	21	13	3	1	0	6	23	0	.263	.325
Tom Colcolough	P22		22	70	10	14	6	2	2	0	5	7	1	.200	.286
Jock Menefee	P13	(2-2)	13	47	6	12	7	1	2	0	3	3	2	.255	.362
Monte Cross	SS13		13	43	14	19	13	1	5	2	5	4	6	.442	.837
Fred Steere	SS10		10	39	3	8	4	0	0	0	2	1	2	.205	.205
George Nicol	P8	(1-2)	8	20	8	9	3	1	0	0	0	1	0	.450	.500
John Easton	P3		3	5	0	0	2	0	0	0	0	0	0	.000	.000
Gene DeMontreville	SS2		2	8	0	2	0	0	0	0	1	4	0	.250	.250
Jim Ritz	3B1		1	4	1	0	0	0	0	0	0	0	1	.000	.000
Phil Knell	P1	(2-2)	1	3	1	0	0	0	0	0	0	0	0	.000	.000

1894 NATIONAL LEAGUE

PITTSBURGH (cont.)
Pirates

BATTERS	POS/GAMES		GP	AB	R	H	BI	2B	3B	HR	BB	SO	SB	BA	SA
Harry Jordan	P1		1	3	0	0	0	0	0	0	1	1	0	.000	.000
Adonis Terry	P1	(1-2)	1	0	0	0	0	0	0	0	0	0	0	----	----
			132	4676	955	1458	803	222	124	48	434	208	256	.312	.443

PITCHERS		W	L	PCT	G	GS	CG	SH	SV	IP	H	BB	SO	ERA
Red Ehret		19	21	.475	46	38	31	1	0	347	441	128	102	5.14
Ad Gumbert		15	14	.517	37	31	26	0	0	269	372	84	65	6.02
Frank Killen		14	11	.560	28	28	20	1	0	204	261	86	62	4.50
Tom Colcolough		8	5	.615	22	14	11	0	0	149	207	70	29	7.08
Jock Menefee	(2-2)	5	8	.385	13	13	13	0	0	112	159	39	33	5.40
George Nicol	(1-2)	3	4	.429	8	5	3	0	0	44	57	33	11	6.50
Harry Jordan		1	0	1.000	1	1	1	0	0	9	10	2	1	4.00
John Easton		0	1	.000	3	1	1	0	0	20	26	4	1	4.12
Adonis Terry	(1-2)	0	1	.000	1	1	0	0	0	1	2	4	0	67.50
Phil Knell	(1-2)	0	0	----	1	0	0	0	0	7	11	6	0	11.57
Elmer Smith		0	0	----	1	0	0	0	0	4	6	1	0	4.50
		65	65	.500	132	132	106	2	0	1165	1552	457	304	5.60

CHICAGO
Colts

57-75   .432   -34   8th   Cap Anson

BATTERS	POS/GAMES		GP	AB	R	H	BI	2B	3B	HR	BB	SO	SB	BA	SA
Cap Anson	1B82,2B1		83	340	82	132	99	28	4	5	40	15	17	.388	.538
Jiggs Parrott	2B123,3B1		124	517	82	128	64	17	9	3	16	35	30	.248	.333
Bill Dahlen	SS66,3B55		121	502	149	179	107	32	14	15	76	33	42	.357	.566
Charlie Irwin	3B67,SS61		128	498	84	144	95	24	9	8	63	23	35	.289	.422
Jimmy Ryan	OF108		108	474	132	171	62	37	7	3	50	23	11	.361	.487
Bill Lange	OF109,SS2		111	442	84	145	90	16	9	6	56	18	65	.328	.446
Walt Wilmot	OF133		133	597	134	197	130	45	12	5	35	23	74	.330	.471
Pop Schriver	C88,SS3,3B3,1B2		96	349	55	96	47	12	3	3	29	21	9	.275	.352
George Decker	1B48,OF29,3B7,2B2		91	384	74	120	92	17	6	8	24	17	23	.313	.451
Mal Kittredge	C51		51	168	36	53	23	8	2	0	26	20	2	.315	.387
Clark Griffith	P36,OF7,SS1		46	142	27	33	15	5	4	0	23	9	6	.232	.324
Bill Hutchinson	P36,OF4		39	136	30	42	16	3	0	6	11	17	2	.309	.463
Adonis Terry	P23,OF7,1B2	(2-2)	30	95	19	33	17	4	2	0	11	12	3	.347	.432
Willie McGill	P27		27	82	10	20	3	5	0	0	15	12	1	.244	.305
Scott Stratton	P15,OF5,1B2	(2-2)	23	96	29	36	23	5	4	3	6	1	3	.375	.604
Bert Abbey	P11		11	39	3	5	4	0	0	0	2	7	1	.128	.128
Sam Dungan	OF10	(1-2)	10	39	5	9	3	2	0	0	7	1	1	.231	.282
Llewellyn Camp	2B8		8	33	1	6	1	2	0	0	1	6	0	.182	.242
John Houseman	SS3,2B1		4	15	5	6	4	3	1	0	5	3	2	.400	.733
Kid Camp	P3		3	11	0	0	0	0	0	0	0	1	0	.000	.000
Fred Clausen	P1		1	1	0	0	0	0	0	0	0	1	0	.000	.000
			135	4960	1041	1555	895	265	86	65	496	298	327	.314	.441

PITCHERS		W	L	PCT	G	GS	CG	SH	SV	IP	H	BB	SO	ERA
Clark Griffith		21	14	.600	36	30	28	0	0	261	328	85	71	4.92
Bill Hutchinson		14	16	.467	36	34	28	0	0	278	373	140	59	6.06
Willie McGill		7	19	.269	27	23	22	0	0	208	272	117	58	5.84
Scott Stratton	(2-2)	8	5	.615	15	12	11	0	0	119	198	40	23	6.03
Adonis Terry	(2-2)	5	11	.313	23	21	16	0	0	163	232	123	39	6.09
Bert Abbey		2	7	.222	11	11	10	0	0	92	119	37	24	5.18
Kid Camp		0	1	.000	3	2	2	0	0	22	34	12	6	6.55
Fred Clausen		0	1	.000	1	1	0	0	0	4	5	3	1	10.38
		57	75	.432	135	134	117	0	0	1148	1561	557	281	5.68

ST. LOUIS
Browns

56-76   .424   -35   9th   Doggie Miller

BATTERS	POS/GAMES		GP	AB	R	H	BI	2B	3B	HR	BB	SO	SB	BA	SA
Roger Connor	1B99	(2-2)	99	380	83	122	79	28	25	7	51	17	17	.321	.582
Joe Quinn	2B106		106	405	59	116	61	18	1	4	24	8	25	.286	.365
Bones Ely	SS126,2B1,P1		127	510	85	156	89	20	12	12	30	34	23	.306	.463
Doggie Miller	3B52,C41,2B18,1B12,OF4,SS1		127	481	93	163	86	9	11	8	58	9	17	.339	.453
Tommy Dowd	OF117,2B7,3B1		123	524	92	142	62	16	8	4	54	33	31	.271	.355
Frank Shugart	OF122,SS7,3B7		133	527	103	154	72	19	18	7	38	37	21	.292	.436

ST. LOUIS (cont.)
Browns

BATTERS	POS/GAMES		GP	AB	R	H	BI	2B	3B	HR	BB	SO	SB	BA	SA
Charles Frank	OF77,1B3,P2		80	319	52	89	42	12	7	4	44	13	14	.279	.398
Heinie Peitz	C39,3B47,1B14,P1		99	338	52	89	49	19	9	3	43	21	14	.263	.399
Ted Breitenstein	P56,OF7		63	182	27	40	13	7	2	0	31	19	3	.220	.280
Duff Cooley	OF39,3B13,SS1,1B1		54	206	35	61	21	3	1	1	12	16	7	.296	.335
Pink Hawley	P53,OF1		53	163	16	43	23	6	6	2	5	16	2	.264	.411
Old Hoss Twineham	C38		38	127	22	40	16	4	1	1	9	11	2	.315	.386
Dad Clarkson	P32		33	88	11	16	7	0	1	0	16	28	1	.182	.205
Marty Hogan	OF29	(2-2)	29	100	11	28	13	3	4	0	3	13	7	.280	.390
Dick Buckley	C27,1B1	(1-2)	29	89	5	16	3	1	2	1	6	3	1	.180	.270
Tim O'Rourke	3B18	(2-3)	18	71	10	20	10	4	1	0	8	3	2	.282	.366
Kid Gleason	P8,1B1	(1-2)	9	28	3	7	1	0	1	0	2	1	0	.250	.321
Joe Peitz	OF7		7	26	10	11	3	2	3	0	6	1	2	.423	.731
Ernest Mason	P4,OF1		4	12	0	3	0	0	0	0	1	1	0	.250	.250
Paul Russell	OF1,2B1,3B1		3	10	1	1	0	0	0	0	0	2	0	.100	.100
Willard Brown	1B3	(2-2)	3	9	0	1	0	0	0	0	0	2	0	.111	.111
Pete Browning	OF2	(1-2)	2	7	1	1	0	0	0	0	0	0	0	.143	.143
George Paynter	OF1		1	4	0	0	0	0	0	0	1	0	1	.000	.000
Art Ball	2B1		1	3	0	1	0	0	0	0	0	1	0	.333	.333
John Ricks	3B1		1	1	0	0	0	0	0	0	0	0	0	.000	.000
			133	4610	771	1320	650	171	113	54	442	289	190	.286	.408

PITCHERS			W	L	PCT	G	GS	CG	SH	SV	IP	H	BB	SO	ERA
Ted Breitenstein			27	23	.540	56	50	46	1	0	447	497	191	140	4.79
Pink Hawley			19	27	.413	53	41	36	0	0	393	481	149	120	4.90
Dad Clarkson			8	17	.320	32	32	24	1	0	233	318	117	46	6.36
Kid Gleason		(1-2)	2	6	.250	8	8	6	0	0	58	75	21	9	6.05
Ernest Mason			0	3	.000	4	2	2	0	0	23	34	10	3	7.15
Charlie Frank			0	0	----	2	0	0	0	0	3	6	7	1	15.00
Heinie Peitz			0	0	----	1	0	0	0	0	3	7	2	0	9.00
Bones Ely			0	0	----	1	0	0	0	0	1	0	3	0	0.00
			56	76	.424	133	133	114	2	0	1161	1418	500	319	5.29

CINCINNATI
Reds

55-75   .423   -35   10th   Charlie Comiskey

BATTERS	POS/GAMES		GP	AB	R	H	BI	2B	3B	HR	BB	SO	SB	BA	SA
Charlie Comiskey	1B60,OF1		61	220	26	58	33	8	0	0	5	5	10	.264	.300
Bid McPhee	2B126		126	474	107	144	88	21	9	5	90	23	33	.304	.418
Germany Smith	SS127		127	482	73	127	76	33	5	3	41	28	15	.263	.371
Arlie Latham	3B127,2B2		129	524	129	164	60	23	6	4	60	24	59	.313	.403
Jimmy Canavan	OF95,SS3,3B2,2B1,1B1		101	356	77	97	70	16	9	13	62	25	13	.272	.478
Dummy Hoy	OF126		126	495	114	148	70	22	13	5	87	18	27	.299	.426
Bug Holliday	OF119,1B1		121	511	119	190	119	24	7	13	40	20	29	.372	.523
Morg Murphy	C74,SS1,3B1		75	255	42	70	37	9	0	1	26	34	6	.275	.322
Farmer Vaughn	C43,1B27,OF8,SS3		72	284	50	88	64	15	5	8	12	11	5	.310	.482
Tom Parrott	P41,OF13,1B12,SS1,3B1,2B1		68	229	51	74	40	12	6	4	17	10	4	.323	.480
Frank Dwyer	P45,OF10,SS2		54	172	31	46	28	9	2	2	15	13	0	.267	.378
John McCarthy	OF25,1B15		40	167	29	45	21	9	1	0	17	6	3	.269	.335
Bill Merritt	C24,3B3,1B1,OF1	(3-3)	29	113	17	37	21	6	1	1	9	3	4	.327	.425
Icebox Chamberlain	P23		23	70	10	22	7	7	1	1	7	5	2	.314	.486
Frank Motz	1B18		18	69	8	14	12	4	0	0	9	1	2	.203	.261
Bill Whitrock	P10,OF7,3B1	(1-2)	18	60	8	13	8	1	0	0	2	4	1	.217	.233
Bill Massey	1B10,2B2,3B1		13	53	7	15	5	3	0	0	3	2	0	.283	.340
Chauncey Fisher	P11	(1-2)	11	43	5	10	4	1	1	1	1	2	0	.233	.372
Lem Cross	P8		9	26	3	6	4	1	1	0	1	4	0	.231	.346
Marty Hogan	OF6	(1-2)	6	23	4	3	3	0	0	0	1	4	2	.130	.130
Henry Fournier	P6		6	19	0	2	1	0	0	0	1	5	0	.105	.105
Jesse Tannehill	P5		5	11	0	0	1	0	0	0	1	2	0	.000	.000
Carney Flynn	P2		2	3	0	0	0	0	0	0	0	0	0	.000	.000
Murray McGuire	P1		1	4	0	1	0	0	0	0	0	0	0	.250	.250
Con Murphy	C1		1	4	0	0	0	0	0	0	1	1	0	.000	.000
Fred Blank	P1		1	3	0	0	0	0	0	0	0	2	0	.000	.000
Bill Pflann	P1		1	1	0	0	0	0	0	0	0	0	0	.000	.000
			132	4671	910	1374	772	224	67	61	508	252	215	.294	.410

PITCHERS		W	L	PCT	G	GS	CG	SH	SV	IP	H	BB	SO	ERA
Frank Dwyer		19	22	.463	45	40	34	1	1	348	471	106	49	5.07
Tom Parrott		17	19	.472	41	36	31	1	1	309	402	126	61	5.60
Icebox Chamberlain		10	9	.526	23	22	18	1	0	178	220	91	57	5.77

1894 NATIONAL LEAGUE

CINCINNATI (cont.)
Reds

PITCHERS		W	L	PCT	G	GS	CG	SH	SV	IP	H	BB	SO	ERA
Lem Cross		3	4	.429	8	7	3	0	0	53	94	21	11	8.49
Bill Whitrock	(2-2)	2	6	.250	10	8	8	0	0	70	110	39	9	6.65
Chauncey Fisher	(2-2)	2	8	.200	11	11	10	0	0	91	134	44	14	7.32
Jesse Tannehill		1	0	1.000	5	1	1	0	1	29	37	16	7	7.14
Henry Fournier		1	3	.250	6	4	4	0	0	45	71	20	5	5.40
Fred Blank		0	1	.000	1	1	1	0	0	8	5	9	1	4.50
Bill Pflann		0	1	.000	1	1	0	0	0	3	10	4	0	27.00
Carney Flynn		0	2	.000	2	1	0	0	0	8	16	10	4	17.61
Murray McGuire		0	0	----	1	0	0	0	0	6	15	5	1	10.50
		55	75	.423	132	132	110	4	3	1147	1585	491	219	5.99

WASHINGTON
Senators

45-87 .341 -46 11th Gus Schmelz

BATTERS	POS/GAMES		GP	AB	R	H	BI	2B	3B	HR	BB	SO	SB	BA	SA
Ed Cartwright	1B132		132	507	88	149	106	35	13	12	57	43	31	.294	.485
Piggy Ward	2B79,OF12,SS3,3B1		98	347	86	105	36	11	7	0	80	31	41	.303	.375
Frank Scheibeck	SS52	(2-2)	52	196	49	45	17	2	4	0	45	24	11	.230	.281
Bill Joyce	3B99		99	355	103	126	89	25	14	17	87	33	21	.355	.648
Bill Hassamaer	OF68,3B31,2B14,SS4		118	494	106	159	90	33	17	4	41	20	16	.322	.482
Charles Abbey	OF129		129	523	95	164	101	26	18	7	58	38	31	.314	.472
Kip Selbach	OF80,SS19		97	372	69	114	71	21	17	7	51	20	21	.306	.511
Deacon McGuire	C104		104	425	67	130	78	18	6	6	33	19	11	.306	.419
Paul Radford	SS47,2B25,OF24		95	325	61	78	49	13	5	0	65	23	24	.240	.311
White Wings Tebeau	OF61	(1-2)	61	222	41	50	28	10	6	0	37	20	17	.225	.324
Win Mercer	P50,OF4		53	164	29	48	29	5	2	2	9	20	9	.293	.384
Al Maul	P29,OF12		42	125	23	30	20	3	3	2	14	11	1	.240	.360
Dan Dugdale	C33,3B3,OF2		38	134	19	32	16	4	2	0	13	14	7	.239	.299
Otis Stocksdale	P18,OF4,2B2,SS1,3B1		24	71	10	23	6	1	0	0	2	5	2	.324	.338
Mike Sullivan	P20,OF1	(1-2)	20	57	4	9	7	1	1	1	2	11	0	.158	.263
Duke Esper	P18	(1-2)	18	54	7	14	4	3	1	1	4	7	0	.259	.407
Joe Sullivan	2B8,SS6,OF1,3B1	(1-2)	17	60	7	15	5	3	0	0	6	2	3	.250	.300
Charlie Petty	P16	(1-2)	16	41	5	8	3	0	1	0	4	8	0	.195	.244
Tim O'Rourke	2B4,SS3	(3-3)	7	25	4	5	2	2	1	0	2	1	0	.200	.360
Jake Boyd	P3,OF3		6	21	1	3	1	0	0	0	1	4	2	.143	.143
George Haddock	P4,OF1	(2-2)	5	16	4	3	3	2	0	0	1	2	1	.188	.313
John Malarkey	P3,OF1		4	14	1	1	0	0	0	0	0	8	0	.071	.071
Kid Mohler	2B3		3	9	0	1	0	0	0	0	2	4	0	.111	.111
Ben Stephens	P3		3	4	0	1	0	0	0	0	0	0	0	.250	.250
Varney Anderson	P2		2	7	2	3	0	0	0	0	0	2	0	.429	.429
Count Campau	OF2		2	7	1	1	0	0	0	0	1	4	0	.143	.143
Rip Egan	P1		1	3	0	0	1	0	0	0	1	0	0	.000	.000
Bill Wynne	P1		1	3	0	0	0	0	0	0	1	1	0	.000	.000
			132	4581	882	1317	762	218	118	59	617	375	249	.287	.425

PITCHERS		W	L	PCT	G	GS	CG	SH	SV	IP	H	BB	SO	ERA
Win Mercer		17	23	.425	50	38	29	0	3	336	442	126	72	3.85
Al Maul		11	15	.423	29	27	21	0	0	205	275	73	34	5.94
Otis Stocksdale		5	9	.357	18	14	11	0	0	117	176	42	10	5.06
Duke Esper	(1-2)	5	10	.333	18	14	7	0	0	116	177	39	24	7.45
Charlie Petty	(1-2)	3	8	.273	16	12	8	0	0	103	156	32	14	5.59
John Malarkey		2	1	.667	3	3	3	0	0	26	42	5	3	4.15
Mike Sullivan	(1-2)	2	10	.167	20	12	11	0	1	118	166	74	21	6.58
Bill Wynne		0	1	.000	1	1	1	0	0	8	10	8	2	6.75
Varney Anderson		0	2	.000	2	2	2	0	0	14	15	6	3	7.07
Jake Boyd		0	3	.000	3	3	3	0	0	19	37	14	3	8.53
George Haddock	(2-2)	0	4	.000	4	4	4	0	0	29	50	17	1	8.69
Ben Stephens		0	0	----	3	2	1	0	0	11	19	8	1	4.91
Rip Egan		0	0	----	1	0	0	0	0	5	8	2	2	10.80
		45	87	.341	132	132	101	0	4	1107	1573	446	190	5.51

LOUISVILLE
Colonels

36-94 .277 -54 12th Billy Barnie

BATTERS	POS/GAMES	GP	AB	R	H	BI	2B	3B	HR	BB	SO	SB	BA	SA
Luke Lutenberg	1B67,2B2	69	250	42	48	23	10	4	0	23	21	4	.192	.264
Fred Pfeffer	2B90,SS15,P1	104	409	68	126	59	12	14	5	30	14	31	.308	.443
Danny Richardson	SS107,2B10	116	430	51	109	40	17	2	1	35	31	8	.253	.309

1894 NATIONAL LEAGUE

LOUISVILLE (cont.)
Colonels

BATTERS	POS/GAMES		GP	AB	R	H	BI	2B	3B	HR	BB	SO	SB	BA	SA
Jerry Denny	3B60		60	221	26	61	32	11	7	0	13	12	10	.276	.389
Larry Twitchell	OF51,P1		52	210	28	56	32	16	3	2	15	20	8	.267	.400
Tom Brown	OF129		129	536	122	136	57	22	14	9	60	73	66	.254	.397
Fred Clarke	OF75		75	310	54	83	48	11	7	7	25	27	25	.268	.416
John Grim	C77,2B24,1B7,3B1		108	410	66	122	70	27	7	7	16	15	14	.298	.449
Farmer Weaver	OF35,C17,1B10,2B1	(1-2)	64	244	19	54	24	5	2	3	7	11	3	.221	.295
Tim O'Rourke	1B30,OF18,SS3,3B3,2B1	(1-3)	55	220	46	61	27	3	3	0	23	9	9	.277	.318
Pat Flaherty	3B38		38	145	15	43	15	5	3	0	9	6	2	.297	.372
Oliver Smith	OF38		38	134	26	40	20	6	1	3	27	15	13	.299	.425
George Hemming	P35,OF1	(1-2)	36	131	20	33	10	2	6	2	5	20	2	.252	.405
Phil Knell	P32		32	113	10	31	13	2	4	1	0	18	1	.274	.389
Jock Menefee	P28,2B1	(1-2)	29	79	7	13	4	1	0	0	8	7	2	.165	.177
Peter Gilbert	3B28		28	108	13	33	14	3	1	1	5	4	2	.306	.380
George Nicol	OF26,P1	(2-2)	27	108	12	38	19	6	4	0	2	3	4	.352	.481
Bill Wadsworth	P22		22	74	9	19	10	5	1	0	4	20	0	.257	.351
Billy Earle	C18,1B1,2B1,3B1,OF1	(1-2)	21	65	10	23	7	1	0	0	9	3	2	.354	.369
Fred Lake	2B6,SS5,C5		16	42	8	12	10	2	0	1	11	6	2	.286	.405
Willard Brown	1B13	(1-2)	13	48	5	10	9	2	0	0	5	7	1	.208	.250
Fred Zahner	C10,OF2,1B1		13	45	7	9	3	0	1	0	3	5	2	.200	.244
Scott Stratton	P7,OF5	(1-2)	13	37	9	12	4	1	2	0	4	2	1	.324	.459
Henry Cote	C10		10	31	7	9	3	2	2	0	5	6	2	.290	.484
Sam Dungan	OF8	(2-2)	8	32	6	11	3	1	0	0	4	1	2	.344	.375
Bert Inks	P8	(2-2)	8	27	4	12	3	0	0	0	1	1	0	.444	.444
Matt Kilroy	P8		8	17	2	2	1	0	0	0	1	6	1	.118	.118
Harrison Peppers	P2		2	4	0	0	0	0	0	0	0	0	0	.000	.000
Bill Whitrock	P1	(1-2)	1	2	0	0	0	0	0	0	0	1	0	.000	.000
			130	4482	692	1206	560	173	88	42	350	364	217	.269	.375

PITCHERS		W	L	PCT	G	GS	CG	SH	SV	IP	H	BB	SO	ERA
George Hemming	(1-2)	13	19	.406	35	32	32	1	1	294	358	133	66	4.37
Jock Menefee	(1-2)	8	17	.320	28	24	20	1	0	212	258	50	43	4.29
Phil Knell		7	21	.250	32	28	25	0	0	247	330	104	67	5.32
Bill Wadsworth		4	18	.182	22	22	20	0	0	173	261	103	57	7.60
Bert Inks	(2-2)	2	6	.250	8	8	8	0	0	60	87	34	8	6.49
Scott Stratton	(1-2)	1	5	.167	7	5	4	0	0	43	72	13	3	8.37
George Nicol	(2-2)	0	1	.000	1	1	1	0	0	9	19	5	3	15.00
Harrison Peppers		0	1	.000	2	1	0	0	0	8	10	4	0	6.75
Bill Whitrock	(1-2)	0	1	.000	1	1	0	0	0	4	8	2	0	9.00
Matt Kilroy		0	5	.000	8	7	3	0	0	37	46	20	11	3.89
Fred Pfeffer		0	0	----	1	0	0	0	0	7	8	6	0	2.57
Larry Twitchell		0	0	----	1	0	0	0	0	3	5	1	0	6.00
		36	94	.277	130	129	113	2	1	1097	1462	475	258	5.45

1895 NATIONAL LEAGUE

Mr. Temple's Cup

Pittsburgh businessman Charles C. Temple was a fan of his hometown baseball team. So much so, that when Pittsburgh finished second in 1893, he spent $800 on a trophy that he instructed would be contested by the first and second place teams in 1894. He further ruled that the winners would receive 65 percent of the gate receipts, while the losers divided the rest. The trophy was named after the donor and was referred to as the Temple Cup.

After the 1894 season, first place Baltimore and second place New York squared off in the inaugural Temple Cup battle. Neither team felt very excited about the prospects. Baltimore, who had already won the pennant, felt that they had nothing to prove, and did not want to risk losing the glory of their championship. The second point of contention regarded the division of spoils. The wording of the Temple Cup agreement that the 65 percent should go to the "champions." The Orioles contended that since they were the champions of the regular season, they were entitled to the larger share, regardless of the series outcome. Other suggestions included the possible provision of a fifty-fifty split of the money.

Once the teams got around to playing, New York made short work of Baltimore, whitewashing them in four straight. New York's pitching duo of Amos Rusie and Jouett Meekin each won a pair of games. The scores of the games were: 4-1, 9-6, 4-1, and 16-3. After the series was over, it was revealed that most, if not all, of the players split their earnings with friends on the other team.

These disagreements concerning the Temple Cup pointed out its basic flaw. Always before, a championship series had pitted one league champion against another. Even in the split season of 1892, it was the two winners of each half who faced one another. With the Temple Cup, no longer was it winner versus winner, it was winner versus second best. The team without the best record could aspire to be the Temple Cup champs. That stipulation certainly took away the meaning of the regular season. Why aspire to finish first, when some upstart could luckily beat you in a short series and thus claim the title of league champion and the Temple Cup?

The league cooled off somewhat in 1895, but the overall batting average remained high with a mark of .296. Once more Baltimore won the pennant, this time by three games over Cleveland. They were led at the plate by Hugh Jennings (.386), Joe Kelley

(.365), and Willie Keeler (.377). Rookie pitcher, Bill Hoffer, won 31 with a league best .838 win percentage.

Cleveland, in second, featured the best hitter. Outfielder Jesse Burkett finished with the best average (.409), and most hits (225). His teammates Ed McKean (.342) and Cy Young (35-10) also contributed to the team's success.

Philadelphia's outfield could not match their .400 average of the previous summer — they had to settle for .394 instead. Sam Thompson (.392), Billy Hamilton (.389) and Ed Delahanty (.404) were joined by catcher Jack Clements (.394) in the stratosphere. In addition, Thompson (18), and Clements (13) finished first and second in the home run derby.

Chicago moved up several notches to fourth, while Brooklyn remained the same in fifth. Chicago was led by Bill Lange (.389) and Bill Everett (.358), while Brooklyn enjoyed the hitting of Mike Griffin (.333).

Boston finished tied with Brooklyn while Pittsburgh finished in seventh. Boston enjoyed the bats of Hugh Duffy (.352) and Jimmy Bannon (.350) while Pittsburgh had Jake Stenzel (.374) to lead the way.

Cincinnati, New York, Washington, St. Louis, and Louisville brought up the rear. Their players of note included Dusty Miller of Cincinnati (.335); George Davis (.343), Mike Tiernan (.347) and George Van Haltren (.340) of New York; Deacon McGuire (.336) and Ed Cartwright (.331) of Washington; Duff Cooley (.339) of St. Louis; and finally rookie Fred Clarke (.347) of Louisville.

The Temple Cup of 1895 is considered by some to be one of the best of the group because it was only one of two series that saw the losing side win a game. Baltimore and Cleveland met in October 1895 for the second installment of the championship series. The first game, played in Cleveland, saw the home team score two in the bottom of the ninth to win 5-4. Cleveland also won the second and third games at home by the scores 7-2, and 7-1. It took eight tries for Baltimore to win a Temple Cup game, but they managed to turn the trick by blanking Cleveland 5-0 in front of a home crowd. However, Cleveland wrapped things up with a 5-2 victory in the deciding fifth game. For the second straight year, the second place team had taken the championship cup.

Mr. Temple's purpose in sponsoring the championship was to see his beloved Pittsburgh team win it. After their strong second place showing in 1893, this seemed a distinct possibility. However, much to Temple's disappointment, Pittsburgh finished no higher than sixth during the four-year reign of the Temple Cup.

1895 NATIONAL LEAGUE

BALTIMORE
Orioles

87-43   .669   1st   Ned Hanlon

BATTERS	POS/GAMES		GP	AB	R	H	BI	2B	3B	HR	BB	SO	SB	BA	SA
Scoops Carey	1B123,OF1,SS1,3B1		123	490	59	128	75	21	6	1	27	32	2	.261	.335
Kid Gleason	2B85,3B12,P9,OF4		112	421	90	130	74	14	12	0	33	18	19	.309	.399
Hugh Jennings	SS131		131	529	159	204	125	41	7	4	24	17	53	.386	.512
John McGraw	3B95,2B1		96	388	110	143	48	13	6	2	60	9	61	.369	.448
Willie Keeler	OF131		131	565	162	213	78	24	15	4	37	12	47	.377	.494
Steve Brodie	OF131		131	528	85	184	134	27	10	2	26	15	35	.348	.449
Joe Kelley	OF131		131	518	148	189	134	26	19	10	77	29	54	.365	.546
Wilbert Robinson	C75		77	282	38	74	48	19	1	0	12	19	11	.262	.337
Heinie Reitz	2B48,3B18,SS1		71	245	45	72	29	15	5	0	18	11	15	.294	.396
Boileryard Clarke	C60,1B6		67	241	38	70	35	15	3	0	13	18	8	.290	.378
Bill Hoffer	P41		41	126	22	27	9	3	1	0	8	15	0	.214	.254
George Hemming	P34		35	117	19	33	16	10	2	1	2	12	0	.282	.427
Duke Esper	P34		34	90	7	16	2	2	0	0	4	12	0	.178	.200
Dad Clarkson	P20	(2-2)	20	57	10	8	4	1	0	1	5	17	0	.140	.211
Sadie McMahon	P15		15	51	5	16	5	1	0	0	3	2	1	.314	.333
Frank Bonner	3B11	(1-2)	11	42	9	14	7	1	1	0	5	1	4	.333	.405
Arlie Pond	P6,OF1		7	6	0	2	0	0	1	0	0	2	0	.333	.667
Dan Brouthers	1B5	(1-2)	5	23	2	6	5	2	0	0	1	1	0	.261	.348
Bill Kissinger	P2	(1-2)	2	5	1	1	0	0	0	0	0	1	0	.200	.200
Frank Bowerman	C1		1	1	0	0	0	0	0	0	0	0	0	.000	.000
			132	4725	1009	1530	828	235	89	25	355	243	310	.324	.427

PITCHERS			W	L	PCT	G	GS	CG	SH	SV	IP	H	BB	SO	ERA
Bill Hoffer			31	6	.838	41	38	32	4	0	314	296	124	80	3.21
George Hemming			20	13	.606	34	31	26	1	0	262	288	96	43	4.05
Dad Clarkson		(2-2)	12	3	.800	20	14	10	0	0	142	169	64	23	3.87
Sadie McMahon			10	4	.714	15	15	15	4	0	122	110	32	37	2.94
Duke Esper			10	12	.455	34	25	16	1	1	218	248	79	39	3.92
Kid Gleason			2	4	.333	9	5	3	0	1	50	77	21	6	6.97
Bill Kissinger		(1-2)	1	0	1.000	2	2	1	0	0	11	18	2	3	3.97
Arlie Pond			0	1	.000	6	1	1	0	2	14	10	12	13	5.93
			87	43	.669	132	131	104	10	4	1134	1216	430	244	3.80

CLEVELAND
Spiders

84-46   .646   -3   2nd   Patsy Tebeau

BATTERS	POS/GAMES		GP	AB	R	H	BI	2B	3B	HR	BB	SO	SB	BA	SA
Patsy Tebeau	1B49,2B9,3B6		63	264	50	84	52	13	2	2	16	18	8	.318	.405
Cupid Childs	2B119		119	462	96	133	90	15	3	4	74	24	20	.288	.359
Ed McKean	SS131		131	565	131	193	119	32	17	8	45	25	12	.342	.501
Chippy McGarr	3B108,2B4		112	419	85	111	59	14	2	2	34	33	19	.265	.322
Henry Blake	OF83		84	315	50	87	45	10	1	3	30	33	11	.276	.343
Jimmy McAleer	OF131		131	528	84	143	68	17	2	0	38	37	32	.271	.311
Jesse Burkett	OF131		131	550	153	225	83	22	13	5	74	31	41	.409	.524
Chief Zimmer	C84,1B3		88	315	60	107	56	21	2	5	33	30	14	.340	.467
White Wings Tebeau	OF49,1B42		91	337	57	110	68	16	6	0	50	28	12	.326	.409
Jack O'Connor	C47,1B41,3B1		89	340	51	99	58	14	10	0	30	22	11	.291	.391
Nig Cuppy	P47		47	140	36	40	25	9	3	0	20	14	2	.286	.393
Cy Young	P47		47	140	20	30	13	5	2	0	11	20	0	.214	.279
Bobby Wallace	P30		30	98	16	21	10	2	3	0	6	17	0	.214	.296
Ed Gremminger	3B20		20	78	10	21	15	1	0	0	5	13	0	.269	.282
Phil Knell	P20	(2-2)	20	55	9	11	5	2	1	0	1	9	1	.200	.273
Zeke Wilson	P8	(2-2)	8	18	2	2	3	0	0	0	1	1	3	.111	.111
Mike Sullivan	P4		4	15	2	2	1	1	0	0	0	3	0	.133	.200
Fred Donovan	C3		3	12	1	1	1	0	0	0	1	2	0	.083	.083
Pussy Tebeau	OF2		2	6	3	3	1	0	0	0	2	1	1	.500	.500
Tom O'Meara	C1		1	1	1	0	0	0	0	0	1	0	0	.000	.000
			131	4658	917	1423	772	194	67	29	472	361	187	.305	.395

PITCHERS			W	L	PCT	G	GS	CG	SH	SV	IP	H	BB	SO	ERA
Cy Young			35	10	.778	47	40	36	4	0	370	363	75	121	3.26
Nig Cuppy			26	14	.650	47	40	36	1	2	353	384	95	91	3.54
Bobby Wallace			12	14	.462	30	28	22	1	1	229	271	87	63	4.09
Phil Knell		(2-2)	7	5	.583	20	13	9	0	0	117	149	53	30	5.40
Zeke Wilson		(2-2)	3	1	.750	8	7	3	0	0	45	63	20	16	4.23
Mike Sullivan			1	2	.333	4	3	2	0	0	31	42	16	5	8.42
			84	46	.646	131	131	108	6	3	1144	1272	346	326	3.91

1895 NATIONAL LEAGUE

PHILADELPHIA Phillies   78-53   .595   -9.5   3rd   Art Irwin

BATTERS	POS/GAMES		GP	AB	R	H	BI	2B	3B	HR	BB	SO	SB	BA	SA
Jack Boyle	1B133		133	565	90	143	67	17	4	0	35	23	13	.253	.297
Bill Hallman	2B122,SS3		124	539	94	169	91	26	5	1	34	20	16	.314	.386
Joe Sullivan	SS89,OF6		94	373	75	126	50	7	3	2	24	20	15	.338	.389
Lave Cross	3B125		125	535	95	145	101	26	9	2	35	8	21	.271	.364
Sam Thompson	OF118		119	538	131	211	165	45	21	18	31	11	27	.392	.654
Billy Hamilton	OF123		123	517	166	201	74	22	6	7	96	30	97	.389	.495
Ed Delahanty	OF103,SS9,2B6,3B1		116	480	149	194	106	49	10	11	86	31	46	.404	.617
Jack Clements	C88		88	322	64	127	75	27	2	13	22	7	3	.394	.612
Tuck Turner	OF55		59	210	51	81	43	8	6	2	25	11	14	.386	.510
Charlie Reilly	SS34,3B11,2B3,OF1		49	179	28	48	25	6	1	0	13	12	7	.268	.313
Mike Grady	C38,OF5,3B1,1B1		46	123	21	40	23	3	1	1	14	8	5	.325	.390
Kid Carsey	P44		44	141	24	41	20	2	0	0	15	12	2	.291	.305
Jack Taylor	P41,OF1		42	155	26	45	35	11	2	3	7	18	3	.290	.445
Dick Buckley	C38		38	112	20	28	14	6	1	0	9	17	2	.250	.321
Willie McGill	P20		20	63	7	14	11	6	0	0	6	3	0	.222	.317
Al Orth	P11		11	45	8	16	13	4	0	1	1	6	0	.356	.511
Art Madison	SS6,2B3,3B2		11	34	6	12	8	3	0	0	1	1	4	.353	.441
Tom Smith	P11		11	33	1	8	3	1	0	0	3	6	0	.242	.273
Con Lucid	P10	(2-2)	10	29	8	10	5	3	1	0	3	5	0	.345	.517
Ernie Beam	P9,OF1		10	11	2	2	0	0	0	0	0	4	1	.182	.182
Henry Lampe	P7		7	16	1	2	0	0	1	0	2	6	0	.125	.250
George Hodson	P4		4	5	1	0	0	0	0	0	1	2	0	.000	.000
Deke White	P3		3	8	0	1	1	0	0	0	0	0	0	.125	.125
Gus Weyhing	P2	(1-3)	2	4	0	0	0	0	0	0	0	1	0	.000	.000
			133	5037	1068	1664	930	272	73	61	463	262	276	.330	.450

PITCHERS			W	L	PCT	G	GS	CG	SH	SV	IP	H	BB	SO	ERA
Jack Taylor			26	14	.650	41	37	33	1	1	335	403	83	93	4.49
Kid Carsey			24	16	.600	44	40	35	0	1	342	460	118	64	4.92
Willie McGill			10	8	.556	20	20	13	0	0	146	177	81	70	5.55
Al Orth			8	1	.889	11	10	9	0	1	88	103	22	25	3.89
Con Lucid		(2-2)	6	3	.667	10	10	7	1	0	70	80	35	19	5.94
Tom Smith			2	3	.400	11	7	4	0	0	68	76	53	21	6.88
Deke White			1	0	1.000	3	1	1	0	1	17	17	13	6	9.87
George Hodson			1	2	.333	4	2	1	0	0	17	27	9	6	9.53
Henry Lampe			0	2	.000	7	3	2	0	0	44	68	33	18	7.57
Ernie Beam			0	2	.000	9	1	1	0	3	25	33	25	3	11.31
Gus Weyhing		(1-3)	0	2	.000	2	2	0	0	0	9	23	13	5	20.00
			78	53	.595	133	133	106	2	7	1161	1467	485	330	5.47

CHICAGO Colts   72-58   .554   -15   4th   Cap Anson

BATTERS	POS/GAMES		GP	AB	R	H	BI	2B	3B	HR	BB	SO	SB	BA	SA
Cap Anson	1B122		122	474	87	159	91	23	6	2	55	23	12	.335	.422
Ace Stewart	2B97		97	365	52	88	76	8	10	8	39	40	14	.241	.384
Bill Dahlen	SS129,OF1		129	516	106	131	62	19	10	7	61	51	38	.254	.370
Bill Everett	3B130,2B3		133	550	129	197	88	16	10	3	33	42	47	.358	.440
Jimmy Ryan	OF108		108	438	83	139	49	22	8	6	48	22	18	.317	.445
Bill Lange	OF123		123	478	120	186	98	27	16	10	55	24	67	.389	.575
Walt Wilmot	OF108		108	466	86	132	72	16	6	8	30	19	28	.283	.395
Tim Donahue	C63		63	219	29	59	36	9	1	2	20	25	5	.269	.347
George Decker	OF57,1B11,3B3,SS1,2B1		73	297	51	82	41	9	7	2	17	22	11	.276	.374
Mal Kittredge	C59		60	212	30	48	29	6	3	3	16	9	6	.226	.325
Clark Griffith	P42,OF1		43	144	20	46	27	3	0	1	16	9	2	.319	.361
Adonis Terry	P38,OF1,SS1		40	137	18	30	10	3	2	1	2	17	1	.219	.292
Bill Hutchinson	P38		38	126	12	25	11	3	3	0	5	23	1	.198	.270
Harry Truby	2B33		33	119	17	40	16	3	0	0	10	7	7	.336	.361
Bill Moran	C15		15	55	8	9	9	2	1	1	3	2	2	.164	.291
Scott Stratton	P5,OF4		10	24	3	7	2	1	1	0	4	2	1	.292	.417
Walter Thornton	P7,1B1		8	22	4	7	7	1	0	1	3	1	0	.318	.500
Doc Parker	P7		7	22	3	7	2	0	1	0	1	1	0	.318	.409
Dan Friend	P5		5	17	4	4	1	0	0	0	1	1	0	.235	.235
Charlie Irwin	SS3		3	10	4	2	0	0	0	0	2	1	0	.200	.200
Jiggs Parrott	OF1,SS1,1B1		3	4	0	1	0	0	0	0	0	0	0	.250	.250
Monte McFarland	P2		2	7	0	1	0	0	0	0	0	3	0	.143	.143
John Dolan	P2		2	3	0	0	0	0	0	0	1	0	0	.000	.000
Bert Abbey	P1	(1-2)	1	3	0	1	0	0	0	0	0	0	0	.333	.333
			133	4708	866	1401	727	171	85	55	422	344	260	.298	.405

1895 NATIONAL LEAGUE

CHICAGO (cont.)
Colts

PITCHERS	W	L	PCT	G	GS	CG	SH	SV	IP	H	BB	SO	ERA
Clark Griffith	26	14	.650	42	41	39	0	0	353	434	91	79	3.93
Adonis Terry	21	14	.600	38	34	31	0	0	311	346	131	88	4.80
Bill Hutchinson	13	21	.382	38	35	30	2	0	291	371	129	85	4.73
Doc Parker	4	2	.667	7	6	5	1	0	51	65	9	9	3.68
Walter Thornton	2	0	1.000	7	2	2	0	1	40	58	31	13	6.07
Monte McFarland	2	0	1.000	2	2	2	0	0	14	21	5	5	5.14
Dan Friend	2	2	.500	5	5	5	0	0	41	50	14	10	5.27
Scott Stratton	2	3	.400	5	5	3	0	0	30	51	14	4	9.60
John Dolan	0	1	.000	2	2	1	0	0	11	16	6	1	6.55
Bert Abbey	0	1	.000	1	1	1	0	0	8	10	2	3	4.50
	72	58	.554	133	133	119	3	1	1151	1422	432	297	4.67

BROOKLYN
Bridegrooms

71-60 .542 -16.5 5th (tie) Dave Foutz

BATTERS	POS/GAMES		GP	AB	R	H	BI	2B	3B	HR	BB	SO	SB	BA	SA
Candy LaChance	1B125,OF3		127	536	99	167	108	22	8	8	29	48	37	.312	.427
Tom Daly	2B120		120	455	89	128	68	17	8	2	52	52	28	.281	.367
Tom Corcoran	SS127		127	535	81	142	69	17	10	2	23	11	17	.265	.346
Bill Shindle	3B116		116	477	91	133	69	21	2	3	47	28	17	.279	.350
George Treadway	OF86		86	339	54	87	54	14	3	7	33	22	9	.257	.378
Mike Griffin	OF131,SS1		131	519	140	173	65	38	7	4	93	29	27	.333	.457
John Anderson	OF101		102	419	76	120	87	11	14	9	12	29	24	.286	.444
John Grim	C91,OF1,1B1		93	329	54	92	44	17	5	0	13	9	9	.280	.362
George Shoch	OF39,2B13,SS6,3B3		61	216	49	56	29	9	7	0	32	6	7	.259	.350
Con Daily	C39,OF1		40	142	17	30	11	3	2	1	10	18	3	.211	.282
Brickyard Kennedy	P39		40	127	18	39	21	3	1	0	4	6	0	.307	.346
Ad Gumbert	P33,OF1		34	97	21	35	13	6	0	2	7	10	0	.361	.485
Ed Stein	P32		32	104	12	26	14	3	2	0	5	15	0	.250	.317
Dave Foutz	OF20,1B8		31	115	14	34	21	4	1	0	4	2	1	.296	.348
Dan Daub	P25		25	71	8	14	8	0	0	0	8	15	3	.197	.197
Con Lucid	P21	(1-2)	21	53	14	13	10	0	3	0	7	9	0	.245	.358
Oyster Burns	OF20	(1-2)	20	76	7	14	7	0	1	0	8	2	0	.184	.211
Joe Mulvey	3B13		13	49	8	15	8	4	1	0	2	0	1	.306	.429
Buster Burrell	C12		12	28	7	4	5	0	0	1	4	3	0	.143	.250
Bert Abbey	P8	(2-2)	8	19	4	5	1	0	1	0	2	4	0	.263	.368
Hunkey Hines	OF2		2	8	3	2	1	0	0	0	2	0	0	.250	.250
Jack Cronin	P2		2	2	1	1	2	0	1	0	0	0	0	.500	1.500
John McDougal	P1		1	1	0	0	0	0	0	0	0	0	0	.000	.000
			133	4717	867	1330	715	189	77	39	397	318	183	.282	.379

PITCHERS		W	L	PCT	G	GS	CG	SH	SV	IP	H	BB	SO	ERA
Brickyard Kennedy		19	12	.613	39	33	26	2	1	280	335	93	39	5.12
Ed Stein		15	13	.536	32	27	24	1	1	255	282	93	55	4.72
Ad Gumbert		11	16	.407	33	26	20	0	1	234	288	69	45	5.08
Con Lucid	(1-2)	10	7	.588	21	19	12	2	0	137	164	72	24	5.52
Dan Daub		10	10	.500	25	21	16	0	0	185	212	51	36	4.29
Bert Abbey	(2-2)	5	2	.714	8	6	5	0	0	52	66	9	14	4.33
Jack Cronin		0	0	----	2	0	0	0	2	5	10	3	1	10.80
John McDougal		0	0	----	1	0	0	0	1	3	3	5	2	12.00
		71	60	.542	133	132	103	5	6	1151	1360	395	216	4.94

BOSTON
Beaneaters

71-60 .542 -16.5 5th (tie) Frank Selee

BATTERS	POS/GAMES	GP	AB	R	H	BI	2B	3B	HR	BB	SO	SB	BA	SA
Tommy Tucker	1B125	125	462	87	115	73	19	6	3	61	29	15	.249	.335
Bobby Lowe	2B99	99	412	101	122	62	12	7	7	40	16	24	.296	.410
Germany Long	SS122,2B2	124	535	109	169	75	23	10	9	31	12	35	.316	.447
Billy Nash	3B132	132	508	97	147	108	23	6	10	74	19	18	.289	.417
Jimmy Bannon	OF122,P1	123	489	101	171	74	35	5	6	54	31	28	.350	.479
Hugh Duffy	OF130	130	531	110	187	100	30	6	9	63	16	42	.352	.482
Tommy McCarthy	OF109,2B9	117	452	90	131	73	13	2	2	72	12	18	.290	.341
Charles Ganzel	C76,SS2,1B2	80	277	38	73	52	2	5	1	24	6	1	.264	.318
Jack Ryan	C43,2B5,OF1	49	189	22	55	18	7	0	0	6	6	3	.291	.328
Fred Tenney	OF28,C21	49	173	35	47	21	9	1	1	24	5	6	.272	.353
Kid Nichols	P48,OF1	49	157	23	37	18	3	2	0	14	28	0	.236	.280

BOSTON (cont.)
Beaneaters

BATTERS	POS/GAMES		GP	AB	R	H	BI	2B	3B	HR	BB	SO	SB	BA	SA
Jack Stivetts	P38,1B5,OF2		46	158	20	30	24	6	4	0	6	18	1	.190	.278
Cozy Dolan	P25,OF1		26	83	12	20	7	4	1	0	6	7	3	.241	.313
Jim Sullivan	P21,OF1		22	85	14	15	8	3	0	0	7	14	2	.176	.212
Joe Harrington	2B18		18	65	21	18	13	0	2	2	7	5	3	.277	.431
Jimmy Collins	OF11	(1-2)	11	38	10	8	8	3	0	1	4	4	0	.211	.368
Charles Nice	SS9		9	35	7	8	9	5	0	2	4	2	0	.229	.543
Frank Sexton	P7,OF1,2B1		9	22	2	5	2	0	0	0	1	1	0	.227	.227
Zeke Wilson	P6	(1-2)	6	19	3	6	6	0	0	1	0	1	0	.316	.474
Otis Stocksdale	P4,OF1	(2-2)	5	15	3	4	1	0	0	0	1	2	0	.267	.267
John Warner	C3	(1-2)	3	7	2	1	1	0	0	0	1	0	0	.143	.143
Bill Banks	P1		1	3	0	0	0	0	0	0	0	2	0	.000	.000
			132	4715	907	1369	753	197	57	54	500	236	199	.290	.391

PITCHERS			W	L	PCT	G	GS	CG	SH	SV	IP	H	BB	SO	ERA
Kid Nichols			26	16	.619	47	42	42	1	3	380	417	86	140	3.41
Jack Stivetts			17	17	.500	38	34	30	0	0	291	341	89	111	4.64
Cozy Dolan			11	7	.611	25	21	18	3	1	198	215	67	47	4.27
Jim Sullivan			11	9	.550	21	19	16	0	0	179	236	58	46	4.82
Otis Stocksdale		(2-2)	2	2	.500	4	4	1	0	0	23	31	8	2	5.87
Zeke Wilson		(1-2)	2	4	.333	6	6	4	0	0	45	54	27	5	5.20
Bill Banks			1	0	1.000	1	1	1	0	0	7	7	4	4	0.00
Frank Sexton			1	5	.167	7	5	4	0	0	49	59	22	14	5.69
Jimmy Bannon			0	0	----	1	1	0	0	0	3	4	2	1	6.00
			71	60	.542	132	132	116	4	4	1175	1364	363	370	4.27

PITTSBURGH
Pirates

71-61   .538   -17   7th   Connie Mack

BATTERS	POS/GAMES		GP	AB	R	H	BI	2B	3B	HR	BB	SO	SB	BA	SA
Jake Beckley	1B129		129	530	104	174	110	31	19	5	24	20	20	.328	.487
Lou Bierbauer	2B117		117	466	53	120	69	13	11	0	19	8	18	.258	.333
Monte Cross	SS107,2B1		108	393	67	101	54	14	13	3	38	38	39	.257	.382
Bill Clingman	3B106		106	382	69	99	45	16	4	0	41	43	19	.259	.322
Patsy Donovan	OF125		125	519	114	160	58	17	6	1	47	19	36	.308	.370
Jake Stenzel	OF129		129	514	114	192	97	38	13	7	57	25	53	.374	.539
Elmer Smith	OF123		124	480	88	145	81	14	12	1	55	25	34	.302	.388
Bill Merritt	C63,1B2	(2-2)	67	239	32	68	27	5	1	0	18	16	2	.285	.314
Frank Genins	OF29,3B16,2B16,SS8,1B2		73	252	43	63	24	8	0	2	22	14	19	.250	.306
Pink Hawley	P56		57	185	33	57	42	14	3	5	3	20	1	.308	.497
Joe Sugden	C49		49	155	28	48	17	4	1	1	16	12	4	.310	.368
Bill Hart	P36		36	106	8	25	11	5	2	0	1	12	1	.236	.321
Bill Stuart	SS17,2B2		19	77	5	19	10	3	0	0	2	6	2	.247	.286
Tom Kinslow	C18		19	62	10	14	5	2	0	0	2	2	1	.226	.258
Brownie Foreman	P19		19	46	6	3	4	0	0	0	7	14	2	.065	.065
Connie Mack	C12,1B1		14	49	12	15	4	2	0	0	7	1	1	.306	.347
Frank Killen	P13		14	38	7	13	5	0	1	0	6	7	2	.342	.395
Bill Niles	3B10,2B1		11	37	2	8	0	0	0	0	5	2	2	.216	.216
Jim Gardner	P11		11	34	5	9	3	2	0	0	3	6	1	.265	.324
Sam Moran	P10		11	26	5	4	1	0	1	1	1	1	0	.154	.346
Tom Colcolough	P6		7	15	4	5	3	1	2	0	2	1	0	.333	.667
John Corcoran	SS4,3B2		6	20	0	3	1	0	0	0	0	2	0	.150	.150
Charles Hewitt	P4		4	6	0	1	0	0	0	0	0	1	0	.167	.167
Harry Jordan	P2		2	7	0	2	1	0	0	0	0	2	0	.286	.286
Jock Menefee	P2		2	0	0	0	0	0	0	0	0	0	0	----	----
Gus Weyhing	P1	(2-3)	1	4	2	1	1	1	0	0	0	0	0	.250	.250
Gussie Gannon	P1		1	2	0	0	0	0	0	0	0	2	0	.000	.000
Dave Wright	P1		1	1	0	0	0	0	0	0	0	0	0	.000	.000
			134	4645	811	1349	673	190	89	26	376	299	257	.290	.386

PITCHERS			W	L	PCT	G	GS	CG	SH	SV	IP	H	BB	SO	ERA
Pink Hawley			31	22	.585	56	50	44	4	1	444	449	122	142	3.18
Bill Hart			14	17	.452	36	29	24	0	1	262	293	135	85	4.75
Jim Gardner			8	2	.800	11	10	8	0	0	85	99	27	31	2.64
Brownie Foreman			8	6	.571	19	16	12	0	2	140	131	64	54	3.22
Frank Killen			5	5	.500	13	11	6	0	0	95	113	57	25	5.49
Sam Moran			2	4	.333	10	6	6	0	0	63	78	51	19	7.47
Charles Hewitt			1	0	1.000	4	2	1	0	2	13	13	2	4	4.15
Gus Weyhing		(2-3)	1	0	1.000	1	1	1	0	0	9	10	5	3	1.00
Tom Colcolough			1	1	.500	6	5	2	0	0	35	38	21	15	5.60

1895 NATIONAL LEAGUE

PITTSBURGH (cont.)
Pirates

PITCHERS	W	L	PCT	G	GS	CG	SH	SV	IP	H	BB	SO	ERA
Jock Menefee	0	1	.000	2	1	0	0	0	2	2	7	0	16.20
Harry Jordan	0	2	.000	2	2	2	0	0	17	24	6	4	4.24
Gussie Gannon	0	0	----	1	0	0	0	0	5	7	2	0	1.80
Dave Wright	0	0	----	1	0	0	0	0	2	6	1	0	27.00
	71	61	.538	134	133	106	4	6	1172	1263	500	382	4.05

CINCINNATI
Reds

66-64   .508   -21   8th   Buck Ewing

BATTERS	POS/GAMES		GP	AB	R	H	BI	2B	3B	HR	BB	SO	SB	BA	SA
Buck Ewing	1B105		105	434	90	138	94	24	13	5	30	22	34	.318	.468
Bid McPhee	2B115		115	432	107	129	75	24	12	1	73	30	30	.299	.417
Germany Smith	SS127		127	503	75	151	74	23	6	4	34	24	13	.300	.394
Arlie Latham	3B108,1B3,2B1		112	460	93	143	69	14	6	2	42	25	48	.311	.380
Dusty Miller	OF132		132	529	103	177	112	31	16	10	33	34	43	.335	.510
George Hogriever	OF66,2B3		69	239	61	65	34	8	7	2	36	17	41	.272	.389
Dummy Hoy	OF107		107	429	93	119	55	21	12	3	52	8	50	.277	.403
Farmer Vaughn	C77,1B15,3B1,2B1		92	334	60	102	48	23	5	1	17	10	15	.305	.414
Tom Parrott	P41,1B14,OF9		64	201	35	69	41	13	7	3	11	8	10	.343	.522
Ed Burke	OF56	(2-2)	56	228	52	61	25	8	6	1	22	14	19	.268	.368
Bill Grey	3B27,2B16,SS5,C5,OF1		52	181	24	55	29	17	4	1	15	8	4	.304	.459
Bill Rhines	P38		38	113	20	25	23	2	2	0	8	7	0	.221	.274
Frank Dwyer	P37		37	113	14	30	16	3	5	1	5	5	2	.265	.407
Bug Holliday	OF32		32	127	25	38	20	9	2	0	10	3	6	.299	.402
Frank Foreman	P32		32	94	14	29	11	7	0	2	4	14	1	.309	.447
Morg Murphy	C25		25	82	15	22	16	2	0	0	11	8	6	.268	.293
Bill Merritt	C20,2B1	(1-2)	22	79	9	14	12	2	0	0	6	5	2	.177	.203
Bill Phillips	P18		19	48	9	15	6	3	1	0	2	4	1	.313	.417
Harry Spies	C12,1B2	(1-2)	14	50	2	11	5	0	1	0	3	2	0	.220	.260
Mike Kahoe	C3		3	4	0	0	0	0	0	0	0	0	0	.000	.000
King Bailey	P1		1	4	2	2	1	1	0	0	0	1	1	.500	.750
			132	4684	903	1395	769	235	105	36	414	249	326	.298	.416

PITCHERS	W	L	PCT	G	GS	CG	SH	SV	IP	H	BB	SO	ERA
Bill Rhines	19	10	.655	38	33	25	0	0	268	322	76	72	4.81
Frank Dwyer	18	15	.545	37	31	23	2	0	280	355	74	46	4.24
Frank Foreman	11	14	.440	32	27	19	0	1	219	253	92	55	4.11
Tom Parrott	11	18	.379	41	31	23	0	3	263	382	76	57	5.47
Bill Phillips	6	7	.462	18	9	6	0	2	109	126	44	15	6.03
King Bailey	1	0	1.000	1	1	1	0	0	8	13	0	0	5.63
	66	64	.508	132	132	97	2	6	1147	1451	362	245	4.81

NEW YORK
Giants

66-65   .504   -21.5   9th   Davis - Doyle - Watkins

BATTERS	POS/GAMES		GP	AB	R	H	BI	2B	3B	HR	BB	SO	SB	BA	SA
Jack Doyle	1B58,2B13,3B5,C4		82	319	52	100	66	21	3	1	24	12	35	.313	.408
General Stafford	2B109,OF12,3B2		123	463	79	129	73	12	5	3	40	32	42	.279	.346
Shorty Fuller	SS126		126	458	82	103	32	11	3	0	64	34	15	.225	.262
George Davis	3B80,2B10,OF7,1B2		99	382	98	131	92	34	8	5	52	11	44	.343	.513
Mike Tiernan	OF119		120	476	127	165	71	23	21	7	66	19	36	.347	.527
George Van Haltren	OF131,P1		131	521	113	177	103	23	19	8	57	29	32	.340	.503
Ed Burke	OF39	(1-2)	39	167	38	43	12	6	2	1	7	9	14	.257	.335
Duke Farrell	C62,3B24,1B2		90	312	38	90	58	16	9	1	38	18	11	.288	.407
Park Wilson	C53,1B11,3B3		67	238	32	56	30	9	0	0	14	16	11	.235	.273
Amos Rusie	P49,OF1		53	179	14	44	19	3	1	1	0	28	2	.246	.291
Yale Murphy	OF33,SS8,3B8,2B1		51	184	35	37	16	6	2	0	27	13	7	.201	.255
Tom Bannon	OF21,1B16		37	159	33	43	8	6	2	0	7	8	20	.270	.333
Dad Clarke	P37		37	121	16	29	10	2	1	0	8	15	0	.240	.273
Les German	P25,3B11		35	111	16	29	16	2	2	2	9	7	1	.261	.369
Oyster Burns	OF31,1B2	(2-2)	33	114	21	35	25	5	3	1	14	6	10	.307	.430
Jouett Meekin	P29		31	96	16	28	16	4	3	1	3	11	2	.292	.427
Pop Schriver	C18,1B6		24	92	16	29	16	2	1	1	9	10	3	.315	.391
Willie Clark	1B23		23	88	9	23	16	3	2	0	5	6	1	.261	.311
Harry Davis	1B18		18	72	11	22	15	2	2	0	5	1	5	.306	.389
Frank Butler	OF5		5	22	5	6	2	1	0	0	1	1	0	.273	.318
Andy Boswell	P5	(1-2)	5	16	1	3	1	0	0	0	1	1	1	.188	.188

1895 NATIONAL LEAGUE

NEW YORK (cont.)
Giants

BATTERS	POS/GAMES		GP	AB	R	H	BI	2B	3B	HR	BB	SO	SB	BA	SA
Ed Doheny	P3		3	10	0	1	3	0	1	0	1	3	0	.100	.300
Larry Battam	3B2		2	4	0	1	0	0	0	0	2	1	0	.250	.250
Frank Knauss	P1		1	1	0	0	0	0	0	0	0	1	0	.000	.000
			132	4605	854	1324	699	191	90	32	454	292	292	.288	.389

PITCHERS			W	L	PCT	G	GS	CG	SH	SV	IP	H	BB	SO	ERA
Amos Rusie			23	23	.500	49	47	42	4	0	393	384	159	201	3.73
Dad Clarke			18	15	.545	37	30	27	1	1	282	336	60	67	3.39
Jouett Meekin			16	11	.593	29	29	24	1	0	226	296	73	76	5.30
Les German			7	11	.389	25	18	16	0	0	178	243	78	36	5.96
Andy Boswell		(1-2)	2	2	.500	5	4	3	0	0	34	41	22	18	5.82
Ed Doheny			0	3	.000	3	3	3	0	0	26	37	19	9	6.66
George Van Haltren			0	0	----	1	0	0	0	0	5	13	2	1	12.60
Frank Knauss			0	0	----	1	1	0	0	0	4	9	2	1	17.18
			66	65	.504	132	132	115	6	1	1147	1359	415	409	4.51

WASHINGTON
Senators

43-85   .336   -43   10th   Gus Schmelz

BATTERS	POS/GAMES		GP	AB	R	H	BI	2B	3B	HR	BB	SO	SB	BA	SA
Ed Cartwright	1B122		122	472	95	156	90	34	17	3	54	41	50	.331	.494
Jack Crooks	2B117		117	409	80	114	57	19	8	6	68	39	36	.279	.408
Frank Scheibeck	SS44,3B2,2B2		48	167	17	31	25	5	2	0	17	21	5	.186	.240
Bill Joyce	3B126		126	474	110	148	95	25	13	17	96	54	29	.312	.527
Bill Hassamaer	OF75,1B9,SS1,3B1	(1-2)	85	358	42	100	60	18	4	1	26	13	8	.279	.360
Charlie Abbey	OF132		132	511	102	141	84	14	10	8	43	41	28	.276	.389
Kip Selbach	OF118,SS6,2B5		129	516	115	166	55	21	22	6	69	28	31	.322	.483
Deacon McGuire	C132,SS1		132	533	89	179	97	30	8	10	40	18	16	.336	.478
Win Mercer	P43,SS7,OF5,3B3,2B1		63	196	26	50	26	9	1	1	12	32	7	.255	.327
Jake Boyd	OF21,P14,2B10,SS8,3B1		51	157	29	42	16	5	1	1	20	28	2	.268	.331
Varney Anderson	P29,OF1		35	97	22	28	16	2	3	0	10	9	0	.289	.371
Tom Brown	OF34	(2-2)	34	134	25	32	16	8	3	2	18	16	8	.239	.388
Dan Coogan	SS18,C5,OF2,3B1		26	77	9	17	7	2	1	0	13	6	1	.221	.273
Jack Glasscock	SS25	(2-2)	25	100	20	23	10	2	0	0	7	3	3	.230	.250
Otis Stocksdale	P20,OF	(1-2)	25	74	12	23	15	4	2	0	3	8	1	.311	.419
Al Maul	P16,OF4		22	72	9	18	16	5	2	0	6	7	0	.250	.375
John Malarkey	P22		22	37	2	5	4	0	0	0	2	8	0	.135	.135
Gene DeMontreville	SS12		12	46	7	10	9	1	3	0	3	4	5	.217	.370
John Gilroy	P8,OF3,3B1		12	29	8	7	4	1	0	0	1	4	0	.241	.276
Parson Nicholson	SS10		10	38	7	7	5	2	1	0	7	4	6	.184	.289
Joe Corbett	P3,OF2,SS2		7	15	1	2	1	0	0	0	0	5	0	.133	.133
Andy Boswell	P6,OF1	(2-2)	7	14	4	4	1	0	0	0	1	2	1	.286	.286
Dan Mahoney	C2,1B1		6	12	2	2	1	0	0	0	0	0	0	.167	.167
Billy Lush	OF5		5	18	2	6	2	0	0	0	2	1	0	.333	.333
Carlton Molesworth	P4		4	7	0	1	0	0	0	0	0	3	0	.143	.143
Doc McJames	P2		2	7	1	1	1	0	0	0	0	0	0	.143	.143
Joe Woerlin	SS1		1	3	1	1	0	0	0	0	0	0	0	.333	.333
F. F. McCauley	SS1		1	2	0	0	0	0	0	0	0	0	0	.000	.000
Oscar Purner	P1		1	1	0	0	0	0	0	0	0	0	0	.000	.000
Ed Buckingham	P1		1	1	0	0	0	0	0	0	0	1	0	.000	.000
----- Wesner	SS1		1	0	0	0	0	0	0	0	0	0	0	----	----
			132	4577	837	1314	713	207	101	55	518	396	237	.287	.412

PITCHERS			W	L	PCT	G	GS	CG	SH	SV	IP	H	BB	SO	ERA
Win Mercer			13	23	.361	43	38	32	0	2	311	430	96	84	4.46
Al Maul			10	5	.667	16	16	14	0	0	136	136	37	34	2.45
Varney Anderson			9	16	.360	29	25	18	0	0	205	288	97	35	5.89
Otis Stocksdale		(1-2)	6	11	.353	20	17	11	0	1	136	199	52	23	6.09
Jake Boyd			2	11	.154	14	12	8	0	0	85	126	35	16	7.07
Doc McJames			1	1	.500	2	2	2	0	0	17	17	16	9	1.59
Andy Boswell		(2-2)	1	2	.333	6	3	3	0	0	30	44	19	12	6.00
John Gilroy			1	4	.200	8	4	2	0	0	41	63	24	2	6.53
Carlton Molesworth			0	2	.000	4	3	1	0	0	16	33	15	7	14.63
Joe Corbett			0	2	.000	3	3	3	0	0	19	26	9	3	5.68
John Malarkey			0	8	.000	22	8	5	0	2	101	135	60	32	5.99
Ed Buckingham			0	0	----	1	1	0	0	0	3	6	2	1	6.00
Oscar Purner			0	0	----	1	0	0	0	0	2	4	3	0	9.00
			43	85	.336	132	132	99	0	5	1102	1507	465	258	5.28

1895 NATIONAL LEAGUE

ST. LOUIS Browns — 39-92 .298 -48.5 11th Buckenberger - Von Der Ahe - Quinn - Phelan

BATTERS	POS/GAMES		GP	AB	R	H	BI	2B	3B	HR	BB	SO	SB	BA	SA
Roger Connor	1B103		103	398	78	131	77	29	9	8	63	10	9	.329	.508
Joe Quinn	2B134		134	543	84	169	74	19	9	2	36	6	22	.311	.390
Bones Ely	SS117		117	467	68	121	46	16	2	1	19	17	28	.259	.308
Doggie Miller	3B46,C46,OF21,SS9,1B6		121	490	81	143	74	15	4	5	25	12	18	.292	.369
Tommy Dowd	OF115,3B17,2B2		129	505	95	163	74	19	17	7	30	31	30	.323	.469
Tom Brown	OF83	(1-2)	83	350	72	76	31	11	4	1	48	44	34	.217	.280
Duff Cooley	OF124,3B5,SS3,C1		132	563	106	191	75	9	20	7	36	29	27	.339	.464
Heinie Peitz	C71,1B11,3B10		90	334	44	95	65	14	12	2	29	20	9	.284	.416
Ted Breitenstein	P54,OF16		72	218	25	42	18	2	0	0	29	22	5	.193	.202
Biff Sheehan	OF41,1B11		52	180	24	57	18	3	6	1	20	6	7	.317	.417
Red Ehret	P37		37	96	13	21	9	2	1	1	6	12	0	.219	.292
Denny Lyons	3B33		33	129	24	38	25	6	0	2	14	5	3	.295	.388
Bill Kissinger	P24,OF4,SS4,3B1	(2-2)	33	97	8	24	8	6	1	0	0	11	1	.247	.330
Joe Otten	C24,OF2		26	87	8	21	8	0	0	0	5	8	2	.241	.241
Ike Samuels	3B21,SS3		24	74	5	17	5	2	0	0	5	7	5	.230	.251
Harry Staley	P23		23	67	4	9	1	0	2	0	4	1	1	.134	.194
Dewey McDougal	P18		18	41	1	6	6	1	0	0	8	16	0	.146	.171
Frank Bonner	3B10,OF5,C1	(2-2)	15	59	3	8	8	0	1	1	1	8	2	.136	.220
Dad Clarkson	P7	(1-2)	7	23	0	1	0	0	0	0	3	4	0	.043	.043
Marty Hogan	OF5		5	18	2	3	2	1	0	0	3	0	2	.167	.222
Guy McFadden	1B4		4	14	1	3	2	0	0	0	0	2	0	.214	.214
Joe Connor	3B2		2	7	0	0	1	0	0	0	0	2	0	.000	.000
Mike Ryan	3B2		2	2	0	0	0	0	0	0	0	0	0	.000	.000
Henry Adkinson	OF1		1	5	1	2	0	0	0	0	0	2	0	.400	.400
John Coleman	P1		1	5	0	1	0	0	0	0	0	1	0	.200	.200
Fred Fagin	C1		1	3	0	1	2	0	0	0	0	0	0	.333	.333
Walt Kinlock	3B1		1	3	0	1	0	0	0	0	0	2	0	.333	.333
Red Donahue	P1		1	3	0	0	0	0	0	0	0	1	0	.000	.000
			135	4781	747	1344	629	155	88	38	384	279	205	.281	.374

PITCHERS			W	L	PCT	G	GS	CG	SH	SV	IP	H	BB	SO	ERA
Ted Breitenstein			19	30	.388	54	50	46	1	1	430	458	178	127	4.44
Harry Staley			6	13	.316	23	16	13	0	0	159	223	39	28	5.22
Red Ehret			6	19	.240	37	32	18	0	0	232	360	88	55	6.02
Bill Kissinger		(2-2)	4	12	.250	24	14	9	0	0	141	222	51	31	6.72
Dewey McDougal			3	10	.231	18	14	10	0	0	115	187	46	23	8.32
Dad Clarkson		(1-2)	1	6	.143	7	7	7	0	0	61	91	26	9	7.38
Red Donahue			0	1	.000	1	1	1	0	0	8	9	3	2	6.75
John Coleman			0	1	.000	1	1	1	0	0	8	12	8	5	13.50
			39	92	.298	135	135	105	1	1	1152	1562	439	280	5.76

LOUISVILLE Colonels — 35-96 .267 -52.5 12th John McCloskey

BATTERS	POS/GAMES		GP	AB	R	H	BI	2B	3B	HR	BB	SO	SB	BA	SA
Harry Spies	1B,C,SS	(2-2)	72	276	42	74	35	14	7	2	11	19	4	.268	.391
John O'Brien	2B125,1B3		128	539	82	138	50	10	4	1	45	20	15	.256	.295
Frank Shugart	SS88,OF27		113	473	61	125	70	14	13	4	31	25	14	.264	.374
Jimmy Collins	3B77,OF17,2B2,SS1	(2-2)	96	373	65	104	49	17	5	6	33	16	12	.279	.399
Tom Gettinger	OF63,P2		63	260	28	70	32	11	5	2	8	15	6	.269	.373
Joe Wright	OF60,C1		60	228	30	63	30	10	4	1	12	28	7	.276	.368
Fred Clarke	OF132		132	550	96	191	82	21	5	4	34	24	40	.347	.425
John Warner	C64,1B3,2B1	(2-2)	67	232	20	62	20	4	2	1	11	16	10	.267	.315
Walt Preston	OF26,3B25		50	197	42	55	24	6	4	1	17	17	11	.279	.365
Tub Welch	C28,1B20		47	153	18	37	8	4	1	1	13	7	2	.242	.301
Ducky Holmes	OF29,SS8,3B4,P2		40	161	33	60	20	10	2	3	12	9	9	.373	.516
Mike McDermott	P33		33	82	12	13	4	2	3	0	13	11	1	.159	.256
Bert Cunningham	P31,OF1		32	100	14	30	13	7	3	0	9	20	0	.300	.430
Tom McCreery	OF18,P8,SS4,3B1,1B1		31	108	18	35	10	3	1	0	8	15	3	.324	.370
Gus Weyhing	P28	(3-3)	28	89	9	20	10	2	0	1	11	27	1	.225	.281
Bert Inks	P28		28	84	9	21	7	4	0	0	6	7	0	.250	.298
Dan Brouthers	1B24	(2-2)	24	97	13	30	15	10	1	2	11	2	1	.309	.495
Bill Hassamaer	1B21,2B1,SS1	(2-2)	23	96	7	20	14	2	2	0	3	4	0	.208	.271
Dan Sweeney	OF22		22	90	18	24	16	5	0	1	17	2	2	.267	.356
Fred Zahner	C21		21	49	7	11	6	1	1	0	6	4	0	.224	.286
Dan McGann	SS8,3B6,OF5		20	73	9	21	9	5	2	0	8	6	6	.288	.411
John Luby	P11,1B5,OF2		19	53	6	15	9	2	2	0	8	3	2	.283	.396
Jack Glasscock	SS13,1B5	(1-2)	18	74	9	25	6	3	1	1	3	1	1	.338	.446
Fred Pfeffer	SS5,2B3,1B3		11	45	8	13	5	1	0	0	5	3	2	.289	.311
Bill Kemmer	3B9,1B2		11	38	5	7	3	0	0	1	2	4	0	.184	.263

LOUISVILLE (cont.)
Colonels

BATTERS	POS/GAMES		GP	AB	R	H	BI	2B	3B	HR	BB	SO	SB	BA	SA
Henry Cote	C10		10	33	10	10	5	0	0	0	3	3	2	.303	.303
Phil Knell	P10	(2-2)	10	26	3	6	6	2	1	0	1	4	1	.231	.385
Dan Minahan	3B7,OF2		8	34	6	13	6	0	0	0	1	1	0	.382	.382
Dan McFarlan	P7		7	21	2	5	1	1	0	0	0	3	0	.238	.286
Tom Morrison	SS3,3B3		6	22	3	6	4	0	2	0	1	1	0	.273	.455
Hercules Burnett	OF4,1B1		5	17	6	7	3	0	1	2	2	2	2	.412	.882
Gil Hatfield	3B3,SS2		5	16	3	3	1	0	0	0	1	1	0	.188	.188
Barry McCormick	SS2,2B1		3	12	2	3	0	0	1	0	0	0	1	.250	.417
Mike Trost	1B3		3	12	1	1	1	0	0	0	0	1	1	.083	.083
Bill Wadsworth	P2		2	4	0	1	0	0	0	0	0	0	0	.250	.250
George Meakim	P1		1	3	1	1	0	0	0	0	0	1	0	.333	.333
Grant Briggs	C1		1	3	0	0	0	0	0	0	0	1	0	.000	.000
Bill Kling	P1		1	1	0	0	0	0	0	0	0	0	0	.000	.000
----- Childers	P1		1	0	0	0	0	0	0	0	0	0	0	----	----
George Borchers	P1		1	0	0	0	0	0	0	0	0	0	0	----	----
			133	4724	698	1320		171	73	34	346	323	156	.279	.368

PITCHERS		W	L	PCT	G	GS	CG	SH	SV	IP	H	BB	SO	ERA
Bert Cunningham		11	16	.407	31	28	24	1	0	231	299	104	49	4.75
Gus Weyhing	(3-3)	7	19	.269	28	25	22	1	0	213	285	66	53	5.41
Bert Inks		7	20	.259	28	27	21	0	0	205	294	78	42	6.40
Mike McDermott		4	19	.174	33	26	18	0	0	207	258	103	42	5.99
Tom McCreery		3	1	.750	8	4	3	1	1	49	51	38	14	5.36
Ducky Holmes		1	0	1.000	2	1	1	0	0	14	16	4	0	5.79
George Meakim		1	0	1.000	1	1	1	0	0	7	7	4	2	2.57
John Luby		1	5	.167	11	6	5	0	0	71	115	19	12	6.81
Bill Wadsworth		0	1	.000	2	0	0	0	0	9	24	7	2	16.00
George Borchers		0	1	.000	1	1	0	0	0	1	1	3	0	27.00
Phil Knell	(1-2)	0	6	.000	10	6	3	0	0	57	75	21	19	6.51
Dan McFarlan		0	7	.000	7	7	6	0	0	46	80	15	10	6.65
Tom Gettinger		0	0	----	2	0	0	0	0	6	13	1	0	7.11
Bill Kling		0	0	----	1	0	0	0	0	1	0	1	0	0.00
----- Childers		0	0	----	1	0	0	0	0	0	2	6	0	inf.
		35	96	.267	133	132	104	3	1	1117	1520	470	245	5.90

1896 NATIONAL LEAGUE

The Baltimore Orioles

The Baltimore Orioles were one of the charter members of the American Association in 1882. During the ten-year existence of the league, Baltimore finished last four times. Their best finish had been in 1887, when they finished third. When the team was absorbed by the National League in 1892, it once again finished in the cellar. However, it was during this dismal season that the team made a move in the right direction, for midway through the season, Baltimore hired Ned Hanlon to be their manager.

Slowly and surely, Hanlon began to assemble a championship team. A shrewd judge of baseball ability, and building on the nucleus of catcher Wilbert Robinson, and pitcher Sadie McMahon, Hanlon started to put the pieces together in 1892. Hanlon saw potential in a young infielder, and John McGraw began to play full-time in the latter half of the year. Also joining the team late in the 1892 season was outfielder Joe Kelley. In 1893, Hanlon added second baseman Heinie Reitz, shortstop Hugh Jennings, and outfielder Steve Brodie. This resulted in the team's jump from last to eighth. Before the 1894 season, Hanlon acquired the last two pieces—first baseman Dan Brouthers, and outfielder Willie Keeler. With these additions, the Orioles soared to the championship.

The Orioles repeated this achievement in 1895. Not standing on a pat hand, Hanlon infused two new starters and a new pitcher into the lineup with no ill effect. One of Hanlon's strengths was his ability to add new players constantly but still keep the quality sound. The only sour taste to these championship years was their quick loss in the Temple Cup series both years.

It was no surprise to anyone when Hanlon led the Orioles in 1896 to their third consecutive pennant. And once again, two new faces graced the starting lineup. Baltimore featured a powerful lineup that batted .328 as a team. There was nary a weak link in the group as evidenced by the following averages: Hugh Jennings (.401), Willie Keeler (.386), Joe Kelley (.364), and Wilbert Robinson (.347). Even the two newcomers first baseman Jack Doyle (.339) and third baseman Jim Donnelly (.328), contributed their share.

For the second straight year, Cleveland finished in the runner-up position. And for the second straight year Jesse Burkett broke the .400 barrier. His average of .410

led the league as did his run (160) and hit (240) totals. Pitcher Cy Young was also in good form as he won 28.

Surprisingly Cincinnati moved up to third behind the strong hitting of Ed Burke (.340) and Dusty Miller (.321). Their pitching was also sound as evidenced by the league's earned run average king Bill Rhines (2.45).

Boston's return to the first division was greatly helped by their acquisition of Billy Hamilton. He batted a robust .365 for his new team while stealing 83 bases to boot. His teammates Germany Long (.343) and Kid Nichols (30-14) also pitched in.

Chicago and Pittsburgh finished in fifth and sixth. Chicago was led by Cap Anson (.331), and Bill Dahlen (.352). Pittsburgh was led by Jake Stenzel (.361) and Elmer Smith (.362).

New York and Philadelphia suffered from significant omissions. Despite the big bats of Mike Tiernan (.369) and George Van Haltren (.351), New York sorely missed the strong arm of Amos Rusie who was a season-long holdout. Philadelphia, despite the bat of Ed Delahanty (.397), sorely missed Billy Hamilton. Philadelphia also saw a changing of the guard. Dan Brouthers was released early in the season, his 19-year career over; a career that saw him win four batting championships and finish with a career mark of .342. His replacement later that year was a youngster named Nap Lajoie. They would eventually be teammates again — in the Hall of Fame.

Brooklyn, Washington, St. Louis, and Louisville finished deep in the second division. Their best players were Fielder Jones of Brooklyn (.354), Bill Joyce of Washington who, while splitting his time with New York, won the home run title with 13, and Louisville's Fred Clarke (.325)

Baltimore exacted sweet revenge on Cleveland in the 1896 Temple Cup. A well-prepared Orioles squad demolished the second place Cleveland team four games to none. And none of the games were close as Baltimore prevailed 7-1, 7-2, 6-2, and 5-0.

Ned Hanlon kept his Orioles in close competition until the dark days of dual ownership at the end of the century, when the team was disbanded. Hanlon had a true gift of being able to judge baseball talent, acquire it, mold it, and not be afraid of changing parts to make it work. That is why history judges his trio of Baltimore champions as among the greatest teams of the nineteenth century and of all time.

1896 NATIONAL LEAGUE

BALTIMORE Orioles   90-39   .698   1st   Ned Hanlon

BATTERS	POS/GAMES		GP	AB	R	H	BI	2B	3B	HR	BB	SO	SB	BA	SA
Jack Doyle	1B118,2B1		118	487	116	165	101	29	4	1	42	15	73	.339	.421
Heinie Reitz	2B118,SS3		120	464	76	133	106	15	6	4	49	32	28	.287	.371
Hugh Jennings	SS130		130	521	125	209	121	27	9	0	19	11	70	.401	.488
Jim Donnelly	3B106		106	396	70	130	71	14	10	0	34	11	38	.328	.414
Willie Keeler	OF126		126	544	153	210	82	22	13	4	37	9	67	.386	.496
Steve Brodie	OF132		132	516	98	153	87	19	11	2	36	17	25	.297	.388
Joe Kelley	OF131		131	519	148	189	100	31	19	8	91	19	87	.364	.543
Wilbert Robinson	C67		67	245	43	85	38	9	6	2	14	13	9	.347	.457
Boileryard Clarke	C67,1B14		80	300	48	89	71	14	7	2	14	12	7	.297	.410
Bill Hoffer	P35		35	125	23	38	15	7	4	0	12	12	8	.304	.424
George Hemming	P25,OF2,1B1		30	97	16	25	11	6	5	0	4	7	4	.258	.423
Arlie Pond	P28		28	81	10	19	8	2	0	0	8	10	1	.235	.259
Joe Quinn	2B8,OF8,3B5,SS1	(2-2)	24	82	22	27	5	1	1	0	6	1	6	.329	.366
John McGraw	3B18,1B1		23	77	20	25	14	2	2	0	11	4	13	.325	.403
Sadie McMahon	P22		22	73	6	9	4	2	0	0	1	5	1	.123	.151
Duke Esper	P20		20	66	7	13	5	3	1	0	1	8	0	.197	.273
Bill Keister	2B8,3B6		15	58	8	14	5	3	0	0	3	5	4	.241	.293
Joe Corbett	P8,3B1		9	22	0	6	3	1	1	0	0	4	0	.273	.409
Dad Clarkson	P7		7	18	4	5	2	0	0	0	2	3	0	.278	.278
Frank Bowerman	C3,1B1		4	16	0	2	4	0	0	0	1	0	0	.125	.125
Jerry Nops	P3	(2-2)	3	9	1	1	1	0	0	0	1	2	0	.111	.111
Otis Stocksdale	P1		2	3	1	1	0	0	1	0	0	1	0	.333	1.000
			132	4719	995	1548	854	207	100	23	386	201	441	.328	.429

PITCHERS			W	L	PCT	G	GS	CG	SH	SV	IP	H	BB	SO	ERA
Bill Hoffer			25	7	.781	35	35	32	3	0	309	317	95	93	3.38
Arlie Pond			16	8	.667	28	26	21	2	0	214	232	57	80	3.49
George Hemming			15	6	.714	25	21	20	3	0	202	233	54	33	4.19
Duke Esper			14	5	.737	20	18	14	1	0	156	168	39	19	3.58
Sadie McMahon			11	9	.550	22	22	19	0	0	176	195	55	33	3.48
Dad Clarkson			4	2	.667	7	4	3	0	0	47	72	18	7	4.98
Joe Corbett			3	0	1.000	8	3	3	0	1	41	31	17	28	2.20
Jerry Nops		(2-2)	2	1	.667	3	3	3	0	0	22	29	2	8	6.14
Otis Stocksdale			0	1	.000	1	0	0	0	0	2	4	2	1	16.20
			90	39	.698	132	132	115	9	1	1168	1281	339	302	3.67

CLEVELAND Spiders   80-48   .625   -9.5   2nd   Patsy Tebeau

BATTERS	POS/GAMES		GP	AB	R	H	BI	2B	3B	HR	BB	SO	SB	BA	SA
Patsy Tebeau	1B122,3B7,2B5,SS1,P1		132	543	56	146	94	22	6	2	21	22	20	.269	.343
Cupid Childs	2B132		132	498	106	177	106	24	9	1	100	18	25	.355	.446
Ed McKean	SS133		133	571	100	193	112	29	12	7	45	9	13	.338	.468
Chippy McGarr	3B113,C1		113	455	68	122	53	16	4	1	22	30	16	.268	.327
Henry Blake	OF103,SS1		104	383	66	92	43	12	5	1	46	30	10	.240	.305
Jimmy McAleer	OF116		116	455	70	131	54	16	4	1	47	32	24	.288	.347
Jesse Burkett	OF133		133	586	160	240	72	27	16	6	49	19	34	.410	.541
Chief Zimmer	C91,3B1		91	336	46	93	46	18	3	3	31	48	4	.277	.375
Jack O'Connor	C37,1B17,OF12		68	256	41	76	43	11	1	1	15	12	15	.297	.359
Cy Young	P51,1B3		53	180	31	52	28	11	3	3	4	15	1	.289	.433
Nig Cuppy	P46,OF1		47	141	29	38	20	5	2	1	20	21	1	.270	.355
Bobby Wallace	OF23,P22,1B1		45	149	19	35	17	6	3	1	11	21	2	.235	.336
Zeke Wilson	P33		33	100	18	27	13	3	2	0	5	18	1	.270	.340
John Shearon	OF16		16	64	6	11	3	0	1	0	4	6	3	.172	.203
Tom Delahanty	3B16	(1-2)	16	56	11	13	4	4	0	0	8	4	4	.232	.304
Tom O'Meara	C9,1B1		12	33	5	5	0	0	0	0	5	7	0	.152	.152
Sport McAllister	OF4,C2,P1		8	27	2	6	1	2	0	0	0	2	1	.222	.296
Dale Gear	P3,1B1		4	15	5	6	3	1	1	0	1	1	0	.400	.600
Lou Criger	C1		2	5	0	0	0	0	0	0	1	0	1	.000	.000
Icebox Chamberlain	P2		2	3	1	0	0	0	0	0	1	1	0	.000	.000
			135	4856	840	1463	712	207	72	28	436	316	175	.301	.391

PITCHERS			W	L	PCT	G	GS	CG	SH	SV	IP	H	BB	SO	ERA
Cy Young			28	15	.651	51	46	42	5	3	414	477	62	140	3.24
Nig Cuppy			25	14	.641	46	40	35	1	1	358	388	75	86	3.12
Zeke Wilson			17	9	.654	33	29	20	1	1	240	265	81	56	4.01
Bobby Wallace			10	7	.588	22	16	13	2	0	145	167	49	46	3.34
Icebox Chamberlain			0	1	.000	2	2	1	0	0	11	21	5	2	7.36

CLEVELAND (cont.)
Spiders

PITCHERS	W	L	PCT	G	GS	CG	SH	SV	IP	H	BB	SO	ERA
Dale Gear	0	2	.000	3	2	2	0	0	23	35	6	6	5.48
Sport McAllister	0	0	----	1	0	0	0	0	4	9	2	0	6.75
Patsy Tebeau	0	0	----	1	0	0	0	0	0	1	0	0	0.00
	80	48	.625	135	135	113	9	5	1196	1363	280	336	3.46

CINCINNATI
Reds

77-50   .606   -12   3rd   Buck Ewing

BATTERS	POS/GAMES		GP	AB	R	H	BI	2B	3B	HR	BB	SO	SB	BA	SA
Buck Ewing	1B69		69	263	41	73	38	14	4	1	29	13	41	.278	.373
Bid McPhee	2B117		117	433	81	132	87	18	7	1	51	18	48	.305	.386
Germany Smith	SS120		120	456	65	131	71	22	9	3	28	22	22	.287	.393
Charlie Irwin	3B127		127	476	77	141	67	16	6	1	26	17	31	.296	.361
Dusty Miller	OF125		125	504	91	162	93	38	12	4	33	30	76	.321	.468
Dummy Hoy	OF120		121	443	120	132	57	23	7	4	65	13	50	.298	.409
Ed Burke	OF122		122	521	120	177	52	24	9	1	41	29	53	.340	.426
Heinie Peitz	C67		68	211	33	63	34	12	5	2	30	15	7	.299	.431
Farmer Vaughn	1B57,C57		114	433	71	127	66	20	9	2	16	7	7	.293	.395
Bill Grey	2B12,C11,SS8,OF3,1B2,3B1		46	121	15	25	17	2	1	0	19	11	6	.207	.240
Frank Dwyer	P36		36	110	17	29	15	4	4	0	11	15	3	.264	.373
Red Ehret	P34,1B1		34	102	10	20	20	2	0	1	10	12	2	.196	.245
Bug Holliday	OF16,1B5,SS1,P1		29	84	17	27	8	4	0	0	9	4	1	.321	.369
Frank Foreman	P27		27	74	9	18	8	2	0	0	4	7	2	.243	.270
Chauncey Fisher	P27		27	57	10	14	9	3	0	0	6	5	1	.246	.298
Bill Rhines	P19		19	52	4	10	6	1	0	0	2	7	0	.192	.212
Brownie Foreman	P4	(2-2)	4	10	0	2	0	0	0	0	1	1	0	.200	.200
Bert Inks	P3	(2-2)	3	7	1	0	0	0	0	0	1	0	0	.000	.000
Wiley Davis	P2		2	1	1	0	0	0	0	0	0	0	0	.000	.000
Hank Gastright	P1		1	2	0	0	0	0	0	0	0	0	0	.000	.000
			128	4360	783	1283	648	205	73	20	382	226	350	.294	.388

PITCHERS		W	L	PCT	G	GS	CG	SH	SV	IP	H	BB	SO	ERA
Frank Dwyer		24	11	.686	36	34	30	3	1	289	321	60	57	3.15
Red Ehret		18	14	.563	34	33	29	2	0	277	298	74	60	3.42
Frank Foreman		14	7	.667	27	22	17	0	1	186	212	62	33	3.97
Chauncey Fisher		10	7	.588	27	15	13	2	2	160	199	36	25	4.45
Bill Rhines		8	6	.571	19	17	11	3	0	143	128	48	32	2.45
Bert Inks	(2-2)	1	1	.500	3	3	2	0	0	20	21	9	2	4.50
Wiley Davis		1	1	.500	2	0	0	0	0	4	8	2	1	8.31
Brownie Foreman	(2-2)	1	3	.250	4	4	3	1	0	23	41	16	9	11.35
Hank Gastright		0	0	----	1	0	0	0	0	6	8	1	0	4.50
Bug Holliday		0	0	----	1	0	0	0	0	1	4	2	0	0.00
		77	50	.606	128	128	105	12	4	1108	1240	310	219	3.67

BOSTON
Beaneaters

74-57   .565   -17   4th   Frank Selee

BATTERS	POS/GAMES	GP	AB	R	H	BI	2B	3B	HR	BB	SO	SB	BA	SA
Tommy Tucker	1B122	122	474	74	144	72	27	5	2	30	29	6	.304	.395
Bobby Lowe	2B73	73	305	59	98	48	11	4	2	20	11	15	.321	.403
Germany Long	SS120	120	501	105	172	100	26	8	6	26	16	36	.343	.463
Jimmy Collins	3B80,SS4	84	304	48	90	46	10	9	1	30	12	10	.296	.398
Jimmy Bannon	OF76,2B6,SS5,3B3	89	343	52	86	50	9	5	0	32	23	16	.251	.306
Billy Hamilton	OF131	131	523	152	191	52	24	9	3	110	29	83	.365	.463
Hugh Duffy	OF120,2B9,SS2	131	527	97	158	112	16	8	5	52	19	39	.300	.389
Marty Bergen	C63,1B1	65	245	39	66	37	6	4	4	11	22	6	.269	.376
Fred Tenney	OF60,C27	88	348	64	117	49	14	3	2	36	12	18	.336	.411
Jack Stivetts	P42,OF12,1B5,3B1	67	221	42	76	49	9	6	3	12	10	4	.344	.480
Joe Harrington	3B49,SS4,2B1	54	198	25	39	25	5	3	1	19	17	2	.197	.268
Kid Nichols	P49,OF2	51	147	27	28	24	3	3	1	12	18	2	.190	.272
Charles Ganzel	C41,1B3,SS2	47	179	28	47	18	2	0	1	9	5	2	.263	.291
Dan McGann	2B43	43	171	25	55	30	6	7	2	12	10	2	.322	.474
Jim Sullivan	P31	31	88	9	19	9	3	0	1	2	21	0	.216	.284
Fred Klobedanz	P10	11	41	4	13	8	1	0	2	0	11	0	.317	.488
Willard Mains	P8	10	22	2	6	4	1	0	0	0	2	0	.273	.318
Jack Ryan	C8	8	32	2	3	0	1	0	0	0	1	0	.094	.125
Ted Lewis	P6	6	18	1	2	2	1	0	0	0	1	0	.111	.167
Cozy Dolan	P6	6	14	4	2	0	0	0	0	0	1	0	.143	.143

1896 NATIONAL LEAGUE

BOSTON (cont.)
Beaneaters

BATTERS	POS/GAMES	GP	AB	R	H	BI	2B	3B	HR	BB	SO	SB	BA	SA
Bill Banks	P4	4	11	0	3	0	0	0	0	1	3	0	.273	.273
George Yeager	1B2	2	5	1	1	0	0	0	0	0	1	0	.200	.200
		132	4717	860	1416	735	175	74	36	414	274	241	.300	.392

PITCHERS		W	L	PCT	G	GS	CG	SH	SV	IP	H	BB	SO	ERA
Kid Nichols		30	14	.682	49	43	37	3	1	372	387	101	102	2.83
Jack Stivetts		22	14	.611	42	36	31	2	0	329	353	99	71	4.10
Jim Sullivan		11	12	.478	31	26	21	1	1	225	268	68	33	4.03
Fred Klobedanz		6	4	.600	10	9	9	0	0	81	69	31	26	3.01
Willard Mains		3	2	.600	8	5	3	0	1	43	43	31	13	5.48
Ted Lewis		1	4	.200	6	5	4	0	0	42	37	27	12	3.24
Cozy Dolan		1	4	.200	6	5	3	0	0	41	55	27	14	4.83
Bill Banks		0	3	.000	4	3	2	0	0	23	42	13	6	10.57
		74	57	.565	132	132	110	6	3	1156	1254	397	277	3.78

CHICAGO
Colts

71-57 .555 -18.5 5th Cap Anson

BATTERS	POS/GAMES		GP	AB	R	H	BI	2B	3B	HR	BB	SO	SB	BA	SA
Cap Anson	1B98,C10		108	402	72	133	90	18	2	2	49	10	24	.331	.400
Fred Pfeffer	2B94	(2-2)	94	360	45	88	52	16	7	2	23	20	22	.244	.344
Bill Dahlen	SS125		125	474	137	167	74	30	19	9	64	36	51	.352	.553
Bill Everett	3B97,OF35		132	575	130	184	46	16	13	2	41	43	46	.320	.403
Jimmy Ryan	OF128		128	489	83	149	86	24	10	3	46	16	29	.305	.413
Bill Lange	OF121,C1		122	469	114	153	92	21	16	4	65	24	84	.326	.465
George Decker	OF71,1B36		107	421	68	118	61	23	11	5	23	14	20	.280	.423
Mal Kittredge	C64,P1		65	215	17	48	19	4	1	1	14	14	6	.223	.265
Tim Donahue	C57		57	188	27	41	20	10	1	0	11	15	11	.218	.282
Barry McCormick	3B35,SS6,2B3,OF1		45	168	22	37	23	3	1	1	14	30	9	.220	.268
Clark Griffith	P36		38	135	22	36	16	5	2	1	9	7	3	.267	.356
Dan Friend	P36,OF1		37	126	12	30	10	3	3	1	3	5	2	.238	.333
Adonis Terry	P30		30	99	14	26	15	4	2	0	8	12	4	.263	.343
Harry Truby	2B29	(1-2)	29	109	13	28	31	2	2	2	6	5	4	.257	.367
George Flynn	OF29		29	106	15	27	4	1	2	0	11	9	12	.255	.302
Buttons Briggs	P26		26	78	5	10	6	0	2	0	7	14	0	.128	.179
Doc Parker	P9,OF1		10	36	4	10	4	0	1	0	1	5	0	.278	.333
Josh Reilly	2B8,SS1		9	42	6	9	2	1	0	0	1	1	2	.214	.238
Algie McBride	OF9		9	29	2	7	7	1	1	1	7	3	0	.241	.448
Con Daily	C9		9	27	1	2	1	0	0	0	1	2	1	.074	.074
Walter Thornton	P5,OF3		9	22	6	8	1	0	1	0	5	2	2	.364	.455
Monte McFarland	P4		4	12	0	0	0	0	0	0	0	3	0	.000	.000
			132	4582	815	1311	660	182	97	34	409	290	332	.286	.390

PITCHERS		W	L	PCT	G	GS	CG	SH	SV	IP	H	BB	SO	ERA
Clark Griffith		23	11	.676	36	35	35	0	0	318	370	70	81	3.54
Dan Friend		18	14	.563	36	33	28	1	0	291	298	139	86	4.74
Adonis Terry		15	14	.517	30	28	25	1	0	235	268	88	74	4.28
Buttons Briggs		12	8	.600	26	21	19	0	1	194	202	108	84	4.31
Walter Thornton		2	1	.667	5	5	2	0	0	24	30	13	10	5.70
Doc Parker		1	5	.167	9	7	7	0	0	73	100	27	15	6.16
Monte McFarland		0	4	.000	4	3	2	0	0	25	32	21	3	7.20
Mal Kittredge		0	0	----	1	0	0	0	0	2	2	1	0	5.40
		71	57	.555	132	132	118	2	1	1161	1302	467	353	4.41

PITTSBURGH
Pirates

66-63 .512 -24 6th Connie Mack

BATTERS	POS/GAMES		GP	AB	R	H	BI	2B	3B	HR	BB	SO	SB	BA	SA
Jake Beckley	1B56,OF3,2B1	(1-2)	59	217	44	55	32	7	5	3	22	28	8	.253	.373
Dick Padden	2B61		61	219	33	53	24	4	8	2	14	9	8	.242	.361
Bones Ely	SS128		128	537	85	153	77	15	9	3	33	33	18	.285	.363
Denny Lyons	3B116		118	436	77	134	71	25	6	4	67	25	13	.307	.420
Patsy Donovan	OF131		131	573	113	183	59	20	5	3	35	18	48	.319	.387
Jake Stenzel	OF114,1B1		114	479	104	173	82	26	14	2	32	13	57	.361	.486

1896 NATIONAL LEAGUE

PITTSBURGH (cont.)
Pirates

BATTERS	POS/GAMES		GP	AB	R	H	BI	2B	3B	HR	BB	SO	SB	BA	SA
Elmer Smith	OF122		122	484	121	175	94	21	14	6	74	18	33	.362	.500
Joe Sugden	C70,1B7,OF4		80	301	42	89	36	5	7	0	19	9	5	.296	.359
Bill Merritt	C62,3B5,2B3,1B3,SS2		77	282	26	82	42	8	2	1	18	10	3	.291	.344
Lou Bierbauer	2B59		59	258	33	74	39	10	6	0	5	7	7	.287	.372
Frank Killen	P52		55	173	29	40	25	4	5	2	26	31	1	.231	.347
Pink Hawley	P49		50	163	19	39	21	9	4	1	1	22	1	.239	.362
Harry Davis	1B35,OF10,SS1	(2-2)	44	168	24	32	23	5	6	0	13	21	9	.190	.292
Connie Mack	1B28,C5		33	120	9	26	16	4	1	0	5	8	0	.217	.267
Jim Hughey	P25		25	65	4	14	5	1	0	0	5	8	0	.215	.231
Charles Hastings	P17		17	37	5	8	3	1	0	0	4	7	0	.216	.243
Joe Wright	OF12,3B1	(2-2)	13	52	5	16	6	2	1	0	1	2	1	.308	.385
Jud Smith	3B10		10	35	6	12	4	2	1	0	2	2	3	.343	.457
Brownie Foreman	P9	(1-2)	9	20	2	3	2	0	0	0	7	7	0	.150	.150
Harry Truby	2B8	(2-2)	8	32	1	5	3	0	0	0	2	4	1	.156	.156
Abe Lezotte	1B7		7	29	3	3	3	0	0	0	2	2	1	.103	.103
Jot Goar	P3		3	6	0	1	0	0	0	0	0	0	0	.167	.167
Elmer Horton	P2		2	7	1	0	0	0	0	0	0	1	0	.000	.000
Eddie Boyle	C2	(2-2)	2	5	0	0	0	0	0	0	0	1	0	.000	.000
Tom Delahanty	SS1	(2-2)	1	3	1	1	0	0	0	0	0	0	0	.333	.333
			131	4701	787	1371	667	169	94	27	387	286	217	.292	.385

PITCHERS			W	L	PCT	G	GS	CG	SH	SV	IP	H	BB	SO	ERA
Frank Killen			30	18	.625	52	50	44	5	0	432	476	119	134	3.41
Pink Hawley			22	21	.512	49	43	37	2	0	378	382	157	137	3.57
Jim Hughey			6	8	.429	25	14	11	0	0	155	171	67	48	4.99
Charles Hastings			5	10	.333	17	13	9	0	1	104	126	44	19	5.88
Brownie Foreman		(1-2)	3	3	.500	9	9	5	0	0	62	73	35	18	6.57
Jot Goar			0	1	.000	3	0	0	0	0	13	36	8	3	16.88
Elmer Horton			0	2	.000	2	2	2	0	0	15	22	9	3	9.60
			66	63	.512	131	131	108	8	1	1159	1286	439	362	4.30

NEW YORK
Giants

64-67　.489　-27　7th　Irwin - Joyce

BATTERS	POS/GAMES		GP	AB	R	H	BI	2B	3B	HR	BB	SO	SB	BA	SA
Willie Clark	1B65		72	247	38	72	33	12	4	0	15	12	8	.291	.372
Kid Gleason	2B130,3B3,OF1		133	541	79	162	89	17	5	4	42	13	46	.299	.372
Frank Connaughton	SS54,OF30		88	315	53	82	43	3	2	2	25	7	22	.260	.302
George Davis	3B74,SS45,OF3,1B3		124	494	98	158	99	25	12	6	50	24	48	.320	.455
Mike Tiernan	OF133		133	521	132	192	89	24	16	7	77	18	35	.369	.516
George Van Haltren	OF133,P2		133	562	136	197	74	18	21	5	55	36	39	.351	.484
General Stafford	OF53,SS6		59	230	28	66	40	9	1	0	13	18	15	.287	.335
Parke Wilson	C71,1B2		75	253	33	60	23	2	0	0	13	14	9	.237	.245
Harry Davis	OF40,1B23	(1-2)	64	233	43	64	50	11	10	2	31	20	16	.275	.433
Duke Farrell	C34,SS13,3B7	(1-2)	58	191	23	54	37	7	3	1	19	7	2	.283	.366
Bill Joyce	3B49	(2-2)	49	165	36	61	43	9	2	5	34	14	13	.370	.539
Dad Clarke	P48		49	147	11	30	10	0	1	0	12	19	0	.204	.218
Jake Beckley	1B45,OF2	(2-2)	46	182	37	55	38	8	4	5	9	7	11	.302	.473
Jouett Meekin	P42		43	144	27	43	16	6	5	2	12	9	2	.299	.451
Mike Sullivan	P25		25	77	10	16	5	1	0	0	1	14	0	.208	.221
Dave Zearfoss	C19		19	60	5	13	6	1	1	0	5	5	2	.217	.267
John Warner	C19	(2-2)	19	54	9	14	3	1	0	0	3	7	1	.259	.278
Shorty Fuller	SS18		18	72	10	12	7	0	0	0	14	5	4	.167	.167
Ed Doheny	P17		17	40	5	6	3	1	0	0	4	8	1	.150	.175
George Ulrich	OF11,3B3		14	45	4	8	1	1	0	0	1	1	0	.178	.200
Cy Seymour	P11,OF1		12	32	2	7	0	0	0	0	0	7	0	.219	.219
Bill Campfield	P6		6	12	2	2	3	1	0	0	1	2	0	.167	.250
Charles Gettig	P6		6	9	3	3	0	1	0	0	0	0	0	.333	.444
Fred Pfeffer	2B4	(1-2)	4	14	1	2	4	0	0	0	1	1	0	.143	.143
Carney Flynn	P3		3	4	1	2	3	0	0	1	0	0	0	.500	1.250
Tom Bannon	OF2		2	7	1	1	0	1	0	0	1	1	0	.143	.286
Bill Reidy	P2		2	5	1	0	0	0	0	0	0	0	0	.000	.000
Cy Bowen	P2		2	3	1	1	1	0	0	0	1	2	0	.333	.333
Reddy Foster	---		1	1	0	0	0	0	0	0	0	0	0	.000	.000
Les German	P1	(1-2)	1	1	0	0	0	0	0	0	0	0	0	.000	.000
			133	4661	829	1383	720	159	87	40	439	271	274	.297	.394

1896 NATIONAL LEAGUE

NEW YORK (cont.)
Giants

PITCHERS		W	L	PCT	G	GS	CG	SH	SV	IP	H	BB	SO	ERA
Jouett Meekin		26	14	.650	42	41	34	0	0	334	378	127	110	3.82
Dad Clarke		17	24	.415	48	40	33	1	1	351	431	60	66	4.26
Mike Sullivan		10	13	.435	25	22	18	0	0	185	188	71	42	4.66
Ed Doheny		6	7	.462	17	15	9	0	0	108	112	59	39	4.49
Cy Seymour		2	4	.333	11	8	4	0	0	70	75	51	33	6.40
Charles Gettig		1	0	1.000	4	1	1	0	1	14	20	8	5	9.64
George Van Haltren		1	0	1.000	2	0	0	0	0	8	5	1	3	2.25
Bill Campfield		1	1	.500	6	2	2	0	0	27	31	6	6	4.00
Bill Reidy		0	1	.000	2	1	1	0	0	13	24	2	1	7.62
Cy Bowen		0	1	.000	2	1	1	0	0	12	12	9	3	6.00
Carney Flynn	(1-2)	0	2	.000	3	2	1	0	0	11	18	8	4	11.81
Les German	(1-2)	0	0	---	1	0	0	0	0	3	9	1	0	13.50
		64	67	.489	133	133	104	1	2	1137	1303	403	312	4.54

PHILADELPHIA 62-68 .477 -28.5 8th Billy Nash
Phillies

BATTERS	POS/GAMES		GP	AB	R	H	BI	2B	3B	HR	BB	SO	SB	BA	SA
Dan Brouthers	1B57		57	218	42	75	41	13	3	1	44	11	7	.344	.445
Bill Hallman	2B120,P1		120	469	82	150	83	21	3	2	45	23	16	.320	.390
Bill Hulen	SS73,OF12,2B2		88	339	87	90	38	18	7	0	55	20	23	.265	.360
Billy Nash	3B65		65	227	29	56	30	9	1	3	34	21	3	.247	.335
Sam Thompson	OF119		119	517	103	154	100	28	7	12	28	13	12	.298	.449
Duff Cooley	OF64	(2-2)	64	287	63	88	22	6	4	2	18	16	18	.307	.376
Ed Delahanty	OF99,1B22,2B1		123	499	131	198	126	44	17	13	62	22	37	.397	.631
Mike Grady	C61,3B7		72	242	49	77	44	20	7	1	16	19	10	.318	.471
Lave Cross	3B61,SS37,2B6,OF2,C1		106	406	63	104	73	23	5	1	32	14	8	.256	.345
Jack Clements	C53		57	184	35	66	45	5	7	5	17	14	2	.359	.543
Joe Sullivan	OF45,SS2,3B1	(1-2)	48	191	45	48	24	5	3	2	18	12	9	.251	.340
Jack Taylor	P45,OF2		47	157	10	29	18	6	0	0	9	18	0	.185	.223
Jack Boyle	C28,1B2		40	145	17	43	28	4	1	1	6	7	3	.297	.359
Nap Lajoie	1B39		39	175	36	57	42	12	7	4	1	11	7	.326	.543
Sam Mertes	OF35,SS1,2B1		37	143	20	34	14	4	4	0	8	10	19	.238	.322
Kid Carsey	P27		27	81	13	18	7	2	2	0	11	12	1	.222	.296
Al Orth	P25		25	82	12	21	13	3	3	1	3	11	2	.256	.402
Phil Geier	OF12,2B3,C2		17	56	12	13	6	0	1	0	6	7	3	.232	.268
Josh Keener	P16		16	51	6	16	7	4	0	0	1	6	3	.314	.392
Bill Gallagher	SS14		14	49	9	15	6	2	0	0	10	0	0	.306	.347
Tuck Turner	OF9	(1-2)	13	32	12	7	0	2	0	0	8	5	6	.219	.281
Willie McGill	P12		12	29	4	6	2	1	1	0	2	3	0	.207	.310
Ad Gumbert	P11	(2-2)	11	34	7	9	7	1	1	1	0	3	1	.265	.441
Con Lucid	P5		5	16	0	2	0	0	0	0	0	3	1	.125	.125
Ben Ellis	SS2,3B2		4	16	0	1	0	0	0	0	3	6	0	.063	.063
George Wheeler	P3		3	9	1	1	0	0	0	0	0	0	0	.111	.111
Bert Inks	P3	(1-2)	3	5	1	1	0	0	0	0	0	0	0	.200	.200
Dan Leahy	SS2		2	6	0	2	1	1	0	0	1	2	0	.333	.500
Ned Garvin	P2		2	6	0	0	1	0	0	0	0	4	0	.000	.000
Bill Whitrock	P2		2	3	0	0	0	0	0	0	0	1	0	.000	.000
Charlie Jordan	P2		2	2	1	1	0	0	0	0	0	0	0	.500	.500
Jerry Nops	P1	(1-2)	1	4	0	0	0	0	0	0	0	3	0	.000	.000
			130	4680	890	1382	778	234	84	49	438	297	191	.295	.413

PITCHERS		W	L	PCT	G	GS	CG	SH	SV	IP	H	BB	SO	ERA
Jack Taylor		20	21	.488	45	41	35	1	1	359	459	112	97	4.79
Al Orth		15	10	.600	25	23	19	0	0	196	244	46	23	4.41
Kid Carsey		11	11	.500	27	21	18	1	1	187	273	72	36	5.62
Ad Gumbert	(2-2)	5	3	.625	11	10	7	1	0	77	99	23	14	4.54
Willie McGill		5	4	.556	12	11	7	0	0	80	87	53	29	5.31
Josh Keener		3	11	.214	16	13	11	0	0	113	144	39	28	5.88
Jerry Nops	(1-2)	1	0	1.000	1	1	1	0	0	7	11	1	1	5.14
George Wheeler		1	1	.500	3	2	2	0	0	16	18	5	2	3.86
Con Lucid		1	4	.200	5	5	5	0	0	42	75	17	3	8.36
Ned Garvin		0	1	.000	2	1	1	0	0	13	19	7	4	7.62
Bert Inks	(1-2)	0	1	.000	3	1	0	0	0	10	21	5	2	7.84
Bill Whitrock		0	1	.000	2	1	1	0	0	9	10	3	1	3.00
Charlie Jordan		0	0	----	2	0	0	0	0	5	9	2	3	7.71
Bill Hallman		0	0	----	1	0	0	0	0	2	4	2	0	18.00
		62	68	.477	130	130	107	3	2	1117	1473	387	243	5.20

1896 NATIONAL LEAGUE

BROOKLYN Bridegrooms
58-73 .443 -33 9th (tie) Dave Foutz

BATTERS	POS/GAMES		GP	AB	R	H	BI	2B	3B	HR	BB	SO	SB	BA	SA
Candy LaChance	1B89		89	348	60	99	58	10	13	7	23	32	17	.284	.448
Tom Daly	2B66,C1		67	224	43	63	29	13	6	3	33	25	19	.281	.433
Tom Corcoran	SS132		132	532	63	154	73	15	7	3	15	13	16	.289	.361
Bill Shindle	3B131		131	516	75	144	61	24	9	1	24	20	24	.279	.366
Fielder Jones	OF103		104	395	82	140	46	10	8	3	48	15	18	.354	.443
Mike Griffin	OF122		122	493	101	152	51	27	9	4	48	25	23	.308	.424
Tommy McCarthy	OF103		104	377	62	94	47	8	4	3	34	17	22	.249	.316
John Grim	C77,1B5		81	281	32	75	35	13	1	2	12	14	7	.267	.342
John Anderson	OF68,1B42		108	430	70	135	55	23	17	1	18	23	37	.314	.453
George Shoch	2B62,OF10,3B3,SS1		76	250	36	73	28	7	4	1	33	10	11	.292	.364
Buster Burrell	C60		62	206	19	62	23	11	3	0	15	13	1	.301	.383
Brickyard Kennedy	P42		42	122	12	23	10	2	0	0	2	15	1	.189	.205
Harley Payne	P34,OF1		38	98	5	21	10	4	1	0	9	3	0	.214	.276
Dan Daub	P32		32	84	9	19	14	1	2	0	10	12	1	.226	.286
Bert Abbey	P25		25	63	7	12	7	1	2	0	6	13	0	.190	.270
Ed Stein	P17		17	39	3	10	2	1	0	0	2	6	0	.256	.282
George Harper	P16		16	37	5	6	3	0	1	0	8	3	0	.162	.216
Frank Bonner	2B9		9	34	8	6	5	2	0	0	2	8	1	.176	.235
Ad Gumbert	P5	(1-2)	5	11	0	2	0	1	0	0	1	2	0	.182	.273
Dave Foutz	OF1,1B1		2	8	0	2	0	1	0	0	1	0	0	.250	.375
			133	4548	692	1292	557	174	87	28	344	269	198	.284	.379

PITCHERS		W	L	PCT	G	GS	CG	SH	SV	IP	H	BB	SO	ERA
Brickyard Kennedy		17	20	.459	42	38	28	1	1	306	334	130	76	4.42
Harley Payne		14	16	.467	34	28	24	2	0	242	284	58	52	3.39
Dan Daub		12	11	.522	32	24	18	0	0	225	255	63	53	3.60
Bert Abbey		8	8	.500	25	18	12	0	0	164	210	48	37	5.15
George Harper		4	8	.333	16	11	7	0	0	86	106	39	22	5.55
Ed Stein		3	6	.333	17	10	6	0	0	90	130	51	16	4.88
Ad Gumbert	(1-2)	0	4	.000	5	4	2	0	0	31	34	11	3	3.77
		58	73	.443	133	133	97	3	1	1144	1353	400	259	4.25

WASHINGTON Senators
58-73 .443 -33 9th (tie) Gus Schmelz

BATTERS	POS/GAMES		GP	AB	R	H	BI	2B	3B	HR	BB	SO	SB	BA	SA
Ed Cartwright	1B133		133	499	76	138	62	15	10	1	54	44	28	.277	.353
John O'Brien	2B73	(2-2)	73	270	38	72	33	6	3	4	27	12	4	.267	.356
Gene DeMontreville	SS133		133	533	94	183	77	24	5	8	29	27	28	.343	.452
Bill Joyce	3B48,2B33	(1-2)	81	310	85	97	51	16	10	8	67	20	32	.313	.506
Bill Lush	OF91,2B3		97	352	74	87	45	9	11	4	66	49	28	.247	.369
Tom Brown	OF116		116	435	87	128	59	17	6	2	58	49	28	.294	.375
Kip Selbach	OF126		127	487	100	148	100	17	13	5	76	28	49	.304	.423
Deacon McGuire	C98,1B1		108	389	60	125	70	25	3	2	30	14	12	.321	.416
Charles Abbey	OF78,P2		79	301	47	79	49	12	6	1	27	20	16	.262	.352
Win Mercer	P46,OF1		49	156	23	38	14	1	1	1	9	18	9	.244	.282
Jim Rogers	3B32,2B6,OF1	(1-2)	38	154	21	43	30	6	4	1	10	9	3	.279	.390
Duke Farrell	C18,3B14	(2-2)	37	130	18	39	30	7	3	1	7	3	2	.300	.423
Doc McJames	P37		37	111	8	18	5	1	0	0	3	19	1	.162	.171
Harvey Smith	3B36		36	131	21	36	17	7	2	0	12	7	9	.275	.359
Les German	P28,OF1,3B1	(2-2)	30	70	11	16	6	1	0	1	5	5	3	.229	.286
Pat McCauley	C24,OF1		26	84	14	21	11	3	0	3	7	8	3	.250	.393
Jack Crooks	2B20,3B4	(1-2)	25	84	20	24	20	3	0	3	16	8	2	.286	.429
Silver King	P22		22	58	9	16	12	6	0	0	8	15	1	.276	.379
Al Maul	P8		8	28	6	8	5	1	1	0	3	2	0	.286	.393
Elisha Norton	P8		8	19	2	4	0	1	0	0	0	2	0	.211	.316
Zeke Wrigley	2B3,SS1		5	9	1	1	2	0	0	0	1	1	0	.111	.111
Jake Boyd	P4		4	13	1	1	1	0	0	0	1	1	0	.077	.077
Carney Flynn	P4	(2-2)	4	8	0	2	0	0	0	0	0	2	0	.250	.250
Varney Anderson	P2		2	5	1	3	2	1	0	0	1	0	0	.600	.800
John Malarkey	P1		1	2	1	1	1	1	0	0	0	0	0	.500	1.000
John Gilroy	P1		1	1	0	0	0	0	0	0	0	1	0	.000	.000
			133	4639	818	1328	702	179	79	45	516	365	258	.286	.388

PITCHERS	W	L	PCT	G	GS	CG	SH	SV	IP	H	BB	SO	ERA
Win Mercer	25	18	.581	46	45	38	2	0	366	456	117	94	4.13
Doc McJames	12	20	.375	37	33	29	0	1	280	310	135	103	4.27
Silver King	10	7	.588	22	16	12	0	1	145	179	43	35	4.09

WASHINGTON (cont.)
Senators

PITCHERS		W	L	PCT	G	GS	CG	SH	SV	IP	H	BB	SO	ERA
Al Maul		5	2	.714	8	8	7	0	0	62	75	20	18	3.63
Elisha Norton		3	1	.750	8	5	2	0	0	44	49	14	13	3.07
Les German	(2-2)	2	20	.091	28	20	14	0	1	167	240	74	20	6.32
Jake Boyd		1	2	.333	4	2	2	0	0	32	45	15	6	6.75
Carney Flynn	(2-2)	0	1	.000	4	1	1	0	0	20	43	10	3	8.55
Varney Anderson		0	1	.000	2	2	1	0	0	9	23	3	0	13.00
John Malarkey		0	1	.000	1	1	0	0	0	7	9	3	0	1.29
John Gilroy		0	0	----	1	0	0	0	0	2	0	1	0	0.00
Charlie Abbey		0	0	----	1	0	0	0	0	2	6	0	0	4.50
		58	73	.443	133	133	106	2	3	1137	1435	435	292	4.61

ST. LOUIS
Browns

40-90   .308   -50.5   11th   Diddlebock - Latham - Von der Ahe - Connor - Dowd

BATTERS	POS/GAMES		GP	AB	R	H	BI	2B	3B	HR	BB	SO	SB	BA	SA
Roger Connor	1B126		126	483	71	137	72	21	9	11	52	14	10	.284	.433
Tommy Dowd	2B78,OF48		126	521	93	138	46	17	11	5	42	19	40	.265	.369
Monte Cross	SS125		125	427	66	104	52	10	6	6	58	48	40	.244	.337
Bert Myers	3B121,SS1		122	454	47	116	37	12	8	0	40	32	8	.256	.317
Tuck Turner	OF51	(2-2)	51	203	30	50	27	7	8	1	14	21	6	.246	.374
Tom Parrott	OF108,P7,1B6		118	474	62	138	70	13	12	7	11	24	12	.291	.414
Klondike Douglass	OF74,C6,SS2		81	296	42	78	28	6	4	1	35	15	18	.264	.321
Ed McFarland	C80,OF2		83	290	48	70	36	13	4	3	15	17	7	.241	.345
Joe Sullivan	OF45,2B7,3B1	(2-2)	51	212	25	62	21	4	2	2	9	12	5	.292	.358
Ted Breitenstein	P44,OF8		51	162	21	42	12	5	2	0	13	26	8	.259	.315
Morg Murphy	C48		49	175	12	45	11	5	2	0	8	14	1	.257	.309
Bill Hart	P42,OF8		49	161	9	30	15	4	5	0	3	15	7	.186	.273
Joe Quinn	2B48	(1-2)	48	191	19	40	17	6	1	1	9	5	8	.209	.267
Duff Cooley	OF40	(1-2)	40	166	29	51	13	5	3	0	7	3	12	.307	.373
Red Donahue	P32,OF1		33	107	5	17	9	2	0	0	3	23	1	.159	.178
Bill Kissinger	P20,OF3,3B1		23	73	8	22	12	4	0	0	0	4	0	.301	.356
Tom Niland	OF13,SS5		18	68	3	12	3	0	1	0	5	4	0	.176	.206
Arlie Latham	3B8		8	35	3	7	5	0	0	0	4	3	2	.200	.200
Biff Sheehan	OF6		6	19	0	3	1	0	0	0	4	0	0	.158	.158
Dewey McDougal	P3		3	3	0	0	0	0	0	0	0	1	0	.000	.000
John Wood	P1		1	0	0	0	0	0	0	0	0	0	0	----	----
			131	4520	593	1162	487	134	78	37	332	300	185	.257	.346

PITCHERS	W	L	PCT	G	GS	CG	SH	SV	IP	H	BB	SO	ERA
Ted Breitenstein	18	26	.409	44	43	37	1	0	340	376	138	114	4.48
Bill Hart	12	29	.293	42	41	37	0	0	336	411	141	65	5.12
Red Donahue	7	24	.226	32	32	28	0	0	267	376	98	70	5.80
Bill Kissinger	2	9	.182	20	12	11	0	1	136	209	55	22	6.49
Tom Parrott	1	1	.500	7	2	2	0	0	42	62	18	8	6.21
Dewey McDougal	0	1	.000	3	1	0	0	0	10	13	4	0	8.10
John Wood	0	0	----	1	0	0	0	0	0	1	2	0	inf.
	40	90	.308	131	131	115	1	1	1131	1448	456	279	5.33

LOUISVILLE
Colonels

38-93   .290   -53   12th   McCloskey - McGunnigle

BATTERS	POS/GAMES		GP	AB	R	H	BI	2B	3B	HR	BB	SO	SB	BA	SA
Jim Rogers	1B60,SS12	(2-2)	72	290	39	75	38	8	6	0	15	14	13	.259	.328
John O'Brien	2B49	(1-2)	49	186	24	63	24	9	1	2	13	7	4	.339	.430
Joe Dolan	SS44		44	165	14	35	18	2	1	3	9	12	6	.212	.291
Bill Clingman	3B121		121	423	57	99	37	10	2	2	57	51	19	.234	.281
Tom McCreery	OF111,2B1,P1		115	441	87	155	65	23	21	7	42	58	26	.351	.546
Ollie Pickering	OF45		45	165	28	50	22	6	4	1	12	11	13	.303	.406
Fred Clarke	OF131		131	517	96	168	79	15	18	9	43	34	34	.325	.476
Charles Dexter	C55,OF47		107	402	65	112	37	18	7	3	17	34	21	.279	.381
Doggie Miller	C48,2B25,OF8,3B8,1B3,SS2		98	324	54	89	33	17	4	1	27	9	16	.275	.361
Peter Cassidy	1B38,SS11		49	184	16	39	12	1	1	0	7	7	5	.212	.228
Ducky Holmes	OF33,P2,SS1,2B1		47	141	22	38	18	3	2	0	13	5	8	.270	.319
Chick Fraser	P43,OF2		45	146	12	22	6	3	2	0	7	34	1	.151	.199
Still Bill Hill	P43		43	116	11	24	5	0	0	0	5	23	1	.207	.207
Jack Crooks	2B39	(2-2)	39	122	19	29	15	5	1	2	20	8	8	.238	.344
John Warner	C32,1B1	(1-2)	33	110	9	25	10	1	1	0	10	10	3	.227	.255

LOUISVILLE (cont.)
Colonels

BATTERS	POS/GAMES		GP	AB	R	H	BI	2B	3B	HR	BB	SO	SB	BA	SA
Frank Shannon	SS28,3B3		31	115	14	18	15	1	1	1	13	15	3	.157	.209
Herm McFarland	OF28,C1		30	110	11	21	12	4	1	1	9	14	4	.191	.273
Bill Hassamaer	1B29		30	106	8	26	14	5	0	2	14	7	1	.245	.349
Bert Cunningham	P27,SS1		29	88	11	22	15	3	2	2	5	14	0	.250	.398
Frank Eustace	SS22,2B3		25	100	18	17	11	2	2	1	6	14	4	.170	.260
Abbie Johnson	2B25		25	87	10	20	14	2	1	0	4	6	0	.230	.276
Tom Smith	P11,1B4		15	39	3	8	1	1	1	0	4	5	0	.205	.282
Sammy Strang	SS14		14	46	6	12	7	0	0	0	6	6	4	.261	.261
Art Herman	P14		14	36	3	5	2	0	0	0	0	11	0	.139	.139
Mike McDermott	P12		12	27	6	8	1	2	0	0	2	2	0	.296	.370
Tom Morrison	3B5,OF2,SS1		8	27	3	4	0	1	0	0	4	4	0	.148	.185
Tom Kinslow	C5,1B1		8	25	4	7	7	0	1	0	1	5	0	.280	.360
Gus Weyhing	P5		5	15	2	2	1	0	0	0	2	2	1	.133	.133
Eddie Boyle	C3	(1-2)	3	9	0	0	0	0	0	0	2	2	0	.000	.000
Joe Wright	OF2	(1-2)	2	7	0	2	0	0	0	0	0	1	0	.286	.286
George Treadway	OF1,1B1		2	7	0	1	1	0	0	0	1	0	0	.143	.143
Frank Friend	C2		2	5	1	1	0	0	0	0	1	1	0	.200	.200
Fred Clausen	P2		2	4	0	0	0	0	0	0	0	0	0	.000	.000
Joe Kostal	P2		2	0	0	0	0	0	0	0	0	0	0	----	----
Charlie Emig	P1		1	3	0	0	0	0	0	0	0	1	0	.000	.000
			134	4588	653	1197	520	142	80	37	371	427	195	.261	.351

PITCHERS	W	L	PCT	G	GS	CG	SH	SV	IP	H	BB	SO	ERA
Chick Fraser	12	27	.308	43	38	36	0	1	349	396	166	91	4.87
Still Bill Hill	9	28	.243	43	39	32	0	2	320	353	155	104	4.31
Bert Cunningham	7	14	.333	27	20	17	0	1	189	242	74	37	5.09
Art Herman	4	6	.400	14	12	9	0	0	94	122	36	13	5.63
Tom Smith	2	3	.400	11	5	4	0	0	55	73	25	14	5.40
Gus Weyhing	2	3	.400	5	5	4	0	0	42	62	15	9	6.64
Mike McDermott	2	7	.222	12	10	4	1	0	65	87	44	12	7.34
Ducky Holmes	0	1	.000	2	1	0	0	0	12	26	8	3	7.50
Charlie Emig	0	1	.000	1	1	1	0	0	8	12	7	1	7.88
Tom McCreery	0	1	.000	1	1	0	0	0	1	4	5	0	36.00
Fred Clausen	0	2	.000	2	2	1	0	0	11	17	6	4	6.55
Joe Kostal	0	0	----	2	0	0	0	0	2	4	0	0	0.00
	38	93	.290	134	134	108	1	4	1149	1398	541	288	5.12

1897 NATIONAL LEAGUE

The Beaneaters Prevail

During the decade of the 1890s, there were not many pennant races. The ungainly 12-team format guaranteed that by July, half of the teams would be buried deep in the second division. And with eleven opponents, chances were not great that a team would face a pennant rival late in the season in a meaningful series. The one big exception occurred in 1897.

Baltimore, fresh on the heels of their three pennants in a row, was the odds-on favorite to win a fourth in 1897. The team got off to a fast start, and by June had a comfortable lead. Boston, nicknamed the Beaneaters, on the other hand started slow, losing six of their first seven. But in June, Boston turned red-hot. The team won 20 of 22 to pull ahead of Baltimore by the end of the month. Boston maintained a narrow lead through August, but the Orioles caught them by the 28th. From here to the end of the season, the two teams seesawed back and forth with never more than one game separating them. When the two teams met in Baltimore in the season's next to last series, Baltimore trailed by one-half game, though they had a one-percentage-point lead (.707) to (.706).

Boston won the opener 6-4 in front of a large crowd on September 24, and pushed the margin to one and one-half games. Baltimore crept back the next day winning by a 6-3 margin. In the pivotal third game, Boston broke open a close game by blasting nine runs in the seventh inning on their way to a 19-10 victory. A demoralized Baltimore, now trailing by one and one-half, lost two of their last four to finish two games behind. The Beaneaters had prevailed and broken the Orioles' stranglehold on the pennant.

Boston's hard-hitting lineup saw seven of their eight starters bat over .300. Newcomers Chick Stahl (.354), and Jimmy Collins (.346), as well as veterans Billy Hamilton (.343) and Hugh Duffy (.340) anchored a lineup that batted .319 and scored 1025 runs. In addition Hamilton scored the league's most runs (152) while Hugh Duffy won his second home run title with 11. Not to be outdone, pitcher Kid Nichols led the league with 31 wins.

Baltimore outhit and outpitched Boston, but still fell short. The peerless Willie Keeler had his finest year, leading the league in batting (.424), and hits (239). Other stars included Jack Doyle (.354), Hugh Jennings (.355), Joe Kelley (.362), and Jake

Stenzel (.353). Their pitching staff was anchored by three twenty-game winners paced by Joe Corbett with 24.

New York, with the return of Amos Rusie, bounced into third. Rusie finished with 28 wins and the league's best earned run average (2.45). Once again the offensive chores fell to the outfield duo of George Van Haltren and Mike Tiernan as each batted .330. George Davis had a fine year as well finishing with a .353 average buttressed by a league best 136 runs batted in.

Cincinnati and Cleveland finished fourth and fifth. Their best players included Dusty Miller (.319) of Cincinnati, and Cupid Childs (.338), Bobby Wallace (.335) and Lou Sockalexis (.338) of Cleveland. (Note: Sockalexis, a very gifted Native-American ball player, had a tragically short career due to the excesses of drink. The Cleveland American League team later honored him by coining "Indians" as their nickname.)

Brooklyn and Washington finished tied for sixth. Brooklyn was bolstered by their outfield of Fielder Jones (.314), Mike Griffin (.316) and John Anderson (.325). Washington, enjoying their best ever National League finish, utilized the services of Gene DeMontreville (.341) and Deacon McGuire (.343).

Pittsburgh, Chicago, Philadelphia, Louisville, and St. Louis finished in the last five spots. Performances of note on these teams included Patsy Donovan (.322) of Pittsburgh, Bill Lange (.340) of Chicago, Ed Delahanty (.377) of Philadelphia, and Fred Clarke (.390) of Louisville.

Also in Chicago, Cap Anson came to the end of the line in 1897. After a glorious 27-year major league career, he was released after the season. Following a brief managerial stint in New York the next year, Anson said good-bye to the world of baseball.

The Temple Cup of 1897 featured close games, although the outcome was far from close. Boston won the first game in a thriller 13-12, while the Orioles knotted the series by triumphing in the second 13-11. Likewise, Baltimore took game three 8-3, and took an 11-run lead in game four before hanging on 12-11. The Orioles continued their domination by whipping Boston 9-3 in the clinching game, thus assuring themselves their second straight Temple Cup victory.

Boston's victory in the 1897 pennant race erased some of the bad feelings of their bitter loss of 1889 in a similar situation. The victory also reestablished the Beaneaters as the dominant team of the 1890s. It is hard to ignore the three-pennant run of the Orioles in the middle of the decade, but before and after, the Beaneaters won five pennants of their own.

1897 NATIONAL LEAGUE

BOSTON
Beaneaters 93-39 .705 1st Frank Selee

BATTERS	POS/GAMES		GP	AB	R	H	BI	2B	3B	HR	BB	SO	SB	BA	SA
Fred Tenney	1B128,OF4		132	566	125	180	85	24	3	1	49		34	.318	.376
Bobby Lowe	2B123		123	499	87	154	106	24	8	5	32		16	.309	.419
Germany Long	SS107,OF1		107	450	89	145	69	32	7	3	23		22	.322	.444
Jimmy Collins	3B134		134	529	103	183	132	28	13	6	41		14	.346	.482
Chick Stahl	OF111		114	469	112	166	97	30	13	4	38		18	.354	.499
Billy Hamilton	OF126		127	507	152	174	61	17	5	3	105		66	.343	.414
Hugh Duffy	OF129,2B6,SS2		134	550	130	187	129	25	10	11	52		41	.340	.482
Marty Bergen	C85,OF1		87	327	47	81	45	11	3	2	18		5	.248	.318
Jack Stivetts	OF30,P18,2B2,1B2		61	199	41	73	37	9	9	2	15		2	.367	.533
Fred Klobedanz	P38,OF2		48	148	29	48	20	8	5	1	5		1	.324	.466
Kid Nichols	P46		46	147	20	39	28	5	0	3	7		4	.265	.361
Ted Lewis	P38		38	113	15	28	8	0	1	0	6		3	.248	.265
Bob Allen	SS32,OF1,2B1		34	119	33	38	24	5	0	1	18		1	.319	.387
Charles Ganzel	C27,1B2		30	105	15	28	14	4	3	0	4		2	.267	.362
George Yeager	C13,OF10,2B4,3B1		30	95	20	23	15	2	3	2	7		2	.242	.389
Fred Lake	C18		19	62	2	15	5	4	0	0	1		2	.242	.306
Jim Sullivan	P13		13	33	3	6	3	0	0	0	0		0	.182	.182
Tommy Tucker	1B4	(1-2)	4	14	0	3	4	2	0	0	2		0	.214	.357
Piano Legs Hickman	P2		2	3	1	2	2	0	0	1	0		0	.667	1.667
Mike Mahoney	C1,P1		2	2	1	1	1	0	0	0	0		0	.500	.500
			135	4937	1025	1574	885	230	83	45	423	262	233	.319	.426

PITCHERS		W	L	PCT	G	GS	CG	SH	SV	IP	H	BB	SO	ERA
Kid Nichols		31	11	.738	46	40	37	2	3	368	362	68	127	2.64
Fred Klobedanz		26	7	.788	38	37	30	2	0	309	344	125	92	4.60
Ted Lewis		21	12	.636	38	34	30	2	1	290	316	125	65	3.85
Jack Stivetts		11	4	.733	18	15	10	0	0	129	147	43	27	3.41
Jim Sullivan		4	5	.444	13	9	8	1	2	89	91	26	17	3.94
Piano Legs Hickman		0	0	----	2	0	0	0	1	8	10	5	0	5.87
Mike Mahoney		0	0	----	1	0	0	0	0	1	3	1	1	18.00
		93	39	.705	135	135	115	8	7	1194	1273	393	329	3.65

BALTIMORE
Orioles 90-40 .692 -2 2nd Ned Hanlon

BATTERS	POS/GAMES		GP	AB	R	H	BI	2B	3B	HR	BB	SO	SB	BA	SA
Jack Doyle	1B114		114	460	91	163	87	29	4	1	29		62	.354	.441
Heinie Reitz	2B128		128	477	76	138	84	15	6	2	50		23	.289	.358
Hugh Jennings	SS117		117	439	133	156	79	26	9	2	42		60	.355	.469
John McGraw	3B106		106	391	90	127	48	15	3	0	99		44	.325	.379
Willie Keeler	OF129		129	564	145	239	74	27	19	1	35		64	.424	.544
Joe Kelley	OF130,SS3,3B2		131	505	113	183	118	31	9	5	70		44	.362	.489
Jake Stenzel	OF131		131	536	113	189	116	43	7	4	36		69	.353	.481
Boileryard Clarke	C59,1B4		64	241	32	65	38	7	1	1	9		5	.270	.320
Joe Quinn	3B37,SS21,2B11,OF6,1B2		75	285	33	74	45	11	4	1	13		12	.260	.337
Tom O'Brien	1B25,OF24		50	147	25	37	32	6	0	0	20		7	.252	.293
Wilbert Robinson	C48		48	181	25	57	23	9	0	0	8		0	.315	.365
Joe Corbett	P37,OF1,SS1		42	150	27	37	22	6	1	0	4		4	.247	.300
Bill Hoffer	P38,OF4		42	139	20	33	16	8	1	1	6		2	.237	.331
Frank Bowerman	C38		38	130	16	41	21	5	0	1	1		3	.315	.377
Arlie Pond	P32,OF1		33	90	16	22	6	3	0	0	11		2	.244	.278
Jerry Nops	P30		30	92	7	18	7	2	2	0	3		0	.196	.261
Doc Amole	P11		11	28	1	3	5	0	0	0	1		0	.107	.107
George Blackburn	P5		5	13	1	1	0	0	0	0	0		0	.077	.077
Al Maul	P2	(2-2)	2	3	0	1	0	0	0	0	0		0	.333	.333
Richard Cogan	P1		1	1	0	0	0	0	0	0	0		0	.000	.000
			136	4872	964	1584	821	243	66	19	437	256	401	.325	.414

PITCHERS		W	L	PCT	G	GS	CG	SH	SV	IP	H	BB	SO	ERA
Joe Corbett		24	8	.750	37	37	34	1	0	313	330	115	149	3.11
Bill Hoffer		22	11	.667	38	33	29	1	0	303	350	104	62	4.31
Jerry Nops		20	6	.769	30	25	23	1	0	221	235	52	69	2.81
Arlie Pond		18	9	.667	32	28	23	0	0	248	267	72	59	3.52
Doc Amole		4	4	.500	11	7	6	0	0	70	67	17	19	2.57
George Blackburn		2	2	.500	5	4	3	0	0	33	34	12	1	6.82
Al Maul	(2-2)	0	0	----	2	2	0	0	0	8	9	8	2	7.04
Richard Cogan		0	0	----	1	0	0	0	0	2	4	2	0	13.50
		90	40	.692	136	136	118	3	0	1198	1296	382	361	3.55

1897 NATIONAL LEAGUE

NEW YORK Giants
83-48 .634 -9.5 3rd Bill Joyce

BATTERS	POS/GAMES		GP	AB	R	H	BI	2B	3B	HR	BB	SO	SB	BA	SA
Willie Clark	1B107,OF7,3B1		116	431	63	122	75	17	12	1	37		18	.283	.385
Kid Gleason	2B129,SS3		131	540	85	172	106	16	4	1	26		43	.319	.369
George Davis	SS129		130	519	112	183	136	31	10	10	41		65	.353	.509
Bill Joyce	3B106,1B2		109	388	109	118	64	15	13	3	78		33	.304	.433
Mike Tiernan	OF127		127	528	123	174	72	29	10	5	61		40	.330	.451
George Van Haltren	OF129		129	564	117	186	64	22	9	3	40		50	.330	.417
Ducky Holmes	OF77,SS1	(2-2)	79	306	51	82	44	8	6	1	18		30	.268	.343
John Warner	C110		110	397	50	109	51	6	3	2	26		8	.275	.320
Tom McCreery	OF46,2B3	(2-2)	49	177	36	53	27	8	5	1	22		15	.299	.418
Parke Wilson	C30,1B10,OF4,2B1		46	154	29	46	22	9	3	0	15		5	.299	.396
Cy Seymour	P38,OF6		44	137	13	33	14	5	1	2	4		3	.241	.336
Jouett Meekin	P37		42	137	22	41	10	6	1	0	5		3	.299	.358
Amos Rusie	P38		40	144	25	40	22	1	3	0	3		1	.278	.326
Jim Donnelly	3B23	(2-2)	23	85	19	16	11	3	0	0	9		6	.188	.224
Mike Sullivan	P23		23	66	6	18	8	1	0	0	2		0	.273	.288
Charles Gettig	3B7,2B6,OF3,SS3,P3		22	75	8	15	12	6	0	0	6		3	.200	.280
Jake Beckley	1B17	(1-2)	17	68	8	17	11	2	3	1	2		2	.250	.412
Walt Wilmot	OF9		11	34	8	9	4	2	0	1	2		1	.265	.412
Ed Doheny	P10		10	35	5	7	0	1	0	0	1		2	.200	.229
General Stafford	OF5,SS2	(1-2)	7	23	0	2	3	0	0	0	3		0	.087	.087
Dad Clarke	P6,OF1	(1-2)	7	18	4	3	1	0	0	0	1		0	.167	.167
Dave Zearfoss	C5		5	10	1	3	0	0	1	0	0		0	.300	.300
Yale Murphy	SS3,2B2		5	8	1	0	1	0	0	0	2		0	.000	.000
			137	4844	895	1449	758	188	84	31	404	327	328	.299	.392

PITCHERS		W	L	PCT	G	GS	CG	SH	SV	IP	H	BB	SO	ERA
Amos Rusie		28	10	.737	38	37	35	2	0	322	314	87	135	2.54
Jouett Meekin		20	11	.645	37	34	30	2	0	304	328	99	83	3.76
Cy Seymour		18	14	.563	38	33	28	2	1	278	254	164	149	3.37
Mike Sullivan		8	7	.533	23	16	11	1	2	149	183	71	35	5.09
Ed Doheny		4	4	.500	10	10	10	0	0	85	69	45	37	2.12
Dad Clarke	(1-2)	2	1	.667	6	4	2	0	0	31	43	11	10	6.10
Charles Gettig		1	1	.500	3	2	2	0	0	19	23	9	7	5.21
		83	48	.634	137	136	118	8	3	1187	1214	486	456	3.47

CINCINNATI Reds
76-56 .576 -17 4th Buck Ewing

BATTERS	POS/GAMES		GP	AB	R	H	BI	2B	3B	HR	BB	SO	SB	BA	SA
Jake Beckley	1B97	(2-2)	97	365	76	126	76	17	9	7	18		23	.345	.499
Bid McPhee	2B81		81	282	45	85	39	13	7	1	35		9	.301	.408
Claude Ritchey	SS70,OF22,2B8		101	337	58	95	41	12	4	0	42		11	.282	.341
Charlie Irwin	3B134		134	505	89	146	74	26	6	0	47		27	.289	.364
Dusty Miller	OF119		119	440	83	139	70	27	1	4	48		29	.316	.409
Dummy Hoy	OF128		128	497	87	145	42	24	6	2	54		37	.292	.376
Ed Burke	OF95		95	387	71	103	41	17	1	1	29		22	.266	.323
Heinie Peitz	C71,P2		77	266	35	78	44	11	7	1	18		3	.293	.398
Tom Corcoran	SS63,2B47		109	445	76	128	57	30	5	3	13		15	.288	.398
Bug Holliday	OF42,SS4,2B3,1B3		61	195	50	61	20	9	4	2	27		6	.313	.431
Pop Schriver	C53		61	178	29	54	30	12	4	1	19		3	.303	.433
Farmer Vaughn	1B35,C15		54	199	21	58	30	13	5	0	2		2	.291	.407
Bill Rhines	P41		41	107	4	17	8	1	1	0	9		0	.159	.187
Ted Breitenstein	P40		40	124	16	33	23	4	6	0	6		5	.266	.395
Frank Dwyer	P37		37	94	13	25	10	1	1	0	5		0	.266	.298
Red Ehret	P34		34	66	6	13	6	2	0	0	4		2	.197	.227
Bill Damman	P16		16	31	4	5	6	0	2	0	4		0	.161	.290
Stub Brown	P2		2	5	0	0	0	0	0	0	0		0	.000	.000
Buck Ewing	1B1		1	1	0	0	0	0	0	0	0		0	.000	.000
			134	4524	763	1311	617	219	69	22	380	218	194	.290	.383

PITCHERS		W	L	PCT	G	GS	CG	SH	SV	IP	H	BB	SO	ERA
Ted Breitenstein		23	12	.657	40	39	32	2	0	320	345	91	98	3.62
Bill Rhines		21	15	.583	41	32	26	1	0	289	311	86	65	4.08
Frank Dwyer		18	13	.581	37	31	22	0	0	247	315	56	41	3.78
Red Ehret		8	10	.444	34	19	11	0	2	184	256	47	43	4.78
Bill Damman		6	4	.600	16	11	7	1	0	95	122	37	21	4.74
Stub Brown		0	1	.000	2	1	1	0	0	13	17	8	2	4.15
Heinie Peitz		0	1	.000	2	1	1	0	0	8	9	4	0	7.88
		76	56	.576	134	134	100	4	2	1157	1375	329	270	4.09

1897 NATIONAL LEAGUE

CLEVELAND Spiders
69-62　.527　-23.5　5th　Patsy Tebeau

BATTERS	POS/GAMES		GP	AB	R	H	BI	2B	3B	HR	BB	SO	SB	BA	SA
Patsy Tebeau	1B92,2B18,3B2,SS1		109	412	62	110	59	15	9	0	30		11	.267	.347
Cupid Childs	2B114		114	444	105	150	61	15	9	1	74		25	.338	.419
Ed McKean	SS125		125	523	83	143	78	21	14	2	40		15	.273	.379
Bobby Wallace	3B130,OF1		130	516	99	173	112	33	21	4	48		14	.335	.504
Louis Sockalexis	OF66		66	278	43	94	42	9	8	3	18		16	.338	.460
Jack O'Connor	OF52,1B36,C13		103	397	49	115	69	21	4	2	26		20	.290	.378
Jesse Burkett	OF127		127	517	129	198	60	28	7	2	76		28	.383	.476
Chief Zimmer	C80		80	294	50	93	40	22	3	0	25		8	.316	.412
Cy Young	P46,1B2		48	153	14	34	19	4	3	0	2		4	.222	.288
Ollie Pickering	OF45,2B1	(2-2)	46	182	33	64	22	5	2	1	11		18	.352	.418
Sport McAllister	OF28,SS4,P4,1B3,C2,2B1		43	137	23	30	11	5	1	0	12		3	.219	.270
Lou Criger	C37,1B2		39	138	15	31	22	4	1	0	23		5	.225	.268
Zeke Wilson	P34,OF2,1B1		37	116	16	26	9	0	1	0	8		3	.224	.241
Henry Blake	OF32		32	117	17	30	15	3	1	1	12		5	.256	.325
Jack Powell	P27,OF1		28	97	10	20	12	1	0	0	6		0	.206	.216
Jimmy McAleer	OF24		24	91	6	20	10	2	0	0	7		4	.220	.242
Nig Cuppy	P19		21	55	5	8	3	0	1	0	5		0	.145	.182
Mike McDermott	P9	(1-2)	9	25	0	8	5	0	1	0	0		0	.320	.400
Ira Belden	OF8		8	30	5	8	4	0	2	0	2		0	.267	.400
Henry Clarke	P5,OF2		7	25	3	7	3	0	0	0	2		0	.280	.280
Dale Gear	OF6		7	24	3	4	2	1	0	0	3		2	.167	.208
Fred Cooke	OF5		5	17	2	5	3	2	0	0	3		0	.294	.412
Charlie Brown	P4		4	11	1	3	1	1	0	0	0		0	.273	.364
John Pappalau	P2		2	5	0	0	1	0	0	0	2		0	.000	.000
			132	4604	773	1374	663	192	88	16	435	344	181	.298	.389

PITCHERS			W	L	PCT	G	GS	CG	SH	SV	IP	H	BB	SO	ERA
Cy Young			21	19	.525	46	38	35	2	0	334	391	49	88	3.80
Zeke Wilson			16	11	.593	34	30	26	1	0	264	323	83	69	4.16
Jack Powell			15	10	.600	27	26	24	2	0	225	245	62	61	3.16
Nig Cuppy			10	6	.625	19	17	13	1	0	139	150	26	23	3.17
Mike McDermott		(1-2)	4	5	.444	9	7	4	0	0	62	75	25	12	4.50
Sport McAllister			1	2	.333	4	3	3	0	0	28	29	9	10	4.50
Charlie Brown			1	2	.333	4	4	2	0	0	24	30	17	8	7.77
John Pappalau			0	1	.000	2	1	1	0	0	12	22	6	3	10.50
Henry Clarke			0	4	.000	5	4	3	0	0	31	32	12	3	6.16
			69	62	.527	132	130	111	6	0	1119	1297	289	277	3.95

BROOKLYN Bridegrooms
61-71　.462　-32　6th (tie)　Billy Barnie

BATTERS	POS/GAMES	GP	AB	R	H	BI	2B	3B	HR	BB	SO	SB	BA	SA
Candy LaChance	1B126	126	520	86	160	90	28	16	4	15		26	.308	.446
George Shoch	2B68,SS13,OF4	85	284	42	79	38	9	2	0	49		6	.278	.324
Germany Smith	SS112	112	428	47	86	29	17	3	0	14		1	.201	.255
Bill Shindle	3B134	134	542	83	154	105	32	6	4	35		23	.284	.387
Fielder Jones	OF135	135	548	134	172	49	15	10	1	61		48	.314	.383
Mike Griffin	OF134	134	534	136	169	56	25	11	2	81		16	.316	.416
John Anderson	OF115,1B3	117	492	93	160	85	28	12	4	17		29	.325	.455
John Grim	C77	80	290	26	72	25	10	1	0	1		3	.248	.290
Broadway Smith	C43,OF18,1B6	66	237	36	71	39	13	1	1	4		12	.300	.376
Jimmy Canavan	2B63	63	240	25	52	34	9	3	2	26		9	.217	.304
Brickyard Kennedy	P44	45	147	10	40	18	4	3	1	3		0	.272	.361
Harley Payne	P40,OF1	41	110	13	26	11	0	1	0	8		0	.236	.255
Jack Dunn	P25,2B4,OF3,3B3,SS1	36	131	20	29	17	4	0	0	4		2	.221	.252
Buster Burrell	C27,1B4	33	103	15	25	18	2	0	2	10		1	.243	.320
Chauncey Fisher	P20	20	59	7	12	8	0	1	0	6		0	.203	.237
Dan Daub	P19	19	49	11	11	4	3	0	0	9		2	.224	.286
Jimmy Sheckard	SS11,OF2	13	49	12	14	14	3	2	3	6		5	.286	.612
Pat Hanafin	OF3,2B2	10	20	4	5	2	0	0	0	1		4	.250	.250
Sadie McMahon	P9	9	25	2	5	2	0	0	0	1		0	.200	.200
John Brown	P1	1	2	0	1	0	0	0	0	0		0	.500	.500
		136	4810	802	1343	644	202	72	24	351	255	187	.279	.366

PITCHERS	W	L	PCT	G	GS	CG	SH	SV	IP	H	BB	SO	ERA
Brickyard Kennedy	18	20	.474	44	40	36	2	1	343	370	149	81	3.91
Jack Dunn	14	9	.609	25	21	21	0	0	217	251	66	26	4.57
Harley Payne	14	17	.452	40	38	30	1	0	280	350	71	86	4.63
Chauncey Fisher	9	7	.563	20	13	11	1	1	149	184	43	31	4.23

1897 NATIONAL LEAGUE

BROOKLYN (cont.)
Bridegrooms

PITCHERS		W	L	PCT	G	GS	CG	SH	SV	IP	H	BB	SO	ERA
Dan Daub		6	11	.353	19	16	11	0	0	138	180	48	19	6.08
John Brown		0	1	.000	1	1	0	0	0	5	7	4	0	7.20
Sadie McMahon		0	6	.000	9	7	5	0	0	63	75	29	13	5.86
		61	71	.462	136	136	114	4	2	1195	1417	410	256	4.60

WASHINGTON
Senators

61-71 .462 -32 6th (tie) Schmelz - Brown

BATTERS	POS/GAMES		GP	AB	R	H	BI	2B	3B	HR	BB	SO	SB	BA	SA
Tommy Tucker	1B93	(2-2)	93	352	52	119	61	18	5	5	27		18	.338	.460
John O'Brien	2B86		86	320	37	78	45	12	2	3	19		6	.244	.322
Gene DeMontreville	SS99,2B33		133	566	92	193	93	27	8	3	21		30	.341	.433
Charlie Reilly	3B101		101	351	64	97	60	18	3	2	34		18	.276	.362
Charlie Abbey	OF80		80	300	52	78	34	14	8	3	27		9	.260	.390
Tom Brown	OF115		116	469	91	137	45	17	2	5	52		25	.292	.369
Kip Selbach	OF124		124	486	113	152	59	25	16	5	80		46	.313	.461
Deacon McGuire	C73,1B6		93	327	51	112	53	17	7	4	21		9	.343	.474
Zeke Wrigley	OF36,SS33,3B30,2B9		104	388	65	110	64	14	8	3	21		5	.284	.384
Duke Farrell	C63,1B1		78	261	41	84	53	9	6	0	17		8	.322	.402
Win Mercer	P44,C1		48	135	22	43	19	2	5	0	6		7	.319	.407
Doc McJames	P44		44	124	12	21	13	1	2	0	5		1	.169	.210
Jake Gettman	OF36		36	143	28	45	29	7	3	3	7		8	.315	.469
Ed Cartwright	1B33		33	124	19	29	15	4	0	0	8		9	.234	.266
Cy Swaim	P27		27	75	8	17	9	1	0	0	1		3	.227	.240
Silver King	P23		24	57	8	11	7	2	0	0	12		0	.193	.228
Tom Leahy	OF10,3B5,2B3,C1	(2-2)	19	52	12	20	7	2	1	0	9		6	.385	.462
Les German	P15,2B2,3B1		19	44	8	15	3	2	0	0	3		0	.341	.386
Elisha Norton	P4,OF3		7	18	0	5	2	2	1	0	0		0	.278	.500
Roger Bresnahan	P6,OF1		6	16	1	6	3	0	0	0	1		0	.375	.375
Bill Fox	SS2,2B2		4	14	4	4	0	0	0	0	1		0	.286	.286
Billy Lush	OF3		3	12	1	0	0	0	0	0	2		0	.000	.000
Al Maul	P1	(1-2)	1	1	0	0	0	0	0	0	0		0	.000	.000
Joe Stanley	P1		1	1	0	0	0	0	0	0	0		0	.000	.000
			135	4636	781	1376	674	194	77	36	374	348	208	.297	.395

PITCHERS		W	L	PCT	G	GS	CG	SH	SV	IP	H	BB	SO	ERA
Win Mercer		20	20	.500	46	42	34	3	3	333	397	103	88	3.24
Doc McJames		15	23	.395	44	39	33	3	2	324	361	137	156	3.61
Cy Swaim		10	11	.476	27	20	15	0	0	193	225	60	55	4.43
Silver King		6	9	.400	23	19	12	0	1	154	196	45	32	4.79
Roger Bresnahan		4	0	1.000	6	5	3	1	0	41	52	10	12	3.95
Les German		3	5	.375	15	5	4	0	0	84	117	33	2	5.59
Elisha Norton		2	1	.667	4	2	1	0	0	17	31	11	3	6.88
Al Maul	(1-2)	0	1	.000	1	1	0	0	0	2	4	1	0	9.00
Joe Stanley		0	0	----	1	0	0	0	0	1	0	0	0	0.00
		61	71	.462	135	133	102	7	6	1148	1383	400	348	4.01

PITTSBURGH
Pirates

60-71 .458 -32.5 8th Patsy Donovan

BATTERS	POS/GAMES		GP	AB	R	H	BI	2B	3B	HR	BB	SO	SB	BA	SA
Harry Davis	1B64,3B32,OF14,SS1		111	429	70	131	63	10	28	2	26		21	.305	.473
Dick Padden	2B134		134	517	84	146	58	16	10	2	38		18	.282	.364
Bones Ely	SS133		133	516	63	146	74	20	8	2	25		10	.283	.364
Jesse Hoffmeister	3B48		48	188	33	58	36	6	9	3	8		6	.309	.484
Patsy Donovan	OF120		120	479	82	154	57	16	7	0	25		34	.322	.384
Steve Brodie	OF100		100	370	47	108	53	7	12	2	25		11	.292	.392
Elmer Smith	OF123		123	467	99	145	54	19	17	6	70		25	.310	.463
Joe Sugden	C81,1B3		84	288	31	64	38	6	4	0	18		9	.222	.271
Bill Merritt	C53,1B7		62	209	21	55	26	6	1	1	9		2	.263	.316
Jesse Tannehill	OF33,P21		56	184	22	49	22	8	2	0	18		4	.266	.332
Jim Donnelly	3B44	(1-2)	44	161	22	31	14	4	0	0	16		14	.193	.217
Frank Killen	P42		42	129	16	32	7	4	0	1	17		2	.248	.302
Pink Hawley	P40		40	130	10	30	9	3	1	0	4		0	.231	.269
Denny Lyons	1B35,3B2		37	131	22	27	17	6	4	2	22		5	.206	.359
John Rothfuss	1B32		35	115	20	36	18	3	1	2	5		3	.313	.409
Jim Gardner	P14,OF6,3B6,2B1		27	76	13	12	8	2	1	1	9		3	.158	.250

1897 NATIONAL LEAGUE

PITTSBURGH (cont.)
Pirates

BATTERS	POS/GAMES		GP	AB	R	H	BI	2B	3B	HR	BB	SO	SB	BA	SA
Jim Hughey	P25		25	63	4	8	3	1	0	0	5		0	.127	.143
Tom Leahy	OF13,C6,3B6	(1-2)	24	92	10	24	12	3	3	0	7		3	.261	.359
Charles Hastings	P16		16	43	7	10	6	0	0	1	11		0	.233	.302
Charles Kuhns	3B1		1	3	0	0	0	0	0	0	1		0	.000	.000
			135	4590	676	1266	575	140	108	25	359	334	170	.276	.370

PITCHERS		W	L	PCT	G	GS	CG	SH	SV	IP	H	BB	SO	ERA
Pink Hawley		18	18	.500	40	39	33	0	0	311	362	94	88	4.80
Frank Killen		17	23	.425	42	41	38	1	0	337	417	76	99	4.46
Jesse Tannehill		9	9	.500	21	16	11	1	1	142	172	24	40	4.25
Jim Hughey		6	10	.375	25	17	13	0	0	149	193	45	38	5.06
Charles Hastings		5	4	.556	16	10	9	0	0	118	138	47	42	4.58
Jim Gardner		5	5	.500	14	11	8	0	0	95	115	32	35	5.19
		60	71	.458	135	134	112	2	2	1153	1397	318	342	4.67

CHICAGO
Colts

59-73 .447 -34 9th Cap Anson

BATTERS	POS/GAMES	GP	AB	R	H	BI	2B	3B	HR	BB	SO	SB	BA	SA
Cap Anson	1B103,C11	114	424	67	121	75	17	3	3	60		11	.285	.361
Jim Connor	2B76	77	285	40	83	38	10	5	3	24		10	.291	.393
Bill Dahlen	SS75	75	276	67	80	40	18	8	6	43		15	.290	.478
Bill Everett	3B83,OF8	92	379	63	119	39	14	7	5	36		26	.314	.427
Jimmy Ryan	OF136	136	520	103	156	85	33	17	5	50		27	.300	.458
Bill Lange	OF118	118	479	119	163	83	24	14	5	48		73	.340	.480
George Decker	OF75,1B38,2B1	111	428	72	124	63	12	7	5	24		11	.290	.386
Mal Kittredge	C79	79	262	25	53	30	5	5	1	22		9	.202	.271
Barry McCormick	3B56,SS46,2B1	101	419	87	112	55	8	10	2	33		44	.267	.348
Nixey Callahan	2B30,P23,OF21,SS18,3B2	94	360	60	105	47	18	6	3	10		12	.292	.400
Walter Thornton	OF59,P16	75	265	39	85	55	9	6	0	30		13	.321	.400
Tim Donahue	C55,SS2,1B1	58	188	28	45	21	7	3	0	9		3	.239	.309
Clark Griffith	P41,OF2,SS2,3B1,1B1	46	162	27	38	21	8	4	0	18		2	.235	.333
Fred Pfeffer	2B32	32	114	10	26	11	0	1	0	12		5	.228	.246
Dan Friend	P24,OF1	25	88	12	25	9	5	0	0	5		1	.284	.341
Buttons Briggs	P22	22	81	5	13	5	0	1	0	3		1	.160	.185
Roger Denzer	P12	12	39	4	6	1	1	0	0	1		0	.154	.179
Jim Korwan	P5	5	12	0	0	0	0	0	0	1		0	.000	.000
Tom Hernon	OF4	4	16	2	1	2	0	0	0	0		1	.063	.063
Dave Wright	P1	1	3	1	1	1	0	0	0	1		0	.333	.333
Adonis Terry	P1	1	3	1	0	0	0	0	0	0		0	.000	.000
		138	4803	832	1356	681	189	97	38	430	317	264	.282	.386

PITCHERS	W	L	PCT	G	GS	CG	SH	SV	IP	H	BB	SO	ERA
Clark Griffith	21	18	.538	41	38	38	1	1	344	410	86	102	3.72
Nixey Callahan	12	9	.571	23	22	21	1	0	190	221	55	52	4.03
Dan Friend	12	11	.522	24	24	23	0	0	203	244	86	58	4.52
Walter Thornton	6	7	.462	16	16	15	0	0	130	164	51	55	4.70
Buttons Briggs	4	17	.190	22	22	21	0	0	187	246	85	60	5.26
Roger Denzer	2	8	.200	12	10	8	0	0	95	125	34	17	5.13
Dave Wright	1	0	1.000	1	1	1	0	0	7	17	2	4	15.43
Jim Korwan	1	2	.333	5	4	3	0	0	34	47	28	12	5.82
Adonis Terry	0	1	.000	1	1	1	0	0	8	11	6	1	10.13
	59	73	.447	138	138	131	2	1	1197	1485	433	361	4.53

PHILADELPHIA
Phillies

55-77 .417 -38 10th George Stallings

BATTERS	POS/GAMES		GP	AB	R	H	BI	2B	3B	HR	BB	SO	SB	BA	SA
Nap Lajoie	1B108,OF19,3B2		127	545	107	197	127	40	23	9	15		20	.361	.569
Lave Cross	2B38,3B47,OF2,SS1		88	344	37	89	51	17	5	3	10		10	.259	.363
Sam Gillen	SS69,3B6		75	270	32	70	27	10	3	0	35		2	.259	.319
Billy Nash	3B79,SS19,2B4		104	337	45	87	39	20	2	0	60		4	.258	.329
Tommy Dowd	OF73,2B19	(2-2)	91	391	68	114	43	14	4	0	19		30	.292	.348
Duff Cooley	OF131,1B2		133	566	124	186	40	14	13	4	51		31	.329	.420
Ed Delahanty	OF129,1B1		129	530	109	200	96	40	15	5	60		26	.377	.538
Jack Clements	C49		55	185	18	44	36	4	2	6	12		3	.238	.378

1897 NATIONAL LEAGUE

PHILADELPHIA (cont.)
Phillies

BATTERS	POS/GAMES		GP	AB	R	H	BI	2B	3B	HR	BB	SO	SB	BA	SA
Phil Geier	OF45,2B37,SS6,3B2		92	316	51	88	35	6	2	1	56		19	.278	.320
Jack Boyle	C50,1B24		75	288	37	73	36	9	1	2	19		3	.253	.313
Al Orth	P36,OF6		53	152	26	50	17	7	4	1	3		5	.329	.447
Jack Taylor	P40,OF1		43	139	12	35	17	6	1	1	7		0	.252	.331
Frank Shugart	SS40		40	163	20	41	25	8	2	5	8		5	.252	.417
Ed McFarland	C37	(2-2)	38	130	18	29	16	3	5	1	14		2	.223	.346
Bill Hallman	2B31	(1-2)	31	126	16	33	15	3	0	0	8		1	.262	.286
Jack Fifield	P27		27	77	11	18	6	3	0	2	9		0	.234	.351
George Wheeler	P26		26	79	11	16	0	7	0	0	4		2	.203	.291
Davey Dunkle	P7		7	23	2	4	1	1	0	0	2		0	.174	.217
Youngy Johnson	P5		5	13	0	1	0	0	0	0	0		0	.077	.077
Bob Becker	P5		5	9	1	1	1	0	0	0	2		0	.111	.111
Kid Carsey	P4	(1-2)	4	13	1	3	1	0	0	0	0		0	.231	.231
Mike Grady	C3	(1-2)	4	13	1	2	0	0	0	0	1		0	.154	.154
Sam Thompson	OF3		3	13	2	3	3	0	1	0	1		0	.231	.385
Bert Miller	2B3		3	11	2	2	1	0	0	0	2		0	.182	.182
Ed Abbaticchio	2B3		3	10	0	3	0	0	0	0	1		0	.300	.300
George Stallings	OF1,1B1		2	9	1	2	0	1	0	0	0		0	.222	.333
Tully Sparks	P1		1	3	0	0	0	0	0	0	0		0	.000	.000
Tom Lipp	P1		1	1	0	1	0	0	0	0	0		0	1.000	1.000
			134	4756	752	1392	633	213	83	40	399	299	163	.293	.398

PITCHERS			W	L	PCT	G	GS	CG	SH	SV	IP	H	BB	SO	ERA
Jack Taylor			16	20	.444	40	37	35	2	2	317	376	76	88	4.23
Al Orth			14	19	.424	36	34	29	2	0	282	349	82	64	4.62
George Wheeler			11	10	.524	26	19	17	0	0	191	229	62	35	3.96
Davey Dunkle			5	2	.714	7	7	7	0	0	62	72	23	9	3.48
Jack Fifield			5	18	.217	27	26	21	0	0	211	263	80	38	5.51
Kid Carsey		(1-2)	2	1	.667	4	4	2	0	0	28	35	16	1	5.14
Youngy Johnson			1	2	.333	5	2	1	0	0	29	39	12	7	4.66
Tully Sparks			0	1	.000	1	1	1	0	0	8	12	4	0	10.13
Tom Lipp			0	1	.000	1	1	0	0	0	3	8	2	1	15.00
Bob Becker			0	2	.000	5	2	2	0	0	24	32	7	10	5.63
			55	77	.417	134	133	115	4	2	1155	1415	364	253	4.60

LOUISVILLE
Colonels

52-78   .400   -40   11th   Rogers - Clarke

BATTERS	POS/GAMES		GP	AB	R	H	BI	2B	3B	HR	BB	SO	SB	BA	SA
Perry Werden	1B131		131	506	76	153	83	21	14	5	40		14	.302	.429
Jim Rogers	2B39,1B3		41	150	22	22	22	3	2	2	22		4	.147	.233
General Stafford	SS103,OF7,3B1	(2-2)	111	432	68	120	53	16	5	7	31		14	.278	.378
Bill Clingman	3B113		113	395	59	90	47	14	7	2	37		14	.228	.314
Tom McCreery	OF89	(1-2)	89	338	55	96	40	5	6	4	38		13	.284	.370
Ollie Pickering	OF63	(1-2)	63	246	34	62	20	5	2	1	25		20	.252	.301
Fred Clarke	OF127		128	518	120	202	67	30	13	6	45		57	.390	.533
Bill Wilson	C103,3B1		105	381	43	81	41	12	4	1	18		9	.213	.273
Charles Dexter	OF32,C23,3B14,SS2		76	257	43	72	46	12	5	2	21		12	.280	.389
Honus Wagner	OF52,2B9		61	237	37	80	39	17	4	2	15		19	.338	.468
Abbie Johnson	2B33,SS12		48	161	16	39	23	6	1	0	13		2	.242	.292
Joe Dolan	2B18,SS18		36	133	10	28	7	2	2	0	8		6	.211	.256
Chick Fraser	P35,OF1		36	112	10	18	11	1	0	2	10		2	.161	.223
Bill Nance	OF35		35	120	25	29	17	5	3	3	20		3	.242	.408
Bert Cunningham	P29,OF2		31	93	13	22	10	0	1	2	1		1	.237	.323
Still Bill Hill	P27		27	74	5	7	4	0	1	0	4		1	.095	.122
Bill Magee	P22		22	62	4	13	9	1	0	0	4		0	.210	.226
Heinie Smith	2B21		21	76	7	20	7	3	0	1	3		1	.263	.342
Major Hach	2B9,3B7		16	51	5	11	3	2	0	0	5		1	.216	.255
Dick Butler	C10		10	38	3	7	2	0	0	0	0		1	.184	.184
George Hemming	P9,1B1		10	28	5	5	2	1	0	0	2		0	.179	.214
LeRoy Evans	P9	(2-2)	9	23	1	3	3	0	0	0	2		0	.130	.130
Dad Clarke	P7	(2-2)	7	22	0	5	2	0	0	0	0		0	.227	.227
Bill Clark	2B3,3B1		4	16	2	3	2	0	0	0	1		1	.188	.188
Henry Dowling	P4		4	10	1	2	0	1	0	0	0		0	.200	.300
Burt Miller	P4		4	6	0	1	0	0	0	0	0		0	.167	.167
Art Herman	P3		3	6	1	2	1	1	0	0	3		0	.333	.500
Frank Martin	2B2		2	8	1	2	0	0	0	0	0		0	.250	.250
Rube Waddell	P2		2	6	0	0	0	0	0	0	0		0	.000	.000
Jim Jones	P1		2	4	2	1	0	1	0	0	1		0	.250	.250
Ducky Holmes	SS1	(1-2)	2	4	0	0	0	0	0	0	1		0	.000	.000

1897 NATIONAL LEAGUE

LOUISVILLE (cont.)
Colonels

BATTERS	POS/GAMES		GP	AB	R	H	BI	2B	3B	HR	BB	SO	SB	BA	SA
Tom Delahanty	2B1		1	4	1	1	2	1	0	0	0		0	.250	.500
Ossie Schreckengost	C1		1	3	0	0	0	0	0	0	0		0	.000	.000
			134	4520	669	1197	563	160	70	40	370	453	195	.265	.358

PITCHERS			W	L	PCT	G	GS	CG	SH	SV	IP	H	BB	SO	ERA
Chick Fraser			15	19	.441	35	34	32	0	0	286	332	133	70	4.09
Bert Cunningham			14	13	.519	29	27	25	0	0	235	286	72	49	4.14
Still Bill Hill			7	17	.292	27	26	20	1	0	199	209	69	55	3.62
LeRoy Evans		(2-2)	5	4	.556	9	8	6	0	0	59	66	24	20	4.10
Bill Magee			4	12	.250	22	16	13	1	0	155	186	99	44	5.39
George Hemming			3	4	.429	9	8	7	0	0	67	80	25	7	5.10
Dad Clarke		(2-2)	2	4	.333	7	6	6	0	0	55	74	10	7	3.95
Henry Dowling			1	2	.333	4	4	2	0	0	26	39	8	3	5.88
Burt Miller			0	1	.000	4	1	1	0	0	17	32	3	3	7.94
Art Herman			0	1	.000	3	2	1	0	0	18	23	5	4	4.00
Rube Waddell			0	1	.000	2	1	1	0	0	14	17	6	5	3.21
Jim Jones			0	0	----	1	0	0	0	0	7	19	5	0	18.90
			52	78	.400	134	133	114	2	0	1138	1363	459	267	4.42

ST. LOUIS
Browns

29-102 .221 -63.5 12th Dowd - Nicol - Hallman - Von der Ahe

BATTERS	POS/GAMES		GP	AB	R	H	BI	2B	3B	HR	BB	SO	SB	BA	SA
Mike Grady	1B83,OF1	(2-2)	83	322	48	90	45	11	3	7	26		7	.280	.398
Bill Hallman	2B77,1B3	(2-2)	79	298	31	66	26	6	2	0	24		12	.221	.255
Monte Cross	SS131		131	462	59	132	55	17	11	4	62		38	.286	.396
Fred Hartman	3B124		124	516	67	158	67	21	8	2	26		18	.306	.390
Tuck Turner	OF102		103	416	58	121	41	17	12	2	35		8	.291	.404
Dick Harley	OF89		89	330	43	96	35	6	4	3	36		23	.291	.361
Bud Lally	OF84,1B3		87	355	56	99	42	15	5	2	9		12	.279	.366
Klondike Douglass	C61,OF43,1B17,3B7,SS1		125	516	77	170	50	15	3	6	52		12	.329	.405
John Houseman	2B41,OF33,SS5,3B3		80	278	34	68	21	6	6	0	28		16	.245	.309
Morg Murphy	C53,1B8		62	207	13	35	12	2	0	0	6		1	.169	.179
Red Donahue	P46,OF2,1B1		49	155	11	33	14	7	2	1	4		1	.213	.303
Bill Hart	P39,OF6,1B1		46	156	14	39	14	1	2	2	1		4	.250	.321
Tommy Dowd	OF30,2B5	(1-2)	35	145	25	38	9	9	1	0	6		11	.262	.338
Ed McFarland	C23,1B3,OF3,2B1	(1-2)	31	107	14	35	17	5	2	1	8		2	.327	.439
Roger Connor	1B22		22	83	13	19	12	3	1	1	13		3	.229	.325
Bill Kissinger	P7,OF7		14	39	7	13	6	3	2	0	3		0	.333	.513
Kid Carsey	P12	(2-2)	13	43	2	13	5	2	2	0	1		1	.302	.442
Lou Bierbauer	2B12		12	46	1	10	1	0	0	0	0		2	.217	.217
Percy Coleman	P12		12	28	2	6	3	0	0	0	1		0	.214	.214
Willie Sudhoff	P11		11	42	7	10	3	1	0	0	1		0	.238	.262
Duke Esper	P8		8	25	2	8	3	0	0	0	1		0	.320	.320
Bill Hutchinson	P6		6	18	1	5	0	0	1	0	1		0	.278	.389
Con Lucid	P6		6	17	2	3	1	0	0	0	4		0	.176	.176
Mike McDermott	P4	(2-2)	4	9	0	2	0	1	0	0	0		0	.222	.333
Ed Beecher	OF3		3	12	1	4	1	0	0	0	0		1	.333	.333
John Grimes	P3		3	7	0	2	1	0	0	0	3		0	.286	.286
LeRoy Evans	P3	(1-2)	3	3	0	0	0	0	0	0	3		0	.000	.000
Frank Huelsman	OF2		2	7	0	2	0	1	0	0	0		0	.286	.429
			132	4642	588	1277	484	149	67	31	354	314	172	.275	.356

PITCHERS			W	L	PCT	G	GS	CG	SH	SV	IP	H	BB	SO	ERA
Red Donahue			10	35	.222	46	42	38	1	1	348	484	106	64	6.13
Bill Hart			9	27	.250	39	38	31	0	0	295	395	148	67	6.26
Kid Carsey		(2-2)	3	8	.273	12	11	11	0	0	99	133	31	14	6.00
Willie Sudhoff			2	7	.222	11	9	9	0	0	93	126	21	19	4.47
Percy Coleman			1	2	.333	12	4	2	0	0	57	99	32	10	8.16
Mike McDermott		(2-2)	1	2	.333	4	4	1	0	0	21	23	19	3	9.28
Bill Hutchinson			1	4	.200	6	5	2	0	0	40	55	22	5	6.07
Con Lucid			1	5	.167	6	6	5	0	0	49	66	26	4	3.67
Duke Esper			1	6	.143	8	8	7	0	0	61	95	12	8	5.28
John Grimes			0	2	.000	3	1	1	0	0	20	24	8	4	5.95
Bill Kissinger			0	4	.000	7	4	2	0	0	31	51	15	5	11.49
LeRoy Evans		(1-2)	0	0	----	3	0	0	0	0	13	33	13	4	9.24
			29	102	.221	12	132	109	1	1	1127	1584	453	207	6.21

1898 NATIONAL LEAGUE

Willie Keeler

One of the most feared hitters during the 1890s was a man who stood five feet, four inches, and weighed 140 pounds. There were other players who could hit more home runs, steal more bases, knock in more runs, but none could hit better than our modestly sized hero. This man posted a higher batting average (.387) than any other player in the decade. His name was Willie Keeler.

Keeler was born in Brooklyn during the years of the National Association. After playing sporadically for Brooklyn and New York in 1892 and 1893, Keeler was acquired by Ned Hanlon for his Baltimore Orioles in 1894. Hanlon proved himself a genius as Keeler ripped off five consecutive seasons of hitting over .370. In two of those seasons, Willie Keeler won the batting title. It was the 1897 season that saw him at his peak, and that earned him adulation and fame. Keeler spread-eagled the batting race by finishing at .424, aided by a 44-game hitting streak.

Willie Keeler's batting style was unique. His stance was awkward, he used the lightest bat in the league, yet he poked and slapped the ball past his startled opponents. His superb bat control and his ability to foul off balls indefinitely, led directly to the rule change of a bunted foul on two strikes being out. He never hit the ball with great power, and his few extra base hits were earned by his speed. Out of Keeler's almost 3,000 hits, more than 85 percent were singles. To sum up his batting technique, Keeler simply said "I hit them where they ain't."

In 1898, Boston won the pennant again. The big guns for the Beaneaters were Jimmy Collins (.328), Billy Hamilton (.369), and Fred Tenney (.328). Collins also won the home run title with 15. Pitcher Kid Nichols once again had a superb year, winning a league best 31.

The Baltimore Orioles once again finished second. They were led by their most diminutive players Willie Keeler and John McGraw. Keeler won his second batting title with a mark of .385, while McGraw batted .342. Gene DeMontreville (.328) and Hugh Jennings (.328) also contributed.

Cincinnati returned to third, while Chicago moved up to fourth. Cincinnati had the services of Elmer Smith (.342) and 27-game winner Pink Hawley, while Chicago was paced by Jimmy Ryan (.323), Bill Lange (.319), and Bill Everett (.319). Pitcher Clark Griffith posted the best earned run average of 1.88.

Cleveland and Philadelphia finished in the next two slots. Cleveland used their stellar duo of Jesse Burkett (.341) and Cy Young (25-13) to achieve fifth, while Philadelphia used Ed Delahanty (.334), and Napolean Lajoie (.324) to achieve sixth.

New York and Pittsburgh finished next in seventh and eighth. New York was led by George Van Haltren (.312) and strikeout champion Cy Seymour (239), while Pittsburgh was led by Patsy Donovan (.302) and Jesse Tannehill's 25 wins.

The last four spots were occupied by Louisville, Brooklyn, Washington, and St. Louis. Their players of note included Fred Clarke (.307) and Dummy Hoy (.304) of Louisville; Fielder Jones (.304) of Brooklyn; John Anderson (.305), Heinie Reitz (.303), and Kip Selbach (.303) of Washington; and Lave Cross (.317) of St. Louis.

There was no great clamor for playing the Temple Cup series after the 1898 season, so it was not played. Its anti-climactic nature led to a lack of fan interest, and the trophy was quietly returned to its owner. People just could not get used to seeing the second best team declared champion, as happened in three of the four Temple Cup series.

After the 1898 season, Willie Keeler played another dozen years in the majors making stops in Brooklyn and in New York. He finished with a batting average of .341, one of the top dozen of all time. And when the Baseball Hall of Fame opened its doors in 1939, Willie Keeler took his rightful place among the greats who played the game.

1898 NATIONAL LEAGUE

BOSTON Beaneaters — 102-47 .685 — 1st — Frank Selee

BATTERS	POS/GAMES		GP	AB	R	H	BI	2B	3B	HR	BB	SO	SB	BA	SA
Fred Tenney	1B117,C1		117	488	106	160	62	25	5	0	33		23	.328	.400
Bobby Lowe	2B145,SS2		147	559	65	152	94	11	7	4	29		12	.272	.338
Germany Long	SS142,2B2		144	589	99	156	99	21	10	6	39		20	.265	.365
Jimmy Collins	3B152		152	597	107	196	111	35	5	15	40		12	.328	.479
Chick Stahl	OF125		125	467	72	144	52	21	8	3	46		6	.308	.407
Billy Hamilton	OF110		110	417	110	154	50	16	5	3	87		54	.369	.453
Hugh Duffy	OF152,3B1,1B1,C1		152	568	97	169	108	13	3	8	59		29	.298	.373
Marty Bergen	C117,1B2		120	446	62	125	60	16	5	3	13		9	.280	.359
George Yeager	C37,1B17,OF9,SS2		68	221	37	59	24	13	1	3	16		1	.267	.376
Kid Nichols	P50,1B1		51	158	26	38	23	3	3	2	4		0	.241	.335
Fred Klobedanz	P35,1B6,OF2		43	127	12	27	15	2	1	3	1		0	.213	.315
Ted Lewis	P41,2B1		42	131	17	37	18	6	0	0	6		0	.282	.328
Vic Willis	P41		41	117	9	17	6	0	0	0	11		0	.145	.145
Jack Stivetts	OF14,1B10,SS4,2B2,P2		41	111	16	28	16	1	1	2	10		1	.252	.333
General Stafford	OF35,1B1	(2-2)	37	123	21	32	8	2	0	1	4		3	.260	.301
Piano Legs Hickman	OF7,P6,1B6		19	58	4	15	7	2	0	0	1		0	.259	.293
David Pickett	OF14		14	43	3	12	3	1	0	0	6		2	.279	.302
Bill Keister	SS4,2B4,OF1		10	30	5	5	4	2	0	0	0		0	.167	.233
Kitty Bransfield	C4,1B1		5	9	2	2	1	0	1	0	0		0	.272	.444
Stub Smith	SS3		3	10	1	1	0	0	0	0	0		0	.100	.100
Mike Sullivan	P3		3	3	0	1	0	0	0	0	0		0	.333	.333
Hi Ladd	OF1	(2-2)	1	4	1	1	0	0	0	0	0		0	.250	.250
			152	5276	872	1531	761	190	55	53	405	303	172	.290	.377

PITCHERS		W	L	PCT	G	GS	CG	SH	SV	IP	H	BB	SO	ERA
Kid Nichols		31	12	.721	50	42	40	5	4	388	316	85	138	2.13
Ted Lewis		26	8	.765	41	33	29	1	2	313	267	109	72	2.90
Vic Willis		25	13	.658	41	38	29	1	0	311	264	148	160	2.84
Fred Klobedanz		19	10	.655	35	33	25	0	0	271	281	99	51	3.89
Piano Legs Hickman		1	2	.333	6	3	3	1	2	33	22	13	9	2.18
Mike Sullivan		0	1	.000	3	2	0	0	0	12	19	9	1	12.00
Jack Stivetts		0	1	.000	2	1	1	0	0	12	17	7	1	8.25
		102	47	.685	152	152	127	9	8	1340	1186	470	432	2.98

BALTIMORE Orioles — 96-53 .644 -6 — 2nd — Ned Hanlon

BATTERS	POS/GAMES		GP	AB	R	H	BI	2B	3B	HR	BB	SO	SB	BA	SA
Dan McGann	1B145		145	535	99	161	106	18	8	5	53		33	.301	.393
Gene DeMontreville	2B123,SS28		151	567	93	186	86	19	2	0	52		49	.328	.369
Hugh Jennings	SS115,B27,OF1		143	534	135	175	87	25	11	1	78		28	.328	.421
John McGraw	3B137,OF3		143	515	143	176	53	8	10	0	112		43	.342	.396
Willie Keeler	OF128,3B1		129	561	126	216	44	7	2	1	31		28	.385	.410
Joe Kelley	OF122,3B2		124	464	71	149	110	18	15	2	56		24	.321	.438
Ducky Holmes	OF112	(2-2)	113	442	54	126	64	10	9	1	23		25	.285	.355
Wilbert Robinson	C77		79	289	29	80	38	12	2	0	16		3	.277	.332
Boileryard Clarke	C70,1B10		82	285	26	69	27	5	2	0	4		2	.242	.274
Jim Hughes	P38,OF15		52	164	23	37	20	7	4	2	12		0	.226	.354
Doc McJames	P45		45	149	12	27	14	7	1	0	5		2	.181	.242
Jake Stenzel	OF35	(1-2)	35	138	33	35	22	5	2	0	12		4	.254	.319
Jerry Nops	P33		33	91	11	20	8	1	2	0	10		0	.220	.275
Art Ball	3B15,SS14,2B2,OF1		32	81	7	15	8	2	0	0	7		2	.185	.210
Frank Kitson	P17,OF11		31	86	13	27	16	1	3	0	5		2	.314	.395
Al Maul	P28,OF1		29	93	21	19	10	3	2	0	16		1	.204	.280
Steve Brodie	OF23	(2-2)	23	98	12	30	19	3	2	0	5		3	.306	.378
Tom O'Brien	OF16	(1-2)	18	60	9	13	14	0	0	0	10		0	.217	.217
Joe Quinn	3B8,2B1,OF1	(1-2)	12	32	5	8	5	1	0	0	1		0	.250	.281
Bill Hoffer	P4,OF4	(1-2)	8	24	2	5	4	1	0	0	4		0	.208	.250
Frank Bowerman	C4	(1-2)	5	16	5	7	1	1	0	0	2		1	.438	.500
Mike Heydon	C3		3	9	2	1	1	0	0	0	2		0	.111	.111
Arlie Pond	P3		3	7	2	2	0	0	0	0	2		0	.286	.286
Henry Wilson	C1		1	2	0	0	0	0	0	0	1		0	.000	.000
			154	5242	933	1584	757	154	77	12	519	316	250	.302	.368

PITCHERS		W	L	PCT	G	GS	CG	SH	SV	IP	H	BB	SO	ERA
Doc McJames		27	15	.643	45	42	40	2	0	374	327	113	178	2.36
Jim Hughes		23	12	.657	38	35	31	5	0	301	268	100	81	3.20
Al Maul		20	7	.741	28	28	26	1	0	240	207	49	31	2.10
Jerry Nops		16	9	.640	33	29	23	2	0	235	241	78	91	3.56

1898 NATIONAL LEAGUE

BALTIMORE (cont.)
Orioles

PITCHERS		W	L	PCT	G	GS	CG	SH	SV	IP	H	BB	SO	ERA
Frank Kitson		8	5	.615	17	13	13	1	0	119	123	35	32	3.24
Arlie Pond		1	1	.500	3	2	1	1	0	20	8	9	4	0.45
Bill Hoffer	(1-2)	0	4	.000	4	4	4	0	0	34	62	16	5	7.34
		96	53	.644	154	153	138	12	0	1323	1236	400	422	2.90

CINCINNATI
Reds

92-60 .605 -11.5 3rd Buck Ewing

BATTERS	POS/GAMES	GP	AB	R	H	BI	2B	3B	HR	BB	SO	SB	BA	SA
Jake Beckley	1B118	118	459	86	135	72	20	12	4	28		6	.294	.416
Bid McPhee	2B130,OF3	133	486	72	121	60	26	9	1	66		21	.249	.346
Tom Corcoran	SS153	153	619	80	155	87	28	15	2	26		19	.250	.354
Charlie Irwin	3B136	136	501	77	120	55	14	5	3	31		18	.240	.305
Dusty Miller	OF152	152	586	99	175	90	24	12	3	38		32	.299	.396
Algie McBride	OF120	120	486	94	147	43	14	12	2	51		16	.302	.393
Elmer Smith	OF123,P1	123	486	79	166	66	21	10	1	69		20	.342	.432
Heinie Peitz	C101	105	330	49	90	43	15	5	1	35		9	.273	.358
Harry Steinfeldt	2B31,OF29,3B22,SS5,1B4	88	308	47	91	43	18	6	0	27		9	.295	.393
Farmer Vaughn	1B39,C33	78	275	35	84	46	12	4	1	11		4	.305	.389
Pink Hawley	P43	43	130	17	24	16	2	1	1	5		1	.185	.238
Ted Breitenstein	P39,OF2	41	121	16	26	17	2	1	0	16		0	.215	.248
Bob Wood	C29,OF1,1B1	39	109	14	30	16	6	0	0	9		1	.275	.330
Bill Damman	P35	35	82	14	16	7	0	4	0	10		0	.195	.293
Still Bill Hill	P33	33	98	10	13	3	1	0	0	5		1	.185	.238
Frank Dwyer	P31	31	85	11	12	5	1	1	0	7		1	.141	.176
Bug Holliday	OF28	30	106	21	25	7	2	1	0	14		5	.236	.274
Herm McFarland	OF17	19	64	10	18	11	1	3	0	7		3	.281	.391
Percy Coleman	P1	1	3	0	0	1	0	0	0	0		0	.000	.000
Jot Goar	P1	1	0	0	0	0	0	0	0	0		0	----	----
		157	5334	831	1448	688	207	101	19	455	300	166	.271	.359

PITCHERS	W	L	PCT	G	GS	CG	SH	SV	IP	H	BB	SO	ERA
Pink Hawley	27	11	.711	43	37	32	3	0	331	357	91	69	3.37
Ted Breitenstein	20	14	.588	39	37	32	3	0	316	313	123	68	3.41
Bill Damman	16	10	.615	35	22	16	2	2	225	277	67	51	3.61
Frank Dwyer	16	10	.615	31	28	24	0	0	240	257	42	29	3.04
Still Bill Hill	13	14	.481	33	32	26	2	0	262	261	119	75	3.98
Percy Coleman	0	1	.000	1	1	1	0	0	9	13	3	2	3.00
Jot Goar	0	0	----	1	0	0	0	0	2	4	1	0	22.50
Elmer Smith	0	0	----	1	0	0	0	0	1	2	3	0	18.00
	92	60	.605	157	157	131	10	2	1385	1484	449	294	3.50

CHICAGO
Orphans

85-65 .567 -17.5 4th Tom Burns

BATTERS	POS/GAMES	GP	AB	R	H	BI	2B	3B	HR	BB	SO	SB	BA	SA
Bill Everett	1B149	149	596	102	190	69	15	6	0	53		28	.319	.364
Jim Connor	2B138	138	505	51	114	67	9	9	0	42		11	.226	.279
Bill Dahlen	SS142	142	521	96	151	79	35	8	1	58		27	.290	.393
Barry McCormick	3B136,SS1,2B1	137	530	76	131	78	15	9	2	47		15	.247	.321
Sam Mertes	OF60,SS14,2B4,1B2	83	269	45	80	47	4	8	1	34		27	.297	.383
Bill Lange	OF111,1B2	113	442	79	141	69	16	11	5	36		22	.319	.439
Jimmy Ryan	OF144	144	572	122	185	79	32	13	4	73		29	.323	.446
Tim Donahue	C122	122	396	52	87	39	12	3	0	49		17	.220	.265
Walter Thornton	OF34,P28	62	210	34	62	14	5	2	0	22		8	.295	.338
Frank Chance	C33,OF17,1B3	53	147	32	41	14	4	3	1	7		7	.279	.367
Walt Woods	P27,OF11,2B6,SS3,3B3	48	154	16	27	8	1	0	0	4		3	.175	.182
Danny Green	OF47	47	188	26	59	27	4	3	4	7		12	.314	.431
Frank Isbell	OF28,P13,3B3,2B3,SS2	45	159	17	37	8	4	0	0	3		3	.233	.258
Nixey Callahan	P31,OF9,SS1,2B1,1B1	43	164	27	43	22	7	5	0	4		3	.262	.366
Clark Griffith	P38	38	122	15	20	15	2	3	0	13		1	.164	.230
Matt Kilroy	P13,OF12	26	96	20	22	10	4	1	0	13		0	.229	.292
Art Nichols	C14	14	42	7	12	6	1	0	0	4		6	.286	.310
Harry Wolverton	3B13	13	49	4	16	2	1	0	0	1		1	.327	.347
Jack Taylor	P5	5	15	4	3	2	2	0	0	3		0	.200	.333
Buttons Briggs	P4	4	14	2	6	1	1	0	0	0		0	.429	.500
Bill Phyle	P3	4	9	1	1	0	0	0	0	2		0	.111	.111

1898 NATIONAL LEAGUE

CHICAGO (cont.)
Orphans

BATTERS	POS/GAMES	GP	AB	R	H	BI	2B	3B	HR	BB	SO	SB	BA	SA
Dan Friend	P2	2	7	0	2	0	1	0	0	0		0	.286	.429
Henry Clarke	P1,OF1	2	4	0	1	0	0	0	0	1		0	.250	.250
John Katoll	P2	2	4	0	0	0	0	0	0	0		0	.000	.000
Frank Martin	2B1	1	4	0	0	0	0	0	0	0		0	.000	.000
		152	5219	828	1431	656	175	84	18	476	394	220	.274	.350

PITCHERS		W	L	PCT	G	GS	CG	SH	SV	IP	H	BB	SO	ERA
Clark Griffith		24	10	.706	38	38	36	4	0	326	305	64	97	1.88
Nixey Callahan		20	10	.667	31	31	30	2	0	274	267	71	73	2.46
Walter Thornton		13	10	.565	28	25	21	2	0	215	226	56	56	3.34
Walt Woods		9	13	.409	27	22	18	3	0	215	224	59	26	3.14
Matt Kilroy		6	7	.462	13	11	10	0	0	100	119	30	18	4.31
Jack Taylor		5	0	1.000	5	5	5	0	0	41	32	10	11	2.20
Frank Isbell		4	7	.364	13	9	7	0	0	81	86	42	16	3.56
Bill Phyle		2	1	.667	3	3	3	2	0	23	24	6	4	0.78
Henry Clarke		1	0	1.000	1	1	1	0	0	9	8	5	1	2.00
Buttons Briggs		1	3	.250	4	4	3	0	0	30	38	10	14	5.70
John Katoll		0	1	.000	2	1	1	0	0	11	8	1	3	0.82
Dan Friend		0	2	.000	2	2	2	0	0	17	20	10	4	5.29
		85	65	.567	152	152	137	13	0	1343	1357	364	323	2.83

CLEVELAND
Spiders

81-68 .544 -21 5th Patsy Tebeau

BATTERS	POS/GAMES	GP	AB	R	H	BI	2B	3B	HR	BB	SO	SB	BA	SA
Patsy Tebeau	1B91,2B34,SS7,3B3	131	477	53	123	63	4	1	53			5	.258	.304
Cupid Childs	2B110	110	413	90	119	31	9	4	1	69		9	.288	.337
Ed McKean	SS151	151	604	89	172	94	23	1	9	56		11	.285	.371
Bobby Wallace	3B141,2B13	154	593	81	160	99	25	13	3	63		7	.270	.371
Henry Blake	OF136,1B2	136	474	65	116	58	18	7	0	69		12	.245	.312
Jimmy McAleer	OF104,2B2	106	366	47	87	48	3	0	0	46		7	.238	.246
Jesse Burkett	OF150	150	624	114	213	42	18	9	0	69		19	.341	.399
Lou Criger	C82	84	287	43	80	32	13	4	1	40		2	.279	.362
Jack O'Connor	1B69,C48,OF15	131	478	50	119	56	17	4	1	26		8	.249	.308
Cy Young	P46	47	154	20	39	13	4	1	2	8		2	.253	.331
Jack Powell	P42	42	136	15	18	9	3	1	0	11		0	.132	.169
Zeke Wilson	P33,OF3	37	118	11	21	9	2	1	0	5		0	.178	.212
Louis Sockalexis	OF16	21	67	11	15	10	2	0	0	1		0	.224	.254
Chief Zimmer	C19	20	63	5	15	4	2	0	0	5		2	.238	.270
John Heidrick	OF19	19	76	10	23	8	2	2	0	3		3	.303	.382
Nig Cuppy	P18	18	48	2	5	0	0	0	0	3		1	.104	.104
Sport McAllister	P9,OF8	17	57	8	13	9	3	1	0	5		0	.228	.316
Fred Frank	OF17	17	53	3	11	3	1	1	0	4		1	.208	.264
Jim Burke	3B13	13	38	1	4	1	1	0	0	2		1	.105	.132
Ossie Schreckengost	C9	10	35	5	11	10	2	3	0	0		1	.314	.543
Cowboy Jones	P9	9	28	1	2	1	0	0	0	3		1	.071	.071
Ed Beecher	OF8	8	25	1	5	0	2	0	0	0		0	.200	.280
Chick Fraser	P6	(2-2)	6	16	2	4	2	1	0	0	0		1	.250	.313
Frank Bates	P4	4	9	2	1	1	0	0	0	3		0	.111	.111
George Kelb	P3	3	5	1	1	0	0	0	0	0		0	.200	.200
Peter McBride	P1	1	2	0	2	2	0	0	0	1		0	1.000	1.000
		156	5246	730	1379	605	162	56	18	545	306	93	.263	.325

PITCHERS		W	L	PCT	G	GS	CG	SH	SV	IP	H	BB	SO	ERA
Cy Young		25	13	.658	46	41	40	1	0	378	387	41	101	2.53
Jack Powell		23	15	.605	42	41	36	6	0	342	328	112	93	3.00
Zeke Wilson		13	18	.419	33	31	28	1	0	255	307	51	45	3.60
Nig Cuppy		9	8	.529	18	15	13	1	0	128	147	25	27	3.30
Cowboy Jones		4	4	.500	9	9	7	0	0	72	76	29	26	3.00
Sport McAllister		3	4	.429	9	7	6	0	0	65	73	23	9	4.55
Frank Bates		2	1	.667	4	4	4	0	0	29	30	11	5	3.10
Chick Fraser		(2-2)	2	3	.400	6	6	6	0	0	42	49	12	19	5.57
George Kelb		0	1	.000	3	1	1	0	0	16	23	1	8	4.41
Peter McBride		0	1	.000	1	1	1	0	0	7	9	4	6	6.43
		81	68	.544	156	156	142	9	0	1334	1429	309	339	3.20

1898 NATIONAL LEAGUE

PHILADELPHIA Phillies   78-71   .523   -24   6th   Stallings - Shettsline

BATTERS	POS/GAMES		GP	AB	R	H	BI	2B	3B	HR	BB	SO	SB	BA	SA
Klondike Douglass	1B146		146	582	105	150	48	26	4	2	55		18	.258	.326
Nap Lajoie	2B146,1B1		147	608	113	197	127	43	11	6	21		25	.324	.461
Monte Cross	SS149		149	525	68	135	50	25	5	1	55		20	.257	.330
Bill Lauder	3B97		97	361	42	95	67	14	7	2	19		6	.263	.357
Elmer Flick	OF133		134	453	84	137	81	16	13	8	86		23	.302	.448
Duff Cooley	OF149		149	629	123	196	55	24	12	4	48		17	.312	.407
Ed Delahanty	OF144		144	548	115	183	92	36	9	4	77		58	.334	.454
Ed McFarland	C121		121	429	65	121	71	21	5	3	44		4	.282	.375
Wiley Piatt	P39		41	122	19	32	9	2	1	0	6		0	.262	.295
Al Orth	P2,OF1		39	123	17	36	14	6	4	1	3		1	.293	.431
Red Donahue	P35		35	112	8	16	10	0	1	0	4		1	.143	.161
Ed Abbaticchio	3B20,2B4,OF1		25	92	9	21	14	4	0	0	7		4	.228	.272
Morg Murphy	C25	(2-2)	25	86	6	17	11	3	0	0	6		0	.198	.233
Jack Fifield	P21		21	64	5	7	4	1	1	0	5		1	.109	.156
Billy Nash	3B20		20	70	9	17	9	2	1	0	11		0	.243	.300
Dave Fultz	OF14,2B3,SS1		19	55	7	10	5	2	2	0	6		1	.182	.291
George Wheeler	P15		15	43	5	8	3	1	0	0	3		0	.186	.209
Sam Thompson	OF14		14	63	14	22	15	5	3	1	4		2	.349	.571
Kid Elberfield	3B14		14	38	1	9	7	4	0	0	5		0	.237	.342
Davey Dunkle	P12		12	28	2	6	1	1	0	0	1		0	.214	.250
Newt Fisher	C8,3B1		9	26	0	3	0	1	0	0	0		1	.115	.154
Bill Duggleby	P9		9	21	4	5	6	1	0	1	4		0	.238	.429
Ed Murphy	P7		7	14	0	5	3	0	0	0	0		0	.357	.357
Jack Boyle	1B4,C3		6	22	0	2	3	0	1	0	1		0	.091	.182
Bert Conn	P1		1	3	1	1	1	0	1	0	0		0	.333	1.000
Bob Becker	P1		1	1	0	0	0	0	0	0	1		0	.000	.000
			150	5118	822	1431	706	238	81	33	472	382	182	.280	.377

PITCHERS		W	L	PCT	G	GS	CG	SH	SV	IP	H	BB	SO	ERA
Wiley Piatt		24	14	.632	39	37	33	6	0	306	285	97	121	3.18
Red Donahue		16	17	.485	35	35	33	1	0	284	327	80	57	3.55
Al Orth		15	13	.536	32	28	25	1	0	250	290	53	52	3.02
Jack Fifield		11	9	.550	21	21	18	2	0	171	170	60	31	3.31
George Wheeler		6	8	.429	15	13	10	0	0	112	155	36	20	4.17
Ed Duggleby		3	3	.500	9	5	4	0	0	54	70	18	12	5.50
Ed Murphy		1	2	.667	7	3	2	0	0	30	41	10	8	5.10
Davey Dunkle		1	4	.200	12	7	4	0	0	68	83	38	21	6.98
Bert Conn		0	1	.000	1	1	0	0	0	7	13	2	3	6.43
Bob Becker		0	0	----	1	0	0	0	0	5	6	5	0	10.80
		78	71	.523	150	150	129	10	0	1288	1440	399	325	3.72

NEW YORK Giants   77-73   .513   -25.5   7th   Joyce - Anson

BATTERS	POS/GAMES		GP	AB	R	H	BI	2B	3B	HR	BB	SO	SB	BA	SA
Bill Joyce	1B130,3B14,2B2		145	508	91	131	91	20	9	10	88		34	.258	.392
Kid Gleason	2B144,SS6		150	570	78	126	62	8	5	0	39		21	.221	.253
George Davis	SS121		121	486	80	149	86	20	5	2	32		26	.307	.381
Fred Hartman	3B123		123	475	57	129	88	16	11	2	25		11	.272	.364
Jack Doyle	OF38,1B24,SS15,3B5,C2	(2-2)	82	297	42	84	43	15	3	1	12		14	.283	.364
George Van Haltren	OF156		156	654	129	204	68	28	16	2	59		36	.312	.413
Mike Tiernan	OF103		103	415	90	116	49	15	11	5	43		19	.280	.405
John Warner	C109,OF1		110	373	40	96	42	14	5	0	22		9	.257	.322
Mike Grady	C57,OF30,1B7,SS3		93	287	64	85	49	19	5	3	38		20	.296	.429
Cy Seymour	P45,OF35,2B1		80	297	41	82	23	5	2	4	9		8	.276	.347
Charles Gettig	OF21,P17,2B12,SS9		64	196	30	49	26	6	2	0	15		5	.250	.301
Amos Rusie	P37,OF1,1B1		41	138	23	29	8	2	4	0	1		2	.210	.283
Jouett Meekin	P38		38	129	16	27	12	5	1	0	9		0	.209	.264
Walt Wilmot	OF34		35	138	16	33	22	4	2	2	9		4	.239	.341
Tom McCreery	OF35	(1-2)	35	121	15	24	17	4	3	1	19		3	.198	.306
Pop Foster	OF21,3B10,SS2		32	112	10	30	9	6	1	0	0		0	.268	.339
Ed Doheny	P28		28	86	11	14	11	1	1	2	4		0	.163	.267
Bill Carrick	P5		5	18	0	3	2	1	0	0	1		0	.167	.222
Tacks Latimer	C4,OF2		5	17	1	5	1	1	0	0	0		0	.294	.353
John Puhl	3B2		2	9	1	2	1	0	0	0	0		0	.222	.222
Joe Regan	OF2		2	5	1	1	2	0	0	0	0		0	.200	.200
Ed Glenn	SS2	(2-2)	2	4	1	1	0	0	0	0	3		1	.250	.250
Jock Menefee	P1		1	5	0	0	0	0	0	0	0		0	.000	.000
Jack Gilbert	OF1	(2-2)	1	4	0	1	0	0	0	0	0		1	.250	.250

1898 NATIONAL LEAGUE

NEW YORK (cont.)
Giants

BATTERS	POS/GAMES	GP	AB	R	H	BI	2B	3B	HR	BB	SO	SB	BA	SA
Parke Wilson	OF1	1	4	0	0	0	0	0	0	0		0	.000	.000
Dave Zearfoss	C1	1	1	0	1	0	0	0	0	0		0	1.000	1.000
		157	5349	837	1422	712	190	86	34	428	372	214	.266	.353

PITCHERS		W	L	PCT	G	GS	CG	SH	SV	IP	H	BB	SO	ERA
Cy Seymour		25	19	.568	45	43	39	4	0	357	313	213	239	3.18
Amos Rusie		20	11	.645	37	36	33	4	1	300	288	103	114	3.03
Jouett Meekin		16	18	.471	38	37	34	1	0	320	329	108	82	3.77
Ed Doheny		7	19	.269	28	27	23	0	0	213	238	101	96	3.68
Charles Gettig		6	3	.667	17	8	7	0	0	115	141	39	14	3.83
Bill Carrick		3	1	.750	5	4	4	0	0	40	39	21	10	3.40
Jock Menefee		0	1	.000	1	1	1	0	0	9	11	2	3	4.82
		77	73	.513	157	156	141	9	1	1354	1359	587	558	3.44

PITTSBURGH
Pirates

72-76 .486 -29.5 8th Bill Watkins

BATTERS	POS/GAMES		GP	AB	R	H	RBI	2B	3B	HR	BB	SO	SB	BA	SA
Willie Clark	1B57		57	209	29	64	31	9	7	1	22		0	.306	.431
Dick Padden	2B128		128	463	61	119	43	7	6	2	35		11	.257	.311
Bones Ely	SS148		148	519	49	110	44	14	5	2	24		6	.212	.270
Bill Grey	3B137		137	528	56	121	67	17	5	0	28		5	.229	.280
Patsy Donovan	OF147		147	610	112	184	37	16	9	0	34		41	.302	.357
Tom O'Brien	OF69,1B21,3B8,2B7,SS4	(2-2)	107	413	53	107	45	10	8	1	25		13	.259	.329
John McCarthy	OF137		137	537	75	155	78	13	12	4	34		7	.289	.380
Pop Schriver	C95,1B1		98	315	25	72	32	15	3	0	23		0	.229	.295
Frank Bowerman	C59,1B9	(2-2)	69	241	17	66	29	6	3	0	7		4	.274	.324
Jesse Tannehill	P43,OF7		60	152	25	44	17	9	3	1	7		4	.289	.408
Harry Davis	1B52,OF6	(1-3)	58	222	31	65	24	9	13	1	12		7	.293	.464
Tom McCreery	OF51	(2-2)	53	190	33	59	20	5	7	2	26		3	.311	.442
Steve Brodie	OF42	(1-2)	42	156	15	41	21	5	0	0	6		3	.263	.295
Jim Gardner	P25,3B8,2B1		35	91	8	14	3	0	0	0	14		1	.231	.308
Bill Rhines	P31		31	100	7	15	5	1	1	0	6		0	.150	.180
Frank Killen	P23	(1-2)	24	65	6	17	4	1	0	0	6		0	.262	.277
Bill Eagan	2B17		19	61	14	20	5	2	3	0	8		1	.328	.459
Charles Hastings	P19		19	43	5	10	4	0	1	0	7		0	.233	.279
Bill Hart	P16		16	50	4	12	3	0	1	0	1		1	.240	.280
John Ganzel	1B12		15	45	5	6	2	0	0	0	4		0	.133	.133
Morg Murphy	C5	(1-2)	5	16	0	2	2	0	0	0	1		0	.125	.125
Fred Lake	1B3		5	13	1	1	1	0	0	0	2		0	.077	.077
Sam Leever	P5		5	12	2	3	1	0	0	0	1		0	.250	.250
Bill Hoffer	P4	(2-2)	4	11	0	1	0	0	1	0	0		0	.091	.273
Jack Cronin	P4		4	10	1	1	1	0	0	0	2		0	.100	.200
Zeke Rosebrough	P4		4	8	0	3	1	0	0	0	1		0	.375	.375
Joe Rickert	OF2		2	6	0	1	0	0	0	0	0		0	.167	.167
Hi Ladd	----	(2-2)	1	1	0	0	0	0	0	0	0		0	.000	.000
			152	5087	634	1313	520	140	88	14	336	343	107	.258	.328

PITCHERS		W	L	PCT	G	GS	CG	SH	SV	IP	H	BB	SO	ERA
Jesse Tannehill		25	13	.658	43	38	34	5	2	327	338	63	93	2.95
Bill Rhines		12	16	.429	31	29	27	2	0	258	289	61	48	3.52
Frank Killen	(1-2)	10	11	.476	23	23	17	0	0	178	201	41	48	3.75
Jim Gardner		10	13	.435	25	22	19	1	0	185	179	48	41	3.21
Bill Hart		5	9	.357	16	15	13	1	1	125	141	44	19	4.82
Charles Hastings		4	10	.286	19	13	12	0	0	137	142	52	40	3.41
Bill Hoffer	(2-2)	3	0	1.000	4	3	3	0	0	31	26	15	11	1.74
Jack Cronin		2	2	.500	4	4	2	1	0	28	35	8	9	3.54
Sam Leever		1	0	1.000	5	3	2	0	0	33	26	5	15	2.45
Zeke Rosebrough		0	2	.000	4	2	2	0	0	22	23	9	6	3.32
		72	76	.486	152	152	131	10	3	1324	1400	346	330	3.41

LOUISVILLE
Colonels

70-81 .464 -33 9th Fred Clarke

BATTERS	POS/GAMES	GP	AB	R	H	BI	2B	3B	HR	BB	SO	SB	BA	SA
Honus Wagner	1B75,3B65,2B10	151	588	80	176	105	29	3	10	31		27	.299	.410
Heinie Smith	2B33	35	121	14	23	13	4	0	0	6		6	.190	.223

1898 NATIONAL LEAGUE

LOUISVILLE (cont.)
Colonels

BATTERS	POS/GAMES		GP	AB	R	H	BI	2B	3B	HR	BB	SO	SB	BA	SA
Claude Ritchey	SS80,2B71		151	551	65	140	51	10	4	5	46		19	.254	.314
Bill Clingman	3B79,SS74,OF1,2B1		154	538	65	138	50	12	6	0	51		15	.257	.301
Charles Dexter	OF95,2B8,C7		112	421	76	132	66	13	5	1	26		44	.314	.375
Dummy Hoy	OF148		148	582	104	177	66	15	16	6	49		37	.304	.416
Fred Clarke	OF149		149	599	116	184	47	23	12	3	48		40	.307	.401
Mal Kittredge	C86		86	287	27	70	31	8	5	1	15		9	.244	.317
General Stafford	2B28,OF22,3B1	(1-2)	49	181	26	54	25	3	0	1	19		7	.298	.331
Bert Cunningham	P44		44	140	21	32	16	3	1	1	10		1	.229	.286
George Decker	1B32,OF6	(2-2)	42	148	27	44	19	4	3	0	9		9	.297	.365
Bill Magee	P38		38	111	10	14	5	1	0	0	2		2	.126	.135
Harry Davis	1B34,2B2,OF1	(2-3)	37	138	18	30	16	5	2	1	7		6	.217	.304
Henry Dowling	P36		36	107	9	21	9	4	4	0	6		1	.196	.308
Mike Powers	C22,1B6,OF1		34	99	13	27	19	4	3	1	5		1	.273	.404
Bill Wilson	C28,1B1		29	102	5	17	13	1	2	1	5		3	.167	.245
Chick Fraser	P26	(1-2)	26	78	8	13	3	0	2	0	6		2	.167	.218
Bill Nance	OF22		22	76	13	24	16	5	0	1	12		2	.316	.421
Topsy Hartsel	OF21		22	71	11	23	9	0	0	0	11		2	.324	.324
Cooney Snyder	C17		17	61	4	10	6	0	0	0	3		0	.164	.164
Red Ehret	P12		13	40	3	9	4	3	1	0	1		0	.225	.350
Nick Altrock	P11		11	29	4	7	2	0	0	0	2		1	.241	.241
Wally Taylor	3B7,2B1		9	24	2	6	2	1	0	0	1		1	.250	.292
Scoops Carey	1B8		8	32	1	6	1	1	1	0	1		0	.188	.281
Joshua Clarke	OF6		6	18	0	3	0	0	0	0	1		0	.167	.167
Tom Stouch	2B4		4	16	4	5	6	1	0	0	1		0	.313	.375
Frank Todd	P4		4	5	1	1	1	0	1	0	0		0	.200	.600
John Richter	3B3		3	13	1	2	0	0	0	0	0		0	.154	.154
Tommy Leach	3B3,2B1		3	10	0	1	0	0	0	0	0		0	.100	.100
Lou Mahaffey	P1		1	4	0	0	0	0	0	0	1		0	.000	.000
Dad Clarke	P1		1	3	0	0	0	0	0	0	0		0	.000	.000
			154	5193	728	1389	601	150	71	32	375	429	235	.267	.342

PITCHERS			W	L	PCT	G	GS	CG	SH	SV	IP	H	BB	SO	ERA
Bert Cunningham			28	15	.651	44	42	41	0	0	362	387	65	34	3.16
Bill Magee			16	15	.516	38	33	29	3	0	295	294	129	55	4.05
Henry Dowling			13	20	.394	36	32	30	0	0	286	284	120	84	4.16
Chick Fraser		(1-2)	7	17	.292	26	26	20	1	0	203	230	100	58	5.32
Nick Altrock			3	3	.500	11	7	6	0	0	70	89	21	13	4.50
Red Ehret			3	7	.300	12	10	9	0	0	89	130	20	20	5.76
Dad Clarke			0	1	.000	1	1	1	0	0	9	10	2	1	5.00
Lou Mahaffey			0	1	.000	1	1	1	0	0	9	10	5	1	3.00
Frank Todd			0	2	.000	4	2	0	0	0	11	23	8	5	13.91
			70	81	.464	154	154	137	4	0	1334	1457	470	271	4.24

BROOKLYN
Bridegrooms

54-91　　.372　　-46　　10th　　Barnie - Griffin - Ebbets

BATTERS	POS/GAMES		GP	AB	R	H	BI	2B	3B	HR	BB	SO	SB	BA	SA
Candy LaChance	1B74,SS48,OF13		136	526	62	130	65	23	7	5	31		23	.247	.346
Bill Hallman	2B124,3B10		134	509	57	124	63	10	7	2	29		9	.244	.303
George Magoon	SS93		93	343	35	77	39	7	0	1	30		7	.224	.254
Bill Shindle	3B120		120	466	50	105	41	10	3	1	10		3	.225	.266
Fielder Jones	OF144,SS2		146	596	89	181	69	15	9	1	46		36	.304	.364
Mike Griffin	OF134		134	537	88	161	40	18	6	2	60		15	.300	.367
Jimmy Sheckard	OF105,3B1		105	408	51	113	64	17	9	4	37		8	.277	.392
Jack Ryan	C84,3B4,1B1		87	301	39	57	24	11	4	0	15		5	.189	.252
Tommy Tucker	1B73	(1-2)	73	283	35	79	34	9	4	1	12		1	.279	.350
Broadway Smith	OF26,C20,3B2,2B2,1B1		52	199	25	52	23	6	5	0	3		7	.261	.342
John Grim	C52		52	178	17	50	11	5	1	0	8		1	.281	.320
Jack Dunn	P41,OF4,SS4,3B2		51	167	21	41	19	0	1	0	7		3	.246	.257
Joe Yeager	P36,OF4,SS2,2B1		43	134	12	23	15	5	1	0	7		1	.172	.224
Brickyard Kennedy	P40		40	135	15	34	13	7	2	0	3		2	.252	.333
John Anderson	OF22,1B2	(1,3-3)	25	90	12	22	10	5	4	0	6		2	.244	.389
Ralph Miller	P23,OF1		24	62	6	12	6	1	0	0	4		1	.194	.210
Tom Daly	2B23		23	73	11	24	11	3	1	0	14		6	.329	.397
Kit McKenna	P14		14	40	5	9	7	3	0	0	2		0	.225	.300
Butts Wagner	3B11	(2-2)	11	38	2	9	3	1	1	0	2		0	.237	.316
Ed Stein	P3		3	10	1	4	1	0	0	0	1		0	.400	.400
Harry Howell	P2		2	8	1	2	1	0	0	0	1		0	.250	.250
Welcome Gaston	P2		2	8	2	1	1	0	1	0	0		0	.125	.375
C.F. Hopper	P2		2	4	1	0	0	0	0	0	0		0	.000	.000

1898 NATIONAL LEAGUE

BROOKLYN (cont.)
Bridegrooms

BATTERS	POS/GAMES		GP	AB	R	H	BI	2B	3B	HR	BB	SO	SB	BA	SA
Harley Payne	P1		1	4	1	3	3	0	0	0	0		0	.750	.750
Elmer Horton	P1		1	4	0	1	0	0	0	0	0		0	.250	.250
F. C. Hansford	P1		1	3	0	0	0	0	0	0	0		0	.000	.000
			149	5126	638	1314	563	156	66	17	328	314	130	.256	.322

PITCHERS		W	L	PCT	G	GS	CG	SH	SV	IP	H	BB	SO	ERA
Jack Dunn		16	21	.432	41	37	31	0	0	323	352	82	66	3.60
Brickyard Kennedy		16	22	.421	40	39	38	0	0	339	360	123	73	3.23
Joe Yeager		12	22	.353	36	33	32	0	0	291	333	80	70	3.65
Ralph Miller		4	14	.222	23	21	16	0	0	152	161	86	43	5.34
Harry Howell		2	0	1.000	2	2	2	0	0	18	15	11	2	5.00
Kit McKenna		2	6	.250	14	9	7	0	0	101	118	57	27	5.63
Harley Payne		1	0	1.000	1	1	1	0	0	9	11	3	2	4.00
Welcome Gaston		1	1	.500	2	2	2	0	0	16	17	9	0	2.81
Elmer Horton		0	1	.000	1	1	1	0	0	9	16	6	0	10.00
Ed Stein		0	2	.000	3	2	2	0	0	23	39	9	6	5.48
C. F. Hopper		0	2	.000	2	2	2	0	0	11	14	5	5	4.91
F. C. Hansford		0	0	----	1	0	0	0	0	7	10	5	0	3.86
		54	91	.372	149	149	134	1	0	1299	1446	476	294	4.01

WASHINGTON
Senators

51-101   .336   -52.5   11th   Brown - Doyle - McGuire - Irwin

BATTERS	POS/GAMES		GP	AB	R	H	BI	2B	3B	HR	BB	SO	SB	BA	SA
Jack Doyle	1B38,2B5	(1-2)	43	177	26	54	26	2	2	2	7		9	.305	.373
Heinie Reitz	2B132		132	489	62	148	47	20	2	2	32		11	.303	.364
Zeke Wrigley	SS97,2B11,OF3,3B1		111	400	50	98	39	9	10	2	20		10	.245	.333
Jud Smith	3B47,SS10,1B7,2B1		66	234	33	71	28	7	5	3	22		11	.303	.415
Jake Gettman	OF139,1B3		142	567	75	157	47	16	5	5	29		32	.277	.349
John Anderson	OF93,1B17	(2-3)	110	430	70	131	71	28	18	9	23		18	.305	.516
Kip Selbach	OF131,SS1		132	515	88	156	60	28	11	3	64		25	.303	.417
Deacon McGuire	C93,1B37		131	489	59	131	57	18	3	1	24		10	.268	.323
Duke Farrell	C61,1B28		99	338	47	106	53	12	6	1	34		12	.314	.393
Win Mercer	P33,SS23,OF19,3B5,2B1		80	249	38	80	25	3	5	2	18		14	.321	.398
Butts Wagner	3B39,OF10,SS8,2B5	(1-2)	63	223	20	50	31	11	2	1	14		4	.224	.305
Gus Weyhing	P45,OF1		46	141	12	25	5	3	0	0	8		2	.177	.199
Wild Bill Donovan	OF20,P17,SS1,2B1		39	103	11	17	8	2	2	2	4		2	.165	.282
Bill Dineen	P29,OF2		32	80	10	8	3	0	1	0	9		1	.100	.125
Bert Myers	3B31		31	110	14	29	13	1	4	0	13		2	.264	.345
Buck Freeman	OF29		29	107	19	39	21	2	3	3	7		2	.364	.523
Doc Casey	3B22,SS4,C3		28	112	13	31	15	2	0	0	2		2	.192	.219
Frank Killen	P17,OF4	(2-2)	21	55	7	15	7	2	0	0	12		1	.273	.309
Charlie Carr	1B20		20	73	6	14	4	2	0	0	3		15	.192	.219
Frank Gatins	SS17		17	58	6	13	5	2	0	0	3		2	.224	.259
Tom Brown	OF15		16	55	8	9	2	1	0	0	5		3	.164	.182
Cy Swaim	P16		16	35	2	5	4	0	0	0	0		0	.143	.143
Tom Leahy	3B12,2B3		15	55	10	10	5	2	0	0	8		6	.182	.218
Bob McHale	OF9,SS1,1B1		11	33	5	6	7	2	0	0	1		1	.182	.242
Doc Amole	P7		7	20	4	2	0	0	0	0	1		0	.100	.100
LeRoy Evans	P7		7	19	2	1	2	0	0	0	2		0	.053	.053
Kirtley Baker	P6		6	18	3	5	3	0	1	0	3		0	.278	.389
Jim Field	1B5		5	21	1	2	0	0	0	0	0		0	.095	.095
Bill Eagle	OF4		4	13	0	4	2	1	0	0	0		0	.308	.308
Tom Kinslow	C3,1B1	(1-2)	3	9	0	1	0	0	0	0	0		0	.111	.111
Pop Williams	P2		2	8	3	3	0	1	0	0	0		0	.375	.500
Jack Gilbert	OF2	(1-2)	2	5	0	1	1	0	0	0	1		1	.200	.200
John Sutthof	P2		2	3	0	1	0	0	0	0	1		0	.333	.333
Jim McQuaid	OF1		1	4	0	0	0	0	0	0	0		0	.000	.000
Ed Glenn	SS1	(1-2)	1	4	0	0	0	0	0	0	0		0	.000	.000
Harry Davis	1B1	(3-3)	1	3	0	0	0	0	0	0	0		0	.000	.000
Charlie Weber	P1		1	2	0	0	0	0	0	0	0		0	.000	.000
			155	5257	704	1423	591	177	80	36	370	386	197	.271	.355

PITCHERS		W	L	PCT	G	GS	CG	SH	SV	IP	H	BB	SO	ERA
Gus Weyhing		15	26	.366	45	42	39	0	0	361	428	84	92	4.51
Win Mercer		12	18	.400	33	30	24	0	0	234	309	71	52	4.81
Bill Dineen		9	16	.360	29	27	22	0	0	218	238	88	83	4.00
Frank Killen	(2-2)	6	9	.400	17	16	15	0	0	128	149	29	43	3.58
LeRoy Evans		3	3	.500	7	6	4	0	0	51	50	25	11	3.38

1898 NATIONAL LEAGUE

WASHINGTON (cont.)
Senators

PITCHERS	W	L	PCT	G	GS	CG	SH	SV	IP	H	BB	SO	ERA
Cy Swaim	3	11	.214	16	13	9	0	1	101	119	28	30	4.26
Kirtley Baker	2	3	.400	6	5	4	0	0	47	56	18	7	3.06
Wild Bill Donovan	1	6	.143	17	7	6	0	0	88	88	69	36	4.30
Charlie Weber	0	1	.000	1	1	0	0	0	4	9	1	0	15.75
Pop Williams	0	2	.000	2	2	2	0	0	17	32	7	3	8.47
Doc Amole	0	6	.000	7	5	4	0	0	49	83	22	11	7.83
John Sutthof	0	0	----	2	1	0	0	0	8	16	8	3	12.96
	51	101	.336	155	155	129	0	1	1307	1577	450	371	4.52

ST. LOUIS
Browns

39-111   .260   -63.5   12th   Tim Hurst

BATTERS	POS/GAMES		GP	AB	R	H	BI	2B	3B	HR	BB	SO	SB	BA	SA
George Decker	1B75	(1-2)	76	286	26	74	45	10	0	1	20		4	.259	.304
Jack Crooks	2B66,3B3,SS2,OF1		72	225	33	52	20	4	2	1	40		3	.231	.280
Germany Smith	SS51		51	157	16	25	9	2	1	1	24		1	.159	.204
Lave Cross	3B149,SS2		151	602	71	191	79	28	8	3	28		14	.317	.405
Tommy Dowd	OF130,2B11		139	586	70	143	32	17	7	0	30		16	.244	.297
Jake Stenzel	OF108	(2-2)	108	404	64	114	33	15	11	1	41		21	.282	.381
Dick Harley	OF141		142	549	74	135	42	6	5	0	34		13	.246	.275
Jack Clements	C86		99	335	39	86	41	19	5	3	21		1	.257	.370
Joe Quinn	2B62,SS41,OF	(2-2)	103	375	35	94	36	10	5	0	24		13	.251	.304
Joe Sugden	C60,OF15,1B8		89	289	29	73	34	7	1	0	23		5	.253	.284
Tommy Tucker	1B72	(2-2)	72	252	18	60	20	7	2	0	18		1	.238	.282
Jack Taylor	P50,OF2		54	157	17	38	18	5	2	1	12		1	.242	.318
Suter Sullivan	SS23,OF10,2B6,1B1,P1		42	144	10	32	12	3	0	0	13		1	.222	.243
Willie Sudhoff	P41		41	120	5	19	4	2	1	0	5		0	.158	.192
Russ Hall	SS35,3B3,OF1		39	143	13	35	10	2	1	0	7		1	.245	.273
Kid Carsey	P20,2B10,OF8		38	105	8	21	10	0	1	1	10		3	.200	.248
Tuck Turner	OF34		35	141	20	28	7	8	0	0	14		1	.199	.255
Jim Hughey	P35		35	97	6	11	6	0	1	1	10		1	.113	.165
Ducky Holmes	OF23	(1-2)	23	101	9	24	0	1	1	0	2		4	.238	.267
Tom Kinslow	C14	(2-2)	14	53	5	15	4	2	1	0	1		0	.283	.358
Duke Esper	P10		11	27	1	10	5	0	0	0	1		0	.370	.370
Pete Daniels	P10		10	17	1	3	1	1	0	0	3		0	.176	.235
George Gilpatrick	P7		7	16	1	2	1	0	0	0	0		0	.125	.125
Lou Bierbauer	2B2,SS1,3B1		4	9	0	0	0	0	0	0	1		0	.000	.000
Harry Maupin	P2		2	7	0	3	1	0	0	0	0		0	.429	.429
Mike Mahoney	1B2		2	7	0	0	0	0	0	0	0		0	.000	.000
Jim Callahan	P2		2	4	0	0	0	0	0	0	0		0	.000	.000
Joe Gannon	P1		1	3	0	0	0	0	0	0	0		0	.000	.000
Tom Smith	P1		1	2	0	1	0	0	0	0	1		0	.500	.500
Jim Donnelly	3B1		1	1	0	1	0	0	0	0	0		0	1.000	1.000
			154	5214	571	1290	470	149	55	13	383	402	104	.247	.305

PITCHERS	W	L	PCT	G	GS	CG	SH	SV	IP	H	BB	SO	ERA
Jack Taylor	15	29	.341	50	47	42	0	1	397	465	83	89	3.90
Willie Sudhoff	11	27	.289	41	38	35	0	1	315	355	102	65	4.34
Jim Hughey	7	24	.226	35	33	31	0	0	284	325	71	74	3.93
Duke Esper	3	5	.375	10	8	6	0	0	65	86	22	14	5.98
Kid Carsey	2	12	.143	20	13	10	0	0	124	177	37	10	6.33
Pete Daniels	1	6	.143	10	6	3	0	0	55	62	14	13	3.62
Tom Smith	0	1	.000	1	1	1	0	0	9	9	5	1	2.00
Joe Gannon	0	1	.000	1	1	1	0	0	9	13	5	2	11.00
George Gilpatrick	0	2	.000	7	3	1	0	0	35	42	19	12	6.94
Harry Maupin	0	2	.000	2	2	2	0	0	18	22	3	3	5.50
Jim Callahan	0	2	.000	2	2	1	0	0	8	18	7	2	16.20
Suter Sullivan	0	0	----	1	0	0	0	0	6	10	4	3	1.50
	39	111	.260	154	154	133	0	2	1324	1584	372	288	4.53

1899 NATIONAL LEAGUE

Winners and Losers

During the decade of the 1890s, no concern was given to governing the twelve owners of the National League teams. As there was no commissioner to oversee their actions, the owners pretty much did as they wanted. To say the least, the results were not conducive to the betterment of the sport.

For example, by 1899, several of the owners owned parts of, or all of, more than one team. The two best examples of this dual ownership were Harry Vanderhorst who headed up the syndicate which owned both Baltimore and Brooklyn, and Frank Robison who owned both Cleveland and St. Louis. With nothing to prevent them, these two sets of owners compounded their conflict of interest by stockpiling all their good players on one team — leaving the dregs for the other.

Brooklyn had been a part of the National League since 1890, winning the pennant in their first year. Since that time, they had done little, dropping all the way to tenth place by 1898. Baltimore had a more storied past. This team had won three pennants in a row (1894–6), and had finished a close second the following two years. All this was to change in 1899. Vanderhorst felt he could earn more money in the larger New York market. And certainly a good team in that market would make more money than a poor one. With that in mind, nine of Baltimore's finest were "traded" to Brooklyn before and during the 1899 season, including Baltimore's two best pitchers (Hughes and McJames) as well as outfielders Willie Keeler and Joe Kelley. Manager Ned Hanlon also made the journey north.

The change was immediately felt. All four of the aforementioned players had their usual good years in 1899, which in turn lifted Brooklyn from tenth to first. Meanwhile, Baltimore fell from second to fourth.

Frank Robison did not meet with the same success. St. Louis had been the league's doormat since it rejoined the National League finishing no better than ninth, and in 1898, bringing up the rear in twelfth place. Cleveland, on the other hand, had been a successful team finishing second three times during the decade. For some reason, Robison felt he had a better chance for success in St. Louis, so he transferred 18 players from Cleveland to St. Louis either before or during the 1899 season. The players included Cleveland's best such as Jesse Burkett, Lave Cross, Cupid Childs and Cy Young.

The addition of these players raised St. Louis from last to fifth in 1899, adding 43 more wins than 1898. This could not offset the suffering of the Cleveland baseball club. Stripped of all their good players, the team managed only 20 wins out of 134 games in 1899. Things got so bad, Cleveland played the second half of their schedule on the road for the simple reason that nobody was coming to see them at home.

New additions Willie Keeler (.379), Joe Kelley (.325), and Jim Hughes (28-6) were the main influence behind Brooklyn's rise to the top. They finished eight games up on Boston, who were led by Fred Tenney (.347), Chick Stahl (.351), and earned run average champion Vic Willis (2.50).

Philadelphia rose several notches to third followed closely by Baltimore who landed in fourth. Philadelphia was paced by Ed Delahanty who won the batting (.410) and runs batted in (137) titles and by Nap Lajoie (.378). Baltimore was led by John McGraw's (.391) fine year and by Joe McGinnity's 28 wins.

Like Brooklyn, St. Louis rode the success of their influx of baseball talent to fifth place, one notch ahead of Cincinnati in sixth. Jesse Burkett of St. Louis hit a robust .396, while Cincinnati was topped by Jake Beckley (.333).

Pittsburgh and Chicago finished in seventh and eighth. Pittsburgh was led by Jim Williams (.355) and Ginger Beaumont (.352), while Chicago enjoyed the services of Bill Everett (.310).

Louisville, New York, and Washington finished in the next three spots. Louisville, enjoying their highest finish in eight years, was bolstered by Fred Clarke (.342) and by emerging star Honus Wagner (.336). New York was boosted by George Davis (.337), while Buck Freeman (.318) did the same for Washington. Freeman also swatted 25 home runs, the most since Ned Williamson's fluke total of 27 in 1884.

Dismal Cleveland finished in the cellar, a record-breaking 84 games behind the leaders. None of their pitchers won more than four games. The team suffered through a 24-game losing streak in August and September. After a win, Cleveland then proceeded to drop their last sixteen games of the season.

Big business was in control of baseball during the 1890s. And with it, came many cutthroat business practices. None of these practices had as profound an effect as the dual ownership issue. The lesson learned was that there always a price for success. For every Brooklyn, there was a Cleveland to go with it.

1899 NATIONAL LEAGUE

BROOKLYN Superbas   101-47   .682   1st   Ned Hanlon

BATTERS	POS/GAMES		GP	AB	R	H	BI	2B	3B	HR	BB	SO	SB	BA	SA
Dan McGann	1B61	(1-2)	63	214	49	52	32	11	4	2	21		16	.243	.360
Tom Daly	2B141		141	498	95	156	88	24	9	5	69		43	.313	.428
Bill Dahlen	SS110,3B11		121	428	87	121	76	22	7	4	67		29	.283	.395
Doc Casey	3B134	(2-2)	134	525	75	141	43	14	8	1	25		27	.269	.331
Willie Keeler	OF141		141	570	140	216	61	12	13	1	37		45	.379	.451
Fielder Jones	OF96		102	365	75	104	38	8	2	2	54		18	.285	.334
Joe Kelley	OF143		143	538	108	175	93	21	14	6	70		31	.325	.450
Duke Farrell	C78	(2-2)	80	254	40	76	55	10	7	2	35		6	.299	.417
John Anderson	OF76,1B41		117	439	65	118	92	18	7	4	27		25	.269	.369
Hugh Jennings	1B50,SS12,2B1	(1,3-3)	67	216	42	64	40	3	10	0	22		18	.296	.417
Deacon McGuire	C46	(2-2)	46	157	22	50	23	12	4	0	12		4	.318	.446
Jack Dunn	P41,SS1		43	122	21	30	16	2	1	0	3		3	.246	.279
Brickyard Kennedy	P40		40	109	14	27	8	5	3	0	7		1	.248	.349
Doc McJames	P37		37	112	8	19	6	4	1	0	2		1	.170	.223
Jim Hughes	P35		35	107	17	27	14	4	2	0	12		1	.252	.327
Joe Yeager	SS11,P10,OF1,3B1		23	47	12	9	4	0	1	0	6		0	.191	.234
Broadway Smith	C17	(1-2)	17	61	6	11	6	0	1	0	2		0	.180	.213
Zeke Wrigley	SS14,3B1	(2-2)	15	49	4	10	11	2	2	0	3		2	.204	.327
John Grim	C12		15	47	3	13	7	1	0	0	1		0	.277	.298
Erv Beck	2B6,SS2		8	24	2	4	2	2	0	0	0		0	.167	.250
Peter Cassidy	3B3,SS2	(1-2)	6	20	2	3	4	1	0	0	1		1	.150	.200
W. B. Donovan	P5		5	13	2	3	0	1	0	0	0		0	.231	.308
Al Maul	P4		4	11	2	3	0	0	0	0	1		0	.273	.273
Still Bill Hill	P2	(3-3)	2	5	1	3	2	0	1	0	0		0	.600	1.000
Bill Reidy	P2		2	3	0	0	0	0	0	0	0		0	.000	.000
Dan McFarlan	P1	(1-2)	1	2	0	0	0	0	0	0	0		0	.000	.000
Welcome Gaston	P1		1	1	0	1	2	1	0	0	0		0	1.000	2.000
			150	4937	892	1436	723	178	97	27	477	263	271	.291	.382

PITCHERS			W	L	PCT	G	GS	CG	SH	SV	IP	H	BB	SO	ERA
Jim Hughes			28	6	.824	35	35	30	3	0	292	250	119	99	2.68
Jack Dunn			23	13	.639	41	34	29	2	2	299	323	86	48	3.70
Brickyard Kennedy			22	9	.710	40	33	27	2	2	277	297	86	55	2.79
Doc McJames			19	15	.559	37	34	27	1	1	275	295	122	105	3.50
Al Maul			2	0	1.000	4	4	2	0	0	26	35	6	2	4.50
Joe Yeager			2	2	.500	10	4	2	1	1	48	56	16	6	4.72
Still Bill Hill		(3-3)	1	0	1.000	2	1	1	0	1	11	11	6	3	0.82
Bill Reidy			1	0	1.000	2	1	1	0	1	7	9	2	2	2.57
W. B. Donovan			1	2	.333	5	2	2	0	1	25	35	13	11	4.32
Dan McFarlan		(1-2)	0	0	----	1	0	0	0	0	6	6	3	0	1.50
Welcome Gaston			0	0	----	1	0	0	0	0	3	3	4	0	3.00
			101	47	.682	150	148	121	9	9	1269	1320	463	331	3.25

BOSTON Beaneaters   95-57   .625   -8   2nd   Frank Selee

BATTERS	POS/GAMES		GP	AB	R	H	BI	2B	3B	HR	BB	SO	SB	BA	SA
Fred Tenney	1B150		150	603	115	209	67	19	17	1	63		28	.347	.439
Bobby Lowe	2B148,SS4		152	559	81	152	88	5	9	4	35		17	.272	.335
Germany Long	SS143,1B2		145	578	91	153	100	30	8	6	45		20	.265	.375
Jimmy Collins	3B151		151	599	98	166	92	28	11	5	40		12	.277	.386
Chick Stahl	OF147,P1		148	576	122	202	52	23	19	7	72		33	.351	.493
Billy Hamilton	OF81		84	297	63	92	33	7	1	1	72		19	.310	.350
Hugh Duffy	OF147		147	588	103	164	102	29	7	5	39		26	.279	.378
Marty Bergen	C72		72	260	32	67	34	11	3	1	10		4	.258	.335
Boileryard Clarke	C60		60	223	25	50	32	3	2	2	10		2	.224	.283
General Stafford	OF41,2B5,SS5	(1-2)	55	182	29	55	40	4	2	3	7		9	.302	.396
Charlie Frisbee	OF40		42	152	22	50	20	4	2	0	9		10	.329	.382
Kid Nichols	P42		42	136	13	26	12	3	0	1	6		1	.191	.235
Vic Willis	P41		41	134	14	29	16	3	0	0	4		0	.216	.239
Ted Lewis	P29		29	96	9	25	9	1	1	0	4		1	.260	.292
Billy Sullivan	C22		22	74	10	20	12	2	0	2	1		2	.270	.378
Piano Legs Hickman	P11,OF7,1B1		19	63	15	25	15	2	7	0	2		1	.397	.651
Jouett Meekin	P13	(2-2)	13	41	4	7	4	1	1	0	2		0	.171	.244
Frank Killen	P12	(2-2)	12	41	3	7	5	1	0	0	1		0	.171	.195
Harvey Bailey	P12		12	34	3	8	2	2	0	0	2		0	.235	.294
Charles Kuhns	SS3,3B3		7	18	2	5	3	0	0	0	2		0	.278	.278
Fred Klobedanz	P5		5	11	3	2	3	0	0	1	3		0	.182	.455
George Yeager	OF2,C1		3	8	1	1	0	0	0	0	1		0	.125	.125
Oscar Streit	P2		2	7	0	0	0	0	0	0	0		0	.000	.000

1899 NATIONAL LEAGUE

BOSTON (cont.)
Beaneaters

BATTERS	POS/GAMES		GP	AB	R	H	BI	2B	3B	HR	BB	SO	SB	BA	SA
Mike Sullivan	P1		1	3	0	1	0	0	0	0	1		0	.333	.333
Mike Hickey	2B1		1	3	0	1	0	0	0	0	0		0	.333	.333
Bill Ging	P1		1	2	0	0	0	0	0	0	0		0	.000	.000
Bill Merritt	C1		1	2	0	0	0	0	0	0	0		0	.000	.000
			153	5290	858	1517	741	178	89	39	431	269	185	.287	.377

PITCHERS			W	L	PCT	G	GS	CG	SH	SV	IP	H	BB	SO	ERA
Vic Willis			27	8	.771	41	38	35	5	2	343	277	117	120	2.50
Kid Nichols			21	19	.525	42	37	37	4	1	343	326	82	108	2.99
Ted Lewis			17	11	.607	29	25	23	2	0	235	245	73	60	3.49
Frank Killen		(2-2)	7	5	.583	12	12	11	0	0	99	108	26	23	4.26
Jouett Meekin		(2-2)	7	6	.538	13	13	12	0	0	108	111	23	23	2.83
Piano Legs Hickman			6	0	1.000	11	9	5	2	1	66	52	40	14	4.48
Harvey Bailey			6	4	.600	12	11	8	0	0	87	83	35	26	3.95
Oscar Streit			1	0	1.000	2	1	1	0	0	15	15	15	0	6.75
Mike Sullivan			1	0	1.000	1	1	1	0	0	9	10	4	1	5.00
Bill Ging			1	0	1.000	1	1	1	0	0	8	5	5	2	1.13
Fred Klobedanz			1	4	.200	5	5	4	0	0	33	39	9	8	4.86
Chick Stahl			0	0	----	1	0	0	0	0	2	2	3	0	9.00
			95	57	.625	153	153	138	13	4	1348	1273	432	385	3.26

PHILADELPHIA   94-58   .618   -9   3rd   Bill Shettsline
Phillies

BATTERS	POS/GAMES		GP	AB	R	H	BI	2B	3B	HR	BB	SO	SB	BA	SA
Duff Cooley	1B79,OF14,2B1		94	406	75	112	31	15	8	1	29		15	.276	.360
Nap Lajoie	2B67,OF5		77	312	70	118	70	19	9	6	12		13	.378	.554
Monte Cross	SS154		154	557	85	143	65	25	6	3	56		26	.257	.339
Bill Lauder	3B151		151	583	74	156	90	17	6	3	34		15	.268	.333
Elmer Flick	OF125		127	485	98	166	98	22	11	2	42		31	.342	.445
Roy Thomas	OF135,1B14		150	547	137	178	47	12	4	0	115		42	.325	.362
Ed Delahanty	OF143		146	581	135	238	137	55	9	9	55		30	.410	.582
Ed McFarland	C94		96	324	59	108	57	22	19	2	36		9	.333	.475
Pearce Chiles	OF46,1B25,2B16		97	338	57	108	76	28	7	2	16		6	.320	.462
Klondike Douglass	C66,3B4,1B4,OF1		77	275	26	70	27	6	6	0	10		7	.255	.320
Joe Dolan	2B61		61	222	27	57	30	6	3	1	11		3	.257	.324
Wiley Piatt	P39		40	122	11	33	10	2	2	0	5		0	.270	.320
Chick Fraser	P35,3B3,OF2		40	117	19	21	11	4	1	0	6		2	.179	.231
Bill Goeckel	1B36		37	141	17	37	16	3	1	0	1		6	.262	.298
Red Donahue	P35		35	111	12	20	7	0	0	0	2		2	.180	.180
Al Orth	P21,OF1		22	62	5	13	5	3	1	1	1		2	.210	.339
Bill Bernhard	P21		21	54	5	13	2	1	0	0	2		1	.241	.259
Jack Fifield	P14	(1-2)	14	35	2	9	2	0	0	0	3		0	.257	.257
Bill Magee	P9	(2-3)	9	31	0	5	2	0	0	0	1		0	.161	.161
Red Owens	2B8		8	21	0	1	1	0	0	0	2		0	.048	.048
George Wheeler	P6		6	17	2	4	3	1	0	1	1		1	.235	.471
Henry Croft	2B2	(2-2)	2	7	0	1	0	0	0	0	1		0	.143	.143
Dave Fultz	2B1,SS1	(1-2)	2	5	0	2	0	0	0	0	0		1	.400	.400
			154	5353	916	1613	787	241	83	31	441	341	212	.301	.395

PITCHERS			W	L	PCT	G	GS	CG	SH	SV	IP	H	BB	SO	ERA
Wiley Piatt			23	15	.605	39	38	31	2	0	305	323	86	89	3.45
Red Donahue			21	8	.724	35	31	27	4	0	279	292	63	51	3.39
Chick Fraser			21	12	.636	35	33	29	4	0	271	278	85	68	3.36
Al Orth			14	3	.824	21	15	13	3	1	145	149	19	35	2.49
Bill Bernhard			6	6	.500	21	12	10	1	0	132	120	36	23	2.65
George Wheeler			3	1	.750	6	5	3	0	0	39	44	13	3	6.00
Bill Magee		(2-3)	3	5	.375	9	9	7	0	0	70	82	32	4	5.66
Jack Fifield		(1-2)	3	8	.273	14	11	9	1	1	93	110	36	8	4.08
			94	58	.618	154	154	129	15	2	1333	1398	370	281	3.47

BALTIMORE   86-62   .581   -15   4th   John McGraw
Orioles

BATTERS	POS/GAMES		GP	AB	R	H	BI	2B	3B	HR	BB	SO	SB	BA	SA
Candy LaChance	1B125		125	472	65	145	75	23	10	1	21		31	.307	.405
Gene DeMontreville	2B60	(2-2)	60	240	40	67	36	13	4	1	10		21	.279	.379

1899 NATIONAL LEAGUE

BALTIMORE (cont.)
Orioles

BATTERS	POS/GAMES		GP	AB	R	H	BI	2B	3B	HR	BB	SO	SB	BA	SA
Bill Keister	SS90,2B46,OF1		136	523	96	172	73	22	16	3	16		33	.329	.449
John McGraw	3B117		117	399	140	156	33	13	3	1	124		73	.391	.446
Jimmy Sheckard	OF146,1B1		147	536	104	158	75	18	10	3	56		77	.295	.382
Steve Brodie	OF137		137	531	82	164	87	26	1	3	31		19	.309	.379
Ducky Holmes	OF138		138	553	80	177	66	31	7	4	39		50	.320	.423
Wilbert Robinson	C105		108	356	40	101	47	15	2	0	31		5	.284	.337
George Magoon	SS62	(1-2)	62	207	26	53	31	8	3	0	26		7	.256	.324
Dave Fultz	OF31,3B20,2B2,1B1	(2-2)	57	210	31	62	18	3	2	0	13		17	.295	.329
Pat Crisham	1B26,C22		53	172	23	50	20	5	3	0	4		4	.291	.355
Joe McGinnity	P48,OF2		50	145	21	28	10	0	0	0	5		4	.193	.193
Frank Kitson	P40		45	134	13	27	8	7	1	0	6		7	.201	.269
Broadway Smith	C36,OF2,1B1	(2-2)	41	120	17	46	25	6	4	0	4		7	.383	.500
John O'Brien	2B39	(1-2)	39	135	14	26	17	4	0	1	15		4	.193	.244
Jerry Nops	P33		34	105	6	29	12	2	0	0	2		0	.276	.295
Charlie Harris	3B21,OF3,2B2,SS1		30	68	16	19	1	3	0	0	3		4	.279	.324
Harry Howell	P28		28	82	4	12	3	2	2	0	3		0	.146	.220
Ed Rothermel	2B5,3B2,SS1		10	21	1	2	3	0	0	0	1		0	.095	.095
Kit McKenna	P8,OF1		9	17	1	1	0	1	0	0	3		0	.059	.118
Still Bill Hill	P8	(2-3)	8	24	2	7	4	0	0	0	2		0	.292	.292
Ralph Miller	P5		5	11	3	2	2	1	1	0	3		0	.182	.455
Hugh Jennings	2B2	(2-3)	2	8	2	3	2	0	2	0	0		0	.375	.875
Jack Ryan	C2		2	4	0	2	1	1	0	0	0		1	.500	.750
			152	5073	827	1509	649	204	71	17	418	383	364	.297	.376

PITCHERS			W	L	PCT	G	GS	CG	SH	SV	IP	H	BB	SO	ERA
Joe McGinnity			28	16	.636	48	41	38	4	2	366	358	93	74	2.68
Frank Kitson			22	16	.579	40	37	34	2	0	328	329	65	75	2.77
Jerry Nops			17	11	.607	33	33	26	2	0	259	296	71	60	4.03
Harry Howell			13	8	.619	28	25	21	0	1	209	248	69	58	3.91
Still Bill Hill		(2-3)	3	4	.429	8	7	6	0	0	61	64	18	17	3.25
Kit McKenna			2	3	.400	8	4	4	0	1	45	66	19	7	4.60
Ralph Miller			1	3	.250	6	4	3	0	0	36	42	14	3	4.50
			86	62	.581	152	151	132	10	4	1304	1403	349	294	3.31

ST. LOUIS
Perfectos

84-67 .556 -18.5 5th Patsy Tebeau

BATTERS	POS/GAMES		GP	AB	R	H	BI	2B	3B	HR	BB	SO	SB	BA	SA
Patsy Tebeau	1B65,SS11,3B1,2B1		77	281	27	69	26	10	3	1	18		5	.246	.313
Cupid Childs	2B125		125	464	73	123	48	11	11	1	74		11	.265	.343
Bobby Wallace	SS100,3B52		151	577	91	170	108	28	14	12	54		17	.295	.454
Lave Cross	3B103	(2-2)	103	403	61	122	64	14	5	4	17		11	.303	.392
John Heidrick	OF145		146	591	109	194	82	21	14	2	34		55	.328	.421
Henry Blake	OF87,2B4,SS1,1B1,C1		97	292	50	70	41	9	4	2	43		16	.240	.318
Jesse Burkett	OF140,2B1		141	558	116	221	71	21	8	7	67		25	.396	.500
Lou Criger	C75		77	258	39	66	44	4	5	2	28		14	.256	.333
Jack O'Connor	C57,1B26		84	289	33	73	43	5	6	0	15		7	.253	.311
Ossie Schreckengost	1B42,C25,2B1,OF1	(1,3-3)	72	277	42	77	37	12	2	2	15		14	.278	.357
Ed McKean	SS42,1B15,2B10		67	277	40	72	40	7	3	3	20		4	.260	.339
Mike Donlin	OF51,1B13,SS3,P3		66	266	49	86	27	9	6	6	17		20	.323	.470
Jack Powell	P48,OF1		49	134	13	27	6	0	2	0	12		0	.201	.231
Cy Young	P44		44	148	22	32	18	5	3	1	2		1	.216	.311
Jake Stenzel	OF33	(1-2)	35	128	21	35	19	9	0	1	16		8	.273	.367
Willie Sudhoff	P26	(2-2)	26	68	10	14	2	1	1	0	8		0	.206	.250
Nig Cuppy	P21		21	70	6	13	3	0	0	0	3		0	.186	.186
Cowboy Jones	P12		12	29	1	5	0	3	0	0	4		0	.172	.276
Peter McBride	P11,2B1		12	27	2	5	5	1	0	1	2		0	.185	.333
Charlie Hemphill	OF10	(1-2)	11	37	4	9	3	0	0	1	6		0	.243	.324
Dusty Miller	OF10	(2-2)	10	39	3	8	3	1	0	0	3		1	.205	.231
Tim Flood	2B10		10	31	0	9	3	0	0	0	4		1	.290	.290
Fred Buelow	C4,OF2		7	15	4	7	2	0	2	0	2		0	.467	.733
Zeke Wilson	P5		5	10	0	0	0	0	0	0	1		0	.000	.000
Tom Thomas	P4		4	12	0	3	2	1	0	0	0		0	.250	.333
Freddy Parent	2B2		2	8	0	1	1	0	0	0	0		0	.125	.125
Jim Burke	2B2		2	6	1	2	0	0	0	0	1		0	.333	.333
John Sutthoff	P2		2	6	0	0	0	0	0	0	0		0	.000	.000
Frank Bates	P2	(1-2)	2	3	2	1	1	0	0	0	2		0	.333	.333
			155	5304	819	1514	699	172	89	46	468	262	210	.285	.377

1899 NATIONAL LEAGUE

ST. LOUIS (cont.)
Perfectos

PITCHERS		W	L	PCT	G	GS	CG	SH	SV	IP	H	BB	SO	ERA
Cy Young		26	16	.619	44	42	40	4	1	369	368	44	111	2.58
Jack Powell		23	19	.548	48	43	40	2	0	373	433	85	87	3.52
Willie Sudhoff	(2-2)	13	10	.565	26	24	18	0	0	189	203	67	33	3.61
Nig Cuppy		11	8	.579	21	21	18	1	0	172	203	26	25	3.15
Cowboy Jones		6	5	.545	12	12	9	0	0	85	111	22	28	3.59
Peter McBride		2	4	.333	11	6	4	0	0	64	65	40	26	4.08
Zeke Wilson		1	1	.500	5	2	2	0	0	26	30	4	3	4.50
Tom Thomas		1	1	.500	4	2	2	0	0	25	22	4	8	2.52
Mike Donlin		0	1	.000	3	1	0	0	0	15	15	14	6	7.63
John Sutthoff		0	2	.000	2	2	1	0	0	13	19	10	4	10.38
Frank Bates	(1-2)	0	0	----	2	0	0	0	0	9	7	5	0	1.04
		84	67	.556	155	155	134	7	1	1341	1476	321	331	3.36

CINCINNATI
Reds

83-67 .553 -19 6th Buck Ewing

BATTERS	POS/GAMES		GP	AB	R	H	BI	2B	3B	HR	BB	SO	SB	BA	SA
Jake Beckley	1B134		134	513	87	171	99	27	16	3	40		20	.333	.466
Bid McPhee	2B104,OF1,3B1		111	373	60	104	65	17	7	1	40		18	.279	.370
Tom Corcoran	SS123,2B14		137	537	91	149	81	11	8	0	28		32	.277	.328
Charlie Irwin	3B78,SS6,2B3,1B1		90	314	42	73	52	4	8	1	26		26	.232	.306
Dusty Miller	OF80	(1-2)	80	323	44	81	37	12	5	0	9		18	.251	.319
Elmer Smith	OF87		87	339	65	101	24	13	6	1	47		10	.298	.381
Kip Selbach	OF140		140	521	104	154	87	27	11	3	70		38	.296	.407
Heinie Peitz	C91,P1		93	290	45	79	43	13	2	1	45		11	.272	.341
Harry Steinfeldt	3B59,2B40,SS8,OF2		107	386	62	94	43	16	8	0	40		19	.244	.326
Algie McBride	OF64		64	251	57	87	23	12	5	1	30		5	.347	.446
Bob Wood	C53,OF2,3B2,1B1		62	194	34	61	24	11	7	0	25		3	.314	.443
Kid Elberfield	SS24,3B18		41	138	23	36	22	4	2	0	15		5	.261	.319
Noodles Hahn	P38		38	109	12	16	11	3	2	0	8		3	.147	.211
Pink Hawley	P34		34	101	11	22	10	4	1	0	2		1	.218	.277
Bill Phillips	P33,OF1		34	92	6	12	7	0	2	0	7		0	.130	.174
Ted Breitenstein	P26,OF7		33	105	18	37	11	4	1	1	10		1	.352	.438
Sam Crawford	OF31		31	127	25	39	20	3	7	1	2		6	.307	.365
Farmer Vaughn	1B21,C7,OF1		31	108	9	19	2	1	0	0	3		2	.176	.185
Jim Barrett	OF26		26	92	30	34	10	2	4	0	18		4	.370	.478
Jack Taylor	P24		24	68	3	17	7	2	0	0	0		0	.250	.279
Socks Seybold	OF22		22	85	13	19	8	5	1	0	6		2	.224	.306
Mike Kahoe	C13		13	42	2	7	4	1	1	0	0		1	.167	.238
Jake Stenzel	OF7	(2-2)	9	29	5	9	3	1	0	0	4		2	.310	.345
John Frisk	P9		9	25	5	7	2	1	0	0	2		0	.280	.320
Bill Damman	P9		9	18	0	1	2	0	0	0	2		0	.056	.056
Lefty Houtz	OF5		5	17	1	4	0	0	1	0	4		1	.235	.353
Jack Cronin	P5		5	17	2	2	2	0	0	0	2		0	.118	.118
Frank Dwyer	P5		5	11	0	4	0	0	0	0	0		0	.364	.364
			156	5225	856	1439	699	194	105	13	485	295	228	.275	.360

PITCHERS	W	L	PCT	G	GS	CG	SH	SV	IP	H	BB	SO	ERA
Noodles Hahn	23	8	.742	38	34	32	4	0	309	280	68	145	2.68
Bill Phillips	17	9	.654	33	27	18	1	1	228	234	71	43	3.32
Pink Hawley	14	17	.452	34	29	25	0	1	250	289	65	46	4.24
Ted Breitenstein	13	9	.591	26	24	21	0	0	211	219	71	59	3.59
Jack Taylor	9	10	.474	24	18	15	2	2	168	197	41	34	4.12
John Frisk	3	6	.333	9	9	9	0	0	68	81	17	17	3.95
Bill Damman	2	1	.667	9	5	3	1	1	48	74	11	2	4.88
Jack Cronin	2	2	.500	5	5	5	0	0	41	56	16	9	5.49
Frank Dwyer	0	5	.000	5	5	2	0	0	33	48	9	2	5.51
Heinie Peitz	0	0	----	1	0	0	0	0	5	6	1	3	5.40
	83	67	.553	156	156	130	8	5	1361	1484	370	360	3.70

PITTSBURGH
Pirates

76-73 .510 -25.5 7th Watkins - Donovan

BATTERS	POS/GAMES		GP	AB	R	H	BI	2B	3B	HR	BB	SO	SB	BA	SA
Willie Clark	1B78		80	298	49	85	44	13	10	0	35		11	.285	.396
John O'Brien	2B79	(2-2)	79	279	26	63	33	2	4	1	21		8	.226	.272
Bones Ely	SS132,2B6		138	522	66	145	72	18	6	3	22		8	.278	.352
Jim Williams	3B152		152	617	126	219	116	28	27	9	60		26	.355	.532

1899 NATIONAL LEAGUE

PITTSBURGH (cont.)
Pirates

BATTERS	POS/GAMES	GP	AB	R	H	BI	2B	3B	HR	BB	SO	SB	BA	SA
Patsy Donovan	OF121	121	531	82	156	55	11	7	1	17		26	.294	.347
Ginger Beaumont	OF102,1B2	111	437	90	154	38	15	8	3	41		31	.352	.444
John McCarthy	OF138	138	560	108	171	67	22	17	3	39		28	.305	.421
Frank Bowerman	C79,1B28	109	424	49	110	53	16	10	3	11		10	.259	.366
Tom McCreery	OF97,SS9,2B7	118	455	76	147	64	21	9	2	47		11	.323	.422
Pop Schriver	C78,1B8	91	301	31	85	49	19	5	1	23		4	.282	.389
Sam Leever	P51	51	146	15	33	18	6	4	0	8		0	.226	.322
Jesse Tannehill	P40,OF1	47	132	17	34	10	5	3	0	8		2	.258	.341
Art Madison	2B19,SS15,3B2	42	118	20	32	19	2	4	0	11		1	.271	.356
Heinie Reitz	2B34	34	130	11	34	15	4	2	0	10		3	.262	.323
Bill Hoffer	P23,OF6,2B1	33	91	12	18	2	2	0	0	1		1	.198	.220
Pop Dillon	1B30	30	121	21	31	20	5	0	0	5		5	.256	.298
Tully Sparks	P28	28	62	8	8	5	2	1	0	9		0	.129	.194
Jack Chesbro	P19	19	58	3	9	3	0	0	0	3		0	.155	.155
Heinie Smith	2B15,SS1	15	53	9	15	12	3	1	0	5		2	.283	.377
George Fox	1B9,C3	13	41	4	10	3	0	1	1	3		2	.244	.366
Bill Rhines	P9	10	23	4	10	2	1	2	0	0		0	.435	.652
Chummy Gray	P9	9	26	2	1	0	0	0	0	3		0	.038	.038
Jim Gardner	P6	6	13	3	3	0	1	0	0	1		0	.231	.308
Harley Payne	P5	5	10	1	1	0	0	0	0	1		0	.100	.100
Zeke Rosebrough	P2	2	2	1	0	0	0	0	0	0		0	.000	.000
Jay Parker	P1	1	0	0	0	0	0	0	0	0		0	----	----
		154	5450	834	1574	700	196	121	27	384	345	179	.289	.384

PITCHERS	W	L	PCT	G	GS	CG	SH	SV	IP	H	BB	SO	ERA
Jesse Tannehill	24	14	.632	40	35	32	3	1	313	354	51	61	2.73
Sam Leever	21	23	.477	51	39	35	4	3	379	353	122	121	3.18
Tully Sparks	8	6	.571	28	17	8	0	0	170	180	82	53	3.86
Bill Hoffer	8	10	.444	23	19	15	2	0	164	169	64	44	3.63
Jack Chesbro	6	9	.400	19	17	15	0	0	149	165	59	28	4.11
Bill Rhines	4	4	.500	9	9	4	0	0	54	59	13	6	6.00
Chummy Gray	3	3	.500	9	7	6	0	0	71	85	24	9	3.44
Jim Gardner	1	0	1.000	6	3	0	0	0	32	52	13	2	7.52
Harley Payne	1	3	.250	5	5	2	0	0	26	33	4	8	3.76
Zeke Rosebrough	0	1	.000	2	2	0	0	0	6	14	3	2	9.00
Jay Parker	0	0	----	1	1	0	0	0	0	0	2	0	inf.
	76	73	.510	154	154	117	9	4	1364	1464	437	334	3.60

CHICAGO
Orphans

75-73   .507   -26   8th   Tom Burns

BATTERS	POS/GAMES		GP	AB	R	H	RBI	2B	3B	HR	BB	SO	SB	BA	SA
Bill Everett	1B136		136	536	87	166	74	17	5	1	31		30	.310	.366
Barry McCormick	2B99,SS3		102	376	48	97	52	15	2	2	25		14	.258	.324
Gene DeMontreville	SS82	(1-2)	82	310	43	87	40	6	3	0	17		26	.281	.319
Harry Wolverton	3B98,SS1		99	389	50	111	49	14	11	1	30		14	.285	.386
Danny Green	OF115		117	475	90	140	56	12	11	6	35		18	.295	.404
Sam Mertes	OF108,1B3,SS1		117	426	83	127	81	13	16	9	33		45	.298	.467
Jimmy Ryan	OF125		125	525	91	158	68	20	10	3	43		9	.301	.394
Tim Donahue	C91,1B1		92	278	39	69	29	9	3	0	34		10	.248	.302
Bill Lange	OF94,1B14		107	416	81	135	58	21	7	1	38		41	.325	.416
Jim Connor	2B44,3B25		69	234	26	48	24	7	1	0	18		6	.205	.244
Frank Chance	C57,OF1,1B1		64	192	37	55	22	6	2	1	15		10	.286	.354
George Magoon	SS59	(2-2)	59	189	24	43	21	5	1	0	24		5	.228	.265
Nixey Callahan	P35,OF9,SS2,2B1		47	150	21	39	18	4	3	0	8		9	.260	.327
Jack Taylor	P41		42	139	25	37	17	9	2	0	16		0	.266	.360
Clark Griffith	P38,SS1		39	120	15	31	14	5	0	0	14		2	.258	.300
Bill Bradley	3B30,SS5		35	129	26	40	18	6	1	2	12		4	.310	.419
Ned Garvin	P24		24	71	1	11	1	0	0	0	1		0	.155	.155
Art Nichols	C15		17	47	5	12	11	2	0	1	0		3	.255	.362
Frank Quinn	OF10,2B1		12	34	6	6	1	0	1	0	6		1	.176	.235
Doc Curley	2B10		10	37	7	4	2	0	1	0	3		0	.108	.162
Bill Phyle	P10		10	34	2	6	1	0	0	0	0		0	.176	.176
Richard Cogan	P5,OF3		8	25	4	5	4	1	2	0	2		0	.200	.400
John Katoll	P2		2	7	1	0	0	0	0	0	1		0	.000	.000
John Malarkey	P1		1	5	0	1	0	1	0	0	0		0	.200	.400
Skel Roach	P1		1	4	0	0	0	0	0	0	0		0	.000	.000
			152	5148	812	1428	661	173	82	27	406	342	247	.277	.359

1899 NATIONAL LEAGUE

CHICAGO (cont.)
Orphans

PITCHERS	W	L	PCT	G	GS	CG	SH	SV	IP	H	BB	SO	ERA
Clark Griffith	22	14	.611	38	38	35	0	0	320	329	65	73	2.79
Nixey Callahan	21	12	.636	35	34	33	3	0	294	327	76	77	3.06
Jack Taylor	18	21	.462	41	39	39	1	0	355	380	84	67	3.76
Ned Garvin	9	13	.409	24	23	22	4	0	199	202	42	69	2.85
Richard Cogan	2	3	.400	5	5	5	0	0	44	54	24	9	4.30
Skel Roach	1	0	1.000	1	1	1	0	0	9	13	1	0	3.00
John Katoll	1	1	.500	2	2	2	0	0	18	17	4	1	6.00
Bill Phyle	1	8	.111	10	9	9	0	1	84	92	29	10	4.20
John Malarkey	0	1	.000	1	1	1	0	0	9	19	5	7	13.00
	75	73	.507	152	152	147	8	1	1331	1433	330	313	3.37

LOUISVILLE
Colonels

75-77   .493   -28   9th   Fred Clarke

BATTERS	POS/GAMES		GP	AB	R	H	BI	2B	3B	HR	BB	SO	SB	BA	SA
Mike Kelley	1B76		76	282	48	68	33	11	2	3	21		10	.241	.326
Claude Ritchey	2B137,SS11		147	536	65	161	71	15	7	4	49		21	.300	.377
Bill Clingman	SS109		109	366	67	96	44	15	4	2	46		13	.262	.342
Tommy Leach	3B80,SS25,2B2		106	406	75	117	57	10	6	5	37		19	.288	.379
Charles Dexter	OF71,SS6		80	295	47	76	33	7	1	1	21		21	.258	.298
Dummy Hoy	OF154		154	633	116	194	49	17	13	5	61		32	.306	.398
Fred Clarke	OF144,SS3		148	602	122	206	70	23	9	5	49		49	.342	.435
Chief Zimmer	C62,1B11	(2-2)	75	262	43	78	22	11	3	2	22		9	.298	.385
Honus Wagner	3B75,OF61,2B7,1B4		147	571	98	192	113	43	13	7	40		37	.336	.494
Mike Powers	C38,1B7	(1-2)	49	169	15	35	22	8	2	0	6		1	.207	.278
Mal Kittredge	C43	(1-2)	45	129	11	26	12	2	1	0	26		3	.202	.233
Bert Cunningham	P39,OF3,SS1		44	154	17	40	17	2	0	2	5		1	.260	.312
Deacon Phillipe	P42,OF2		44	128	17	26	10	5	0	0	8		3	.203	.242
Walt Woods	P26,2B11,SS3,OF2		42	126	15	19	14	1	1	1	10		5	.151	.198
George Decker	1B38	(1-2)	38	135	13	36	18	8	0	1	12		3	.267	.348
Henry Dowling	P34		34	116	10	27	9	4	0	0	2		1	.233	.267
Topsy Hartsel	OF22		30	75	8	18	7	1	1	1	11		1	.240	.320
Dave Wills	1B24		24	94	15	21	12	3	1	0	2		1	.223	.277
Fred Ketchem	OF15		15	61	13	18	5	1	0	0	0		2	.295	.311
Bill Magee	P12	(1-3)	12	27	1	3	5	1	1	0	0		0	.111	.222
Rube Waddell	P10		10	34	2	8	3	2	0	0	0		0	.235	.294
Tacks Latimer	C8,1B1		9	29	3	8	4	1	0	0	2		1	.276	.310
Patsy Flaherty	P5,OF2		7	24	3	5	6	1	1	0	3		0	.208	.333
Harry Wilhelm	P5		5	12	1	3	2	0	1	1	1		0	.250	.667
Farmer Steelman	C4		4	15	2	1	2	0	1	0	2		0	.067	.200
Tom Messitt	C3		3	11	0	1	0	0	0	0	0		0	.091	.091
Kitty Brashear	P3		3	2	0	1	0	0	0	0	0		0	.500	.500
Henry Croft	---	(1-2)	2	2	0	0	0	0	0	0	0		0	.000	.000
Bob Langsford	SS1		1	4	0	0	0	0	0	0	0		0	.000	.000
Clay Fauver	P1		1	4	0	0	0	0	0	0	0		0	.000	.000
Burley Bayer	SS1		1	3	0	0	0	0	0	0	0		0	.000	.000
Rudy Hulswitt	SS1		1	0	0	0	0	0	0	0	0		0	----	----
			155	5307	827	1484	640	192	68	40	436	375	233	.280	.364

PITCHERS		W	L	PCT	G	GS	CG	SH	SV	IP	H	BB	SO	ERA
Deacon Phillipe		21	17	.553	42	38	33	2	1	321	331	64	68	3.17
Bert Cunningham		17	17	.500	39	37	33	1	0	324	385	75	36	3.84
Henry Dowling		13	17	.433	34	32	29	0	0	290	321	93	88	3.11
Walt Woods		9	13	.409	26	21	17	0	0	186	216	37	21	3.28
Rube Waddell		7	2	.778	10	9	9	1	1	79	69	14	44	3.08
Bill Magee	(1-3)	3	7	.300	12	10	6	1	0	71	91	28	13	5.20
Patsy Flaherty		2	3	.400	5	4	4	0	0	39	41	5	5	2.31
Kitty Brashear		1	0	1.000	3	0	0	0	0	8	8	2	5	4.50
Clay Fauver		1	0	1.000	1	1	1	0	0	9	11	2	1	0.00
Harry Wilhelm		1	1	.500	5	3	2	0	0	25	36	3	6	6.12
		75	77	.493	155	155	134	5	2	1352	1509	323	287	3.45

NEW YORK
Giants

60-90   .400   -42   10th   Day - Hoey

BATTERS	POS/GAMES	GP	AB	R	H	BI	2B	3B	HR	BB	SO	SB	BA	SA
Jack Doyle	1B113,C5	118	448	55	134	76	15	7	3	33		35	.299	.384
Kid Gleason	2B146	146	576	72	152	59	14	4	0	24		29	.264	.302

1899 NATIONAL LEAGUE

NEW YORK (cont.)
Giants

BATTERS	POS/GAMES		GP	AB	R	H	BI	2B	3B	HR	BB	SO	SB	BA	SA
George Davis	SS108		108	416	68	140	57	21	5	1	37		34	.337	.418
Fred Hartman	3B50		50	174	25	41	16	3	5	1	12		2	.236	.328
Pop Foster	OF84,SS1,3B1		84	301	48	89	57	9	7	3	20		7	.296	.402
George Van Haltren	OF151		151	604	117	182	58	21	3	2	74		31	.301	.356
Tom O'Brien	OF127,3B21,SS2,2B1,1B1		150	573	100	170	77	21	10	6	44		23	.297	.400
John Warner	C82,1B3		88	293	38	78	19	8	1	0	15		15	.266	.300
Parke Wilson	C31,1B29,SS19,3B15,OF6		97	328	49	88	42	8	6	0	43		16	.268	.329
Mike Grady	C43,3B35,OF4,1B4		86	311	47	104	54	18	8	2	29		20	.334	.463
Cy Seymour	P32,OF8,1B3,3B1		50	159	25	52	27	3	2	2	4		2	.327	.409
Bill Carrick	P44		44	130	7	18	10	2	1	0	11		1	.138	.169
Mike Tiernan	OF35		35	137	17	35	7	4	2	0	10		2	.255	.314
Ed Doheny	P35		35	112	13	27	9	2	0	0	4		2	.241	.259
Charles Gettig	P18,3B8,2B3,1B3,OF1		34	97	7	24	9	3	0	0	7		4	.247	.278
Tom Fleming	OF22		22	77	9	16	4	1	1	0	1		1	.208	.247
Scott Hardesty	SS20,1B2		22	72	4	16	4	0	0	0	1		2	.222	.222
Orville Woodruff	OF19,1B1		20	61	11	15	7	1	1	2	9		3	.246	.393
Jouett Meekin	P18	(1-2)	18	58	7	12	4	2	1	1	3		1	.207	.328
Frank Martin	3B17		17	54	5	14	1	2	0	0	2		0	.259	.296
Tom Colcolough	P11,OF1		14	37	3	10	6	1	0	0	1		0	.270	.297
Ira Davis	SS3,1B2		6	17	3	4	2	1	1	0	0		1	.235	.412
Kid Carsey	3B3,SS2	(3-3)	5	18	2	6	1	1	0	0	2		2	.333	.389
Zeke Wrigley	3B4	(1-2)	4	15	1	3	1	0	0	0	1		1	.200	.200
Will Garoni	P3		3	4	0	0	0	0	0	0	0		0	.000	.000
John O'Neill	C2		2	7	0	0	0	0	0	0	0		0	.000	.000
Leo Fishel	P1		1	4	0	1	0	0	0	0	0		0	.250	.250
Bill Stuart	2B1		1	3	0	0	0	0	0	0	0		0	.000	.000
John Puhl	3B1		1	2	0	0	0	0	0	0	0		0	.000	.000
Pete Cregan	OF1		1	2	0	0	0	0	0	0	0		0	.000	.000
Frank McPartlin	P1		1	1	1	0	0	0	0	0	0		0	.000	.000
Youngy Johnson	P1		1	1	0	0	0	0	0	0	0		0	.000	.000
Doc Sechrist	P1		1	0	0	0	0	0	0	0	0		0	----	----
			152	5092	734	1431	607	161	65	23	387	360	234	.281	.352

PITCHERS			W	L	PCT	G	GS	CG	SH	SV	IP	H	BB	SO	ERA
Bill Carrick			16	27	.372	44	43	40	3	0	362	485	122	60	4.65
Ed Doheny			14	17	.452	35	33	30	1	0	265	282	156	115	4.51
Cy Seymour			14	18	.438	32	32	31	0	0	268	247	170	142	3.56
Charles Gettig			7	8	.467	18	15	12	0	0	128	161	54	25	4.43
Jouett Meekin		(1-2)	5	11	.313	18	18	16	0	0	148	169	70	30	4.37
Tom Colcolough			4	5	.444	11	8	7	0	0	82	85	41	14	3.97
Will Garoni			0	1	.000	3	1	1	0	0	10	12	2	2	4.50
Leo Fishel			0	1	.000	1	1	1	0	0	9	9	6	6	6.00
Frank McPartlin			0	0	----	1	0	0	0	0	4	4	3	2	4.50
Youngy Johnson			0	0	----	1	0	0	0	0	2	0	2	1	0.00
Doc Sechrist			0	0	----	1	0	0	0	0	0	0	2	0	----
			60	90	.400	152	151	138	4	0	1278	1454	628	397	4.29

WASHINGTON
Senators

54-98   .355   -49   11th   Art Irwin

BATTERS	POS/GAMES		GP	AB	R	H	BI	2B	3B	HR	BB	SO	SB	BA	SA
Dan McGann	1B76	(2-2)	76	280	65	96	58	9	8	5	14		11	.343	.486
Frank Bonner	2B85		85	347	41	95	44	20	4	2	18		6	.274	.372
Dick Padden	SS85,2B48		134	451	66	125	61	20	7	2	24		27	.277	.366
Charlie Atherton	3B63,OF1		65	242	28	60	23	5	6	0	21		2	.248	.318
Buck Freeman	OF155,P2		155	588	107	187	122	19	25	25	23		21	.318	.563
Jimmy Slagle	OF146		147	599	92	163	41	15	8	0	55		22	.272	.324
Jack O'Brien	OF121,3B4		127	468	68	132	51	11	5	6	31		17	.282	.365
Deacon McGuire	C56,1B1	(1-2)	59	199	25	54	12	3	1	1	16		3	.271	.312
Win Mercer	3B62,P23,OF16,SS1,1B1		108	375	73	112	35	6	7	1	32		16	.299	.360
Shad Barry	OF23,1B22,SS13,3B13,2B7		78	247	31	71	33	7	5	1	12		11	.287	.368
Pete Cassidy	1B37,3B6,SS3	(2-2)	46	178	21	56	32	13	0	3	9		5	.315	.438
Mal Kittredge	C43	(2-2)	44	133	14	20	11	3	0	0	10		2	.150	.173
Gus Weyhing	P43		43	126	13	26	12	3	1	0	8		2	.206	.246
Bill Dineen	P37,OF1		37	119	9	36	4	2	0	0	8		0	.303	.319
Dan McFarlan	P32	(2-2)	32	86	6	16	4	2	3	0	5		0	.186	.279
General Stafford	2B17,SS13,3B2	(2-2)	31	118	11	29	14	5	1	1	5		4	.246	.331
Frank Scheibeck	SS27		27	94	19	27	9	4	1	0	11		5	.287	.351
Mike Roach	C20,1B3		24	78	7	17	7	1	0	0	3		3	.218	.231
Bill Hulen	SS19		19	68	10	10	3	1	0	0	10		5	.147	.162

WASHINGTON (cont.)
Senators

BATTERS	POS/GAMES		GP	AB	R	H	BI	2B	3B	HR	BB	SO	SB	BA	SA
Jake Gettman	OF16,1B2		19	62	5	13	2	1	0	0	4		4	.210	.226
Harry Davis	1B18		18	64	3	12	8	2	3	0	8		2	.188	.313
Jim Duncan	C14	(1-2)	15	47	5	11	5	2	0	0	4		1	.234	.277
Mike Powers	C12,1B1	(2-2)	14	38	3	10	3	2	0	0	1		0	.263	.316
Dick Butler	C11		12	36	4	10	1	0	1	0	2		1	.278	.333
Kirtley Baker	P11		12	19	1	3	1	0	0	0	1		0	.158	.158
Doc Casey	3B9	(1-2)	9	34	3	4	2	2	0	0	2		1	.118	.176
Bill Magee	P8	(3-3)	8	15	1	5	2	1	0	0	1		0	.333	.400
Frank McManus	C7		7	21	3	8	2	1	0	0	2		3	.381	.429
LeRoy Evans	P7		7	20	2	4	2	0	0	0	1		0	.200	.200
Jack Fifield	P6	(2-2)	7	20	0	4	2	1	0	0	2		0	.200	.250
Bill Coughlin	3B6		6	24	2	3	3	0	1	0	1		1	.125	.208
Arlie Latham	OF1,2B1		6	6	1	1	0	0	0	0	1		0	.167	.167
Duke Farrell	C4	(1-2)	5	12	2	4	1	1	0	0	2		1	.333	.417
Davey Dunkle	P4		4	11	0	3	2	0	0	0	0		0	.273	.273
Kid Carsey	P4	(2-3)	4	11	1	0	0	0	0	0	0		0	.000	.000
George Decker	OF1,2B1	(2-2)	4	9	0	0	0	0	0	0	0		0	.000	.000
Mike Heydon	C2		3	3	0	0	0	0	0	0	2		0	.000	.000
Frank Killen	P2	(1-2)	2	5	0	1	1	0	0	0	0		0	.200	.200
Lefty Herring	P2		2	1	1	1	0	0	0	0	1		0	1.000	1.000
Bill Leith	P1		1	1	0	0	0	0	0	0	0		0	.000	.000
Dorsey Riddlemoser	P1		1	1	0	0	0	0	0	0	0		0	.000	.000
			155	5256	743	1429	613	162	87	47	350	341	176	.272	.363

PITCHERS			W	L	PCT	G	GS	CG	SH	SV	IP	H	BB	SO	ERA
Gus Weyhing			17	21	.447	43	38	34	2	0	335	414	76	96	4.54
Bill Dineen			14	20	.412	37	35	30	0	0	291	350	106	91	3.93
Dan McFarlan		(2-2)	8	18	.308	32	28	22	1	0	212	268	64	41	4.76
Win Mercer			7	14	.333	33	21	21	0	0	186	234	53	28	4.60
LeRoy Evans			3	4	.429	7	7	6	0	0	54	60	25	27	5.67
Jack Fifield		(2-2)	2	4	.333	6	6	6	0	0	47	73	17	12	6.13
Kid Carsey		(2-3)	1	2	.333	4	3	2	0	0	29	27	4	3	3.72
Bill Magee		(3-3)	1	4	.200	8	7	4	0	0	42	54	28	11	8.57
Kirtley Baker			1	7	.125	11	6	3	0	0	54	79	22	6	6.83
Davey Dunkle			0	2	.000	4	2	2	0	0	26	46	14	9	10.04
Frank Killen		(1-2)	0	2	.000	2	2	1	0	0	12	18	4	3	6.00
Buck Freeman			0	0	----	2	0	0	0	0	7	15	3	0	7.71
Lefty Herring			0	0	----	2	0	0	0	0	2	0	2	0	0.00
Bill Leith			0	0	----	1	0	0	0	0	2	4	2	1	18.00
Dorsey Riddlemoser			0	0	----	1	0	0	0	0	2	7	2	0	18.00
			54	98	.355	155	155	131	3	0	1300	1649	422	328	4.93

CLEVELAND
Spiders

20-134 .130 -84 12th Cross - Quinn

BATTERS	POS/GAMES		GP	AB	R	H	BI	2B	3B	HR	BB	SO	SB	BA	SA
Tommy Tucker	1B127		127	456	40	110	40	19	3	0	24		3	.241	.296
Joe Quinn	2B147		147	615	73	176	72	24	6	0	21		22	.286	.345
Harry Lochead	SS146,2B1,P1		148	541	52	129	43	7	1	1	21		23	.238	.261
Suter Sullivan	3B101,OF20,SS3,1B3,2B2		127	473	37	116	55	16	3	0	25		16	.245	.292
Sport McAllister	OF79,C17,3B7,1B6,SS3,P3,2B1		113	418	29	99	31	6	8	1	19		5	.237	.297
Tommy Dowd	OF147		147	605	81	168	35	17	6	2	48		28	.278	.336
Dick Harley	OF142		142	567	70	142	50	15	7	1	40		15	.250	.307
Joe Sugden	C66,OF4,1B3,3B1		76	250	19	69	14	5	1	0	11		2	.276	.304
Charlie Hemphill	OF54	(2-2)	55	202	23	56	23	3	5	2	6		3	.277	.371
Ossie Schreckengost	C39,1B1,SS1,OF1	(2-3)	43	150	15	47	10	8	3	0	6		4	.313	.407
Lave Cross	3B38	(1-2)	38	154	15	44	20	5	0	1	8		2	.286	.338
Jim Hughey	P36		36	111	9	18	5	1	0	0	5		0	.162	.171
Jim Duncan	1B17,C14	(2-2)	31	105	9	24	9	2	3	2	4		0	.229	.362
Charlie Knepper	P27		27	89	6	12	2	2	1	0	4		0	.135	.180
Crazy Schmit	P20,OF6		25	70	6	11	1	0	0	0	6		2	.157	.157
Harry Colliflower	P14,OF6,1B4		23	76	5	23	9	4	0	0	2		0	.303	.355
Frank Bates	P20,OF1	(2-2)	21	65	5	14	3	1	0	0	7		0	.215	.231
Chief Zimmer	C20	(1-2)	20	73	9	25	14	2	1	2	5		1	.342	.479
Jack Stivetts	P7,OF7,SS1,3B1		18	39	8	8	2	1	1	0	6		0	.205	.282
Art Krueger	3B9,SS2,2B2		13	44	4	10	2	1	0	0	8		1	.227	.250
Willie Sudhoff	P11	(1-2)	11	31	1	2	6	0	1	0	4		0	.065	.129
Kid Carsey	P10,SS1	(1-3)	11	36	5	10	4	0	0	0	3		0	.278	.278
Still Bill Hill	P11	(1-3)	11	31	2	4	0	0	0	0	1		0	.129	.129
Louis Sockalexis	OF5		7	22	0	6	3	1	0	0	1		0	.273	.318
Jack Harper	P5		5	11	2	2	1	0	0	0	4		0	.182	.182

CLEVELAND (cont.)
Spiders

BATTERS	POS/GAMES		GP	AB	R	H	BI	2B	3B	HR	BB	SO	SB	BA	SA
Harry Maupin	P5		5	10	0	0	0	0	0	0	0		0	.000	.000
Jack Clements	C4		4	12	1	3	0	0	0	0	0		0	.250	.250
George Bristow	OF3		3	8	0	1	0	1	0	0	0		0	.125	.125
Charles Ziegler	SS1,2B1		2	8	2	2	0	0	0	0	0		0	.250	.250
Ed Kolb	P1		1	4	1	1	0	0	0	0	0		0	.250	.250
Highball Wilson	P1		1	3	0	1	0	1	0	0	0		0	.333	.667
			154	5279	529	1333	454	142	50	12	289	280	127	.253	.305

PITCHERS			W	L	PCT	G	GS	CG	SH	SV	IP	H	BB	SO	ERA
Charlie Knepper			4	22	.154	27	26	26	0	0	220	307	77	43	5.78
Jim Hughey			4	30	.118	36	34	32	0	0	283	403	88	54	5.41
Still Bill Hill		(1-3)	3	6	.333	11	10	7	0	0	72	96	39	26	6.97
Willie Sudhoff		(1-2)	3	8	.273	11	10	8	0	0	86	131	25	10	6.98
Crazy Schmit			2	17	.105	20	19	16	0	0	138	197	62	24	5.86
Jack Harper			1	4	.200	5	5	5	0	0	37	44	12	14	3.89
Kid Carsey		(1-3)	1	8	.111	10	9	8	0	0	78	109	24	11	5.68
Harry Colliflower			1	11	.083	14	12	11	0	0	98	152	41	8	8.17
Frank Bates			1	18	.053	20	19	17	0	0	153	239	105	13	7.24
Sport McAllister			0	1	.000	3	1	1	0	0	16	29	10	2	9.56
Highball Wilson			0	1	.000	1	1	1	0	0	8	12	5	1	9.00
Ed Kolb			0	1	.000	1	1	1	0	0	8	18	5	1	10.13
Harry Maupin			0	3	.000	5	3	2	0	0	25	55	7	3	12.60
Jack Stivetts			0	4	.000	7	4	3	0	0	38	48	25	5	5.68
Harry Lochead			0	0	----	1	0	0	0	0	4	4	2	0	0.00
			20	134	.130	154	154	138	0	0	1264	1844	527	215	6.37

1900 NATIONAL LEAGUE

Consolidation

By the end of the 1899 season, it was clear to the baseball owners that their 12-team format was not a success. There were simply not enough strong franchises to fill out a 12-team circuit. An idea was proposed to downsize the National League to eight teams. This would save the league the expense of buttressing the weaker teams. To save the whole, the National League knew it had to cut out some of the dead wood.

A natural solution presented itself with the existence of the dual ownership teams. Since the owners of the Baltimore and Cleveland teams had already sold their talent down the river, those two were a logical choice to be axed. Another choice was the Louisville club. Although the team had improved its lot over the latter part of the 1890s, it still was in weak financial shape, and was currently up for sale. In addition, the team's ballpark had burned down the summer before, putting a further financial burden on the team. The fourth team whose demise was discussed was Washington, a perennial tailender in the field and in the box office.

In March of 1900, the National League's Circuit Reduction Committee voted the four teams out of the league. Washington, Baltimore and Cleveland were paid off in cash. Louisville was paid less because it merged with Pittsburgh. What remained to play the 1900 season was an eight-team league consisting of Boston, Brooklyn, Chicago, Cincinnati, New York, Philadelphia, Pittsburgh, and St. Louis.

For the second time in a row, Brooklyn won the pennant. Among their better players were Willie Keeler (.362), Joe Kelley (.319), Tom Daly (.312), and Fielder Jones (.310). Joe McGinnity joined his former Baltimore brethren on Brooklyn and responded with a 28-win season.

Pittsburgh climbed to second thanks to the addition of Louisville's finest. None performed better than Honus Wagner (.381) who won his first batting title, while leading the league in doubles (45) and triples (22).

Philadelphia stayed put in third with their usual array of batting stars featuring Ed Delahanty (.323), Nap Lajoie (.337), Elmer Flick (.367) and Roy Thomas (.316). In addition, Flick had the most runs batted in (110), while Thomas plated the most runs (132).

Boston slipped to fourth, finishing six games under .500. Their best included Billy

Hamilton (.333), Jimmy Collins (.304), and via defunct Washington, Buck Freeman (.301). Teammate Germany Long won the home run title with 12.

Chicago and St. Louis finished in a tie for fifth. Chicago was topped by Danny Green (.298) and Jack McCarthy (.294), while St. Louis enjoyed the talents of Jesse Burkett (.363), and John McGraw (.344).

Cincinnati finished seventh just ahead of New York who finished eighth. Cincinnati was led by Jake Beckley (.341) and Jim Barrett (.316) while New York was bested by Kip Selbach (.337), George Davis (.319), and George Van Haltren (.315).

After the season, Brooklyn faced second place Pittsburgh in a series sponsored by a Pittsburgh newspaper. The Chronicle-Telegraph Cup, named after the newspaper, was to be a best of five series, with all games to be played in Pittsburgh. Despite this handicap, Brooklyn won the first two games, 5-2, and 4-2. Pittsburgh blanked the visitors 10-0 in game three, but Brooklyn came back and clinched the series with a 6-1 win in game four.

The National League achieved its goals by consolidating the league. The eight franchises were fiscally sound, and the only debt that remained was the buyout fees for the four extinct franchises. The competitiveness had also returned to the league. Last place New York had only finished 23 games out of first, the second closest last place finish ever. But tempering the era of good feelings was a new threat — a threat that would not be easily dismissed.

1900 NATIONAL LEAGUE

BROOKLYN 82-54 .603 1st Ned Hanlon
Superbas

BATTERS	POS/GAMES		GP	AB	R	H	BI	2B	3B	HR	BB	SO	SB	BA	SA
Hugh Jennings	1B112,2B2		115	441	61	120	69	18	6	1	31		31	.272	.347
Tom Daly	2B93,1B3,OF2		97	343	72	107	55	17	3	4	46		27	.312	.414
Bill Dahlen	SS133		133	483	87	125	69	16	11	1	73		31	.259	.344
Lave Cross	3B117	(2-2)	117	461	73	135	67	14	6	4	25		20	.293	.375
Willie Keeler	OF136,2B1		136	563	106	204	68	13	12	4	30		41	.362	.449
Fielder Jones	OF136		136	552	106	171	54	26	4	4	57		33	.310	.393
Joe Kelley	OF77,1B32,3B13		121	454	90	145	91	23	17	6	53		26	.319	.485
Duke Farrell	C74		76	273	33	75	39	11	5	0	11		3	.275	.352
Jimmy Sheckard	OF78		85	273	74	82	39	19	10	1	42		30	.300	.454
Deacon McGuire	C69		71	241	20	69	34	15	2	0	19		2	.286	.365
Gene DeMontreville	2B48,SS12,3B7,OF1,1B1		69	234	34	57	28	8	1	0	10		21	.244	.286
Joe McGinnity	P44,OF1		46	145	18	28	16	4	1	0	1		4	.193	.234
Brickyard Kennedy	P42		43	123	10	37	15	8	2	0	5		0	.301	.398
Frank Kitson	P40,OF1		43	109	20	32	16	5	1	0	6		2	.294	.358
Harry Howell	P21		22	42	6	12	6	2	0	1	6		1	.286	.405
Jack Dunn	P10	(1-2)	10	26	2	6	1	0	0	0	1		0	.231	.231
Jerry Nops	P9		9	25	0	4	1	0	0	0	3		0	.160	.160
Gus Weyhing	P8	(2-2)	8	18	2	4	2	0	0	0	1		0	.222	.222
Broadway Smith	3B6,C1		7	25	2	6	3	0	0	0	1		2	.240	.240
Wild Bill Donovan	P5		5	13	0	0	2	0	0	0	0		0	.000	.000
Joe Yeager	P2,3B1	(1,3-3)	3	9	0	3	0	0	0	0	0		0	.333	.333
Farmer Steelman	C1		1	4	0	0	0	0	0	0	0		0	.000	.000
Doc Casey	3B1	(1-2)	1	3	0	1	1	0	0	0	0		0	.333	.333
			142	4860	816	1423	676	199	81	26	421	272	274	.293	.383

PITCHERS		W	L	PCT	G	GS	CG	SH	SV	IP	H	BB	SO	ERA
Joe McGinnity		28	8	.778	44	37	32	1	0	343	350	113	93	2.94
Brickyard Kennedy		20	13	.606	42	35	26	2	0	292	316	111	75	3.91
Frank Kitson		15	13	.536	40	30	21	2	4	253	283	56	55	4.19
Harry Howell		6	5	.545	21	10	7	2	0	110	131	36	26	3.75
Jerry Nops		4	4	.500	9	8	6	1	0	68	79	18	22	3.84
Jack Dunn	(1-2)	3	4	.429	10	7	5	0	0	63	88	28	6	5.57
Gus Weyhing	(2-2)	3	4	.429	8	8	3	0	0	48	66	20	8	4.31
Joe Yeager	(1,3-3)	1	1	.500	2	2	2	0	0	17	21	5	2	6.88
Wild Bill Donovan		1	2	.333	5	4	2	0	0	31	36	18	13	6.68
		82	54	.603	142	141	104	8	4	1226	1370	405	300	3.89

PITTSBURGH 79-60 .568 -4.5 2nd Fred Clarke
Pirates

BATTERS	POS/GAMES		GP	AB	R	H	BI	2B	3B	HR	BB	SO	SB	BA	SA
Duff Cooley	1B66		66	249	30	50	22	8	1	0	14		9	.201	.241
Claude Ritchey	2B123		123	476	62	139	67	17	8	1	29		18	.292	.368
Bones Ely	SS130		130	475	60	116	51	6	6	0	17		6	.244	.282
Jim Williams	3B103,SS4		106	416	73	110	68	15	11	5	32		18	.264	.389
Honus Wagner	OF118,3B9,2B7,1B3,P1		135	527	107	201	100	45	22	4	41		38	.381	.573
Ginger Beaumont	OF138		138	567	105	158	50	14	9	5	40		27	.279	.362
Fred Clarke	OF104		106	399	84	110	32	15	12	3	51		21	.276	.396
Chief Zimmer	C78,1B2		82	271	27	80	35	7	10	0	17		4	.295	.395
Tom O'Brien	1B65,OF25,2B4,SS2		102	376	61	109	61	22	6	3	21		12	.290	.404
Tommy Leach	3B31,SS8,2B7,OF4		51	160	20	34	16	1	2	1	21		8	.213	.263
Jack O'Connor	C40,1B2	(2-2)	43	147	15	35	19	4	1	0	3		5	.238	.279
Tom McCreery	OF35,P1		43	132	20	29	13	4	3	1	16		2	.220	.318
Deacon Phillipe	P38		38	105	7	19	7	3	1	0	1		0	.181	.229
Pop Schriver	C24,1B1		37	92	12	27	12	7	0	1	10		0	.293	.402
Jesse Tannehill	P29,OF4		34	110	19	37	17	7	0	0	5		2	.336	.400
Jack Chesbro	P32,OF1		32	85	10	15	9	4	1	0	6		1	.176	.247
Sam Leever	P30		30	88	9	18	5	2	2	1	2		1	.205	.307
Rube Waddell	P29	(1,3-3)	30	81	6	14	9	2	3	0	0		1	.173	.272
Pop Dillon	1B5	(1-2)	5	18	3	2	1	1	0	0	0		0	.111	.167
Tacks Latimer	C4		4	12	1	4	2	1	0	0	0		0	.333	.417
Patsy Flaherty	P4		4	9	0	1	0	0	0	0	1		0	.111	.111
Jiggs Donahue	C2,OF1		3	10	1	2	3	0	1	0	0		1	.200	.400
Ed Poole	P1,OF1		2	4	1	2	3	0	1	1	0		0	.500	1.750
Jouett Meekin	P2		2	4	0	0	0	0	0	0	0		0	.000	.000
Bert Husting	P2	(2-2)	2	3	0	0	0	0	0	0	0		0	.000	.000
Walt Woods	P1		1	1	0	0	0	0	0	0	0		0	.000	.000
			140	4817	733	1312	602	185	100	26	327	321	174	.272	.368

PITTSBURGH (cont.)
Pirates

PITCHERS		W	L	PCT	G	GS	CG	SH	SV	IP	H	BB	SO	ERA
Jesse Tannehill		20	6	.769	29	27	23	2	0	234	247	43	50	2.88
Deacon Phillipe		20	13	.606	38	33	29	1	0	279	274	42	75	2.84
Sam Leever		15	13	.536	30	29	25	3	0	233	236	48	84	2.71
Jack Chesbro		15	13	.536	32	26	20	3	1	216	220	79	56	3.67
Rube Waddell	(1,3-3)	8	13	.381	29	22	16	2	0	209	176	55	130	2.37
Ed Poole		1	0	1.000	1	0	0	0	0	7	4	0	3	1.29
Jouett Meekin		0	2	.000	2	2	1	0	0	13	20	8	3	6.92
Patsy Flaherty		0	0	----	4	1	0	0	0	22	30	9	5	6.14
Bert Husting	(2-2)	0	0	----	2	0	0	0	0	8	10	5	7	5.63
Honus Wagner		0	0	----	1	0	0	0	0	3	3	4	1	0.00
Tom McCreery		0	0	----	1	0	0	0	0	3	3	1	0	12.00
Walt Woods		0	0	----	1	0	0	0	0	3	9	1	1	21.00
		79	60	.568	140	140	114	11	1	1229	1232	295	415	3.06

PHILADELPHIA
Phillies

75-63 .543 -8 3rd Bill Shettsline

BATTERS	POS/GAMES		GP	AB	R	H	BI	2B	3B	HR	BB	SO	SB	BA	SA
Ed Delahanty	1B130		131	539	82	174	109	32	10	2	41		16	.323	.430
Nap Lajoie	2B102,3B1		102	451	95	152	92	33	12	7	10		22	.337	.510
Monte Cross	SS131		131	466	59	94	62	11	3	3	51		19	.202	.258
Harry Wolverton	3B101	(2-2)	101	383	42	108	58	10	8	3	20		4	.282	.373
Elmer Flick	OF138		138	545	106	200	110	32	16	11	56		35	.367	.545
Roy Thomas	OF139,P1		140	531	132	168	33	4	3	0	115		37	.316	.335
Jimmy Slagle	OF141		141	574	115	165	45	16	9	0	60		34	.287	.347
Ed McFarland	C93,3B1		94	344	50	105	38	14	8	0	29		9	.305	.392
Joe Dolan	3B31,2B29,SS12		74	257	39	51	27	7	3	1	16		10	.198	.261
Klondike Douglass	C47,3B2		50	160	23	48	25	9	4	0	13		7	.300	.406
Al Orth	P33,OF3		39	129	6	40	21	4	1	1	2		2	.310	.380
Pearce Chiles	1B16,2B12,OF3		33	111	13	24	23	6	2	1	6		4	.216	.333
Bill Bernhard	P32		32	91	7	14	6	1	0	0	3		0	.154	.165
Red Donahue	P32		32	90	9	20	12	0	0	0	3		1	.222	.222
Chick Fraser	P29		29	85	8	22	10	4	1	0	5		2	.259	.329
Wiley Piatt	P22		22	68	8	17	7	0	1	0	4		1	.250	.279
Morg Murphy	C11		11	36	2	10	3	0	1	0	0		0	.278	.333
Jack Dunn	P10	(2-2)	10	33	3	10	5	1	0	0	0		1	.303	.333
Bert Meyers	3B7		7	28	5	5	2	1	0	0	3		1	.179	.214
Bert Conn	P4		6	9	4	3	1	1	0	0	0		0	.333	.444
Al Maul	P5		5	15	2	3	1	0	0	0	2		0	.200	.200
Fred Jacklitsch	C3	(1,3-3)	5	11	0	2	3	1	0	0	0		0	.182	.273
Charles Ziegler	3B3		3	11	0	3	1	0	0	0	0		0	.273	.273
Warren McLaughlin	P1		1	2	0	1	0	0	0	0	1		0	.500	.500
			141	4969	810	1439	694	187	82	29	440	374	205	.290	.378

PITCHERS		W	L	PCT	G	GS	CG	SH	SV	IP	H	BB	SO	ERA
Chick Fraser		15	9	.625	29	26	22	1	0	223	250	93	58	3.14
Red Donahue		15	10	.600	32	24	21	2	0	240	299	50	41	3.60
Bill Bernhard		15	10	.600	32	27	20	0	2	218	284	74	49	4.77
Al Orth		14	14	.500	33	30	24	2	1	262	302	60	68	3.78
Wiley Piatt		9	10	.474	22	20	16	1	0	161	194	71	47	4.71
Jack Dunn	(2-2)	5	5	.500	10	9	9	1	0	80	87	29	12	4.84
Al Maul		2	3	.400	5	4	3	0	0	38	53	3	6	6.16
Bert Conn		0	2	.000	4	1	1	0	0	17	29	16	2	8.31
Warren McLaughlin		0	0	----	1	0	0	0	0	6	4	6	1	4.50
Roy Thomas		0	0	----	1	0	0	0	0	3	4	0	0	3.38
		75	63	.543	141	141	116	7	3	1249	1506	402	284	4.12

BOSTON
Beaneaters

66-72 .478 -17 4th Frank Selee

BATTERS	POS/GAMES	GP	AB	R	H	BI	2B	3B	HR	BB	SO	SB	BA	SA
Fred Tenney	1B111	112	437	77	122	56	13	5	1	39		17	.279	.339
Bobby Lowe	2B127	127	474	65	132	71	11	5	3	26		15	.278	.342
Germany Long	SS125	125	486	80	127	66	19	4	12	44		26	.261	.391
Jimmy Collins	3B141,SS1	142	586	104	178	95	25	5	6	34		23	.304	.394
Buck Freeman	OF91,1B19	117	418	58	126	65	19	13	6	25		10	.301	.452
Billy Hamilton	OF136	136	520	103	173	47	20	5	1	107		32	.333	.396

1900 NATIONAL LEAGUE

BOSTON (cont.)
Beaneaters

BATTERS	POS/GAMES		GP	AB	R	H	BI	2B	3B	HR	BB	SO	SB	BA	SA
Chick Stahl	OF135		136	553	88	163	82	23	16	5	34		27	.295	.421
Billy Sullivan	C66,SS1,2B1		72	238	36	65	41	6	0	8	9		4	.273	.399
Shad Barry	OF24,SS18,2B16,1B10,3B1		81	254	40	66	37	10	7	1	13		9	.260	.366
Boileryard Clarke	C67,1B8		81	270	35	85	30	5	2	1	9		0	.315	.359
Hugh Duffy	OF49,2B1		55	181	27	55	31	5	4	2	16		11	.304	.409
Bill Dineen	P40		44	125	14	35	9	1	0	0	9		6	.280	.288
Vic Willis	P32		32	88	8	12	11	2	1	0	3		0	.136	.182
Ted Lewis	P30		30	73	10	10	5	0	0	0	11		0	.137	.137
Kid Nichols	P29		29	90	14	18	7	0	0	1	7		1	.200	.233
Togie Pittinger	P18		18	46	2	6	2	0	0	0	0		0	.130	.130
Nig Cuppy	P17		17	42	7	11	6	3	0	0	4		0	.262	.333
Jack Clements	C10		16	42	6	13	10	1	0	1	3		0	.310	.405
Joe Connor	C7		7	19	2	4	4	0	0	0	2		1	.211	.211
Harvey Bailey	P4	(1-2)	4	9	2	2	1	0	1	0	0		0	.222	.444
Rome Chambers	P1		1	1	0	0	0	0	0	0	0		0	.000	.000
			142	4952	778	1403	676	163	68	48	395	278	182	.283	.373

PITCHERS	W	L	PCT	G	GS	CG	SH	SV	IP	H	BB	SO	ERA
Bill Dineen	20	14	.588	40	37	33	1	0	321	304	105	107	3.12
Ted Lewis	13	12	.520	30	22	19	1	0	209	215	86	66	4.13
Kid Nichols	13	16	.448	29	27	25	4	0	231	215	72	53	3.07
Vic Willis	10	17	.370	32	29	22	2	0	236	258	106	53	4.19
Nig Cuppy	8	4	.667	17	13	9	0	1	105	107	24	23	3.08
Togie Pittinger	2	9	.182	18	13	8	0	0	114	135	54	27	5.13
Harvey Bailey	0	0	----	4	1	0	0	0	20	24	11	9	4.95
Rome Chambers	0	0	----	1	0	0	0	1	4	5	5	2	11.25
	66	72	.478	142	142	116	8	2	1240	1263	463	340	3.72

CHICAGO
Orphans

65-75 .464 -19 5th (tie) Tom Loftus

BATTERS	POS/GAMES		GP	AB	R	H	BI	2B	3B	HR	BB	SO	SB	BA	SA
John Ganzel	1B78	(1-2)	78	284	29	78	32	14	4	4	10		5	.275	.394
Cupid Childs	2B137		137	531	67	128	44	14	5	0	57		15	.241	.286
Barry McCormick	SS84,3B21,2B5		110	379	35	83	48	13	5	3	38		8	.219	.303
Bill Bradley	3B106,1B15		122	444	63	125	49	21	8	5	27		14	.282	.399
Jimmy Ryan	OF105		105	415	66	115	59	25	4	5	29		19	.277	.393
Danny Green	OF102		103	389	63	116	49	21	5	5	17		28	.298	.416
John McCarthy	OF123		124	503	68	148	48	16	7	0	24		22	.294	.354
Tim Donahue	C66,2B1		67	216	21	51	17	10	1	0	19		8	.236	.292
Sam Mertes	OF88,1B33,SS7		127	481	72	142	60	25	4	7	42		38	.295	.407
Frank Chance	C51,1B1		56	149	26	44	13	9	3	0	15		8	.295	.396
Bill Clingman	SS47	(1-2)	47	159	15	33	11	6	0	0	17		6	.208	.245
Charles Dexter	C22,OF13,2B1		40	125	7	25	20	5	0	2	1		2	.200	.288
Nixey Callahan	P32		32	115	16	27	9	3	2	0	6		5	.235	.296
Clark Griffith	P30		30	95	16	24	7	4	1	1	8		2	.253	.347
Ned Garvin	P30		30	91	12	14	4	1	0	0	3		0	.154	.165
Jack Taylor	P28		28	81	7	19	6	3	1	1	3		1	.235	.333
Sammy Strang	3B16,SS9,2B2		27	102	15	29	9	3	0	0	8		1	.284	.314
Bill Everett	1B23		23	91	10	24	17	4	0	0	3		2	.264	.308
Jocko Menefee	P16		17	46	5	5	4	0	0	0	2		0	.109	.109
John Kling	C15		15	51	8	15	7	3	1	0	2		0	.294	.392
Cozy Dolan	OF13		13	48	5	13	2	1	0	0	2		2	.271	.292
Bert Cunningham	P8		8	27	5	4	1	1	0	0	1		1	.148	.185
Art Nichols	C7	(1,3-3)	8	25	1	5	0	0	0	0	3		1	.200	.200
Frank Killen	P6	(1-2)	6	20	0	3	2	0	0	0	1		0	.150	.150
Sam Dungan	OF3	(1-2)	6	15	1	4	1	0	0	0	1		0	.267	.267
Harry Wolverton	3B3	(1-2)	3	11	2	2	0	0	0	0	2		1	.182	.182
Long Tom Hughes	P3		3	6	0	0	0	0	0	0	2		0	.000	.000
Erwin Harvey	P1	(1,3-3)	2	3	0	0	0	0	0	0	0		0	.000	.000
Roger Bresnahan	C1		2	2	0	0	0	0	0	0	0		0	.000	.000
Mal Eason	P1		1	3	0	0	0	0	0	0	0		0	.000	.000
			146	4907	635	1276	519	202	51	33	343	383	189	.260	.342

PITCHERS	W	L	PCT	G	GS	CG	SH	SV	IP	H	BB	SO	ERA
Clark Griffith	14	13	.519	30	30	27	4	0	248	245	51	61	3.05
Nixey Callahan	13	16	.448	32	32	32	2	0	285	347	74	77	3.82
Jack Taylor	10	17	.370	28	26	25	2	1	222	226	58	57	2.55

CHICAGO (cont.)
Orphans

PITCHERS		W	L	PCT	G	GS	CG	SH	SV	IP	H	BB	SO	ERA
Ned Garvin		10	18	.357	30	28	25	1	0	246	225	63	107	2.41
Jock Menefee		9	4	.692	16	13	11	0	0	117	140	35	30	3.85
Bert Cunningham		4	3	.571	8	7	7	0	0	64	84	21	7	4.36
Frank Killen	(1-2)	3	3	.500	6	6	6	0	0	54	65	11	4	4.67
Mal Eason		1	0	1.000	1	1	1	0	0	9	9	3	2	1.00
Long Tom Hughes		1	1	.500	3	3	3	0	0	21	31	7	12	5.14
Erwin Harvey		0	0	----	1	0	0	0	0	4	3	1	0	0.00
		65	75	.464	146	146	137	9	1	1271	1375	324	357	3.23

ST. LOUIS
Cardinals

65-75 .464 -19 5th (tie) Tebeau - Heilbroner

BATTERS	POS/GAMES		GP	AB	R	H	BI	2B	3B	HR	BB	SO	SB	BA	SA
Dan McGann	1B121,2B1		121	444	79	132	58	10	9	4	32		26	.297	.387
Bill Keister	2B116,SS7,3B3		126	497	78	149	72	26	10	1	25		32	.300	.398
Bobby Wallace	SS126		126	485	70	130	70	25	9	4	40		7	.268	.381
John McGraw	3B99		99	334	84	115	33	10	4	2	85		29	.344	.416
Patsy Donovan	OF124		126	503	78	159	61	11	1	0	38		45	.316	.342
John Heidrick	OF83		85	339	51	102	45	6	8	2	18		22	.301	.383
Jesse Burkett	OF141		141	559	88	203	68	11	15	7	62		32	.363	.474
Lou Criger	C75,3B1		80	288	31	78	38	8	6	2	4		5	.271	.361
Mike Donlin	OF47,1B21		78	276	40	90	48	8	6	10	14		14	.326	.507
Wilbert Robinson	C54		60	210	26	52	28	5	1	0	11		7	.248	.281
Pat Dillard	OF26,3B21,SS3	(1-2)	57	183	24	42	12	5	2	0	13		7	.230	.279
Cy Young	P41		41	124	13	22	13	5	1	1	3		1	.177	.258
Cowboy Jones	P39		39	117	12	21	7	0	2	0	7		0	.179	.214
Jack Powell	P38		38	109	15	31	12	4	4	1	10		3	.284	.422
Willie Sudhoff	P16,OF12,3B7		35	106	15	20	6	1	1	0	11		8	.189	.217
Joe Quinn	2B14,SS6,3B1	(1-2)	22	80	12	21	11	2	0	1	10		4	.262	.325
Jim Hughey	P20		20	41	6	7	2	0	0	0	8		0	.171	.171
Lave Cross	3B16	(1-2)	16	61	6	18	6	1	0	0	1		1	.295	.311
Art Krueger	2B12		12	35	8	14	3	3	2	1	10		0	.400	.686
Jack O'Connor	C10	(1-2)	10	32	4	7	6	0	0	0	2		0	.219	.219
Gus Weyhing	P7	(1-2)	7	21	1	2	0	0	0	0	0		0	.095	.095
Fred Buelow	C4,OF1		6	17	2	4	3	0	0	0	0		0	.235	.235
Tom Thomas	P5	(1-3)	5	11	1	1	0	0	0	0	2		0	.091	.091
Patsy Tebeau	SS1		1	4	0	0	0	0	0	0	0		0	.000	.000
Jack Harper	P1		1	1	0	0	0	0	0	0	0		0	.000	.000
Harry Stanton	C1		1	0	0	0	0	0	0	0	0		0	----	----
			142	4877	744	1420	602	141	81	36	406	318	243	.291	.375

PITCHERS		W	L	PCT	G	GS	CG	SH	SV	IP	H	BB	SO	ERA
Cy Young		19	19	.500	41	35	32	4	0	321	337	36	115	3.00
Jack Powell		17	16	.515	38	37	28	3	0	288	325	77	77	4.44
Cowboy Jones		13	19	.406	39	36	29	3	0	293	334	82	68	3.57
Willie Sudhoff		6	8	.429	16	14	13	2	0	127	128	37	29	2.76
Jim Hughey		5	7	.417	20	12	11	0	0	113	147	40	23	5.19
Gus Weyhing	(1-2)	3	2	.600	7	5	3	0	0	47	60	21	6	4.63
Tom Thomas		2	2	.500	5	1	1	0	0	26	38	4	7	3.76
Jack Harper		0	1	.000	1	1	0	0	0	3	4	2	0	12.00
		65	75	.464	142	141	117	12	0	1217	1373	299	325	3.75

CINCINNATI
Reds

62-77 .446 -21.5 7th Bob Allen

BATTERS	POS/GAMES		GP	AB	R	H	BI	2B	3B	HR	BB	SO	SB	BA	SA
Jake Beckley	1B140		141	558	98	190	94	26	10	2	40		23	.341	.434
Joe Quinn	2B74	(2-2)	74	266	18	73	25	5	2	0	16		7	.274	.308
Tom Corcoran	SS124,2B5		127	523	64	128	54	21	9	1	22		27	.245	.325
Harry Steinfeldt	3B67,OF2,2B64,SS2		134	510	57	125	66	29	7	2	27		14	.245	.341
Algie McBride	OF110		112	436	59	120	59	15	8	4	25		12	.275	.374
Jim Barrett	OF137		137	545	114	172	42	11	7	5	72		44	.316	.389
Sam Crawford	OF95		101	389	68	101	59	15	15	7	28		14	.260	.429
Heinie Peitz	C80,1B8		91	294	34	75	34	14	1	2	20		5	.255	.330
Charlie Irwin	3B61,SS16,OF6,2B3		87	333	59	91	44	15	6	1	14		9	.273	.363
Mike Kahoe	C51,SS1		52	175	18	33	9	3	3	1	4		3	.189	.257
Bob Wood	C18,3B15,OF1	(1-2)	45	139	17	37	22	8	1	0	10		3	.266	.338

1900 NATIONAL LEAGUE

CINCINNATI (cont.)
Reds

BATTERS	POS/GAMES		GP	AB	R	H	BI	2B	3B	HR	BB	SO	SB	BA	SA
Ed Scott	P43		43	127	9	20	11	3	2	1	1		0	.157	.236
Ted Breitenstein	P24,OF12		41	126	12	24	12	1	1	2	9		0	.190	.262
Noodles Hahn	P38		38	111	12	23	9	3	1	2	2		0	.207	.306
Doc Newton	P35		35	86	11	17	7	0	1	0	6		2	.198	.221
Phil Geier	OF27,3B2	(1,3-3)	30	113	18	29	10	1	4	0	7		3	.257	.336
Elmer Smith	OF27	(1-2)	29	111	14	31	18	4	4	1	18		5	.279	.414
Bill Phillips	P29		29	79	8	13	3	0	0	0	3		1	.165	.165
Topsy Hartsel	OF18	(2-2)	18	64	10	21	5	2	1	2	8		7	.328	.484
Dick Harley	OF5	(2-2)	5	21	2	9	5	1	0	0	1		4	.429	.476
Bob Allen	SS5		5	15	0	2	1	1	0	0	0		0	.133	.200
Arch Stimmell	P2	(1-2)	2	5	1	1	2	0	0	0	0		0	.200	.200
			144	5026	703	1335	591	178	83	33	333	408	183	.266	.354

PITCHERS		W	L	PCT	G	GS	CG	SH	SV	IP	H	BB	SO	ERA
Ed Scott		17	20	.459	42	35	31	0	1	315	370	65	87	3.86
Noodles Hahn		16	20	.444	39	37	29	4	0	311	306	89	132	3.27
Ted Breitenstein		10	10	.500	24	20	18	1	0	192	205	79	39	3.65
Bill Phillips		9	11	.450	29	24	17	3	0	208	229	67	51	4.28
Doc Newton		9	15	.375	35	27	22	1	0	235	255	100	88	4.14
Arch Stimmell		1	1	.500	2	1	1	0	0	13	18	4	2	6.92
		62	77	.446	144	144	118	9	1	1275	1383	404	399	3.83

NEW YORK
Giants

60-78　　.435　　-23　　8th　　Ewing - Davis

BATTERS	POS/GAMES		GP	AB	R	H	BI	2B	3B	HR	BB	SO	SB	BA	SA
Jack Doyle	1B133		133	505	69	135	66	24	1	1	34		34	.267	.325
Kid Gleason	2B111,SS1		111	420	60	104	29	11	3	1	17		23	.248	.295
George Davis	SS114		114	426	69	136	61	20	4	3	35		29	.319	.406
Piano Legs Hickman	3B120,OF7		127	473	65	148	91	19	17	9	17		10	.313	.482
Elmer Smith	OF83	(2-2)	85	312	47	81	34	9	7	2	24		14	.260	.353
George Van Haltren	OF141,P1		141	571	114	180	51	30	7	1	50		45	.315	.398
Kip Selbach	OF141		141	523	98	176	68	29	12	4	72		36	.337	.461
Frank Bowerman	C75,SS2		80	270	25	65	42	5	3	1	6		10	.241	.293
Mike Grady	C41,1B12,SS11,3B7,OF5,2B2		83	251	36	55	27	8	4	0	34		9	.219	.283
Win Mercer	P32,3B19,OF14,SS7,2B3		75	248	32	73	27	4	0	0	26		15	.294	.310
Bill Carrick	P45		45	115	14	20	5	1	1	0	9		1	.174	.200
Pink Hawley	P41		41	123	9	25	11	1	1	1	3		0	.203	.252
John Warner	C31		34	108	15	27	13	4	0	0	8		1	.250	.287
Pop Foster	OF12,SS7,2B5		31	84	19	22	11	3	1	0	11		0	.262	.321
Cy Seymour	P13,OF3,1B1	(1,3-3)	23	40	9	12	2	0	0	0	3		0	.300	.300
Danny Murphy	2B22		22	74	11	20	6	1	0	0	8		4	.270	.284
Curt Bernard	OF19,SS1		20	71	9	18	8	2	0	0	6		1	.254	.282
Ed Doheny	P20	(1,3-3)	20	54	7	12	7	3	0	0	1		4	.222	.278
Dummy Taylor	P11		11	22	2	3	1	0	0	0	1		0	.136	.136
Christy Mathewson	P6		6	11	1	2	1	2	0	0	1		0	.182	.364
Charlie Frisbee	OF4	(1-2)	4	13	2	2	3	1	0	0	2		0	.154	.231
Richard Cogan	P2,SS1		3	8	0	1	0	0	0	0	1		0	.125	.125
Tommy Sheehan	SS1	(2-2)	1	2	0	0	0	0	0	0	0		0	.000	.000
			141	4724	713	1317	564	177	61	23	369	343	236	.279	.357

PITCHERS		W	L	PCT	G	GS	CG	SH	SV	IP	H	BB	SO	ERA
Bill Carrick		19	22	.463	45	41	32	1	0	342	415	92	63	3.53
Pink Hawley		18	18	.500	41	38	34	2	0	329	377	89	80	3.53
Win Mercer		13	17	.433	33	29	26	1	0	243	303	58	39	3.86
Ed Doheny	(1,3-3)	4	14	.222	20	18	12	0	0	134	148	96	44	5.45
Dummy Taylor		4	3	.571	11	7	6	0	0	62	74	24	16	2.45
Cy Seymour	(1,3-3)	2	1	.667	13	7	2	0	0	53	58	54	19	6.96
Christy Mathewson		0	3	.000	6	1	1	0	0	34	37	20	15	5.08
Richard Cogan		0	0	----	2	0	0	0	0	8	10	6	1	6.75
George Van Haltren		0	0	----	1	0	0	0	0	3	1	3	0	0.00
		60	78	.435	141	141	113	4	0	1207	1423	442	277	3.96

1900 AMERICAN LEAGUE

A New Threat

In 1894, Cincinnati sportswriter Ban Johnson was approached to become the president of a minor league calling itself the Western League. Intrigued, Johnson accepted the challenge.

By the late 1890s, Johnson had molded the Western League into the strongest minor league in the land. Featuring teams in Detroit, Indianapolis, Kansas City, and other midwestern cities, Johnson and the league cracked down on the rowdier elements in the game by strengthening the role of the league president, supporting the umpire crew, and by not tolerating rough play. These tactics, while going against the grain of baseball trends of the times, gained him the support of the public.

By the end of the 1899 season, Johnson wanted more. He felt he was ready to play with the National League as equals. When the Nationals trimmed their league from twelve to eight teams, Johnson moved in. He shifted a franchise into the vacated National League city of Cleveland and brazenly placed a team in the National League stronghold of Chicago. To deregionalize his league, Johnson christened it as the American League.

The American League opened the 1900 season with eight teams in Buffalo, Chicago, Cleveland, Detroit, Indianapolis, Kansas City, Milwaukee, and Minneapolis. All but Minneapolis had seen major league baseball before.

Most of the players stocking the teams were major league veterans who had been playing in the Western League, or been cut adrift by the downsizing of the National League. Ostensibly, the American League was considered a minor league circuit in 1900, but the percentage of its major league caliber players exceeded both the first year of the major league American Association and the only year of the major league Union Association.

Chicago pulled away from the pack during the summer and won the inaugural American League flag by four and one-half games. Their best hitters, Joe Sugden (.289), Dick Padden (.284), and Bill Shugart (.283) could not top the .300 mark, as the team finished with the worst hitting in the league. Their top pitcher was Roger Denzer who won twenty.

Second place Milwaukee featured the batting of John Anderson (.309) and Dave Fultz (.298), while third place Indianapolis enjoyed the hitting of George Magoon

(.309), Socks Seybold (.304) and Topsy Hartsel (.300). The top pitchers for these clubs were respectively Bill Reidy who won 19 and Win Kellum who won 20.

Detroit finished in fourth while Kansas City finished fifth. Detroit was led by Dick Harley (.325) and three 19-game winners, Roscoe Miller, Joe Yeager, and Jack Cronin. Kansas City possessed the batting champion Sam Dungan (.337) and the league's winningest and losingest pitcher, Arnold Lee (23-22).

Cleveland, Buffalo, and Minneapolis brought up the rear. Good performances on these teams included Candy LaChance of Cleveland (.302), Doc Amole's 22 wins for Buffalo, and Perry Werden (.316) of Minneapolis.

Ban Johnson was pleased with the result of the American League's first season. He felt that he had given the public a well-disciplined viable alternative to the rowdy National League.

Following the season, Johnson ended the pretense of the American League's minor league status. He announced early in 1901 that the American League would henceforth be a major league on equal footing with the National League. This would be the fourth time this claim would be made against the senior circuit. And unlike the other three attempts, this claim and threat would not go away. That is, until the National League granted the American League equality three years later, whereupon the two leagues became joint participants in major league baseball — a partnership that has endured for over 90 years.

1900 AMERICAN LEAGUE

CHICAGO White Stockings 82-53 .608 1st Charlie Comiskey

BATTERS	POS/GAMES		GP	AB	R	H	BI	2B	3B	HR	BB	SO	SB	BA	SA
Frank Isbell	1B54,OF18,3B15,P7		109	399	49	99							22	.248	.343
Dick Padden	2B130		130	482	84	137							36	.284	.361
Frank Shugart	SS98		98	377	54	107							16	.283	.385
Fred Hartman	3B116		116	450	71	124							15	.275	.356
Dummy Hoy	OF137		137	547	115	139							32	.254	.311
Herm McFarland	OF120		120	460	81	111							31	.241	.341
Steve Brodie	OF64		64	229	41	60							8	.262	.314
Joe Sugden	C74,1B43		121	459	47	133							15	.289	.357
Dick Buckley	C34		40	139	10	28							0	.201	.245
John Katoll	P37		38	109	6	17							0	.155	.193
Chauncey Fisher	P35		38	120	10	27							0	.225	.283
Tommy Dowd	1B26	(1-2)	36											.235	
Roger Denzer	P36		36	108	8	23							0	.212	.250
Bob Wood	C28	(2-2)	35	127	15	39							3	.307	.417
John Shearon	OF34	(2-2)	34											.285	
Roy Patterson	P29		33	96	12	19							0	.191	.219
Bob Dillard	OF16	(2-2)	28	98	13	19							5	.193	.245
Charlie O'Leary	SS26		26	92	4	15							0	.163	.196
Bud Lally	1B7	(1-2)	10											.238	
Dave Brain	3B7,2B1		8											.240	
Frank McManus	OF4	(1-2)	7											.143	
Willie McGill	P6		6											.200	
Ed Doheny	P5	(2-3)	6											.214	
Tom Thomas	P3	(3-3)	3											.200	
Cy Seymour	P2	(2-3)	2											.000	
G. E. Clayton	1B2		2											.333	
Ed Burke		(1-3)	1											.000	
Frank Killen	P1	(2-2)	1											.000	
			137	4690	667	1205							183	.257	

PITCHERS		W	L	PCT	G	GS	CG	SH	SV	IP	H	BB	SO	ERA
Roger Denzer		20	10	.667	36			3						
Chauncey Fisher		19	9	.679	35			6						
Roy Patterson		17	8	.680	29			4						
John Katoll		16	14	.533	37			6						
Frank Isbell		5	2	.714	7			0						
Willie McGill		3	2	.600	6									
Cy Seymour	(2-3)	1	1	.500	2			0						
Tom Thomas	(2-2)	1	2	.333	3									
Frank Killen	(2-2)	0	1	.000	1									
Ed Doheny	(2-3)	0	4	.000	5									
		82	53	.608	137			19						

MILWAUKEE Brewers 79-58 .577 -4 2nd Connie Mack

BATTERS	POS/GAMES		GP	AB	R	H	BI	2B	3B	HR	BB	SO	SB	BA	SA
John Anderson	1B90,OF44		134	542	94	168							63	.309	.417
Dave Fultz	2B57,SS49		114	430	85	128							36	.298	.421
Wid Conroy	SS89		116	431	58	101							42	.234	.304
Jim Burke	3B127		127	456	47	112							23	.245	.300
Irv Waldron	OF139		139	579	92	170							34	.293	.370
Tom Carey	OF78		79	320	45	79							6	.246	.294
Fred Ketcham	OF73		73	316	42	83							12	.231	.297
Harry Smith	C79		80	273	25	71							10	.260	.348
Bill Diggins	C50,1B13	(2-2)	63											.297	
Tommy Dowd	OF48,1B14	(2-2)	62											.278	
Jim Garry	OF60	(1-2)	60											.264	
Lou Bierbauer	2B45	(2-3)	45											.183	
Henry Dowling	P37		38	105	9	28							1	.267	.324
Tully Sparks	P34		34	104	9	24							1	.231	.288
Bill Reidy	P32		32	104	7	22							2	.212	.231
Bill Hallman	OF29	(2-2)	29	105	13	23							2	.219	.229
George Rettger	P23		29	82	11	17							0	.207	.293
George Yeager	C16		25	80	16	31							2	.387	.500
Harry Clark	1B19		19	76	10	20							3	.263	.382
Henry Spies	C17	(2-2)	17											.317	
George Wheeler	P16		16	46	4	8							0	.173	.196
Ed Abbaticchio	2B13,1B1	(2-2)	16											.180	
Rube Waddell	P15	(2-3)	15	49	6	12							0	.244	.367

MILWAUKEE (cont.)
Brewers

BATTERS	POS/GAMES		GP	AB	R	H	BI	2B	3B	HR	BB	SO	SB	BA	SA
Henry Reitz	2B8		8											.370	
Bert Husting	P5	(1-2)	5											.118	
----- O'Rourke	SS1		1											.000	
Fred Raymer	2B1		1											.000	
			139	4846	635	1283							237	.265	

PITCHERS			W	L	PCT	G	GS	CG	SH	SV	IP	H	BB	SO	ERA
Bill Reidy			19	9	.679	32			1						
Tully Sparks			16	12	.571	34			1						
Henry Dowling			16	19	.471	37			4						
Rube Waddell		(2-3)	10	3	.769	15			2						
George Wheeler			7	3	.700	16			0						
George Rettger			7	11	.389	23			2						
Bert Husting		(1-2)	4	1	.800	5			0						
			79	58	.577	139			10						

INDIANAPOLIS   71-64   .526   -11   3rd   Bill Watkins
Hoosiers

BATTERS	POS/GAMES		GP	AB	R	H	BI	2B	3B	HR	BB	SO	SB	BA	SA
Mike Kelley	1B108		108	418	52	86							11	.206	.273
George Magoon	2B120		120	449	81	139							36	.309	.390
Art Madison	SS98		98	378	51	100							8	.264	.333
Mike Hickey	3B126		126	454	62	111							30	.244	.297
George Hogriever	OF138		138	524	116	132							15	.252	.338
Socks Seybold	OF107		115	444	72	135							7	.304	.450
Topsy Hartsel	OF101	(1-2)	104	406	86	122							31	.300	.426
Mike Powers	C99		110	416	42	124							0	.298	.356
Phil Geier	SS32,OF27	(2-3)	80	326	39	105							14	.322	.405
Mike Heydon	C45		61	208	32	52							1	.250	.351
George Flynn	OF29		53	175	29	38							13	.217	.280
Win Kellum	P43		43	127	17	26							0	.205	.276
Fred Barnes	P25		32	94	10	20							1	.213	.255
Bill Damman	P26		27	67	6	10							0	.149	.179
Jim Gardner	P20		23	76	5	20							0	.263	.276
William Grey	SS18	(2-2)	18											.217	
Bill Milligan	P13	(2-2)	13											.225	
Arch Stimmel	P11	(2-2)	11											.118	
Jot Goar	P10		10											.211	
Ted Guese	P9		9											.250	
John Richter	OF3		3											.000	
War Sanders	P2		2											.667	
Ace Stewart	2B1	(1-2)	1											.333	
John Doscher	P1		1											.000	
Norwood Gibson	P1	(1-2)	1											.000	
			139	4797	718	1261							167	.263	

PITCHERS			W	L	PCT	G	GS	CG	SH	SV	IP	H	BB	SO	ERA
Win Kellum			20	18	.526	43			3						
Fred Barnes			13	10	.565	25			0						
Bill Damman			10	12	.455	26			0						
Jim Gardner			8	8	.500	20			1						
Jot Goar			7	2	.778	10			0						
Bill Milligan		(2-2)	6	6	.500	13			0						
Arch Stimmel		(2-2)	5	4	.556	11			2						
Ted Guese			2	3	.400	9									
John Doscher			0	1	.000	1									
Norwood Gibson		(1-2)	0	0	----	1									
War Sanders			0	0	----	2									
			71	64	.526	139			6						

DETROIT   71-67   .514   -12.5   4th   George Stallings
Tigers

BATTERS	POS/GAMES		GP	AB	R	H	BI	2B	3B	HR	BB	SO	SB	BA	SA
Pop Dillon	1B123	(2-2)	123	470	57	137							25	.291	.379
Jack Ryan	2B91,C20,1B15		126	462	71	119							15	.258	.333

1900 AMERICAN LEAGUE

DETROIT (cont.)
Tigers

BATTERS	POS/GAMES		GP	AB	R	H	BI	2B	3B	HR	BB	SO	SB	BA	SA
Kid Elberfield	SS109		109	396	61	104							28	.262	.316
Doc Casey	3B115	(2-2)	115	469	75	122							37	.260	.307
Dick Harley	OF123	(1-2)	123	486	77	158							47	.325	.372
Ducky Holmes	OF111		112	433	64	126							29	.291	.367
George Nicol	OF73		73	283	31	73							10	.258	.353
Al Shaw	C87		88	294	60	76							4	.259	.323
Sport McAllister	C48,2B32		109	382	63	112							40	.293	.377
Jack Cronin	P46		46	141	21	28							1	.199	.362
Joe Yeager	P33	(2-3)	45	141	16	30							5	.213	.291
George Stallings	OF42		42	147	17	37							7	.251	.347
Charles Jones	OF32		32	121	14	28							6	.231	.314
Roscoe Miller	P30		30	98	7	10							0	.163	.235
John Frisk	P21		30	70	11	20							2	.286	.371
Tommy Sheehan	SS19	(1-2)	22	75	7	17							2	.226	.253
Suter Sullivan	3B12	(1-2)	22											.226	
Bill Grey	OF9,3B7,SS4,2B3	(1-2)	21											.282	
Ed Siever	P14		14											.263	
Harry Bay	OF12		12											.200	
Welcome Gaston	P8	(1-3)	8											.167	
Jack Fifield	P5		5											.167	
Still Bill Hill	P5		5											.375	
Frank Owen	P3,1B1		4											.600	
Ed Wheeler	3B2		2											.000	
			140	4781	663	1276							258	.267	

PITCHERS			W	L	PCT	G	GS	CG	SH	SV	IP	H	BB	SO	ERA
Roscoe Miller			19	9	.679	30			4						
Joe Yeager		(2-3)	19	12	.613	33			6						
Jack Cronin			19	22	.463	46			3						
Ed Siever			6	5	.545	14			1						
John Frisk			6	9	.400	21			1						
Still Bill Hill			1	3	.250	5			1						
Welcome Gaston		(1-2)	1	4	.200	5									
Frank Owen			0	1	.000	3									
Jack Fifield			0	2	.000	5									
			71	67	.514	140			16						

KANSAS CITY
Blues

69-70 .496 -13 5th Jim Manning

BATTERS	POS/GAMES		GP	AB	R	H	BI	2B	3B	HR	BB	SO	SB	BA	SA
Sam Dungan	1B115	(2-2)	117	469	63	158							6	.337	.433
Germany Schaefer	2B84,SS19		110	398	62	102							30	.256	.342
Butts Wagner	SS76		76	312	58	86							14	.275	.375
Bill Coughlin	3B130		130	510	60	134							20	.263	.335
Jack O'Brien	OF140		140	573	81	171							26	.298	.398
Charlie Hemphill	OF131		131	517	113	165							26	.319	.412
John Farrell	OF124		125	478	88	129							28	.269	.349
John Gonding	C73		73	246	18	46							4	.187	.211
Dale Gear	P35,OF34		79	252	47	70							5	.277	.369
Ace Stewart	2B54	(2-2)	54	190	21	34							13	.179	.210
Arnold Lee	P48		50	150	15	34							0	.227	.273
Case Patten	P45		45	136	16	28							0	.206	.235
Parke Wilson	C39		42	154	17	45							7	.292	.338
Bill Clingman	SS41	(2-2)	41	155	18	48							5	.309	.335
Frank McManus	C33	(2-2)	33											.297	
John Ganzel	1B22		22	92	15	36							4	.391	.565
Chummy Gray	P13	(2-2)	13											.190	
Otto Thiel	3B12		12											.111	
Eli Cates	P11		11											.172	
Dan Daub	P7,OF1		8											.278	
Norwood Gibson	P8	(2-2)	8											.111	
----- Nagle	OF7		7											.233	
John Sullivan	C7		7											.260	
Kid Carsey	P3	(2-2)	3											.286	
Tom Thomas	P2	(2-3)	2											.250	
----- Carroll	OF1		1											.000	
			141	4949	670	1357							188	.274	

1900 AMERICAN LEAGUE

KANSAS CITY (cont.)
Blues

PITCHERS		W	L	PCT	G	GS	CG	SH	SV	IP	H	BB	SO	ERA
Arnold Lee		23	22	.511	48			1						
Dale Gear		19	11	.633	35			2						
Case Patten		17	20	.459	45			3						
Chummy Gray	(3-3)	3	3	.500	13									
Dan Daub		2	3	.400	7									
Norwood Gibson	(2-2)	2	4	.333	8									
Eli Cates		2	5	.286	11			0						
Kid Carsey	(2-2)	1	0	1.000	3									
Tom Thomas	(2-3)	0	2	.000	2									
		69	70	.496	141			6						

CLEVELAND
Spiders

63-73   .463   -19.5   6th   James McAleer

BATTERS	POS/GAMES		GP	AB	R	H	BI	2B	3B	HR	BB	SO	SB	BA	SA
Candy LaChance	1B116		116	457	60	138							29	.302	.396
Tim Flood	2B91	(2-2)	91											.247	
Dan Shay	SS61		61	219	29	49							7	.224	.324
Suter Sullivan	3B66	(2-2)	66											.298	
Ollie Pickering	OF140		140	599	117	194							13	.324	.386
Frank Genins	OF110		140	566	84	166							21	.293	.357
Charlie Frisbee	OF60	(2-2)	60	233	33	54							12	.231	.300
Harry Spies	C74	(1-2)	74											.216	
Pat Crishman	C39,OF28,1B24		93	354	31	90							8	.254	.316
Rooney Viox	SS48		48	165	20	37							2	.224	.279
Lou Bierbauer	2B35	(1-3)	43											.217	
Bill Hoffer	P29		43	126	19	24							1	.190	.238
Bill Hart	P34		37	135	17	34							3	.251	.326
Charles Buelow	3B22		31	130	24	36							2	.353	.531
Jim Jones	OF27		27	113	12	27							1	.239	.239
Jim Tamsett	3B24		24	85	6	12							3	.141	.200
Jimmy McAleer	OF20		20	77	8	18							0	.233	.233
Kit McKenna	P20		20	61	2	9							1	.147	.164
Frank Cross	C16		19	64	10	15							1	.234	.297
John White	OF15		19	72	11	20							4	.277	.306
Charles Baker	P17	(2-2)	17											.231	
Bill Diggins	C13	(1-2)	13											.170	
Dick Braggins	P10,OF2		12											.200	
Clay Fauver	P10		10											.206	
Roxy Walters	3B10		10											.151	
Farmer Weaver	OF8		8											.233	
Charlie Chech	P5,OF2		7											.200	
S. A. Reust	P6		6											.190	
Al Smythe	P6		6											.250	
Zeke Wilson	P6		6											.353	
Tom Delahanty	2B3		3											.200	
Bumpus Jones	P3		3											.222	
Frank Martin	3B3	(2-2)	3											.000	
Rip Egan	P2		2											.250	
Arch Kern	P2	(2-2)	2											.143	
Welcome Gaston	P1	(2-2)	1											.667	
			140	4867	647	1259							108	.259	

PITCHERS		W	L	PCT	G	GS	CG	SH	SV	IP	H	BB	SO	ERA
Bill Hart		18	15	.545	34			2						
Bill Hoffer		16	12	.571	29			3						
Kit McKenna		8	10	.444	20			3						
Charles Baker	(2-2)	6	7	.462	17			1						
Dick Braggins		5	5	.500	10			0						
Clay Fauver		4	6	.400	10			1						
Bumpus Jones		2	1	.667	3									
S. A. Reust		2	4	.333	6			0						
Rip Egan		1	1	.500	2									
Zeke Wilson		1	4	.200	6									
Welcome Gaston	(2-2)	0	1	.000	1									
Arch Kern	(2-2)	0	2	.000	2									
Charlie Chech		0	2	.000	5									
Al Smythe		0	3	.000	6									
		63	73	.463	140			9						

1900 AMERICAN LEAGUE

BUFFALO Bisons   61-78   .439   -23   7th   Dan Shannon

BATTERS	POS/GAMES		GP	AB	R	H	BI	2B	3B	HR	BB	SO	SB	BA	SA
Scoops Carey	1B116		135	543	66	147							13	.270	.377
Charles Atherton	2B46		49	193	38	65							7	.337	.534
Bill Hallman	SS80	(1-2)	100	397	53	111							11	.279	.368
Jay Andrews	3B117		122	456	51	114							15	.250	.342
Jocko Halligan	OF126		127	519	82	139							13	.268	.378
Jake Gettman	OF121		121	516	82	154							35	.298	.407
John Shearon	OF80	(1-2)	80											.274	
Ossie Schreckengost	C95,1B24		125	503	71	142							14	.282	.370
George Speer	C57		57	192	21	45							3	.234	.266
Doc Amole	P47		47	134	13	24							0	.179	.216
Matt Broderick	SS45		45	146	12	34							2	.233	.267
Lou Bierbauer	2B33,3B6,SS1	(3-3)	40											.295	
John Kerwin	P27		35	119	15	33							0	.277	.361
Warren Hart	OF31		34	141	17	33							14	.234	.284
James Garry	OF19	(2-2)	19											.182	
Frank Foreman	P15		18	50	9	18							1	.360	.460
Bill Hooker	P17		17	45	5	8							0	.177	.289
Charles Hastings	P15	(2-2)	15											.184	
Jud Smith	3B14		14											.176	
Hub Knoll	OF14		14											.321	
Charles Baker	P13	(1-2)	13											.375	
Tim Flood	2B12	(1-2)	12											.283	
Kid Carsey	SS5,P4	(1-2)	11											.188	
Jack Crooks	2B8		8											.100	
Arch Kern	P8	(1-2)	8											.154	
Ed Burke	OF7	(3-3)	7											.103	
Bill Milligan	P7	(1-2)	7											.467	
Ed Fertsch	P4		4											.100	
Dad Clarke	P3		3											.143	
Frank Martin	2B2	(1-2)	2											.000	
Jacob Jimeson	P1		1											.250	
Chummy Gray	P1	(1-2)	1											.000	
			140	4995	678	1324							128	.265	

PITCHERS		W	L	PCT	G	GS	CG	SH	SV	IP	H	BB	SO	ERA
Doc Amole		22	22	.500	47			2						
John Kerwin		12	14	.462	27			2						
Charles Hastings	(2-2)	8	5	.615	15									
Frank Foreman		7	6	.538	15			1						
Bill Hooker		4	13	.235	17			1						
Archie Kern	(1-2)	3	1	.750	8									
Kid Carsey	(1-2)	2	1	.667	4									
Charles Baker	(1-2)	2	5	.286	13			0						
Jocko Milligan	(1-2)	1	4	.200	7									
Chummy Gray	(1-2)	0	1	.000	1									
Jacob Jimeson		0	1	.000	1									
Dad Clarke		0	2	.000	3									
Ed Fertsch		0	3	.000	4									
		61	78	.439	140			6						

MINNEAPOLIS Millers   53-86   .381   -31   8th   Walt Wilmot

BATTERS	POS/GAMES		GP	AB	R	H	BI	2B	3B	HR	BB	SO	SB	BA	SA
Perry Werden	1B127		127	511	64	161							13	.316	.468
Ed Abbaticchio	2B101	(1-2)	101											.238	
Germany Smith	SS129		129	492	65	127							13	.258	.321
Bill Nance	3B129		129	489	69	151							14	.268	.360
Walt Wilmot	OF129		129	511	76	136							42	.267	.342
Bud Lally	OF127	(2-2)	128	555	71	146							21	.263	.333
Al Davis	OF101		101	418	82	118							22	.282	.368
Newt Fisher	C114		118	501	57	106							15	.211	.240
Erwin Harvey	OF26,P22	(2-3)	51	193	33	58							5	.300	.389
Red Ehret	P39		44	139	14	35							1	.252	.309
Art Nichols	2B23	(2-3)	44	165	15	42							14	.254	.303
Fred Jacklitsch	C25	(2-3)	32	87	21	16							2	.183	.230
Doc Parker	P30		32	93	7	22							0	.237	.268
Harvey Bailey	P28	(2-2)	28	91	6	23							0	.253	.319
Mike McCann	P23		24	61	4	12							0	.197	.230
Oscar Bandeline	OF16,P5		22	66	8	17							4	.258	.303

MINNEAPOLIS (cont.)
Millers

BATTERS	POS/GAMES		GP	AB	R	H	BI	2B	3B	HR	BB	SO	SB	BA	SA
Ed Dixon	C16		16	48	9	12							1	.250	.333
John Grim	1B14	(2-2)	14											.318	
Charles Hastings	P12	(1-2)	12											.219	
Dan Higgins	2B11		11											.175	
Bill Krause	2B9		9											.193	
David McAndrews	3B8		8											.093	
Joe Schrall	OF8		8											.167	
Ed Burke	OF6	(2-3)	6											.348	
John Burns	OF5		5											.237	
----- Campbell	3B2		2											.375	
Joe Corbett	P1		1											.000	
			142	4929	674	1304							<u>154</u>	.265	

PITCHERS			W	L	PCT	G	GS	CG	SH	SV	IP	H	BB	SO	ERA
Harvey Bailey		(2-2)	14	11	.560	28			1						
Doc Parker			12	15	.444	30			1						
Red Ehret			12	23	.343	39			1						
Erwin Harvey		(2-3)	7	14	.333	22			1						
Mike McCann			4	13	.235	23			1						
Charles Hastings		(1-2)	3	6	.333	12			0						
Oscar Bandeline			1	4	.200	5									
Joe Corbett			0	0	----	1									
			53	86	.381	142			<u>5</u>						

EPILOGUE

The Century Turns

By 1900, baseball had grown up. The growing pangs were sharp as evidenced by the turmoil on and off the field. Constant changes in management, league alignments, and bankruptcies kept the sport in a constant state of flux. Dozens of rule changes added to the mix an aura of uncertainty. Baseball weathered the scandal of players throwing games, teams throwing games, even leagues throwing out teams. Despite all this, most of the players played well and they played hard.

Major league baseball was played in 36 cities in the previous century. The cities ranged in size from small (Middletown) to large (New York), and stretched from Iowa to Massachusetts. In some cases, the fans watched in droves and followed their favorites with great interest. In other cases, they watched in driblets, forcing the teams to relocate. Most of the time, the fans of baseball reveled in their team's successes and were bitterly disappointed when they came up short.

Statistically, the nineteenth century saw it all. All of the winningest teams in baseball history played before 1900. Conversely, so did the poorest. The 1890s saw the greatest hitting bonanza the game has ever known, while the 1880s witnessed some of the weakest batting. Ironman pitchers routinely pitched more than 500 innings, but some could not make the jump ten feet back in 1893. Whole outfields batted over .400, yet some entire teams failed to hit half that average. In all, the game was a series of contrasts before the century turned.

The nineteenth century saw baseball evolve from pastures to palaces, from poverty to wealth, from fun to serious business. In all, nineteenth century baseball is a fascinating story that deserves to be heard.

SELECTED BIBLIOGRAPHY

ARTICLES

Ahrens, Arthur. "Chicago White Sox of 1900." *Baseball Research Journal*, 1978. Society for American Baseball Research.

Ahrens, Arthur. "The Chicago NL Champs of 1876." *Baseball Research Journal*, 1982. Society for American Baseball Research.

Bailey, Bob. "Four Teams Out: The NL Reduction of 1900." *Baseball Research Journal*, 1990. Society for American Baseball Research.

Brock, Darryl. "1869 Red Stockings." *Baseball Research Journal*, 1987. Society for American Baseball Research.

Davids, L. Robert. "The 1892 Split Season." *Baseball Research Journal*, 1981. Society for American Baseball Research.

Ivor-Campbell, Frederick. "Jim Devlin." *Nineteenth Century Stars*, 1989. Society for American Baseball Research.

Malloy, Jerry. "Moses Walker." *Nineteenth Century Stars*, 1989. Society for American Baseball Research.

Miller, Jim. "The Orioles' First Flag." *The National Pastime*, 1990. Society for American Baseball Research.

O'Malley, John J. "Jim Mutrie." *Nineteenth Century Stars*, 1989. Society for American Baseball Research.

Phelps, Frank V. "Ross Barnes." *Nineteenth Century Stars*, 1989. Society for American Baseball Research.

Rygelski, Jim. "Chris Von der Ahe." *Nineteenth Century Stars*, 1989. Society for American Baseball Research.

Shipley, Robert. "19th Century Pitching Changes." *Baseball Research Journal*, 1994. Society for American Baseball Research.

Tiemann, Robert L. "Curt Welch." *Nineteenth Century Stars*, 1989. Society for American Baseball Research.

Tiemann, Robert L. "Forgotten 1891 Winning Streak." *Baseball Research Journal*, 1989. Society for American Baseball Research.

Tiemann, Robert L. "The National League in 1893: Adjusting and Repeating." *Baseball Research Journal*, 1993. Society for American Baseball Research.

Voight, David Q. "Denny Lyons' 52-Game Hitting Streak." *The National Pastime*, 1993. Society for American Baseball Research.

BOOKS

Charlton, James, editor. *The Baseball Chronology*. New York: Macmillan Publishing Company, 1991.
Lowry, Philip J. *Green Cathedrals*. Cooperstown: The Society for American Baseball Research, 1986.
James, Bill. *The Bill James Historical Baseball Abstract*. New York: Villard Books, 1987.
Neft, David S., editor. *The Baseball Encyclopedia*, First Edition. New York: The Macmillan Company, 1969.
Phillips, John. *The Fall Classics of the 1890s*. Cabin John: Capital Publishing Company, 1989.
Reichler, Joseph L., editor. *The Baseball Encyclopedia*, Fourth Edition. New York: Macmillan Publishing Company, 1979.
Ryczek, William J. *Blackguards and Red Stockings*. Jefferson: McFarland & Company, Inc., 1992.
Seymour, Harold. *Baseball: The Early Years*. New York: Oxford University Press, 1960.
Thompson, S. C. *All-Time Rosters of Major League Baseball Clubs*. New York: A. S. Barnes and Co., 1974.
Thorn, John and Palmer, Peter, editors. *Total Baseball*, Third Edition. New York: Harper Perennial, 1993.
Thorn, John and Palmer, Peter, editors. *Total Baseball*, Fourth Edition. New York: Viking, 1995.
Wolff, Rick, editor. *The Baseball Encyclopedia*, Ninth Edition. New York: Macmillan Publishing Company, 1993.

GUIDES

Beadle's Dime Base Ball Player, 1860–1862, 1864–1867, 1869–1871.
DeWitt's Base-ball Guide, 1876.
Players National League Baseball Guide, 1890.
Reach's Official Baseball Guide, 1883–1887, 1889, 1891–1892, 1894–1896, 1898.
Spalding's Official Baseball Guide, 1878–1879, 1881, 1887.

NEWSPAPERS

The Sporting News, 1886–1900.

INDEX

(Key to Abbreviations: AA — American Assocation; AL — American League; NA — National Assocation; NL — National League; PL — Players' League; UA — Union Association)

Abadie, John 37, 38
Abbaticchio, Ed 288, 295, 320, 324
Abbey, Bert 238, 247, 248, 257, 264, 265, 278
Abbey, Charlie 249, 259, 268, 278, 279, 286
Abbot, Dan 211, 212
Abercrombie, Dave 9
Adams, George 59
Adams, Jim 211
Addy, Bob 10, 21, 29, 34, 41, 49
Adkinson, Henry 269
Ahearn, Charlie 64
Ake, John 108
Alberts, Gus 111, 120, 177, 226
Alexander, Nin 107, 122
Alleghenys (AA, Pittsburgh) 82, 95, 111, 133, 147
Alleghenys (NL, Pittsburgh) 156, 170, 184, 206
Allen, Bob 204, 219, 234, 244, 254, 283, 317
Allen, Ham 16
Allen, Hezekiah 102
Allen, Jack 59
Allen, Myron 89, 142, 165, 178, 179
Allen, Pete 244
Allison, Andy 17
Allison, Art 10, 16, 23, 33, 36, 42

Allison, Bill 17
Allison, Doug 9, 15, 17, 22, 23, 27, 33, 41, 47, 52, 53, 57, 96
Altoona (UA) Mountain Citys 122
Altrock, Nick 297
Alvord, Billy 130, 192, 211, 220, 229, 244
Amole, Doc 283, 298, 299, 324
Anderson, Bill 193
Anderson, Dave 183, 204, 207
Anderson, John 255, 265, 278, 285, 297, 298, 302, 320
Anderson, Varney 185, 259, 268, 278, 279
Andrews, Ed 101, 127, 141, 154, 169, 183, 185, 196, 228
Andrews, Jay 324
Andrews, Jim 203
Andrews, Wally 106, 178
Andrus, Fred 41, 100
Andrus, Wyman 127
Annis, Bill 99
Anson, Cap 11, 15, 22, 27, 33, 41, 48, 53, 58, 63, 69, 75, 87, 100, 126, 140, 155, 168, 183, 203, 218, 236, 247, 257, 264, 275, 287
Ardner, Joe 102, 206
Armstrong, Sam 10
Arnold, Billy 16
Arundel, Harry 38, 82, 99

Arundel, Tug 81, 109, 157, 172
Atherton, Charlie 308, 324
Athletics (AA, Philadelphia) 81, 93, 109, 134, 149, 163, 176, 190, 214, 227
Athletics (NA, Philadelphia) 8, 15, 22, 27, 33
Athletics (NL, Philadelphia) 43
Atkinson, Al 109, 117, 118, 119, 120, 150, 163
Atkinson, Ed 23
Atlantics (NA, Brooklyn) 15, 22, 28, 37
Austin, Henry 23
Aydelotte, Jake 112, 150

Bahret, Frank 112, 117
Bailey, Harvey 302, 303, 315, 324, 325
Bailey, King 267
Bakely, Jersey 93, 121, 122, 123, 177, 178, 184, 199, 227, 230
Baker, Charles 323, 324
Baker, Charlie 119, 120
Baker, George 96, 116, 130, 143
Baker, Kirtley 207, 247, 253, 298, 299, 309
Baker, Norm 96, 135, 136, 213
Baker, Phil 96, 119, 143
Baldwin, Kid 120, 122, 133, 149, 161, 176, 190, 204, 214

INDEX

Baldwin, Lady 116, 128, 129, 140, 154, 170, 199, 203
Baldwin, Mark 155, 168, 191, 197, 222, 235, 236, 243, 245
Ball, Art 258, 292
Baltimore 14, 21, 24, 29, 83, 96, 108, 117, 136, 151, 162, 177, 191, 212, 226, 239, 247, 253, 263, 273, 283, 292, 303
Baltimore (NA) Lord Baltimores 14, 21, 29; Marylands 24; (NL) Orioles 239, 247, 253, 263, 273, 283, 292, 303; (AA) Orioles 83, 96, 108, 136, 151, 162, 177, 191, 212, 226; (UA) Monumentals 117
Bancker, Stud 36
Bandeline, Oscar 324, 325
Banks, Bill 266, 275
Banning, Jim 172, 186
Bannon, Jimmy 248, 254, 265, 266, 274
Bannon, Tom 267, 276
Barber, Charlie 117
Barker, Al 11
Barkley, Sam 109, 133, 147, 156, 178, 192
Barlow, Tom 15, 23, 29, 36, 38
Barnes, Bill 121
Barnes, Fred 321
Barnes, Ross 8, 14, 21, 27, 33, 41, 48, 58, 71
Barnie, Billy 29, 35, 38, 96, 151
Barr, Bob 95, 96, 112, 113, 143, 144, 212, 219
Barrett, Bill 10, 15, 17, 21
Barrett, Jim 305, 316
Barrett, Marty 99, 112
Barron, ----- 29
Barrows, Frank 8
Barry, Shad 308, 315
Bartson, Charles 197
Bass, John 10, 15, 47
Bassett, Charley 99, 127, 143, 157, 171, 185, 205, 219, 237
Bastian, Charlie 122, 123, 126, 141, 154, 169, 183, 197, 220, 228
Bates, Bush 192
Bates, Frank 294, 304, 305, 309, 310
Battam, Larry 268
Battin, Joe 10, 22, 27, 34, 41, 48, 82, 95, 96, 111, 116, 120, 213
Bauers, Al 106, 142
Bausewine, George 190

Bay, Harry 322
Bayer, Burley 307
Beach, Jack 112
Beals, Tommy 9, 17, 23, 27, 33, 63
Beam, Alex 184
Beam, Ernie 264
Beaneaters (NL, Boston) 87, 99, 128, 141, 156, 169, 182, 205, 218, 233, 243, 254, 265, 274, 283, 292, 302, 314
Beard, Oliver 190, 204, 229
Beatin, Eb 154, 170, 184, 206, 220, 221
Beatle, Dave 103
Beaumont, Ginger 306, 313
Beavens, E. P. 9, 15
Becannon, Jim 106, 136, 155
Bechtel, George 8, 14, 21, 28, 33, 34, 37, 42, 43
Beck, Erv 302
Beck, Frank 111, 117, 118
Becker, Bob 288, 295
Beckley, Jake 170, 184, 198, 222, 235, 243, 256, 266, 275, 276, 284, 293, 305, 316
Beecher, Ed 156, 185, 199, 200, 226, 229, 289, 294
Begley, Ed 101, 136
Begley, Gene 141
Behel, Steve 116, 150
Belden, Ira 285
Bell, Charlie 192, 228, 229
Bell, Frank 135
Bellan, Steve 9, 15, 22
Bellman, John 189
Benedict, Art 90
Benners, Ike 110, 123
Bennett, Charlie 54, 64, 70, 77, 89, 103, 128, 140, 154, 170, 182, 205, 218, 233, 243
Bentley, Cy 16
Bergen, Marty 274, 283, 292, 302
Berger, Tun 207, 222, 238
Bergh, John 43, 65
Berkelbach, Frank 108
Berkenstock, Nate 8
Berman, Charlie 10
Bernard, Curt 317
Bernhard, Bill 303, 314
Berry, Charlie 119, 120, 122
Berry, Tom 8
Berthrong, Harry 9
Bestick, ----- 17
Bickham, Dan 149

Bielaski, Oscar 18, 23, 29, 35, 41
Bierbauer, Lou 149, 163, 176, 190, 196, 222, 235, 243, 256, 266, 276, 289, 299, 320, 323, 324
Bignal, George 116
Birchall, Jud 81, 93, 109
Bird, Frank 239
Bird, George 11
Birdsall, Dave 8, 14, 21
Bishop, Bill 147, 156, 157, 183
Bishop, Frank 119
Bisons (AL, Buffalo) 324
Bisons (NL, Buffalo) 57, 65, 69, 75, 88, 100, 129
Bisons (PL, Buffalo) 199
Bittman, Henry 192
Black, Bob 122, 123
Blackburn, George 283
Blair, Bill 176
Blaisdell, Howard 122, 123
Blake, Henry 256, 263, 273, 285, 294, 304
Blakiston, Bob 81, 93, 109, 112
Blank, Fred 258, 259
Blauvelt, Henry 212
Bligh, Ned 151, 176, 191, 210
Bliss, Frank 54
Blogg, Wes 96
Blong, Joe 37, 41, 48
Blue Stockings (AA, Toledo) 109
Blues (AA, Cleveland) 164, 177
Blues (AL, Kansas City) 322
Blues (NL, Cleveland) 59, 63, 71, 76, 88, 102
Boardman, Fred 30
Bohn, Charlie 82
Boland, ----- 38
Bond, Tommy 28, 29, 33, 41, 47, 52, 57, 65, 71, 78, 112, 118
Bonner, Frank 253, 263, 269, 278, 308
Boone, George 229
Booth, ----- 36
Booth, Amos 44, 49, 66, 82
Booth, Eddie 15, 16, 23, 28, 35, 43
Borchers, George 168, 270
Borden, Joe 34, 35, 42
Boston 8, 14, 21, 27, 33, 42, 47, 52, 57, 65, 71, 76, 87, 99, 118, 128, 141, 156, 169, 182, 196, 205, 218, 225, 233, 243, 254, 265, 274, 283, 292, 302, 314

INDEX

Boston (NA) Red Stockings 8, 14, 21, 27, 33; (NL) Red Caps 42, 47, 52, 57, 65, 71, 76; Beaneaters 87, 99, 128, 141, 156, 169, 182, 205, 218, 233, 243, 254, 265, 274, 283, 292, 302, 314; (AA) Reds 225; (UA) Reds 118; (PL) 196 Reds
Boswell, Andy 267, 268
Bowen, Cy 276, 277
Bowerman, Frank 263, 273, 283, 292, 296, 306, 317
Bowes, Frank 215
Bowman, Bill 218
Bowman, Sumner 204, 207, 226
Boyd, Bill 14, 23, 29, 37, 38
Boyd, Frank 244
Boyd, Jake 259, 268, 278, 279
Boyle, Eddie 276, 280
Boyle, Henry 116, 129, 130, 142, 157, 158, 171, 185
Boyle, Jack 149, 161, 175, 189, 197, 225, 237, 244, 254, 264, 277, 288, 295
Bradley, Bill 306, 315
Bradley, George 34, 41, 42, 48, 60, 63, 70, 71, 72, 76, 88, 93, 116, 150, 177
Bradley, Nick 120
Brady, ----- 35
Brady, Steve 29, 36, 94, 106, 136, 150
Brady, Tom 33
Braggins, Dick 323
Brain, Dave 320
Brainard, Asa 9, 16, 17, 21, 22, 29, 30
Brannock, Mike 8, 35
Bransfield, Kitty 292
Brashear, Kitty 307
Breitenstein, Alonzo 90
Breitenstein, Ted 225, 226, 239, 248, 258, 269, 279, 284, 293, 305, 317
Brennan, James 116, 130, 179, 190, 199
Bresnahan, Roger 286, 315
Brewers (AA, Milwaukee) 226
Brewers (AL, Milwaukee) 320
Bridegrooms (AA, Brooklyn) 189
Bridegrooms (NL, Brooklyn) 203, 221, 234, 245, 255, 265, 278, 285, 297
Briggs, Buttons 275, 287, 293, 294

Briggs, Charlie 119
Briggs, Grant 213, 229, 239, 270
Brill, Frank 103
Briody, Fatty 64, 76, 88, 101, 116, 129, 143, 154, 179
Bristow, George 310
Britt, Jim 15, 16, 23
Broderick, Matt 324
Brodie, Steve 205, 218, 239, 247, 248, 253, 263, 273, 286, 292, 296, 304, 320
Brooklyn 15, 17, 22, 28, 37, 110, 135, 148, 163, 175, 189, 196, 203, 214, 221, 234, 245, 255, 265, 278, 285, 297, 302, 313
Brooklyn (NA) Atlantics 15, 22, 28, 37; Eckfords 17; (NL) Bridegrooms 203, 221, 234, 245, 255, 265, 278, 285, 297; Superbas 302, 313; (AA) Trolley Dodgers 110, 135, 148, 163, 175; Bridegrooms 189; Gladiators 214; (PL) Wonders 196
Brooks, Harry 150, 151
Broughton, Cecil 88, 96, 116, 133, 136, 170
Brouthers, Dan 59, 60, 64, 69, 75, 88, 89, 100, 129, 140, 154, 170, 182, 196, 225, 234, 245, 253, 263, 269, 277
Brown, ----- 29
Brown, Charlie 285
Brown, Ed 83, 109, 110
Brown, James 101, 121, 122, 150
Brown, Joe 100, 137
Brown, John 285, 286
Brown, Lewis 42, 47, 52, 53, 57, 58, 69, 70, 87, 95, 118
Brown, Oliver 15, 37
Brown, Stub 247, 253, 284
Brown, Tom 83, 84, 95, 106, 134, 147, 156, 157, 169, 182, 196, 225, 237, 249, 260, 268, 269, 278, 286, 298
Brown, Willard 155, 168, 182, 197, 219, 247, 249, 258, 260
Brown Stockings (AA, St. Louis) 83
Brown Stockings (NA, St. Louis) 34
Brown Stockings (NL, St. Louis) 41, 48
Browning, Pete 82, 94, 106, 107, 135, 148, 162, 178, 192, 198, 221, 222, 235, 237, 249, 255, 258

Browns (AA, St. Louis) 93, 107, 133, 147, 161, 175, 189, 211, 225
Browns (NL, St. Louis) 238, 248, 257, 269, 279, 289, 299
Browns (UA, Chicago) 119
Bryant, George 128
Brynan, Tod 168, 169, 218
Buckeyes (AA, Columbus) 95, 106, 191, 210, 227
Buckingham, Ed 268
Buckley, Dick 171, 185, 205, 219, 239, 248, 254, 258, 264, 320
Buckley, John 199
Budd, ----- 199
Buelow, Charles 323
Buelow, Fred 304, 316
Buffalo 57, 65, 69, 75, 88, 100, 129, 199, 324
Buffalo (NL) Bisons 57, 65, 69, 75, 88, 100, 129; (PL) Bisons 199; (AL) Bisons 324
Buffinton, Charles 76, 87, 99, 128, 142, 154, 169, 183, 198, 225, 240
Buker, Harry 103
Bullas, Sim 109
Bunce, Josh 47
Burch, Ernie 102, 148, 163
Burdick, Bill 171, 185
Burdock, Jack 15, 22, 27, 33, 41, 47, 52, 57, 65, 71, 76, 87, 99, 128, 141, 156, 169, 175, 221
Burghers (PL, Pittsburgh) 198
Burke, Dan 212, 213, 233
Burke, Ed 204, 207, 226, 235, 237, 245, 253, 267, 274, 284, 320, 324, 325
Burke, Jim 294, 304, 320
Burke, Joe 211, 228
Burke, Mike 58
Burke, Walter 75, 76, 88, 118, 154
Burkett, Jesse 205, 206, 220, 233, 244, 256, 263, 273, 285, 294, 304, 316
Burnett, Hercules 178, 270
Burns, Dick 89, 116, 130
Burns, Jim 179, 192, 230
Burns, John 325
Burns, Oyster 108, 123, 136, 137, 162, 175, 177, 189, 203, 221, 234, 245, 255, 265, 267
Burns, Pat 108, 117
Burns, Tom 63, 69, 75, 87,

100, 126, 140, 155, 168, 183, 203, 218, 235
Burrell, Buster 219, 265, 278, 285
Burrell, Harry 225, 226
Burris, Al 254, 255
Burroughs, Henry 9, 17
Burt, Frank 83
Bushong, Doc 38, 43, 64, 72, 78, 88, 102, 133, 147, 161, 175, 189, 203
Butler, Bill 112
Butler, Dick 288, 309
Butler, Frank 118, 267
Buttery, Frank 16

Cady, Charles 88, 119, 123
Cahill, John 106, 142, 157, 158
Cahill, Tom 229
Calihan, Wil 212, 227
Callahan, Ed 116, 118, 123
Callahan, Jim 299
Callahan, Nixey 254, 255, 287, 293, 294, 306, 307, 315
Callahan, Pat 111
Camp, Kid 236, 257
Camp, Llewellyn 239, 247, 257
Campau, Count 170, 211, 259
Campbell, ----- 325
Campbell, Hugh 23, 24
Campbell, Mat 23
Campbell, Sam 214
Campfield, Bill 276, 277
Canavan, Jimmy 226, 228, 236, 246, 258, 286
Cannell, Pete 150
Cantz, Bart 177, 191, 214
Carbine, Jack 38, 42
Cardinals (NL, St. Louis) 316
Carey, Fred 52, 53
Carey, Scoops 263, 297, 324
Carey, Tom 10, 14, 21, 27, 33, 41, 47, 52, 59, 320
Cargo, Chick 236
Carl, Fred 193
Carl, Lew 30
Carleton, Jim 10, 16
Carmen, George 214
Carney, John 185, 199, 226, 228
Carpenter, Hick 59, 66, 72, 81, 94, 108, 133, 149, 161, 176, 190, 239
Carr, Charlie 298
Carrick, Bill 295, 296, 308, 317

Carroll, ----- 322
Carroll, Chick 120
Carroll, Cliff 75, 87, 99, 127, 143, 157, 171, 203, 218, 239, 243
Carroll, Fred 106, 134, 147, 156, 171, 184, 198, 222
Carroll, Pat 121, 122
Carroll, Scrappy 121, 129, 165
Carsey, Kid 230, 234, 244, 254, 255, 264, 277, 288, 289, 299, 308, 309, 310, 322, 323, 324
Cartwright, Ed 211, 259, 268, 278, 286
Caruthers, Bob 107, 133, 147, 161, 175, 189, 203, 221, 239, 246, 247
Casey, Bill 163
Casey, Bob 77
Casey, Dan 123, 128, 129, 141, 154, 169, 183, 213
Casey, Dennis 108, 123, 136, 155
Casey, Doc 298, 302, 309, 313, 322
Caskin, Ed 59, 65, 70, 89, 101, 129, 141
Cassian, Ed 220, 230
Cassidy, John 36, 37, 38, 41, 47, 48, 53, 60, 64, 70, 77, 87, 110, 135
Cassidy, Peter 279, 302, 308
Cates, Eli 322, 323
Cattanach, John 99, 116
Centennials (NA, Philadelphia) 37
Chamberlain, Icebox 148, 162, 175, 178, 189, 210, 211, 227, 235, 246, 258, 273
Chambers, Rome 315
Chance, Frank 293, 306, 315
Chapman, Fred 163
Chapman, Jack 28, 34, 42
Chatterton, James 122, 123
Chech, Charlie 323
Chesbro, Jack 306, 313, 314
Chicago 8, 28, 35, 41, 48, 53, 58, 63, 69, 75, 87, 100, 119, 126, 140, 155, 168, 183, 197, 203, 218, 236, 247, 257, 264, 275, 287, 293, 306, 315, 320
Chicago (NA) White Stockings 8, 28, 35; (NL) White Stockings 41, 48, 53, 58, 63, 69, 75, 87, 100, 126, 140, 155, 168, 183, 203, 218, 236, 247;

Colts 257, 264, 275, 287; Orphans 293, 306, 315; (UA) Browns 119; (PL) Pirates 197; (AL) White Stockings 320
Childers, ----- 270
Childs, Cupid 169, 213, 220, 233, 244, 256, 263, 273, 285, 294, 304, 315
Chiles, Pearce 303, 314
Church, Hi 215
Cincinnati 44, 49, 52, 58, 66, 81, 93, 107, 117, 133, 149, 161, 176, 190, 204, 221, 228, 235, 246, 258, 267, 274, 284, 293, 305, 316
Cincinnati (NL) Red Stockings 44, 49; Reds 52, 58, 66, 204, 221, 235, 246, 258, 267, 274, 284, 293, 305, 316; (AA) Red Stockings 81, 93, 107, 133, 149, 161, 176, 190; Kellys 228; (UA) Outlaw Reds 117
Clack, Bobby 28, 37, 44
Clapp, John 16, 22, 27, 33, 41, 48, 53, 57, 66, 71, 89
Clare, Denny 15
Clark, Bill 288
Clark, Bob 148, 163, 175, 189, 203, 221, 249
Clark, Ed 150, 228
Clark, Harry 320
Clark, Spider 185, 199, 200
Clark, Willie 267, 276, 284, 296, 305
Clarke, Archie 205, 219
Clarke, Boileryard 247, 253, 263, 273, 283, 292, 302, 315
Clarke, Dad 168, 169, 228, 253, 267, 268, 276, 277, 284, 288, 289, 297, 324
Clarke, Fred 260, 269, 279, 288, 297, 307, 313
Clarke, Harry 186
Clarke, Henry 285, 294
Clarkson, Dad 219, 233, 248, 258, 263, 269, 273
Clarkson, John 78, 100, 126, 140, 155, 169, 170, 182, 205, 218, 233, 244, 256
Clausen, Fred 237, 247, 248, 249, 257, 280
Clayton, G. E. 320
Clements, Ed 207
Clements, Jack 101, 121, 127, 141, 154, 169, 183, 204, 219, 234, 244, 254, 264, 277, 287, 299, 310, 315

Cleveland, Elmer 117, 168, 171, 228
Cleveland 10, 16, 59, 63, 71, 76, 88, 102, 164, 177, 184, 198, 206, 220, 233, 244, 256, 263, 273, 285, 294, 309, 323
Cleveland (NA) Forest Citys 10, 16; (NL) Blues 59, 63, 71, 76, 88, 102; Spiders 184, 206, 220, 233, 244, 256, 263, 273, 285, 294, 309; (AA) Blues 164, 177; (PL) Infants 198; (AL) Spiders 323
Cline, Monk 83, 106, 136, 178, 229
Clingman, Bill 204, 228, 266, 279, 288, 297, 307, 315, 322
Clinton, Jim 17, 23, 29, 37, 38, 42, 78, 96, 108, 133, 151
Clusman, Billy 169
Clymer, Bill 227
Cobb, George 239, 240
Cogan, Richard 283, 306, 307, 317
Cogswell, Ed 57, 64, 78
Colcolough, Tom 243, 256, 257, 266, 308
Coleman, Jack 90, 101, 102, 109, 134, 135, 147, 149, 150, 156, 170, 190
Coleman, John 204, 269
Coleman, Percy 289, 293
Colgan, Bill 111
Colliflower, Harry 309, 310
Collins, ----- 239
Collins, Bill 190, 214, 220
Collins, Chub 100, 112, 128
Collins, Dan 28, 42
Collins, Hub 148, 162, 175, 178, 189, 203, 221, 234
Collins, Hugh 164
Collins, Jimmy 266, 269, 274, 283, 292, 302, 314
Colliver, Bill 128
Colonels (AA, Louisville) 135, 148, 162, 178, 192, 210, 229
Colonels (NL, Louisville) 237, 249, 259, 269, 279, 288, 297, 307
Colts (NL, Chicago) 257, 264, 275, 287
Columbus 95, 106, 191, 210, 227
Columbus (AA) Buckeyes 95, 106, 191, 210, 227
Comiskey, Charlie 83, 93, 107, 133, 147, 161, 175, 189, 197, 225, 235, 246, 258

Cone, Fred 8
Conley, Ed 99
Conn, Bert 295, 314
Connally, Red 142
Connaughton, Frank 254, 276
Connell, Terry 28
Connor, Jim 236, 287, 293, 306
Connor, Joe 269, 315
Connor, John 99, 129, 136
Connor, Roger 64, 70, 77, 89, 101, 126, 141, 155, 168, 182, 196, 219, 234, 245, 253, 257, 269, 279, 289
Connors, Jerry 234
Connors, Joe 122, 123
Connors, Ned 9
Conover, Ted 190
Conroy, Ben 214
Conroy, Wid
Conway, Bill 102, 151
Conway, Dick 151, 156, 169, 170
Conway, Jim 110, 134, 135, 192
Conway, Peter 129, 140, 143, 154, 170, 184
Coogan, Dan 268
Cook, Paul 101, 148, 162, 178, 192, 196, 225, 229
Cooke, Fred 285
Cooley, Duff 248, 258, 269, 277, 279, 287, 295, 303, 313
Coon, William 34, 43
Cooney, Jim 203, 218, 236, 238
Corbett, Joe 268, 273, 283, 325
Corcoran, John 110, 266
Corcoran, Larry 63, 69, 75, 87, 100, 126, 141, 143, 144, 158
Corcoran, Mike 100
Corcoran, Tom 198, 227, 234, 245, 255, 265, 278, 284, 293, 305, 316
Corey, Fred 64, 65, 72, 77, 93, 109, 134, 135
Corkhill, Pop 94, 108, 133, 149, 161, 175, 176, 189, 203, 221, 222, 227, 235
Corridan, Phillip 119
Cote, Henry 260, 270
Cotter, Dan 199
Cotter, Tom 225
Coughlin, Bill 309, 322
Coughlin, Dennis 18
Coughlin, Ed 100
Coughlin, Roscoe 203, 219

Cowboys (AA, Kansas City) 178, 192
Cowboys (NL, Kansas City) 143
Cox, Frank 103
Coyle, Bill 243
Cramer, Dick 89
Crane, Cannonball 118, 127, 129, 143, 144, 168, 182, 197, 221, 222, 228, 237, 245, 246
Crane, Fred 23, 37
Crane, Sam 65, 94, 117, 128, 140, 142, 157, 205, 207
Craver, Bill 9, 14, 21, 28, 33, 37, 42, 47
Crawford, George 214
Crawford, Sam 305, 316
Cream Citys (NL, Milwaukee) 54
Cream Citys (UA, Milwaukee) 116
Creamer, George 54, 59, 64, 72, 77, 95, 111
Creegan, Marty 120
Creely, Gus 211
Cregan, Pete 308
Criger, Lou 273, 285, 294, 304, 316
Crisham, Pat 304, 323
Critchley, Morrie 82, 83
Croft, Art 37, 48, 53
Croft, Henry 303, 307
Cronin, Dan 116, 119
Cronin, Jack 265, 296, 305, 322
Crooks, Jack 191, 210, 227, 238, 248, 268, 278, 279, 299, 324
Crosby, George 100
Cross, Amos 135, 148, 162
Cross, Clarence 121, 122, 164
Cross, Frank 323
Cross, Lave 162, 178, 190, 198, 227, 234, 244, 254, 264, 277, 287, 299, 304, 309, 313, 316
Cross, Lem 246, 258, 259
Cross, Monte 240, 256, 266, 279, 289, 295, 303, 314
Crothers, Doug 122, 123, 136
Crotty, Joe 82, 83, 117, 135, 150
Crowell, Bill 165, 177, 178
Crowley, Bill 34, 47, 57, 65, 71, 88, 93, 99, 129
Crowley, John 101
Cudworth, James 122, 123
Cuff, John 117
Cullen, John 123
Cummings, Candy 14, 21, 22, 28, 33, 41, 49

INDEX

Cunningham, Bert 163, 164, 177, 191, 198, 199, 226, 227, 269, 270, 280, 288, 289, 297, 307, 315, 316
Cuppy, Nig 233, 244, 256, 263, 273, 285, 294, 304, 305, 315
Curley, Doc 306
Curren, Pete 43
Curry, Wes 110, 111
Curtis, Jim 221, 230
Cushman, Ed 88, 116, 134, 136, 150, 151, 164, 211, 212
Cusick, Tony 101, 123, 127, 141, 154
Cuthbert, Ned 8, 15, 21, 28, 34, 41, 49, 83, 93, 117

Dahlen, Bill 218, 236, 247, 259, 264, 275, 287, 293, 302, 313
Dailey, John 36, 37
Dailey, Vince 206
Daily, Con 121, 127, 142, 156, 171, 185, 196, 221, 234, 246, 255, 265, 275
Daily, Ed 127, 141, 154, 157, 172, 191, 192, 205, 206, 210, 214, 215, 229, 230
Daily, One Arm 75, 76, 88, 119, 120, 130, 143, 144, 165
Daisey, George 122
Daley, Bill 182, 196, 225
Dalrymple, Abner 54, 58, 63, 69, 75, 87, 100, 126, 140, 156, 170, 226
Daly, Joe 214, 220, 233
Daly, Sun 240
Daly, Tom 155, 168, 185, 203, 221, 234, 245, 255, 265, 278, 297, 302, 313
Damman, Bill 284, 293, 305, 321
Daniels, Charlie 118
Daniels, Law 162, 179
Daniels, Peter 207, 299
Darby, George 246
Dark Blues (NA, Hartford) 29, 33
Dark Blues (NL, Hartford) 41, 47
Darling, Dell 88, 155, 168, 183, 197, 225
Darragh, Jack 229
Daub, Dan 235, 246, 255, 265, 278, 285, 286, 322, 323

Daugherty, Charles 122
Davies, George 226, 233, 244, 245
Davis, Al 324
Davis, Daisy 99, 107, 128
Davis, George 206, 220, 221, 233, 245, 253, 267, 276, 284, 295, 308, 317
Davis, Harry 267, 276, 286, 296, 297, 298, 309
Davis, Ira 308
Davis, Jumbo 122, 151, 162, 178, 189, 192, 211, 214, 230
Davis, Wiley 274
Day, Bill 183, 204, 207
Deagle, Ren 94, 107, 108
Dealy, Pat 121, 128, 142, 157, 213
Dean, Dory 44
Deane, Harry 10, 29
Deasley, Jim 119, 122
Deasley, Pat 71, 76, 93, 107, 126, 141, 155, 172
Decker, Frank 59, 83
Decker, George 236, 247, 259, 264, 275, 287, 297, 299, 307, 309
Decker, Harry 112, 122, 140, 143, 183, 204, 207
Dee, Jim 111
Dehlman, Dutch 15, 22, 28, 34, 41, 48
Delahanty, Ed 169, 183, 198, 219, 234, 244, 254, 264, 277, 287, 295, 303, 314
Delahanty, Tom 254, 273, 276, 289, 323
Delancy, Bill 206
De Marais, Fred 203, 204
DeMiller, Henry 239
DeMontreville, Gene 256, 268, 278, 286, 292, 303, 306, 313
Denny, Jerry 69, 75, 87, 99, 127, 142, 157, 171, 185, 205, 219, 220, 249, 260
Denzer, Roger 287, 320
DePangher, Mark 101
Derby, Gene 137
Derby, George 70, 77, 88
Detroit 70, 77, 89, 102, 128, 140, 154, 170, 321
Detroit (NL) Wolverines 70, 77, 89, 102, 128, 140, 154, 170; (AL) Tigers 321
Devine, Jim 141
Devine, Walt 96
Devlin, James 141, 154, 175, 189

Devlin, Jim 21, 28, 35, 42, 47
Dewald, Charles 199
Dexter, Charles 279, 288, 297, 307, 315
Dickerson, Buttercup 52, 58, 64, 72, 95, 107, 108, 116, 129
Diggins, Bill 320, 323
Dignan, Steve 65
Dillard, Bob 320
Dillard, Pat 316
Dillon, John 37
Dillon, Packy 37
Dillon, Pop 306, 313, 321
Dineen, Bill 298, 308, 309, 315
Dixon, Ed 325
Doe, Al 198, 199
Doheny, Ed 268, 276, 277, 284, 295, 296, 308, 317, 320
Dolan, Cozy 238, 266, 274, 275, 315
Dolan, Joe 279, 288, 303, 314
Dolan, John 204, 205, 228, 248, 264, 265
Dolan, Tom 58, 75, 93, 107, 116, 130, 142, 151, 175
Dole, Lester 36
Donahue, Jiggs 313
Donahue, Jim 150, 164, 178, 192, 227
Donahue, Red 245, 269, 279, 289, 295, 303, 314
Donahue, Tim 225, 264, 275, 287, 293, 306, 315
Donlin, Mike 304, 305, 316
Donnelly, Frank 247, 248
Donnelly, Jim 112, 122, 128, 143, 157, 172, 185, 211, 228, 273, 284, 286, 299
Donnelly, John 23, 28
Donnelly, Peter 10
Donohue, Joe 220
Donovan, Fred 263
Donovan, Patsy 203, 205, 229, 230, 235, 238, 243, 256, 266, 275, 286, 296, 306, 316
Donovan, Wild Bill 298, 299, 302, 313
Dooms, Harry 237
Doran, John 229
Dorgan, Jerry 64, 81, 110, 112, 128
Dorgan, Mike 48, 59, 63, 70, 72, 89, 101, 126, 141, 155, 213
Dorr, Bert 83
Dorsey, Jeremiah 117, 118
Doscher, Herm 15, 23, 36, 58, 59, 71, 76

INDEX

Doscher, John 321
Doty, Babe 212
Douglass, Klondike 279, 289, 295, 303, 314
Dow, Clarence 118
Dowd, Tommy 225, 229, 238, 248, 259, 269, 279, 287, 289, 299, 309, 320
Dowie, Joe 191
Dowling, Henry 288, 289, 297, 307, 320, 321
Dowse, Tom 206, 228, 234, 235, 237, 238
Doyle, Connie 90, 111
Doyle, Ed 83
Doyle, Jack 191, 210, 220, 233, 237, 245, 253, 267, 273, 283, 295, 298, 307, 317
Doyle, Joe 18
Drake, Lyman 113
Drauby, Jake 238
Drew, David 119, 121
Driscoll, Denny 65, 66, 82, 95, 96, 107, 129
Drissel, Mike 133
Duffee, Charlie 189, 211, 227, 238, 246
Duffy, Ed 8
Duffy, Hugh 168, 183, 197, 225, 233, 243, 254, 265, 274, 283, 292, 302, 315
Dugan, Bill 110, 123
Dugan, Ed 110
Dugdale, Dan 143, 259
Duggleby, Bill 295
Duke, Martin 230
Duncan, Jim 309
Dundon, Ed 95, 106
Dungan, Sam 236, 247, 259, 260, 315, 322
Dunkle, Davey 288, 295, 309
Dunlap, Fred 63, 71, 76, 88, 116, 129, 140, 142, 154, 170, 184, 197, 207, 230
Dunn, Jack 285, 297, 298, 302, 313, 314
Dunn, Stephen 121
Dunning, Andy 184, 219
Duryea, Jesse 190, 204, 205, 221, 222, 225, 226, 235, 238, 249, 250
Duzen, Bill 199, 200
Dwight, Al 122
Dwyer, Frank 168, 183, 197, 226, 228, 235, 239, 246, 258, 267, 274, 284, 293, 305

Dwyer, John 76
Dyler, John 82

Eagan, Bill 225, 247, 296
Eagle, Bill 298
Earl, Howard 203, 226
Earle, Billy 190, 211, 236, 243, 255, 260
Eason, Mal 315, 316
East, Harry 83
Easterday, Henry 121, 178, 191, 210, 214
Easton, John 191, 210, 225, 226, 228, 239, 256, 257
Ebright, Buck 185
Eckfords (NA, Brooklyn) 17
Eclipse (AA, Louisville) 82, 94, 106
Eden, Charles 48, 59, 111, 134
Edwards, ----- 38
Egan, James 77
Egan, Rip 259, 323
Eggler, Dave 9, 14, 22, 28, 33, 43, 48, 57, 88, 96, 100, 129
Ehret, Red 179, 192, 193, 210, 229, 235, 236, 243, 256, 257, 269, 274, 284, 297, 324, 325
Eiteljorg, Ed 203, 204, 230
Eland, ----- 24
Elberfield, Kid 295, 305, 322
Elizabeth 23
Elizabeth (NA) Resolutes 23
Ellick, Joe 37, 54, 64, 117, 119, 120, 123
Ellis, Ben 277
Elm Citys (NA, New Haven) 35
Ely, Bones 100, 148, 213, 221, 240, 248, 257, 258, 269, 275, 286, 296, 305, 313
Emig, Charlie 280
Emslie, Bob 96, 108, 134, 135, 137
Esper, Duke 204, 207, 214, 219, 220, 234, 236, 249, 253, 259, 263, 273, 289, 299
Esterbrook, Dude 65, 76, 94, 106, 126, 141, 164, 171, 178, 192, 205, 221
Eustace, Frank 280
Evans, ----- 36
Evans, Jake 59, 64, 70, 78, 88, 102, 137
Evans, LeRoy 288, 289, 298, 309

Everett, Bill 264, 275, 287, 293, 306, 315
Evers, Tom 83, 119
Ewell, G. 10
Ewing, Buck 64, 70, 77, 89, 101, 126, 141, 155, 168, 182, 197, 219, 237, 244, 256, 267, 274, 284
Ewing, John 93, 117, 126, 178, 192, 193, 197, 219

Faatz, Jay 111, 177, 184, 199
Fagan, Bill 164, 179
Fagin, Fred 269
Falch, Anton 116
Fanning, John 185, 254, 255
Farley, Tom 112
Farmer, Bill 171, 176
Farrar, John 110
Farrar, Sid 90, 101, 126, 141, 154, 169, 183, 197
Farrell, Bill 81, 96
Farrell, Duke 168, 183, 197, 225, 235, 249, 253, 267, 276, 278, 286, 298, 302, 309, 313
Farrell, Jack 29, 57, 59, 63, 69, 75, 87, 99, 127, 141, 143, 157, 177, 191
Farrell, Joe 77, 89, 102, 151
Farrell, John 322
Farrow, John 23, 28
Fast, ----- 158
Fauver, Clay 307, 323
Fee, John 185
Fennelly, Frank 108, 112, 133, 149, 161, 176, 190, 215
Ferguson, Bob 9, 15, 22, 23, 28, 29, 33, 41, 47, 48, 53, 60, 64, 70, 77, 90, 111
Ferguson, Charlie 101, 102, 127, 141, 154
Ferson, Alex 185, 186, 199, 240
Fertsch, Ed 324
Field, Jim 95, 106, 133, 137, 212, 298
Field, Sam 36, 37, 44
Fields, George 16
Fields, Jocko 156, 157, 171, 184, 198, 220, 222, 237
Fifield, Jack 288, 295, 303, 309, 322
Figgemeier, Frank 254, 255
Finley, Bill 141
Firth, Ted 110, 111
Fishel, Leo 308

INDEX

Fisher, ----- 193
Fisher, Charles 121, 123
Fisher, Chauncey 244, 256, 258, 259, 274, 285, 320
Fisher, Cherokee 11, 14, 22, 29, 34, 44, 48, 52, 53
Fisher, George 102, 119, 122, 129
Fisher, Newt 295, 324
Fisler, Wes 8, 15, 22, 27, 33, 43
Fitzgerald, Dennis 214
Fitzgerald, John 212, 225, 229, 237, 238
Flaherty, Marty 72
Flaherty, Pat 260
Flaherty, Patsy 307, 313, 314
Flanagan, Ed 163, 193
Fleet, Frank 9, 17, 23, 24, 28, 34, 37, 38
Fleming, Tom 308
Fletcher, George 17
Flick, Elmer 295, 303, 314
Flint, Silver 37, 53, 58, 63, 69, 75, 87, 100, 126, 140, 155, 168, 183
Flood, Tim 304, 323, 324
Flowers, Dickie 9, 10, 15
Flynn, Carney 258, 259, 276, 277, 278, 279
Flynn, Clipper 9, 17
Flynn, Ed 165
Flynn, George 275, 321
Flynn, Joe 118, 121
Flynn, John 140, 155
Flynn, Mike 225
Fogarty, Jim 101, 102, 127, 141, 154, 169, 183, 197
Fogarty, Joe 130
Foley, Curry 57, 65, 69, 70, 75, 76, 88, 89
Foley, John 127
Foley, Tom 8
Foley, Will 35, 44, 49, 54, 58, 70, 119
Foran, Jim 10
Force, Davy 9, 14, 15, 21, 22, 28, 33, 43, 48, 57, 65, 69, 75, 88, 100, 129, 143
Ford, Ed 110
Ford, Tom 210, 215
Foreman, Brownie 266, 274, 276
Foreman, Frank 119, 123, 137, 191, 204, 205, 221, 230, 238, 240, 245, 267, 274, 324
Forest Citys (NA, Cleveland) 10, 16

Forest Citys (NA, Rockford) 10
Forster, Tom 77, 111, 136, 150
Fort Wayne 10
Fort Wayne (NA) Kekiongas 10
Foster, Elmer 109, 121, 150, 168, 182, 203, 218
Foster, Pop 295, 308, 317
Foster, Reddy 276
Fournier, Henry 258, 259
Fouser, Bill 43
Foutz, Dave 107, 133, 147, 161, 175, 189, 203, 221, 234, 245, 246, 255, 265, 278
Fox, Bill 286
Fox, George 229, 306
Fox, John 71, 96, 111, 143, 144
France, Ossie 203, 204
Frank, Charles 248, 258
Frank, Fred 294
Franklin, ----- 120
Fraser, Chick 279, 280, 288, 289, 294, 297, 303, 314
Freeman, Buck 230, 298, 308, 309, 314
Freeman, Julie 175
French, Bill 24
Fricken, Hon 205
Friel, Pat 213, 227
Friend, Dan 264, 265, 275, 287, 294
Friend, Frank 280
Fries, Peter 95, 112
Frisbee, Charlie 302, 317, 323
Frisk, John 305, 322
Fuller, Ed 143, 144
Fuller, Harry 226
Fuller, Shorty 172, 189, 211, 225, 237, 245, 253, 267, 276
Fulmer, Chick 11, 14, 21, 28, 34, 42, 57, 65, 81, 94, 107, 108
Fulmer, Chris 119, 151, 162, 177, 191
Fulmer, Washington 38
Fultz, Dave 295, 303, 304, 320
Fusselbach, Ed 83, 117, 134, 178

Gagus, Charlie 119, 120
Gallagher, Bill 90, 121, 277
Gallagher, Jim 143
Gallagher, John 96
Galligan, John 193
Galvin, John 16, 29
Galvin, Louis 121
Galvin, Pud 34, 57, 58, 65, 66, 69, 70, 75, 76, 88, 100, 129,

134, 147, 156, 171, 184, 198, 222, 236, 239
Gamble, Robert 176
Gannon, Gussie 266, 267
Gannon, Joe 299
Ganzel, Charles 121, 127, 140, 141, 154, 170, 182, 205, 218, 233, 243, 254, 265, 274, 283
Ganzel, John 296, 315, 322
Gardner, Alex 113
Gardner, Fred 162
Gardner, Gid 60, 63, 64, 96, 108, 117, 119, 120, 137, 157, 169, 172
Gardner, Jim 266, 286, 287, 296, 306, 321
Garfield, Bill 184, 206
Garoni, Will 308
Garry, James 243, 320, 324
Garvin, Ned 277, 306, 307, 315, 316
Gastfield, Ed 103, 126, 128
Gaston, Welcome 297, 298, 302, 322, 323
Gastright, Hank 191, 210, 228, 238, 243, 255, 274
Gatins, Frank 298
Gaule, Mike 193
Gear, Dale 273, 274, 285, 322, 323
Gedney, Count 15, 17, 22, 27, 35
Geer, Billy 27, 36, 52, 65, 110, 121, 135
Geier, Phil 277, 288, 317, 321
Geis, Emil 83, 84, 155
Geiss, Bill 102, 103
Genins, Frank 235, 239, 266, 323
George, William 155, 156, 168, 182, 191, 192
Gerhardt, Joe 23, 29, 35, 42, 47, 52, 58, 70, 94, 106, 126, 141, 155, 164, 211, 214, 229
German, Les 213, 245, 253, 267, 268, 276, 277, 278, 279, 286
Gessner, Charlie 150
Gettig, Charles 276, 277, 284, 295, 296, 308
Gettinger, Tom 189, 211, 269, 270
Gettman, Jake 286, 298, 309, 324
Getzien, Pretzels 103, 128, 140,

INDEX

154, 170, 185, 205, 218, 220, 239
Giants (NL, New York) 126, 141, 155, 168, 182, 205, 219, 237, 245, 253, 267, 276, 284, 295, 307, 317
Giants (PL, New York) 196
Gibson, Bob 203, 207
Gibson, Norwood 321, 322, 323
Gibson, Whitey 176
Gilbert, Bill 240
Gilbert, Harry 207
Gilbert, Jack 295, 298
Gilbert, John 207
Gilbert, Pete 212, 226, 240, 255, 260
Gilks, Bob 165, 177, 178, 184, 206, 247
Gill, Jim 189
Gillen, Sam 243, 287
Gillen, Tom 121, 140
Gillespie, Jim 199
Gillespie, Pete 64, 69, 77, 89, 101, 126, 141, 155
Gilligan, Barney 38, 59, 63, 69, 75, 87, 99, 127, 143, 157, 170
Gilman, Jim 244
Gilman, Pit 102
Gilmore, Frank 143, 144, 157, 172
Gilmore, Jim 36
Gilpatrick, George 299
Gilroy, ----- 28, 34
Gilroy, John 268, 278, 279
Ging, Bill 303
Gladiators (AA, Brooklyn) 214
Gladman, Buck 90, 112, 143
Glasscock, Jack 59, 63, 71, 76, 88, 102, 117, 129, 142, 157, 158, 171, 185, 205, 219, 238, 243, 248, 256, 268, 269
Gleason, Bill 83, 93, 107, 133, 147, 161, 176, 193, 199, 204
Gleason, Jack 48, 83, 93, 94, 116, 130, 149
Gleason, Kid 169, 183, 219, 220, 239, 248, 253, 258, 274, 263, 284, 295, 307, 317
Glenalvin, Bob 203, 247
Glenn, Ed 110, 147, 169, 179, 298
Glenn, Ed 298
Glenn, John 9, 17, 18, 23, 28, 35, 41, 48
Goar, Jot 276, 293, 321
Godar, John 240

Goeckel, Bill 303
Goetz, George 191
Golden, Mike 35, 38, 54
Goldsby, Walt 107, 110, 112, 143, 177
Goldsmith, Fred 36, 60, 63, 69, 75, 87, 100, 108
Goldsmith, Wally 10, 17, 24, 38
Gonding, John 322
Goodall, Herb 210
Goodenough, Bill 248
Goodfellow, Mike 161, 177
Goodman, Jake 54, 82
Gore, George 58, 63, 69, 75, 87, 100, 126, 140, 155, 168, 182, 197, 219, 237, 239
Gorman, John 93, 111, 122
Gormley, Ed 73
Gothams (NL, New York) 89, 101
Gould, Charlie 8, 14, 29, 36, 44, 49
Grady, John 122
Grady, Mike 254, 264, 277, 288, 289, 295, 308, 317
Graff, John 249, 250
Graff, Louis 213
Graham, Barney 190
Graham, Bernard 117, 119
Graulich, Lew 220
Graves, Frank 142
Gray, Charlie 207
Gray, Chummy 306, 322, 323, 324
Gray, Jim 111
Gray, Reddy 198, 207, 243
Grays (NL, Louisville) 42, 47
Grays (NL, Providence) 52, 57, 63, 69, 75, 87, 99, 127
Green, Danny 293, 306, 315
Green, Ed 214
Green, Jim 120
Greening, John 172
Greenwood, Bill 81, 110, 162, 177, 191, 212
Greer, Ed 136, 149, 151, 163
Gremminger, Ed 263
Grey, Bill 204, 219, 267, 274, 296, 321, 322
Greyson, ----- 23
Griffin, Mike 162, 177, 191, 197, 221, 234, 245, 255, 265, 278, 285, 297
Griffin, Sandy 101, 212, 230, 248
Griffin, Thomas 116
Griffith, Clark 225, 226, 247,

248, 259, 264, 265, 275, 287, 293, 294, 306, 307, 315
Griffith, Ed 236
Griffith, Frank 256
Grim, John 169, 212, 226, 237, 249, 260, 265, 278, 285, 297, 302, 325
Grimes, John 289
Gross, Emil 57, 63, 69, 90, 119
Gruber, Henry 154, 170, 184, 199, 220
Guese, Ted 321
Guiney, Ben 103
Gumbert, Ad 168, 169, 183, 196, 218, 236, 243, 256, 257, 265, 277, 278
Gumbert, Bill 207, 236, 249
Gunkle, Fred 59
Gunning, Tom 99, 128, 142, 154, 176, 190
Gunson, Joe 119, 192, 239, 244, 248
Guth, Charlie 63

Hach, Major 288
Hackett, Mert 87, 99, 128, 143, 157
Hackett, Walter 118, 128
Haddock, George 172, 185, 186, 199, 225, 234, 246, 254, 255, 259
Haffner, Bill 179
Hagan, Art 88, 89, 90, 100
Hague, Bill 29, 42, 47, 52, 57
Hahn, Noodles 305, 317
Haigh, Ed 239
Halbriter, Ed 81
Haldeman, John 47
Haley, Fred 64
Hall, Al 59, 64
Hall, Charlie 164
Hall, George 9, 14, 21, 27, 33, 43, 47
Hall, Jim 15, 29, 38
Hall, Russ 299
Halligan, Jocko 199, 221, 235, 239, 324
Hallinan, Jim 10, 35, 38, 42, 49, 53
Hallman, Bill 169, 183, 198, 227, 234, 244, 254, 264, 277, 288, 289, 297, 320, 324
Hallman, Jim 48
Hallstrom, Charles 127
Halpin, Jim 78, 119, 128
Ham, Ralph 11, 16

INDEX

Hamburg, Charlie 210
Hamill, John 112, 113
Hamilton, Billy 179, 192, 204, 219, 234, 244, 254, 264, 274, 283, 292, 302, 314
Handiboe, Jim 147
Hanifan, Pat 285
Hankinson, Frank 53, 58, 63, 64, 70, 89, 101, 136, 150, 164, 179
Hanlon, Ned 63, 70, 77, 89, 102, 128, 140, 154, 170, 184, 198, 222, 240
Hanna, John 110, 112
Hansford, F. C. 298
Harbridge, Bill 33, 41, 47, 53, 58, 64, 77, 90, 117
Hardesty, Scott 308
Hardie, Lew 101, 140, 205, 227
Harding, Louis 147
Harkins, John 102, 135, 148, 163, 164, 177
Harley, Dick 289, 299, 309, 317, 322
Harper, George 254, 255, 278
Harper, Jack 309, 310, 316
Harrington, Jerry 204, 221, 235, 249
Harrington, Joe 266, 274
Harris, Charlie 304
Harris, Frank 122
Harrison, Rit 36
Hart, Bill 150, 163, 211, 234, 266, 279, 289, 296, 323
Hart, Tom 230
Hart, Warren 324
Hartford 29, 33, 41, 47
Hartford (NA) Dark Blues 29, 33; (NL) Dark Blues 41, 47
Hartman, Fred 256, 289, 295, 308, 320
Hartnett, Pat 211
Hartsel, Topsy 297, 307, 317, 321
Harvey, Erwin 315, 316, 324, 325
Hassamaer, Bill 259, 268, 269, 280
Hastings, Charles 244, 276, 287, 296, 324, 325
Hastings, Scott 11, 14, 16, 21, 29, 35, 42, 49
Hatfield, Gil 129, 155, 168, 182, 197, 229, 230, 246, 270
Hatfield, John 9, 14, 22, 27, 35, 43
Hautz, Charlie 37, 111

Hawes, Bill 57, 117
Hawke, Dick 239, 247, 248, 253
Hawkes, Thorny 59, 112
Hawley, Pink 239, 248, 258, 266, 276, 286, 287, 293, 305, 317
Hawley, Scott 254
Hayes, Jack 78, 95, 110, 111, 135, 143, 162, 196
Hayes, Mike 43
Haymakers (NA, Troy) 9, 15
Haynes, Peter 214
Healey, Tom 52, 53
Healy, Egyptian 130, 142, 157, 158, 171, 183, 185, 186, 211, 212, 227, 237, 238, 240
Heard, Charlie 207
Hecker, Guy 82, 94, 95, 107, 135, 136, 148, 162, 178, 192, 193, 206, 207
Heidrick, John 294, 304, 316
Heifer, Frank 33
Heintzman, John 148
Hellings, ----- 38
Hellman, Tony 151
Helmbold, Horace 214
Hemming, George 196, 199, 221, 235, 237, 238, 249, 253, 260, 263, 273, 288, 289
Hemp, Ducky 162, 207, 213
Hemphill, Charlie 304, 309, 322
Henderson, Hardie 90, 96, 108, 136, 137, 148, 151, 163, 164, 171
Hengle, Emery 119, 121, 129
Henry, George 246
Henry, John 102, 137, 143, 144, 205
Herman, Art 280, 288, 289
Hernon, Tom 287
Herr, Ed 165, 175, 211
Herring, Lefty 309
Hess, Tom 240
Heubel, George 8, 17, 43
Hewitt, Charles 266
Heydon, Mike 292, 309, 321
Heyner, John 207
Hibbard, John 100
Hickey, Mike 303, 321
Hickman, Ernest 122, 123
Hickman, Piano Legs 283, 292, 302, 303, 317
Hicks, Nat 14, 22, 28, 35, 43, 49
Higby, ----- 16
Higgins, Bill 169, 211, 213

Higgins, Dan 325
Higham, Dick 9, 14, 22, 27, 35, 41, 52, 64
Hiland, John 127
Hill, Belden 213
Hill, Still Bill 279, 280, 288, 289, 293, 302, 304, 309, 310, 322
Hilsey, Charles 90, 109
Hines, Hunkey 265
Hines, Mike 87, 99, 127, 128, 135, 170
Hines, Paul 17, 23, 28, 35, 41, 48, 52, 57, 63, 69, 75, 87, 99, 127, 143, 157, 171, 185, 205, 229
Hodes, Charlie 8, 15, 28
Hodnett, Charles 93, 116
Hodson, George 254, 264
Hoffer, Bill 263, 273, 283, 292, 293, 296, 306, 323
Hoffman, Frank 179
Hoffman, Hickey 59
Hoffmeister, Jesse 286
Hofford, John 134, 147
Hogan, Eddie 83, 116, 164, 177
Hogan, Marty 258, 269
Hogriever, George 267, 321
Holbert, Bill 42, 54, 59, 60, 64, 71, 77, 94, 106, 136, 150, 164, 175
Holdsworth, Jim 16, 17, 22, 28, 35, 43, 47, 77, 112
Holland, Will 191
Holliday, Bug 190, 204, 221, 235, 246, 258, 267, 274, 284, 293
Hollingshead, Holly 17, 23, 36
Hollison, John 236
Holmes, Ducky 269, 270, 279, 280, 284, 288, 292, 299, 304, 322
Honan, Marty 203, 218
Hooker, Bill 324
Hooper, Mike 24
Hoosiers (AA, Indianapolis) 111
Hoosiers (AL, Indianapolis) 321
Hoosiers (NL, Indianapolis) 53, 157, 171, 185
Hoover, Buster 101, 121, 151, 235
Hoover, Charlie 179, 192
Hop Bitters (AA, Rochester) 212
Hopper, C. F. 297, 298
Horan, John 119
Horner, Frank 253
Hornung, Joe 57, 65, 66, 71,

INDEX

76, 87, 99, 128, 142, 156, 169, 191, 205
Horton, Elmer 276, 298
Hotaling, Pete 58, 63, 71, 76, 88, 102, 135, 165, 177
Houck, Sadie 57, 63, 65, 70, 89, 109, 134, 143, 151, 164
Householder, Charles 83, 110, 119, 120
Houseman, Frank 151
Houseman, John 259, 289
Houtz, Lefty 305
Howe, Shorty 205, 245
Howell, Harry 297, 298, 304, 313
Hoy, Dummy 172, 185, 199, 225, 238, 249, 258, 267, 274, 284, 297, 307, 320
Hubbard, Allen 93
Hudson, Nat 147, 161, 175, 189
Huelsman, Frank 289
Hughes, Bill 119, 134, 135
Hughes, Jim 292, 302
Hughes, Long Tom 315, 316
Hughes, Mickey 175, 189, 203, 214
Hughey, Jim 226, 247, 248, 276, 287, 299, 309, 310, 316
Hulen, Bill 277, 308
Hulswitt, Rudy 307
Humphries, John 89, 101, 112
Hunt, Dick 17
Hunter, Bill 107
Hunter, Lem 88
Hurley, Dick 17
Hurley, Jerry 182, 198, 228
Husted, Bill 198
Husting, Bert 313, 314, 321
Hutchinson, Bill 123, 183, 203, 218, 236, 247, 248, 259, 264, 265, 289
Hutchinson, Ed 203
Hyndman, Jim 150

Indianapolis 53, 111, 157, 171, 185, 321
Indianapolis (NL) Hoosiers 53, 157, 171, 185; (AA) Hoosiers 111; (AL) Hoosiers 321
Infants (PL, Cleveland) 198
Ingraham, Charles 96
Inks, Bert 221, 234, 238, 253, 260, 269, 270, 274, 277
Irwin, Art 64, 72, 77, 87, 99, 127, 141, 154, 169, 183, 185, 186, 196, 225, 255
Irwin, Bill 149
Irwin, Charlie 247, 257, 264, 274, 284, 293, 305, 316
Irwin, John 78, 118, 150, 157, 172, 185, 199, 225, 229
Isbell, Frank 293, 294, 320

Jacklitsch, Fred 314, 324
Jackson, Henry 157
Jackson, Sam 8, 15
Jacoby, Harry 83, 137
Jennings, Al 54
Jennings, Hugh 229, 237, 247, 249, 253, 263, 273, 283, 292, 302, 304, 313
Jewett, Nat 17
Jimeson, Jacob 324
Johns, Tom 24
Johnson, Abbie 280, 288
Johnson, Abe 248
Johnson, Bill 121, 157, 212, 226, 240
Johnson, Caleb 10
Johnson, John 254, 255
Johnson, Spud 191, 210, 220
Johnson, Youngy 288, 308
Johnston, Dick 110, 128, 142, 156, 169, 182, 196, 197, 228
Jones, ----- 24, 29
Jones, ----- 112
Jones, Alex 184, 237, 238, 254, 255
Jones, Bill 83, 121
Jones, Bumpus 235, 245, 246, 323
Jones, Charles 110, 136, 322
Jones, Charlie 38, 44, 48, 49, 52, 57, 65, 94, 108, 133, 149, 161, 164, 179
Jones, Cowboy 294, 304, 305, 316
Jones, Fielder 278, 285, 297, 302, 313
Jones, Frank 103
Jones, Henry 103
Jones, Jack 89, 93, 95, 117
Jones, Jim 288, 323
Jones, Mike 210
Jordan, Charlie 277
Jordan, Harry 257, 266, 267
Jordan, Mike 207
Joy, Pop 119
Joyce, Bill 196, 225, 234, 259, 268, 276, 278, 284, 295

Kahoe, Mike 267, 305, 316
Kalbfuss, Charlie 120
Kane, Jerry 211
Kansas City 122, 143, 178, 192, 322
Kansas City (NL) Cowboys 143; (AA) Cowboys 178, 192; (UA) Unions 122; (AL) Blues 322
Kappel, Heinie 161, 176, 191
Kappel, Joe 101, 214
Karl, George 35
Katoll, John 294, 306, 307, 320
Kavanaugh, ----- 17
Kearns, Tom 66, 77, 103
Keas, Ed 177, 178
Keating, Ed 162
Keefe, George 143, 144, 157, 172, 185, 186, 199, 230
Keefe, John 213
Keefe, Tim 64, 71, 77, 94, 106, 126, 141, 155, 168, 182, 197, 219, 220, 234, 244
Keeler, Willie 237, 245, 246, 253, 263, 273, 283, 292, 302, 313
Keenan, Jim 36, 66, 82, 112, 133, 149, 161, 176, 190, 204, 221
Keenan, Kid 228
Keener, Josh 277
Keffer, Frank 213
Keinzil, Bill 81, 121
Keister, Bill 273, 292, 304, 316
Kekiongas (NA, Fort Wayne) 10
Kelb, George 294
Kelley, Joe 218, 235, 240, 247, 253, 263, 273, 283, 292, 302, 313
Kelley, Mike 307, 321
Kellogg, Nat 128
Kellum, Win 321
Kelly, Bill 10
Kelly, Charles 90
Kelly, John 59, 60, 76, 90, 96, 117, 120
Kelly, King 52, 58, 63, 69, 75, 87, 100, 126, 140, 155, 169, 182, 196, 218, 225, 228, 233, 245
Kellys (AA, Cincinnati) 228
Kelty, John 207
Kemmer, Bill 269
Kemmler, Rudy 57, 71, 81, 82, 95, 106, 134, 147, 191

Kennedy, Brickyard 234, 246, 255, 265, 278, 285, 297, 298, 302, 313
Kennedy, Charles 117, 150
Kennedy, Doc 59, 63, 71, 76, 88
Kennedy, Ed 94, 106, 136, 148
Kennedy, Ted 126, 148, 150
Kenney, John 15
Kent, Ed 109
Keokuk 38
Keokuk (NA) Westerns 38
Kerins, John 111, 135, 148, 162, 178, 191, 193, 211
Kern, Archie 323, 324
Kernan, Joe 24
Kerwin, John 324
Kessler, Henry 23, 28, 37, 44, 49
Ketchem, Fred 307, 320
Keystones (UA, Philadelphia) 121
Kiley, John 112, 218
Killeen, Henry 220
Killen, Frank 226, 238, 243, 256, 257, 266, 276, 286, 287, 296, 298, 302, 303, 309, 315, 316, 320
Kilroy, Matt 151, 162, 177, 191, 196, 228, 238, 249, 260, 293, 294
Kilroy, Mike 177, 220
Kimball, Gene 10
Kimber, Sam 110, 127
King, Mart 8, 15
King, Sam 112
King, Silver 143, 161, 175, 189, 197, 222, 237, 245, 246, 278, 286
King, Steve 9, 15
Kinlock, Walt 269
Kinsler, ----- 245
Kinslow, Tom 143, 164, 196, 221, 234, 245, 255, 266, 280, 298, 299
Kinzie, Walt 77, 100, 107
Kirby, John 123, 130, 142, 157, 158, 165, 179
Kissinger, Bill 263, 269, 279, 289
Kitson, Frank 292, 293, 304, 313
Kittredge, Mal 203, 218, 236, 247, 257, 264, 275, 287, 297, 307, 308
Kling, Bill 220, 240, 270
Kling, John 315

Klobedanz, Fred 274, 275, 283, 292, 302, 303
Klusman, Billy 211
Knauss, Frank 210, 220, 221, 235, 256, 268
Knell, Phil 171, 198, 228, 234, 238, 256, 257, 260, 263, 270
Knepper, Charlie 309, 310
Knight, George 36
Knight, Joe 101, 102, 204
Knight, Lon 34, 43, 64, 70, 77, 93, 109, 127, 134, 135
Knoll, Hub 324
Knouff, Ed 134, 151, 161, 162, 175, 177, 178, 190
Knowdell, Jake 28, 37, 54
Knowles, Jimmy 143, 164, 212, 237
Knowles, Tim 110, 111
Knox, Andrew 214
Kohler, Henry 10, 24, 29
Kolb, Ed 310
Koons, Harry 119, 122
Korwan, James 255, 287
Kostal, Joe 280
Krause, Bill 325
Krehmeyer, Charles 107, 130, 135
Krieg, Bill 119, 120, 126, 135, 143, 157
Krieger, ----- 123
Krock, Gus 168, 183, 185, 186, 199, 200
Krueger, Art 309, 316
Krumm, Al 184
Kuehne, Bill 95, 106, 134, 147, 156, 170, 184, 198, 227, 229, 235, 237, 239
Kuhns, Charles 287, 302

LaChance, Candy 246, 255, 265, 278, 285, 297, 303, 323
Ladd, Hi 292, 296
LaDew, Scott 192
Lafferty, Flip 43, 47
Lajoie, Nap 277, 287, 295, 303, 314
Lake, Fred 218, 260, 283, 296
Lally, Bud 222, 289, 320, 324
Lampe, Henry 254, 264
Landis, Doc 81, 83, 84
Lane, Chappy 82, 109
Lange, Bill 247, 257, 264, 275, 287, 293, 306
Langsford, Bob 307
Larkin, Henry 109, 134, 150, 163, 176, 190, 198, 227, 238, 249
Larkin, Terry 43, 47, 48, 53, 58, 64, 110, 119
LaRoque, Sam 170, 206, 222, 229
Latham, Arlie 65, 93, 107, 133, 147, 161, 175, 189, 197, 204, 221, 235, 246, 258, 267, 279, 309
Latham, Juice 33, 36, 47, 81, 94, 106
Latimer, Tacks 295, 307, 313
Lauder, Bill 295, 303
Lauer, Chuck 111, 184, 203
Laughlin, Ben 23
Laughlin, Bill 96
Laury, John 36
Lavin, John 107
Lawlor, Mike 64, 120
Lawson, Al 205, 207
Leach, Tommy 297, 307, 313
Leahy, Dan 277
Leahy, Tom 286, 287, 298
Leary, Jack 65, 70, 82, 83, 84, 94, 96, 119, 122
Ledwith, Mike 29
Lee, Arnold 322, 323
Lee, Leonidas 48
Lee, Tom 100, 117, 118
Leever, Sam 296, 306, 313, 314
Lehane, Mike 120, 210, 227
Leighton, John 213
Leiper, John 228
Leith, Bill 309
Leitner, Doc 157, 158
Lennon, Bill 10, 18, 24
Leonard, ----- 239
Leonard, Andy 9, 14, 21, 27, 33, 42, 47, 52, 66
Letcher, Tom 226
Leutz, ----- 17
Levis, Charles 112, 117, 120, 137
Lewis, ----- 199, 200
Lewis, Fred 71, 90, 93, 107, 116, 129, 149
Lewis, Ted 274, 275, 283, 292, 302, 303, 315
Lezotte, Abe 276
Libby, Stephen 58
Lillie, Jim 88, 89, 100, 129, 143
Lincoln, Ezra 206, 213
Lipp, Tom 288
Little, George 48

INDEX

Little, Harry 47
Lochead, Harry 309, 310
Locke, Marsh 112
Lockwood, Milo 119, 120
Loftus, Tom 48, 93
Lohman, Pete 230
Long, Dan 212
Long, Germany 192, 205, 218, 233, 243, 254, 265, 274, 283, 292, 302, 314
Long, Harry 178
Long, James 229, 247
Lord Baltimores (NA, Baltimore) 14, 21, 29
Loughran, ----- 101
Louisville 42, 47, 82, 94, 106, 135, 148, 162, 178, 192, 210, 229, 237, 249, 259, 269, 279, 288, 297, 307
Louisville (NL) Grays 42, 47; Colonels 237, 249, 259, 269, 279, 288, 297, 307; (AA) Eclipse 82, 94, 106; Colonels 135, 148, 162, 178, 192, 210, 229
Lovett, Len 23, 24, 37
Lovett, Tom 134, 189, 203, 221, 246, 254
Lowe, Bobby 205, 218, 233, 243, 254, 265, 274, 283, 292, 302, 314
Lowe, Charlie 15
Lowe, Dickie 103
Luby, John 203, 218, 236, 269, 270
Lucid, Con 249, 255, 264, 265, 277, 289
Luckey, Howard 214
Luff, Henry 36, 77, 81, 95, 121, 122
Lukens, Al 254, 255
Lush, Billy 268, 278, 286
Lutenberg, Luke 259
Lynch, Henry 247
Lynch, Jack 69, 70, 94, 106, 136, 150, 151, 164, 215
Lynch, Thomas 100
Lynch, Tom 101, 123, 127
Lyons, Denny 127, 150, 163, 176, 190, 214, 225, 237, 243, 256, 269, 275, 286
Lyons, Harry 154, 161, 175, 182, 212, 237, 245
Lyons, Pat 206
Lyons, Toby 213
Lyston, Bill 228, 256
Lytle, Dad 203, 207

McAleer, Jimmy 184, 198, 220, 233, 244, 254, 263, 273, 285, 323
McAllister, Sport 273, 274, 285, 294, 309, 310, 322
McAndrews, David 325
MacArthur, Mal 112
McAtee, Bub 8, 15
McBride, Algie 275, 293, 305, 316
McBride, Dick 8, 15, 22, 27, 33, 34, 42
McBride, John 214
McBride, Peter 294, 304, 305
McCaffery, Harry 82, 83, 93, 133
McCaffrey, Sparrow 191
McCann, Mike 324, 325
McCarthy, John 246, 258, 296, 306, 315
McCarthy, Tommy 118, 128, 141, 154, 175, 189, 211, 225, 226, 233, 243, 254, 265, 278
McCarton, Frank 16
McCarty, John 192
McCauley, Allen 112, 204, 230
McCauley, F. F. 268
McCauley, Jim 107, 126, 129, 148
McCauley, Pat 248, 278
McClellan, Bill 53, 69, 90, 101, 135, 148, 163, 175, 177
McCloskey, ----- 36
McCloskey, W. 123
McClure, Hal 76
McCormick, Barry 270, 275, 287, 293, 306, 315
McCormick, Harry 59, 72, 94
McCormick, Jerry 96, 119, 121
McCormick, Jim 53, 59, 63, 64, 71, 72, 76, 88, 102, 117, 126, 127, 140, 156, 157, 239
McCormick, Pat 81
McCoy, Art 186
McCreery, Tom 269, 270, 279, 280, 284, 288, 295, 296, 306, 313, 314
McCuller, John 81
McCullough, Charles 213, 215
McDermott, Joe 10, 17
McDermott, Mike 193, 269, 270, 280, 285, 289
McDonald, Jack 15, 17
McDonald, Jim 111, 120, 129
McDoolan, ----- 24
McDougal, Dewey 269, 279
McDougal, John 265

Mace, Harry 230
Macey, ----- 214
McElroy, James 101, 102, 123
McFadden, Guy 269
McFarlan, Dan 270, 302, 308, 309
McFarland, Alex 237
McFarland, Claude 117, 118
McFarland, Ed 244, 279, 288, 289, 295, 303, 314
McFarland, Herm 280, 293, 320
McFarland, Monte 264, 265, 275
McFettridge, John 204
McGann, Dann 269, 274, 292, 302, 308, 316
McGarr, Chippy 119, 149, 163, 175, 191, 192, 205, 244, 256, 263, 273
McGeachey, Jack 140, 142, 157, 158, 171, 185, 196, 225, 227
McGeary, Mike 9, 15, 22, 27, 34, 41, 48, 57, 63, 71, 77
McGee, F. 120
McGee, Pat 28, 35, 37
McGill, Willie 199, 225, 226, 228, 235, 247, 248, 257, 264, 277, 320
McGinley, Tim 36, 37, 42
McGinn, Frank 207
McGinnis, Gus 244, 245, 247, 248
McGinnis, Jumbo 83, 93, 107, 133, 147, 151, 161
McGinnity, Joe 304, 313
McGlone, John 143, 165, 177
McGraw, John 226, 239, 247, 253, 263, 273, 283, 292, 304, 316
McGrillis, Mark 239
McGuckin, Joe 213
McGuiness, John 43, 59, 121
McGuire, Deacon 109, 128, 141, 154, 169, 170, 177, 212, 229, 238, 249, 259, 268, 278, 286, 298, 302, 308, 313
McGuire, Murray 258, 259
McGunnigle, William 57, 58, 65, 66, 76
McHale, Bob 298
McIntyre, Frank 89, 90, 95
McJames, Doc 268, 278, 286, 292, 302
Mack, Connie 143, 157, 172, 185, 199, 222, 235, 243, 256, 266, 276

INDEX

Mack, Denny 10, 11, 15, 21, 28, 41, 65, 82, 95
Mack, Reddy 135, 148, 162, 178, 191, 212
McKean, Ed 164, 177, 184, 206, 220, 233, 244, 256, 263, 273, 285, 294, 304
McKee, ----- 120
McKeever, Jim 118
McKelvey, John 36
McKelvy, Russ 53, 82
McKenna, Ed 28, 48, 119
McKenna, Kit 297, 298, 304, 323
McKeon, Larry 112, 133, 143, 149
McKeough, Dave 212, 227
McKinnon, Alex 101, 129, 142, 156
McLaughlin, Barney 122, 123, 154, 213
McLaughlin, Frank 78, 95, 96, 117, 119, 122, 123
McLaughlin, Jim 108, 119
McLaughlin, Tom 94, 106, 135, 150, 230
McLaughlin, Warren 314
McMahon, John 237, 245
McMahon, Sadie 190, 213, 214, 226, 227, 239, 240, 247, 253, 263, 273, 285, 286
McManus, Frank 309, 320, 322
McManus, Pat 60
McMillan, Reddy 205
McMullen, George 164
McMullin, John 9, 10, 14, 22, 27, 34, 35
McNabb, Ed 247
McPartlin, Frank 308
McPhee, Bid 81, 94, 107, 133, 149, 161, 176, 190, 204, 221, 235, 246, 258, 267, 274, 284, 293, 305
McQuaid, Jim 225, 298
McQuery, Mox 117, 128, 143, 213, 229
McRemer, ----- 120
McShannic, Pete 171
McSorley, Trick 37, 109, 130, 147
McSweeney, Paul 225
McTamany, Jim 135, 148, 163, 178, 191, 210, 227
Macullar, Jimmy 59, 94, 108, 136, 151
McVey, Cal 8, 14, 21, 27, 33, 41, 48, 52, 58

McVey, George 135
Madden, Kid 156, 169, 170, 182, 196, 225, 226, 227
Madigan, Pony 143, 144
Madison, Art 264, 306, 321
Magee, Bill 288, 289, 297, 304, 307, 309
Magner, John 58
Magoon, George 297, 304, 306, 321
Mahaffey, Lou 297
Mahoney, Dan 235, 268
Mahoney, Mike 283, 299
Mains, Willard 168, 169, 226, 228, 274, 275
Malarkey, John 259, 268, 278, 279, 306, 307
Malone, ----- 17
Malone, Fergy 8, 15, 21, 28, 34, 43, 121
Maloney, John 43, 47
Manlove, Charles 101, 122
Mann, Fred 78, 81, 95, 106, 134, 147, 163, 165
Manning, Jack 21, 29, 30, 33, 42, 49, 52, 66, 70, 90, 127, 151
Manning, Jim 99, 128, 140, 154, 192
Manning, Tim 75, 96, 108, 127, 136
Mansell, John 81
Mansell, Mike 59, 66, 82, 95, 109, 110, 111
Mansell, Tom 59, 89, 90, 93, 106, 108
Mansfields (NA, Middletown) 16
Mappes, George 137, 142
Maroons (NL, St. Louis) 129, 142
Maroons (UA, St. Louis) 116
Marr, Lefty 149, 191, 204, 221, 228
Mars, Ed 213
Martin, Al 17, 29, 37
Martin, Frank 288, 294, 308, 323, 324
Martin, Phonney 15, 17, 22
Marylands (NA, Baltimore) 24
Maskrey, Harry 82
Maskrey, Leech 82, 94, 107, 135, 148, 149
Mason, Charlie 36, 37, 93
Mason, Ernest 258
Massey, Bill 258
Mathews, Bobby 10, 14, 22, 27, 35, 43, 49, 57, 69, 71, 76, 93, 109, 134, 150, 163, 227

Mathewson, Christy 317
Matterson, C.V. 116
Matthias, Steve 119
Mattimore, Mike 155, 156, 176, 190, 192, 215
Mauck, Al 247, 248
Maul, Al 121, 154, 171, 184, 198, 222, 249, 259, 268, 278, 279, 283, 286, 292, 302, 314
Maumees (AA, Toledo) 211
Maupin, Harry 299, 310
Mayer, Ed 204, 219
Mays, Al 135, 136, 150, 151, 164, 175, 191, 210
Meakim, George 210, 227, 235, 236, 270
Meegan, Peter 110, 134
Meek, Dad 189, 211
Meekin, Jouett 229, 237, 238, 249, 253, 267, 268, 276, 277, 284, 295, 296, 302, 303, 308, 313, 314
Meinke, Frank 102, 128, 129
Meister, George 109
Meister, John 150, 164
Menefee, Jock 236, 249, 256, 257, 260, 266, 267, 295, 296, 315, 316
Mercer, Win 259, 268, 278, 286, 298, 308, 309, 317
Merrill, Ed 78, 111
Merritt, Bill 218, 237, 243, 254, 256, 258, 266, 267, 276, 286, 303
Mertes, Sam 277, 293, 306, 315
Messitt, Tom 307
Metcalf, Bob 35
Metropolitans (AA, New York) 94, 106, 136, 150, 164
Meyerle, Levi 8, 15, 21, 28, 34, 43, 49, 121
Meyers, Henry 214
Middletown 16
Middletown (NA) Mansfields 16
Millard, Frank 211
Miller, Bert 288, 289
Miller, Bob 212, 230
Miller, Burt 288
Miller, Cyclone 99, 101, 102, 119, 150
Miller, Doggie 111, 134, 147, 156, 170, 184, 207, 222, 235, 243, 257, 269, 279
Miller, Dusty 191, 211, 267, 274, 284, 293, 304, 305
Miller, Ed 109
Miller, Fred 238

INDEX

Miller, George 49, 108
Miller, Henry 236
Miller, Joe 18, 35, 38, 109, 135
Miller, Ralph 297, 298, 304
Miller, Reddy 27, 34
Miller, Roscoe 322
Millers (AL, Minneapolis) 324
Milligan, Bill 321, 324
Milligan, Jocko 109, 134, 150, 163, 175, 189, 198, 227, 238, 245, 247
Mills, Charlie 9, 14
Mills, Everett 9, 14, 21, 29, 33, 41
Milwaukee 54, 116, 226, 320
Milwaukee (NL) Cream Citys 54; (AA) Brewers 226; (UA) Cream Citys 116; (AL) Brewers 320
Minahan, Dan 270
Mincher, Ed 10, 18
Minneapolis (AL) Millers 324
Mitchell, Robert 49, 52, 59, 83
Moffett, Joe 109
Moffett, Sam 102, 157, 158, 171
Mohler, Kid 259
Molesworth, Carlton 268
Monroe, Frank 112
Monumentals (UA, Baltimore) 117
Moolic, George 140
Moore, Harry 119
Moore, Jerry 102, 122, 128
Moore, Molly 37
Moran, Bill 239
Moran, Sam 266
Morelock, Harry 220, 234
Morgan, Bill 37, 54, 82, 95, 110, 112
Moriarity, Gene 99, 112, 128, 129, 239
Morrill, John 42, 47, 52, 57, 65, 71, 76, 87, 99, 128, 142, 156, 169, 185, 186, 196
Morris, E. 118
Morris, Ed 106, 134, 147, 156, 171, 184, 198
Morris, P. 120
Morrison, Hank 158
Morrison, John 111, 164
Morrison, Mike 165, 177, 178, 213
Morrison, Tom 270, 280
Morrissey, John 69, 77
Morrissey, Tom 116
Morton, Charlie 82, 83, 109, 128

Morton, Sparrow 101, 102
Motz, Frank 204, 246, 258
Mountain, Frank 64, 70, 78, 81, 95, 106, 134, 147
Mountain Citys (UA, Altoona) 122
Mountjoy, Bill 94, 108, 133, 137
Moynahan, Mike 65, 70, 71, 93, 102, 109
Mueller, John 43
Muldoon, Mike 76, 88, 102, 136, 151
Mullane, Tony 70, 82, 93, 109, 149, 161, 176, 190, 204, 205, 221, 222, 235, 246, 247, 253, 256
Mullen, ----- 16
Mulligan, ----- 120
Mullin, Henry 112, 118
Mulvey, Joe 87, 90, 101, 127, 141, 154, 169, 183, 197, 227, 234, 249, 265
Munce, John 123
Mundinger, George 112
Munn, Horatio 38
Munyan, John 165, 210, 211
Murnane, Tim 16, 22, 27, 34, 42, 47, 52, 118
Murphy, ----- 118
Murphy, Bob 206
Murphy, Clarence 148
Murphy, Con 101, 102, 196, 215, 258
Murphy, Connie 246
Murphy, Dan 237
Murphy, Danny 317
Murphy, Ed 295
Murphy, Joe 142, 147, 149, 161
Murphy, John 122, 123
Murphy, Larry 229
Murphy, Morg 196, 225, 235, 246, 258, 267, 279, 289, 295, 296, 314
Murphy, Pat 155, 168, 182, 205
Murphy, Tony 106
Murphy, Willie 102, 112
Murphy, Yale 253, 267, 284
Murray, Miah 99, 135, 171, 230
Murray, Tom 255
Mutuals (NA, New York) 9, 14, 22, 27, 35
Mutuals (NL, New York) 42
Myers, Al 116, 126, 143, 157, 171, 183, 185, 204, 219
Myers, Bert 279, 298, 314
Myers, George 100, 129, 142, 157, 171, 185

Myers, Henry 69, 83, 84, 123
Myers, Lewis 117

Nagle, ----- 322
Nagle, Tom 203, 218
Nance, Bill 288, 297, 324
Nash, Billy 110, 128, 142, 156, 169, 182, 196, 218, 233, 243, 254, 265, 277, 287, 295
Nationals (AA, Washington) 112
Nationals (NA, Washington) 17
Nationals (UA, Washington) 119
Nava, Sandy 75, 87, 99, 137, 151
Neagle, John 58, 90, 96, 111
Neale, Joe 148, 162, 211, 225, 226
Nelson, Bill 111
Nelson, Candy 15, 17, 22, 27, 35, 53, 60, 72, 94, 106, 136, 150, 155, 164, 214
Nevins, Al 23
New Haven 35
New Haven (NA) Elm Citys 35
New York 9, 14, 22, 27, 35, 42, 89, 94, 101, 106, 126, 136, 141, 150, 155, 164, 168, 182, 196, 205, 219, 237, 245, 253, 267, 276, 284, 295, 307, 317
New York (NA) Mutuals 9, 14, 22, 27, 35; (NL) Mutuals 42; Gothams 89, 101; Giants 126, 141, 155, 168, 182, 205, 219, 237, 245, 253, 267, 276, 284, 295, 307, 317; (AA) Metropolitans 94, 106, 136, 150, 164; (PL) Giants 196
Newell, John 222
Newell, T. E. 48
Newman, Charles 236, 237
Newton, Doc 317
Nice, Charles 266
Nichol, Sam 171, 210
Nichols, Al 37, 42, 47
Nichols, Art 293, 306, 315, 324
Nichols, Kid 205, 218, 233, 243, 254, 265, 266, 274, 275, 283, 292, 302, 303, 315
Nichols, Tricky 36, 42, 48, 52, 53, 65, 83, 84
Nicholson, Parson 170, 211, 268
Nicol, George 211, 218, 219, 256, 257, 260, 322

INDEX

Nicol, Hugh 69, 75, 93, 107, 133, 147, 161, 176, 190, 204
Niland, Tom 279
Niles, Bill 266
Noftsker, George 122
Nolan, The Only 53, 71, 72, 96, 123, 127
Nops, Jerry 273, 277, 283, 292, 304, 313
Norton, Elisha 278, 279, 286
Norton, Pete 9
Nusz, Emory 120

Oberbeck, Henry 93, 96, 117, 118, 122, 123
Oberlander, Hart 177, 178
O'Brien, Billy 121, 122, 157, 171, 185, 214
O'Brien, Darby 164, 175, 189, 203, 221, 234
O'Brien, Jack 81, 93, 109, 134, 150, 163, 177, 214, 308, 322
O'Brien, Jerry 157
O'Brien, John 177, 178, 184, 199, 221, 225, 247, 269, 278, 279, 286, 304, 305
O'Brien, Peter 203
O'Brien, Tom 78, 96, 118, 137, 164, 212, 283, 292, 296, 308, 313
O'Connell, John 227
O'Connell, Pat 151, 215
O'Connor, Dan 210
O'Connor, Frank 244, 245
O'Connor, Jack 161, 176, 191, 210, 228, 233, 244, 256, 263, 273, 285, 294, 304, 313, 316
O'Day, Hank 109, 134, 143, 144, 157, 172, 182, 185, 186, 197
O'Donnell, ----- 121
O'Hagan, Hal 238
Oldfield, Dave 96, 135, 143, 148
O'Leary, Charlie 320
O'Leary, Dan 57, 65, 70, 78, 117
Olin, Frank 109, 112, 120, 128
Olympics (NA, Washington) 9, 17
O'Meara, Tom 263, 273
O'Neal, ----- 29
O'Neil, Dennie 248
O'Neil, Ed 211, 212, 214
O'Neill, Fred 164
O'Neill, J. 37, 38
O'Neill, John 308
O'Neill, Tip 89, 107, 133, 147, 161, 175, 189, 197, 225, 235
Oran, Tom 37
Orioles (AA, Baltimore) 83, 96, 108, 136, 151, 162, 177, 191, 212, 226
Orioles (NL, Baltimore) 239, 247, 253, 263, 273, 283, 292, 303
O'Rourke, ----- 17
O'Rourke, ----- 321
O'Rourke, Jim 16, 21, 27, 33, 42, 47, 52, 57, 65, 69, 75, 88, 89, 100, 126, 141, 155, 168, 182, 197, 219, 237, 249
O'Rourke, John 57, 65, 94
O'Rourke, Mike 213
O'Rourke, Tim 213, 228, 239, 247, 249, 258, 259, 260
O'Rourke, Tom 156, 169, 206, 213
Orphans (NL, Chicago) 293, 306, 315
Orr, Dave 89, 94, 106, 136, 150, 164, 175, 191, 196
Orth, Al 264, 277, 288, 295, 303, 314
Osborne, Fred 207
Osterhout, Charles 59
Ottarson, Bill 163
Otten, Joe 269
Outlaw Reds (UA, Cincinnati) 117
Owen, Frank 322
Owens, Red 303
Oxley, Henry 101, 106

Pabor, Charlie 10, 16, 22, 28, 36, 37, 38
Pabst, Ed 211, 214
Padden, Dick 275, 286, 296, 308, 320
Palmer, ----- 130
Pappalau, John 285
Parent, Freddy 304
Parker, Doc 248, 264, 265, 275, 324, 325
Parker, Jay 306
Parks, Bill 34, 35, 36, 42
Parrott, Jiggs 236, 247, 257, 264
Parrott, Tom 246, 247, 248, 258, 267, 279
Parsons, Charles 142, 164, 206
Parsons, John 108
Patten, Case 322, 323
Patterson, Dan 9, 17, 27, 37
Patterson, Roy 320
Pattison, George 121
Paul, Lou 43
Payne, Harley 278, 285, 298, 306
Paynter, George 258
Peak, Elias 118, 121
Pearce, Dickey 9, 14, 22, 28, 34, 41, 48
Pearce, Frank 42
Pears, Frank 192, 248
Pearson, Dave 44
Pechiney, George 133, 149, 165
Peitz, Heinie 239, 248, 258, 269, 274, 284, 293, 305, 316
Peitz, Joe 258
Pelouze, Bill 142
Peltz, John 112, 177, 211, 213, 215
Peoples, Jim 107, 133, 135, 148, 163, 175, 191
Peppers, Harrison 260
Perfectos (NL, St. Louis) 304
Petee, Pat 229
Peters, John 28, 35, 41, 48, 54, 58, 63, 69, 82, 96, 111
Pettit, Bob 155, 168, 226
Petty, Charlie 190, 245, 256, 259
Pfeffer, Fred 77, 87, 100, 101, 126, 140, 155, 168, 183, 197, 218, 237, 238, 249, 259, 260, 269, 275, 276, 287
Pflann, Bill 258, 259
Phelan, Dan 210
Phelan, James 117, 129, 130
Phelps, Neal 10, 22, 27, 35, 43
Philadelphia 8, 15, 21, 22, 27, 28, 33, 34, 37, 43, 81, 90, 93, 101, 109, 121, 126, 134, 141, 149, 154, 163, 169, 176, 183, 190, 197, 204, 214, 219, 227, 234, 244, 254, 264, 277, 287, 295, 303, 314
Philadelphia (NA) Athletics 8, 15, 22, 27, 33; Philadelphias 21, 28, 34; Centennials 37; (NL) Athletics 43; Quakers 90, 101, 126, 141, 154, 169,183; Phillies 204, 219, 234, 244, 254, 264, 277, 287, 295, 303, 314; (AA) Athletics 81, 93, 109, 134, 149, 163, 176, 190, 214, 227; (UA) Keystones 121; (PL) Quakers 197
Philadelphias (NA, Philadelphia) 21, 28, 34
Phillies (NL, Philadelphia) 204,

219, 234, 244, 254, 264, 277, 287, 295, 303, 314
Phillipe, Deacon 307, 313, 314
Phillips, Bill 59, 63, 71, 76, 88, 102, 135, 148, 163, 178, 207, 267, 305, 317
Phillips, Marr 111, 128, 134, 212
Phyle, Bill 293, 294, 306, 307
Piatt, Wiley 295, 303, 314
Pickering, Ollie 279, 285, 288, 323
Pickett, Dave 292
Pickett, John 192, 197, 239
Pierce, Gracie 82, 83, 89, 95
Pierce, Maury 120
Piercy, Andy 69
Pierre, Dick 90
Pierson, Dick 136
Pike, Jay 47
Pike, Lip 9, 14, 21, 29, 34, 41, 49, 52, 72, 164
Pinkham, Ed 8
Pinkney, George 102, 135, 148, 163, 175, 189, 203, 221, 238, 249
Pirates (NL, Pittsburgh) 222, 235, 243, 256, 266, 275, 286, 296, 305, 313
Pirates (PL, Chicago) 197
Pittinger, Togie 315
Pittsburgh 82, 95, 111, 120, 133, 147, 156, 170, 184, 198, 206, 222, 235, 243, 256, 266, 275, 286, 296, 305, 313
Pittsburgh (NL) Alleghenys 156, 170, 184, 206; Pirates 222, 235, 243, 256, 266, 275, 286, 296, 305, 313; (AA) Alleghenys 82, 95, 111, 133, 147; (UA) Stogies 120; (PL) Burghers 198
Pitz, Herm 213, 215
Plock, Walt 220
Polhemus, Mark 157
Pond, Arlie 263, 273, 283, 292, 293
Poole, Ed 313, 314
Poorman, Tom 63, 65, 66, 109, 128, 142, 163, 176
Popplein, George 24
Porter, Henry 116, 135, 148, 163, 179, 192
Porter, Matt 122
Potts, Dan 238
Powell, Abner 119, 120, 149, 151
Powell, Jack 285, 294, 304, 305, 316

Powell, Jim 110
Powell, Martin 70, 77, 89, 117, 134
Power, Tom 212
Powers, Jim 215
Powers, Mike 297, 307, 309, 321
Powers, Phil 53, 65, 71, 81, 94, 108, 133, 137
Pratt, Al 10, 16
Pratt, Tom 8
Preston, Walt 269
Price, Bill 214
Prince, Walt 95, 103, 112, 120
Proeser, George 177, 178, 213
Providence 52, 57, 63, 69, 75, 87, 99, 127
Providence (NL) Grays 52, 57, 63, 69, 75, 87, 99, 127
Puhl, John 295, 308
Purcell, Blondie 58, 59, 66, 69, 70, 71, 75, 76, 90, 101, 102, 128, 134, 135, 151, 162, 176, 177, 190, 214
Purner, Oscar 268
Pyle, Shadow 101, 102, 155

Quakers (NL, Philadelphia) 90, 101, 126, 141, 154, 169, 183
Quakers (PL, Philadelphia) 197
Quarles, Bill 230, 243
Quest, Joe 10, 53, 58, 63, 69, 75, 89, 93, 107, 111, 128, 150
Quicksteps (UA, Wilmington) 123
Quincy, Ben 89
Quinlan, ----- 28
Quinlan, Frank 225
Quinn, ----- 48
Quinn, ----- 71, 72
Quinn, Frank 306
Quinn, Joe 10, 33, 35, 38, 116, 129, 142, 169, 182, 196, 218, 233, 248, 257, 269, 273, 279, 283, 292, 299, 309, 316
Quinn, Paddy 38
Quinn, Tom 147, 191, 198
Quinton, Marsh 110, 134

Radbourn, George 89, 90
Radbourn, Old Hoss 66, 69, 75, 87, 88, 99, 127, 142, 156, 169, 170, 182, 196, 221, 222
Radcliff, John 8, 14, 21, 28, 37
Radford, Paul 87, 99, 127, 143,
164, 175, 184, 198, 199, 225, 238, 249, 250, 259
Rainey, John 155, 199
Ramsey, Toad 135, 136, 148, 162, 178, 189, 193, 211
Ray, Irv 169, 182, 191, 212, 226
Raymer, Fred 321
Raymond, Harry 178, 192, 210, 229, 236, 238
Reach, Al 8, 15, 22, 27, 34
Reach, Bob 17, 23
Reardon, Jim 142, 149
Reccius, John 82, 95
Reccius, Phil 82, 94, 107, 135, 136, 148, 162, 164, 165, 178, 212
Red Caps (NL, Boston) 42, 47, 52, 57, 65, 71, 76
Red Stockings (AA, Cincinnati) 81, 93, 107, 133, 149, 161, 176, 190
Red Stockings (NA, Boston) 8, 14, 21, 27, 33
Red Stockings (NL, Cincinnati) 44, 49
Redmon, Billy 37, 49, 54
Reds (AA, Boston) 225
Reds (NA, St. Louis) 36
Reds (NL, Cincinnati) 52, 58, 66, 204, 221, 235, 246, 258, 267, 274, 284, 293, 305, 316
Reds (PL, Boston) 196
Reds (UA, Boston) 118
Reed, Hugh 29
Reeder, Icicle 108, 120
Reeder, Nick 229
Regan, Joe 295
Reid, William 96, 111
Reidy, Bill 276, 277, 302, 320, 321
Reilley, Charlie 59, 66, 70, 72, 75
Reilly, Charlie 191, 210, 222, 234, 244, 254, 264, 286
Reilly, Joe 118, 136
Reilly, Josh 275
Reilly, Long John 66, 94, 107, 133, 149, 161, 176, 190, 204, 221
Reipschlager, Charles 94, 106, 136, 150, 165
Reis, Laurie 48, 53
Reising, Charlie 112
Reitz, Heinie 247, 253, 263, 273, 283, 298, 306, 321
Remsen, Jack 15, 23, 27, 33, 41, 48, 53, 58, 71, 101, 110
Resolutes (NA, Elizabeth) 23

Ressler, Larry 36
Rettger, George 225, 226, 233, 235, 320, 321
Reust, S. A. 323
Reville, Henry 30
Rexter, Bill 38
Reynolds, Charles 189, 192
Reynolds, Charlie 81
Rhines, Bill 204, 205, 221, 222, 235, 249, 267, 274, 284, 296, 306
Rhodes, Bill 249
Richardson, Art 119
Richardson, Danny 101, 126, 141, 155, 156, 168, 182, 197, 219, 238, 246, 259
Richardson, Hardy 57, 65, 69, 75, 88, 100, 129, 140, 154, 170, 182, 196, 225, 237, 238
Richmond, John 33, 59, 65, 71, 76, 81, 95, 106, 134
Richmond, Lee 57, 64, 65, 72, 78, 87, 88, 149
Richmond 110
Richmond (AA) Virginians 110
Richter, John 297, 321
Rickert, Joe 296
Rickley, Chris 121
Ricks, John 225, 258
Riddle, John 185, 214
Riddlemoser, Dorsey 309
Riley, Billy 38, 59
Ringo, Frank 90, 101, 109, 128, 134, 143, 147
Ritchey, Claude 284, 297, 307, 313
Ritter, Charles 129
Ritter, Floyd 212
Ritterson, Whitey 43
Ritz, Jim 256
Roach, John 155, 156
Roach, Mike 308
Roach, Skel 306, 307
Roat, Fred 207, 236
Robinson, Charlie 112, 135
Robinson, Fred 117
Robinson, Val 17
Robinson, Wilbert 150, 163, 176, 190, 213, 214, 226, 239, 247, 253, 263, 273, 283, 292, 304, 316
Robinson, Yank 77, 117, 118, 133, 147, 161, 175, 189, 198, 225, 228, 238
Rocap, Adam 33
Rochester (AA) Hop Bitters 212
Rockford 10

Rockford (NA) Forest Citys 10
Rogers, Emmett 211
Rogers, Fraley 14, 21
Rogers, Jim 278, 279, 288
Rollinson, ----- 120
Rooks, George 218
Rosebrough, Zeke 296, 306
Roseman, Chief 77, 94, 106, 136, 150, 151, 163, 164, 210, 211
Rothermel, Ed 304
Rothfuss, John 286
Routcliffe, Phillip 207
Rowe, Dave 48, 76, 96, 116, 130, 143, 179
Rowe, Jack 58, 65, 69, 75, 88, 100, 129, 140, 154, 170, 184, 199
Rowen, Ed 76, 93, 109
Roxburgh, Jim 108, 163
Ruby Legs (NL, Worcester) 64, 72, 77
Rudderham, John 118
Rusie, Amos 185, 205, 206, 219, 237, 245, 253, 267, 268, 284, 295, 296
Russell, Paul 258
Rust, ----- 83, 84
Ryan, Cyclone 164, 218
Ryan, Jack 193, 210, 229, 254, 265, 274, 297, 304, 321
Ryan, Jimmy 126, 140, 155, 168, 183, 197, 218, 219, 236, 247, 248, 257, 264, 275, 287, 293, 306, 315
Ryan, John 117, 118, 120, 123
Ryan, Johnny 21, 29, 30, 36, 42, 49
Ryan, Mike 269
Ryder, Tom 116

Sage, Henry 211
Sager, Pony 11
Sales, Ed 206
Salisbury, Harry 60, 82
Samuels, Ike 269
Sanders, Ben 169, 183, 198, 227, 237
Sanders, War 321
Santry, Ed 103
Sauters, Al 214
Sawyer, Will 88
Say, Jim 81, 82, 123, 165
Say, Louis 24, 29, 36, 66, 81, 96, 117, 122
Saylor, Lefty 220
Scanlon, Mort 205
Scannell, John 118

Schaefer, Germany 322
Schafer, Harry 8, 14, 21, 27, 33, 42, 47, 52
Schafer, John 150, 151, 164
Schappert, Jack 83
Scharf, Nick 83, 96
Scheffler, Ted 170, 212
Scheibeck, Frank 165, 170, 211, 256, 259, 268, 308
Scheible, John 244, 255
Schellhasse, Art 205, 229
Schenk, Bill 82, 110, 135
Scherer, Harry 193
Schmit, Crazy 207, 240, 245, 247, 309, 310
Schoeneck, Jumbo 117, 119, 120, 171, 185
Schomberg, Otto 147, 157, 171
Schrall, Joe 325
Schreckengost, Ossie 289, 294, 304, 309, 324
Schriver, Pop 148, 169, 183, 204, 236, 247, 257, 267, 284, 296, 306, 313
Schultz, John 226
Schultze, John 220
Schwartz, Pop 95, 117
Scott, ----- 117
Scott, Ed 317
Scott, Milt 75, 102, 128, 134, 151
Sechrist, Doc 308
Seery, Emmett 117, 123, 129, 142, 157, 171, 185, 196, 228, 237
Selbach, Kip 259, 268, 286, 298, 305, 317
Selman, Frank 10, 17, 24, 29, 36
Senators (NL, Washington) 238, 249, 259, 268, 278, 286, 298, 308
Sensenderfer, Count 8, 15, 22, 27
Serad, Billy 100, 129, 161, 176
Seward, Ed 127, 163, 176, 190, 214, 220
Seward, George 34, 43, 83
Sexton, Frank 266
Sexton, Tom 116
Seybold, Socks 305, 321
Seymour, Cy 276, 277, 284, 295, 296, 308, 317, 320
Seymour, Jake 82
Shaffer, ----- 38
Shaffer, Frank 117, 122
Shaffer, Orator 27, 29, 34, 47, 53, 58, 63, 71, 76, 88, 116, 129, 134, 150, 214
Shaffer, Taylor 214

INDEX

Shallix, Gus 108, 133
Shandly, Jim 43
Shannon, Dan 192, 196, 198, 230
Shannon, Frank 238, 280
Sharpe, John 60
Sharrott, George 246, 255
Sharrott, John 205, 206, 219, 237, 244, 245
Shaw, Al 322
Shaw, Dupee 89, 103, 118, 127, 143, 144, 157, 172
Shaw, Sam 177, 247, 248
Shay, Dan 323
Shea, Mike 161
Shearon, John 220, 273, 320, 324
Sheckard, Jimmy 285, 297, 304, 313
Sheehan, Biff 269, 279
Sheehan, Dan 322
Sheehan, Tommy 317
Sheppard, John 24
Sheridan, ----- 38
Shetzline, John 83
Shindle, Bill 140, 154, 177, 191, 197, 219, 239, 247, 255, 265, 278, 285, 297
Shinnick, Tim 210, 229
Shoch, George 143, 157, 172, 185, 226, 239, 245, 255, 265, 278, 285
Shoupe, John 83, 120
Shreve, Ledell 157, 158, 162, 171, 185
Shugart, Frank 197, 222, 235, 243, 248, 257, 269, 288, 320
Siefke, Fred 215
Siegel, John 121
Siever, Ed 322
Siffel, Frank 109, 134
Sigsby, Seth 245
Silch, Ed 175
Simmons, Joe 8, 16, 38
Simon, Henry 165, 213, 215
Simpson, Marty 24
Sixsmith, Ed 102
Skinner, Al 118, 119
Sladen, Art 118
Slagle, Jimmy 308, 314
Slagle, John 228, 229
Slattery, Mike 118, 168, 182, 197, 221, 230
Smalley, Will 206, 230
Smiley, Bill 29, 83
Smith, ----- 117, 118
Smith, ----- 149
Smith, Bill 24, 140

Smith, Bill 102
Smith, Broadway 285, 297, 302, 304, 313
Smith, Charlie 9
Smith, Edgar 87, 90, 112, 113, 127, 206
Smith, Elmer 149, 161, 176, 190, 235, 236, 243, 256, 257, 266, 276, 286, 293, 305, 317
Smith, Frank 111
Smith, Fred 211, 212
Smith, Germany 102, 122, 135, 148, 163, 175, 189, 203, 221, 235, 246, 258, 267, 274, 285, 299, 324
Smith, Harry 48, 49, 193, 320
Smith, Harvey 278
Smith, Heinie 288, 296, 306
Smith, John 24, 29, 36, 77, 78
Smith, Jud 246, 248, 276, 298, 324
Smith, Leo 212
Smith, Oliver 260
Smith, Phenomenal 109, 111, 117, 118, 134, 135, 140, 162, 176, 177, 190, 204, 207, 220
Smith, Pop 66, 69, 71, 72, 82, 83, 95, 106, 133, 147, 156, 170, 182, 184, 205, 230
Smith, Reggie 150
Smith, Skyrocket 178
Smith, Stub 292
Smith, Tom 37, 81, 254, 264, 280, 299
Smythe, Al 323
Sneed, John 112, 210, 211, 227
Snow, Charlie 29
Snyder, Charlie 214
Snyder, Cooney 297
Snyder, George 81
Snyder, Jim 17
Snyder, Josh 17
Snyder, Pop 23, 29, 34, 42, 47, 52, 57, 71, 81, 94, 108, 133, 149, 165, 177, 184, 199, 230
Snyder, Redleg 44, 123
Sockalexis, Louis 285, 294, 309
Somerville, Andy 255
Somerville, Ed 36, 37, 42
Sommer, Joe 66, 81, 94, 108, 136, 137, 151, 162, 177, 191, 206, 212
Sommers, Kid 248
Sommers, Pete 164, 170, 183, 185, 205, 206
Sowders, Bill 169, 170, 182, 184, 207
Sowders, John 158, 192, 196

Sowders, Len 151
Spalding, Al 8, 14, 21, 27, 33, 41, 48, 53
Sparks, Tully 288, 306, 320, 321
Speer, George 324
Spencer, ----- 18
Spiders (AL, Cleveland) 323
Spiders (NL, Cleveland) 184, 206, 220, 233, 244, 256, 263, 273, 285, 294, 309
Spies, Harry 267, 269, 320, 323
Sprague, Charles 155, 184, 211, 212
Springer, Ed 193
Spurney, Ed 222
St. Louis 34, 36, 41, 48, 83, 93, 107, 116, 129, 133, 142, 147, 161, 175, 189, 211, 225, 238, 248, 257, 269, 279, 289, 299, 304, 316
St. Louis (NA) Brown Stockings 34; Reds 36; (NL) Brown Stockings 41, 48; Maroons 129, 142; Browns 238, 248, 257, 269, 279, 289, 299; Perfectos 304; Cardinals 316; (AA) Brown Stockings 83; Browns 93, 107, 133, 147, 161, 175, 189, 211, 225; (UA) Maroons 116
St. Paul 121
St. Paul (UA) White Caps 121
Stafford, Bob 214
Stafford, General 199, 245, 253, 267, 276, 284, 288, 292, 297, 302, 308
Stafford, John 244
Stahl, Chick 283, 292, 302, 303, 315
Stalberger, Bill 127
Staley, Harry 171, 184, 198, 218, 222, 233, 243, 254, 269
Stallings, George 203, 288, 322
Stanley, Joe 117, 286
Stanton, Harry 316
Staples, Joe 129
Stars (AA, Syracuse) 213
Stars (NL, Syracuse) 59
Start, Joe 9, 14, 22, 27, 35, 42, 47, 53, 57, 63, 69, 75, 87, 99, 127, 143
Statesmen (AA, Washington) 229
Statesmen (NL, Washington) 143, 157, 171, 185
Stearns, Dan 65, 70, 81, 96, 108, 129, 136, 192

INDEX

Stearns, William 9, 18, 23, 29, 36
Stecher, Charlie 214
Stedronsky, John 58
Steelman, Farmer 307, 313
Steere, Fred 256
Stein, Ed 203, 218, 219, 233, 246, 255, 265, 278, 297, 298
Steinfeldt, Harry 293, 305, 316
Stemmeyer, Bill 128, 142, 156, 177, 178
Stenzel, Jake 203, 236, 243, 256, 266, 275, 283, 292, 299, 304, 305
Stephens, Ben 259
Stephens, Clarence 149, 221, 222, 235
Stephens, George 240, 249, 250
Stephenson, Dummy 234
Sterling, John 214
Stewart, Ace 264, 321, 322
Stimmell, Arch 317, 321
Stine, Harry 214
Stines, Gat 11
Stivetts, Jack 189, 211, 225, 226, 233, 243, 254, 266, 274, 275, 292, 309, 310
Stocksdale, Otis 249, 250, 259, 266, 268, 273
Stockwell, Leonard 59, 107, 206
Stoddard, ----- 37
Stogies (UA, Pittsburgh) 120
Stouch, Tom 297
Stovey, Harry 64, 65, 72, 77, 93, 109, 134, 149, 150, 163, 176, 190, 196, 218, 233, 239, 246, 247
Strang, Sammy 280, 315
Stratton, Asa 72
Stratton, Ed 24
Stratton, Scott 178, 192, 193, 210, 222, 229, 237, 249, 257, 260, 264, 265
Straub, Joe 64, 81, 95
Strauss, Joseph 122, 136, 148, 149
Streit, Oscar 302, 303
Strick, John 82
Stricker, Cub 81, 93, 109, 134, 164, 165, 177, 178, 184, 198, 225, 239, 249
Strief, George 59, 82, 93, 102, 107, 120, 122, 134
Strike, John 141
Struve, Al 107
Stuart, Bill 266, 308
Studley, Seem 18
Stultz, George 254

Stynes, Neil 199
Suck, Tony 88, 117, 119, 120
Sudhoff, Willie 289, 299, 304, 305, 309, 310, 316
Sugden, Joe 243, 256, 266, 276, 286, 299, 309, 320
Sullivan, ----- 36
Sullivan, Bill 53, 213
Sullivan, Billy 302, 315
Sullivan, Chub 49, 52, 64
Sullivan, Dan 82, 95, 107, 133, 135, 147
Sullivan, Denny 57, 65
Sullivan, Fleury 111
Sullivan, Jim 218, 228, 266, 274, 275, 283
Sullivan, Joe 249, 254, 259, 264, 277, 279
Sullivan, John 322
Sullivan, Marty 155, 168, 185, 205, 218, 220
Sullivan, Mike 176, 185, 186, 203, 219, 227, 235, 246, 256, 259, 263, 276, 277, 284, 303
Sullivan, Pat 122, 123
Sullivan, Sleeper 69, 83, 93
Sullivan, Suter 299, 309, 322, 323
Sullivan, Ted 123
Sullivan, Tom 106, 116, 148, 179, 192
Sunday, Art 196
Sunday, Billy 87, 100, 126, 140, 155, 170, 184, 204, 207
Superbas (NL, Brooklyn) 302, 313
Sutcliffe, Sy 100, 126, 130, 170, 184, 198, 230, 239
Sutthoff, John 298, 299, 304, 305
Sutton, Ezra 10, 16, 22, 27, 33, 43, 47, 52, 57, 65, 71, 76, 87, 99, 128, 142, 156, 169
Swabach, William 155, 156
Swaim, Cy 286, 299
Swan, Andy 110, 112
Swandell, Marty 17, 23
Swartwood, Ed 70, 82, 95, 111, 135, 148, 163, 211, 212, 236
Swartzel, Parke 192
Sweasy, Charlie 9, 16, 21, 28, 29, 37, 44, 52
Sweeney, Bill 81, 117, 118
Sweeney, Charlie 75, 87, 88, 99, 116, 129, 130, 142, 165
Sweeney, Dan 269
Sweeney, Jerry 122

Sweeney, Peter 172, 185, 189, 210, 211, 214
Sweeney, Rooney 96, 117, 130
Sweigert, Ham 214
Swett, Pop 196
Sylvester, Lou 117, 148, 149, 161
Syracuse 59, 213
Syracuse (NL) Stars 59; (AA) Stars 213

Taber, John 205
Tamsett, Jim 323
Tannehill, Jesse 258, 260, 286, 287, 296, 306, 313, 314
Tate, Pop 128, 142, 156, 169, 191, 213
Taylor, ----- 29
Taylor, Bill 70, 71, 72, 82, 95, 96, 109, 116, 134, 135, 151, 163
Taylor, Dummy 317
Taylor, Harry 210, 229, 237, 247
Taylor, Jack 219, 234, 244, 245, 254, 255, 264, 277, 288, 293, 294, 299, 305, 306, 307, 315
Taylor, Oak 47, 111
Taylor, Sandy 60
Taylor, Wally 297
Tebeau, Patsy 155, 184, 198, 220, 233, 244, 256, 263, 273, 274, 285, 294, 304, 316
Tebeau, Pussy 263
Tebeau, White Wings 161, 176, 190, 211, 212, 256, 259, 263
Tener, John 137, 168, 183, 198
Tenney, Fred 118, 119, 123, 254, 265, 274, 283, 292, 302, 314
Terrell, Tom 148
Terry, ----- 36
Terry, Adonis 110, 135, 148, 163, 175, 189, 203, 221, 235, 236, 240, 243, 257, 264, 265, 275, 287
Thake, Al 15
Thayer, Ed 43
Thiel, Otto 322
Thomas, Roy 303, 314
Thomas, Tom 304, 305, 316, 320, 322, 323
Thompson, Andrew 36
Thompson, Art 120
Thompson, Frank 38
Thompson, John 81
Thompson, Sam 128, 140, 154,

INDEX

170, 183, 204, 219, 234, 254, 264, 277, 288, 295
Thompson, Tug 112
Thompson, Will 236
Thornton, John 186, 219, 220, 234, 239
Thornton, Walter 264, 265, 275, 287, 293, 294
Tiernan, Mike 155, 156, 168, 182, 205, 219, 237, 245, 253, 267, 276, 284, 295, 308
Tierney, William 81, 117
Tigers (AL, Detroit) 321
Tilley, John 76, 109, 121
Tipper, Jim 16, 29, 36
Titcomb, Ledell 141, 155, 156, 163, 168, 182, 212
Tobin, Bill 64
Todd, Frank 297
Toledo (AA) Blue Stockings 109; Maumees 211
Tomney, Phil 178, 192, 210
Toole, Steve 148, 163, 179, 215
Townshend, George 163, 176, 212, 226
Toy, Jim 164, 215
Traffley, Bill 53, 94, 108, 136, 151
Traffley, John 193
Tray, Jim 112
Treacey, Fred 8, 15, 21, 28, 34, 37, 43
Treacey, Pete 43
Treadway, George 247, 255, 265, 280
Trenwith, George 36, 37
Trojans (NL, Troy) 59, 64, 70, 77
Trolley Dodgers (AA, Brooklyn) 110, 135, 148, 163, 175
Trost, Mike 211, 270
Trott, Sam 65, 70, 77, 89, 108, 136, 162, 177
Troy, Dasher 70, 75, 77, 89, 106, 136
Troy (NA) Haymakers 9, 15; (NL) Trojans 59, 64, 70, 77
Truax, Fred 207
Truby, Harry 264, 275, 276
Trumbull, Ed 112, 113
Tucker, Tommy 162, 177, 191, 205, 218, 233, 243, 254, 265, 274, 283, 286, 297, 299, 309
Turbidy, Jeremiah 122
Turner, Tuck 244, 254, 255, 264, 277, 279, 289, 299
Twineham, Old Hoss 248, 258

Twitchell, Larry 140, 154, 170, 184, 199, 228, 238, 249, 260
Tyng, Jim 57, 169

Ulrich, George 238, 246, 276
Underwood, Fred 255
Unions (UA, Kansas City) 122

Vadaboncoeur, E. 101
Valentine, Bob 43
Valentine, John 95
Van Dyke, Bill 211, 243
Van Haltren, George 155, 168, 183, 196, 226, 227, 236, 239, 240, 243, 253, 267, 268, 276, 277, 284, 295, 308, 317
Van Zant, Dick 177
Vaughn, Farmer 149, 178, 192, 197, 228, 229, 235, 246, 258, 267, 274, 284, 293, 305
Veach, Peek A Boo 122, 123, 162, 206, 207
Viau, Leon 176, 190, 204, 205, 206, 220, 233, 237, 238
Vickery, Tom 204, 218, 219, 240, 244, 245
Vinton, Bill 101, 102, 127, 134
Viox, Rooney 323
Virginians (AA, Richmond) 110
Virtue, Jake 206, 220, 233, 244, 256
Visner, Joe 137, 189, 198, 225, 230
Voss, Alex 119, 120, 122, 123

Waddell, Rube 288, 289, 307, 313, 314, 320, 321
Wadsworth, Bill 247, 260, 270
Wadsworth, Jack 206
Wagenhurst, Woodie 169
Wagner, Butts 297, 298, 322
Wagner, Honus 288, 296, 307, 313, 314
Waitt, Charlie 34, 48, 83, 90
Waldron, Irv 320
Walker, Fleet 109
Walker, George 177
Walker, Oscar 38, 57, 65, 83, 110
Walker, Wallie 103
Walker, Walt 137
Walker, Welday 109
Wall, Howard 23
Wallace, Bobby 256, 263, 273, 285, 294, 304, 316

Walsh, Joe 226
Walters, Roxy 323
Ward, Jim 43
Ward, John 120, 127
Ward, Monte 52, 53, 57, 63, 69, 75, 89, 101, 126, 141, 155, 168, 182, 196, 221, 234, 245, 253
Ward, Piggy 90, 183, 222, 239, 246, 247, 259
Warner, Fred 37, 53, 59, 90
Warner, John 266, 269, 276, 279, 284, 295, 308, 317
Washington 9, 17, 23, 36, 112, 119, 143, 157, 171, 185, 229, 238, 249, 259, 268, 278, 286, 298, 308
Washington (NA) Olympics 9, 17; Nationals 17; Washingtons 23, 36; (NL) Statesmen 143, 157, 171, 185; Senators 238, 249, 259, 268, 278, 286, 298, 308; (AA) Nationals 112; Statesmen 229; (UA) Nationals 119
Washingtons (NA, Washington) 23, 36
Waterman, Fred 9, 17, 23, 35
Watkins, Bill 112
Watson, Mother 161
Weaver, Farmer 178, 192, 210, 229, 237, 249, 256, 260, 323
Weaver, Sam 34, 35, 54, 81, 94, 95, 121, 150
Weber, Charlie 298, 299
Weber, Harry 103, 112
Weckbecker, Pete 185, 210
Weidman, Stump 65, 66, 70, 77, 89, 102, 103, 128, 143, 154, 155, 156, 164, 168
Weihe, Podgie 94, 111
Welch, Curt 109, 133, 147, 161, 176, 190, 213, 214, 226, 235, 239, 249
Welch, Mickey 64, 71, 77, 89, 101, 126, 141, 155, 168, 182, 205, 206, 219, 237
Welch, Tub 211, 269
Wells, Jake 211
Wentz, John 229
Werden, Perry 116, 172, 211, 226, 238, 248, 288, 324
Werrick, Joe 121, 148, 162, 178
Wesner, ----- 268
West, Billy 28, 43
West, Buck 108, 206
West, Frank 254
Westerns (NA, Keokuk) 38

Westervelt, Huyler 253
Wetzel, George 137
Weyhing, Gus 163, 176, 190, 196, 227, 234, 244, 254, 255, 264, 266, 269, 270, 280, 298, 308, 309, 313, 316
Weyhing, John 176, 191, 192
Wheeler, Ed 322
Wheeler, George 277, 288, 295, 303, 320, 321
Wheeler, Harry 52, 53, 58, 64, 66, 81, 95, 107, 117, 119, 120, 122, 123
Wheelock, Bobby 156, 210, 227
Whistler, Lew 205, 219, 237, 239, 248, 249
Whitaker, Bill 177, 191
White, Bill 57, 111, 148, 149, 162, 175, 178
White, C. B. 90
White, Deacon 10, 16, 21, 27, 33, 41, 47, 52, 58, 66, 69, 75, 88, 100, 129, 140, 154, 170, 184, 199, 200
White, Deke 264
White, Elmer 10
White, John 323
White, Warren 9, 18, 23, 29, 35
White, Will 47, 52, 58, 66, 70, 81, 94, 108, 133, 149
White, William 120
White Caps (UA, St. Paul) 121
White Stockings (AL, Chicago) 320
White Stockings (NA, Chicago) 8, 28, 35
White Stockings (NL, Chicago) 41, 48, 53, 58, 63, 69, 75, 87, 100, 126, 140, 155, 168, 183, 203, 218, 236, 247
Whitehead, Milt 116, 122
Whitely, Gurd 102, 128
Whiting, Ed 83, 94, 107, 143
Whitney, Art 64, 70, 75, 77, 111, 134, 147, 156, 168, 182, 197, 225, 228
Whitney, Frank 42
Whitney, Jim 71, 76, 87, 99, 128, 143, 157, 172, 185, 214
Whitrock, Bill 211, 249, 258, 259, 260, 277
Widner, Wild Bill 161, 172, 191, 210, 228
Wiley, ----- 120
Wilhelm, Harry 307
Williams, Dale 44
Williams, Gus 215

Williams, Jim 305, 313
Williams, Pop 298, 299
Williams, Tom 233, 244
Williams, Wash 110, 126
Williamson, Ned 53, 58, 63, 69, 75, 87, 100, 101, 126, 140, 155, 168, 183, 197
Willigrod, Julius 76, 77
Willis, Vic 292, 302, 303, 315
Wills, ----- 112, 122
Wills, Dave 307
Wilmington (UA) Quicksteps 123
Wilmot, Walt 172, 185, 203, 218, 236, 247, 257, 264, 284, 295, 324
Wilson, Bill 207, 288, 297
Wilson, Henry 292
Wilson, Hickie 110
Wilson, Highball 310
Wilson, Parke 245, 253, 267, 276, 284, 296, 308, 322
Wilson, Zeke 263, 266, 273, 285, 294, 304, 305, 323
Wilsonholm, ----- 90
Winkelman, George 95, 143, 144
Wise, Bill 83, 84, 119, 120, 143, 144
Wise, Nick 170
Wise, Sam 70, 76, 87, 99, 128, 141, 156, 169, 185, 199, 226, 249
Witherow, ----- 36
Woerlin, Joe 268
Wolf, Chicken 82, 94, 106, 135, 136, 148, 149, 162, 178, 192, 210, 229, 239
Wolters, Rynie 9, 16, 23, 24
Wolverines (NL, Detroit) 70, 77, 89, 102, 128, 140, 154, 170
Wolverton, Harry 293, 306, 314, 315
Wonders (PL, Brooklyn) 196
Wood, ----- 29
Wood, Bob 293, 305, 316, 320
Wood, Fred 103, 129
Wood, George 64, 70, 77, 89, 90, 103, 128, 129, 141, 154, 169, 183, 191, 198, 227, 235, 240
Wood, Jimmy 8, 15, 17, 21
Wood, John 279
Wood, Peter 129, 183
Woodcock, Fred 236
Woodhead, Red 24, 59
Woodruff, Orville 308

Woods, Walt 293, 294, 307, 313, 314
Worcester 64, 72, 77
Worcester (NL) Ruby Legs 64, 72, 77
Wordsworth, Favel 23
Worth, Herb 16
Woulfe, Jim 108, 111
Wright, Dave 266, 267, 287
Wright, George 8, 14, 21, 27, 33, 42, 47, 52, 57, 65, 71, 75
Wright, Harry 8, 14, 21, 27, 33, 42, 47
Wright, Joe 269, 276, 280
Wright, Pat 203
Wright, Rasty 206, 213
Wright, Sam 36, 42, 66, 71
Wright, William 157
Wrigley, Zeke 278, 286, 298, 302, 308
Wylie, Ren 82
Wyman, Frank 119, 122, 123
Wynne, Bill 259

Yaik, Henry 171
Yeager, George 275, 283, 292, 302, 320
Yeager, Joe 297, 298, 302, 313, 322
Yeatman, Bill 18
Yewell, Ed 112, 120
Yingling, Joe 143, 144, 254
York, Tom 9, 14, 21, 28, 33, 41, 47, 52, 57, 63, 69, 75, 88, 108, 137
Yost, Gus 248
Young, Cy 206, 220, 233, 243, 256, 263, 273, 285, 294, 304, 305, 316
Young, J. D. 239
Youngman, Henry 207

Zahner, Fred 260, 269
Zay, ----- 151
Zearfoss, Dave 276, 284, 296
Zettlein, George 8, 15, 17, 21, 28, 34, 35, 43
Ziegler, Charles 310, 314
Ziegler, George 207
Zies, Bill 225
Zimmer, Chief 103, 150, 165, 177, 184, 206, 220, 233, 244, 256, 263, 273, 285, 294, 307, 309, 313
Zinn, Frank 176